AINSLIE'S
COMPLETE GUIDE TO
HARNESS RACING

The Trotting Season at Prospect Park Fair Grounds, Long Island—Race between "Fullerton" and "Goldsmith Maid," Monday, June 8th, 1874.
—Woodcut, The Bettmann Archive

ALSO BY TOM AINSLIE

The Compleat Horseplayer
Ainslie's Jockey Book
Ainslie's Complete Guide to Thoroughbred Racing
The Handicapper's Handbook
Theory and Practice of Handicapping

Ainslie's Complete Guide to

HARNESS RACING

By TOM AINSLIE

SIMON AND SCHUSTER • NEW YORK

ISBN 0-671-27065-6
Library of Congress Catalog Card Number 74–122433
Manufactured in the United States of America

6   7   8   9   10   11

Contents

PREFACE

A Game of Prediction

SPEED EXCITES MAN. He craves it. He equates it with beauty. He prizes it above strength. He tests his own speed aground, in water and on ice and snow, envying the superior speed of others. He is an avid helmsman and eager passenger, enchanted by the speed of vehicles wheeled, winged and waterborne. As a spectator, he revels in the extreme speed of athletes, including the speed of racing animals.

Nothing could be more natural. When our subhuman ancestors resided in trees and had fingers on their feet, the ability to get from one place to another in an enormous hurry was basic to survival. Speed remained decisive during the eons in which hand-to-hand combat determined who owned what and who ruled whom. The first sporting games were war exercises, combat rehearsals from which most of the harm was subtracted. One boxed or wrestled or dueled, but not necessarily to the death. One ran as quickly as possible, but not to escape or overtake a murderous foe.

In due course, the connection between sport and war became remote. Survival no longer depends on bear hugs, parries or speed afoot. But the sporting tradition and the craving for speed are deeply ingrained. They are part of our psychological luggage. They are in our bones. They may even be instincts.

Whatever they are, they coexist in a state of sublime compatibility with another of man's profoundest inclinations, the urge to bet. It is an urge associated with the desire for material gain, but not entirely. Just as often, betting expresses a wish to test one's powers of prediction or, in some cases, a yen to question fate and get a refreshingly prompt, uncomplicated answer.

All of which accounts for the durable prosperity of horse racing. Older than history, the sport and the betting which accompanies it now flourish on an industrial scale in West and East, under flags and

Ayres approaches the finish wire in the 1964 Hambletonian at DuQuoin, Ill., trotting to a record 1:56:4 with John Simpson, Sr., in the bike. Big John, driven by Eddie Wheeler, was second.

ideologies of all hues, wherever men have leisure and spare cash to show for their toil. Continuing popularity and growth seem assured. The atmosphere has never been more favorable. The lunatic view of racing as a vice has receded from fashion in most parts of the world. Few nations any longer mistake joylessness for morality.

The earliest form of horse racing, harness racing probably came into being before the invention of the wheel the very first time a couple of prehistoric teamsters found themselves driving their sledges in the same direction. Pedestrians fortunate enough to witness the great event would have been less than Neanderthal if they had neglected to form opinions about the outcome, make bets, and have the time of their lives. Such enjoyments led inevitably to formal contests in pastures or overland and finally to the stadium spectacles which have beguiled mankind for ages.

More than thirty-five centuries ago, professional horsemen—inheritors of an already ancient tradition—were breeding, training and racing trotters for the entertainment of Near Eastern royalty. Horses large enough to be mounted by grown men would not evolve for another six or seven hundred years. But the equine midgets of history's dawn were sufficiently swift and sturdy to make the two-wheeled chariot the fastest vehicle on earth, a prime accessory for battle, hunt or sport.

At every stage of harness racing's development, betting and its proceeds have had more than a trifle to do with making the mare go. To sharpen the savor of competition and to substantiate their pride in themselves and their animals, the horsemen of old posted stakes, or side bets, and the winner took all. Nowadays the posting of stakes remains a routine precondition of the sport's most important events. For some races, staking begins before the horses are born and continues periodically until the day of competition. These side bets form a substantial proportion of the purse that ultimately is divided among the first five finishers in such a race.

The major concern of this book is, of course, the kind of betting that occurs in the game of prediction played at the pari-mutuel windows by fans, horsemen and raceway personnel. Pari-mutuel betting is central to the pleasure experienced by the customers of the industry. It is the industry's fundamental source of revenue and growth. Yet the otherwise impressive literature of harness racing is usually silent about it. Among the many works of scholarship in which enthusiasts of the sport have celebrated its past and heralded its future, not one so much as mentions the principles and techniques of handicapping —the business of trying to pick a winner—on which intelligent, fully enjoyable betting depends.

This book corrects the omission. It devotes itself entirely to the fascinations of handicapping, recognizing that the fan pays his way into a track not only to watch races but to bet on them. It assumes without fear of contradiction that he would rather win than lose. Bearing this in mind, it explores the world of harness racing from tack room to board room, dwelling on the backstage activities, tendencies and trends that influence raceway performance and, therefore, affect the reader's powers of prediction.

The race that engages the fan's speculative interest is in a very real sense the result of years of activity by breeders, trainers, grooms, drivers, raceway officials and, lest we forget, horses. For some of these, the race may be the turning point or even the climax of a career. To understand the race and, more to the point, predict its outcome with any degree of confidence, one must know the industry of which the race is a product. One must even know its traditions, the molds in which its procedures are shaped. And, while knowledge of the exploits of bygone champions cannot possibly help the player to pick the winner of the fifth at Pompano Park, he is likely to be more comfortable if he understands what others are talking about when they mention certain hallowed names.

Aside from brief, occasional samplings of relevant history, the reader will spend his time in the present, behind the scenes, where horsemen form the strategies and tactics that lead to the winner's circle and the mutuel cashier's window. Knowing that handicapping is effective only to the degree that it encompasses the actualities of the sport, we shall study those actualities in comprehensive detail. At the finish, we shall be able to pick winners. The more success-oriented among us will even be able to show a profit at it.

Horsemen Are Handicappers

As anyone must realize after overhearing the kinds of conversation that resound in raceway grandstands and clubhouses, many fans regard the racing itself as merely an incidental ceremony preceding the announcement of the winning numbers. Indeed, some players behave as if a race were the spin of a roulette wheel, with each number as likely to win as any other. But racing is not that way at all. Horses and drivers are living creatures, not numbers. Some have virtually no chance to win their races. Others are so superior to the competition that they remain attractive after the odds drop below even money.

To make dependable evaluations of that sort, one must be a good handicapper. The handicapper bases his judgments on what he knows about the sport's likelihoods. He knows about the variables of Standardbred class and fitness; the problems presented by the length and contours of the particular track; the nuances of the phenomenon called "pace"; the disparate talents of trainers and drivers; the significance of an animal's behavior during the preliminary warm-ups.

Horsemen make evaluations of the same kind. The success of any trainer or driver is largely measurable in terms of his own handicapping ability. He may never gamble (except when he posts the stakes required for entry in a major race). But he simply must be able to assess his horse and himself and their rivals in light of the opportunities and challenges presented by each new race. This is handicapping, pure and unembellished. If the horseman is not good at it, he almost surely will enter his livestock in the wrong races. And he will worsen matters by driving unintelligently, allowing better tacticians—better handicappers, if you please—to anticipate his every move and cut each race to their own cloth.

The reader may be surprised to learn that an overwhelming majority of trainers and drivers labor under the disadvantage just described, or under others even more severe. The ability to sit at home or in the stands and differentiate such horsemen from their superiors is among the most essential components of harness-race handicapping. Almost anyone with an attention span of five minutes can learn to do this with a high degree of skill. Neither are the other phases of handicapping forbiddingly difficult.

Why, then, are handicappers such rare birds? Why do so many fans persist in playing numbers instead of horses and drivers? Why do thousands haunt the mutuel booths, the washrooms, the refreshment stands and, if they can arrange it, the paddocks and barns, seeking hot tips? Is it not true that the past-performance records published in the raceway's nightly program contain far more substantial information?

Yes, it is true. Unfortunately, many racegoers are mystified by the past-performance records. Others are able to decipher the printed abbreviations and symbols, but are at a loss to interpret their significance. Doubtful of their own judgments, or unable to make judgments at all, innumerable fans look elsewhere for help. This is the main reason why raceway crowds are so easily excited by rumors and false reports. And why, in consequence, some natural 5 to 1 shots leave the starting gate at odds of 7 to 5.

The Oldest New Sport

I concede that one need not be a winning bettor to enjoy an occasional outing at the local raceway. Horse races are incomparably exciting. Moreover, these are prosperous times. Millions of men and women can afford the very minor misfortunes with which racing penalizes innocence. Unless the customer gambles insanely, his losing excursion to the track costs no more than a night on the town.

Nevertheless, it is more fun to win than to lose. Nobody with normal emotions can possibly be indifferent to the outcome of his bets. Because human beings favor pastimes in which they are skilled and avoid those in which they take a thumping, one might ask why harness racing has not attempted to educate its own clientele. Why the huge omissions from the tons of literature issued by the industry and its able publicists? Has harness racing's emergence as a major "spectator" sport blinded it to the fact that most of its patrons, however enthusiastic they may be, are transients? And that, aside from a small minority of neurotically compulsive losers, persons who attend the races regularly do so because they have learned how to avoid serious financial loss?

Public ignorance of the principles of handicapping accounts for much of the profligate gambling at racetracks. By neglecting to teach people how to play the game, the tracks perpetuate gambling. Ironically, nobody benefits from this—least of all the tracks. Uninformed bettors depart the scene for good after losing more than they can afford. Tracks, horsemen and state treasuries suffer because pari-mutuel revenues are not as large as they would be if more people understood racing well enough to embrace it as a hobby. Contrary to a widespread misconception, racegoers do not bet against the track but against each other. Regardless of who wins or loses, the track and the taxing state get a fixed percentage of the wagered money. The more that is bet, the higher the revenue.

To understand why all forms of American horse racing persist in a self-defeating reluctance to educate their customers, one must realize that Puritanism is not yet extinct on this continent. Pari-mutuel betting exists by sufferance of state legislatures. The legislators welcome the tax receipts and political sinecures that derive from the betting, but they are easily unnerved by the shrill noises of which North America's vestigial, diminishing antigambling elements remain capable.

Therefore, no matter how festively cordial a legislator may be while enjoying some track operator's brandy and cigars, and no matter how readily he may vote to extend the track's season, he remains primly aloof in public. In turn, as if by treaty, the track operator attempts to conduct his business inoffensively. Which is not always possible. Should a track's advertising campaign emphasize too plainly that there are pari-mutuel machines on the premises, the piping outcries of bluenoses reverberate like thunder in the state capital. Obviously, handicapping instruction by racetracks might be regarded as the encouragement of "gambling"—a gross breach of the treaty.

Certain stirrings in Thoroughbred and Standardbred racing suggest that this ridiculous situation will end sooner rather than later. The printed programs sold to harness-racing fans at Sportsman's Park and Hollywood Park contain handicapping advice. A few running tracks have been conducting useful seminars. Every little bit helps. Pending a real breakthrough, however, it would be unfair to chide harness racing for a failure to lead the way. The sport may have its roots in antiquity, but the present American form of it is scarcely out of knee britches. It is the new kid on the block. In some major cities, neither press, television nor radio give it the emphasis and promotional assistance accorded to other sports. Successful though it may be, the industry is still struggling for acceptance. Where encouragement of "gambling" is concerned, its leaders hardly can be expected to rush in where the very senior tycoons of Thoroughbred racing have long feared to tread.

Until 1940, there was no such thing as night harness racing with pari-mutuel wagering. Then came World War II. In effect, the industry as we now know it is barely twenty-five years old. It has spent virtually the entire time trying to gain popular footholds, win legislative approval, and build new plants—jobs which are by no means completed as of 1970, although the sport has long since achieved major economic standing. Business now proceeds at the rate of almost 4,000 separate evenings and afternoons of pari-mutuel betting per year, with at least 25 million paid admissions and wagering in the neighborhood of $2 billion, of which about $150 million enrich the treasuries of state governments.

Everything about harness racing is in transition, as befits a youthful, expanding industry. None of the sport's customs or procedures is held sacredly exempt from debate and change. With new raceways opening and old ones extending their seasons, an influx of young horsemen and administrators enlivens the stable areas and front offices. Many of these newcomers are ambitious, bright and competent, and their capacity for experimentation and innovation helps to intensify an atmosphere of controversy and ferment unique in major professional sport. Harness racing is an environment in which hardly anyone can afford to rest on his laurels, lest someone else whisk them out from under him.

Some of the most keenly debated issues in the sport bear substantially on the picking of winners. I shall review them now for that reason and to introduce the reader to some of the frames of reference in which he will be trying to handicap races.

For example, major tracks vary in length from one mile to ⅝-mile to a half-mile, producing three different kinds of racing. Each type of track has its staunch supporters, disagreements among whom make the walls tremble whenever the subject arises. Meanwhile, regardless of the length of anyone's favorite raceway, the chances are that its season grows longer each year and that its racing circuit, if near a metropolitan area, operates practically the entire year round—a fundamental change from the summer entertainment of the past, and a challenge to handicappers.

With the longer season and the prudent tendency of horsemen to send better animals to the farm before the snow flies and the racing strip freezes, track managements do what they can to make the lesser winter competition as attractive as the summer. Some tinker with quinellas, exactas, twin doubles and twin exactas—forms of pie-in-the-sky betting which pay large returns to bettors lucky enough to pick two or four successful horses at a time. These lures often have the desired effect, increasing the raceway's mutuel handle. But they arouse apprehension among conservatives in the industry, who hold that the sport should stand on its own feet, unsupported by gimmicks. Behind this attitude is a wholesome dread of scandal. Hoodlums and would-be fixers gravitate like maggots to any sport on which people bet. Far from concentrating their ingenious efforts on basketball and football, they have caused many a gray hair in racing. It goes without saying that they are powerfully attracted to propositions like the twin double, in which odds of 10,000 to 1 are not unusual.

Whether a raceway features gimmick bets or not, its effort to improve attendance and increase the mutuel handle rests mainly on the presentation of close, exciting races. This responsibility is the racing secretary's, and he wears a furrowed brow. Horses are not created equal, yet any owner with a horse good enough to race at the particular track is entitled to a fair share of opportunities to win. To provide such opportunities without adulterating the nightly programs is quite a task. Estimating the quality of the available livestock, the racing secretary writes conditions which specify the kinds of horses eligible for entry in each race. Methods of doing this vary greatly without approaching perfection. They are in a state of rapid flux and promise to remain so for years. They differ so widely from place to place that even an experienced handicapper may find himself in deep water on his first visit to an unfamiliar raceway. Reading the eligibility conditions printed in the evening's program, and looking at the past-performance records of the horses, he may be unable to tell whether a particular animal's latest races were against better or poorer opposition than it faces tonight.

Raceway managements fret, frown and ruminate over more than one aspect of those printed programs. Details that appeared in the program records published at your track last season may be missing this year, having been replaced with other material. Should a horse arrive at your track from a circuit where the programs employ unfamiliar notations or contain unsatisfactorily incomplete data, the record may appear in your program untranslated and unexpanded, leaving you helpless to evaluate the horse. Improvement and standardization of the past-performance records is a slow and troublesome process when each racing circuit has its own formula and the incentive of printers and track program departments is often to provide a minimum of information.

Another focus of concern is the rule book. Revised frequently to keep pace with the sport's evolving challenges, the rules are enforced with varying degrees of flexibility and competence from circuit to circuit. Some presiding judges are so knowing and so uncompromisingly firm in their administration of racing law that certain tricky drivers are afraid to perform at their tracks, having enough trouble in life without incurring more. In recent years, for example, a few top judges have been fining and suspending drivers who take the early lead and then slow the pace sufficiently to make the outcome a matter of tactics and luck rather than of Standardbred speed and fitness. These judges are even more severe with drivers who perform incompetently or, if competent, neglect to produce the best effort of which a horse seems capable. While some drivers avoid such judges, others plead to race at their tracks, hoping to prove that they can win fairly and honestly and thus live down black marks earned elsewhere. Needless to say, the standardization of racing law and its enforcement engrosses those who run the industry.

When I set forth toward the unprecedented goal of supplying harness-racing enthusiasts with a decently comprehensive book about handicapping, I found the industry cooperative. Racing secretaries, presiding judges, breeders, trainers, drivers, publicists, raceway directors, professional handicappers and national organizations were uniformly helpful. Nobody attempted to evade controversial topics. Nobody tried to sell me the Brooklyn Bridge. I was welcome to pick brains, rifle files and peek under rugs from one end of the country to the other.

The relaxed candor with which harness-racing folk discuss the prospects and problems of their sport is attributable to their utter confidence in its worth. They believe quite rightly that they are involved in something good. They foresee nothing but progress. Accordingly, they regard existing controversies as the temporary pains of growth. I praise their refreshingly mature attitudes so early in my book because I am eager to establish a positive tone. I admire the sport and its people—this book's later complaints and criticisms notwithstanding.

Not Everybody Bets

Although everyone in the harness-raceway sport is obsessed with trends in the pari-mutuel handle (from which comes the money for purses and profits), a high proportion of horsemen and executives are otherwise indifferent to betting. The industry derives from and retains much of the character of a freakish kind of horse racing in which betting, while sometimes present, has seldom been the heart of the matter.

North American harness racing was for hundreds of years an essentially rural pastime. Its participants were farmers, with a sprinkling of professional barnstormers who had forsaken the hoe in favor of full-time horsemanship, either independently or as employees of various well-funded stables owned by landed gentry.

The main locale was the country fair, where the pet that towed the family trap during the week raced to a sulky on Saturday afternoon, occasionally defeating more expensive, professionally managed livestock. Betting was largely an expression of loyalty to a particular horse, or to the family or friend or hometown that represented one's link with the animal.

During certain fairs, local billiard emporiums and taverns were sometimes the scenes of wheeling and dealing. I have been told of auction-betting pools that amounted to tens of thousands of dollars, rivaling the Calcutta pools that later troubled professional golf. And old-fashioned bookmaking was not unheard of. But at most fairs the race was the thing and gambling was hardly anyone's main reason for attending.

To this day, some of the richest and most important American harness races are conducted in that spirit. The renowned Hambletonian, comparable in prestige to the Epsom Derby or the Belmont Stakes of Thoroughbred racing, takes place each year without noticeable betting. No pari-mutuel facilities exist at the Du Quoin, Ill., State Fair. The stray bookie who turns up to solicit Hambletonian action is quickly banished. Yet each year at least 40,000 lovers of harness racing trek to this prairie community, cheer the Hambletonian and depart without complaint about the lack of betting opportunities. At the Indianapolis Fair Grounds, the crucial Fox Stake for two-year-old pacers, the Horseman Stake for trotters of that age and the famous Horseman Futurities for three-year-old trotters and pacers are conducted in identical style, betless. So are the important stakes races at Bloomsburg and Carlisle, Pa.

These classic events are by no means the only bonds between the raceway sport and the country recreation from which it so recently emerged. The racing at pari-mutuel tracks is heavily influenced by men who were breeding, training, and driving Standardbreds before anyone dreamed of installing lights and mutuel machines to create a new industry. With surprisingly few exceptions, today's top raceway drivers and trainers are the sons or grandsons of harness horsemen. For many such persons, the horse comes first, the race is second and betting is irrelevant. Some bet comfortably small amounts for fun, when not working. Others get a few hundred down on their own horses when they think they have exceptionally bright chances to win.

The driver is a marked man as soon as he shows more interest in cashing a bet than in winning part of a purse. The world of the sulky driver-trainer is small. Everybody knows everybody else. In fact, everybody knows a good deal about everybody else's business, training methods and driving talents. These men not only drive against each other but frequently drive each other's horses. They sometimes even train each other's horses. They cannot fool each other. The occasional driver who tries to lose this week in hope of winning at a good mutuel price next week quickly falls from grace among his colleagues. Also, he attracts the attention of the hawkeyes in the judges' stand and the racing secretary's office. Major tracks lose no time denying stall space to a driver whose horses specialize in dramatic reversals of form.

Not that the sport is overrun with such characters. Neither is it congested with Eagle Scouts and avenging angels. But raceway operators and leading horsemen are the stewards of huge capital investments from which they and their partners extract substantial profits. They believe with good reason that their continuing prosperity depends on their ability to satisfy the public's standards of sporting rectitude. With press, prosecutors and legislators perpetually ready to make hay of athletic scandal, and with so much at stake, harness racing's severity toward wrongdoers is an expression of sheer practicality. Because the risks are so considerable, cheating is much less frequent than one might think after spending a few minutes at the raceway bar, a center of intrigue to which we shall return in a later chapter.

Is It Gambling?

By popular consent, the purchaser of common stock is entitled to call himself an investor. Depending on his choice of stock, others may refer to him as a speculator. But hardly anyone calls him a gambler. Good. Assuming that the stock transaction results from the buyer's study of the national economy, the particular industry, the specific corporation and the stock market itself, he has committed an act of speculative investment. He has made an informed decision. He is playing a game of skill with all the skill he can muster. It is, to be sure, a game from which the element of chance is not entirely absent. But it is a game in which the informed fare better than the uninformed. It is no activity for gamblers, whom I may as well define as persons who trust to luck even when engaged in games of skill.

The only place for a gambler is a properly supervised gambling casino. Craps and roulette are games of pure chance in which the only permissible skill is knowledge of the odds. The extra penalties that befall a gambler in contests of skill are spared him in the casino. There he can entrust himself to luck, hunch and superstition. If he wins, he is lucky. If he loses, he is not, but he has had as much chance to win as any other patron of the resort.

Place that same gambler at a poker table and he is a helpless pigeon. Poker is a game of skill in which chance plays only a minimal role. Unaware of this, or unable to acknowledge it, the gambler takes his customary refuge in superstition, neurosis, guess and hope. He hasn't a prayer of success against players who know the complicated probabilities and psychological tricks of the game.

The gambler is similarly disadvantaged at a harness raceway. Here again he attempts to win by luck what seldom can be won except through skill and knowledge. The occupant of yonder box seat may be a bulwark of his community, but unless his bets derive from competent handicapping analysis, his behavior is that of a common gambler and he surely will lose more money than necessary.

I am not sure that anyone has ever emphasized this kind of thing in print before. Yet the differences between shrewd speculation and impulsive gambling are as real at the raceway as in any brokerage office or poker game. Indeed, the skills of the handicapper compare quite comfortably with those of the expert poker or bridge player and are rewarded with gratifying consistency at the counters where mutuel clerks cash winning tickets.

Why then the familiar notion that all horseplayers are nothing but gamblers? It arises partly because of a popular failure to differentiate between games of chance and games of skill: In many minds, any wager is gambling (unless, of course, the wager takes the socially exalted form of a life insurance premium, or an investment in hog futures, or the like). Also, as we have seen, many horseplayers actually *are* gamblers.

But of all contributing factors, the most important is the belief that nobody can beat the races. Though not true, this notion is so widely accepted that the friends and relatives of the racegoer may well look upon him as an eccentric (or worse) who persists in playing a game he cannot win. The logical conclusion is that he enjoys losing. Which is exactly what the Freudians have been saying about gamblers for years.

Postponing for a while our discussion of whether the reader can beat the races, I think it useful to repeat my earlier observation that normal persons do not like to lose large sums of money. They prefer to win. Ultimately, they measure their enjoyment of the harness races in terms of whether the entertainment, excitement, and suspense are worth the financial cost. Handicappers of even middling competence win enough or lose so little that they can justly claim to have profited, even if they have not exactly beaten the races.

Such a person may take his wife to the track twenty times in a season and incur a total net loss of $200 after all that transportation and all those admission tickets, expensive dinners and bets. Even if he were a less capable selector and spent $300 more than he took in, the entertainment would be rather considerably cheaper than an equal number of pilgrimages to the theater or to nightclubs or, for that matter, to restaurants without pari-mutuel facilities.

In offering to explore the principles of Standardbred handicapping with my reader, I hold forth the prospect of an unparalleled hobby, one that often pays for itself. It even yields net profits, but only to persons who approach it with the studious care that marks the expert players of any great game. I believe, perhaps with more optimism than may be warranted by the facts, that these same possibilities exist for a substantial fraction of racegoers who now bet as if racing were a game of chance. It seems to me that many such persons would prefer to behave sensibly if someone would only do them the courtesy of showing them how. Which is why I am here.

For some men and women, of course, the track is a kind of pagan temple in which to commune with fate, test hunches, obey horoscopes and respond to the vibrations of lucky numbers. Whatever else such folks may be, they emote like gamblers, act like gamblers and lose like gamblers. I doubt that I can abolish their superstitions, but I can at least show them a more effective way to confront fate.

Getting Down to Cases

The earliest chapters of the book review the history and the economic realities of the harness-racing industry, the tremendously important mathematics of the pari-mutuel system—the likelihood that anyone can beat the percentages—and the nature and background of the Standardbred horse, with special attention to the mysterious subjects of breeding and conformation and their places in handicapping.

The next chapter describes the materials necessary or useful to the development of expert handicapping technique. It contains the most thorough analysis of past-performance programs ever published, including full directions for reading and understanding the types of program notations used on various racing circuits. Actual samples of the different programs are reproduced.

The differences among raceways, including the all-important factor of track size, are covered in Chapter 2, guaranteed to elicit howls of indignation in certain quarters. The purpose is not to stir up the natives but to arm the reader for his future visits to tracks of all sizes.

Succeeding chapters discuss handicapping factors such as form, class, age, sex, consistency, time, post position, pace, the racing stable, the driver and prerace warm-ups. The section devoted to trainers and drivers not only takes the measure of North America's leading conditioners and reinsmen but also offers insights into professional problems that affect the performance of horses and should, therefore, concern the handicapper.

In these chapters on the principles of handicapping, the reader will find ample guidance about the kinds of races most suitable for play; the effects of rain, wind and seasonal changes; ways to recognize an improving horse or a deteriorating one; coping with fields that include horses that frequently break stride; clocking the warm-ups; the significance of driver switches; cheating, drugging and "stiffing"; recognizing lameness and other manifestations of unreadiness to win.

The book explores the perplexing differences among conditioned, classified and claiming races, indicating the limits within which the reader may be able to appraise the relative quality of a horse entered for the first time in one type of race after having competed in either or both of the other types.

It is one of the fundamental truths of handicapping that principles are more important than procedures. Regardless of the individual's method or "system," his success depends on the fidelity with which he adheres to the established likelihoods of the sport. Nevertheless, it seems to me that orderly handicapping procedures are convenient and efficient. They are especially useful to fans who do not spend every evening at the races and must rely on the information contained in the program rather than on prior observations of their own.

With this in mind, I have included a systematic procedure (*not* a "system") which should enable the reader to handicap any playable race in not more than five minutes. Its chief virtue is the use of pencil and paper to arrive at numerical ratings for the logical contenders in the race. Many good handicappers believe that the art cannot be mechanized successfully—and are correct in that belief—but this book's numerical method does not abolish the need for judgment. It simply eliminates the mental juggling that causes fans so much difficulty and leads them into so many errors. The efficacy of the method will become apparent enough toward the end of the book, when we handicap entire programs at Hollywood Park, Sportsman's Park, Liberty Bell, Yonkers Raceway and Roosevelt Raceway.

Acknowledgments

It is impossible to write a book free of factual error, but I try and I usually come quite close. It also is impossible to write a completely unbiased book, and I never try. In the present case, my allegiance is to the racegoer, the consumer who pays his money and takes his choice. I am prejudiced in his behalf. I approve of anything that increases his enjoyment of the sport—especially anything that enlarges his powers of prediction. I detest and deplore the notion that he is a dunce, fit only to be misled and exploited.

If harness racing were not worth the attention of its present following and of the new fans likely to be recruited by a book of this kind, I would not have written the book at all. I am satisfied that the sport compares more than favorably with other stadium diversions. Its attitudes toward the public are more decent than most.

This does not mean that whatever is convenient or profitable for the management of a particular raceway is necessarily a boon to its customers. As one conspicuous example among several, I might cite the inadequacy of the information contained in the printed programs sold at certain tracks. To the degree that a track's program booklet fails to offer clear, comprehensive summaries of the records of horses and drivers, mystery prevails, handicapping is virtually impossible and the bettor might just as well play Bingo.

As self-appointed champion of the paying customer, I shall deal in vigorous terms with this and other matters of dissatisfaction. I shall examine various controversial issues in terms of my own consumer-oriented prejudices. Although the total effect of the book will be to promote the industry and enlarge its mutuel revenues, not everyone in the business will take kindly to every word.

For that reason, I want to make absolutely clear that the opinions expressed in this book are my own. They derive from my own experience and thought. Of the hundreds of harness-racing officials, administrators and horsemen with whom I have chatted while preparing the book, none can be justly accused of having implanted or encouraged any of these opinions. All they supplied were facts.

Among those whose generous courtesy enabled me to compile my facts with a minimum of difficulty I am most deeply indebted to Stanley F. Bergstein, vice-president for publicity and public relations of the United States Trotting Association and executive secretary of Harness Tracks of America. Although he is one of the busiest executives in all sport, he gave his time lavishly and helped to open numerous doors for me. All of Stan's colleagues were helpful, notably Edward F. Hackett, executive vice-president of USTA and the following USTA functionaries: Dale Bordner, Al Buongiorne, Dick Conley, Larry Evans, Earl Flora, Walter Adamkosky, Darrell Foster, Dave Garland, Joe Goldstein, George Smallsreed and Dennis Nolan. I thank them all and absolve each of responsibility for any errors or excesses which someone might otherwise blame on him.

I thank the all-time great driver, trainer, breeder and goodwill ambassador, Delvin C. Miller, for allowing me to poke around his barns, train the stakes-winning Tarport Birdie and absorb fundamentals of the sport that are invisible from the stands. Among the racing secretaries who submitted to my inquiries with only occasional alarm or dismay, I thank the dean of them all, Bill Connors of Hazel Park, Wolverine, The Meadows and Pompano Park. Also Phil Langley of Sportsman's Park, Jim Lynch of Liberty Bell, Ed Parker of Yonkers Raceway, and Larry Mallar of Roosevelt Raceway.

James C. Harrison, the nation's foremost authority on the breeding of Standardbreds, has my gratitude for his attentive help. I have pilfered freely from his monumental volume, *Care and Training of the Trotter and Pacer.* The generously given ideas of Billy Haughton, Stanley Dancer, Del Miller, Ralph Baldwin, John Simpson, Sr., Frank Ervin, Joe O'Brien, Bob Farrington, Harry Pownall and Sanders Russell represent an absolute totality of existing knowledge about the training, conditioning, driving and general management of Standard-breds. I thank them for their contributions.

I thank presiding judge John Broderick and the greatest of all, Milt Taylor, for the privilege of watching many races with them and learning on the inside how rules are interpreted and enforced. I thank Philip A. Pines, director of the Hall of Fame of the Trotter at Goshen, N.Y., author of the splendid *Complete Book of Harness Racing,* for . his kindness in allowing me to borrow otherwise unobtainable materials from the Hall of Fame library.

Harness-racing publicists to whom I owe thanks are Mort Berry and Ed Hogan of Liberty Bell, Bob Cox of Pompano Park and the Red Mile, Bob Wellman of Hollywood Park, and Sam Anzalone and his predecessor Irving Rudd of Yonkers.

I found expert handicappers remarkably unsecretive. Those who shared their ideas with me and allowed me to orate about my own were Dolly (Harness Hattie) Boyer, the most successful public selector in Florida; Wally Rottkamp, who publishes *Trotter Weekly* and is a leading selector in New York; Nick Saponara, tops in Philadelphia; and Kurt Stehmann, the sharpest in the Midwest.

For permission to reproduce materials from the printed programs of Yonkers Raceway and Roosevelt Raceway, I thank the M. I. (Doc) Robins program department and, for many extra kindnesses, that organization's program manager, Ray Harris. For materials from the Liberty Bell programs, my gratitude to Edward J. Dougherty, president of the Liberty Bell Racing Association. And for the Sportsman's Park and Hollywood Park materials, I thank my friends and associates on *The Daily Racing Form.*

Finally, I honor the memory of Lew Burton, who knew harness racing completely, having been its foremost journalist and later one of its most creative raceway executives. I do not know what he would have thought of this book, but I'd prefer to believe that the time he gave me was not wasted.

Ainslie's
Complete Guide to
Harness Racing

1

Arming the Handicapper

IN THE TYPICAL NORTH AMERICAN harness race the horses go one mile. The winning trotter or pacer usually completes its journey in slightly more than two minutes, arriving at the finish wire perhaps a fifth of a second before its closest pursuer. Often the margin is one of inches—hundredths of a second—and the officials must examine a magnified photograph to decide which horse won.

The best horse does not necessarily finish first. Its defeat often is attributed to racing luck, and properly so. Crowding and careening around sharp turns at upward of thirty miles an hour with sulkies and drivers behind is an invitation to ill fortune. Yet luck does not dominate the sport. Far from it.

What often is explained as luck is not necessarily luck at all, but the proceeds of human frailty. In the first place, the race is only in part a test of equine speed and stamina. It is mainly a competition among men. For better or worse, the unequal talents of men affect the performances of the horses. Handicapping wisdom begins with the realization that the best drivers have the best luck.

The paramount importance of the driver is literally built into the oval design of the racing strip. Every few seconds the sulkies tear around one of the two semicircles that lie at either end of the oval. To take one of these turns even a few feet away from the inside rail adds yards to a horse's journey. Because the final result of the race is measured in inches and split seconds, one does not willingly waste yards. Yet the time comes when yards and the limited energies of the horse must be traded for favorable position at or near the head of the pack. The best drivers know when to attempt these rapid transactions. In carrying them off, they inflict bad luck on other drivers. By contrast, lesser drivers tend to make their bids at unfavorable times. Their attempts fail not because of bad luck but because someone else tricks them into the ill-advised action or beats them to it or hems them in or parks them out and exhausts their horses.

To the inexperienced observer, it may seem that the race actually is won in the homestretch, the final straight dash to the money. But why did the winner enter the stretch with sufficient reserve energy to retain its lead against all challenge? Or why did it have enough energy and enough racing room to overtake and pass the leader in the last yards? From the instant the race begins, every move of every horse and driver is part of a struggle for final striking position. The best drivers manage to achieve such position more often, even while conserving the stamina of their horses more efficiently.

Because he is so adept, the top reinsman wins many races in which he does not have the best horse. In fact, it is fair to say that the third most-conspicuous patsy at any track is the driver who seldom wins unless he happens to have much the best horse. The second most-conspicuous is the driver who seldom wins even when he *does* have much the best horse. And the patsiest patsy of all is the poor soul who bets money on such people.

Lindy's Pride (center) storms between the leading Gun Runner and Dayan (left) to wrap up the $173,455 Dexter Trot at Roosevelt Raceway in 1969. Trained and driven by Howard Beissinger, the brilliant animal swept all five major stakes races for three-year-old trotters that season.

So much for the kind of racing (and betting) luck that has little to do with luck. Unforeseeable and unavoidable mischance does arise and does affect the outcome of races. From the outside of one rubber-tired bicycle wheel to the outside of the other, a racing sulky is more than four feet wide. It cannot go wherever the horse can go, a truth that is fundamental to the education of horses and drivers alike. Let two drivers steer toward the same opening on the rail and one must inevitably give way, very likely leaving himself and his animal in poor position. He probably has only himself to blame, and is not our concern. The problem is the domino effect of his mistake. Any driver racing directly behind a horse that swerves, slows or breaks stride is out of luck. If the resultant tumult costs him the race, he seldom is responsible for the loss. Furthermore, in trying to collect himself and his horse, he may complicate the traffic jam, leaving other horses hopelessly boxed in, and others so depleted that they have nothing left for the stretch drive. This is bad, bad luck. Yet the final winner may well be the best horse in the race. Or the fourth best horse, with the best driver.

As must now be clear, the goal of the handicapping racegoer is to find the best combination of horse and driver. Having done so, his chances of cashing a bet are as bright as possible. But he had better not make his down payment on that tropical island until the race is over. The horse's ability to trot or pace in full accordance with expectations may have been undermined minutes or hours or days before the race begins. The excellent performance last week and the splendid workout the other day may have dulled the horse's competitive edge. The attentions of a new or overzealous or negligent groom may have upset the animal. An item in the elaborate harness may be a trifle too tight or too lose or too stiff. The minor discomfort may cost a tenth of a second of speed—the difference between winning and finishing fourth by almost a half-length.

Perhaps the sulky has not been disassembled and cleaned and oiled. The accumulated debris in the wheels may act as a brake. Perhaps the horse has never taken an unsound step in its life but is thrown off tonight by new shoes that fail by the tiniest fraction of an inch or ounce to support the balanced stride on which racing success depends.

The Standardbred is a remarkably sturdy and courageous animal, frequently as docile and untemperamental as a good dog. When training and conditioning provide even half the chance to which his breeding entitles him, he will race his heart out for the men who tend him. But he cannot confer with them. If they do not notice the bruise on his leg, or the heat of strained or damaged tissue; if they attribute some inconvenient change in his manner to animal perversity, and ignore or punish it; if they regard him as a racing implement, a thing, he must go to pieces sooner rather than later. The night on which he shapes up as the sharpest horse in the race may be the night of his decline.

Or something may frighten him during the race. Perhaps a discarded sandwich wrapper suddenly blows across his field of vision. Or a clod of earth kicked backward by a hoof hits his face like a projectile. Or a horse breaking stride in front of him causes him to panic at the threatened collision and break stride himself before his driver can do anything to prevent it.

Or with everything in his favor and clear sailing ahead, he may skid slightly on a fault in the racing surface, thereby losing momentum and composure long enough to be passed by luckier rivals. Or a tiring horse may duck toward the rail at the instant that a second horse moves up on the outside. The best horse in the race may be boxed between such animals for four or five seconds and lose all chance.

Racing luck and human error, including his own errors of judgment, make it impossible for even the shrewdest handicapper to be right all the time. Strive as he will, no bettor is even remotely sure of coming home from the track tonight with more money than he had when he went. But a really good judge of horses and drivers who keeps his wits about him has every reason to expect more winning nights than losing ones. Reliable statistics on the performance of harness-racing handicappers do not exist. However, my own experiences at the raceways have persuaded me that four winners in every ten bets are a realistic goal for a sensible player.

Not knowing how familiar my reader is with harness racing or its galloping relative, Thoroughbred racing, I intend to compare the two as infrequently as possible. Nevertheless, I feel compelled to make one small comparison now. In more than three decades as a follower of the runners, including several recent years as a rather widely accepted authority on Thoroughbred handicapping, I can recall mighty few afternoons on which I have been able to pick as many as six winners. Indeed, I seldom find as many as six playable races on a program of nine. I go home in a mood of insufferable arrogance if I catch three or four winners in that many attempts. In Thoroughbred handicapping, to maintain a winning average in the neighborhood of 40 percent, year in and year out, requires study, application and self-control of an extremely high order.

Harness racing is more generous to the handicapper. Naturally, everything goes wrong on some nights and one's only winner pays a wretched $3.80. But the fit Standardbred is a fantastically reliable and consistent performer. When the weather is right and the quality of the horseflesh good, a sound handicapper's selections are there or thereabouts in almost every race. As subsequent illustrations will show, five or six winners are by no means impossible on a good night.

Before taking leave of mischance, the subject with which this chapter began, we had better dispose of the most bothersome and by all odds the most seriously misunderstood mischance of them all— the hated lapse from gait known as the "break."

Gaits and Breaks

The pacer is the perkiest of race horses. Its front legs move in perfect step with the hind pair. As if connected by a piston, left front and left hind stride forward in unison and then come the right front and right hind, equally precise. The animal's weight swings from side to side in an amusing swagger, the self-important appearance of which is mightily enhanced by a bouncing, flowing mane and an impressive cargo of straps, boots, patches, poles, pads, blinkers and hobbles.

A good trotter is more elegant. Its front legs move in a marvelously symmetrical, rolling motion, the sight of which has been likened to a barrel going downhill. Its hind legs are rigorously out of step with the front. Left front and right hind strike the ground almost simultaneously and then give way to right front and left hind. A good horse of this kind is all grace and power. A bad one looks from the rear like one of those horse costumes used in school plays, with a boy fore and another boy aft and feet flying all over the place at random.

It is said that both the trot and pace are artificial gaits, but I doubt it. Horses seem to have been trotting and pacing instinctively for thousands of years. What is artificial is not the gaits themselves but the rules, which require the Standardbred to maintain the trot or pace while racing as swiftly as possible. In normal circumstances, any horse asked for speed will go into a gallop. But galloping violates the rules of harness racing and fetches intermittent grief to horsemen and bettors.

When a racing trotter or pacer forgets or ignores its training and breaks into a gallop, the driver is obliged—on pain of disqualification —to restrain the animal until it recovers the proper gait. The gallop-

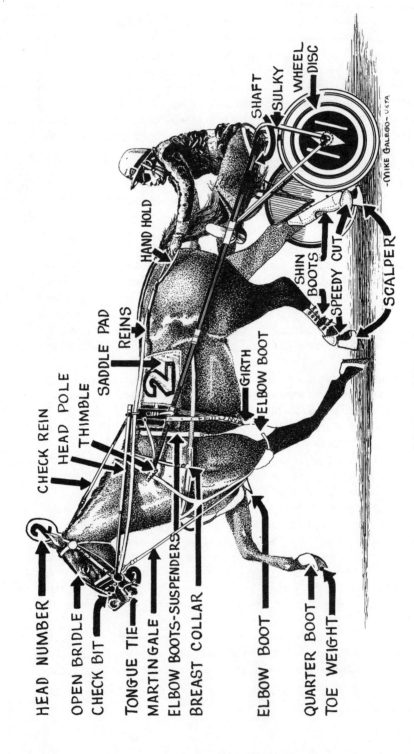

A trotter and his equipment.

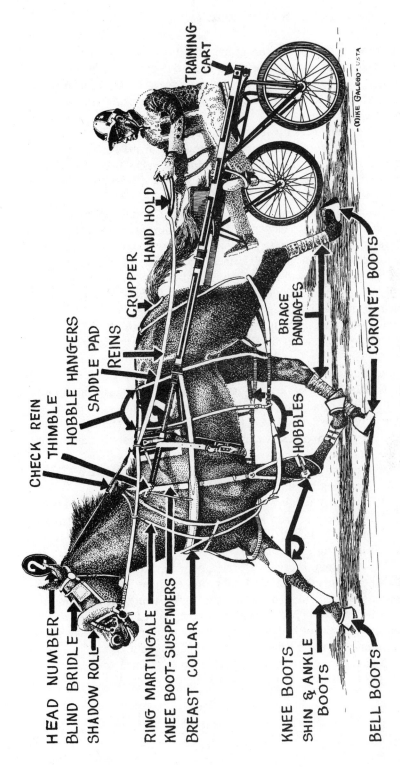

HEAD NUMBER
BLIND BRIDLE
SHADOW ROLL

CHECK REIN
THIMBLE
HOBBLE HANGERS
SADDLE PAD
REINS

RING MARTINGALE
KNEE BOOT-SUSPENDERS
BREAST COLLAR

CRUPPER
HAND HOLD

TRAINING CART

KNEE BOOTS
SHIN & ANKLE BOOTS

HOBBLES

BRACE BANDAGES

CORONET BOOTS

BELL BOOTS

—MIKE GALEGO— USTA

A pacer and his regalia.

ing horse is forbidden to gain ground. If the driver has room, he is expected not only to take the horse back but move it outside, away from other horses. The delay usually costs the galloper all chance in its race, although extremely sharp Standardbreds occasionally recover from a break in time to win.

As anyone could testify after merely one evening at a harness raceway, a breaking horse causes great annoyance in the stands. The ire multiplies in ratio to the amount of money that has been bet on the animal. After the race the driver is likely to be booed, as if he had encouraged the horse to break.

Awful rumors circulate. Especially among persons who do not realize that, of all the many ways to try to lose a harness race, the deliberate break is the least plausible. Not only does a break attract unfavorable attention; it is extremely dangerous for the horse, the driver and for others with whom they might collide. The skeletal structure of any seasoned sulky driver is a collage of healed fractures, most of them acquired in accidents caused by breaking horses. A driver suspected of encouraging horses to break stride could not survive the vengeance to which other horsemen would promptly subject him.

What explains breaks? The causes are these:

1. A horse may break while leaving the starting line, if it has not yet settled into proper stride and traffic problems impel the driver to ask for more—or less—speed than the animal can manage.

2. A horse may break when too fatigued to respond in any other way to the driver's urging.

3. A horse may break under stress when other horses are breaking, or when there is a pile-up on the track.

4. A horse may break when bumped by another horse or sulky.

5. A horse may break when an unsound gait causes it to strike a leg with one of its hooves. This sometimes happens if the driver attempts to cut a turn too sharply.

6. A horse may break if deprived of racing room when eager to go, as when trapped behind a leader whose driver deliberately slows the pace, or when trapped behind and inside tiring, slowing horses.

7. A horse may break if an item of equipment fails and the driver no longer can control its gait. For example, harness straps may separate or chafe, or the bit may hurt the animal's teeth.

8. A horse may break when frightened by overzealous whipping or a wind-borne piece of paper or the splatter of mud.

As can be imagined, nobody in harness racing is fond of the break. Breeders measure their success at least in part by the increasing number of foals that prefer trotting or pacing to running. Conservative bettors refuse to bet on a horse with a history of breaking, and even avoid betting on races in which two or three such animals take part, for fear that their galloping may block the path and ruin the chances of a more reliable horse.

I don't like the break either, but I am unable to become lathered up about it. The point of harness racing, after all, is to move rapidly and bravely on the trot or pace, resisting all temptation to run. Accordingly, the breaking horse deserves to lose, and so does the unfortunate who bets on the animal. Viewed in this light, the breaking Standardbred is closely comparable to the Thoroughbred runner that gets left at the post or is disqualified for failing to run in a straight line. To contend that the rules about breaks spoil the racing is like arguing that the dribble spoils basketball—because the most sensible way to take a basketball down court is to tuck it under an arm and run. Or that the matador should be equipped with a machine gun. Or that the best way to send a tennis ball across a net is by throwing it.

Obviously, there are no pari-mutuel machines at basketball games, bullfights or tennis matches. But there is a certain amount of betting, and the failure of a competitor to perform well under the limitations imposed by rules is, often enough, the reason that his supporters lose bets.

Pacers break far less frequently than trotters do. Side-wheelers (as pacers are called) are not more virtuous, and often are not as carefully trained or shod. Their salvation is the help they get from hobbles, which are leather or plastic loops, one encircling each leg. The hobble on the right hind leg is connected by a strap to the hobble on the right front. An identical arrangement keeps things secure on the left. Thus, when the pacer extends a front leg, the hind leg on the same side is hauled forward. Trotting becomes impossible and galloping also is inhibited, even if not prevented entirely. Free-legged pacers, which race without hobbles, do so either because they are more talented or because hobbles chafe and discourage them.

Forced by the nature of their gait to race without the effective kind of hobbles that keep most pacers out of trouble, trotters are the main problem in the breaking department. The bettor's protection is to read the past performances carefully and steer clear of chronic breakers. Moreover, extreme caution is advisable in one's approach to important races for two- and three-year-old trotters. Being green, these young animals are most likely to break in the heat of the stern competition they face when racing for a large purse. The fact that a young trotter has not broken into a gallop in any of the minor races detailed in its past-performance record is no guarantee that it will stay flat tonight, with the $50,000 purse and the gold cup on the line and all that speed to contend with.

The Communications Gap

We have been touching on some of the uncertainties of harness racing. They keep the handicapping fan on the alert, where he belongs. To the extent that he enlarges his understanding of the sport's surprises, his expectations become more realistic and his handicapping and betting procedures become more sophisticated.

Completely accurate prediction is impossible. Intermittent disappointment is unavoidable. But the good handicapper is equipped to minimize uncertainty. He concentrates his efforts on situations in which uncertainty is least likely to arise. Unlike the promiscuous gambler, who ricochets all evening between elation and prostration, the handicapper invests no more emotion (or money) in one bet than he comfortably can afford. His view is long. His deepest pleasure lies in the knowledge that he can select a high enough percentage of winning Standardbreds to fare very well in the end. To find these truths attractive and reasonable is the first long stride toward the agreeable business of converting a casual pastime into a rewarding hobby.

As part of the process, we now consider a state of affairs which is in no way fundamental to harness racing but happens to be—at this stage in the sport's history—a frustration for the occasional racegoer. I assume that most followers of the sport are in that category. Regardless of his enthusiasms, man seldom is in complete command of his leisure time. Even when he is, he probably does not choose to spend six evenings a week at the races. If he is a good handicapper and a sensible bettor, he probably does quite nicely at major raceways, even if he visits them irregularly. But his prospects do not compare with those of the good handicapper who manages to get to the races five or six evenings a week.

The reasons for this are not good, or necessarily permanent, but they are inescapably real. In most cities, the sport is so scantily covered in the press that the fan has no hope of knowing what happens at the track unless he is there to see for himself. If the local newspaper publishes raceway results, it usually does so in a minimum of space, without information about post positions, drivers' names, fractional times, breaks and other material which might give the results more meaning.

The conscientious follower of any other major sport is able to keep fairly well abreast of developments by reading the daily press, fan magazines and trade papers. But the harness-racing enthusiast has few resources other than the past-performance program vended at the track. It would be possible to make these programs so comprehensive that the occasional racegoer who knew the sport would be able to wager on virtually an equal footing with the nightly regulars. Nobody has yet bothered to make the programs quite that comprehensive. The person who gets to the raceway only once in a while must therefore compensate for his lack of information by wagering with extreme caution, if winning is the name of his game.

In my conversations with professional handicappers, I have been struck by the care with which they take note of significant racing incidents. They watch every race closely, making written or mental records of happenings that reveal the improving or declining form of a horse. Much of this material could be included in the published past-performance summaries but seldom is.

For example, a horse might rough it on the outside for the better part of a half-mile, sometimes traveling as many as three horses wide of the rail. The professional who sees this takes pains to remember it. Why? Because the programs sold at most tracks do not show that a horse was parked three wide. Many programs might show that the horse was parked for only a quarter-mile, even though he raced on the outside much farther than that. Thousands of fans who did not see the particular race, or who made no note of what they saw, are likely to underestimate the form of such a horse when they read its published record before its next race.

For another example, a horse might encounter interference, break stride and be 20 lengths behind the leader at the half-mile call. He might then make up 15 lengths during the next three-eighths of a mile. The program's past-performance chart would show that he was five lengths behind at the stretch call, but only regular racegoers would know how well he had performed to gain that much ground—because programs do not tell how far horses lead or trail at the half-mile.

To compete on anything like even terms with the regular clients, the average handicapping fan needs to milk every available drop of significance from the available records. In the few localities where general newspapers or *The Daily Racing Form* publish detailed result charts, he is well advised to clip, save and consult those pages. Later, I shall suggest some good uses for a handicapper's notebook. For now, I think it important to become acquainted with the types of program past-performance records available at leading tracks. On the pages that follow you will find the decoding instructions published in the programs of Hollywood Park, Sportsman's Park, Liberty Bell and the two big New York tracks, Yonkers and Roosevelt Raceways. I recommend that you read the instructions carefully. The rest of this book will be of small help to anyone unable to understand a past-performance record.

To substantiate my complaints about the average past-performance program and to help the reader appreciate the variety of factors that are blended in handicapping, I shall now list the major factors, showing how the programs might offer better service than they do.

FORM: A Standardbred's physical condition is the index to his readiness. The best evidence of fitness is a bravely vigorous recent performance. The little circle which means "parked out" should appear in the proper place in the record of a horse that raced on the outside through the major portion of a turn. If it raced three wide, the symbol should be doubled. If an animal's performance was not as poor as the record makes it seem, words to that effect should appear somewhere on the past-performance page. For example, "Disliked mud," or "Boxed in," or "Flushed out" (terms we shall explore later) would constitute alibis substantial enough to excuse a poor finish. On the other hand, "Sucked along," "Hung," "Passed tired ones" or "Others broke" would warn the player that the animal's performance had not been as good as it looks in the record.

CLASS: The class structure of harness racing being in a state of development and experimentation, it often is difficult to tell whether a horse is moving up in class, or down, or merely sideways. The programs should tell not only what major conditions governed eligibility for the horse's recent races but also what the purses were. Thus, when an animal goes from a conditioned or classified race to a claimer, or vice versa, the player might have some idea of the nature of the move. If a past race was for females only, or for horses in a certain age range, the past performances should show it.

SPEED: The ultimate measure of a Standardbred is the time it takes him to go a winning mile. But an individual track's inherent

TYPES OF RACES.

Free-For-All, Invitational and Preferred Races

Invitational (Inv.), Free-For-All (FFA) and Preferred (Pref.) races are for the fastest horses at the meeting. These groups are graded by the Racing Secretary based on their performance in previous races. These races are similar to Handicaps and Graded Allowances in Thoroughbred racing. The aforementioned groups are posted and normally not eligible to conditioned races, unless specifically so stated by conditions written by the Racing Secretary. However, any horse is permitted to start in any claiming race if the owner so chooses.

Conditioned Races

In conditioned races, horses are grouped by certain conditions published by the Racing Secretary. These conditions always include gait (trotter or pacer) and may include age, sex, money winnings and number of races won. The condition on earnings and number of races won may apply to the meeting in progress, the current season, a previous season or possibly the lifetime earnings or victories of the horses involved. For example, a condition might read, "For 3-year-old pacing fillies, non-winners of $2,500 in 1968 or two races at this meeting." This condition specifies gait (pacing), age (3-year-olds), sex (fillies), money earnings in a previous season (less than $2,500 in 1968) and number of races won at the current meeting (less than two).

Conditions also may put a narrow limit on money or races won. For example: "For 4-year-old trotters that won $5,000 but less than $7,500 in 1968." This type of condition limits the number of horses eligible and provides the Racing Secretary with finer selection. Generally speaking, the more conditions placed on a race, the smaller the number of horses eligible to that race.

Conditions are written by the Racing Secretary to provide regular opportunities for the horses competing at Hollywood Park. The secretary surveys the horses available, writes conditions to fit these and brings together fields of equal ability, and then offers the conditions to the horsemen in the form of a "condition book." The horsemen then select the conditioned races they think best for their horses and enter three days prior to race day. Following are the abbreviations developed to aid our patrons in determining the approximate class of horses in the indicated race.

Cd/1 — Will signify that the horse started in a race where the basic money won condition was under $3,500.

Cd/2 — Basic condition was between $3,500 and $5,000.

Cd/3 — Basic condition was between $5,000 and $7,500.

Cd/4 — Basic condition was between $7,500 and $10,000.

Cd/5 — Basic condition was in excess of $10,000.

Mdn — Maiden Races.

Nw/2 — Non-winners of 2 races.

Nw/3 — Non-winners of 3 races.

2yo — Two-year-old.

3yo — Three-year-old.

Qua — Qualifying Race. These races do not count in the number of starts a horse may make during a year.

Claiming Races

In claiming races, horses are grouped by value and entered by the owner or his agent at the price they feel best suits the particular horse. Claiming races are written in various price brackets ($2,500, $3,500, $7,500, $20,000 and up) by the Racing Secretary to accommodate the horses available at the track.

Any horse in a claiming race may be claimed (bought) for the amount designated, provided the purchaser meets the rules in effect.

Note: Conditions may be written for claiming races exactly as they are for conditioned races.

Stakes and Futurities

In stakes and futurities horses are entered, or nominated, in a year prior to the year of racing.

There is usually a nominating fee and subsequent sustaining payments to keep the horse eligible, but all of these payments must be paid out, along with the amount of money put up by the track, to the winner or winners when the race is contested.

Head Numbers

Head numbers on the horses warming up will show a color combination. These colors indicate a specific race and number of the horse in that race; such as YELLOW and GREEN, first race. Please refer to the bottom of the page for each race identifying colors. These combinations may also be found on the totalizator board.

Saddle Numbers

For the first time, saddle numbers will be used for horses warming up and each number will be of a different color and may be easily followed around the track.

Saddle Number Combinations

1. Arc Orange
2. Green
3. White
4. Pink
5. Black
6. Light Yellow
7. Blue
8. Green-Orange
9. Blue-Orange
10. Red and White

HOW TO READ THE PROGRAM.

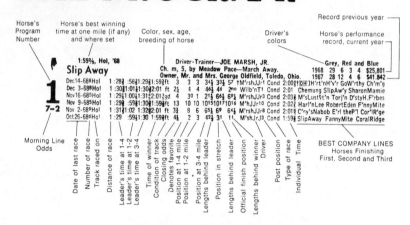

Horse's Program Number	Horse's best winning time at one mile (if any) and where set	Color, sex, age, breeding of horse		Driver's colors	Record previous year Horse's performance record, current year

```
                  1:59⅖, Hol, '68          Driver-Trainer—JOE MARSH, JR.              Grey, Red and Blue
        Slip Away                    Ch. m, 5, by Meadow Pace—March Away.       1968  29  6  3  4  $25,801
                               Owner, Mr. and Mrs. George Oldfield, Toledo, Ohio.  1967  28 12  4  6  $41,842
        Dec14-688Hol  1 :28⅗ :58⅖1:29⅖1:59⅖ft   3    3  3  3½  33½ 5⁷ ⁴M'rshJJr·¹ Cond 2:00⁴⁺DHⁱJH'rt'nH'v'r GoW'rthy Ch'm'g
        Dec  3-688Hol  1 :30⅘1:01⅘1:30⅘2:01 ft 2½   4  4  46½ 46  2ᴺᴼ Wilb'nT¹ Cond 2:01  Chemung SlipAw'y SharonMamie
        Nov16-685Hol  1 :29⅘1:00⅘1:31⅗2:01⅗gd  4   30 1  2½  66⅝ 69½ M'rshJJr³ Cond 2:03⅘ M'sLust⅛t'n Torj'n D'styH.F'rbes
        Nov  9-685Hol  1 :29⅖ :59⅘1:30⅘1:59⅘ft 13  10 10 10¹⁵10¹⁷10¹⁶ M'hJJr¹⁰ Cond 2:02⁷ Harl'nLee RobertEden F'nnyMite
        Nov  2-689Hol  1 :31⅗1:02 1:32⅘2:01 ft 3⅘   8  6  65½ 6⁹  64½ M'rshJJr⁸ Cond 2:01⅘ C'ny'sNabob E'rl theP'l Cor'lR'ge
        Oct26-686Hol  1 :29  :59⅘1:30 1:59⅖ft 4½   2  3  42½ 3¹  1¹  M'shJrJ³ Cond 1:59⅖ SlipAway FannyMite CoralRidge
```

1 7-2

Morning Line Odds	Date of last race	Number of race	Track raced on	Distance of race	Leader's time at 1-4	Leader's time at 1-2	Leader's time at 3-4	Time of winner	Condition of track	Closing odds	Denotes favorite	Position at 1-4 mile	Position at 1-2 mile	Position at 3-4 mile	Lengths behind leader	Position in stretch	Lengths behind leader	Official finish position	Lengths behind winner	Driver	Post position	Type of race	Individual Time	BEST COMPANY LINES Horses Finishing First, Second and Third

STANDARD ABBREVIATIONS AND SYMBOLS

Horse's Color
b—bay
blk—black
br—brown
ch—chestnut
gr—gray
ro—roan

Horse's Sex
c—colt
f—filly
g—gelding
h—horse
m—mare
r—ridgeling

Track Conditions
ft—fast
gd—good
sl—slow
sy—sloppy
m—muddy
hy—heavy

Finish Information
no—nose
h—head
nk—neck
dis—distanced (more than 25 lengths)
dnf—did not finish
acc—accident

Class Of Race*
Qua—Qualifying
Mat—Matinee
Mdn—Maiden
2000—Claiming (actual value on horse)

   *Occasionally a horse will race where according to his earnings it appears that he was not eligible. However this horse qualified under a secondary

condition (also eligible). The past performance line will carry the main condition of the race as it shows the actual class of competition.

Racing Information
o—parked out
x—break
ix—interference break
ex—equipment break
‡—free-legged

⊛—won on other than fast or good track

Wagering Information
N. B.—Non-betting
N. R.—Not reported
▲—favorite
e—entry
f—field
c—claimed out of that race for the amount specified.

[From the Hollywood Park Program]

speed may vary by several seconds from one night to another. The programs might well offer their customers figures that would reflect such variations. Every insider knows to within a few fifths of a second how rapidly each grade of Standardbred gets the mile under ideal conditions at the local track. It would be simple enough to determine how greatly the time of each race on an evening's program deviated from the norm for its class. The average deviation would be the track's speed variant for that night. Included with the past-per-

HOW TO READ THE PROGRAM:

In reading the top past performance line on Earl Laird, below, the information from left to right indicates: the most recent start was July 28, 1966, in the 9th race at Sportsman's Park, a 5/8ths mile track. The distance was one mile and the leading horse reached the quarter-mile in 31-3/5 seconds, the half-mile in 1:03, the three-quarters in 1:33-1/5 and the mile in 2:02. The track was fast and Earl Laird, at even money, was the favorite. He was sixth and parked outside at quarter, second and still outside at the half, second 1¼ lengths behind the leader at the three-quarters, second 1 length behind the leader at the head of the stretch, and first by 2½ lengths at the finish. He was driven by R. Williams and had post position 1. The race was a stake with a $7,500 purse, Earl Laird's actual time was 2:02, and he was first with Volcanic Dan second and Be Sweet third.

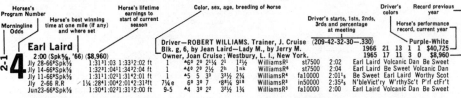

STANDARD ABBREVIATIONS AND SYMBOLS:

Horse's Color
b—bay
blk—black
br—brown
ch—chestnut
gr—gray
ro—roan

Horse's Sex
c—colt
f—filly
g—gelding
h—horse
m—mare ·
r—ridgeling

Track Conditions
ft—fast
gd—good
sl—slow
sy—sloppy
m—muddy
hy—heavy

Finish Information
no—nose
h—head
nk—neck
di—distanced (more than 25 lengths)
dnf—did not finish
acc—accident

CLASS OF RACE*
Qua—Qualifying
Mat—Matinee
Mdn—Maiden
2000—Claiming (actual value on horse)
nw1000—Non-winners of $1,000 etc. lifetime
w1000—Winners of $1,000, etc. lifetime
n2R—Non-winners of two races
nw1000⁶⁵—Non-winners of $1,000 in 1965
nw10000⁶⁵⁶⁶—Non-winners of $10,000 in 1965 and 1966
nw10000¹⁰—Non-winners of $10,000 in their last ten starts
3y5000—3-year-olds, etc. with purse value
pr4000—Preferred with purse value

in5000—Invitational with purse value
hp7500—Handicap with purse value
jfa7500—Junior Free-For-All with purse value
fa10000—Free-For-All with purse value
st7500—Stake with purse value

*Occasionally a horse will race where according to his earnings it appears that he was not eligible. However this horse qualified under a secondary condition (Also eligible). The past performance line will carry the main condition of the race as it shows the actual class of competition.

RACING INFORMATION
o—parked out

x—break
ix—interference break
ex—equipment break
‡—free-legged
⊕—won on other than fast or good track
†—footnote
(P) Provisional license—Drivers not possessing one year driving experience and 25 satisfactory starts at extended pari-mutuel meetings.

WAGERING INFORMATION
N.B.—Non-betting
N.R.—Not reported
▲—favorite
e—entry
f—field
c—claimed out of that race for the amount specified

[From the Sportsman's Park Program]

formance data, the variant would put a horse's times into better perspective.

PACE: One of the basics of Standardbred handicapping, pace is most effectively analyzed if the player knows how far behind or ahead a horse was at each stage of his race. Most programs show this

HOW TO READ THE PROGRAM

The horse's head number, saddle cloth number, program number, mutuel number and post position are the same except where there is an entry in the race. The initials immediately following the horse's name represent color and sex, figures denote age. The names following are the horse's sire, dam, dam's sire and trainer in that order. In parentheses under the horse's name is the horse's lifetime earnings up to Jan. 1 of the current year. Also, lifetime win record, age when made and size of track, except half-mile track, through Dec. 31 of previous year. Then come the driver's name, weight and his colors. Alongside of that are the horse's last year's best winning time and track where made. Then his number of starts, how many times he finished first, second or third and his money winnings. Beneath the horse's earnings are records of his eight most recent races. They read from bottom to top, therefore the top is the horse's latest race .

The date of the race is followed by the name of the track. All tracks are half-mile unless followed by the figure (1) which means that it is a mile track; or (¾) which is a three-quarter mile track, etc. Then is noted the condition of the track on the day of the race and the type of the race. Where money figures follow track condition it denotes price of horse in claiming race. Race distance, time of leading horse at ¼, ½ and ¾ follow, then comes the winner's time. The figures that follow in order show the post positions of the horse, his position at the ¼, ½, ¾, stretch with lengths behind except for the leading horse whose number denotes lengths ahead; and finish with beaten lengths. If he was the winner it shows how far he was ahead of the second horse and the losers' show how far they were behind the winning horse. The next figure shows the horse's actual time in that race. Wherever a small "°" appears after the calls, it denotes that the horse raced on the outside at least one quarter of a mile. In some instances these figures won't appear because the track at which the horse raced did not have its races charted. Then follows the closing odds to the dollar, the horse's driver, and order of finish, giving the names of the first three horses.

In all races of ¾ mile or less, the fractional times will be carried for the ¼, ½, and time of race. In races of 1 1/16 and 1⅛ miles the times will be carried for ¼, ¾, Mile, and finish. In 1½ mile races the times will be at ¼, Mile, 1¼ and finish. Positions of the horses will correspond with the times in 1¼ and 1½ mile races.

ABBREVIATIONS AND SYMBOLS

HORSES COLOR AND SEX

b g—bay gelding
blk c—black colt
br m—brown mare
ch h—chestnut horse
gr f—grey filly
ro—roan

TRACK SIZE

(5/8)—5/8 mile track
(3/4)—3/4 mile track
(1)—one mile track

TRACK CONDITIONS

ft—fast
gd—good
sy—sloppy
sl—slow
hy—heavy
my—muddy

TYPE OF RACE

Cd 2,000—Conditioned & Purse
Stk—Stake
clm 3000—$3,000 claiming race (act. value on this horse)
nw 3000 (non-winners $3,000; etc.); Opt—optional claimer
cl—classified
ec—early closer
lc—late closer
qua—qualifying
mdn—maiden
Opn—Open
alw—Allowance Races
hcp—Handicap
Pref—Preferred
Inv—Invitational
tp—Trot and Pace

RACING INFORMATION

x—Break
ix—Interference Break
ex—Equipment Break
°—Parked Out
°°—Parked out 3 wide
wkt—Workout
be—Broken Equipment
(P)—Provisional Driver
‡—Free-legged Pacer
‡—Hobbled Trotter
m—One Mile
Z.—Horse Claimed
dr qua—Driver Qualifying
(NY)—N.Y. State Bred

WAGERING INFORMATION

f—mutuel field
e—entry
*—favorite
NB—No Betting
NR—Not Reported
DNF—Did Not Finish

FINISH INFORMATION

ns—nose
hd—head
nk—neck
dh—dead heat
dis—distanced
dq—Disqualification

PROGRAM and HEAD NUMBER | Free Legged | Horse's Name | Lifetime Win Record | Age When Made | Size of Track | Horse's color | Sex | Age | Sire | Dam | Dam's Sire | Best Win Time This Year | Name of Trainer

2 ‡**PAPPY'S JOY** (NY) blk h, 6, by Flow Up, Jenny VI by Jay Guy (Tr.-J. Jones)
Owner-Gay Stables, New York, N.Y. Lex(1) 2:02:4 1969 3 1 0 0 1,080.
($36,243) 3, 2:02:4 (1) (P) ABE SMITH (150) Green-White YR 2:03:1 1968 26 5 6 3 24,162.
5-16 YR‡ ft Cd A2000 m 30:1 1:03 1:35:2 2:05:3 3 1° 2x 4 3/3 5x/4dq 2:06:3 *1.20e(A.Smith)MacHugh,BabeHeir,MssTllyLee
5-5 YR‡ ft clm 4000 m 30:1 1:03 1:35:2 2:05:3 3 1° 2x 4 3/3 5x/4dq 2:06:3 *1.20e(A.Smith)MacHugh,BabeHeir,MssTllyLee

Date of Race | Track Raced On | Track Condition | Age, Type of Race, Purse | Distance of Race | Time at 1/4 | Time at 1/2 | Time at 3/4 | Time of Winner | Post Position | Position at 1/4 | Position at 1/2 | Position at 3/4 | Stretch Position and Lengths | Finish Position and Lengths | Actual Time | Odds to 1.00 | Best Win Time Last Year | Driver | Name of Winner | Second Horse | Third Horse

[From the Yonkers Raceway Program]

margin only at the stretch call and finish. A few show it only at the finish. A very few show it at the three-quarter-mile call, stretch and finish.

TRAINER: In recent years, some good trainers have begun to concentrate on training, employing so-called "catch drivers" to handle the reins in actual competition. No program tabulates the records of nondriving trainers, although such statistics are tremen-

HOW TO READ THE PROGRAM

The horse's head number, saddle cloth number, program number, mutuel number and post position are the same except where there is an entry in the race. The initials immediately following the horse's name represent color and sex, figures denote age. The names following are the horse's sire, dam and sire of dam in that order. Under the horse's name are his lifetime earnings and lifetime record preceded by his age when record was made up to January 1 of the current year. Following the lifetime earnings is the name of the driver, his date of birth, weight and his colors. Next is the horse's best winning time on a half-mile, five-eighths, three-quarter or mile track for last year and the current racing season, followed by his starts and the number of wins, seconds, thirds in purse races and his money winnings. Beneath the horse's name are records of his seven most recent races. They read from bottom to top, therefore the top line is the horse's last race.

The date of the race is followed by the name of the track. All tracks are half-mile unless followed by the figure (1) which means that it is a mile track or (⅝) which is a three-quarter mile track, etc. Then is noted the Purse, condition of the track on the day of the race, the Conditions of the race or if a Claiming Race the Claiming Price. Race distance, time of leading horse at the ¼, ½ and ¾ follow, then comes the winner's time. The figures that follow in order show the post position of the horse, his position at the ¼, ½, ¾, stretch with lengths behind except for the leading horse whose number denotes lengths ahead, and finish with beaten lengths. If he was a winner, it shows how far ahead of the second horse and the losers show how far they were behind the winning horse. The next figure shows the horse's actual time in that race. Whenever a small "o" appears after the calls, it denotes that the horse raced on the outside at least one-quarter of a mile. In some instances these figures won't appear because the track at which the horse raced did not have its races charted. Then follows the closing odds to the dollar, the horse's driver, and the order of finish, giving the names of the first three horses.

KEY TO ABBREVIATIONS

Horses' Colors	Horses' Sex	Track Conditions	Finish Information	Wagering Information	Race Classes
b—bay	c—colt	ft—fast	ns—nose	N.B.—No Betting	Cd.—Condition Race
blk—black	f—filly	gd—good	hd—head	N.R.—Not Reported	3000 clm—Actual claiming
br—brown	g—gelding	sy—sloppy	nk—neck	*—favorite	price on this horse
ch—chestnut	h—horse	sl—slow	dh—dead heat	e—entry	Clm.Al.—Claiming Allowance
gr—gray	m—mare	my—muddy	dis—distanced (over 25	f—field	Ec—early closing event
ro—roan		hy—heavy	lengths behind winner)		FA—Free for all
			P—Placing		JFA—Junior Free for all
					Hcp.—Handicap Race

Racing Information
- Inv.—Invitational Race
- °—raced on outside for at least ¼ mile
- (1)—Mile Track
- ax—break caused by accident
- Mdn.—Maiden Race
- x—horse broke at this point
- (⅝)—⅞ Track
- acc—accident
- Mat.—Matinee Race
- ‡—races without hopples
- B.E.—broken equipment
- ex—equipment break
- NW—Non-Winners
- ix—break caused by interference
- H.N.—head number
- dnf—did not finish
- Opn.—Open To All
- †—moved up in position at finish due to the disqualification of another horse.
- Opt.Clm.—Optional Claiming
- Qua. (Dr.)—Qualifying Race for driver.
- Pref.—Preferred
- Qua. (h-d)—Qualifying Race for both horse and driver.
- Qua.—Qualifying Race
- (P)—before driver's name indicates driver holds Provisional License issued to those with
- Stk.—Stake Race
- limited experience and subject to the approval of the Judges.
- T—Time Trial
- Z—horse claimed.
- W—Winners
- BAR—Barred in wagering.
- T.Dis.—Time for race was disallowed on this horse because of a placing due to other than a lapped on break at finish.

PROGRAM and HEAD NUMBER	Date of Race	Track Raced On	Purse	Track Condition	Type of Race Condition or Claiming Price	Distance of Race	Time at ¼	Time at ½	Time at ¾	Time of Winner	Post Position	Position at ¼	Position at ½	Position at ¾	Stretch Position and Lengths	Finish Position and Lengths	Horse's Actual Time	Equivalent odds to 1.00	Driver	Best Win Time of Year	Name of Winner	Name of Second Horse	Name of Third Horse
6																							

OVERTRICK   b c, 3, by Solicitor—Overbid by Hal Dale   Trainer-J. Patterson
$40,129 — 2, 1:59⁴ (1)   Mrs. Leonard J. Buck, Far Hills, N.J.   (⅝)1:57¹ 1963 9 6 1 0 34,283
7-27 LB⅜   Driver-JOHN PATTERSON, 6-14-20   (125)   GREY-YELLOW   (1)1:59⁴ 1962 16 10 3 0 40,129
10000 ft 3yr Stk mi 28² :58³¹:27²¹:57¹   6   3   3   1   1⁵   1⁶   1:57¹   *.30 (J.Patterson)   Overtrick,FrankT.Ace,JamesB.Han.

[From the Liberty Bell Program]

dously revealing. By the same token, most catch drivers are themselves trainers. Tabulated trainer standings would disclose whether these drivers do as well with their own horses as with those from other barns.

DRIVER: Most programs include listings of the track's leading drivers, showing how many starts, victories and seconds and thirds each has had during the current meeting. After a meeting has been under way for a week or so, and active reinsmen have had a representative number of starts, these listings are helpful. Considerably more helpful are programs that summarize the record of every driver in every race, or list the records of all local drivers in a separate tabulation. Still more helpful would be a method that not only revealed the driver's record at the current meeting but also showed how he had been doing elsewhere on the circuit or—if it still be early in the season—how he fared last year.

POST POSITION: At all half-mile and ⅝-mile tracks, inside post positions are advantageous and outside ones are handicaps. Something is missing from the program that neglects to reveal how many horses have started in each post position, how many have won from each position and what the percentages have been. Statistics for recent meetings would be helpful, especially during the first weeks of a new season.

Although I consider all those deficiencies regrettable, and could mention others, I do not think that they incapacitate the player. Fortunately, the Standardbred is such a reliable beast, and some drivers are so much more dependable than others, that the information contained in most programs is sufficient for intelligent play. Knowing the kinds of facts that probably are missing from the program, the handicapper simply treads carefully if he has not been at the raceway for a while. This may not be a bad thing in itself, encouraging the prudence for which no amount of information can substitute.

Nevertheless, I think most racegoers will agree with me that it would be nice to have all relevant information in the program. It would be an encouragement and a reassurance. It would increase the handicapping fan's pleasure by permitting him greater confidence in his judgments. Which would mean more frequent visits to the raceway and more frequent bets. Nothing could be fairer than that.

Periodicals

Lean pickings await the fan who goes to the average newsstand for help with his raceway handicapping. Having developed during an era of prohibitively expensive publishing costs, harness racing lacks national periodicals comparable to baseball's *The Sporting News,* Thoroughbred racing's *Daily Racing Form, Morning Telegraph* and *Thoroughbred Record,* and the flock of magazines that help to arouse and maintain informed awareness of what goes on in professional football, basketball, tennis and golf.

Significant changes in driver-trainer-owner relationships, the emergence of promising new horses and drivers, news of fines and suspensions, expertly detailed analyses of past and upcoming races—matters of this kind would be food and drink for someone interested in harness racing. Little or none is available. In the largest racing centers, the determined fan sometimes can find a newspaper sporting page on which dribs and drabs appear, but they are local in character. Out-of-town developments of the greatest importance go unreported. Horses break speed records while racing for enormous purses, and scarcely anyone outside the industry itself hears about it—perhaps not even in the city where the event occurs!

The lack of national news creates in every major racing center a weird insularity. The Yonkers fan assumes that if the feat did not take place in New York it did not take place at all. Which is why brilliant trainer-drivers such as Herve Filion and Bob Farrington, after setting incredible records at first-class raceways elsewhere, have been able to win at inflated mutuel prices in New York.

Among existing magazines, the following are worth attention:

Hoof Beats: Official monthly of the U.S. Trotting Association, this magazine is well edited, well written and magnificently illustrated with color photographs. Apart from short reports on matters of USTA policy, including occasional brief peeks at subjects of controversy, the magazine consists largely of personality profiles, historical reviews and technical advice on the care and training of Standardbreds. From these pieces and from the column, "In Harness," written by editorial director Stan Bergstein, the fan learns a good deal about the ideals, concerns and botherations of horsemen, and about current trends. None of this is vital to one's handicapping, but it makes the sport more enjoyable by bridging the gulf between the racing strip and the stands. The subscription rate is $6 a year from USTA, 750 Michigan Avenue, Columbus, Ohio 43215.

The Harness Horse: This weekly is one means of learning who has been winning what, and where. Not much detail, but a way of keeping up. Available at $12 a year from Box 1831, Harrisburg, Pa. 17105.

The Horseman and Fair World: Information similar to that in *The Harness Horse,* plus lists of the leading drivers at current meetings. Weekly, for $12 a year from Box 886, Lexington, Ky. 40501.

Trotter Weekly: As far as I know, this is the only weekly periodical that tries to enlarge its readers' knowledge of handicapping. Edited by Walter J. Rottkamp, an excellent selector in his own right, the magazine is of uneven quality but frequently contains useful advice and is always in there pitching with the names of horses and drivers expected to perform well. Available for $10 a year from Box 2300, Wantagh, N.Y. 11793.

Racing Star Weekly: I would not mention this weekly paper at all if its New York edition did not contain an excellent column by one "Hap Mason." In real life, he is harness-racing expert for a daily newspaper and one of the sharpest journalists in the field. His column in the *Star* is extremely informative about horses and the men who train and drive them. Otherwise the paper is exclusively for Thoroughbred racing fans. It is obtainable for $14 a year from Amerpub, Inc., 505 Eighth Avenue, New York, N.Y. 10018.

Sulky: Semiannual handicap ratings of all active Standardbreds and leading drivers, plus a method of adjusting the figures to the particular circumstances of the race. While I doubt that an accurate handicap rating of the average horse is likely to remain accurate for six weeks, much less six months, this booklet's driver ratings are fairly good. And the overall approach to handicapping a race is sound enough. The reader might enjoy trying to compare the results of his own handicapping methods with those of *Sulky*. It costs $10 a year from P.O. Box 5156, Lighthouse Point, Fla. 33064.

Books

Numerous books have been published about the handicapping of harness races. Most of them offer unproductive ideas in unreadable prose. The trouble with handicapping advice, of course, is that any charlatan can handicap a race after it is over. If he hopes to deceive the public or—as seems to be the case more often than not— if he is unable to resist deluding himself, he is perfectly free to confect unsupportable theories and generalizations. Two exceptions are these:

Win at the Trotters, by Warren Pack and Richard Davison. Before the newspaper that employed him gave up the ghost, Warren Pack was a highly competent and refreshingly opinionated harness-racing reporter and commentator. With Richard Davison, who owns Standardbreds, he put together this nice little manual, a reading of which will reward anyone interested in handicapping. Aside from an overemphasis on New York racing, the book's sole drawback is its brevity. Scarcely longer than a pamphlet, it gives only a lick and a promise to subjects about which the authors would have had more to say in a more adequate volume. Published at $1 in 1967 by Essandess Special Editions, a division of Simon & Schuster, Inc., 630 Fifth Avenue, New York, N.Y. 10020.

Success at the Harness Races, by Barry Meadow. The merits of this enthusiastic book outweigh its defects. Meadow seems a capable handicapper and communicates his ideas clearly. All his handicapping examples are drawn from New York races, and some cannot be made to conform with his theories without a good deal of stretching. But he takes pains to cover a wide range of possibilities and, in doing so, offers material more substantial than that of his predecessors in the field. Published at $4.95 in 1967 by Citadel Press, Inc., 222 Park Avenue South, New York, N.Y. 10003.

As I remarked much earlier, few sports have been the subject of more distinguished, scholarly literature than harness racing has. Unfortunately, most of the best historical works are already out of print and seldom can be obtained from libraries without difficulty. Among these, the finest is *The American Trotter,* by John Hervey, published in 1947 by Coward-McCann, Inc. Hervey was an absolutely first-rate historian and his book is a joy, full of names, atmosphere, exploits and the glamour of the past. Of good books still available, the best are:

Care and Training of the Trotter and Pacer, by James C. Harrison. Incomparably the finest work ever published about the techniques of a sport, this enormous volume is compulsory reading for whoever wants to know harness racing. All-time great drivers and trainers join Harrison in exploring every relevant subject from shoeing to feeding to driving tactics to paying stable expenses. Handicapping and betting are beyond the scope of the book, but it surely will improve the reader's selection procedures by expanding his knowledge of the sport. Published at $7.50 in 1968 by the USTA.

The Complete Book of Harness Racing, by Philip A. Pines. The director of the Hall of Fame of the Trotter, Goshen, N.Y., is Standardbred racing's foremost living historian. His large and lively book tells the fascinating story of the breed and the game. Nothing on handicapping, but rich in the background information which every handicapper should have.

Inside Information

In 1969, the celebrated quarterback of the New York *Jets,* Joe Namath, fell into an unseemly public wrangle with the American Football League. His New York saloon having become a hangout of hoodlums, the league demanded that Namath sell his partnership in the place. Almost simultaneously, owners of big-league baseball teams unloaded their stock in Las Vegas gambling casinos, having been prodded to do so by the commissioner of baseball.

To maintain the public confidence on which prosperity rests, all sports take pains to police the conduct of competitors both on and off the field. Recurrent hullabaloo about sports personalities and hoodlums, or suspected hoodlums, is occasioned by the well-documented belief that some characters go to great lengths to bet on sure things and are not above bribing or coercing susceptible athletes.

Harness racing's main problems with the underworld have been occasioned by the energetic, even violent resourcefulness with which thugs try to cash tickets on twin doubles, twin exactas and other bonanza bets. Bullyboys have been known to make life unpleasant for fans who declined to sell "live" twin tickets (potential winning ones) at bargain prices. Drivers foolish enough to associate with hoods have been roughed up for unsatisfactory performances, such as winning key races that their chums expected them to lose.

Obviously, if shenanigans of this kind were permitted to get out of hand, the only people at raceways would be gangsters. To produce the opposite effect, the industry has been vigorous about expelling undesirables from its grandstands, clubhouses and stable areas. Horsemen, including a few talented ones, have been booted out of the business or, in lesser cases, exiled for long periods. In punishing waywardness, and preventing it, the tracks are assisted by a USTA security staff and by Harness Tracks Security, Inc., a national investigative network headed by John L. Brennan, a former FBI administrator who spent many years doing similar work in Thoroughbred racing.

In implying that the worst is over, I should be careful to emphasize that the worst was not really all that dreadful. The underworld never made connections with more than an infinitesimal number of horsemen. The bullying of customers by goons who wanted to buy up all the live twin-double tickets did not dominate the atmosphere in the stands. Anyhow, a decent human being can now pay his way into a harness track with no expectation of being jostled by thieves and with every expectation of seeing honestly competitive sport.

But the appetite for a sure thing is not entirely an underworld phenomenon. Pillars of commerce, industry and the professions are capable of extraordinary behavior when they leave the office to seek pleasure. Hundreds of otherwise sensible persons have bought Standardbred horses, incurring the heavy financial burdens of stable ownership, for no reason other than their screw-loose belief that owners get hot tips.

Amusingly, some rather prominent stables are owned by folks who started as bettors and whose affection for horses, though increasing, does not yet surpass their interest in betting. Some of them wear iridescent suits, speak raucously and make a big thing of their familiarity with the famous horsemen whom they employ. The horsemen put up with this, and are even deferential to it, so long as the Johnny-come-latelies pay the bills promptly and refrain from causing embarrassment about bets.

Most horsemen are close-mouthed, even with their owners. They keep their own counsel because they were brought up that way, in the rural tradition, and because they know that Hell hath no fury like that of a fool who has been steered into a few losing bets. Obviously, a competent horseman knows when his own animal has a good chance of winning, and when it does not. Alas, he also realizes that it sometimes wins when he least expects it to, and loses when he least expects it to. He knows, furthermore, that he cannot pick a higher percentage of winners than a decent handicapper can, and that he could not do so even if he were to question every other trainer before every race.

The most that anyone can get out of the typical trainer or driver about a race in which he is involved is, "I think I've got a shot at it." Or, "I don't think so. That other filly is real tough." Most are even less communicative than that. A few are willing to confide their frank opinions to persons whom they trust not to embarrass them. But their opinions are emphatically not more dependable than those of a good handicapper.

In disputing this perhaps disappointing fact with me recently, a racegoing friend demanded, "What if the best horse in the race has gone sour in the last day or so, and only the trainer knows it? Wouldn't you want to know it, too? Wouldn't it help you to know it?"

Answer: If a horse goes seriously sour, its people scratch it from the race. If it goes only middling sour, but badly enough to endanger its chances, the change in its condition often is plainly noticeable during the prerace warm-ups and parade. Finally, it may win when sour or lose when fit. The purpose of this chapter is to arm the reader with the attitudes and insights that are basic to good handicapping. The present section of the chapter should be read and understood in that light. Inside information, or what passes for it, may sometimes help the handicapper to confirm his own judgments but should never be permitted to unhorse those judgments.

One of the most colorful bettors of modern times was active at eastern raceways. In fact, he became an owner of horses, both as employer and partner of some of the sport's foremost trainer-drivers. What made him colorful was the enormous amounts of money he won when he was hot, and the enormous sums he lost when he was not. He was notorious for this before he owned horses, and he remained so after he began chumming around with top horsemen. He would make a small fortune, then lose it and disappear for a while until he accumulated a fresh stake. Everybody liked him. Nobody mistrusted him. If any bettor had access to inside information, it was he. It did him absolutely no good. At this writing he has been absent from the raceways for years, presumably in pursuit of a new bankroll.

A horseman I know remembers him well. The horseman is a brilliant trainer and driver who was born and brought up in the sport. A fun-loving fellow, he enjoys betting when his duties permit him to leave the paddock and frolic in the clubhouse. I have been to the races with him more than a few times, and can certify that he is a good handicapper. That is, he wins almost as many bets as he loses. In discussing the colorful bettor mentioned above, this horseman says affectionately, "A nice guy. And a pretty sharp handicapper. Did I ever tell you about the time he talked me into betting on one of my own horses and the damned thing won?"

Please note that the handicapper gave "inside information" to the horseman. And please remember that whatever inside information the handicapper got from horsemen was not dependable enough to make a long-term winner of him. He was an inconsistent selector before he ever became an owner, and inconsistent he remained.

Alleged inside information abounds at raceway bars, coffee counters and mutuel windows. Everybody is forever "giving winners" to everybody else. So-and-so says that such-and-such stable is going to bet with both hands tonight. Hot tip! The report spreads through the place and shortly is reflected in the decreasing odds on the horse.

The tips are not always false. Stables do bet, and news does leak. But stables lose bets, too. And the race is not unusual in which as many as three stables bet heavily on their own horses. How hot can a tip be if other stables ignore it to bet on their own animals?

Inside information is sometimes interesting, but is almost invariably worthless. In no circumstances is it as useful to the good handicapper as his own interpretation of the facts contained in the past-performance records. To disbelieve this is to discount handicapping and commit oneself to the great fraternity of those who spend their time prospecting for tips, and lose and lose and lose.

Tip Sheets

Some excellent handicappers peddle their racing selections in the tip sheets sold at raceway entrances. So do some mediocre handicappers. And handicappers of both kinds prepare selections for daily newspapers. The best of these public selectors develop substantial followings. Their loyal customers flock to the mutuel windows to bet as advised, and the odds drop.

A racegoer who knows nothing about the horses is undoubtedly better off with a popular tip sheet than with a hat pin. But nobody can stay ahead of the game by playing these selections, no matter how bright the tip-sheet handicapper may be.

The reason for this apparent contradiction is that the traditions of the tip-sheet trade require the handicapper to make selections in every race on every program. Moreover, to increase the number of winning selections, he often picks three or four horses per race, listing them in order of preference but claiming victory even when the second or third or fourth preference wins. Thus, to hit as many winners as the tip sheet claims for itself, the innocent customer must play three or four horses in every race, which is a recipe for disaster.

Even if he plays only the top selections, the customer courts insolvency by playing every race. Nobody can show a profit through play on every race on every program. Some races are too full of breakers to play. Others are too close for firm decision. But the tip sheets fail to make these distinctions.

All this being so, the tip sheet is of no value to a handicapper. Neither are newspaper selections. Neither, for that matter, are the track handicapper's selections published in some programs. And neither, by the way, are the "best bets" of public selectors. In naming a horse as "best bet" of the night, the tip sheet or newspaper usually singles out an animal which has a splendid chance of winning, but whose odds are too low. "Best bets" invariably lead to long-run financial loss, the percentage of winners not being high enough to overcome the skimpy mutuel prices.

The Handicapper's Notebook

On Friday evening, December 20, 1968, the seventh race at Hollywood Park offered a $5,000 purse to pacers that had won more than $5,000 during the year but had been unable to win any of their three most recent starts.

Leaving from post position two was this gelding:

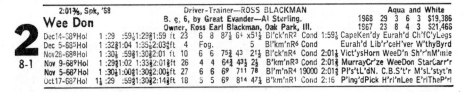

Though ignored in the betting on December 14, when it went off at 23 to 1, the six-year-old had made up considerable ground in the final quarter-mile. It apparently broke stride near the finish, yet crossed the wire only a length and a half behind the winner.

The leader at the three-quarter-mile call had been timed in 1:29:2,* and the final time of the race was 1:59—meaning that the last quarter had been covered in :29:3. Yet Wee Don had paced the final quarter more swiftly than that, gaining six full lengths. Calculating a length as equivalent to one-fifth of a second, as is customary, one can assume that Wee Don traveled the final quarter-mile in :28:2, which is high speed. Perhaps the horse broke stride from exhaustion.

But what kind of race was it? The past-performance line said only "Cond"—for "conditioned." What were the conditions? California harness-race fanciers are able to solve riddles of that kind. Their editions of *The Daily Racing Form* publish complete result charts, including footnote commentary about the way races are contested and how various key animals perform.

* One minute, twenty-nine and two-fifths seconds. The harness-racing industry has not yet achieved agreement on how best to translate this kind of statistic into numbers. Depending on local preference, the time is presented as 1:29⅖, or 1:29² or 1:29:2 (which would mean 1:29 plus two-tenths to anyone unfamiliar with the ways of this sport).

Let us now look at the chart of Wee Don's December 14 race:

NINTH RACE **1 MILE PACE. (Adios Butler [E.Cobb]—1:55⅗—10-29-60.)**
Hol Har **Conditioned. Purse $5,000. All ages. For winners of over $5,000 in 1968.**
Dec. 14, 1968
Value to winner, $2,500; second, $,1250; third, $600; fourth, $400; fitfh, $250. Mutuel Pool, $137,938.

Index	Horses	PP	St	¼	½	¾	Str	Fin	Driver	Time	Owners	Odds to $1
12- 9-68[1]	—Cape Kennedy	5	7	$7^{1½}$	5^{h}	5½	5^{h}	1¾	T Wilburn	1:59.00	Green Hornet Stable Inc	2.90
12- 5-68[1]	—Eurahead	6	3	2½	6^{1}	6^{1}	4^{1}	2no	J O'Brien	1:59.16	J Alderman	4.30
11-30-68[3]	—Chief Crazy Legs	8	4	5^{2}	$1^{1½}$	1^{2}	$1^{1½}$	3¾	R Williams	1:59.18	Genevieve Riley	2.40
11-28-68[1]	—Victorys Horn	7	8	8	7½	$7^{1½}$	8	4no	J W'iamsJr.	1:59.36	B N Redden	15.50
12- 5-68	—Wee Don	2	6	6^{2}	8	8	6^{1}	x$5^{2½}$	R Blackman	1:59.37	R E Blackman	23.50
21- 9-68[2]	—Sharon Mamie	1	5	4½	$4^{1½}$	3½	$7^{1½}$	6½	W Long	1:59.80	Bobby-Ken Stable-King	12.30
11-29-68	—Meadow Brick	3	2	1^{1}	3^{h}	4^{1}	3½	7	J Dennis	1:59.90	Grant-Miller	4.90
12- 4-68[4]	—Cardinal King	4	1	3^{1}	$2^{1½}$	2^{1}	2^{2}	xDNF	W Cameron		Nevele Acres	11.10

Time, :29, :59⅕, 1:29⅖, 1:44, 1:59. Track fast.

$2 Mutuel Prices				
	5-CAPE KENNEDY	7.80	4.00	3.20
	6-EURAHEAD		4.40	3.20
	8-CHIEF CRAZY LEGS			3.00

B. c, 3, by Capetown—Kitty Bird. Trainer, T. Wilburn.
AT GATE—10:51. OFF AT 10:51 PACIFIC STANDARD TIME. START GOOD. WON DRIVING.
CAPE KENNEDY lacked early speed, rallied in the drive and finished fast to wear down the leaders in the closing stages. EURAHEAD was blocked on the final turn, got clear and rallied late. CHIEF CRAZY LEGS set the pace and slackened. SHARON MAMIE had to check in the stretch while searching for room. WEE DON was interfered wi th.CARDINAL KING broke stride and fell at the finish.

First off, we see that the eligibility conditions of the race were identical with those of the December 20 race. The footnotes disclose that Wee Don suffered interference. Apparently the gelding broke stride because Cardinal King was staggering around in front of him, or causing other horses to. Very good. Wee Don's race was even better than the past-performance program suggested, and the break in stride was completely excusable.

The result chart revealed enough to enable many handicappers to recognize Wee Don as a sound choice. The horse won at a generous mutuel price of $10.60. Later, we shall handicap an entire Hollywood Park program which occurred almost a year later, in November, 1969. We shall see that the California raceway's program by then had become more communicative about the class differences among conditioned races. Nevertheless, result charts remain extremely useful—especially when they are as detailed as the kind that explained Wee Don's break in stride. Players unable to get the track program every day may be fortunate enough to live where the sporting page of the daily newspaper publishes charts. If the charts show nothing more than the purse, eligibility conditions and fractional times of the races, plus the post positions, drivers and stage-by-stage racing positions of the horses, they are valuable. Conscientious handicappers collect them.

Are they a necessity? Only to someone who hates to lose a bet he might have won. Players with a more casual attitude toward the hobby can manage without the charts, but might be interested in experimenting with them. Where the program is silent about the actual class of a previous race, a file of charts becomes a blessing. Where the program shows that a horse raced unexpectedly well at high odds, the chart may show that the driver simply benefited from a pile-up among other horses, or that one of the top contenders in the race was trapped on the rail during the decisive stages, or was forced to race too far on the outside.

On the other hand, if a horse's latest performance seemed poor, the chart helps the handicapper to decide whether the animal had gone off form or was merely a victim of circumstances. Note how many pacers in Wee Don's December 14 race emerged from it with legitimate excuses for losing.

A convenient place for charts is the pocket of a loose-leaf binder, unless the fan is willing to paste each on a separate page of the notebook. On those pages he also might want to calculate nightly track variants. This method of interpreting the true significance of speed will be described in a later chapter.

Still another function of the notebook comes into play during winter months, when extreme cold not only affects fractional and final times but also makes apparent quitters of perfectly game Standardbreds. The handicapper who records the temperature solves many winter mysteries and cashes some nice tickets. More on weather later, of course.

Among the most intriguing sights at any raceway are handicappers who make their own charts. Usually working in teams, they log everything they can about every horse, from the moment it emerges from the paddock for its first jogging warm-up. Present every night, some of these handicappers work with plywood panels on which eight or nine stopwatches are mounted, so that they can time the warm-ups. I shall have more to say about the timing of warm-ups when the subject falls due. I mention it now to suggest the lengths to which a human being may go when in the grip of a hobby.

Binoculars

Although one of the main virtues of half-mile tracks is good visibility from the stands, binoculars make a significant difference, even in the best seats. Whether or not you are interested in crossing every "t" and dotting every "i" to make your handicapping supremely successful, a pair of seven- or eight-power binoculars will increase your enjoyment of the sport. Seeing more, you understand more about driving tactics and the problems of the parked or boxed-in horse.

When to Handicap

Advance copies of the past-performance records are available on the day of the race at newsstands in many cities. Some tracks distribute the material a day earlier than that. On the Illinois–California circuit, *The Daily Racing Form* publishes the past performances, and usually can be obtained on the morning of the races, if not the night before.

Although important late developments like scratches and driver changes are not included in these advance materials, they offer the handicapper a chance to work in peace. Twenty minutes before post time is a difficult time and the track a difficult place for handicapping. The sights and sounds, the distracting remarks, the changes on the tote board and most especially the prerace performances of the horses all deserve attention, sometimes for fun and sometimes for handicapping purposes. One can't have one's nose in a program and one's eyes and ears open to other stimuli without spoiling something.

Because I enjoy the challenge of handicapping, and resent interference with that pleasure, I take pains to get most of the work done before I arrive at the track. There I quickly catch up on the late changes and adjust my figures accordingly. This leaves me free to heckle my companions, if any, while watching the warm-ups, the tote board and the races themselves.

A particularly pleasant approach is to go to the track early for dinner at a table with a good view. If alone or accompanied by someone blessed with the gift of silence, you can down the drinks and the food and do your handicapping before the action starts. As I hope to convince everyone, the handicapping itself does not take long, if done in an orderly way.

2

Know Your Track

MODERN TIMES BEGAN for harness racing in 1940, when
George Morton Levy, a New York lawyer with tremendous political
clout, obtained legislative approval for night racing with pari-mutuel
betting at Roosevelt Raceway, a sometime motordrome at Westbury,
Long Island.

Under less intrepid auspices, the new era might have ended almost
as soon as it began. Harness racing had been mildly popular in New
York at the turn of the century, but hardly anyone remembered and
fewer cared. The sports fans of the metropolitan area avoided Roosevelt Raceway with great determination during its first seasons, belying
the theory that they would bet on anything if given the chance.

The races were dreary. The drivers' main strategy seemed to consist
of trying to gain unfair advantage by leaving the starting line ahead of
everyone else, or by tricking other drivers into trying it. Repeated
false starts and recalls delayed some races for more than a half-hour,
leaving many horses too exhausted or unnerved to perform well. A
shrewdly handled animal able to get to the first turn on the lead was a
mortal cinch to finish no worse than third. Because the track was
hungry for every dollar it could get at the betting windows, wagering
often continued until the horses had reached that turn, a state of
affairs which permitted larcenous syndicates to make last-second
place and show bets on whatever nag was in front at the time.

The indomitable Levy and his faithful associates put a stop to that
nonsense in 1946, when they began using the mobile starting gate, on
the development of which they had invested $50,000 of their own
dwindling capital. The inventor, Steve Phillips, had introduced the
idea in 1937, after watching movie cameramen shoot head-on pictures
of races from the back of a moving truck. His device was an auto-
mobile equipped with a barrier behind which trotters and pacers

moved rapidly and fairly to the starting line, whereupon the car would speed away, leaving the animals on their own.

In 1940, a total of 59 programs of pari-mutuel harness racing had been attended by 126,000 customers in the United States. These high-rolling tourists had bet an average of less than $15 each, making the sport's total mutuel handle for that year a bit more than $1.7 million. In 1950, with the mobile gate firmly established and the sport finally becoming believable as honest competition, 1,181 programs of racing attracted almost 6.5 million customers and a handle above $245 million. And in 1970, about 26 million clients will bet upward of $2 billion on more than 4,000 programs. Levy and his partners were the first but by no means the last raceway operators to count their profits in the millions.

Nighttime pari-mutuels and the mobile gate were fundamental to urban acceptance of the sport. Other innovations have enhanced its popularity by heightening its excitement or, more substantially, by improving its quality and consistency. Some of these innovations, like

Pacers approach the start behind mobile gate at Delaware, Ohio Fair Grounds, home of the classic Little Brown Jug.

year-round racing and multiple bets of the exacta variety, have already been mentioned. Others are of quite considerable meaning to the handicapper, because they lead to the formful competition which rewards handicapping. The reader should know of these developments:

1. *Improved equipment:* Wheel discs now prevent the miserable accidents caused when hooves become fouled in wheel spokes. A new type of sulky places the driver's weight behind the wheels rather then directly above them, preventing downward thrust by the sulky shafts and sparing horses this extra burden, on which some of their leg ailments and more than a few of their racing inconsistencies have been blamed. At this writing, the new design is still regarded as experimental.

Leading Harness Raceways

Mile Tracks
BAY MEADOWS, San Mateo, Cal.
DU QUOIN STATE FAIR, Du Quoin, Ill.
FAIRMOUNT PARK, Collinsville, Ill.
HAWTHORNE, Cicero, Ill.
HOLLYWOOD PARK, Inglewood, Cal.
ILLINOIS STATE FAIR, Springfield.
INDIANA STATE FAIR, Indianapolis.
LATONIA RACEWAY, Florence, Ky.
NEW YORK STATE FAIR, Syracuse.
THE RED MILE, Lexington, Ky.
SCARBOROUGH DOWNS, Scarborough, Me.
WASHINGTON PARK, Homewood, Ill.
WOLVERINE RACEWAY, Livonia, Mich.

Thirteen-sixteenths-mile Track
ASSINIBOIA DOWNS, Winnipeg, Man.

Three-quarter-mile Tracks
CAHOKIA DOWNS, East St. Louis, Ill.
VERNON DOWNS, Vernon, N.Y.

Eleven-sixteenths-mile Track
RACEWAY PARK, Toledo, O.

Five-eighths-mile Tracks

ATLANTIC CITY RACEWAY, Atlantic City, N.J.
BAY STATE RACEWAY, Foxboro, Mass.
BLUE BONNETS, Montreal, Que.
BRANDYWINE RACEWAY, Wilmington, Del.
DOVER DOWNS, Dover, Del.
GARDEN CITY, St. Catherine's, Ont.
GREEN MOUNTAIN PARK, Pownal, Vt.
GREENWOOD RACEWAY, Toronto, Ont.
HAZEL PARK, Hazel Park, Mich.
LAUREL RACEWAY, Laurel, Md.
LIBERTY BELL PARK, Philadelphia, Pa.
MOHAWK RACEWAY, Campbellville, Ont.
POCONO DOWNS, Wilkes-Barre, Pa.
POMPANO PARK, Pompano Beach, Fla.
RIDEAU-CARLETON, Ottawa, Ont.
SCIOTO DOWNS, Columbus, O.
SPORTSMAN'S PARK, Cicero, Ill.
THE MEADOWS, Meadow Lands, Pa.
WINDSOR RACEWAY, Windsor, Ont.

Half-mile Tracks

AUDUBON PARK, Henderson, Ky.
AURORA DOWNS, North Aurora, Ill.
BALMORAL PARK, Crete, Ill.
BANGOR RACEWAY, Bangor, Me.
BATAVIA DOWNS, Batavia, N.Y.
BLOOMSBURG FAIR, Bloomsburg, Pa.
BUFFALO RACEWAY, Hamburg, N.Y.
CARLISLE FAIR, Carlisle, Pa.
CHARLOTTETOWN, Prince Edward Island
COLDBROOK, New Brunswick
CONNAUGHT PARK, Lucerne, Que.
CUMBERLAND RACEWAY, Cumberland, Me.
DELAWARE FAIR, Delaware, O.
EXHIBITION PARK, Sherbrooke, Que.
FREDERICTON, New Brunswick
FREEHOLD RACEWAY, Freehold, N.J.
GEORGETOWN RACEWAY, Georgetown, Del.
HARRINGTON RACEWAY, Harrington, Del.
HINSDALE RACEWAY, Hinsdale, N.H.

HISTORIC TRACK, Goshen, N.Y.
INVERNESS, Nova Scotia
JACKSON RACEWAY, Jackson, Mich.
JACQUES CARTIER, Quebec City, Que.
LAVIOLETTE, Three Rivers, Que.
LEBANON RACEWAY, Lebanon, O.
LEWISTON RACEWAY, Lewiston, Me.
LOUISVILLE DOWNS, Louisville, Ky.
LOWER SACKVILLE, Nova Scotia
MAYWOOD PARK, Maywood, Ill.
MONCTON, New Brunswick
MONTICELLO RACEWAY, Monticello, N.Y.
NORTHFIELD PARK, Northfield, O.
NORTHLANDS PARK, Edmonton, Alberta
NORTHVILLE DOWNS, Northville, Mich.
OCEAN DOWNS, Ocean City, Md.
RICHELIEU PARK, Montreal, Que.
ROCKINGHAM PARK, Salem, N.H.
ROOSEVELT RACEWAY, Westbury, N.Y.
ROSECROFT RACEWAY, Oxon Hill, Md.
SAGUENAY RACEWAY, Jonquiere, Que.
SAINT JOHN'S, Newfoundland
SARATOGA HARNESS, Saratoga Springs, N.Y.
SKOWHEGAN RACEWAY, Skowhegan, Me.
SUFFOLK DOWNS, East Boston, Mass.
SUMMERSIDE, Prince Edward Island
SYDNEY, Nova Scotia
TRURO, Nova Scotia
WESTERN FAIR RACEWAY, London, Ont.
WHEELING DOWNS, Wheeling, W.Va.
WOODSTOCK, New Brunswick
YONKERS RACEWAY, Yonkers, N.Y.

But the extra speed produced by certain horses when racing to it would seem to promise eventual acceptance. Another useful innovation are mud guards or fenders which permit more formful racing in wet weather by protecting horses and drivers from blinding splashes of muddy slop. Also promising are plastic horseshoes, lighter and more comfortable than metal. The lighter the shoe, the fleeter the horse.

    2. *Improved surfaces:* Harness raceways have pioneered in the use of synthetic racing surfaces. The Meadows and Laurel and Windsor

Raceways have plastic strips. Roosevelt Raceway uses a rubber one. The artificial surfaces are uniformly fast, regardless of weather. When slightly cushioned with sand, they seem to cause less soreness and lameness than do other kinds of footing. With rare exception, modern raceways have installed advanced drainage systems and fast-drying surfaces, making for fewer reversals of form after a rain.

   3. *Segregated paddocks:* Modern raceway design includes a fully enclosed paddock large enough to accommodate every horse on the program. The rules expressly bar the area to anyone not needed there, while keeping all animals in one place, safe from tamperers but visible to the audience.

   4. *Prerace testing:* Simple, rapid, harmless blood tests now reveal before the race whether a horse's system contains unlawful medication. Compulsory at Ohio raceways, these tests should become standard everywhere. The conventional post-race urine test should remain in use to discourage malpractice during the interval between the prerace blood sampling and the race itself. The familiar saliva test is of little use and should be abandoned.

   5. *Qualifying races:* These purseless engagements are required for horses that break stride too often or that behave badly before or during races or that fail to produce speed up to the local standard or that have been sidelined by illness or injury. At major tracks, no such horse is allowed into a betting race until demonstrating readiness in a qualifier. The "Qua" notation in the past-performance record often causes handicapping problems—but not insoluble ones, as we shall see. The chief effect on the qualifying races (where they are properly conducted), is to assure the public that a horse permitted to start in a betting event is fit for competition.

   6. *U.S. Trotting Association:* Formed in 1939 after years of chaos in which rival factions had been competing for national control of the sport, the USTA provides big-league continuity and uniformity where cannibalism once reigned. All but a very few raceways are members of the association. The nonmembers avail themselves of its indispensable services through contracts. The USTA licenses officials, drivers, trainers and owners, and maintains computerized records of all races and all horses. No unregistered, uncertified Standardbred can compete at any USTA track. Wherever a trotter or pacer may travel, he is accompanied by his USTA eligibility certificate, which itemizes his breeding, the names of his owners, his time and earnings records and the details of all his race performances during the current year, plus equal detail on at least six of his races during the previous year.

   State regulations governing the conduct of the sport tend to conform with the USTA's own developing standards, but not in all particulars, at all times, in all places. For example, a horseman suspended at one USTA track is unlikely to find work at another, although exceptions occur.

The USTA is dictatorial neither in its powers nor preferences, but it does so well that no serious proposal has been made to decorate harness racing with the kind of "czar" resorted to by other sports. Interestingly, the USTA is the only supervisory body in major professional sport that is not fully controlled by the sport's promoters. Horsemen, owners, breeders and racing officials all are members and all, in accordance with USTA regulation, are duly represented on the board of directors. Each member has one vote, which counts as much as the vote allowed someone who owns stock in a raceway or is employed in raceway management. USTA pronouncements represent a consensus in which raceway management, while understandably influential, is far from dominant. Unlike their counterparts in professional baseball, basketball, football and flat racing, harness-raceway owners cannot cause edicts to be issued in the name of the sport.

One important feature of modern harness racing has been called an innovation, but really is not. The half-mile track has been, furthermore, a sore point among trainers and drivers since the earliest days of country-fair competition. On the other hand, it has always been a source of delight for spectators. Because the length of a track can be a problem for handicappers, the time has come for us to examine the half-miler, and then the ⅝-mile and mile tracks.

The Half-Milers

Before the pari-mutuel era, championships were decided on one-mile tracks. Horsemen acknowledged their long stretches and gradual turns as supreme tests of Standardbred speed and heart. Racing luck was a minimal factor. Wherever else trotters and pacers might have competed during the season, their moments of ultimate truth occurred in classic confrontations on mile-long ovals at Lexington, Ky., Indianapolis, Ind., Springfield, Ill., and Goshen and Syracuse, N.Y.

Then as now, the title of "champion" had two meanings. For practical purposes, a harness-racing champion has always been the horse that went out and whipped the best of its age and gait, winning lots of purse money. But in the record books and other communications of the sport, "champion" also designates the animal that travels the fastest mile of the year for its age, gait and sex. A "world champion" is one that sets an all-time speed record. Moreover, seasonal and world championships are recorded for each age and sex and for trips at distances other than a mile, and for performances at various distances on half-mile, ⅝-mile and mile tracks. Literally dozens of speed champions are crowned each year, some for records set not in actual races but in time trials.

Timed speed is more than the stuff of which record books are compounded and championships confected. It is the essence of harness racing. It is the sport's fundamental measure. It is the main standard whereby horsemen identify potentially valuable breeding stock. Because the most impressive times are achieved and competition is fairest in trips that involve only two turns, the one-mile tracks retain an exalted place in the sport.

Classic trotting races like the Hambletonian and the Kentucky Futurity are still held at one-mile tracks, although competition for enormous purses at half-mile and ⅝-mile raceways invariably affects the national rankings. In pacing, the shift of championship emphasis to shorter tracks is even more noticeable. The so-called "Big Four" races for three-year-old pacers take place at three half-milers and one ⅝-mile track. Horsemen continue to prize young pacers that win in good time or set new records at Indianapolis, Du Quoin, Lexington or Springfield, but the biggest purses and headlines are elsewhere. Inasmuch as two half-mile plants, Yonkers and Roosevelt Raceways, account for about a third of the total mutuel handle in the United States each year, the change is understandable.

Among the hundreds of racing strips at country fairgrounds, half-milers have always been overwhelmingly numerous. Few fair associations could afford to construct and maintain the mile tracks required for nationally significant competition. Half-milers occupied less real estate and were more practical for all but the largest fairs. Good horses often raced at those half-milers, but not usually when important issues were at stake.

The epochal success of Roosevelt Raceway demonstrated that urban audiences did not consider a half-mile track inferior. Indeed, it is suggested with vehemence that Roosevelt's success was due substantially to the pell-mell excitement of races that begin directly in front of the stands and end there after the horses have scrambled around four hairpin turns. When Yonkers Raceway was erected on the site of the old Empire City course, what had been a mile track was converted into a half-miler and became more lucrative than Roosevelt. This, plus the economics of raceway construction, encouraged most

Bret Hanover goes three wide half-way through first heat of the 1965 Little Brown Jug, which he won in a record 1:57—fastest mile ever paced on a half-mile track.

other operators to build half-milers during the sport's period of rapid expansion.

With agreement that verges on unanimity, horsemen point out that the best horse is less likely to prevail on a half-miler than on a longer track. Where races involve four turns and the stretches are short, luck and post position play unnaturally important roles, they say. They add that powerful, long-striding Standardbreds are at serious disadvantages on the tight bends. And that horses of all kinds tend to break down under the strain. And that it's a crying shame when an animal with the great heart needed for a real stretch drive loses to nimbler horses which can skip around the turns at a half-miler and need no stretch kick because there's no stretch worth mentioning. And so on.

To all such complaints, the standard answer long has been that half-mile tracks are ideal for the spectator, who pays the bills. He can see everything. The horses pass before him three times—at the start, halfway and at the finish. And competition is keen. The short straightaways force the drivers to stay as close to the pace-setter as they can. Knowing that large amounts of lost ground seldom are recoverable in the short homestretch, they hustle for the early lead and keep hustling for position throughout. This makes for an exciting spectacle.

What excites the spectator, however, may depress the handicapper. Horses get in each other's way more frequently at half-mile tracks. Regardless of whether the drivers use unfair tactics, the contours of the oval guarantee jams. Moreover, a horse with the slightest tendency to grab a knee with a hoof is going to do it sooner or later on one of those turns and lose a race he figured to win.

Fortunately, there is more to the question of the half-mile track than one might think after reading the foregoing review of conventional pros and cons. In harness racing, as in all other earthly pursuits, man and animal tend to adapt to the challenges of environment. A striking example of such adaptation occurred in 1950, when a 23-year-old named Stanley Dancer invaded Yonkers, won everything in sight and began what has amounted to a revolution in the racing and training of Standardbreds, not only at half-milers but everywhere else.

As implied earlier, good horses used to be educated for the competition at mile tracks. In those races, the first three-quarters of the mile were merely prelude, the all-out racing coming in the final quarter. At the start, the drivers would find positions on the rail and then would travel Indian file until the home turn, where the action began. Although these tactics were impracticable at half-mile tracks, the tendency of drivers was to modify them but slightly, reserving as much horse for the final drive as the competition would permit. And then along came Dancer.

He trained his horses to leave quickly and go as far as they could, as fast as they could. He won race after race this way, his horses often finishing on their hands and knees but with insurmountable leads. He won so often that the only recourse for other drivers was to leave with him, fight him for the lead, make him earn his way. In the process, they had to leg up their own horses for that kind of racing. The spectacle at half-mile tracks became more spectacular than ever.

Curiously, a kind of equilibrium set in. With the development and establishment of sprinting tactics especially suited to half-mile tracks, it became evident that certain horses and a small minority of drivers could sustain such tactics, whereas others could not. In light of this fact, successful handicapping became possible.

Dancer's great rival in the topmost echelon of Standardbred racing is Billy Haughton, who says, "For a horse to do any real good in New

York he has to be able to rough it for five-eighths of a mile on the outside. This is a fact of life and you have to learn to live with it."

Another fact of life at half-mile tracks is that the horse may be able to rough it but may be a poor betting risk unless his driver is a certified topnotcher. The barns at Yonkers and Roosevelt are full of horses that can rough it when in shape. But relatively few drivers can be relied on to make best use of that ability in the helter-skelter of the race.

The handicapper and his onrushing competitor, the would-be handicapper, are urged to consider the following fundamental truths about half-mile tracks:

1. The short stretches and the four sharp turns enlarge the problem of racing luck. But the best drivers have the best luck.

2. Post position is important. Horses with the five inside holes enjoy pronounced advantages. If the horse marooned in position 7 or 8 is not considerably faster and fitter than any of its rivals, the handicapper prefers an animal with an inside spot.

3. Yet the talents of the driver often are more significant than the advantages of post position. As we shall see, the top driver who leaves from berth 7 or 8 is a better bet than the lesser driver who tries to navigate an equally fit horse from an inside spot in the same race.

4. If a horse has been racing at mile and ⅝-mile tracks without displaying early speed, it may be at a severe disadvantage in its first race or two at a half-miler, where slow leavers suffer.

5. A horse is seldom worth attention at a half-miler unless its record suggests readiness to rough it on the outside without perishing in the stretch. Or—and this amounts to the same thing—the horse should seem ready to produce enough early speed to stay out of trouble all the way, while reserving some wallop for the finish.

The ⅝-Milers

Recognizing the costs of constructing and maintaining a mile track, leading horsemen advocate the ⅝-miler as a fitting compromise. On a strip of this length, the traditional mile race involves only three turns, each of which is less precipitous than those at a half-mile track. Furthermore, the stretches are long enough to permit a strong horse to overtake a tiring leader in the final strides, which means that a wide range of racing tactics is possible. The driver more often can design the tactics to suit the horse and its opposition, rather than employ the sometimes unsuitable tactics dictated by the tighter contours of half-mile tracks.

As if additional elbow room and fewer problems of racing luck were not sufficient, drivers and trainers declare that horses remain sounder on ⅝-mile tracks. Also, animals with a tendency to knock knees do perfectly well on these slightly longer ovals, but encounter bad trouble on the turns at half-milers.

Although the sport's biggest mutuel handles and purses are found at Yonkers and Roosevelt, these great half-mile operations have no part of a monopoly on the best racing stock or the best drivers and trainers. The top ⅝-mile tracks, Sportsman's Park, Liberty Bell and Brandywine, offer purses that compare favorably with New York's— especially in the bread-and-butter races that predominate on any track's nightly program. It is argued, furthermore, that a fleet, reasonably sound animal of average quality can make more money on the ⅝-mile tracks because it holds its form for longer periods.

In the mid-1950's, when Roosevelt Raceway was about to renovate, eminent horsemen tried to persuade George Morton Levy and his associates that conversion to a ⅝-mile oval would benefit one and all. Levy doubted it, but agreed to investigate. The only ⅝-mile track with a race meeting in progress at the time was Hazel Park, near Detroit. Levy and his party arrived there on a night so wet, dark and foul that it would have made the Taj Mahal look bad. And Hazel Park is not the Taj Mahal. To put it mildly, Levy was unimpressed. What really finished the idea, however, was not the weather. The death blow was the remoteness of the starting line.

At a ⅝-mile track, the traditional mile race begins on the backstretch at the five-eighths pole, three-eighths of a mile from the finish line. The horses pass directly in front of the stands only twice. Those who favor half-mile tracks regard the backstretch start as a serious drawback. They believe that fans accustomed to the excitement of seeing races start under their noses would not take kindly to the other plan. In response to the observation that most Thoroughbred races start out of sight of any customer who lacks binoculars, and that the running-horse industry is not exactly on the rocks, the adherents of half-mile tracks declare that the flats would be better off if their races began in front of the stands.

The sincerity of these views is absolutely beyond question. Managements of half-mile tracks truly believe that their patrons would dislike ⅝-mile racing, even though such racing may involve fewer

upsets of form. Indeed, if the belief were not genuine, these managements might be attracted to certain other advantages of the ⅝-mile
design. For one thing, Sportsman's Park can accommodate nine-horse
fields, without requiring the ninth horse to start from a second tier
on the rail. This extra entry means additional differences of betting
opinion, helpful to the mutuel handle.

Even more helpful to trade at the windows is the fact that a horse
that leaves from post position 7 at Sportsman's Park is at no great
disadvantage. But at most half-milers, anything further from the rail
than post 5 is in a poor situation. In fact, at certain half-milers, the
four inside posts are overwhelmingly favorable. Where fields of seven
and eight horses are customary, but three or four of the starters are
handicapped by their post positions, competition is less keen than it
might be, and betting must reflect it.

Although half-milers outnumber other pari-mutuel raceways, it is
interesting to note that only two of the short ovals—the mighty Yonkers
and Roosevelt—consistently offer programs of top quality. A third
big-league half-miler, Brandywine, converted to a ⅝-mile strip during
1969.

If you are content with your own raceway and have no intention
of traveling elsewhere to try your skill at tracks of other dimensions,
these matters may not inflame your interest. But they are important
to an understanding of the sport and, above all, they involve issues
vital to handicapping.

At this stage of our discussion, the handicapper should keep the
following facts in mind about ⅝-mile tracks:

1. Their longer stretches and fewer, more gradual turns mean
winning opportunities for horses capable of stout finishes. Animals
with high early speed can still win, but are less likely to back into
first money than at tracks where the homestretches are shorter.
2. As at half-milers, the driver is more important than the post
position. Top drivers win more than their share of races.
3. A horse that has done well at one-mile tracks while showing
good early foot is seldom at a disadvantage on a ⅝-mile track.
4. A horse that has been showing insufficient early speed but some
finishing courage at half-mile tracks may improve by several lengths
on a ⅝-mile track.
5. A speed horse unable to withstand challenge at half-mile tracks
should be watched—but not bet on—in its first starts at a ⅝-mile
track. It may lack the necessary heart and stamina. But on the other

hand, the tighter turns at the half-miler may have been its only problem, and it may race well on the longer oval.

The One-Milers

At a mile track, the race begins in front of the stands and ends there, after the horses travel the course once. Times are fastest, interference least likely, form most reliable. However, it is highly unlikely that new one-mile raceways will be constructed, because they are too expensive.

Among North America's major raceways, Hollywood Park is the premier one-miler. Its purses compare with those of Roosevelt Raceway and Sportsman's Park, if not with those of Yonkers, and the quality of its racing is first-rate. Another mile track that qualifies as major is Washington Park, near Chicago.

The vastness of mile tracks seems forbidding to a fan accustomed to the bullring intimacy of the half-milers. The strangeness has a way of wearing off in a hurry, however. Form stands up beautifully and nothing is more exciting than a long stretch drive.

Interestingly, the all-out sprinting style introduced at Yonkers by Stanley Dancer has influenced the tactics everywhere else. Races at the one-mile ovals no longer are the single-file processions they used to be. Not long ago, I spent a few evenings at Washington Park and noticed that many drivers were ready, willing and able to shoot at least part of the works on the first turn—and were winning their races. Times do change.

The handicapper should absorb the following facts about racing at one-mile tracks:

1. Unless a horse has demontsrated its readiness to produce speed in the homestretch, it probably is not worth a bet.

2. Post position is of little consequence.

3. Although these tracks surpass all others as fair tests of equine quality and fitness, with interference and luck at irreducible minimums, the top driver is still a pronounced asset. If he has the best horse, so much the better. But he need not have the best horse to outmaneuver a less resourceful driver.

The Grand Circuit

As drivers, Stanley Dancer, Billy Haughton and Del Insko each win over $1 million in purses during an average year. As owners and trainers, they account for much more than that. To compete for every available major prize, powerful stables maintain separate divisions on two or more racing circuits at a time. Dancer commutes from New York to New Jersey to Liberty Bell or Brandywine or Chicago or California. So does Haughton. Insko favors New York and Chicago–California. Herve Filion and his several brothers race in New York, New Jersey, Liberty Bell–Brandywine, New England and Canada. If the boss is driving his horses at Track "A," assistants take the reins at "B" and "C." And at the height of the season, the big stables have divisions on the Grand Circuit, the most lucrative barnstorming operation in American sport.

The Roarin' Grand, as it is called, was organized in 1873, to provide a continuous schedule of suitably rich purses for the leading stables of the time. In short order, Grand Circuit Week became the most exciting period of the year for any track able to get on the schedule. Almost a century later, interest remains high. The Hambletonian is the highlight of Grand Circuit Week at the Du Quoin, Illinois Fair. The Little Brown Jug climaxes the week at the Delaware, Ohio Fair. Over the 23-week season, Grand Circuit stakes events involve purses that total almost $5 million.

This makes all the shuttling back and forth highly worthwhile for Haughton, Dancer, Insko, Joe O'Brien, George Sholty, Del Miller and other handlers of first-class stock. In the bargain, these drivers and their prize animals bring to tracks like Wolverine Raceway, Saratoga, Buffalo, Blue Bonnets, Monticello, Rosecroft, The Meadows, Greenwood, Hazel Park and Lexington a quality of competition far more distinguished than can be found in those places during other phases of the season. By imparting a big-league atmosphere, the Grand Circuit heightens interest in the sport and, in a real sense, upgrades the standing of many tracks that might otherwise be written off as minor.

The first half-mile track to play host to Grand Circuit racing was the celebrated Historic Track at Goshen, N.Y., in 1911. Roosevelt Raceway became a Grand Circuit stop in 1941. In 1969, it was the only track on the continent to be awarded two Grand Circuit weeks, a distinction it earned by helping to make the 1969 Messenger Stakes the richest event in history—more than $203,000 for three-year-old pacers.

Being concerned not only with fat purses but with the record book and its implications about the future value of their horses as sires and broodmares, Grand Circuiteers continue to emphasize the importance of their races on one-mile tracks, where times are faster and excuses fewer. Yet the realities are such that only five of the 1969 Grand Circuit stops were at mile ovals: Springfield, Du Quoin, Indianapolis, Lexington, and Hollywood Park. One was at Vernon Downs, a ¾-mile raceway. Six were at ⅝-mile tracks: Blue Bonnets, Greenwood, The Meadows, Sportsman's Park, Hazel Park and Liberty Bell. And eleven were at half-milers: Roosevelt (twice), Wolverine, Brandywine, Rosecroft, Saratoga, Goshen, Buffalo, Monticello, Delaware (Ohio), and Yonkers.

Right Way—Wrong Way

No matter how early you arrive at the track, horses will be jogging, pacing and trotting around it, some moving counterclockwise as in a race, others going in the opposite direction. If you have done your handicapping in advance and know which animals on the program are the likeliest candidates for your support, you might want to keep an eye out for them during the warm-ups. I say "might" but I mean "should." It is possible to handicap quite well without looking at the horses, but the percentage of success increases for someone who bets on animals that behave like winners before they race.

An inexperienced racegoer can make evaluations of that kind. The techniques are explained in this book's chapter on warm-ups. But the newcomer must first become accustomed to the bewildering comings and goings on the track. The first step is to identify the horses. The second is to recognize what they are doing.

How things look as you move out of the paddock for the final warm-ups at The Meadows, in Meadowlands, Pa.

At some tracks, the color of the horse's saddle cloth identifies the number of the race in which he is entered. The number on the cloth is his program number. At other tracks, the cloth bears a large number (his program number) and a small number (the number of his race). The color of the cloth designates his post position. At still other tracks, the horses wear numbered tags on their heads. Again, color and number identify the animal and race. The printed program explains the various color and number codes, which may also be described on a board posted in the infield.

Customarily, the horses take their first warm-ups about two hours before they race, jogging a mile or two or three "the wrong way of the track" (clockwise) and then turning for a moderate workout "the right way of the track," after which they turn again and jog to the paddock to be washed, cooled and rested. An hour later they return outdoors for another jog and a stiffer workout, and then back to the paddock to cool down. After the post parade come two "scores," which are final warm-up dashes of perhaps a quarter-mile each, the right way of the track. Whether jogging, warming up or scoring, and whether moving the right or wrong way of the track, every horse is in the process of cranking up for its race. It is fun to evaluate a horse's appearance and behavior, especially when the effort is repaid at the windows.

Seats and Eats

The people least likely to know what is happening in a race are those who cluster along the rail. Everyone should do that occasionally, to hear the rattling hooves and see the flying clods and sense the competitive tension and listen to bettors berating drivers. But the place to be is high up. As high as possible, for the sharpest, clearest view of the entire track.

The clubhouse dining room is usually the best place to sit. It is high, and it is athwart the finish line. The highest of its tables are, unfortunately, the farthest removed from the track, but compromises are possible. Make advance reservations. Specify a table that is close to the finish line and from which the entire racing strip can be seen while seated. Get to the track early. If the table is not as specified, refuse to accept it. If the maître d' responds unpleasantly, offering another table that turns out to be worse, you are dealing with a bandit. Bribe him, if you feel like it, and you may get a proper table. Next time, do not make reservations in the usual way. Instead, write a letter to the president of the track (whose name will be in the program), describe your disagreeable experience with the restaurant people, name the date you want to return and ask if the track management can't arrange civilized treatment for you.

Now that track managements are annoyed and restaurant concessionaires infuriated from coast to coast, I'd like to go a step further. The truth is that I have experienced sublime courtesy and splendid meals in numerous racetrack restaurants, but seldom unless I was accompanied by the president of the track and/or the public relations director and/or the racing secretary and/or a leading horseman. I do not count the times I bought courtesy giving large tips before they had been earned. The pleasure of watching races while dining at a good table is so considerable that it is worth struggling for. I now have told you how to do it.

If you prefer to eat at home, or in some other setting less expensive than the track restaurant, you might want a reserved seat. At most tracks, unreserved seats are poorly situated and few in number. Except at extremely modern plants in which the clubhouse occupies entire upper levels of the stands on both sides of the finish line, you will notice that the best reserved seats are not in the clubhouse but in the grandstand. Clubhouses usually are located beyond the finish line, whereas grandstands tend to be right on the line, offering seats in that ideal position or a few yards to the left. Since you pay extra for reserved seats, you should investigate the possibilities and prefer a seat on the finish line or slightly to its left. The farther beyond the line you are, the poorer your view of the stretch drive and finish.

Having obtained a roost, you should forthwith determine the location of the mutuel windows and settle on the best route there and back. If you become knowledgeable about mutuel prices, as I hope, you sometimes will want to delay your betting until the final couple of minutes before the race starts. On crowded nights, you leave your seat sooner, because the ticket lines are longer. On any night, the height of foolishness is to bet too soon, yet the height of frustration is to arrive on line too late to bet. A little experience and knowledge of the traffic patterns between seat and windows will make you an expert maneuverer.

The Tote Board

Roosevelt Raceway has the finest totalizator board in the world. It stands out there behind the inside rail just like any other

tote board, but it communicates more information. It shows the shifting patterns of wagering in terms of actual mutuel prices, rather than
old-fashioned bookmaking odds. It also gives the highest and lowest
prices each horse could pay for place and show if the race were to
take place immediately.

Conventional tote boards show the bookmaking odds for win, and
the amounts of money bet on each horse for win, place and show,
plus the totals acumulated in the win, place and show pools. Arith-
meticians can calculate whether a horse listed at 3 to 1 will pay $8.00,
$8.20, $8.40, $8.60 or $8.80. The ability to do this toward the end
of the betting period is a great comfort. If the horse in question has
suddenly become popular with the crowd, it might drop from 3 to 1
to 9 to 5. The chances of it doing that at the last minute are slight
if the 3 to 1 actually means $8.80. Similarly, the mental wizard can
tell what kind of price to expect for place if the horse and another
likely contender finish 1–2. If everyone were an arithmetician, the
Roosevelt tote board would be an ostentatious luxury. As matters
stand, it is a great boon and should be imitated everywhere.

Other vital information on the tote board includes late scratches
and driver changes, the condition of the racing strip, the time of day
and the time at which the next race is scheduled to start. During each
race, its elapsed time is displayed on the board, ticking off automatically. As each quarter-mile ends, the official clocking up to that
point appears at once, enabling the handicapper to tell whether some
driver is setting an unusually fast or slow pace. All these kinds of tote-
board data are helpful in handicapping and make the races more fun.

Judge Hanley's Maneuver

After thousands of afternoons and evenings at racetracks of all kinds, I can recall perhaps a half-dozen occasions on which mutuel sellers yelled at customers to come back and pick up forgotten change. When getting change while buying a $5 ticket with a $20 bill, I have seldom received the $10 bill before the $5 bill, and have not often been given both at once. Standard procedure is to toss the customer whatever number of small bills is due him as part of his change and, with exquisitely casual timing, withhold the large bill until it becomes evident that he plans to wait for it.

Having been bored by this glorious tradition for many a year, a friend of mine known as Judge Hanley came up with the antidote. He is not really a judge, but is called that because he is full of wisdom, as I am about to demonstrate. When the Judge buys, let us say, a $2 ticket with a $10 bill, and the seller throws him three singles at the instant the ticket emerges from the slot, Judge Hanley's Maneuver begins.

He touches neither the ticket nor the bills. He just lets them lie there. This is highly unusual. Think about it for a second. The typical bettor, full of adrenalin and hope, grabs the ticket as soon as it appears at the mouth of the slot, seizes the singles, realizes that something is absent, looks inquiringly at the seller and gets the missing five. And the untypical bettor is in such haste that he runs away with the ticket and the singles, contributing five dollars to the seller.

But Judge Hanley touches nothing. This bewilders the seller.

Unique tote board at Roosevelt Raceway shows changing odds in terms of actual pari-mutuel prices, including maximum and minimum price each horse would pay for place and show.

"Whaddya want?" inquires the seller. "More tickets?"

"No," says Judge Hanley. "I want more money."

The implication enrages the seller, who could not hold a position of trust at the track if his honesty were not world-renowned. Rather than argue the point, delay the line and attract unwelcome attention, he disgorges the extra five. The next time the Judge appears at his window, the seller, having forgotten, may well go through the traditional routine again. Once more, Judge Hanley keeps his hands at his sides, touching neither the mutuel ticket nor the insufficient change, By the third race, at the latest, the seller is completely tamed. If the Judge buys a $2 ticket with a $10 bill, the ticket and three singles have scarcely hit the counter when the five arrives. Then, and not before, Judge Hanley picks up the lot, murmurs his thanks and departs.

I have tried it myself. The results are invigorating. Remember, the key to the Maneuver is to touch nothing. Let the ticket lie there. Let the singles lie there. Remain silent unless spoken to. The Maneuver is useful not only at racetracks but when purchasing tickets at theaters, stadiums and railway and bus terminals. Welcome to the club.

The Jargon

The more comfortable you are, the more you will enjoy yourself. A great aid to comfort at the raceway is to know the terminology of the sport and, rather especially, to avoid exposing oneself as a novice by employing the wrong lingo. Be advised that the unmistakable mark of harness-racing ignorance is to speak of a horse that "ran" a good or bad race. Standardbreds trot or pace. Unless they break stride, they do not run. Although harness horsemen have managed to achieve a state of profitable coexistence with the urban types who have invaded their sport, they turn a thin-lipped purple when they hear the word "run" misused. Indeed, some of them take vengeful pleasure from hornswoggling new owners who say "run" instead of "trot" or "pace." They assume that someone who does *not* say "run" may know a bit about the sport.

A comparable but less widespread offense is the use of the word "rider." Harness horsemen are drivers, not riders, although some of the loudest, most ferocious noises at Chicago, California and New York raceways issue from paying customers who bellow that "the rider run the horse too wide. If he gets a better ride, he wins."

In the final analysis, your sense of belonging increases with the frequency of your visits to the cashier's window. Pending the night when you finally hit five or six winners, and deserve to, you can feel more at home by saying "trot" or "pace" or "race" or "driver." For "front-runner" say "quick-leaver." And understand what the knowledgeable mean by terms like "brush," "score," "hung-out," "covered up," "jump" and "colt."

3

The Arithmetic of Winning

HOW DO HUMAN BEINGS make their decisions? Among the legions of scientists who seek answers to that question, my favorites are a group of research psychologists who had the misfortune to read a book of mine called *The Compleat Horseplayer,* in which I describe a fairly cut-and-dried method of picking winners at Thoroughbred tracks. To facilitate their study of handicapping decisions, the psychologists converted the book's written advice into diagrams—thickets of circles and connecting lines in patterns which resembled giant hydrocarbon molecules. After counting all the circles and lines, the scholars advised me that the suggested handicapping procedure involved decisions five times as complex as those made by the average Wall Street securities analyst. And twelve times as complex as those of a neurosurgeon diagnosing a brain tumor.

They were impressed by the complexity. I am not. Handicapping decisions are much less complex than those made by a woman when she selects her clothing for a major social event. Neither she nor anyone else often faces quandaries more elaborate than those that arise when she stares at the contents of her closet. Yet she survives.

Putting it another way, handicapping is complicated, but not forbiddingly so. Unlike neurosurgery and the planning of investment portfolios, handicapping is a game. Its complexity is that of a good game, worth the time and effort of adults. A game (as I keep saying) much like poker, the enormous complexities of which are endlessly stimulating but in no sense burdensome.

The harness-racing handicapper uses his informed experience to find logic in the multitude of facts displayed in the printed program and on the tote board and racing strip. Some of the facts are clear, others obscure. But each relates to all the others in ways that vary from horse to horse, driver to driver, race to race and night to night.

Because the raw materials of handicapping are abundant, changeable and deceptive, the game becomes a highly personal exercise in approximation—closer to an art than to a science. Which is why the predictions and decisions of experts coincide only part of the time.

Handicapping formulas are a dime a dozen, and are no substitute for informed judgment. The best of them, in fact, are not really formulas at all, but procedures for the orderly application of judgment. No matter which method the handicapper adopts, he inevitably places his own stamp on it. Formula or not, he attempts to predict the future by interpreting past events of uncertain character and inexact significance. Yet success at the raceway demands predictions of considerable accuracy.

If certainty about the past is so limited, must not certainty about the future be terribly fragile? How can anyone profit from such confusion?

By dealing in probabilities. Likelihoods. Or, as they say at the track, by working *with* the percentages instead of against them.

Beating the Percentages

It so happens that the old saw, "You can beat a race, but you can't beat the races," is quite wrong. It turns reality upside down. The truth is that nobody can be sure of beating an individual race, but lots of people win more than they lose in a season's activity at the track. There is nothing peculiar about this. In any game worth playing, the outcome of any one play is rarely a matter of absolute certainty. But someone who plays well finishes ahead in the long run.

Take poker as an example. No matter how expert the player, nothing short of a royal flush provides certainty of a winning bet. The expert is lucky if he holds one royal flush in forty years of play. In other words, he can't necessarily beat the race. But he is an expert and he makes out fine, losing a little, winning a little more. He beats the game.

Let us suppose that our poker expert competes with six of his peers in a game of jackpots. After he has been at the table with them a few times, he knows a great deal about their courage, wiles and weaknesses. He undoubtedly knows more than any handicapper can know about a field of horses. The usefulness of this knowledge varies from session to session, of course. In poker, last week's tabby is this week's tiger, his mood having modified his style for the time being. A further limitation on the expert's success is that his opponents also are experts and know a great deal about *his* style.

In the end, therefore, the poker expert's main armor against uncertainty is his knowledge of the game itself—more particularly, his knowledge of the percentages that give the game its central character. As long as he is faithful to the laws—the probabilities—embodied in those percentages, he seldom loses. And, when he combines knowledge of the probabilities with accurate guesses about the tactics of his opponents, he becomes a big winner.

Allow me to pursue the matter further. By reminding the reader how the percentages are used in poker, I hope to whet his appetite for discussion of the sparser, less familiar, but equally important percentages in harness racing.

A 52-card poker deck contains slightly less than 2.6 million five-card hands. The exact probability of drawing any specific hand is a matter of established mathematical knowledge. So is the probability of improving any hand on the draw. If the expert has a chance to convert his hand into a straight by discarding one card and drawing either a nine or an ace, will he bet the money required for the gamble? It all depends.

He knows that the odds against drawing either an ace or nine are 5 to 1. He may draw the right card and lose the pot to someone who has a flush or a full house. But he will win in the long run on hands of this kind if he respects the percentages of the game. He will win in the long run if he takes the risk *only when the pot is large enough to repay him for it.* If he draws the one card on occasions when the pot pays less than a 5 to 1 gamble should, he eventually must lose. Winning one such hand in every six or seven he plays, he will take in less money than he spends on the losing hands.

Identical principles apply to horseplaying. Certain percentages are as firmly established in racing as in cards, and deserve comparable respect. They occur with astonishing uniformity year after year. They affect the handicapper's choice of horse. They affect the size and frequency of his bets.

What is more, racing is so patterned that a handicapper's own methods are sure to embody percentages of their own. If his procedures are consistent (regardless of whether they are profitable or not), they find winning horses at a rate that fluctuates hardly at all from one year to the next. Likewise, his annual rate of profit or loss on each wagered dollar varies but slightly from year to year. He may encounter long losing streaks and incredible strings of winners, but in the end his handicapping settles at its own percentage level. When he knows this percentage, and the accompanying rate of profit or loss,

At Yonkers and wherever else people bet on horses, some players get on line before they have made up their minds about the race. They continue to study the form until they find themselves eye-to-eye with the mutuel clerk, whereupon handicapping terminates and money changes hands.

he is able to judge the efficiency of his methods. He remains uncertain about the outcome of an individual bet, but knows with considerable certainty that, in due course, he can expect to win a predictable minimum percentage of bets, with a predictable minimum profit or loss per invested dollar.

A life insurance company does the same kind of thing on an incomparably larger scale. It hitches its treasury to the laws of probability. It does not have the vaguest idea when you will die. But it knows, within the practical limits of earthly certainty, the percentage of people your age who will die this year, or next, or twelve years from now. It designs its premium rates accordingly. In the long run its ledgers show a predictable percentage of deaths, a predictable percentage of surviving premium-payers, and a predictable rate of profit.

Although good handicappers are faithful to the established percentages of the game, and to the percentages achieved by their own methods, handicapping is not really a mathematical pastime. Some of the best selectors use pencils only to cross out the names of horses they think will lose. Other good handicappers do simple arithmetic, but not much of it. Still others devise rather elaborate arithmetical formulas in an attempt to introduce reassuring order into the hodge-podge of information with which they deal. In harness racing, dom-inated by the factor of timed speed, formulas of that kind are particularly useful. They require no arithmetical skill beyond the ability to add, subtract, multiply, and divide.

Even the numbers contained in this chapter need not be committed to memory. Far more important than the numbers are the conclusions they permit about the nature of the game.

The Magic Number

Anybody who bets $1,000 on the races and emerges from the experience with less than $830 is doing something dreadfully wrong. A $2 bettor who selected horses with a hatpin, or by using numer-ology, or by consulting tea leaves, would probably lose no more than $170 in a series of 500 bets—an investment of $1,000.

It is, of course, more than theoretically possible to go broke at the track. Desperate gamblers do it every day. And victims of inefficient selection methods or wasteful betting systems also manage to run out of cash long before they should.

The shortest route to disaster is to bet too much of one's money at a time. The man with a $1,000 bankroll who plays it all on one horse has a splendid chance of losing it. The man who bets the $1,000 in five installments of $200 each also risks extinction: In any given series of five bets, no handicapper on earth can be sure of winning so much as one!

How, then, can a less-than-expert player expect to have $830 left after betting $1,000?

The magic number is 17.

Without knowing the slightest thing about horses, and betting entirely at random, the player's long-term losses should not exceed 17 percent of the total amount he bets. To limit his losses to that extent, he need only bet in amounts small enough to assure himself of a large, representative number of bets.

It works like this. Of all money bet on a race, most tracks deduct approximately 17 percent for taxes and their own revenue. The re-maining 83 percent is disbursed to the holders of winning mutuel tickets.

This means that, regardless of how the individual fares with his own bet, the crowd as a whole loses 17 percent of its wagered dollar on every race, every night, every week, every year. A random bettor, playing horses at random, should do no worse. A selection system employing daisy petals or playing cards or dice or anything else entirely unrelated to handicapping should leave the bettor with close to 83 percent of his wagered money after a series of 500 or more bets.

Any handicapping procedure that results in annual losses as high as 17 percent of all money wagered is, therefore, no better than the hatpin method. And anyone who loses more than 17 cents of every dollar he bets in a season is—whether he realizes it or not—going far out of his way to find trouble.

The 17 percent "take" of racetracks has been compared unfavorably with the smaller levies imposed by gambling casinos. A roulette player, for example, should lose only slightly more than a nickel of each dollar he bets, assuming that the computation is made after a long, representative series of plays. The difference between roulette and racing is, however, a matter of frequency. The wheel spins every few seconds, all night. The roulette fanatic makes hundreds of plays in one session. No matter how conservatively he bets, the house "take" of 5 percent-plus nibbles away at his capital, and he finally has nothing left.

But the horseplayer encounters only nine or ten races a night. If each wager involves the smallest possible fraction of his betting capital, he might play for months or years before emptying his pocket. For example, a man who allocates $500 to raceway betting and bets $2 on every race should have about $414 left after 28 visits to the track. He might have much more or much less, but the track "take" *should* siphon off only $86 or so from the 252 bets he makes. If he knows absolutely nothing about horses and makes no attempt to learn, he very probably will do just about that well.

It follows that anything useful he learns about horses and drivers should enable him to begin reducing the percentage of loss. In this chapter we shall see that he can begin to reduce that percentage merely by learning some of the probabilities of the game, and without learning a thing about horses or drivers!

Betting on Favorites

An infallible guide to the reliability or intelligence, or both, of a racing expert is his attitude toward persons who bet on favorites. All experts know that, in a representative series of harness races, about one in every three will be won by the betting favorite—the horse on which the crowd bets the most money. The conclusions various writers achieve in light of this statistic are a dead giveaway to their knowledge of probability. Anyone ignorant of probability is unable to evaluate his own chances at the track and is hopelessly unqualified to advise anyone else.

It is fashionable to sneer at "chalk players" and "bridge jumpers" —the conservative types who play nothing but favorites. Observing that favorites win approximately a third of the time, many sages proclaim, with flawless arithmetic, that the crowd is wrong two-thirds of the time. They insist that the secret of success at the track is to part company with the crowd, avoid favorites and, presumably, begin winning a lion's share of the two races in three which find the crowd wrong. Such advice is crude nonsense. Whatever truth it contains is strictly coincidental.

Any child will understand this after a few facts are presented. At major raceways, the usual race involves eight or nine horses. This means that about 80 horses perform on a representative evening. The crowd picks nine of these animals as betting favorites. Typically, about three of the nine win. Anyone who thinks it easier to find winners among 71 non-favorites than among nine favorites is thinking backward.

The fact that non-favorites win almost two-thirds of all races does not mean that non-favorites have twice as good a chance to win as favorites do. Quite the contrary. Until we handicap the entire field and see which horse is the likeliest of the lot (a task few players can perform), we know nothing about the non-favorite except that it is one of seven or eight non-favorites in its race. But we know more than that about the favorite. Without doing any handicapping, we know that the statistical expectation of victory by the favorite is one in three, which is convertible into odds of 2 to 1. But the statistical expectation of victory by a non-favorite in a nine-horse race is one in twelve—odds of 11 to 1! These figures are obtained by dividing the fraction of races that non-favorites win ($\frac{2}{3}$) by the number of non-favorites in the race (8).

We now have established that it is foolish to reject a horse simply because it is the favorite, or to stab at another horse simply because it is not. We therefore are in a better position to appreciate some interesting statistics. We begin with a blazer:

To cut the magic number of 17 by more than half and bring wagering losses within striking distance of the break-even point, one need only confine one's bets to horses that are the favorites in certain types of races!

During 1968, raceways sent the official result charts of 40,628 harness races to the recordkeepers at the USTA. The USTA computer tells me that favorites won 36.1 percent of those races, at average odds of slightly more than 7 to 5. A flat bet on each of the favorites would have cost a player 12.3 cents per wagered dollar. That is, if someone visits twenty random raceways for as many evenings of entertainment and bets $2 on the favorite in each of 180 races, he can expect to lose $44.28—or $2.21 per outing.

As the accompanying tabulation shows, however, some favorites are much better risks than others. The hypothetical tourist described above could cut his losses to $26.40 for the twenty evenings, simply by making no bets on the favorites in claiming races.

These are fantastic figures. The $2 bettor who plays favorites only, and avoids claiming races, has a statistically valid expectation of losing about $1.32 on each visit to a harness raceway. It should be apparent that the player can reduce these losses and, indeed, take profits

The Arithmetic of Favorites

The material below derives from a study unprecedented in American horse racing. At my request, the USTA programmed its computer to show the number of races won by betting favorites, and the mutuel prices they paid. The study encompassed all 40,628 harness races charted during 1968.

Type of Race	Percentage of Winning Favorites		Average Odds (To 1)		Net Loss per $1 Bet	
	Trot	Pace	Trot	Pace	Trot	Pace
Invitational*	38.1	39.6	1.41	1.27	8.2¢	10.1¢
Preferred	38.2	37.7	1.41	1.47	7.9	6.9
Conditioned	35.8	38.3	1.40	1.35	14.1	11.0
Claiming	31.0	32.9	1.58	1.60	20.0	14.5
All	35.1	36.4	1.43	1.43	14.7	11.5

* This and other terms are explained in Chapter 8, pages 181 to 212.

home if he learns enough handicapping to discriminate among favorites, betting on the more solid ones and avoiding the others.

For example, a player of favorites can win substantial sums at leading half-mile tracks if he confines his speculation to pacers and high-class, seasoned trotters, making no bet unless the horse has an outstanding driver and an advantageous post position and is favored by a comfortable margin. This last point is important for several reasons, not the least of which is the difficulty of identifying the favorites in some races until after the races are over. If you study chart books published by the program departments at leading tracks (a useful study, by the way), you will have no trouble "showing" that a flat bet on certain kinds of favorites would have made you a fortune. Beware. All too often, the favorite reported in the chart was not the favorite two or three minutes before post time. Sometimes the issue is unresolved until the final flash, when it is too late to get on line and make a bet. Where two or more horses are that closely matched, the would-be player of favorites should abstain. Not only is he likely to bet on a horse that winds up as second or third choice in the betting, but also he is likely to bet on a horse whose chances are not quite as bright as a favorite's should be. To avoid this, it is best to delay betting until the last possible moment, and to return to one's seat without a ticket if the favorite is not clearly established at that time. Considering the frequency with which insiders and other heavy bettors at leading tracks alter the odds pattern during the final seconds before the betting windows close, the average racegoer cannot be sure that a horse is the favorite unless its odds are much the lowest in the field three minutes before the race starts. To illustrate, if the animal is odds-on at 4 to 5 in an eight-horse field, nothing else should be listed at less than 8 to 5. If the horse is at even money, the second choice should be at least 9 to 5. If the horse is posted at 6 to 5, the second choice should be at least 2 to 1. And so on.

In checking result charts to see how one or another method of betting on solid favorites would have fared, the reader should be scrupulous about tossing out all races in which the odds reported for the second choice were close to those on the favorite. Chances are excellent that someone trying to apply a chalk-playing method would have put his money on that second choice often enough to throw the system entirely out of kilter. On the evening before these words were written, a horse won at Roosevelt Raceway as a 5 to 2 favorite, having dropped from 4 to 1 on the very last flash of the tote board. Obviously, the horse was favored by relatively few bettors, whose enormous late wagers more than offset the $2 and $5 contributions of the crowd at large. For a horse to drop from 4 to 1 to 5 to 2, bypassing 7 to 2 and 3 to 1, is not at all unusual in the last two or three minutes of betting at major tracks. So be guided accordingly in all your thinking about favorites.

The Tote Board and the Price

This table shows the mutuel prices represented by the figures posted on racetrack odds boards. Horses posted at 4 to 5 or higher may pay more than the minimum mutuel price, but they never pay less. The computations are revised at frequent intervals until post time.

Odds	Price	Odds	Price	Odds	Price
1-9	$2.20	2-1	$6.00	18-1	$38.00
1-8	2.20	5-2	7.00	19-1	40.00
1-7	2.20	3-1	8.00	20-1	42.00
1-6	2.20	7-2	9.00	21-1	44.00
1-5	2.40	4-1	10.00	22-1	46.00
1-4	2.40	9-2	11.00	23-1	48.00
1-3	2.60	5-1	12.00	24-1	50.00
2-5	2.80	6-1	14.00	25-1	52.00
1-2	3.00	7-1	16.00	30-1	62.00
3-5	3.20	8-1	18.00	35-1	72.00
3-4	3.40	9-1	20.00	40-1	82.00
4-5	3.60	10-1	22.00	45-1	92.00
1-1	4.00	11-1	24.00	50-1	102.00
6-5	4.40	12-1	26.00	60-1	122.00
7-5	4.80	13-1	28.00	75-1	152.00
3-2	5.00	14-1	30.00	99-1	200.00
8-5	5.20	15-1	32.00		
9-5	5.60	16-1	34.00		
		17-1	36.00		

Another aspect of betting on favorites seldom gets attention in print, except from oracles who manage to get the facts backward. I refer to the concept of "short price." To say that even money is a "short price" and that much more profit is to be made by betting on horses at 4 to 1 is to recite gibberish. In the first place, a winning bet at even money returns the bettor a profit of 100 percent. Second, almost half of all horses that go at even money win their races. Someone who were to bet on all of them would lose about 3 cents per wagered dollar, year after year. But horses that go at 4 to 1 are riskier. About 16 percent of them win, yielding a net loss in the vicinity of 13 cents on the wagered dollar.

Obviously, one would not—or should not—bet on a horse just because its price is short. But if one is "looking for a good price" and is not a real handicapper, the best available price is even money or thereabouts, because the long-term losses are negligible. And stabbing at horses with higher odds is financially ruinous. The few studies that have been made of pari-mutuel patterns prove beyond doubt that horses held at low odds win higher percentages of their races than do horses that go at higher odds. In fact, horses at 2 to 1 win a higher percentage of their races than horses at 3 to 1. And horses at 6 to 1 win a higher percentage than horses at 7 to 1. And so forth. It all graphs out. The lower the odds, the higher the statistical likelihood of victory.

I sound very much like an incurable bridge jumper, but I am not. My goal at the moment is to nullify the effects of all the nonsense that is spoken and written about short-priced horses, so that the reader will approach his own handicapping with a firmer understanding of the mathematics of the game. When he becomes a good selector, he will land on favorites and non-favorites—not because of their odds but because of their records as sharp animals, fit to win in the particular circumstances that confront them.

Before moving to other matters, I must emphasize that the poor showing of favorites in claiming races is a temporary phenomenon. The industry was slow to adopt this kind of competition, in which the conditions of eligibility specify the price at which any horse that races can be bought (claimed) by a bona fide owner. Reluctant to lose fit animals in that way, horsemen have tended to accept claiming races only as a last resort, and only with hopelessly inferior horses. One hallmark of Standardbred inferiority is inconsistency, of course, which is why so many favorites come up empty in claiming races. Even as I write this, however, the picture is improving. In 1970, leading tracks were presenting more claiming races than ever, and better horses than ever were participating. Horsemen had begun to discover that fortunes were to be made by entering decent horses to race at claiming prices roughly equivalent to their actual market value. By 1975, or thereabouts, when horsemen, racing secretaries, and bettors will be thoroughly at ease with this type of racing, the percentage of winning favorites undoubtedly will be in phase with the 36 to 37 percent that is typical in other kinds of harness competition.

Attainable Profits

Regardless of the individual's handicapping style, the percentages of the game govern his results. The more often he bets on longshots, the fewer tickets he cashes. And the more often he bets on low-priced horses, the more often he wins. But his rate of profit—the only meaningful index to his success—depends on whether he wins frequently enough or at odds high enough to compensate for his losses.

It has long been taken for granted in racing that a first-class handicapper can win about four bets in ten if he is extremely conservative, bets on relatively few races and inclines toward horses whose odds average about 2 to 1. Such play yields a profit of about 20 cents for every wagered dollar, increasing the handicapper's capital at a tremendous rate. For example, if he starts with $2,000 and makes an average of two $100 bets a night for 200 racing nights (spread over a period of years, perhaps), his operations return a profit of $8,000, enlarging his capital to $10,000.

Players of such accomplishment are more numerous at running tracks (where handicapping is relatively intricate) than at harness raceways (where handicapping is relatively simple). There is nothing paradoxical about this. A shrewd handicapper of Thoroughbreds can pick his spots, avoiding races in which factors like distance, weight, class and current form resist firm analysis. But the handicapper of Standardbreds often is confronted with a program of nine pacing races, each at a mile, and each with three or four logical contenders whose adequate class and superior form are clearly evident. It sometimes becomes extremely difficult, even unrealistic, to decide that one such race is more suitable for betting than another. Accordingly, the good handicapper is likely to find himself betting on six or seven races a night, a level of activity that seldom pays off at running tracks, and is no guarantee of profits at raceways, either.

If he bears in mind some of the mutuel statistics discussed earlier, the handicapper may derive some bright ideas from the following:

To earn a profit of 20 cents on the wagered dollar, a handicapper must:

1. Win half of his bets, at average odds not lower than 7 to 5, or
2. Win 40 percent of his bets, at average odds of 2 to 1, or

3. Win a third of his bets, at average odds of 13 to 5, or

4. Win 30 percent of his bets, at average odds of 3 to 1.

Anyone who hopes to do twice that well, earning profits at the rate of 40 cents on the wagered dollar, must:

1. Win half of his bets, at average odds of 9 to 5, or

2. Win 40 percent of his bets, at average odds of 5 to 2, or

3. Win a third of his bets, at average odds of more than 3 to 1, or

4. Win 30 percent of his bets, at average odds exceeding 7 to 2.

Any of the formulas on those two lists is theoretically attainable at a raceway. But the practicalities of the game, and of human self-control, suggest that the handicapper deserves a medal if he can achieve results in the neighborhood of items 2 and 3 on the first of the lists. If he does that well, he will be able to buy his own medal.

Beware the Law of Averages

Statisticians and others acquainted with the laws of probability try, wherever possible, to measure situations in precise terms. They know that averages are misleading. The classic example is a man who needs to cross a river. Being six feet tall, and having learned that the average depth of the river is only five feet, he starts to wade across. In midstream he sinks like a stone and drowns. A river with an average depth of five feet may be 12 feet deep at midstream.

Or take the following series of numbers: 1, 2, 3, 4, 5, 6, 7, 8, 9, 75. The average of those numbers is 12. But, if the numbers represent the results of something or other—like the odds paid by a series of winning bets—the average distorts reality. Nine of the ten horses ran at odds of 9 or less, yet the striker of averages struts around under the delusion that he can expect an average return of about 12 from his next series of ten winners. Unless the horse that returned 75 —and threw the average out of whack—was a normal, predictable, usual selection, a statistician would prefer to say that the *median* of the series was between 5 and 6. In other words, he would look for the point that falls midway in the series. Five of the numbers in this particular series were 6 or more. The other five were 5 or less. The median is, therefore, around 5.5. Which ain't 12.

In the handicapping of Standardbreds it is essential to remember the illusory character of averages. For an extreme example, the player sometimes notices that a horse has won over $200,000 in 40 starts—an average of about $5,000 per race. To decide that the horse is the class of its race because it has the highest average earnings might be a serious mistake. It might have won most of its money last year, in so-called sire stakes competition, which offers high purses to animals bred in the particular state. The horse might never have won a race against the tougher stock it encountered in less lucrative events. Another horse in tonight's race, with average earnings of only $3,000, might have an enormous edge in class and condition.

Knowing that averages can never be more than rough yardsticks, the good handicapper looks beyond them. Above all, he pays no heed whatever to the racetrack superstition known as "the law of averages."

Example: If favorites win slightly more than one of every three races, and nine races in succession have been won by nonfavorites, it is incorrect to suppose that the favorite in the tenth race has a better-than-ordinary chance to win. The favorite is *not* "due." Aside from what the handicapper may think of the animal's quality, which is quite another matter, its status as favorite tells only one thing about its chances. That one thing is a generality: In the long run, favorites win about one race out of three.

The long run is sometimes very long. Persons who base their play on the inevitability of victory by favorites sometimes increase the amount of their bets after every loss. They lose more than they should. In fact, if they go the route of doubling the bet after each loss, they end in ruin.

It is not unusual for ten consecutive favorites to lose. The man who bets $2 on a favorite loses it, bets $4 on the next, and $8 on the next and continues to double up in hope that the favorite is "due," will have parted with $1,022 after nine successive losses. His system will require a bet of $1,024 on the next race. If he has that much money and the courage to risk it, the bet positively will lower the odds on the favorite. If the horse wins, which is by no means inevitable, and pays as much as even money, which is problematical, the bettor emerges with a profit of $2 on an investment of $2,046.

The law of averages is equally unreliable in connection with the performances of drivers. The driver does not live who does not suffer intermittent losing streaks. Thirty or forty losses in succession are neither excessive nor unusual. A betting system based on the concept that some highly rated driver is "due" is a betting system sure to fail. Unless the player's capital and endurance are unlimited.

Similarly, the handicapper's knowledge that his selections win almost twice in every five attempts is poor grounds for an assumption that seven losses in a row will probably be followed by an immediate winner. Or that seven winners in a row make the next selection a likely loser.

Unawareness of probability causes severe harm at every raceway, every night. After a longshot wins, a disappointed player consults his program and discovers that the horse was driven and trained by its owner. No other horse in the race had been owned, driven and trained by one man. Eureka! A new system! If the horse is the only one in its race that is driven and trained by its owner, and if it has had a race in ten days, and if its last race was at this track, and if, and if, and if! The player now loses eight bets in succession on owner-driven horses.

I am trying to emphasize that one cannot determine probabilities without a large, representative series of cases. One robin does not make a spring. And, even after the probabilities have been determined, they remain nothing but probabilities. In no way do they guarantee the outcome of a single, isolated event. Nor do they guarantee the outcome of a short series of events. The feeblest handicapper enjoys winning nights and winning weeks. The only inevitability in his situation is that he will end as a heavy loser if he persists in his usual methods. And the best handicapper suffers losing nights and losing weeks, but recovers the ground if he continues to play in his usual, sensible style.

As I have insisted before, and as may now seem more agreeable, you can't necessarily beat a race, but you may be able to beat the races. To do so, you will have to overcome the unfavorable percentages of the game. You will have to develop a style of play in which (1) your handicapping knowledge reveals animals with especially good chances and (2) the long-term returns on your winnings are more than sufficient to repair your long-term losses.

The House Percentage

In poker, the odds are 4 to 1 against filling a flush by drawing one card. Unless the pot contains at least four times as much money as he must pay for the one card, the good poker player drops out.

Suppose that the owner of the card table were charging the players 20 cents for every dollar in every pot, deducting that percentage before each payoff. The odds against filling a four-flush would remain

4 to 1, but the player no longer would be able to break even on such gambles unless the pots contained at least five times as much money as he paid for his fifth card.

Chances are that the player would quit the game. Or, if it were the only game in town, he would revise his methods. He would play more conservatively, incurring fewer risks. Where winning probabilities decrease, losses become more costly, more difficult to overcome.

This is exactly what has happened in horse racing. The "house"— a partnership of raceway management and the state treasury—cuts every pari-mutuel pool with a cleaver, lowering the payoff prices and making profitable handicapping much more difficult than it might be if the house percentage were lower.

The principle of pari-mutuel betting is eminently fair. The odds paid by the winning horse are—in principle—the ratio between the amount of money bet on it and the amounts bet on all the losers.

Theoretically, if members of the crowd bet $30,000 on Horse "A" and other players bet a total of $60,000 on all other horses in the race, "A" is a 2 to 1 shot (60 to 30). The mutuel price should be $6, representing the bettor's original $2 plus his $4 profit. In actuality, "A" pays nothing like $6. At Yonkers and Roosevelt and Washington Park and Hollywood, the horse pays only $5, having been cut from 2 to 1 to 3 to 2 by the house percentage. In Pennsylvania, where the cut is larger, the horse pays only $4.80—7 to 5.

The so-called house deductions are known as take and breakage. They finance track operations and provide tax revenues to the state and other governments. Tracks need funds with which to pay purses, hire employees and keep themselves spruce. Governments are undoubtedly entitled to a slice, too. It would be idle to deplore any of this. But certain trends are questionable.

At Yonkers and Roosevelt, for example, the State of New York makes more money from the mutuel pools than the tracks do. At every opportunity, the state enlarges its racing revenues by increasing the percentage of takeout. It is a kind of confiscation unmatched in American industry. Desperately in need of more money with which to pay wages and post the purses that attract good stables, the tracks would prefer that states content themselves with smaller shares. But states seldom agree. So the take rises and rises and rises, and the outlook darkens.

The following tables show what happens to the natural profits of a winning bet, where the legal take is 15 percent, 16 percent and 17 percent.

The 15-percent Bite

Natural Odds	Natural Mutuel Price	Actual Mutuel Price	Reduction of Proft (%)
7–1	$16.00	$13.60	16
6–1	14.00	11.80	18
5–1	12.00	10.20	18
4–1	10.00	8.40	20
3–1	8.00	6.80	20
2–1	6.00	5.00	25
1–1	4.00	3.40	30
4–5	3.60	3.00	37

The 16-percent Bite

Natural Odds	Natural Mutuel Price	Actual Mutuel Price	Reduction of Proft (%)
7–1	$16.00	$13.40	19
6–1	14.00	11.60	20
5–1	12.00	10.00	20
4–1	10.00	8.40	20
3–1	8.00	6.60	23
2–1	6.00	5.00	25
1–1	4.00	3.20	40
4–5	3.60	3.00	37

The 17-percent Bite

Natural Odds	Natural Mutuel Price	Actual Mutuel Price	Reduction of Proft (%)
7–1	$16.00	$13.20	20
6–1	14.00	11.60	20
5–1	12.00	9.80	24
4–1	10.00	8.20	23
3–1	8.00	6.60	23
2–1	6.00	4.80	30
1–1	4.00	3.20	40
4–5	3.60	2.80	50

Alert readers may have noticed apparent discrepancies in those tables. They are explained by the curiosity known as breakage, which we shall discuss in a moment. For now, it is useful to notice that an increase of as little as 1 percent in the takeout means a substantial loss of profit for the winning bettor.

The following states required a 15-percent takeout as of 1969: Illinois and Michigan.

The following had a 16-percent takeout: Maryland, New Jersey and New York.

17 percent: Florida, Kentucky, Massachusetts, New Hampshire and Pennsylvania.

17½ percent: Delaware and Ohio.

18 percent: Maine and Vermont.

I have saved the best for last. At this writing, the take in California is only 14 percent. I doubt it will remain at that level. So long as it does, however, West Coast racegoers will have an easier time than the rest of us. Look at the following comparison of Pennsylvania or Kentucky mutuel prices with what the same horses would pay in California:

Natural Odds	Ky. or Pa. Mutuel	Calif. Mutuel
7–1	$13.20	$13.60
6–1	11.60	12.00
5–1	9.80	10.20
4–1	8.20	8.60
3–1	6.60	6.80
2–1	4.80	5.00
1–1	3.20	3.40
4–5	2.80	3.00

Note that the 20- and 40-cent differences in these mutuel prices represent differences of 10 and 20 percent on the bettor's investment, although the difference in take is only 3 percent.

The Truth about Breakage

Let us now return to Horse "A," on which $30,000 has been bet. The natural odds against him are 2 to 1, because $60,000 has been wagered on the other horses. The win pool is $90,000.

First off, the track attends to the takeout. Assuming a 15-percent takeout, as in Illinois and Michigan, the track removes $13,500 from the mutuel pool. This leaves $76,500, including the $30,000 bet on the winning horse. The remainder of $46,500 is supposed to be the profit for the winning bettors, but is not. Look at what happens:

30,000 ⌐46,500.00
            1.55

The $30,000 has been divided into the $46,500 to see how much money is due per dollar bet on the winning horse. Another way of saying it is that the division gives the "dollar odds" on "A."

Inasmuch as nobody can make a $1 bet at a track, mutuel prices always are stated in terms of a $2 bet. Therefore, the next step should be to multiply 1.55 by 2. The product, 3.10, would be the profit on a $2 bet—the odds in terms of $2. To compute the actual mutuel pay-off, one then would add the bettor's original $2 to the $3.10, giving a mutuel price of $5.10 on "A."

But it is not done that way, except in Delaware.

Everywhere else, the dollar odds of 1.55 are reduced to 1.50. If the odds had been 1.51 or anything else up to and including 1.59, they also would have been cut to 1.50. This is known as "dime break-age." Unless dollar odds turn out by themselves to end in a string of zeroes, they are always cut to the next lower dime. Track and state pocket the leftover pennies—millions of dollars a year.

Back again now to Horse "A" and the poor soul who bet on it to win. Now that the dollar odds are only 1.50, the odds on the $2 bet are 3 to 2 and the mutuel price becomes $5.

The procedure lacks logic except as a pretext for inflating the take-out without seeming to. The usual practice is to divide the breakage equally between state treasury and track. In California, major tracks get none of the loot. The state takes it all. New Jersey also takes 100 percent. In New York, the track gets half the state gets one-quarter and the other quarter goes into a Horse Breeders Fund, from which large purses are paid in a sire stakes program. In Maryland, the track retains none of the breakage, but in Delaware it takes it all.

This legalized pilferage from the rightful proceeds of a winning bet began years ago, when mutuel prices were computed by a slightly different method. Instead of dividing the amount bet on the *winner* into the amount bet on all the *losers,* and coming up with the basic dollar odds, the tracks worked in terms of $2 units. They divided the amount of the entire betting pool by a figure representing the number of $2 tickets sold on the winner. The answer was the winner's mutuel price. This is worth exploring further, since it shows how breakage blossomed into the larceny that it now is. Let us therefore take another look at Horse "A," this time using the old-fashioned method of cal-culating his mutuel price.

The $30,000 bet on him represents 15,000 mutuel tickets. The pool, after the 15-percent take, is $76,500. The arithmetic:

15,000 | 76,500.00
      ‾‾‾‾‾‾
        5.10

Under this old method, the track would have paid $5.10 to any holder of a winning $2 ticket on "A." In those days, furthermore, the track take was no higher than 10 percent, so the mutuel would have been at least $5.40. But that's another story.

Breakage arose because few mutuel prices came out in round numbers. The correct payoff on "A" might have been $5.12. Rather than bother their mutuel clerks with the chore of making chicken-feed change, the tracks adopted dime breakage, reducing the $5.12 to $5.10. As I now have shown, dime breakage under the old method was less exploitative than dime breakage as now practiced. Under the old method, the winning player collected a higher mutuel.

At some point, a procedure called nickel breakage came into vogue. Odds were computed at the dollar level, as they now are. If a ticket on "A" was worth 1.55 to 1.00, the mutuel remained $5.10. If the ticket was worth 1.59 to 1.00, the dollar odds were cut to 1.55 and the mutuel remained $5.10. Dollar odds that ended in anything but a zero or a 5 were always reduced to the next lower nickel.

Which paved the way for dime breakage calculated in terms of the dollar odds. A whopping increase over the old-style dime breakage. Take a horse whose dollar odds are 2.19. Under nickel breakage the odds become 2.15 and the mutuel price is $6.30. But the new, unreasonable dime breakage reduces the dollar odds from 2.19 to 2.10. The horse pays only $6.20. Breakage that used to be 8 cents has become 18 cents.

Consider what this means to the holder of a ticket on a short-priced horse. If the dollar odds come out at .99, they are reduced to .90 and the mutuel payoff is 18 cents less than it should be. For any horse in the even-money range, breakage reduces the profit on a winning ticket by as much as 18 percent!

Place and Show Betting

As most racegoers—but not all—understand, the holder of a show ticket collects a profit if the horse wins or finishes second or third. A place ticket wins if the horse finishes first or second. A win ticket loses unless the horse wins.

Obviously, the best horse in the race has a better chance of finishing second or third than of winning. Some excellent handicappers try to capitalize on this truth, playing for only place or show. The profits on a successful place or show bet are low, but the players hope to compensate by winning many more bets than they lose.

Place bets pay relatively little because the money contributed to the pool by losing bettors must be divided between two groups of winners—those who hold place tickets on the winner and those who backed the horse that finished second. The profits on show bets are even lower, because the money must be divided three ways.

Consider the arithmetic:

1. To win money on horses that pay $2.20, it is necessary to cash 91 of every 100 bets.

2. To win money on horses that pay $2.40, it is necessary to cash more than 83 of every 100 bets.

3. To win money on horses that pay $2.60, it is necessary to cash more than 77 of every 100 bets.

4. To win money on horses that pay $3.00, it is necessary to cash more than 66 of every 100 bets.

Those are large orders.

The following statements about place and show betting can be accepted as maxims. They derive from the facts of raceway life, the patterns and percentages of the game:

1. It is harder to make money by betting for place and show than for win.

2. The number of correct predictions necessary to produce a profit in a representative series of place or show bets is unattainable except by a supremely expert, supremely patient handicapper.

3. The relatively low natural odds on place and show bets are drastically reduced by take and breakage, making the task of the place or show bettor even more difficult.

4. Anyone able to show a profit from a long series of place or show bets has the ability to make important money on straight betting—betting to win.

Calculating Place and Show Prices

The place pool consists of all the money bet on all the horses for place. Like the win pool, it is subject to take and breakage. Unlike the win pool, it is divided (after take and breakage) between two groups of bettors. Those who bet on the winning horse for place share the profits with those who bet on the runner-up for place. Here is an example:

Total amount in place pool: $48,000
Remainder after 15-percent take: $40,800
Total bet on "A" to place: $20,000
Total bet on "B" to place: $12,000

The total profit to be returned to the successful place bettors on this race is $8,800. That figure is obtained by subtracting from the net pool of $40,800 the $12,000 that was bet on "A" and "B." The remainder is what the losing bettors have lost.

The $8,800 is now divided in half, leaving $4,400 in profits for distribution to the backers of "A" and $4,400 for those who bet on "B."

Take "A" first:

$$20,000 \mid \frac{4,400.00}{.22}$$

The correct dollar odds on "A" to place are .22. Breakage transforms this to .20, making "A" a 1 to 5 shot for place. The mutuel is $2.40.

Without take and breakage, the mutuel would be $2.80. The natural profits on "A" have been reduced by 50 percent! Cut in half!

Now for "B":

$$12,000 \mid \frac{4,400.00}{.36}$$

Breakage reduces the odds to .30 to 1.00, making the mutuel price $2.60. But the natural price, without take and breakage, would be $3.33. The profits have been cut by 55 percent.

The difficulties of place and show betting are even more pronounced than these examples indicate. Most notably, the purchaser of a place or show ticket buys a pig in a poke. He may have reason for confidence in the horse's ability to finish second or third, but he cannot know what the ticket will be worth until the race is over—except at Roosevelt, where an unusual totalizator board displays the full possibilities. If he must share the profits with holders of place tickets on an odds-on favorite, his own ticket will be worth relatively little. If his horse wins the race and a longshot finishes second—or vice versa—the place ticket will be worth more. Thus, his position is comparable to that of a poker player with a bobtail straight who agrees to buy a card without knowing how much money is in the pot. He might as well play a slot machine.

To make this clear, let us now see what happens to the place price on the well-backed "A" if longshot "C" wins the race or finishes second. The pool remains $40,800, after deduction of the take. The crowd has bet $5,000 on "C" to place. That amount, plus the $20,000 bet on "A," is now deducted from the pool, leaving $15,800 for distribution. Holders of tickets on "A" will get $7,900. So will the supporters of "C." Compute the price on "A":

$$20,000 \mid \overline{7,900.00} \atop .39$$

The correct odds are slashed to .30 by breakage, making the mutuel price $2.60. This is more than "A" paid when the pool was shared with backers of the fairly well-supported "B." But now that "B" has failed to finish first or second, the $12,000 bet on him has been lost, and the losses have increased the profits distributed to owners of cashable place tickets.

I doubt that it is necessary to work out the computations on a show pool. After the take, the amounts bet on all three horses are subtracted from the net pool. The remainder is divided into three equal parts, and the show price on each horse is then calculated in the usual way.

Place Overlays

By definition, an overlay is a horse whose chances of winning are greater than the odds indicate. A competent handicapper can tell whether a horse's chances are good, bad or indifferent. He may even have a method of describing its chances numerically, telling himself that "A" should be a 2 to 1 shot, because it can beat tonight's field 33 percent of the time, and "B" should be 10 to 1 because it hardly could be expected to win more than once in eleven tries. Needless to say, such figures are only personal estimates. Without a good computer (and years of data processing), it will not be possible to refine handicapping to the point where a horse's chances might be expressed in accurate mathematical terms.

Nevertheless, the good handicapper usually recognizes an overlay when he sees one. If he likes a horse's chances and it turns out to be a longshot, it is an overlay. If he thinks the horse should be an odds-on favorite, and its odds remain above even money, it is an overlay. If he thinks it will win in a walk and would be a good bet at 1 to 10, he considers it a big overlay at 2 to 5.

If one is capable of recognizing overlays and bets on no other kind of horse, profits are inevitable. "Any time I can get 20 to 1 on a natural 10 to 1 shot, I grab it," bellows the sage of the grandstand bar. But he is not talking about overlays, even though he thinks he is. No horse is worth a bet unless it has a reasonable chance to win. I doubt that anyone can tell whether an outsider should be 10 to 1 or 20 to 1.

At smaller raceways, one frequently finds that the likeliest horse in the race is noticeably underbet for place or show. That makes the horse an overlay for place or show. If it wins, or finishes second or third, it will pay a higher mutuel price for place or show than it should.

It is easy enough to spot these opportunities. If the tote board shows that the amount of money bet on the horse to win is about a quarter of the total win pool, but that the animal accounts for only about a sixth of the place pool, it is underbet for place. Whether it is worth a place bet depends largely on what the mutuel patterns have been at the particular track. At tracks like Yonkers, Roosevelt, Hollywood, Sportsman's Park, Washington Park and Liberty Bell, the crowds include numerous punters who watch the board closely for discrepancies, and hasten to bet whenever a good prospect is underbet in the place or show pool. Elsewhere, the crowds often neglect such overlays, permitting shrewd operators to cash in.

In my opinion, it makes no sense to bet on horses for show, regardless of overlays. Place bets are understandable in the following circumstances:

1. When the best horse in the race is an odds-on favorite and all other likely contenders in the race are longshots. In circumstances of that kind the favorite may pay as much for place as for win.

2. When the two best horses in the race are coupled as a betting entry and the handicapper believes that they have an unusually good chance to finish first and second, a place bet may return a higher price than a win bet.

3. When the best horse in the race is a big overlay at odds of 4 to 1 or better, it often pays even money or better for place, justifying the handicapper's decision to bet for win and place.

Obviously, to make such decisions profitably, one must be capable of recognizing the best horse in the race a substantial percentage of the time.

Hedging

In connection with place bets on horses presumed to be the top contenders in their races, it is important to understand the thinking processes of players who try to minimize their losses by hedging their bets. They bet each of their selections across the board, or for win and place or win and show.

Their success depends, as usual, on handicapping ability and is limited by the effects of take and breakage. These effects, as we have seen, are most severe when the odds are short. If a player backs a horse for win and show and the animal finishes third, there is no doubt that the proceeds of the show ticket reduce the overall loss. Indeed, if the player bets six or seven times as much for show as for win, he may turn a nice profit on such a deal.

However, when the horse substantiates the player's handicapping ability by winning the race, the return on combined win and show betting is severely less than it would be if all the money were bet to win.

The inherent problem of all such maneuvering at the mutuel windows is the near-impossibility of making money on place or show bets. Unless the player is able to make a profit for place or show, his hedging merely prevents him from making as much on his win bets as he otherwise might. Or, if he also is incapable of making money on win bets, the hedges will tend to reduce his overall rate of loss to some extent, while increasing his total investment. Finally, if he is good enough to break even or make a small profit on place or show bets, he almost certainly wastes time and money in the effort: He is good enough to make considerably more money than that by betting to win only!

Betting More than One Horse to Win

"I never bet against myself," declaims the sage. "Betting two horses in a race is betting against yourself."

I have been hearing that line since I was in knickerbockers and have yet to discover any logic in it. Neither is there any mathematics in it. As nearly as I can tell, the horror of "betting against yourself" derives from superstition—the idea that conflicting wishes might antagonize the gods. Or that if you bet on Horse "A" you should not weaken the potency of your wishes by also betting on Horse "B."

When it comes to the pell-mell of harness racing on half-mile tracks, however, the player can lose more money through vain wishes than through betting on two horses—each to win—in certain races. In fact, there are occasions when it is intelligent to bet on three horses, each to win. Situations of this kind arise less often at one-mile and ⅝-mile tracks, where the contention is less hectic and a horse that figures best, even if narrowly, can be counted on to arrive home first a satisfactory percentage of the time.

In a later chapter we shall discuss the kinds of races in which bets on more than one horse are the difference between profit and loss or —for a good handicapper—the difference between betting and passing the race entirely. I hardly need point out that multiple bets never are made unless each of the horses, if it wins, is likely to return a mutuel price large enough to make the total investment profitable.

Booking Percentages

In olden times, a hustler could shop among the trackside book-makers for the best odds. Good handicappers made money that way by betting on every horse except rank outsiders, overrated favorites and other animals that figured to lose.

BOOKING PERCENTAGES

Odds	Percentage	Odds	Percentage	Odds	Percentage
1–9	90.00	8–5	38.46	13–1	7.14
1–8	88.89	9–5	35.71	14–1	6.66
1–7	87.50	2–1	33.33	15–1	6.25
1–6	85.68	5–2	28.57	16–1	5.88
1–5	83.33	3–1	25.00	17–1	5.55
1–4	80.00	7–2	22.23	18–1	5.26
1–3	75.00	4–1	20.00	19–1	5.00
2–5	71.42	9–2	18.19	20–1	4.76
1–2	66.67	5–1	16.67	25–1	3.85
3–5	62.50	6–1	14.29	30–1	3.23
3–4	57.14	7–1	12.50	40–1	2.44
4–5	55.55	8–1	11.11	50–1	1.96
1–1	50.00	9–1	10.00	60–1	1.64
6–5	45.45	10–1	9.09	75–1	1.32
7–5	41.67	11–1	8.33	99–1	.99
3–2	40.00	12–1	7.69		

The practice was known variously as "booking against the book" and "dutching." Its basis was the bookmaker's scale of percentages, which showed how odds rose or fell in conformity with the fraction of the betting pool represented by the amount bet on each horse. For an easy example, if the player felt that an even-money choice could not win, he would operate as if half the betting pool—the proportion represented by the bets on that horse—were up for grabs. Simply by betting all other horses in the race in amounts equal or proportionate to their booking percentages, he would win. Provided that the favorite lost.

I understand that some players try the same kind of thing at the mutuel windows. However, mutuel bets are made not at the fixed odds of the bookmaking days, but at final odds. These can only be approximated when betting is in progress and are not announced until the race is over. Despite this disadvantage and the difficulties to which it leads, people persist in trying to book against the mutuel book. Knowing that the pool adds up to about 117 percent (the extra 17 being take and breakage), they try to eliminate horses whose odds represent 30 or 40 percent of the pool. They then bet on the remaining horses in proportions indicated by the table of booking percentages. If any of the horses on which they bet happens to win, they show a profit. Theoretically, that is.

Bets must be made at the last possible moment, in amounts that require lightning calculation. Enormous capital and outstanding ability as a handicapper are needed. The player cannot operate alone, because bets have to be made at more than one window. How could a solo bettor get down bets of $33, $19, $11, and $7 in the same race—and all in the final seconds before the race starts? To bet any earlier would be to risk having the entire deal thrown awry by last-second changes in the odds.

I do not say that profitable betting of this kind is impossible. But it requires betting partners of such reliability, capital of such magnitude and handicapping talent so well developed that the rare person able to carry it off would probably do better by playing alone, betting on his own choices to win.

Progressive and System Betting

Most betting systems are mathematically unsound. They require the player to increase his bet after every losing attempt. Their theory is that the player is "due" to win at some point, and that the increased bet will return enough to make up for prior losses. We have already discussed the disaster that awaits anyone who, relying on a "law" of averages, doubles his bet after every loss on a favorite, or on a top driver. One need not double the bets, of course. Modifications of the double-up method are used by many players. But these systems only modify losses. They cannot produce profits except briefly and accidentally. Also, they require investment outlays beyond all proportion to the returns.

A pet approach of some players is called "due-column betting." The bettor decides that the raceway owes him a nightly stipend—say, $100. He therefore bets as much on each of his selections as will produce the desired return. Let us say that he likes a 4 to 1 shot in the first race. He bets $25. If the horse loses, the raceway now "owes" him $125, so he bets $63 on a 2 to 1 shot in the second race. If the horse wins, the player has about $101 in profit and goes home. Otherwise, he now needs $188 to replace his losses and supply his intended profit.

The chief shortcoming of that procedure is the supposition that anyone can make a profit at any raceway on any given night. Or in any given week. Thus, due-column betting multiplies one's losses during a losing streak, requiring bets of steadily increasing and, in time, prohibitively large size. Few players can afford such outlays.

A far more intelligent plan is to abandon due columns and double-ups and the like, allocating a *fixed percentage* of betting capital to each transaction. As capital decreases, so do the bets, enabling the player to withstand a long succession of losses. As capital increases, the bets do also, in a gratifying upward spiral.

The notion that a player should risk more when he is winning and less when he is losing is accepted as wisdom in every game that involves betting. Players who adhere to that principle make more—or lose less—than players who defy it. If two handicappers are capable of showing a 20 percent profit on flat bets, and each starts with a bankroll of $100, the one who bets 5 percent of capital on each of his selections will end the year with far more money than the one who favors due-column betting or progressive betting or other upside-down methods that violate the percentages of the game, the principles of sound investment and the tenets of common sense.

The player who bets 5 percent of capital can stay in business at a raceway for months, without winning a dime. If he goes there with $100 and loses his first twenty bets in succession, he will have $45 left. If he actually is capable of a long-term profit in the 20-percent range, he could go to the harness races for years without encountering a losing streak as awful as that, but the point is made.

The due-column or progressive bettor would be ruined by such a losing streak, even though he were just as good a handicapper as the other man. By the same token, neither the due-column bettor nor the believer in progressive betting makes as much money in a series of winning bets as the man who bets a fixed fraction of his capital.

To demonstrate, let us analyze the occasional blessing of five winners in succession. For simplicity, let us assume that each winner pays 5 to 2. The due-column bettor has a bankroll of $400 and wants to make $50 per race. He bets $20 on each of the five successive winners, netting $250 in profit and raising his bankroll to $650. He is as happy as a clam.

The adherent of progressive betting also has a $400 bankroll. He bets $20 on the first horse, planning to apply his magic formula in such a way as to bet more on the second, if the first loses. But the first wins, and so do the next four. He ends by making $250 on the winning streak. His bankroll is also $650 and he is perfectly satisfied.

The man who bets 5 percent of capital also has a $400 bankroll. His first bet nets $50, making his capital $450.

His second bet is $22, netting $55. Bankroll: $505.

His third bet is $25, netting $62.50. Bankroll: $567.50.

His fourth bet is $28, netting $70. Bankroll: $637.50.

His fifth bet is $32, netting $80. Bankroll: $717.50.

He has done better than the others. Even if his next two horses lose, he will remain in excellent condition.

He will bet $36 on the first loser, reducing his capital to $681.50.

He will bet $34 on the second loser, reducing his capital to $647.50.

The due-column bettor will lose $20 on the first unsuccessful bet and, assuming that we still are dealing with 5 to 2 shots, will drop $28 on the second. His bankroll is now down to $602.

The progressive bettor, no matter how conservative his methods, will lose at least $50 on the two bets, reducing his capital to $600 or less, with losses mounting at an unendurable rate if the unhappy streak continues.

Daily Doubles and the Like

It is hard enough to pick a winner without contracting to pick two in succession, as in the daily double. Or four in succession, as in the twin double. Or the first two finishers in exact order, as in the perfecta (exacta). Or the first two finishers in exact order in two races (twin perfecta or twin exacta). Or the first two finishers, regardless of order (quinella).

The trouble with all those multiple bets, apart from the difficulty of making selections, is that the player does not have the faintest idea what the payoff will be. All too often, the return is much smaller than the risk warrants. For a typical example, a player likes a horse in the first or second race, and "wheels" it in the daily double—buying tickets that couple it with each horse in the other race. This probably costs $16 or $18. The horse wins its race at odds, let's say, of 5 to 2. The daily double pays $24. The player makes $6 or $8 on his large bet. Had he put the same amount of money on the horse he liked, it would have returned about $60, a much higher profit for a much more sensible investment.

I could carry on in this vein for pages, covering every miserable contingency, but I won't detain you any longer. The truth is that multiple, gimmick bets are here to stay and are becoming more numerous every season. The customers love them.

If you consider the evening incomplete on which you fail to play the daily double and all available exactas and quinellas, I cannot hope to dissuade you, but perhaps you might be willing to accept one small bit of advice. Play the gimmicks without hope of making substantial money. Reserve your biggest bets for the regular windows, where you can invest in one well-handicapped selection at a time. Play the doubles for fun—pairing three horses in one race with four in another, trying to break even or almost. Never spend more than $2 for a ticket. Treat the exactas the same way. If you can narrow contention to two horses in a race, play them both ways, for $4. If you find that three horses have approximately equal chances, box them for $12, betting that each will finish first and second in tandem with the other two.

You would do better to use all that money for straight win betting on standout selections, but I suppose that you would miss some important fun. Or something.

The Cost of the Hobby

They say that the school of experience offers no free scholarships and that one must suffer the painful lessons of loss before becoming a winner. This may be so. One does not master the principles of handicapping and betting without practice, which can be expensive.

How expensive? Transportation, admission, program and moderate refreshment are likely to cost $10 an outing. Plus the cost of mutuel tickets. In my opinion, the beginning handicapper should make no bets whatever until he has become acustomed to the tense hullabaloo of the track and until, above all, he has demonstrated through dry runs that he can pick himself some winners.

At that stage, the $2 bet becomes appropriate. Penalizing the player for his mistakes, the $2 bet is an experience quite unlike the dry run, which permits second thoughts, benefits of the doubt and other forms of self-deception. After proving that one can take in at least as much on $2 bets as one spends for the tickets, it is time to abandon the $2 window.

To be sure, $2 bets are the least expensive at the raceway. But they offer virtually no chance to make back one's "overhead" expenses, such as transportation and admission. Assuming that the handicapper is capable of a 20-percent profit and bets on six races a night, his $12 outlay would net him about $2.40. This is less than he spends to get into the place and buy his program. Now that he is a good handicapper, he might as well make real money.

During the period of education and experimentation—the period of dry runs—the player should squirrel money away in a capital fund. When finally ready to play for profit, he should have not less than $500 in his fund, and should make bets of not less than $20—but also not more than 5 percent of the fund.

Where the handicapper might net $2.40 on a typical evening of $2 bets, he carries off $24 after an equally typical evening on which he increases the bets to $20 each. His hobby has begun to pay for itself. It promises to become even more remunerative as his capital resources multiply.

How long does it take to achieve this enviable state of being? A straight answer is impossible. Some players never achieve it at all, begrudging the effort demanded for careful handicapping. At the opposite extreme, some players seem to become excellent handicappers in a few weeks—if their letters to me can be believed. On balance, I'd guess that a person who combines keen interest with moderate talent should be able to get along nicely after a couple of months of study, including at least a half-dozen betless visits to the track.

4

The Breeding Factor

THE STANDARDBRED is uniquely American, a product of the celebrated melting pot. Its emergence as a recognizable type began during the earliest years of the new republic, when matings of Thoroughbred runners with light-harness horses of uncertain origin produced some phenomenal young.

Many of these off-bred horses were more compact and docile, less leggy and fragile than the Thoroughbred, yet no less brave. Some could trot more swiftly than any horse known previously, and were gluttons for work. A few had the mysterious gift of prepotency, transmitting their high speed, deep stamina and affinity for the trot to generation after generation of their descendants.

These few were the progenitors, the founders. Their blood upgraded what had been a kind of genetic hash into what now is recognized universally as a true breed. Although official registration did not begin until 1871, the U.S. Standardbred has already made a heavy imprint on harness racing throughout the world. The breed is still new and vigorous, still evolving. Its greatest exploits lie ahead.

The name, "Standardbred," arose from rules adopted in 1879 by the National Association of Trotting Horse Breeders: "In order to define what constitutes a trotting-bred horse, and to establish a breed of trotters on a more intelligent basis. . . ."

The Association decreed that a horse would be acceptable as "a standard trotting-bred animal" if it went a mile in 2:30 or better, or was parent or progeny of a "standard" animal. Nowadays the standard is 2:20 for two-year-olds and 2:15 for older horses.

Some harness-race enthusiasts wish the breed had another name. "Standard" sounds too standard, as if the horses were not *deluxe*. "Thoroughbred," on the other hand, has an aristocratic ring to it. Nonsense. All race horses come from the same seed.

Hambletonian, from whom all Standardbreds descend.

Examine pedigrees and you discover that the winner of the Hambletonian is a blood cousin of the winner of the Kentucky Derby and of
every other duly registered trotter, pacer, and runner on earth. The
lineage of each is traceable to the late seventeenth and early eighteenth
centuries, when British horsemen sought to invigorate their ancient
racing stock with infusions of North African and Near Eastern blood.
Three imported stallions established dominant lines—the Darley
Arabian, Byerly Turk and Godolphin Barb (so called because it was
thought to come from the Barbary Coast of Morocco). One of the
Darley Arabian's foremost sons, Flying Childers, an undefeated runner,
founded the line that led to our modern trotters and pacers, by way
of the legendary Messenger and Hambletonian. A full brother to Flying Childers, called Bartlett's Childers, founded the Eclipse line, which
includes most leading North American Thoroughbreds. All these
descendants of the Darley Arabian are also descendants, through
cross-breeding, of the Byerly Turk and Godolphin Barb.

Messenger, the spirited grey with which the whole thing is believed to have started in North America, never trotted or paced in competition. He had been an outstanding runner in England, as befitted a descendant of Flying Childers and Matchem (forebear of Man O' War). His racing career behind him, he came to Philadelphia in 1788 and went to stud, begetting not only some top runners but the line of trotters and pacers that now occupy stalls from Hollywood to Du Quoin to Hinsdale to Melbourne. The preeminence of Messenger became unmistakable as early as 1845, when his granddaughter, a twelve-year-old mare named Lady Suffolk, became the first horse in history to haul a sulky a mile in less than 2:30.

The great Hambletonian was foaled in 1849, full of Messenger blood. Like most of his era, he also was full of unidentifiable blood. His sire, Abdallah, was by a Thoroughbred out of a mare of unknown breeding. His dam was a descendant of Norfolk-Hackney road trotters. It all added up, somehow. Between 1851 and 1875, the incredible Hambletonian sired 1,331 sons and daughters whose descendants literally have obliterated every other strain of trotter and pacer in North American racing. Every single harness racer on the continent traces directly to Hambletonian, as do many of the best in other parts of the world.

On a mare descended from Diomed (winner of the first British Derby), Hambletonian got Dexter, who trotted in 2:17¼, a new world record. A Hambletonian granddaughter, Goldsmith Maid, broke that record seven times in a spectacular thirteen-year career, finally going in 2:14.

Goldsmith Maid was a remarkable horse, a national celebrity. As a gate attraction and a living advertisement for harness racing, she was a forerunner of the immortal Dan Patch, who toured the land in a private railroad car and paced in 1:55. The Maid was foaled in 1855, sired by a son of Hambletonian out of a mare of unknown lineage. She did no racing—except on roads at a gallop—until she was eight. Finally broken to harness, she made her competitive debut in a setting we now can appreciate as appropriately symbolic—the Orange County Fair at Goshen, N.Y. Before she was retired on her twentieth birthday, the mare won 119 races (332 separate heats in all), was second in 16, third in 5, fourth in 1 and unplaced only once. Her earnings of $364,200 were unequalled by any horse until 1931, when Sun Beau (a Thoroughbred descendant of Messenger) reached $376,744 on running tracks.

The awesome mare did all that in harness to lumbering, sixty-pound, high-wheeled sulkies over racing strips that would never pass muster today. She was a barnstormer. She traversed the continent several times, drawing huge crowds at fairs and on streets and even at railroad sidings. Her lithographed likeness adorned the walls of parlors, barns and saloons. Many historians think that she was the making of American harness racing.

After retirement, the Maid dropped only three foals, none of which contributed much to the advancement of the breed. But she had done enough. Four of her relatives—all sons of Hambletonian—attended to the improvement of the breed with such vigor that all of our leading trotters and pacers carry their blood in tail male (the male side of the pedigree). These great stallions were George Wilkes, Dictator, Happy Medium and Electioneer.

George Wilkes founded the Axworthy line, represented today by the outstanding trotting sires Florican and Hickory Smoke and the pacing sires Knight Dream, Duane Hanover, and Torpid.

From Dictator came the Billy Direct line of pacers, represented in current sire lists by Tar Heel and Thorpe Hanover.

Happy Medium founded the greatest of trotting lines, headed by Peter the Great and then by Peter Volo and Peter Scott and their sons, Volomite and Scotland. From these came leading trotting sires such

Nevele Pride at the grave of Goldsmith Maid.

as Star's Pride, Hoot Mon, Speedster, Hickory Pride and Sharpshooter, plus pacing sires like Bye Bye Byrd, Bullet Hanover, Sampson Hanover, Poplar Byrd and Capetown.

The world's outstanding line of pacers was seeded by Hambletonian's son, Electioneer, whose descendants include such contemporary sires as Good Time, Gene Abbe, Adios Boy, Greentree Adios, Dale Frost, Bullet Hanover, Meadow Skipper and the late Adios, who deserves a book of his own.

Adios

Bought at auction for $21,000 by Del Miller in 1948, Adios, who had paced in 1:57½, presently became the most successful stallion of any breed in the history of horse racing. Before his death in 1965, he sired more than 600 foals. By 1969, the best of these had won over $18 million in purses—about $3 million more than the winnings credited to the get of Bull Lea, the all-time great Thoroughbred sire.

Of four champions that have paced the mile in 1:55 or faster, three were sons of Adios: Bret Hanover (1:53:3), Adios Butler (1:54:3), and Adios Harry (1:55). No fewer than 78 of his sons and daughters

Adios, most successful racing sire in history.

took records of 2:00 or less, among them famous competitors like Bullet Hanover, Shadow Wave, Dancer Hanover, Dottie's Pick, Henry T. Adios, Countess Adios, Adios Boy, Lehigh Hanover, Meadow Ace, Adios Vic, Cold Front, and the 1:55 marvels mentioned above.

Adios sired the dams of 77 performers with records of 2:00 or less. His 365 yearlings sold at public auction brought almost $7 million —an average of $18,512. It is taken for granted that his descendants will form the most powerful Standardbred dynasty of all, dominating the pacing scene both on the track and at the breeding farms.

Standardbred Ruggedness

Newcomers to harness racing are sometimes appalled by the demands made on the horses. Their prerace workouts are strenuous enough to leave the animals lathered in sweat, their heads down, ears drooping and tails extended, as if in utter exhaustion. In no other sport do the athletes expend so much energy in so-called warm-ups. One wonders how the trotters and pacers can have anything left for the race itself.

The fact is that many trainers now work their horses less sternly on the night of the race than they used to. Horses that race once a week for months on end seem to hold their edge longer if asked for less effort between races. But the total output of energy remains about the same as it was in the days when seasons were shorter and races fewer. Standardbreds not only are capable of fantastic exertion but require it. Their neuromuscular systems produce top speed with minimum breaks of stride only after a degree of fatigue has been established. This characteristic is comparable to that of the baseball pitcher whose control suffers if he gets more than four days of rest between starts. Asked what was wrong, he explains, "I was just too strong. Too much rest."

Associated with the Standardbred's strength is his incredible equanimity. He is as intelligent as any other racehorse, and as aware of the difference between a night of racing and a night in the barn. But he rarely gets fussed. Unless something hurts him, he stands placidly in his paddock stall, often so quietly that he seems to be dozing. A harness-race paddock, full of horses and their handlers, is quieter than the average insurance office. Some horses are more temperamental than others, but few cause real problems.

In shape, these solid equine citizens produce the same speed week after week after week. The 2:05 pacer arrives within a few ticks of that mark in every race, seldom going much faster unless sucked along behind swifter animals, and seldom going much slower unless delayed by an off track or interference or a poor drive. When the horse has an unobstructed trip and finishes it in much slower time than expected, the trainer knows that wear and tear have set in and that a vacation is indicated.

Some of the most remarkable demonstrations of Standardbred ruggedness and consistency occur on the Grand Circuit. Some of these involve three heats on the same afternoon. Each entrant has been racing about once a week, all summer. Yet now they race two or three times in one day against the best of their age, gait and sex— and the winning time in the decisive, final heat may vary by less than a second from the times recorded in the preliminary heats.

Old-timers are full of lore about the endurance of bygone trotters and pacers. The Columbian Trot of 1893 lasted nine heats (on three successive days) before Alix won it. To warm up for an exhibition at Agawam, Mass., Greyhound jogged five miles the wrong way of the track, turned and trotted six more, the last two briskly. He then was timed in 1:57.

In future decades, senior citizens of the sport will undoubtedly brag about Cardigan Bay, as sturdy a horse as ever pulled a sulky. His immortality is assured because he was the first harness horse to win more than $1 million in purses. But there was more to Cardigan Bay than that. He was a model of Standardbred courage.

When Stanley Dancer and an American syndicate bought the eight-year-old gelding for $100,000 in 1964, he was the greatest pacer in New Zealand and Australia, having won everything in sight and recording some amazing times. For example: 1:56:1 on a $\frac{9}{16}$-mile track. In 1962, a sulky wheel collapsed during a training jog, and the frightened animal had bolted to his stall, dragging the cart behind him and tearing a bone-deep hole in his right hip when he crashed into a wall. Lesser horses are put to death after such injuries, but means were found to ease this one's pain during four months of treatment which shifted Cardy's weight to his sound side. The gelding emerged barely able to walk, his right hip six inches lower than his left. But he soon was back in training.

Stanley Dancer once told Lou Effrat of *The New York Times:* "I saw Cardigan Bay win the 1964 Inter-Dominions. What actually convinced me to go ahead happened one morning while Peter Wolfenden was training him for the Final. I had the stopwatch on Old Cardy and was amazed to see him go two miles, the second in 2:02:3 and the final half in one minute flat. When I heard that Wolfenden had jogged him seventeen miles that same morning, I knew the deal had to be made."

Through much of his epochal career in the United States, the gelding was an orthopedic case. In June, 1965, after winning at Roosevelt Raceway, he underwent surgery for removal of a fractured splint bone. But on July 23, he was sound enough to go 1:58:3 at Roosevelt, be-

Cardigan Bay defeats Bret Hanover at Yonkers Raceway, as Stanley Dancer glances back triumphantly at Frank Ervin.

hind Fly Fly Byrd. During the following year, when he was beating the likes of Bret Hanover, he was plagued with an ailing suspensory ligament. When Bret beat the gelding in June, Dancer blamed the injured ligament and decided that the old horse was through. But Cardigan Bay again recovered sufficiently to return to the wars. In 1968, he pushed his earnings to $1,000,671, winning in 2:01 at Freehold Raceway, and promptly was retired for keeps.

Is Breeding a Science?

All great Standardbred sires of recent years have also been good race horses. But not all good race horses distinguish themselves in the boudoir. Until a stallion's offspring begin racing, nobody can be sure whether he is capable of begetting youngsters as sound and swift as he was. The suspense is enormous, and so is the cost. The breeding industry is no place for the timid, the impatient or the poor.

Our foremost authority on the breeding of trotters and pacers is James C. Harrison, who used to be general manager of the nation's premier nursery, Hanover Shoe Farms, and now is developing Lana Lobell Farm as a power in the field. He says:

> I do not know of any way in which the sire potential of a horse can be assessed positively in advance. I suppose I have probably devoted more time to this problem than any living person. I have spent hundreds of hours running up charts and laying out check lists covering the factors of speed, early speed, gait, disposition, size, general conformation, breeding, racing manners, courage, endurance, opportunity and other items of interest covering page after closely typed page. In the end, nothing came of it. I recall that on one occasion I proved conclusively that Volomite could not be a successful sire. It was then that I gave it up as a bad job and reverted to the basic philosophy of so many of the most successful breeders, "Breed the best to the best and hope for the best."

Nothing could be more reasonable. Mated with mares of high quality, Nevele Pride, Overcall, Laverne Hanover, Adios Vic, Best Of All, Carlisle, Romeo Hanover, Romulus Hanover, and other leading racers of recent seasons may beget champions. But they may not. Nobody will be competent to pass judgment on them as sires until they have sent several crops to the races for years of testing. All anyone knows is that some great racers become great sires and dams. And on this fact reposes the "hope for the best" to which Jim Harrison refers.

Most leading breeders sell their yearlings at auction, where prices naturally are highest on animals that represent matings of the best with the best. Sometimes the promise is fulfilled with minimum delay. In 1965, for example, Speedy Streak fetched a then-record auction price of $113,000 and, after early difficulties, went on to win the 1967 Hambletonian. The previous record price for an auctioned yearling was $105,000, which Stanley Dancer paid in 1958 for Dancer Hanover, by Adios. The horse came up with a bad shoulder and never

Dancer Hanover during his racing days, with Del Miller in the sulky. Dancer later sired champions Romeo Hanover and Romulus Hanover, and two of the highest-priced yearlings of all time, Nevele Bigshot and Froehlich Hanover.

earned his way as a competitor, though he showed signs of greatness on occasion. He finally went to Hanover Shoe Farms, where he had been foaled, and began to get foals of his own.

One of these was Romeo Hanover, who sold for a mere $8,500 in 1964, was voted Pacer of the Year in 1965 and retired with earnings of $658,505. Romeo's full brother (by Dancer Hanover out of Romola Hanover) was Romulus Hanover, a $35,000 yearling who won purses of $483,750. In 1969, another full brother, Froehlich Hanover, fetched an all-time high of $125,000 at the Harrisburg yearling auction. This exceeded by $10,000 the record price paid in 1968 for a fourth brother, Nevele Bigshot.

Complete returns are not yet in on Nevele Bigshot, Menges Hanover, Bart Hanover, Brad Hanover, and Nevele Major, each of which brought $100,000 at yearling auctions in recent years. If, as seems possible at this writing, some of the five perform woefully in competition, perhaps they will make up for it later, earning themselves out as studs. With well-bred sires in extreme demand, a $100,000 stallion has a fair chance to earn his price in the breeding stall, even if he fails to do so at the raceway. Horsemen who pay huge sums for glamorous yearlings know this full well.

Does it seem, then, that breeding may be a precise art, even a science? I would not hasten to such a conclusion. If breeders and buyers were capable of uniformly accurate evaluations of Standard-bred stock, certain winning horses could sell for many times the low prices they bring at the yearling auctions.

The fastest pacer of all time, Bret Hanover, by Adios, cost a rela-tively moderate $50,000, but retired with earnings of $922,616. Kerry Way, two-year-old Trotter of the Year with earnings of over $100,000 in 1965, and three-year-old Trotter of the Year in 1966, when she won the Hambletonian, was a $16,000 yearling. Carlisle went for $5,500 and won a hundred times that much in his first five seasons of racing. Nardin's Byrd sold for $2,500, won $136,261 as a two-year-old and remained among the top money winners during the succeeding two years.

Fresh Yankee, by Hickory Pride, was a fantastic bargain. After being sold for $900 as a yearling, all she did was become a world champion trotting mare with a record of 1:57:1, earnings well up in six figures, victories on both sides of the Atlantic and bright prospects as a broodmare.

It would be possible to fill hundreds of pages with rags-to-riches tales like these. They prove conclusively that the quality of a Standard-bred is not always discernible in its pedigree, or even in the impres-sions it arouses by its physical appearance at a yearling auction. If breeding were even a moderately exact science, there would be fewer surprises. Horses with the most impressive parentage not only would command the highest sales prices, as they now do, but would also win all the big races, which they do not.

Early Speed

The racegoer uses the term "early speed" to describe horses that leave quickly, reach the first turn on the lead or in competition for it, and try to cut out the pace of the race, sometimes helping and sometimes wrecking opponents that begin less rapidly. Standardbred horsemen have two other meanings for the term. One, which need not concern us here, refers to horses that seem capable of winning early in the year, while other horses are still training or racing into shape. And the third meaning, which has to do with breeding, describes horses able to perform at high speed when only two or three years old.

Now that many of the richest races are for two- and three-year-olds, and most champions retire to stud at five, it is interesting to realize that early speed is of comparatively recent origin. Until an opinionated tycoon named Leland Stanford demonstrated some revolutionary breeding and training theories in the final quarter of the nineteenth century, few trotters were deemed ready for competition before age four or five.

The reasons for keeping young horses away from the races were traditional and, before Stanford, were practical as well. The original job of the road-racing harness horse, after all, had been to haul passengers and cargo, heavy labor for which mature, full-grown animals were best suited. Secondly, while the Standardbreds of the time could almost always be taught to trot at speed, they did not usually learn rapidly. This was due partly to the uncertainties of their breeding and partly to drawn-out schooling methods which were scaled to the lowest common denominator.

Stanford considered all this idiotic. Variously president of the Union Pacific Railroad, governor of California and U.S. senator from that state, he could afford to dispute any tradition he pleased and seek proof for any upstream theory he held. It seemed to him that horses properly bred to trot would produce early speed if asked for it. So he bought Electioneer, son of Hambletonian, for $12,500, and installed the stallion with an expensive harem of trotting mares on his farm at Palo Alto, where Leland Stanford University now stands.

The foals were not subjected to heavy work, for which only mature horses were suited. All they were asked to do was abide by their heredity and trot swiftly. In the parlance of harness racing, they were "brushed"—asked for high speed over short distances. It worked.

Fifteen years after the 17-year-old Goldsmith Maid set her world's record of 2:14, a three-year-old named Sunol, by Stanford's Electioneer, went a mile in 2:10¾. A stablemate named Arion recorded the same time at two. Stanford's trotters accumulated so many world's records for their ages that controversy ended.

Nowadays, many horsemen wish that early speed could be deemphasized, so that Standardbreds might be spared all-out effort before their bone structures mature. No doubt, animals unraced until age four might last longer, but the already hazardous economics of Standardbred ownership would become prohibitively risky. As matters stand, the purchaser of a yearling has some expectation of beginning to recover his investment within a year, when the animal goes to the races. To delay competition an additional two years would increase expenses greatly without necessarily increasing the possibility of profit. Indeed, illnesses and injuries suffered in training—or even in farm pastures—disable more horses than racing accidents do. The longer a horse remains unraced, the less the likelihood that he ever will race.

Another reason why the classic events for colts (the term applied to horses less than four, regardless of sex) attract so much attention is that fresh, well-bred, two- and three-year-olds are the soundest, most spirited and least battleworn of racing animals. Because they are in mint condition, their performances are likely to imply much about the breeding value of their parents—to say nothing of their own potential value in that department. To this consideration must be added the psychological fact that in racing, as elsewhere in life, the young and new invariably excite more interest than the old and familiar.

Mares and foals in pasture at Castleton Farm, Lexington, Ky.

Finally, as Leland Stanford demonstrated so long ago, and as has become increasingly manifest with the evolution of the breed, Standardbreds are capable of speed at ages two and three which were totally beyond the reach of their ancestors, regardless of age. Bred to race, they seem ready to prove it almost as soon as they are foaled. They now learn in weeks what could be taught to their forebears only in months or years. It's in their blood.

Trotting versus Pacing

An ironic footnote to the achievements of Leland Stanford is that the descendants of his great trotting stallion, Electioneer, have turned out to be the foremost pacers in the sport. Stanford detested pacers and would not have one on his premises. His purist attitude was widely shared: Good horses raced on the trot. The pace was for culls. And horses that could not pace unless strapped in hobbles were beneath notice.

Trotters remain the aristocrats of the breed. By comparison with pacers, they are hard to educate. They are more difficult to shoe. They are more difficult to maintain in winning condition. They are much more difficult to drive. They have the cherished early speed, but at two and three even the best of them are prone to break stride, causing as much agony in the barn as in the grandstand. Important stakes races for young trotters frequently turn into jumping fiascos, with horse after horse breaking stride and the race going not necessarily to the swiftest but to the luckiest. Among trotters of less talent, breaking often remains a lifelong problem.

Because many bettors hesitate to risk money on a horse that may lose because it galloped, or because another breaker got in its way, the mutuel handle suffers. As a class, trotters are not good for business and will not be until the absolutely inevitable day when the breed improves sufficiently to make breaking a rarity.

Among the few stables that have no pacers is the renowned Arden Homestead Stable of Goshen, N.Y. Its master, E. Roland Harriman, is uninfluenced by considerations of commerce. He has been known to deplore the material factors which account for the growing predominance of hobbled pacers. The time may come when his staunch dedication to the trotter will be listed among his main contributions to the stability and respectability of harness racing.

In any event, he already is revered as the sport's most devoted benefactor. In the twenties, when a crisis of disorganization threatened to wreck the system of foal registration on which Standardbred breeding and racing depend for order and continuity, Harriman and his Trotting Horse Club of America shouldered the burden at enormous expense. In the thirties, he was powerfully instrumental in forming the USTA, of which he now is honorary chairman. He also helped to develop the Hall of Fame of the Trotter into the flourishing institution it is. He is as close to a patron saint as can be found in any sport.

Most owners and trainers praise Harriman's commitment to the trotting gait, but regard it as a luxury. Some statistics will illustrate how economic realities have affected trotting. In 1948, the USTA issued eligibility certificates for 4,563 trotters. In 1968, it issued certificates for 8,046. In 1969, the figure was 8,229. Trotters are more abundant than they were twenty years ago, during the infancy of the raceway sport. But see how pacers have proliferated. In 1948, only 5,709 certificates were issued for them. In 1968, the total was 22,725. And in 1969, it rose to 24,503. In two decades, trotters had diminished from 45 percent of the active Standardbred population to about 25 percent.

The 40,628 harness races charted by the USTA during 1968 reflected this imbalance. Only 7,695 were trotting events—fewer than one in five.

Many of the hobbled pacers that perform at our raceways were bred to trot. For years, it has been customary in most stables to make a pacer of any animal whose development as a trotter involves more than ordinary difficulty. As one old-time horseman says with prejudiced distaste for newcomers in his field, "It takes *skill* to train a trotter. Your average used-car salesman who decides to be a trainer hasn't the know-how, the talent, the patience or the time and money it takes to gait a trotter properly and shoe it properly and hang it up properly and get it balanced so it will race flat. So he saves himself the sweat. He hangs hobbles on the horse and there he is, the trainer of a pacer."

Being truly bred to the pacing gait, descendants of Adios and Billy Direct arouse nothing but admiration among horsemen. The attitude is somewhat less favorable toward pacers with a trotting heritage. The reasoning in some quarters is that a natural-born trotter converted to pacing must have something wrong with it, ranging from physical unsoundness to inadequate early schooling. Whatever the flaw, it must ultimately take its toll, the skeptics say.

The argument may hold up in the case of a seriously unsound horse. But Gerry Mir, a 2:00 trotter at three, turned pacer and took a record of 1:59:3 at seven. The eight-year-old Reed's Waylay was voted Aged Pacing Mare of 1968, after winning 17 of 26 starts, banking $58,393 and taking a record of 1:59:2f (the "f" refers to a ⅝-mile track). Until that year, she had been a trotter, with career earnings of $20,105.

Sometimes pacers become trotters. The classic example was Steamin' Demon, a 1:57 pacer which became a 1:59:1 trotter.

Jim Harrison and other breeding authorities are confident that indecision about whether to train Standardbreds to pace or trot will diminish in the future. With increased refinement of the breed, the progeny of trotters will trot, requiring less elaborate management to produce the gait. Indeed, the few trainers now fully expert in the development of trotters seem to agree that the trotting heritage has become stronger than it used to be. In years past, many horses could be made to trot only after being weighed down with extremely heavy shoes. Lighter ones now suffice. And all hands acknowledge that more foals than ever "hit the ground trotting"—moving on that gait at an early age, without prompting and, bless them, without ever galloping. Well, hardly ever.

And now let us get down to the meat and potatoes. Is the horse's family tree of any significance to a handicapper?

Breeding and Handicapping

I might as well be blunt. The bettor lurches headlong toward a dead end when he attempts to forecast the outcome of a race in terms of the horses' breeding.

Handicapping is a matter of assessing fitness to win a particular race on a particular evening. It is entirely a process of evaluating the competitive records of horses, drivers and trainers, plus noting the prerace appearance and deportment of the animals. The likeliest contender in the race is the horse whose record and driver seem best suited to the situation. Its record may be best because its breeding made it capable of achieving such a record, but the handicapper hardly will accept breeding as a substitute for performance.

Given knowledge of the horse's parents and of the paternal lines and maternal families combined in its pedigree, the handicapper knows only that the animal once had a certain potential. Within minutes after it was conceived in the womb of the dam, things began to happen which, for better or worse, affected that potential. The mysterious lottery of inheritance may actually have endowed it with the spirit and physique that the breeder had in mind. Or with better. Or worse. Its prenatal development may have been affected adversely by congenital illness or injury. It might flourish as a foal, bring $100,000 at a yearling auction and never win a dime at a raceway. Or, as we have seen, it might bring $900 as a yearling and turn out to be Fresh Yankee.

The only races in which breeding is even slightly useful as a handicapping factor are those involving green horses whose competitive records are too scanty for confident evaluation. If only one entrant is of outstanding parentage, and if it hails from a top barn, it may be best. But it probably is nothing to risk money on. Green horses are forever breaking stride and getting in each other's way and making life miserable for bettors.

The man with the plump tweed jacket and streamlined binoculars smiles indulgently at you when some plug pays $32.40 after staggering home first. The man implies that the outcome was inevitable because the horse is, after all, a son of So-and-so. Waste no time envying the man. He does not possess the secrets of the universe. Chances are that he's just another name dropper. Past performances are the key to handicapping. Breeding is merely interesting conversation.

You should read the following lists of leading sires, not for use in your handicapping but for the pleasure of knowing some names significant in the sport. Later in this book, when we handicap entire programs at leading raceways, you will notice that offspring of these great sires include numerous animals that can't beat cheap stock.

Leading Sires

In terms of money won by their offspring, the following stallions have been the most successful sires in each of the indicated years.

1967	1968	1969
Gene Abbe	Good Time	Tar Heel
Good Time	Gene Abbe	Star's Pride
Star's Pride	Tar Heel	Gene Abbe
Tar Heel	Star's Pride	Good Time
Speedster	Bye Bye Byrd	Bye Bye Byrd
Bye Bye Byrd	Speedster	Speedster
Sharpshooter	Adios Boy	Hickory Smoke
Hickory Smoke	Hickory Smoke	Adios Boy
Sampson Hanover	Hickory Pride	Capetown
Knight Dream	Thorpe Hanover	Greentree Adios

Leading Maternal Grandpas

The records show that a two- or three-year-old by a top sire out of a dam by one of the following stallions has at least a potential class advantage over an animal of lesser pedigree.

Adios	King's Counsel
Knight Dream	Poplar Byrd
Hoot Mon	Worthy Boy
Tar Heel	The Widower
Victory Song	Florican
Nibble Hanover	Rodney
Titan Hanover	Royal Napoleon
Good Time	Volomite
Dean Hanover	Star's Pride
Darnley	Ensign Hanover
Scotland	Bombs Away

Leading Breeders

The reason that so many Standardbreds are named Something-or-Other Hanover is that they were bred at Hanover Shoe Farms, the sport's largest, most successful nursery. The establishment is in Hanover, Pa., and was named after a shoe manufacturing company owned by its founders.

In 1968, Hanover-bred trotters and pacers won purses of $3,798,853, an industry record. Among Hanover stallions are Tar Heel, Star's Pride, Ayres, Hickory Smoke, Dancer Hanover, Bullet Hanover, Gamecock, Best Of All, Caleb, Knight Dream, and Sampson Hanover.

The second most successful breeding operation is that of Castleton Farm, Lexington, Ky., with studs such as Bret Hanover, Good Time, Florican, Speedy Scot, Right Time, Diller Hanover, Scottish Pence, Worthy Boy, Speedster, Dartmouth, Matastar, Walter McKlyo, Spectator, Prince Victor, and Ensign Hanover.

Walnut Hall Farm, Donerail, Ky., is home for Duane Hanover, Florlis, Coffee Break, Sampson Direct, and Kimberly Kid.

Stoner Creek Stud, Paris, Ky., has Nevele Pride, Meadow Skipper, Henry T. Adios, and Porterhouse.

At Lana Lobell Farm, Hanover, Pa., are A.C.'s Viking, Adios Don, Adios Vic, Airliner, Bengazi Hanover, Noble Victory, Overtrick, and Solicitor.

Almahurst Farm, Lexington, Ky., has Shadow Wave and Golden Money Maker. At Hempt Farms, Mechanicsburg, Pa., stand Hickory Pride, Bye Bye Byrd, and Harlan Dean. White Devon Farm, Geneseo, N.Y., has Egyptian Candor, Thorpe Hanover, Great Lullwater, Greentree Adios, Adora's Dream, Trowbridge, and Tactile. Blue Chip Farm, Wallkill, N.Y., is the court of Gene Abbe and All Aflame.

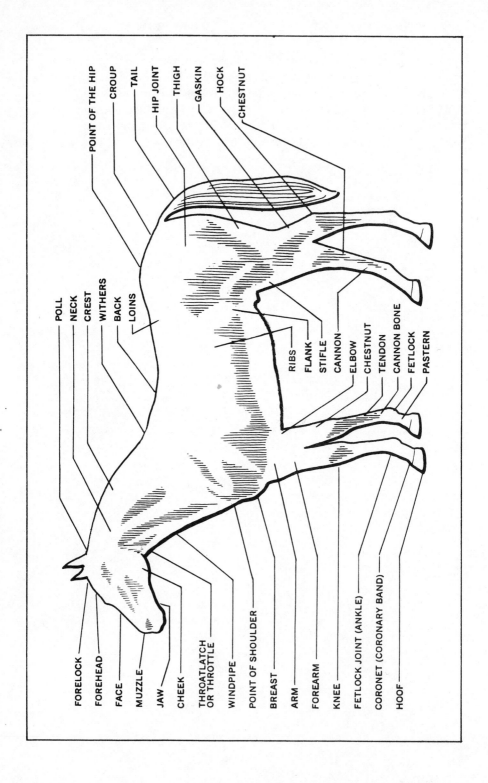

5

Standardbred Conformation

"I DO NOT BELIEVE that we have established a definitive type of Standardbred," writes Jim Harrison. "I think that we have taken but a tiny step along the evolutionary path. . . . I cannot conceive that nature will permit the establishment of a breed of horses that are required to trot and pace and yet constantly hit their shins, cross-fire and rap their knees. I envision, instead, trotters that will never hit their shins, pacers that will never cross-fire and horses of both gaits that will never touch their knees.

"In order to establish these desirable characteristics, we must probe for a type. The type is a long-barreled trotter that will permit positive clearance between the legs on the same side. The type is a pacer that will be wider-bodied and will never cross-fire. The type is a horse, either trotter or pacer, that will pick his front foot up and lay it down again in an absolutely straight line, thus eliminating the knee-knockers."

Some Standardbreds are so well constructed that they can pace or trot at top speed without cutting or bruising their knees or legs with their own hooves or, as in so-called cross-firing, rapping one hoof with another. If they also have ample lungs and air passages and sturdy joints, tendons, ligaments and feet, they are ideal prospects. Properly schooled and equipped, these sound animals can withstand the strains of training and racing for years on end.

Such horses are a precious minority. They are the ones that, with a little bit of luck, become champions and near-champions. At the opposite extreme is another, larger minority of Standardbreds short-changed by evolution. Some are so badly made that they break down in training. Others are able to get to the races, but cannot generate high speed without hurting themselves. To avoid the pain, they develop awkward gaits, subjecting their muscles and tendons to extra strain and becoming slower and less sound than ever.

A majority of Standardbreds fall between these extremes. Their physiques are flawed, but not so gravely that productive racing careers are out of the question. In the hands of genuinely expert horsemen who understand the nuances of corrective shoeing and "hanging up" (equipping), horses with noticeable physical imperfections win millions of dollars a year, holding their own in the best company, suffering no unusual aches and pains and remaining essentially sound for years. Lower on the scale, horses with unsound feet, ligaments, tendons, or joints are able to qualify as "racing sound," remaining competitive enough to earn their way in claiming, conditioned and classified races at tracks of all kinds.

Pending the day when the entire breed will be free of the inherited defects which now prevent so many horses from racing long and well, horsemen are constrained to be wary when they look over the merchandise at yearling sales. In assessing the conformation of a Standardbred, they do not demand utter perfection—never having seen it except in the mind's eye. But they are quick to lose interest in a youngster whose fashionable breeding will mean a high purchase price, unless his conformation is good enough to promise relative freedom from trouble. They are far more likely to gravitate to less expensive yearlings. It is relatively easy to balance the books on a $5,000 purchase whose orthopedic problems condemn it to an undistinguished career. But when a $50,000 animal goes bad at two or three, the red ink flows.

The experts seldom disagree about horses of hopelessly poor conformation. And they drool in unison over animals that approach perfection. But disagreements arise when the boys enter the vast middle ground, the area where doubts gnaw, disappointments lurk and opportunities are missed. Billy Haughton, who has few peers as a judge of yearlings, thought that Romeo Hanover's full brother, Romulus Hanover, was the better constructed of the two. He was astounded when he was able to get Romulus for $35,000 at the 1965 Harrisburg auction.

Some mighty sharp operators did not like Romulus at all. He had a dished (slightly concave) hoof, suggesting cramped bones and possible future soreness. Also, his pasterns were longer than ideal, implying a susceptibility to tendon troubles. Haughton doubted that the foot was all that bad and was entirely unperturbed by the pasterns, which were set at a sound, strong angle. He was right. Romulus won $483,750 in three years.

Race Time, by Good Time, would have cost a fortune if the buyers had not mistrusted the shape of his knees. He went for $19,000 and paced his way to a record of 1:57 and career earnings of almost $500,000. Thorpe Hanover, another pacer with suspect knees, not only developed into a prime performer but also became a highly successful sire, his knees no longer a puzzle.

Trotters are considered safer investments when they have long bodies. Yet Star's Pride, the top trotting sire, is short-barreled and begets more of the same. Evidently a trotter that picks up and puts down its feet properly can prosper despite close-coupled construction. And another animal's knees, feet or hocks may look weak without barring its access to the winner's circle. Furthermore, some horses outgrow slight deviations from acceptable conformation which drive

The sales ring at the celebrated Tattersalls yearling auction in Lexington, Ky.

down prices at yearling auctions. Either that, or they develop strong characteristics which compensate for the defects, as when a short-barreled trotter goes for years without rapping himself.

As already implied, good trainers often pick up where nature leaves off, keeping a relatively sound horse in shape and preventing a relatively unsound horse from going bad. On the other hand, inexpert trainers dependably fail to get the best from good horses and hasten the worst in poor ones.

Ayres, by Star's Pride out of the Hoot Mon mare, Arpege, was born to win and did. John F. Simpson, Sr., president and general manager of Hanover Shoe Farms and an all-time great trainer-driver, won trotting's triple crown with this fine animal, thereby substantiating breeding theory and adding another remarkable chapter to the extraordinary history of Hanover. To do his best, Ayres required special shoes. Nothing elaborate or, strictly speaking, corrective. Shoes of the standard half-inch width were a mite too narrow. The next wider standard size, $\frac{5}{8}$ of an inch, was a trifle too wide. So Simpson had his horseshoer make $\frac{9}{16}$-inch shoes for Ayres. A $\frac{1}{16}$-inch difference in width made championship performance routine for the superb animal. Under less astute management, Ayres might have gone a few ticks slower on some occasions, failing to realize his great potential. Mind you, he had the conformation. But there is more to harness racing, obviously, than conformation.

Jimmy Cruise proves the same point every couple of years, winning important stakes races with trotters which under other auspices can barely stand, much less trot. He makes them racing sound, winning sound. Another genius, Herve Filion, makes winners of claiming racers unable to earn their hay in other stables. These are horses whose inborn defects have been magnified by the wear and tear of racing. But Filion sees something in them, claims them from cheap races and makes money with them.

A season or two ago, one of the nation's outstanding trainers said that he was going to claim The Rabbit, a Filion reclamation project which had been winning consistently at Liberty Bell. "Okay," said the Canadian. "But before you waste your money, take him on a trip." The other trainer wheeled the horse around the track once and returned to the paddock aghast. "You can keep him!" he exclaimed. "He's as lame as a billy goat!" Filion nodded gravely, and continued to win races with the horse, having determined the combination of special equipment, feed, care and driving technique which kept the animal in high gear, lameness notwithstanding.

I have strayed from the subject of Standardbred conformation because I want to put it in meaningful perspective for the handicapping racegoer. Clearly, conformation, like breeding, is of utmost importance to buyers at yearling sales. Equally clearly, conformation is of almost no relevance to the handicapper faced with the problem of analyzing the records of horses and drivers. Whatever is wrong with the horse is reflected in its past performances. If the records show that a particular animal has the class, current form, driver and post position to beat its field, and if it looks spry and fit during its pre-race exercises, you probably have located a bet, whether you like its pasterns or not.

In a race for green two- or three-year-olds, you occasionally may spot a winner on grounds of superior physique, especially if the youngster is well bred, from a top barn, with a top driver, and behaves nicely before the race. I doubt you can make any money that way, but you may enjoy the attempt.

On a muddy track, small, nimble horses usually perform more reliably than large, long-striding ones. Players who remember this can cash tickets at excellent prices on the rare evenings when modern raceways come up muddy.

Another reason to learn a little about conformation is somewhat frivolous but is worth points in certain social situations. If a horse has been racing dismally and your companion is enchanted by its high odds, it is mighty satisfying to be able to say, "Look at his hind legs. No wonder he can't win anything. He's cow-hocked." We'll come to cow hocks shortly.

Size and Weight

Measured at the withers—the high point of the torso, directly rearward of the neck—a Standardbred usually stands between 15 and 16 hands, a hand being four inches. The term, "15-1" means 15 hands plus an inch. Horses as short as 14 or as tall as 17 hands turn up once in a while. So do Standardbreds that weigh upward of half a ton, although 900 pounds is more typical.

Lou Dillon, world's champion trotter from 1903 to 1912, stood one-half inch higher than 15 hands. Nevele Pride, who became champion in 1969, was only an inch and a half taller. Greyhound, whose trotting record stood from 1937 until 1969, was unusually tall —16-1¼.

Feet and Ankles

Many horsemen inspect Standardbreds from the ground up. No foot, no horse. If the hoof is too narrow, it must absorb extra pounds of impact per square inch of its limited surface. At high speeds on hard tracks, the probability of trouble multiplies, not only in the narrow foot but also in the ankles and knees to which the concussion is transmitted.

The best forelegs are those with feet that toe straight ahead, leaving hoofprints almost exactly parallel with each other. Horses that toe in slightly are forgiven the defect, but pronounced pigeon toes can mean undue strain on ligaments and tendons—a prescription for lameness. Pigeon-toed trotters tend to rap their hind shins, a problem which sometimes can be corrected by proper shoeing.

A horse that toes out may do so because his hooves have not been trimmed correctly or, more likely, because he is badly put together. Pacer or trotter, he probably knocks his knees, the outward-pointing toe of one foreleg swinging inward and rapping the knee of the other foreleg. Really bad knee-knockers cannot race at all. Others do all right on tracks with gradual turns but come to grief at the half-milers.

As much attention is paid to pasterns as to feet. The ideal pastern slopes from fetlock to hoof at an angle of 45 degrees. If more upright than that, it is less springy than it should be. It transmits too much concussion to ankle and knee, which eventually go bad. Such a horse is said to be "up on his ankles," and his condition is regarded as more serious if the pasterns are short as well as upright. A horse whose pasterns are long or slope lower than they should is "down on his fetlocks." His pasterns are too springy, subjecting leg tendons to excessive strain.

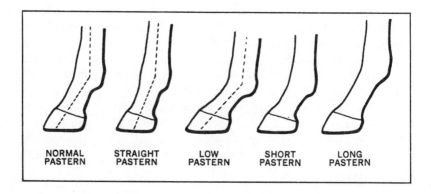

| NORMAL PASTERN | STRAIGHT PASTERN | LOW PASTERN | SHORT PASTERN | LONG PASTERN |

Knee, Hock and Tendon

A horse has knees in his forelegs only. The corresponding joint in the hind legs looks like an elbow but is called a hock (horses' elbows are in the forelegs). The knee contains seven or eight bones, depending on the individual. It is so delicate and so slow to develop that good stables keep two-year-olds out of hard training until X rays show that it is fully formed.

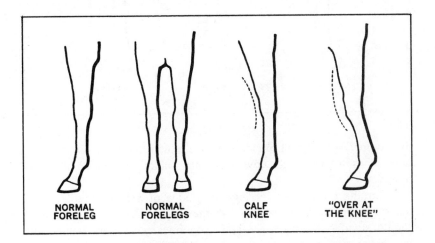

NORMAL FORELEG   NORMAL FORELEGS   CALF KNEE   "OVER AT THE KNEE"

The normal knee is situated directly below the elbow, permitting even dispersal of concussion and proper attachment of tendons. Horses whose forelegs bend backward at the knees are called "calf-kneed" or "back at the knee." They seldom last long. Unable to absorb and disperse the stress of concussion, these knees tend to chip and to develop arthritic conditions. Also, the misshapen tendons associated with them often deteriorate rapidly.

Some horses are "over at the knee" or "buck-kneed," the joint protruding forward. Such forelegs are less handsome than straight ones but are otherwise no detriment.

Horsemen prefer Standardbreds whose hind legs drop almost straight down from the hocks. If the hoof is noticeably forward of the hock, the animal is slightly downgraded for sickle hocks, which may lead to serious difficulties with tendons, but usually do not.

The worst malformation of the hocks is known as cow hock. The horse looks knock-kneed from the rear. His hind feet toe outward when walking but fly inward on the trot, virtually guaranteeing that

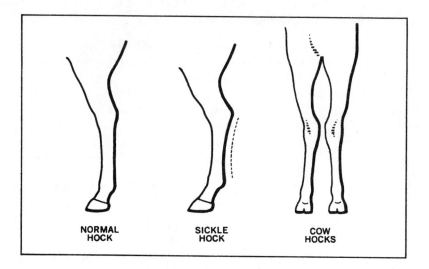

NORMAL HOCK   SICKLE HOCK   COW HOCKS

the hoof of one leg will interfere painfully with the flesh, muscle and bone of the other. Slight cow hocks are unlikely to bother a pacer, however.

Returning now to the forelegs, the judge of Standardbred conformation is especially concerned with the shape of the flexor tendon. It should stand out, firm, tight and economically straight, behind the leg, between knee and fetlock. Fat, spongy tendons are anathema. Even in an otherwise well-formed leg, they tend to rupture under strain. Such afflictions of tendon fiber or sheath are known as bows—bowed tendons—and often mean the end of a racer's usefulness.

From Chest to Hips

A narrow-chested horse not only lacks lung capacity but also suffers the handicap of forelegs that are too close to each other and too likely to interfere with each other.

A broad, deep chest keeps the legs apart and provides plenty of space for lungs. It should be accompanied by a powerful, sloped shoulder for the full extension of the forelegs that produces a good, long stride. Upright shoulders cramp the stride and, worse than that, absorb shock as inefficiently as the upright pasterns with which they often combine in a poorly endowed horse.

The withers should be fairly prominent, indicating the long spinal muscles of powerful stride. The muscles of the loin should also be

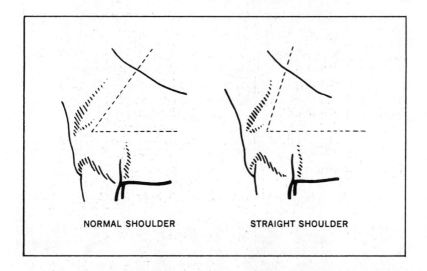

NORMAL SHOULDER   STRAIGHT SHOULDER

evident. They tie the horse's rear to his front, creating the "close-coupled" appearance of well-coordinated trotters and pacers. If "light over the kidney" or "wasp-waisted"—slender-loined and slack in the coupling—a horse is less able to transmit power from rear to front.

Head and Neck

A wide forehead suggests an adequate brain pan and, in fact, is seldom found on a stupid, unmannerly horse. Large, clear, dark eyes are another sign of kindly, manageable intelligence.

Large nostrils and a broad space between the jawbones mean ample breathing passages. Billy Haughton places four fingers under the jaws. If the fingers do not fit comfortably in the space between the bones, he rejects the animal. He says no good horse has ever flunked that test.

A long, limber neck is far preferable to a short one. Long-necked horses stride out more decisively, have better balance and more stamina.

Color and Markings

The official colors:

BAY—Brownish body and black "points" (mane, tail and lower legs). The body color ranges from a yellowish tan to a deep, red mahogany or a dark brown.

DARK BAY OR BROWN—If the hairs on muzzle or flank are tan or brown, the horse is in this category.

CHESTNUT—Mane and tail are brown or flaxen, never black, although a few black hairs may be noticeable. Body color varies from a dark liver to reddish gold, copper and light yellow.

BLACK—Sometimes completely black, but as likely to look dark brown, with fine black hairs on the muzzle.

GRAY—A mixture of white and black hairs.

ROAN—A mixture of black, white and yellow hairs, or black, white and red.

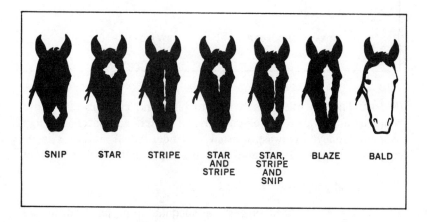

SNIP   STAR   STRIPE   STAR AND STRIPE   STAR, STRIPE AND SNIP   BLAZE   BALD

Because the patches known as "markings" are always white, they never are referred to by color.

A *snip* is a small patch of bare skin or white hairs on lip or nose.

A *star* is a small patch of white on the forehead.

A *stripe* is a narrow mark running down the face to the nose or lower.

A *blaze* is a larger patch. When it covers the entire face, the horse is called white-faced or bald-faced.

Markings also are found on the heels, the coronet of the hoof, the pasterns, ankles (half-ankle or full-ankle), and above, where they are known as socks, half-stockings or stockings. Many horsemen distrust the bone structure of horses with white legs, ankles or pasterns.

6

The Beatable Race

"THE HORSE IS ONLY a convenience. He is not a necessity," announced a wry acquaintance of mine as we watched customers stampede to the betting windows before a race so wide open that only a guru could have handicapped it.

"These people are betting on numbers, not horses," complained my friend. "They would just as soon bet on cockroaches. The day someone discovers how to make cockroach races visible in a large stadium, the horse will become obsolete."

He was joking in earnest. Some racegoers are more eager to bet than to win. They bet on every race, every double, every exacta, every quinella in a promiscuous frenzy. The horses might as well be cockroaches. The Constitution guarantees every citizen absolute freedom to make an ass of himself, and the raceway is there to help.

In some respects, the tracks are surprisingly decent about trying to protect the player from his own worst excesses. Early in the year, races for green two- and three-year-olds are conducted without betting. This gives the youngsters a chance to get their legs under them. When they finally appear in betting races, some (but not many) have settled down a bit and have established sufficient form to deserve the attention of the handicapping fan. Another contribution to sanity is the qualifying race, a nonbetting affair in which horses show whether they have the speed and manners to compete for purses at the particular track.

Otherwise, raceway managements do their utmost to keep the customer in a state of hysterical confusion. Visualizing themselves accurately as purveyors of entertainment, they try to generate maximum excitement and suspense. From their viewpoint, the ideal race is one in which (a) contention is so close that nobody can make head or tail of it, (b) the start has to be delayed because so many customers want to make last-minute bets at the high odds which distinguish races of this kind and (c) the excitement ends with a wall of horses roaring down the stretch, nose to nose in a photo finish. The worst calamity of all, the ineradicable stain on the racing secretary's record, is the evening on which several standout horses lay over their fields and win by city blocks. That sort of thing is not considered exciting enough.

Track managements offer bookkeeping statistics to support their outlook. At most tracks, the mutuel handle seems to rise when contention is close and the races become more difficult to handicap. If the percentage of winning favorites approaches 40, as it sometimes does, and if few close finishes occur, as sometimes happens, the front office goes into deep mourning and the racing secretary develops painful digestive disturbances.

Fair competition among evenly matched athletes being the blood and bone of sport, one cannot begin to criticize the raceways for the emphasis they place on it. But one can take care not to be swept up in all the suspense and excitement, which tend to become expensive.

Sooner or later, every racegoer decides what kind of player he is going to be. Consciously or not, he decides what kind of play is the most fun. To me, and I hope to my reader, maximum fun derives from ending the season with more cash in hand than was there to begin with. The only way to scale this pinnacle of joy is to pick spots. Instead of squandering $2 or $5 or whatever on each of nine races plus a daily double and exactas and other blandishments, the spot player concentrates his attention and money on races that offer a fighting chance. Races that can be handicapped. Playable races. Beatable ones.

I do not think that you should bet less money than you now do. I think you should bet less frequently, managing the money more wisely so that you will place larger amounts on solid choices, and avoid other transactions altogether.

The Handicapper's View

Readers who accept the principles set forth in this book will find that harness-race handicapping is a rather straightforward process. Using the past-performance records published in the program, the handicapper compares the horses in terms of current condition, pace, class, driver, and post position. Factors like career speed records, age, sex, career earnings, and winning percentage are all matters of class.

They vary in relevance from race to race and horse to horse. Pace, about which much is said and little is understood, often has more to do with the ability of the driver than with the character of his horse.

The primary handicapping factors are interrelated. To judge class adequately, one must study it in its relationship to current condition. And vice versa. Similarly, the driver factor is meaningless except in its relationship to class, condition and post position.

How, then, does the handicapper deal with a race in which any of these inseparable factors is obscure? Easily. He passes the race. He refuses to bet on it. Here is a useful rule:

Avoid any race in which the relative abilities of the horses are not clearly evident.

Do not expect every race to yield a selection. To the extent that temperament permits, wait in ambush until a good opportunity comes along. A good opportunity is a race in which the past-performance records permit sober judgments unpolluted by wish or guess. Here are some of the fundamentals of this approach:

1. *A race is likely to be playable if every horse in it has raced on the present track or present raceway circuit recently enough to provide a substantial indication of its current form.*

You cannot handicap a pig in a poke. Smart players bet sparingly at the beginning of the season, when some horses arrive from tracks of varying size and quality elsewhere, and others make their first efforts of the year. Until they compete on the present track, valid comparisons of their form are difficult.

This truth practically compels abstention from betting on big stakes and invitational races at any stage of the season. If some of the glamorous contestants have been strutting their stuff elsewhere, their current form remains a matter of surmise until the race is over. One can only guess whether the recent victory of Horse "A" at the Yonkers half-miler was a more impressive display of strength than the victory of Horse "B" at the Sportsman's Park ⅝-miler, especially if neither has yet been tested at tonight's track. An added complication is the effect of shipping on equine form. Most good horses ship comfortably, barnstorming being an integral part of the sport. Yet all good horses do not ship well all the time.

2. *A race probably is playable if most of the horses have raced recently at the present track and if those without recent local starts can be regarded as losers even if they prove to be in top condition.*

If the top contenders in the stakes or invitational are racing to-night on their home grounds and have already thumped the others in races elsewhere, chances are that you needn't worry too much about the invaders. Likewise, if a horse making its local debut in a conditioned, classified or claiming race has been losing in lesser company elsewhere, you can proceed as if it were not in the race. Problems arise only when no judgment can be made about the present class and form of a horse—as when an animal returns from a long layoff to face the kind that it can beat when in shape. Lacking evidence about its present condition, one should pass the race.

3. *A race probably is not playable if the two or three top contenders seem so closely matched that no real distinction can be made among them.*

Handicapping is a process of approximation. It cannot be made precise. Therefore, occasions arise when the handicapper really cannot separate one leading contender from the other one or two. Unless the odds are generous enough to permit a bet on both contenders, or all three, the race should be passed. Bets should never be forced.

4. *The race may be playable if the leading contender is not a breaker and neither are any quick-leaving horses with post positions inside his.*

It makes little sense to bet on a horse with a tendency to break stride. If it is the best horse in the race, abstain entirely. Moreover, having found a nonbreaker, it pays to make reasonably sure that the horse's own performance won't be spoiled by interference from breakers. The problem arises most often in trotting races, obviously, and is especially severe among younger ones and cheaper ones. If you insist on playing such a race, your best bet is likely to be a horse quick enough to be comfortably in front and out of trouble when the rest begin their jumping. Be particularly cautious if the jumpers seem to be early-speed types and are leaving from positions inside your choice. Their efforts to prevent him from getting the rail may be all it takes to throw them off stride. In the resulting melée, he may be piled up, backed up or hung out. Which could lose your bet for you.

5. *The race may not be playable if it is for the cheapest horses on the grounds.*

To deserve a bet, a horse should be capable of two good per-formances in succession. The manes and tails that appear in the cheapest races at most tracks seldom qualify in that sense. They are chronic losers, or chronic breakers, or chronic quitters, or otherwise so unsound that consistency is entirely beyond them. Their records show it. If an animal has lost fifteen consecutive races and displays improvement this week, there seldom is the slightest reason to expect additional improvement next week. Seen in light of its inconsistency, such a horse no longer shapes up as the "least bad" prospect in a bad field, and you pass the race. Unless a horse has winning qualities and has demonstrated them recently, betting is inadvisable.

6. *The race may not be playable if the leading contender has a weak or inexperienced driver.*

Beware the losing driver. He may cancel whatever advantages of class, form and post position the horse should have. Handicapping dilemmas that arise when a losing driver gets the best horse are often resolved most satisfactorily by passing the race.

Winter Racing

A handicapper's problems multiply in the freezing tempera-tures of a northern winter. The sport becomes a gasping, stiff-jointed parody of itself. Playable-beatable races are infrequent and immensely difficult to recognize. The fan's approach to the game under those conditions is as much a test of his character as of his handicapping skill.

Raceways remain open during the northern winter beause it is profitable to do so and they need every dollar they can get. Many leading trainer-drivers risk their necks and jeopardize some of their less valuable livestock in winter competition for the same reason. Most of them detest every minute of it.

Good horses campaign when weather is kind and purses high, in the prime months of spring, summer and fall. Some remain active through December at Hollywood Park, safe from the hazards of winter. Sound horses with bright futures are seldom found at northern tracks between November and March.

The very presence of a trotter or pacer at a winter track is a black mark against it. If it comes from a prominent stable, it undoubtedly belongs to the outfit's secondary, expendable division—the group with which the trainer appeases raceway management during winter

Defying the elements at Roosevelt Raceway.

so that he may be assured of ample stall space for his better stock when the real racing begins in late spring.

Horses do not warm up properly in frigid air. They seem unable to absorb sufficient oxygen through their lungs. They tucker out in the stretch. Their racing times are wildly inconsistent, because the footing varies considerably from night to night and air temperature affects speed. The lower the temperature the slower the race. A horse capable of 2:09 at 40°F. is lucky to do 2:12 at 20°F. Wind, which bothers many good horses in summer, is devastating in winter.

The handicapper sits snug and warm in the glass-enclosed clubhouse, looks at his program and sees gibberish. Did Horse "A" go in 2:12 last week because of the weather or because they finally have worn him to the nub? Did his rival, Horse "B," go in 2:10:1 because of favorable footing or because of improving form or both? Considering that each animal was getting home in 2:07 only a few months ago, what is the handicapper to make of the program information? What can a handicapper do about winter racing?

One thing he can do is stay home, renew acquaintances with his wife and family and spare himself some trouble. If he is determined not only to go racing in winter but to make summer-style wagers, he had better obtain special equipment, a winter survival kit. For example, he had better keep daily notes on the state of the racing strip, the air temperature, the wind velocity, and the time and class of each race. These notes may supplement the conventional program information enough to show him the way to an occasional good bet. At the very least, he will be able to adjust the past-performance data to compensate for the probable effects of weather.

I doubt very much that winter handicapping can be profitable without such notes. Players unable or unwilling to compile them and equally unwilling to stay home with a good book should go to the track not to bet but to eat. Regard the place as a restaurant. Get a good table and a good meal and enjoy both. Limit bets to a minimum, risking nothing unless the horses are better than usual and the records less contradictory than usual. Spring is sure to come.

When It Rains

Innovations in the design and maintenance of raceway ovals have greatly minimized the problem of mud. In the old days, heavy rain transformed the clay surfaces into bogs. Entire programs had to be canceled because the horses were unable to pull the sulkies safely But modern drainage systems and racing surfaces impregnated with stone dust combine to provide good footing under all but the worst conditions. With the slowly growing acceptance of plastic tracks and the inevitability of covered stadiums, weather can be regarded as an obsolescent factor.

The description of a track as "fast," "sloppy," "good," "slow," "muddy," or "heavy" is not as precise as one might think. Even in rainless periods, varying humidity does not liberate the handicapper from the necessity of remaining hawk-eyed and prudent when trying to interpret what happened last week on an off track, or to predict what might happen tonight on another one.

Knowing the variations in speed, texture and puddled water that are encompassed by artibrary terms like "sloppy," "good," "slow," "muddy" and "heavy," and knowing that a horse might like tonight's allegedly "sloppy" track while going frantic on next week's, the handicapper must choose between the following alternatives:

1. Make no bets when the track is anything but fast, and handicap from past performances on fast tracks only.

2. Compile and maintain long-term records showing how off tracks of various kinds have affected the form of individual horses. Confronted with a sloppy track tonight, the player uses such records to eliminate animals that have disliked slop, while upgrading others that seem to enjoy that kind of going.

Besides being easier, the first method is much less risky. The long-term records of the alternate method can produce bonanzas on occasion, but can also cause dismal disappointment. For example, the six or eight races included in a horse's program record may all have taken place on fast tracks, and may indicate that his form is improving. Lo and behold! The player's notebook reveals that the beast performed superbly in the slop six months ago, in a race not included in the pro-

Jimmy Larente after a race in the mud.

gram summary. The horse looks like a splendid prospect under tonight's wet conditions. The reasoning is beyond fault, the prediction sound. But the bet is less likely to pay off than if the track were fast. Here is why.

When a pacer goes at full speed on a dry, fast surface, its steel-shod feet come within a quarter-inch of its knees. A trotter's feet clear by an almost equally small margin. Let the animal slip or skid on a moist surface and it raps itself. The resultant break kills its chances and contradicts the notebook. Even if the notebook's choice remains flat, something else may flounder in the slippery going, cause interference, touch off a mass break and affect the outcome of the race. Adversely.

The footing is fast on so many evenings at the height of the season that nobody should feel compelled to bet when conditions are inferior. Sometimes, of course, the racegoer is betrayed by the Weather Bureau, finds himself in the grandstand staring at the "muddy" sign and hates to waste the evening. That is, he hates not to bet, even if he wastes a few bob in the bargain. In such circumstances, he should handicap the races as if the track were dry and fast. Having done so, he should bet on animals that (a) figure best in their races and (b) are quick types able to race in front where no mud can hit them and no breakers can obstruct them. When in doubt, favor an older horse with high career earnings that has been dying in the stretch on fast tracks, especially if a top driver is to be in the bike. The horse did not earn big money by quitting in the stretch. Chances are reasonable that his aches and pains have been defeating him. It is possible—although much less than a cinch—that the softer footing will help. Certainly, the top driver will do no harm. He and his peers owe some of their success to the skill with which they hold tiring or ouchy horses together in the stretch. Also, they are bravely unruffled by the very real hazards of wet tracks.

7

The Time Factor

HERE IS A REASONABLY SOUND six-year-old pacer capable of a mile in 2:05. I can buy him for $6,000. In the adjoining stall is another six-year-old pacer. I cannot buy him for $6,000. He earned more than that the other night when he won a race in 2:02. The two horses may dwell under the same roof but they are worlds apart. The clock says so.

This is a sport in which time reigns supreme and the clock is executioner. Horsemen may approve the breeding, conformation, and manners of a Standardbred, but they suspend final judgment of its quality until they see how fast it can go the mile. Its speed at the distance determines the kind of purses for which raceway managements permit it to compete. Its earning power and market value therefore stand in direct proportion to its speed. Later in life, its record—the word given to the fastest official mile of its career—helps breeders to assess its potential worth as a stallion or broodmare.

With horsemen and racing secretaries dancing to the tune of the clock, it is logical that handicappers follow suit. Harness-race handicapping comes in many packages, but after all the ribbons and tissue paper are removed, you find a step-by-step procedure in which speed analysis is the main component.

Handicapping would be more complicated and speed analysis less dependable if the horses did not race at more-or-less weekly intervals for months on end, and if their form fluctuated sharply from race to race, Obviously, nobody could assign a meaningful speed rating to an inconsistent horse if the freshest evidence of its speed were a performance four weeks ago.

Similarly, speed analysis would become impractical, if not impossible, if the races varied in distance. As followers of Thoroughbred racing may know, the distance of the race affects each horse differently. Speeds recorded at mixed distances seldom make for useful comparison.

Fortunately, the harness-racing fan can count on several races per evening in which relatively consistent, recently active animals race at the customary distance of one mile. The fan has every reason to expect that the times of their recent races will help him to evaluate the horses' class and condition. And the fractional times—the clockings of each quarter-mile of each race—will permit him to study speed more discriminatingly, in terms of the phenomenon known as pace.

Fractional and final times are by-products of interacting elements such as class, condition, post position, driving tactics and luck. Recognizing this, many successful handicappers urge fans to go beyond raw time and examine the fundamentals from which time derives. They point out that some races are unrepresentatively fast and others are equivalently slow and that a player goes astray when he accepts such times at face value. They argue that trouble arises even when times fall within a normal range. For example, a middling horse might win a race in 2:03 on the same evening that a better horse loses another race in 2:04. But if the two engage each other next week, the better horse occasions no surprise by winning in 2:04:2, with this week's 2:03 performer finishing nowhere.

The points are unarguably valid. The good handicapper does not simply compare raw times. He tries to understand how they came about. Chances are excellent that he can predict the defeat of the 2:03 horse and the victory of the better animal when they race each other, having been able to analyze the previous races. Yet the fact

Nevele Pride blazes to the fastest mile in trotting history—1:54:4—at Indianapolis on August 31, 1969. Driver Stanley Dancer is hidden behind a galloping prompter driven by Billy Haughton.

remains that his handicapping is keyed to time and is most conveniently carried out in terms of time. And so, for that matter, are the handicapping methods of the very experts who properly warn against an uncritical emphasis on time! Time is the beginning, middle, and end of handicapping.

There is no other approach. The sport is organized that way. The past-performance records are designed that way. On some race circuits, class designations in the past-performance programs are so unintelligible that equine quality can be evaluated only in terms of time. On other circuits, where programs make clearer class distinctions among past races, time tells whether an animal is likely to succeed when he tackles a relatively high-grade field, or whether his descent to a lower-grade field might mean a win. In addition, time helps the player to understand why a horse might have faded in the stretch last week and might hold together tonight. Or why the horse that led from start to finish last week might show nothing much tonight.

We shall look beyond time, but shall be careful never to let it out of our sight.

Taking a Record

In the literature of harness racing one seldom sees a Standardbred's name without a coded appendage that summarizes its quality in terms of speed. Lehigh Hanover was not just Lehigh Hanover. He was Lehigh Hanover, p, 3, 1:58:4h. That is, he was a pacer, and at age 3 he won a race in 1:58:4 on a half-mile track.

If he had been a trotter, the "p" would have been missing, but no "t" would have been used, it being understood that the horse is a trotter unless the letter "p" appears after its name. The age at which the career record was taken always appears next, followed by the time itself. If the mark was recorded in a time trial—a speed test against the clock rather than in an actual race—the letters "TT" precede the time figure, as in Bret Hanover, p, 4, TT, 1:53:3m. The size of the track is given as "h" for half-miler, "f" for ⅝-miler and either "m" or no letter at all for a one-miler.

Time trials are important because the sport measures its progress in fifths of a second, and the horse capable of great speed may improve the breed when he goes to stud. So the horseman takes his top animal to Springfield or Lexington or Du Quoin or Indianapolis, cranks him up as if for a $200,000 race and goes with him against the fence. That is, against time, under conditions likely to produce maximum

Ralph Baldwin has Kimberly Duchess tucked into the two hole on the rail behind Frank Ervin and Speed Model at Goshen in 1966. In due course Ralph pulled out and won the Grand Circuit trot.

speed. "Fence" signifies that the horse has the rail all the way and need waste no energy maneuvering to get there, as in a real race. To push the record-seeker to his limit, running horses serve as prompters or pace-pressers, rushing alongside (but never ahead of him) in relays and keeping his mind on his business. If the horse is in top condition and the driver's calculations pan out, the final time may be several ticks faster than anything the animal has been able to achieve in the tumult of actual competition.

The USTA accepts time trials as official Standardbred records, but only when an automatic timer is used. It seems that time-trial clockers used to suffer from a profitable affliction, "Kentucky Thumb" or "Indiana Paralysis," which caused them to start their watches after a friend's horse began its mile, rather than at the instant it crossed the starting line. Times tended to be faster than accurate, which was rewarding for horsemen and clockers but bothered purists.

Most horses have no occasion to take time-trial records. Their career marks are taken in competition. Here again, the rules are significant. A horse may race in 1:59 without improving its career record of 2:03. How and why? Because time does not count as an individual record unless the horse wins the race.

This is of basic importance to the racing fan. Its implications extend far beyond the taking of records, applying directly to the handicapping of ordinary races every night in the week, everywhere.

The central fact of the matter is that horses often race to better times when losing than when winning. An impartial record-keeping organization like the USTA can hardly decide that a losing effort in 1:59 was truly demonstrative of a horse's quality and that its lifetime mark should forthwith be lowered from 2:03. What would the Association then do about all other 2:03 horses whose owners argued that their own recent losses in 1:59 should also be accepted as career records? Or about the chronic 2:11 horse that finally chases other horses home in 2:09? The USTA has no choice. It must limit records to times set while winning or while competing against the stopwatch.

Handicappers are not bound by such considerations, however. They are free to differentiate among a horse's losing races, sometimes accepting and sometimes rejecting the times recorded in the past-performance chart. Before getting to this important phase of handicapping, however, it will be best to dispose of the subject of lifetime speed records.

Handicapping the Records

With regional variations which need not concern us, the past-performance programs tell the player what each horse's career record is, when it was taken, and on what kind of track. They may also show the horse's fastest winning time of the current year and its fastest winning time of the previous year. Naturally, they also show the times of the horse's most recent six or eight races.

The question before the house is whether any of these historical statistics are useful in handicapping. And if so, when and how.

A career record taken two or more years ago means only that the horse once was capable of a performance in 1:58 or 2:04 or whatever the figure is. It is of no earthly use in the handicapping of tonight's race. Too much water has trickled under the bridge. No horse, regardless of quality, is the same in 1971 as in 1969 and no 1971 race can be handicapped off 1969 figures. Needless to say, if you go to the raceway often enough you inevitably will see a longshot plod home first and will hear some clown say, "I shoulda had him. Look. He did two-oh-two in 1965. Nothing else in the race has ever done two-oh-two."

What if the career record was taken last year? And what, for that matter, if the horse's best time last year was extremely fast by comparison with any other time notations on the page?

Last year's mark bears some attention early in the season, especially in races for better horses and, most especially, when the horse in question has been out often enough and/or has performed well enough this year to suggest a resumption of last year's form. But after the doldrums of late winter and early spring are over and the weather turns fair and all six or eight races in the detailed chart are recent races, last year's record should be allowed to recede into history.

Some horses need four or five early-season efforts before achieving their best form. A few are ready to swing after a tightening race or two. If the animal is from a top stable, is racing in the kind of company suitable to a horse of its particular time credentials, and displayed an amount of lick in its race last week, you often can draw comfort and confidence from its previous year's mark. But if it is facing animals of a lower grade than might be expected from a reading of its previous year's record, and if it has been performing indifferently, it probably is a troubled horse. The prudent approach is to handicap entirely in terms of this year's form. And, as emphasized in the last chapter, pass the race if your predominant feeling is one of doubt.

What about the horse's fastest race this year? In general, your most effective handicapping will be based on the six or eight races the program summarizes in detail. Indeed, greatest emphasis should be placed on the latest race or two. So the horse's fastest race of the current year may well be irrelevant to what happens tonight. An exception might be the horse that went sour from illness, injury or overwork, turned in several poor performances after taking its record, was dropped in class, lost again and finally was given an overdue vacation. After returning to action, such a horse often recovers its form, destroying cheap fields and beginning to ascend the class ladder again. If recent efforts show steady improvement, further improvement might be predictable for tonight, especially if the animal has not yet approached the time it recorded earlier in the year.

No rule can be extracted from all this, but a principle can: A horse's most recent performances are the most eloquent forecast of what it might do tonight. However, fast time recorded earlier in the season or last year may sometimes be significant in the case of a horse that is rounding into good form after a layoff. Unless the animal has given solid evidence of improvement, its old records should be ignored.

Although few good handicappers dispute my emphasis on recent form, some of the shrewdest in the sport are careful to check the final times credited to every starter in all of its listed races. If one animal did a faster mile in one of those six or eight starts than has been credited to any of its rivals in their listed performances, these experts regard the horse as a serious threat—even though the swift performance took place a month or two or three ago. It has been argued, indeed, that a player can do very well by confining his bets to such horses, asking only that they have favorable post positions and good drivers.

I am unable to refute the theory (and its supporters are unable to substantiate it), because no thorough statistical study has ever been made. There can be little doubt, however, that the horse with the best final time in the six or eight listed races is often (for additional reasons) the wisest choice in the race. Moreover, when there is nothing else on which to base a selection, this wrinkle sometimes produces a longshot winner. Casual fans interested in betting on every race may find the notion helpful.

Misleading Times

When a horse races on the front end against the rail or moves up on the outside to challenge for the lead, it must cut its own hole in the wind. In doing so, it provides a protective airfoil for any horse racing directly behind it. Sheltered behind the leader on the rail or covered up on the outside, an animal moves with less effort than usual, encountering less air resistance. In the jargon of the sport, such a horse is "sucked along." If it travels that way behind inherently faster horses for most of the journey, its final time is quite sure to be better than it could achieve without the windshields.

For this reason, smart handicappers discount the times recorded for a horse in a race that found it lollygagging behind other animals without making any real moves of its own. A racehorse should get away from the fence and bid for the lead once in a while. It should be amenable to use. If it makes no move in a race, its failure to do so may be attributable to traffic problems or a misjudged drive, but more often means poor form and should be accepted as a warning.

Horsemen and handicappers sometimes philosophize about the number of moves various kinds of horses can be induced to make in a race. Theoretically, an ordinary horse can be brushed vigorously—hard-used—only once in a race. A middling horse supposedly has two moves in it and a really good horse can come up with three. The pell-mell, sprinting style of race driving, which started at half-mile tracks and has been spreading therefrom, has tended to throw the move theory into the discard. Unless he wants to be left behind at the start, every driver makes some kind of move for early position, and one or two more to improve or hold that position, after which comes the crucial, exhausting move in the stretch.

I am bandying words, I suppose. It is true enough that a move to the outside on a turn is likely to take more out of a horse than its move to the rail at the start, or the move it may attempt on the backstretch. But it also is true that veteran horsemen have been counting three and four real moves per mile in the performances of mediocre animals at half-mile and ⅝-mile ovals. The breed is improving, racing tactics are changing and, withal, the definition of "move" probably is undergoing alterations. In any event, a horse that does nothing but ride the coattails of other horses is not making moves and is not really earning the occasionally good times in which it coasts past tired horses at the finish.

According to horsemen, some Standardbreds "don't like air." They race best behind other horses and can be trusted to win only when steered into the open in the final yards of the race, too late to balk or sulk and—hopefully but not invariably—too late to break stride. Horses of this kind often show splendid times in their past-performance charts, but their wins are few by comparison with their seconds and thirds. And the past-performance lines seldom show any attempt to reach the front end before the finish.

To demonstrate the pulled-along horse and the illusions he fosters, I have just taken a random program from a nearby stack and have found the inevitable example, a pacer that went as the 2.10 to 1 favorite in the third race at Yonkers on June 4, 1969. The animal's latest race looked, in part, like this:

29:4   1:00:3   1:33   2:03:4   1 4 5 6 6/2¼   3/1½   2:04:1

Leaving from the ordinarily advantageous rail position, the horse had been shuffled back to fourth at the quarter, and was no better than fifth after a half-mile, which the leader completed in 1:00:3. At the three-quarter call, the pacer was sixth. He was still sixth at the head of the stretch, whereupon he improved his position by less than a length, finishing third and completing his journey in 2:04:1. So far as the record showed, he had not budged from the rail throughout the trip. He apparently had taken third money by default when tired horses backed past him. If this had been his first race of the season, improvement might have been expected. But he had been competing at regular intervals. The race was simply a lackadaisical effort, a sign of unpromising form. And on June 14, the horse endorsed that sign by finishing seventh.

The forecast would have been brighter, and so might have been the result, if the pacer's past-performance line had differed slightly. The fractional and final times would have been the same, but the racing positions would have included some signs of life:

1 6 5⁰ 5⁰ 5/2¼ 3/1½

The two little circles would have meant that the horse got out there and roughed it for half a mile, finally battling his way to a position only 2¼ lengths behind the leader at the stretch call and gaining a bit more to place third. A wholesome race, offering promise of better.

Another entrant in the June 14 race was Charter, whose last race looked better than it had been:

31   1:03   1:33   2:03:1   1 2 2 2 2/1½   2/2   2:03:3

Another suckalong. The program's morning line predicted that this colt would go at 6 to 1, but the crowd sent it at 4.60 to 1, probably because its final time of 2:03:3 on June 7 had been at least ⅗-second faster than the times of any of the other starters in their latest outings. This must be what some of the experts mean when they call time a booby trap.

Analyze Charter's race. He had settled into the second slot on the rail right at the beginning—no great feat, inasmuch as he had left from the inside post. He had remained in that same position all the way, safe and snug, doing nothing to improve his situation. The grand climax came in the stretch, where he remained second on the rail, losing half a length to the leader.

As often happens after a performance of this kind, Charter did nothing on June 14. He finished eighth and last. His 2:03:3 clocking of June 7 had been spurious. Interestingly, his career record up to that point showed victories in 2:06 and 2:07:4, offering no suggestion that he could do better than that unless pulled along behind other horses.

A more spectacular example of how a horse's losing times often look better than its winning ones occurred at Liberty Bell on April 12, 1969, in the Pennsbury Pace, an invitational affair with a $20,000 purse. Rum Customer won it in a blazing 1:58:3. The horse that finished seventh and last was clocked in 1:59:2, making the race one of the more fantastically swift in history. In sixth place, timed in 1:59:1, was Afton Day, a six-year-old with a career record of 2:01:2.

His time behind Rum Customer was quite beyond his capabilities in a situation that put him on the lead or on the outside, where the action is.

The horse that finished second to Rum Customer was Little Jerry Way, whose performance in that remarkable race can be summarized in this way:

29:3   58:4   1:28:1   1:58:3   7 7 7 7 7/4   2/2   1:59

Was Little Jerry Way an example of a sucked-along horse? Not at all. In the first place, Liberty Bell is a ⅝-mile track with a 596-foot homestretch—long enough for a come-from-behind horse to exploit when he is fit and well handled. A horse that saves ground on the rail, racing dead last until the dash for home, may well be doing so because the driver chooses that tactic—a state of affairs less likely to occur at a half-miler. Secondly, a clocking of 1:59 was well within Little Jerry Way's capabilities, and his record showed as much. Finally, a horse that moves from seventh to second in a stretch battle against high-grade competition, gaining 2¾ lengths in the process, is not susceptible to charges that he lucked into the money.

In discussing the phenomenon of the sucked-along horse, we have been dealing not only with time but also with current form, and what last week's race implies for tonight's. It would be tidier to discuss

Rum Customer winning the Pennsbury Pace at Liberty Bell in April, 1969. Little Jerry Way (7) comes on to take second, and Nardin's Byrd is third. Winning driver was Alix Winger, sitting in for Billy Haughton.

each aspect of handicapping separately, covering time now and current form later. But it would be artificial to do so. The elements of handicapping are inseparable. You cannot mention one without immersing yourself in another.

A sidelight on the sucked-along horse is the general belief among Standardbred horsemen that equine psychology often is as influential as wind resistance in producing performances of that kind. The herd instinct runs high in these animals. Most of them would rather trot or pace with other horses than be far in front or far behind. Thus, when the field as a whole cuts out rapid fractions, an inferior member of it may keep up quite well, losing in much better time than it has ever managed while winning

The Perfect Trip

To horsemen the perfect trip is one in which the horse arrives at the head of the stretch full of energy and in position for a clear, straight sail to the wire. During the early stages of such a race, everything develops as if the driver had blueprinted it. Other animals knock each other off, but the lucky one ambles along in unobstructed comfort, being used scarcely at all. He then wins as the driver pleases.

To a considerable extent, the sucked-along horse has a splendid trip, benefiting from the exertions of others without being tested severely itself. Sometimes it actually wins its race, taking a new career record and paying a land-office mutuel. With experience, handicappers learn to mistrust these sudden reversals of form, attributing them to racing luck and doubting the likehood of repetition.

At the same time, one should not forget that every driver seeks the perfect trip for his horse, wanting to spare it all the effort he can. If it is a good horse and has been racing well, the player should not downgrade a performance in which the driver was able to save the animal, out-think other drivers, and win without taxing the horse's courage and stamina.

The foxy Joe O'Brien provided an example in August, 1969, when he and Fresh Yankee defeated the great French mare Une de Mai. A week earlier, Une de Mai had humiliated Nevele Pride in the Roosevelt International and was now a prohibitive favorite. Her driver, Jean-Rene Gougeon, acted as if he were out for a drive in the park, setting a ridiculously slow pace, behind which O'Brien sat and sat and sat. Until the stretch, that is, when Joe took Fresh Yankee out

Joe O'Brien brings Fresh Yankee home first against a straining Nevele Pride at Liberty Bell on September 19, 1969.

and won. A perfect trip, and an embarrassment for Gougeon, who not only had allowed Fresh Yankee to reach the stretch with a full tank of fuel but also had pulled his own horse into hopeless lethargy.

Incidentally, Une de Mai's victory over Nevele Pride was a crushing refutation of the old move theory. The mare raced on the outside all the way, making no fewer than four moves at the American horse before passing and winning.

Track Variants

A type of misleading time about which few racegoers can do anything is recorded on evenings when an ostensibly fast track is unusually slow, or on other evenings when the track is much faster than usual. Without the kind of daily notations mentioned earlier in this book, the player inevitably arrives at a false estimate of some horse's ability. If the problem arose frequently enough to make handicapping a waste of effort for the occasional racegoer who lacked daily notes, I would insist either that notes be kept or the races avoided. Fortunately, the problem is uncommon. I doubt that the track labeled "fast" at a major raceway will be seriously slow or exceedingly fast more than five or six times a year.

Those who wish to keep notes, hoping to catch every possible winner and avoid every possible loser, must first form a reliable estimate of the time predictable on an ordinary evening for each grade of race. That subject is dealt with in the next chapter. After working out a schedule of normal, or par times—a laborious job— the player then goes through the results of the evening's races, noting how the time of each race differed from par. By adding these figures and dividing the total by the number of races, an average is achieved. The figure can be regarded as the track variant for the night, and the times recorded for each horse that raced that night can be adjusted accordingly.

For convenience, it is best to make the par figures unrealistically fast, so that the actual times will be slower. Thus, if $8,000 claiming races, or Class B-3 races, or conditioned races with purses of $3,000, usually are timed in about 2:05 at your track, you might set par for that class at 2:03. This probably would mean that $10,000 claiming races, or Class B-2 races, or conditioned races with purses of $3,500 —whatever the next higher local class might be—would be assigned a par of 2:02:3.

On the night an $8,000 claiming race ends in 2:04:4, you note that its time is $1\frac{4}{5}$ over par. Add the corresponding figures for all the races on the card and divide by the number of races to produce the average, the nightly variant. If, as suggested above, the variant turns out to be $+1\frac{2}{5}$, you simply write it in a notebook and subtract it from the time of a horse that raced on that evening when next you encounter the horse's record in a program.

When I described the compilation of par figures as a laborious job, I understated the case. At tracks that feature conditioned racing (to be described in the next chapter), constant vigilance is necessary lest you confuse one set of conditions with another and assign the wrong par to a field of horses. The best method, indicated above, is to deal in terms of the purse values of the conditioned races, being alert to keep pace with the changing purse structure, which tends to fluctuate at various stages of a long season.

If I seem less than enthusiastic about computing the track variant, it is because I doubt it is worth all the trouble. I have described it because such information is a duty of this book. Also, some handicapping hobbyists are remarkably studious. They seem to enjoy the toil of hair-splitting computation as much as the occasional fat mutuels to which it leads.

I think the track program departments should calculate daily variants and incorporate them in the post-performance records. Their figures would be more reliable than those compiled by racegoers.

The 2:00 Mile

In 1897, an eight-year-old pacer named Star Pointer achieved the first 2:00 mile in the history of harness racing—1:59¼, in fact. In 1903, Lou Dillon, a five-year-old mare, trotted a flat 2:00, the first of her gait to go that fast.

The 2:00 mile remains the watershed, sound barrier, timberline of the sport. It is the chief credential of a good horse. As of the beginning of 1969, only 992 horses had been able to register miles in 2:00 or better, accounting for 2,371 such performances among them. During the 73 years since Star Pointer paved the way, hundreds of thousands of trotters and pacers had tried and failed, but only 14 horses reached the 2:00 mark in an average year.

In 1968, however, 84 new horses joined the breed's elite, going in 2:00 or better for the first time in their lives. The year saw more than 200 performances in 2:00 or less. Never had the clock taken such a battering. Is the breed becoming swifter? Some experts doubt it, observing that the very fastest modern horses rarely surpass the speed records of their greatest predecessors. Yet modern Standardbreds enjoy the incalculable advantages of light, well-balanced sulkies, super-resilient tracks, vitamin-enriched feeds and improved methods of training and conditioning.

It is unsettling to realize that Greyhound set his all-time trotting record of 1:55¼ in 1938, when the sport was barely out of its Dark Ages. The record remained beyond serious challenge for 31 years, until Nevele Pride trotted 1:54:4 in 1969. Dan Patch's pacing mark of 1:55 endured from 1905 to 1960, when Adios Butler went in 1:54:3. The Butler's record stood until Bret Hanover lowered it to 1:54 and again to 1:53:3 in 1966.

The supposition is that legendary Standardbreds like Greyhound, Dan Patch, Lou Dillon, Uhlan and Peter Manning would earn millions if they could return to race for modern purses under modern conditions. It sounds plausible. But they would encounter challenges unknown in their eras. They now would be called on to beat not two or three good horses a year but dozens. Moreover, they would be required to do it under the incorruptible eye of an electronic timing device which, untouched by human thumb, is relentlessly accurate to the last tick.

The amazing Greyhound, with Sep Palin.

Electronics aside, hundreds of today's North American Standardbreds go the mile in times that few horses of the past could match. The breed as a whole is improving at a phenomenal rate, especially in its early (age) speed. Continued improvement is assured in early speed and, finally, in the high speed from which all-time records come. Just as human footracers finally made the 4:00 mile a commonplace, so will the evolving breed of trotters and pacers overwhelm the records of Nevele Pride and Bret Hanover. It is not visionary to predict records of less than 1:50. And it is certain that, with increasing multitudes of horses going the mile in 2:00, the figure will lose its magic. The standard of major-league speed will become 1:55.

Fastest Trotters of All Time

Nevele Pride, 4, TT 1:54:4, Indianapolis, Ind., 1969
Greyhound, 6, TT 1:55¼, Lexington, Ky., 1938
Noble Victory, 4, 1:55:3, Du Quoin, Ill., 1966
Matastar, 4, TT 1:55:4, Lexington, 1962
Peter Manning, 6, TT 1:56¾, Lexington, 1922
Rosalind, mare, 5, TT 1:56¾, Lexington, 1938
Ayres, 3, 1:56:4, Du Quoin, 1964
Speedy Scot, 3, 1:56:4, Lexington, 1963
Carlisle, 4, TT 1:57, Lexington, 1967
Fresh Yankee, mare, 4, TT 1:57:1, Lexington, 1967
Star's Pride, 5, 1:57:1, Du Quoin, 1952

Fastest Pacers of All Time

Bret Hanover, 4, TT 1:53:3, Lexington, 1966
Adios Butler, 4, TT 1:54:3, Lexington, 1960
Billy Direct, 4, TT 1:55, Lexington, 1938
Adios Harry, 4, 1:55, Vernon, N.Y., 1955*
Meadow Skipper, 3, 1:55:1, Lexington, 1963
Dan Patch, 9, TT 1:55¼, Lexington, 1905
Honest Story, 3, TT 1:55:2, Lexington, 1967
Meadow Paige, 3, TT 1:55:2, Lexington, 1967
Bullet Hanover, 3, TT 1:55:3, Lexington, 1960
Sampson Direct, 4, TT 1:56, Lexington, 1961
Rum Customer, 3, 1:56, Indianapolis, 1968

* ¾-mile track.

Lengths per Second

Just as the final time of a race is the winner's time, each of the fractional times represents the official clocking on whatever horse happened to be in the lead at the end of each quarter-mile. Thus, if a horse led all the way in one of its recent outings, the past-performance line shows its exact time at the quarter, half, three-quarters and finish. If it was behind at any of those calls, the fractional times in its record remain the same but refer to performances by another horse or two or three—depending on how often and at what points the early lead shifted.

Putting it another way, the past-performance line shows what kind of speed was afoot in the early stages of the race but does not disclose the individual horse's own early speed. Unless, of course, he was in the lead at one or more of the calls.

Final times are handled differently. The program gives the final time of the race, plus a final time for the individual horse, whether it won or not. At most raceways, a loser's final time is estimated by the program department, employing a traditional formula which equates a beaten length with $\frac{1}{5}$ second.

Thus, if a winner is timed in 2:04, a horse that trailed by two lengths is credited with a time of 2:04:2. Margins of $\frac{1}{2}$ length or less are disregarded, so that a horse that finished $3\frac{1}{2}$ lengths behind the 2:04 winner would be awarded a final time of 2:04:3.

The formula is incorrect. It probably is not incorrect enough to warrant a major fuss, but it is sufficiently off the mark to justify review. The rather trivial handicapping defects to which it leads are compounded, sometimes gravely, by a tangle of related confusions:

1. Program departments disagree over what constitutes a length.

2. Unaware of the disagreement, the public mistakenly believes that the lengths recorded in one past-performance line are equivalent to those in any other.

3. Many players defeat themselves through reckless attempts to extend an already doubtful and inconsistent time-length formula into handicapping areas where it is inapplicable.

The USTA and all but a few program departments (notably the Doc Robins establishment at Yonkers, Roosevelt and Monticello) define a length as the length of a horse—something less than eight feet. The additional length of the sulky is not included in this majority definition.

Peculiar difficulties arise. After all, horse and sulky race as an indivisible unit. For purposes of charting lengths, horse and sulky are observed most easily and accurately as a unit. When a horse races directly behind another, on the rail or elsewhere, it is both convenient and sensible to regard it as a length behind. But the prevailing wisdom insists that such a horse is $1\frac{1}{4}$ or $1\frac{1}{2}$ lengths behind. Accordingly, when a typical raceway program describes a horse as having been a length behind the leader, it means that the horse was racing either inside or outside the leader—it being impossible to cram a horse and its sulky into the space of one official length.

Now consider this: No matter whether a length be that of a horse or of a horse plus its sulky, the five-lengths-per-second formula is wrong.

All self-respecting raceways have a film patrol which takes movies or television tapes of every race, for scrutiny by the judges when fouls or other malpractices are suspected. These tapes show that the trotter or pacer travels across the finish line at a rate of about six lengths per second—if a length be defined in the conventional way, without regard to the presence of the sulky. That is, every beaten length represents about $\frac{1}{6}$ second. And the horse travels about $1\frac{1}{4}$ lengths in $\frac{1}{5}$ second.

Among the very few programs that accept $1\frac{1}{4}$ lengths as equivalent to $\frac{1}{5}$ second are the ones published in California by *The Daily Racing Form*. Other programs charge a horse more for its margin of defeat than the facts justify, adding extra fifths of seconds to the finishing times.

In New York, that outpost of independence and unrest, the programs not only see a length as the distance between the nose of the horse and the rear of the sulky but also count finishing time at the rate of four lengths per second. Where other programs disregard a margin of half a length or less, the New York program adds a fifth of a second for each half-length or more. Thus, if a horse wins by half a length in 2:02, the second horse is given a final time of 2:02:1. A four-length margin is, of course, counted as a time superiority of one second. Three lengths is counted as $\frac{4}{5}$ second. The New York formula is quite accurate.

When New York horses ship elsewhere for a race, the out-of-town program reproduces its record in terms of New York lengths and New York final times, as if no discrepancies existed. The same thing happens when a horse ships into New York. If you agree that it usually is senseless to analyze form recorded at tracks other than the one on which the race is to take place, this particular phenomenon may impress you as additional support for your opinion.

Having taken an overall look at the time-length rigamarole, let us now return to the question of fractional times. We already know that the program contains the fractional times of each recent race but not the fractional times of a trailing horse. Neither do the programs enable the player to calculate those times. They do not disclose the number of lengths by which a horse was racing behind the leader at the quarter, half or three-quarter calls (Illinois and California programs give this information for the three-quarter call). It therefore is impossible to apply a time-length formula to a past-performance line to estimate how rapidly a horse went the early fractions when racing behind the pace-setter.

It is impossible, but some people try. They assume that a horse was a length behind at the half if the program says it was second. It was two lengths behind if third, and so on, at the rate of one length per position. If the program shows that the horse was parked out, they assume that it was a length closer than it would have been on the rail. Thus, if the program says "3⁰," the horse is thought to have been no worse than a length behind. Its time for the half is estimated at 1:03:1 instead of the 1:03 given in the program as the half-mile clocking of the race.

This is bad business, a real trap for the handicapper. While it is true that horses tend to bunch up during a race, the dimensions of the bunch are anything but uniform. Margins vary considerably. Suppose the leader at the half was in front by a nose. Where was the fifth horse? He might have been behind by half a length or half a block. Without access to detailed charts of every race, the handicapper dare not deal in matters about which the program is silent.

Similar objections apply to the widespread practice of estimating a horse's time for the final quarter in terms of the number of lengths by which it led or trailed at the stretch call and finish. There can be no doubt that the time of the final quarter would be vitally useful to the handicapper. But to calculate it, he would have to know where the horse was at the three-quarter call. Except in California and Illinois, the information is not given. Except in those places, therefore, the calculation should not be attempted.

To know that the horse was third at the three-quarter call is, as we have seen, to know very little. To know that it was second on the outside (2⁰) may be helpful, if the program actually means that the animal was on the outside *at that point*. If so, the player who assumes that the horse was a length or less behind the leader will be right more often than wrong. But the fact remains that one must have a clear idea where the horse was at the three-quarter call. To know where it was in the stretch is insufficient.

Why? In the first place, the stretch represents only a minor fraction of the final quarter-mile at most tracks. In the second place, a horse may lose or gain several lengths between the time it leaves the three-quarter pole and reaches the stretch. Yet innumerable handicappers, noticing that the horse gained two lengths in the stretch, decide that its time for the final quarter was $\frac{2}{5}$-second faster than the official time for that decisive portion of the race.

The fact might well be that the horse's actual time was a full second faster. Perhaps it gained considerable ground between the three-quarter call and the stretch call. Or it might have lost ground at that stage while seeking position for the stretch drive, thereby making its time for the final quarter not much faster than the official clocking.

The pleasant pastime of trying to pick winners is quite difficult enough without the complications caused by wild guesses about time and lengths. Handicapping is sound only when carried on in terms of existing information. To the degree that the handicapper depends on surmise, he borrows grief. The scantiness of past-performance records may be cruel deprivation for the player, but the programs have one redeeming feature: they make elaborate handicapping procedures an unsupportable, unproductive waste of time.

I hope readers of this book will agree that handicappers cannot work with facts they do not have. I hope they also will agree that simple procedures based on known fact are easier and more dependable than some of the fanciful methods in which losers become ensnarled.

In that spirit, let's now consider a simple, factual approach to the basic factor of pace. No aspect of harness racing is misrepresented more widely and misunderstood so lamentably as pace. Yet none is more fundamental to the outcome of a race.

Simplifying Pace

If a Standardbred is broken to harness by a patient, able horseman, and is competently schooled and trained from that point onward, the chances are good that it will come to the races as a brave, cheerful, thoroughly manageable creature, devoid of serious temperamental quirks. It may never beat 2:06, but when it is in form it will produce that kind of time in race after race. Moreover, in the hands of a good driver it will put the time together in whatever style seems suitable to the circumstances of the individual race. On occasion it will leave quickly and try to hold the lead all the way. In another situation it will travel covered up, not too far off the pace, until the driver takes out for the front end. And there will be times when it will drop back to the rear, saving ground on the rail, until tiring leaders open holes through which it can make its bid.

A minority of trotters and pacers are less kindly. Sometimes through inheritance, but more often after heavy-handed treatment, they turn out to be "pullers." The harder the driver tries to restrain them, the harder they lean on the bit, frantic to go too fast too soon. Such horses cannot be rated—their energies cannot be conserved. All they can do is go until exhaustion sets in. Another unhappy type is the horse that hates air, quitting or breaking stride if asked to battle outside or in front for more than a few hundred feet. Such horses must be kept under cover, their chances of winning limited by the driver's luck in finding room for a dramatic burst of speed at the very end of the race.

And then there are horses that dislike racing against the rail. And others that hate having a horse between them and the rail. And horses that will stay neck-and-neck for the lead all day but stop as soon as they get in front. And horses that quit when whipped or not whipped.

But the majority of Standardbreds have no eccentricities that prevent a good driver from taking a fair shot at the purse. This is important. Among other things, it means that most Standardbreds have no set style of racing. They dispense their energy to the driver's order. Some are known as quick-leavers which perform well when setting the pace, but tonight's quick-leaver may come from behind next week, the driver having decided to cut the pattern that way.

Because so many of the horses are so pliable to their drivers, the handicapper cannot always look at the past performances and tell how the pace of the race is likely to develop. For example, the records might seem to make Horse "A" a cinch for the early lead. If the driver can hold "A" together at the end, he will be a wire-to-wire winner. Indeed, the race turns out that way quite often. "A" remains on top all the way or fades in the stretch and is beaten. But the handicapper has foreseen the basic pattern of the race.

I do not trust that kind of harness-race handicapping. When it works, it makes the expert look like a super-swami who can blueprint races in advance. But it does not work often enough. To see why, let us return to "A."

The quick-leaving "A" frequently does not have things all his own way in the early stages. Another horse unveils more early speed than has recently been asked of him and battles "A" from the very outset. What happens next is a matter of driving ability. If the driver of "A" is bright, he may retreat from the speed duel as soon as it starts, hoping that someone else will take out after the other horse and make life easier for him later. If this happens, the pace handicapper's forecast is wrong, whether his choice wins or not. He picked a horse to lead all the way, but it raced behind the pace, upending the predicted pattern.

When pace handicappers find more than one horse with sufficient early speed for an all-the-way victory, they usually expect the two or three pace-setting types to exhaust each other. In such a situation, they prefer to back a sharply conditioned animal that can come off the pace to beat the tiring leaders.

The theory is absolutely valid, but handicappers cannot be sure when it will apply. No good driver deliberately incurs the consequences of a speed duel unless he thinks he has enough animal to endure the duel without losing the race. By the same token, there is no great assurance that a supposed come-from-behind horse will come from behind on a given night. If the expected sprint for the early lead does not develop on schedule, because the drivers are playing possum, the pilot of the come-from-behind horse might make his move at the half and lead all the way home.

Another doctrine of the pace handicapper holds that a slow early pace favors the front horse, enabling it to save itself for the stretch. Uncountable races confirm this. The driver who wins the early lead applies the brakes in the second quarter to give his horse a long breather and retain juice for later use. Yet it is in precisely this kind of tactical situation that the biggest reversals of form occur. A horse lucky enough to have adequate racing room behind a slow pace may benefit more than the leader does and may come on at the end, as Fresh Yankee did against Une de Mai. And as longshot winners do every now and again at all raceways.

At this writing, a trend is developing which will inhibit the tactic of the slow early pace and will make conventional pace handicapping even less reliable than it now is. Milt Taylor of Liberty Bell, the foremost presiding judge in the sport, suspends the license of any driver who slows the early pace enough to place other horses at an unsporting disadvantage.

"We don't want any of those second quarters in thirty-four around here," says Taylor. "The public is paying for formful, competitive racing in which the best horse wins. If a driver is not willing to go the first half-mile in legitimate race-horse time, we tell him to go race somewhere else.

"The driver on the lead holds the stick," Taylor explains. "If he slows the pace away down and somebody tries to pass him, he can speed up just enough to keep the other man parked out. He also can cause accidents behind him when horses begin breaking because they have no place to go. It's evil. It's not competitive racing. Just suppose you are a driver. You leave from the outside and tuck in behind and then some wise guy slows the pace so that they go the first half in 1:05. Naturally, they go the second half in something like 1:01 and you have to grow wings to catch them."

Some of the very best drivers in the business conform to Taylor's rules when at Liberty Bell, gleefully relapsing when they move to raceways where their tactics are supervised less stringently. The second quarter of a Liberty Bell race is quite likely to be slower than the first, but not by much. With drivers required to maintain racing speed at all times, they rarely try to hang each other on the outside, knowing that skirmishes of that sort can exhaust both horses. Thus, when a horse comes alongside to challenge for the early lead, the driver of the front horse usually lets him pass, giving his own animal a breather before bidding for the lead once more.

Other tracks are not yet as vigorous about discouraging slow second quarter-miles and the curious upsets that sometimes result. But it is fair to say that all leading tracks have been discouraging extreme forms of that tactic. The headlong, formful racing at Liberty Bell has been attracting sober attention throughout the industry. So has its remarkable freedom from accidents, a happy by-product of what might as well be called Taylor's Law. What with one thing and another, the extremely slow second quarter is doomed.

Pending that development, the student of pace should know that a slow first half-mile usually favors the pace-setter, but sometimes does not and rarely can be foreseen. He also should know that the fast early pace usually benefits a come-from-behind horse. But beyond all else he should know that pace handicapping of the early-speed-versus-late-speed variety is an infirm basis on which to operate. With so many horses able to yield their speed in sequences improvised by the drivers, it is not possible for handicappers to foresee the surprising patterns that sometimes result from that improvisation.

Which brings us to the big question. Can a harness-racing fan use the past-performance records for pace handicapping?

The answer is yes. Vehemently. The guiding principle can be summarized:

Among horses that qualify as possible contenders because they seem to be in fit condition, the likeliest is one that recently demon-

*strated its ability to produce the best final time after setting or over-
coming the fastest early pace.*

"Best final time" and "fastest early pace" refer to comparisons of
(a) the final times recorded for the possible contenders in their respective good, recent races, plus (b) comparisons of the half-mile
times of those races.

Note that the individual horse's racing style, if any, is not involved.
The handicapper's sole concern is to find the animal, regardless of its
supposed early speed, that seems able to complete the mile in comparatively good time after a race in which the half-mile clocking was
relatively fast.

To oversimplify, ignoring other relevant factors, a horse that went
in 2:03 last week in a race with a half-mile time of 1:01:2 would be
regarded as an inherently better prospect than one that went in
2:02:3 off a half-mile time of 1:02:1.

My study of thousands of races at tracks of all sizes has satisfied
me that this principle is the basis of a consistently successful approach
to harness-race handicapping. When applied to the recent past performances of apparently fit and ready trotters or pacers, it turns up
the horse or horses with which top drivers can get the best results,
*entirely without regard to the unforeseeable developments that affect
driving tactics during a race.*

Of all Standardbred handicapping concepts, this may be the most
useful. Let me linger over it a bit, even at risk of repetition. The
horse with sufficient form and class to get the fastest mile off the most
demanding early pace is a top candidate to do just that in whatever
style the driver may choose—or may have thrust on him—during the
race itself.

This approach spares the player the necessity of trying to predict
the pattern of a race before the drivers form that pattern themselves.
It directs the player to a horse most likely to produce a vigorous
stretch kick if the early pace proves unusually slow. And it directs
him to the horse—the very same horse—that probably will be best
able to hold together in the late stages if the early pace is unusually
fast.

The key, of course, is to eliminate apparently unready horses,
sucked-along horses and other probable non-contenders before analyzing pace. Then, after rating the potential pace of each probable
contender, the handicapper simply adjusts the ratings in light of
fundamental influences such as class, driver and post position. We

shall explore those techniques in later chapters. To prepare the way, we should now agree on means of arriving at actual pace ratings.

Pace Ratings

Numbers are a useful convenience in Standardbred handicapping. The numbers used in this book's handicapping have no significance beyond convenience. We are not dealing in magical formulas, but only in simple, orderly methods of comparing the past-performance records of horses.

The pace-rating chart on the facing page offers one easy way to compare the apparent pace potentialities of horses. It assigns an arbitrary point value to each official half-mile time and another point value to the final time of each horse. The assigned numbers could be larger or smaller than they are without affecting the principle. Our concern is simply to establish recognizable *differences* among recent, comparable performances.

The chart is for comparison of pace figures recorded in races on dry, fast surfaces. It can be used to rate performances on good tracks, provided the handicapper is careful to do so only when all races under comparison took place on such a footing.

To pace-rate a contender that went in 2:05:3 in a race timed at 1:03:1 to the half-mile, use the chart as follows:

1. Find the value for a half in 1:03—110.
2. Find the value for a mile in 2:05—90.
3. Add the numbers—110 + 90 = 200.
4. *Subtract* the fifths of seconds, if any, in the official half-mile and final times—200 − 4 = 196.

To recapitulate: *Set aside* whatever fifths of seconds appear in the half-mile and final times. Find the value for the remaining half-mile and final time figures. Add them, and then *subtract* from that total the fifths of seconds that had been set aside.

Another easy way to compute pace ratings is to compare the horses directly on a different scale, as follows:

```
Horse "A": 1:02:4 (20) + 2:05:3 (12) = 32
Horse "B": 1:03:1 (18) + 2:04:4 (16) = 34
Horse "C": 1:03:1 (18) + 2:04  (20) = 38
```

The fastest half-mile time is given a value of 20. One point is subtracted from the rating of each horse for every $\frac{1}{5}$ second of difference between the official half-mile time of its race and the fastest half-mile

Pace-Rating Table

½ Mile	Points	Final Time	½ Mile	Points	Final Time
:55	150	1:53	1:10	75	2:08
:56	145	1:54	1:11	70	2:09
:57	140	1:55	1:12	65	2:10
:58	135	1:56	1:13	60	2:11
:59	130	1:57	1:14	55	2:12
1:00	125	1:58	1:15	50	2:13
1:01	120	1:59	—	45	2:14
1:02	115	2:00	—	40	2:15
1:03	110	2:01	—	35	2:16
1:04	105	2:02	—	30	2:17
1:05	100	2:03	—	25	2:18
1:06	95	2:04	—	20	2:19
1:07	90	2:05	—	15	2:20
1:08	85	2:06	—	10	2:21
1:09	80	2:07	—	5	2:22

time. The same is done with the horses' final times—20 to the fastest and one point less for each $\frac{1}{5}$ second of difference recorded for the slower finishers. The two figures are then added. If you use the pace-rating chart for this example, you will find that it produces the same result as was achieved through direct comparison: the numbers are different, but "C" is four points better than "B" and six points better than "A."

Comparative Track Speeds

Pace handicapping or, for that matter, any other kind of handicapping is most effective when the horses have all been racing at the same track. But the temptation is great to handicap races in which some of the horses have been performing elsewhere. To encourage and assist this practice, the programs publish tables of comparative track speeds. The speed assigned each track is based on USTA figures developed from race times at the track's most recent meeting. Recent changes in footing are not likely to be encompassed in the ratings.

While I doubt that anyone can win money on races of that kind, I admit that it sometimes is fun to try. I would be more than ordinarily reluctant to tackle the problem at a half-mile track, however, unless the out-of-town shippers had also been performing at a track of that size or unless their records showed that they recently had managed well at a half-miler. At a miler or ⅝-miler, I'd be reluctant to fool with a horse from a half-miler unless it had been showing some willingness to come on in the stretch.

From that point forward, the table of comparative track speeds tells the player whether to adjust the out-of-town times upward or downward, and by how much. In doing so, it is important to adjust the half-mile times as well. If tonight's raceway is rated at 2:05 and the other at 2:06, I would deduct a full second from the horse's final time and ⅖ second from its half-mile time. If the first half of the race was clocked in slower figures than the second, I would deduct ⅗ from the half-mile time.

If track programs included track variants in the past-performance records, pace rating would be an even more dependable tool than it is. Nevertheless, I believe that pace rating is the safest, most profitable basis on which the occasional racegoer can build his handicapping method. Relying entirely on information contained in the program, his comparison of half-mile times and final times enables him to hold his own against handicappers who are out there every night and work with private charts. The trick, of course, is to concentrate on playable races (already discussed) and to make astute appraisals of class, form, post position and driver, adjusting the basic ratings accordingly. Let us now consider class.

8

The Class Factor

CLASS IS QUALITY. It expresses itself as speed, soundness, stamina, gameness, stability of gait and consistency of performance. In whatever proportions these traits appear, they represent the individual Standardbred's physical and temperamental heritage, as affected by persons and events. Among environmental influences on class are nutrition, illness and injury, the variable wisdom of grooms, trainers, veterinarians and drivers and, above all, the exertions of training and racing.

Horses of the highest class not only are faster than most other horses but also are sound enough and/or game enough to produce the speed when it counts—on the night of the race, in head-to-head confrontation with the best of their era. They are more likely than others to remain on gait even when pressed to the farthest limits of their speed and endurance. Indeed, when taxed in that way they reach into their reserves of energy for the extra yards of sustained speed that win close races and break records.

The lower the class, the smaller are these reserves of energy or the greater the disabilities which prevent the horse from drawing on them. The cheapest fields at raceways include expensively bred animals condemned to slowness at the mile by some inherited or acquired defect—a muscular, skeletal or organic flaw which limits stride or shortens breath. In the same fields are horses of former speed whose class has deteriorated with age and use.

As the lifetime speed and earnings records of horses in these cheap fields demonstrate, Standardbred class is transient. A breeder or historian evaluates a horse in light of its total achievements, including those of its distant past, but a handicapper concentrates on the present. Without present soundness and condition, class is inoperative. The glories of the past are pleasant to reminisce about but costly to bet on.

By the same criteria, if a horse of superior class has a competent driver and is in good enough shape to demonstrate its class, it is the best bet of the night, the week or the year. A slight class advantage can mean decisive victory.

Obsessed as they are with the desire for close races among evenly matched Standardbreds, raceways take great pains to prevent situations in which one horse of conspicuously superior quality lays over a soft field. Yet sometimes it happens. More often, condition-related differences in current ability make the outcome predictable in a race among animals of ostensibly equal class.

To recognize these differences when they glimmer beneath the surface of the past-performance charts, it is necessary to understand the harness-racing industry's own evolving conceptions of how horses and races should be classified, and how conditions of eligibility for entry should be determined. The class notations on the program page reflect these conceptions and the raceway's method of implementing them. To a great extent, the notations also reflect the standards whereby horsemen evaluate and manipulate their own stock.

The class patterns of harness racing have been in flux for many years. Eligibility conditions and classification methods prevalent at today's tracks differ remarkably from those of a decade ago. Each new season brings horsemen a wider and more equitable assortment of racing opportunities. Today's greater variety of races—some of which overlap or coincide in class without seeming to—challenges the knowledge and judgment of the handicapping fan. More than ever, the ability to draw fine class distinctions is crucial at the mutuel windows. The past-performance chart sometimes obscures these distinctions. The racegoer can begin to sort things out for himself when he learns how race-classification methods developed to their present state, and where they seem to be going from here.

Classified Racing

Time at the mile being the fundamental measure of a North American Standardbred's ability, racing secretaries never stray far from that statistic in deciding whether horses belong on their programs and, if so, in what kinds of races. The same criterion serves horsemen when they make their own decisions about where and when their animals should race, and in what kind of company.

The *when* is crucial. A 2:10 horse is not endlessly capable of the 2:10 mile. It is a living creature, not a robot. It cannot produce 2:10

unless fit. Minor illness, injury or plain lapses from form may affect its speed for weeks, influencing the management decisions of its trainer.

On one side, then, the racing secretary and his expert opinion of each horse's ability. On the other, the horseman and his intimate view of how the horse's *present* ability compares with its *previous* ability or, perhaps, with its *potential* ability. In the middle sits the raceway operator, whose financial outlook brightens to the degree that he can offer the public (a) exciting races and (b) races in which the results are believable because the form stands up. To achieve these goals, the industry has been tinkering for decades with the terms and conditions under which horses compete against each other.

It has not been easy. Horsemen want maximum freedom to enter each animal in the race best suited to its current abilities. Translation: the easiest race with the best purse. Raceway operators need to restrict such freedom so that fields will be as evenly matched as possible. And the public needs to understand the ground rules so that it can compare one past performance with another and assess the current class of each horse on that basis.

During the formative years of the sport, logic decreed that horses be matched on the basis of their time records. Just as a farmer with a 2:17 horse might solicit a race against a 2:20 horse, and might accept a race against some other 2:17 horse, but would avoid losing money to the owner of a 2:12 horse, the programs at country fairs and other early raceways presented fields of animals whose lifetime speed records were competitive. Horses with better records raced for better purses.

This was the logic of innocence. Horsemen quickly realized that it was more profitable to beat cheap horses in slow time than to be beaten by good horses in fast. On occasion, it was most profitable not to win at all. Listen to a veteran racing official who was there:

> The big money was for aged horses in those days. Very little was done with them at two or three. They began at four. If you had a precocious four-year-old, you wanted him to get experience. So you kept him under wraps, letting him finish second to win 25 percent of the purse, but not letting him win. In that way he got no record and could stay in easy races. Sometimes you put him into heat races and could win the first heat in fast enough time to win second money on the overall results of the three or four heats. But the horse still had no record, because he still had not been an official winner. When you finally got ready to shoot with him, you really could make hay. Per-

haps he was good enough to beat everything in the state but was still eligible to race against soft fields. You could win four, five, six races in succession, never going a tick faster than necessary.

This kind of cheating, and the crude maneuvering that caused interminable delays at the start of each race, gave the sport a reputation not greatly superior to that of the wheels of fortune and shell games with which it vied for public attention at fairs. After the war, with pari-mutuel betting and night programs offering promise of riches beyond all precedent, the USTA outlawed the so-called time bar, substituting a classification system less conducive to larceny. Without this reform, harness racing could scarcely have established itself in metropolitan areas and might even have worn out its welcome in the boondocks.

The new system divided horses into 30 classes on the basis of lifetime earnings. Class 30, the lowest, was for nonwinners of $100 (the minimum was increased by USTA amendment in later years). The top class, FFA (Free-for-All), was for horses that had earned more than $50,000. Class 20 was for nonwinners of $2,000; Class 11 was for nonwinners of $20,000, and so forth.

The shortcomings of the class system soon became expensively apparent to horsemen. A horse was imprisoned in its class even after injury, sickness or the deterioration of age left it unable to keep up with sounder animals whose career earnings were no higher. In fact, a horse unable to win in its prescribed class often was boosted to a higher and even more impossible class after having earned a little money when it backed into a few second- or third-place finishes. Or a three-year-old would win so much against easy fields of its own age that its useful career would end at four, when it was obliged not only to face older horses but also faster ones, and no longer could win.

Despite efforts to remedy these defects by making allowances for illness or age, the class system remained unsatisfactory. By winning, horses inevitably earned their way into company too formidable for them. They then were required to lose repeatedly before qualifying for the class demotion which might enable them to resume winning. The horseman found himself in the position of racing his good animal to sure defeat during the very months when it should have been repaying him for all the time and money expended on its early training.

Class racing withered away and was replaced with classified racing, in which the racing secretary assigns the horse to whatever class he considers appropriate. The classes are designated by letter, D being the lowest. The pecking order proceeds through C to B to A to AA and then to JFA (Junior Free-for-All) and FFA. At Yonkers, Roosevelt and Monticello, where letter-classified racing is firmly entrenched, the classes are subdivided. The lowest is C-3, followed in ascending order by C-2, C-1, B-3, B-2, B-1, A-3, A-2, A-1, AA, JFA and FFA.

Acknowledging in 1955 that a racing secretary's classification of a horse was nothing but his handicapping estimate of its speed at the

BILL CONNORS
Racing secretary at Pompano Park,
Hazel Park, The Meadows,
and Wolverine.

mile, the USTA issued a schedule of speeds by which the secretaries were required to abide. At a track where FFA pacers—the best in the country—went in about 2:03, a 2:13 pacer was assigned to D, the poorest of the ten listed classes. Each step up the scale represented about one second of improvement. Trotters were assumed to go $1\frac{3}{5}$ seconds slower than pacers of equal class. Formulas were available for adjusting the table to the relative speed of the individual track.

The old time-bar system had pitted horsemen against an inflexible set of rules. By penalizing achievement and rewarding deceit, the time bar virtually guaranteed that trainers and drivers would be under economic compulsion to fleece each other and fool their rural public. Class racing abolished the rewards of deceit while leaving intact the penalties for achievement. Letter classification falls between its two predecessors. By its very nature it propels horsemen into a ceaseless game of truth or consequences with the racing secretary, who holds most of the trumps.

Although common sense requires the secretary to classify the horses on the basis of their speed, it also dictates that he "move up" a frequent winner, even if its speed is below normal for the higher class. By the same logic, he refuses to "back up" a losing horse to a lower class until satisfied that it cannot earn its way in the higher class. He may demote an animal after one or two losses, or may defer action for many weeks, until persuaded by additional evidence.

Because his decisions directly affect the revenues of racing stables, the secretary's burden is heavy. But the rules offer horsemen no incentive to lighten it. Sooner or later, each trainer finds himself sincerely convinced that one of his horses is misclassified. He knows more about the animal's current condition than the secretary does, but he cannot reasonably expect that official to demote the horse until its predicament is made visible in a few poor races. Temptation arises to lose as abjectly as possible, in hope of hastening the secretary's decision. Similarly, the trainer with a fairly sharp horse must decide whether to win and be moved into a class where purses are higher but the horse's earning capacity may be less. The alternative is to lose and be allowed to remain for a few more races where the pickings are easier.

In self-defense, and in the interest of the all-out competition which he is paid to produce, the racing secretary watches every performance with a cold and critical eye. If he suspects that a horse's people have abandoned hope of winning and have stopped trying, he calls them onto his tear-stained carpet and says as much. To be backed up in class, a horse not only must lose but also must lose in a manner convincing to the secretary. He wants to be sure that the driver is trying.

The notion that horsemen might find it more expedient to lose than to win was rampant in raceway grandstands during the years when letter classes were the national mode. The industry found the idea intolerable. It trembled over rumors about drivers "going" or not. It feared the eventual effects on mutuel receipts of the strange last-minute odds fluctuations which accompanied some of the rumors. Furthermore, horsemen were chronically disgruntled. They wanted latitude to enter races of their own choosing.

To promote public confidence and restore tranquility backstage, the USTA has abolished classified racing in its own sphere of influence, that is, everywhere but the southern part of New York State.

At Yonkers and Roosevelt, the two wealthiest raceway operations in North America, letter classes remain in full force. The same is true at Monticello.

New York raceway managements cling to classified racing for the elemental reason that they consider it good for their business. They maintain that firm control of entries by an astute racing secretary assures close, exciting competition, which stimulates lively betting. Furthermore, their audiences are used to the A-B-C classes. No other method offers such simple, understandable designations. The New York fan knows that a horse moving from C-1 to B-3 is rising in class, and forms his judgments accordingly. When the New York tracks tried to operate without this system between 1963 and 1966, the financial results were branded unsatisfactory. And, finally, New York is unconvinced that chicanery waxes or wanes with changes in classification methods. Where the racing secretary and presiding judge know their business and are supported by a muscular state racing commission, cheating is no particular problem.

It is possible to muster a rebuttal for each of the foregoing arguments, and it is quite easy to rebut each rebuttal. That, in fact, is what has been going on in the industry for years. Controversy about the secessionist character of New York harness racing is deep, bitter and incessant. Although I enjoy playing the oracle, I must decline the pleasure of predicting how this debate will end. The truth is that nobody has the vaguest idea on that score. All we can do at this stage of events is see where each form of harness racing is, and where it seems to be going, and what may be implied for the handicapping enthusiast.

Conditioned Racing

At all North American raceways save the three in downstate New York, conditioned racing has supplanted classified racing. In principle, conditioned racing frees the horseman from bondage to the racing secretary. With the same blow, it liberates that functionary from responsibility for managing the careers of other people's horses. No longer required to classify them according to his assessment of their abilities, he relinquishes the power to type-cast some of them in races more difficult than their trainers and owners might consider suitable. All he does, at least in principle, is write conditions of eligibility for entry in races. The horseman is free to pick and choose among a variety of races, thus managing his animal as he sees fit.

PHIL LANGLEY
Racing secretary
at Sportsman's Park.

The realities of conditioned racing do not coincide at all points with the principle, but they come quite close. Racing secretaries keep a careful census of the kinds of horses ready to race at their tracks, and write conditions designed to produce close contests among the available stock. The conditions are concerned mainly with earnings—lifetime, or last year, or this year, or in each horse's most recent starts. Number, frequency and recency of victories may be among the primary conditions, as may age or sex or both.

When the racing secretary is willing and able to adapt his procedures to the varying talents and credentials of the horses on his grounds, every fit animal has ample opportunities to win, or at least to cash occasional checks. And handicapping fans can tell rather accurately what grade of horse is involved in each race. Where the secretary is short on such ability, or begrudges the effort, or where the equine population is poor, the eligibility conditions tend toward the incomprehensible and so do the results of some of the races.

For example, consider an April race in which the conditions specify nonwinners of $10,000 during the previous year. Some racing secretaries persist in writing such conditions, which attract wildly incompatible fields of horses. Entrants might include animals that already have won *more* than $10,000 during the *current* year, as well as animals that do not belong on the same track with them, having done little last year and less this. Similarly, a race programmed for non-

TED LEONARD
Racing secretary at Maywood,
Rockingham, Pocono Downs,
and Rosecroft.

winners of $4,000 during the current year might prove a soft touch for a classy animal in its second or third start of the season.

Most horsemen admire the conditions written by Phil Langley, racing secretary at Sportsman's Park. He concentrates—as trainers and handicappers must—on recent performances. Eligibility for his races is governed by the amount of money won or the number and purse values of races won in the horse's six, eight or ten most recent starts. Conditions of this kind are easily understood, inspiring the confidence of horsemen and bettors alike.

Obviously, as a horse's earnings increase, so does the quality of the opposition it faces. Sooner or later it must enter conditioned races in which its chances are slim. But if it is in good physical shape, its prospects rarely are hopeless: The recent records of the other horses are, after all, similar to its own. It is astonishing to realize that here, for the first time in the history of this sport, the rules contain nothing that might be interpreted as a penalty for winning or a reward for losing.

Although the racing secretary no longer has the power to classify every horse in the park, he remains responsible for the presentation of closely contested races. The conditions he writes, however ingenious they may be, do not always accomplish this. Some horses, though eligible under the conditions, are not good enough for their races. Others are too good. The secretary negotiates for the withdrawal of such horses. Bargaining of that kind between secretaries and horsemen is most prevalent at tracks where, for one reason or another, relatively good horses and/or relatively poor ones have few opportunities to compete against stock of their own quality.

When the USTA adopted conditioned racing, it suffered no illusion that the new system would be appropriate for all kinds of horses. Its plan was double edged. On the one hand, the association sought to escape the problems attributed to classified racing. On the other, it sought to promote industry-wide acceptance of claiming races. This was a large hope. Claiming races were at odds with some cherished traditions.

Despite large obstacles, claiming races have become an integral feature of the game. More numerous every season, they are bringing about decisive changes in the arts of raceway programming, Standardbred management and handicapping. By establishing clearly delineated classes of competition for cheap horses, they help to bring order and reason to all other aspects of classified and conditioned racing. Suddenly we can see the emerging outlines of a logical gradation, or hierarchy, of Standardbred class. As the class structure becomes clearer and more rational, some of the worst perplexities of harness-race handicapping disappear.

Claiming Races

The owner of a professional baseball or football team invests millions of dollars but dares not enter his own clubhouse without an invitation. The owner of a Thoroughbred runner has a remote and cautious relationship with the animal. But the proprietor of a Standardbred really *belongs*. He has things to *do*.

Any able-bodied man, woman or adolescent can climb into a sulky and drive the average trotter or pacer. It is one of the incomparable pleasures of Standardbred ownership to get all dolled up in horseman's regalia and actually train one's animal. Proudly, and as comfortably as if he were in his easy chair, the owner jogs the horse the wrong way of the track for a couple of miles, then turns it around for a timed trip. Afterward, mud-spattered, he gives the trainer a great deal of advice about its form.

Enchanted owners develop deep attachments to their horses. So do trainers, most of whom entered the sport as the sons and grandsons of owners. The modern horse may no longer be quite the family pet that grazed in the yard between races, but it is credited with intelligence, personality and feelings. It therefore is not often treated as if it were a mere racing tool, an item of merchandise.

This warmly possessive attitude accounts for the reluctance with which harness-racing folk have accepted claiming races. Any horse entered in such a contest is automatically for sale at whatever price is stated in the eligibility conditions. A bona fide horseman can post a claim and a check before the race and lead the animal to his own stable afterward.

The main virtue of these races is fair competition among horses of equal market value, equal class. A horse entered at an unrealistically high price attracts no claims but wins no races, either. When entered at the proper level, it might win but it might also be claimed, a possibility upsetting to many owners.

What finally has tipped the balance in favor of the claiming race is that no other formula assures winning opportunities to mediocre and inferior stock. Young or old, improving or deteriorating, the average horse is best off in a claiming race against its own kind. No matter how cleverly the racing secretary drafts eligibility conditions or, in New York, classifies the horses, the average trotter or pacer is at a disadvantage. Most often, it takes a drubbing from a higher-grade animal headed for better things. If it warms out of its aches and pains enough to score an upset victory, it helps its owner and a handful of longshot fanciers, but contributes nothing to the sport's hard-earned reputation for formful competition. Its victory does not alter the fundamental truths that (a) cheap horses should race against their own kind and (b) that the only known way to assure keen competition among them is to write claiming races for them.

Claiming races were tried and abandoned fifty years ago. They were revived in 1959 at Sportsman's Park, and, in 1965, the USTA began campaigning for their widespread adoption. By 1969, more than a third of all raceway events in the United States were claimers—a phenomenal growth.

Sportsman's Park, which enjoys the third-highest mutuel handle in the country and offers purses to match, programs about 60 claiming races for every 40 races of other kinds. Horses that appear in conditioned or classified races elsewhere race in claimers at Sportsman's Park, sometimes because their abilities are too moderate to qualify them for anything else, and sometimes because the track promotes claimers by offering higher purses than in conditioned races of comparable speed.

This sweetening of the kitty to encourage the segregation of inferior horses may be warranted as a temporary expedient. Eventually, the stability of the sport's class structure will rest on orderly patterns wherein the size of the purse will be an accurate index to the class of the race. All tracks will not have identical purse structures, of course. But the quality of any horse will be comparable to that of any other in terms of the purses won by each in recent races over the same track. And claiming races will be not less than 75 percent of the seasonal fare at the typical raceway.

To show how various tracks have been handling (or detouring) the challenge of the claiming race, I have just checked through some programs of March, 1969. During one week, Washington Park offered 15 claimers, Rockingham Park had 10, Liberty Bell had 4 and Roosevelt Raceway had 2. In another week, Washington Park presented 16, Rockingham had 7, Liberty Bell offered 6 and Roosevelt managed just 1.

Ed Parker, racing secretary at Yonkers, usually puts together 15 or 16 claimers in a week. He requires any male horse aged six or more to race with a claiming tag unless it is classified at B-2 or better. This

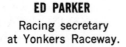

ED PARKER
Racing secretary
at Yonkers Raceway.

leaves the lower end of the letter-class ladder unobstructed for fillies, mares and younger males. More formful competition results, not only in C-3 through B-3 racing, but also in the claimers themselves.

Later in this chapter, I shall offer some handicapping materials helpful in comparing claiming, classified and conditioned races. For now, we can agree that higher claiming prices indicate higher class at any given track, but may be misleading if two tracks are involved. The horse that races with a $5,000 label at Freehold may be perfectly comfortable in $6,000 circles at Brandywine or Yonkers. Market values and claiming prices tend to rise where purses are higher.

Contradictorily, claiming prices also are inflated at tracks where claiming races have not yet come into full fashion. A horse able to win no more than $3,000 a year in cheap company is not a $7,500 horse but a $3,000 one. If it is only four or five years old, or has any kind of breeding potential, its proper claiming level may be as high as $5,000. But the aged gelding that appears in the average claiming race is worth just about what it can win in a year, and its claiming price should reflect that.

By the same standard, the handicapper knows at a glance that a horse entered to be claimed for $5,000 is a horse in physical trouble if it has earned that much or more during the current year, or even during the previous year. Horsemen give nothing away for $5,000 if they can sell it for more.

The Preferred List

One kind of classified racing is accepted throughout the industry. The racing secretary posts what is known as a preferred list, which names the fastest horses on the grounds. These logical contenders for the meeting's richest feature races are not permitted to enter conditioned or letter-class races except in special circumstances. With similar exceptions, lesser animals are not eligible for the big features.

At most tracks, races among the listed horses are identified in the programs as "Preferred." When out-of-town stars and larger purses are involved, the term usually is "Invitational." At Yonkers and Roosevelt, the "Preferred" designation is not used and "Invitational" embraces a wider range of purses and horses.

Every season, a few mature horses of each gait prove routinely capable of 2:00 miles and are hailed as free-for-allers—the animals that confront the best in the world for the highest purses, with no holds barred. Depending on the track, their races are known as FFA (Free-for-All), open, invitational, classic, international or the like.

JFA (Junior Free-for-All) designates a race among stock too good for the average preferred field but not good enough to beat free-for-allers. A horse that races in A or AA company at Yonkers may be

Training in winter quarters at Pompano Park, Florida.

granted an occasional fling at a JFA purse. Moreover, if it ships to a smaller raceway, it probably competes in preferred affairs, even invitationals.

All these types of feature races are comparable with each other in terms of the purses they offer—provided that the handicapper is careful to compare races that occurred at the same track or, at least, on the same racing circuit. A $25,000 invitational almost certainly is a more severe test than a $15,000 one at the same track. But the handicapper makes unwarranted assumptions if he guesses that a $25,000 race at one track was of higher quality than a race of less value at a distant track. Purses vary with the time of year and the customs of the individual raceway. Unless the fan recognizes the names of the animals in an out-of-town race and has means of appraising the form they were in at the time, he has little to go on.

Stakes and Such

Major stakes and futurities of the type that feature Grand Circuit meetings often require nominations and entry fees while the animals still are foals. To nominate a well-bred infant to all the stakes for which it is eligible, and to maintain its eligibility until it proves as a two-year-old that it has been overrated, costs not less than $10,000. The rare creature that justifies such risks throughout its two-, three, and four-year-old form—like a Laverne Hanover or Nevele Pride— repays the enormous investments many times over. But it is sobering to realize that most Standardbreds nominated for stakes never fulfill the early hope. Some never race at all, much less compete in top company. The huge purses awarded to stakes winners consist primarily of nomination fees contributed in behalf of animals that are nowhere to be seen on the day of the race.

The most promising colts actually go onto the Grand Circuit. If they withstand those severe tests as two- and three-year-olds, they become FFA and JFA competitors at four and five. They are the best. It is no trick to recognize their quality in the past-performance records, even in the unlikely event that their names are unfamiliar.

In recent years, however, it has become increasingly possible for a careless bettor to make horrible mistakes about certain young horses whose records include high earnings in stakes races. Without reading those records carefully, the racegoer might assume that the animals were of Grand Circuit quality. He would be dead wrong.

The complicating factor is a type of racing subsidized by rebates from the state treasury's share of the mutuel take or breakage. Devised to encourage the home state's breeding industry and related forms of agriculture, the races are open only to the get of sires that stand in the state. The most extravagant and successful sire stakes program is the one in New York, which offers purses of $3 million a year and has become an instant bonanza for breeders and stable owners sharp enough to establish themselves on the ground floor.

Examples: Duchess Rose, a trotting mare that never beat 2:03:3, won over $200,000 in three years of New York sire stakes racing. Fine Shot was second only to Nevele Pride as a money-winning three-year-old trotter during 1968, accumulating over $144,000 with a mediocre record of 2:02:3. His earnings in two years of sire stakes competition were $259,359, seven or eight times what a horse of his ability might have been expected to make under the best of circumstances in open competition.

Neon Rodney (2:06:3!) earned $62,708 during 1968—more than any other three-year-old trotting filly in North America. She earned it in New York sire stakes. That's Great (2:05), led all two-year-old male trotters with $97,877 during 1968, whereas the future Hambletonian winner, Lindy's Pride (2:00:1) earned only $62,781, being ineligible for the sire stakes in which That's Great took refuge. Also during 1968, Sunnie Tar paced a mile in 1:56:4 and earned $69,564, which put her only in second place among the continent's three-year-old fillies of her gait. The champ was Tar Boy's Dream, who won $81,525 in New York sire stakes without beating 2:02:3.

With millions of dollars going practically by default to lower-grade horses whose chief qualifications are the names and whereabouts of their sires, breeders are doing their utmost to produce livestock that not only will be eligible for the programs but also will be able to pace or trot at high speed. Good horses would win these races without effort. And that is exactly what sire stakes programs are all about— incentive to improve breeding in the sponsoring states.

Under this impetus, outstanding stallions like Overcall, Gene Abbe, Torpid, Speedy Streak, Egyptian Candor, Greentree Adios, Fly Fly Byrd, Thorpe Hanover, Romeo Hanover, Adora's Dream, Speedy Rodney, All Aflame and Adios Boy have turned up as official residents of New York. Their get will inevitably upgrade the racing. In fact, it is possible that the quality of New York or Ohio or Illinois sire stakes may someday be only one cut below that of Grand Circuit competition.

The shape of the future became unmistakably obvious in 1969 when the two-year-old New York-bred trotter, Gunner, not only prospered in sire stakes events but also won the $90,986 Roosevelt Futurity, the sport's foremost open-class stakes race for juvenile trotters. In winning, Gunner defeated top Grand Circuit colts, including the season's champion, Victory Star.

Pending the emergence of other Gunners, the racegoer should be terribly careful not to be misled by the high earnings and apparent stakes credentials of mediocre raceway horses. The tip-off, of course, is their lack of authentic speed.

Other stakes races with which the reader should be acquainted are known as early closers and late closers. Nominations and entry fees for an early closer are posted by the horseman at least six weeks— frequently many months—before the race. Subsequent changes in physical condition and improvements or deteriorations in class give these contests a sporting air akin to that of the more celebrated stakes affairs. Late closers involve less financial adventure, with entries closing from four days to six weeks before the race. In attempting to estimate the probable class of such a race, when one is listed in a past-performance record, the safest criteria remain the final and fractional times.

Overcall, free-for-all pacing champion, undefeated in 21 races during 1969, defeats Miss Conna Adios in $50,000 National Championship Pace at Yonkers Raceway. Del Insko drives Overcall, and Tom Lewis navigates the great mare.

Gunner, product of the New York Sire Stakes, wears down the national champion Victory Star to register an upset in the 1969 Westbury Futurity at Roosevelt.

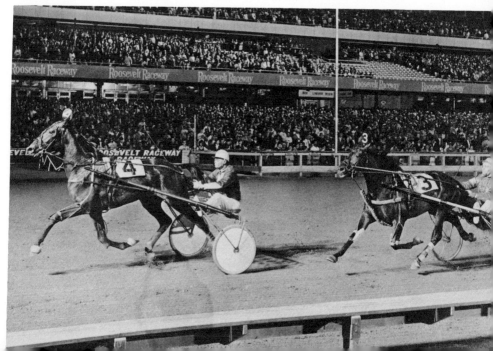

"Big Five" and "Big Four"

The classic tests for three-year-old trotters are the Hambletonian, held at Du Quoin, Ill., and the Kentucky Futurity, at Lexington. In recent years, the Yonkers Futurity, the Dexter Cup (Roosevelt Raceway) and the Colonial (Liberty Bell), have been regarded as the other jewels in a quintuple crown.

Three-year-old pacers of top quality vie for their own "Big Four" —the Little Brown Jug, at Delaware, O., the Messenger Stake, at Roosevelt, the William H. Cane Futurity, at Yonkers, and the Adios, at The Meadows.

Class and Age

The precocious Nevele Pride set world's records at age four, thereby establishing himself as a paragon of the early speed with which modern breeding and training are preoccupied. He was more horse at four than at three, however. And he almost certainly would have been even more horse at five than at four, if he had not been trundled off to make millions at stud, after going lame.

Barring accident, a Standardbred approaches its full racing powers late in its fourth year and should be at its absolute best when five and six. Nothing in the nature of the breed decrees that a trotter or pacer should go into decline at seven, but most of them do by then, if not sooner. Training and racing use them up.

The rules of the sport protect young horses from ruination in races against older animals, which are known in the trade as "aged," as in "aged in the wood." Racing secretaries are forbidden to put horses less than five years of age on their preferred lists, except when (a) the younger ones have demonstrated supremacy in their own local age groups or (b) the horse's stable wants to compete against the best.

In New York, the rules permit entry of a three-year-old in classified races only if the racing secretary thinks it can compete *and* if the stable requests classification, or if the horse has already won some purses in its own age group. The three-year-old is required to begin its classified racing career at a level no higher than C, against the feeblest available opposition.

Every season, good barns make important money with young horses of less than Grand Circuit calibre by taking advantage of these rules. The newcomers to routine raceway competition are unable to beat the best of their own generation and would be destroyed by good older horses, but are much better than the stock they meet in C and B racing.

The same happens elsewhere in the country, with decent three-year-olds swamping the culls they face in races conditioned for life-time non-winners of $3,000. A young horse that hails from a top stable and has a leading driver should always be regarded as a threat in its first few starts against undistinguished raceway stock. It may win five or more races in succession before encountering older horses with sufficient energy to put it in its place.

These young animals usually pay low odds, and lose frequently enough to keep the handicappers in extreme suspense. But they are fun to follow. They are extra-special fun when their records disclose no speed comparable to that of some of the hacks opposing them. Often enough to justify attention, they go several seconds faster in raceway company than they did in their earlier efforts. Age three is the time of life when horses are capable of the most rapid and dramatic improvement.

As a matter of handicapping principle, it is bad judgment to bet *against* a lightly raced three-year-old with a first-rate driver in a conditioned or classified field of cheap, older horses. The youngster may have a pronounced class advantage. If it has not raced recently, or if its only late effort was a qualifying race in unpromisingly slow time, the safest procedure is to pass the race altogether.

Such a horse becomes a more dependable bet in its second conditioned or classified race, especially if its first was a good effort. The odds are low, but a mutuel price of $3.00 is, after all, a profit of 50 cents on the dollar.

In classified and conditioned races restricted to three- and four-year-olds, it pays to assume that the older animal will be strong enough to prevail over the younger, unless its own record is one of chronic slowness and repeated defeat. Putting it another way, if all else is equal (including the drivers and post positions), a 2:05 four-year-old should defeat a 2:05 three-year-old. And a 2:05 five-year-old in good form should upend both of them.

At the opposite end of the Standardbred spectrum are the relics that appear in claiming races. No horse older than 14 is allowed to compete nowadays, but steady animals of 11 and 12 win race after race. Usually geldings of former high class, they often race at claiming prices below their actual market value, because nobody dares to invest in the doubtful future of an ancient horse by claiming it. Hence, the handicapper watches for an oldster whose recent record proves it still capable of putting together successively vigorous performances against cheaper stock. If the record also shows that it has been going the mile as rapidly as any of its opponents, it probably has an edge, on grounds of its competitive honesty.

Before moving to another aspect of class, it might be well to attend to some of the technical terminology employed by Standardbred horsemen in describing age and sex. Until age four, horses of either sex are referred to in some circumstances as "colts." "Colt races" are races for young horses, usually of superior class. On the other hand, in speaking of an individual, young female horse, the word "filly" is used. And a de-sexed male of any age is a gelding. At four, the filly becomes a mare, the colt becomes a horse and the gelding remains a gelding. Also at four, the animals are described as "aged"—although the rules specifically protect them from unfair competition with five-year-olds.

Class and Sex

It is taken for granted that male Standardbreds are stronger competitors than females, but the record disproves that theory. Between 1845, when Lady Suffolk became the first trotter to go in less than 2:30, and 1969, when Nevele Pride became world's champion in 1:54:4, the record had been held by ten mares, ten geldings and only two stallions, of whom Nevele Pride was the second and Cresceus (2:02¼ in 1901) was the first.

Moreover, during the very season in which he set his historic mark, Nevele Pride was defeated by Une de Mai, Fresh Yankee and Lady B. Fast, females all. Indeed, Une de Mai trounced him only one week before he broke all the watches at Indianapolis.

No fewer than eight fillies have won the Hambletonian. And you can get an argument from many a good horseman if you try to name two male trotters of any era who would have been better than even money against Roquepine or Armbro Flight when those ladies were at their best.

What is true among championship trotters is no less true when the humble go at it for ordinary purses. Fillies and mares compete on absolutely equal terms with colts, geldings and entire horses. Some females seem to fade in the heat of summer, but so do some stallions and geldings. There may be a basis for the theory that mares are especially dependable in cold weather, but nobody has ever been able to document it. Stanley Dancer says that some are, some are not and no sweeping generalizations should be made.

It is fairly well agreed that geldings are among the least skittish members of the breed. In fact, many horsemen prefer to geld male trotters and pacers that are below top quality and lack potential breeding value. No longer subject to flights of romantic interest, geldings undoubtedly are the steadiest and most easily managed of Standardbreds. Bob Farrington says that the 2:06 gelding might have been a 2:05 stallion, but it produces the 2:06 consistently, whereas some 2:05 stallions "can throw a 2:07 at you when you least want it."

The steadiness of the gelding is worth knowing about, but I would not build a handicapping method on it. If a gelding and a sexed horse shape up as equals in terms of form, pace, class, driver and post position, the race either is too close for betting, or the fan should bet on them both. Or if the past performances of one horse reveal it as steadier than the other, and worth a bet, it matters little whether the bet is on a gelding, a mare or a stallion. What counts in handicapping is the past-performance record itself, regardless of the animal's sex.

For reasons unexplained, females are scarce among first-rate pacers. The last female able to make trouble in free-for-all competition at that gait was Countess Adios, who won more than $300,000 between 1959 and 1962. Belle Acton was leading money-winning pacer of 1958. Dottie's Pick, Phantom Lady and His Lady managed to win heats in their bids for the Little Brown Jug, but no filly has ever taken it all.

Despite male supremacy in the very top pacing events, the handicapper can overlook sex differences when dealing with other races at that gait. If the mare has the best record, she is a bet. A recent example was Miss Conna Adios, who showed her heels to all but the best male pacers of 1969, and set a world's record for females of 1:57:4f at Liberty Bell. Filly and mare pacers do splendidly in claiming, conditioned, classified, preferred and many invitational races.

Class and Earnings

Racegoers love the horse of former class that suddenly reverts to type and defeats an inferior field. It is easy to identify horses of former class, but difficult to foresee the rare occasion on which one might recover its sea legs and produce something like its old speed.

Every night in the week, horses that once traveled in 2:01 are predictable losers in 2:09. Just as a Standardbred's lifetime mark seldom tells the handicapper much about its next race, its earnings record also bears small relevance to its present form and class.

Career earnings indicate bygone class. But tonight's issue is settled by tonight's class, which is evaluated in terms of the six or eight performances summarized in the program record. If these races offer no hint of ability to win in tonight's circumstances, it is a gross mistake to look for clues in the dead statistics of the past.

Every now and again, fans harvest splendiferous payoffs by betting on career earnings rather than current ability. That is not handicapping, but wishful thinking. There is no long-range profit in it. To be sure, when everything else is equal, it makes sense to go to the horse with high career earnings. But everything else seldom is equal.

Here are some ideas about the significance of earnings in various kinds of races.

CLAIMERS: If the horse drops in claiming price after a succession of poor showings and wins its race at a big mutuel, someone may be able to point out that it had the highest career earnings in the field. If you wish, you probably will be able to show that the horse had lower average annual earnings than some other did, making its career statistic meaningless. You may also be able to argue that the animal lucked into the winner's circle, as big longshots so often do. In any case, you should be calmly confident that horses win on their present ability, which if not recognizable in recent performance is not recognizable at all.

If the entire field seems to be in poor form, the race is unplayable, although I suppose one sometimes might justify a tiny bet on the one horse that is dropping in claiming price. It has been racing no more terribly than the others but at least has been doing so in relatively good company. If the driver is a big winner and the post position is adequate, the bet becomes more understandable. But career earnings remain an unreliable guide.

CLASSIFIED RACES: New York racing secretaries are mighty sharp. Horses win there when moved up in class, substantiating the secretary's judgment. They also win when backed up in class, but not often without some prior sign of imminent improvement.

Since letter classifications are assigned on the basis of current ability, without regard to historical data like career earnings, New York handicapping fans should operate accordingly. Early in the season, classified races do occur in which current ability is unclear and the racing secretary has been guided by factors not included in the printed program. Rather than handicap such races—or any races— off last year's form, including last year's earnings, I prefer to sit them out until the animals have shown what they can do this season.

CONDITIONED RACES: Here again, current ability outweighs the accomplishments of the past. This is particularly noticeable when the conditions limit the field to horses that earned less than a stated amount during the *previous* calendar year. Conditions of that kind are made to order for animals of current sharpness.

If the conditions are silent about last year's earnings but restrict eligibility to horses whose earnings during the present year are below a stated amount, a different approach may pay off. For example, one entrant may have earned a good deal of loot last year and may have performed like his old self in his latest race or two. He deserves some extra points for class.

Earnings become especially misleading when the conditions create a soft touch for a fast horse that has been racing at smaller tracks, winning relatively little money in each start. If, as is often the case, the horse is from a good barn, has been active lately and figures to perform at somewhere near its best, it could be worth a nice bet. Even recent earnings are not always a reliable index to current ability.

Class and Consistency

A sound Standardbred, properly trained, entered in the right races and driven competently, should win at least 20 percent of its starts and should be out of the money not much more than half the time. The horse has less bearing on this part of its record than its owner, trainer and driver do. By placing horses where they have fair shots at purses, stables like those of Bob Farrington and Herve Filion reach levels of consistency unapproachable by other methods. It follows that a horse may develop a good percentage of winning starts in one barn, but become inconsistent in another.

Concerned though they are with what each horse has been doing lately, good handicappers are aware that a good recent race means little unless the animal is the kind that is able to repeat its good performances or, better yet, improve them.

Consistency becomes relevant when a horse's latest effort promises winning form, the pace statistics are lively and the driver and post position are acceptable. If the horse is a chronic loser, or an habitual runner-up, little reliance can be placed in its recent good performance. The odds are extreme that it will revert to type and finish nowhere.

Exceptions occur when the horse's poor record is attributable to bad management. Perhaps it had been hopelessly outclassed for years —which happens—but began to show signs of life after entering lesser races, or shipping to a lesser track, or coming into the hands of a smarter horseman, or all three. Before betting on a chronic loser, the player should take pains to determine whether its apparent improvement might trace to new influences in its racing career. If so, the improvement can be accepted as genuine.

Consistency is not only a matter of winning or finishing close to winners a satisfactory percentage of the time. Like other manifestations of Standardbred talent, it can be clocked. When an expert handicapper decides that a horse's recent performance indicates an ability to win in good time tonight after setting or overcoming the fastest probable early pace, he has passed judgment on the horse's consistency. If its record contained no evidence that it could be *depended on* to produce winning time when fit, the record would be one of inconsistency, and the good recent performance would be dismissed as untypical.

Consistency in winning when properly placed and physically fit is a reassuring feature in the record of a Standardbred, proclaiming its reliability and the honest competence of its stable. It makes the sharpest horse in the race a better bet than he otherwise might be. But it is secondary to the fundamentals of pace, current form, driver and post position. Horses with mediocre winning averages frequently defeat horses with higher averages, and the victories often are predictable.

Class and Pace

After defining class and asserting that it is decisive, I have been trying to call attention to the vital differences between former and present class. The program record's statistical summaries tell about the previous quality of a horse. The detailed recapitulations of the animal's latest races are more useful than that. They permit inference as to whether its present ability is up to its former standard. They also show how its present ability compares with that of each of the other horses in the race.

Conventional handicappers regard the current class of a Standard-bred as equivalent to the class of race in which it recently has been able to win or come close. A horse that has been winning in Class B-2 but not in B-1 is labeled, logically enough, as something less than B-1 stock. This kind of reasoning is adequate for the racing secretary's classification purposes: He keeps the horse in B-2 so long as it continues to earn occasional paychecks at that level. But a handicapping racegoer needs to make finer distinctions.

Every B-2 field is composed primarily of established B-2 horses, plus one or two from B-3 or B-1 that are being tested in a class higher or lower than usual. The player cannot assume that the refugee from B-1 outclasses the others, or that the interloper from B-3 is over its head. He might be able to single out one of the confirmed B-2 animals as a contender on grounds that it defeated the others last week, or that it has been in the money consistently, or that it has been finishing in better time. But he really does not penetrate the subject of current class until he compares the contenders in terms of pace.

Through pace analysis, the player measures contending animals with one yardstick. Above all, he assesses recent performances—the ones most likely to offer fresh clues about present abilities. We have already decided, I hope, that a fit horse of comparatively high present class can go the mile in good time after setting or overcoming a comparatively fast early pace. A fit horse of slightly lower present class might sometimes go in equally good time, but seldom after trying to cope with quite so rigorous an early pace. The probability is that it will react to the fast early pace by finishing in slower time than would be expected of a better horse. An accompanying probability is that it will be unable to match the final time of the better horse even if the early pace is slow.

Of all arguments against this approach, the most familiar emphasizes the well-known fact that horses and drivers usually go no faster than the occasion demands. The true potential of a horse remains concealed, iceberg-fashion, until the evening when it is forced to give everything it has in an effort to withstand opposition of its own quality.

The fact is well known, but does not often apply to raceway situations involving small advances or reductions in class, as from C-2 to C-3, or from a race for non-winners of $4,000 to one for non-winners of $5,000. Or from a $6,000 claimer to $6,500. Most raceway horses have long since been exposed to tests of their basic quality and have gone on from there, upward or downward. What now counts are the small fluctuations in physical condition that affect present class.

As to the improving young horse moving up through the raceway ranks, it sometimes wins in time good enough to defeat far better fields. When it wins in ordinary time, having been asked for no more exertion than necessary, it frequently does so with great authority. If its higher class is not obvious in the pace figures, it can be deduced from the margin of victory, or the strong move in the stretch, or on one or more of the turns. In the next chapter, we shall show how to modify pace figures to give credit for vigorous showings of that kind.

In suggesting that pace ratings indicate which of several fit horses is best able to cope with tonight's kind of opposition, I do not propose that class analysis be left at that. The most precise evaluations of current ability are made when the handicapper adjusts the pace ratings *to reflect the quality of the race in which the pace figures were registered.*

The reasoning here is that the opposition in a relatively cheap race is invariably less powerful than in an even slightly better race. Regardless of whether the horse's pace figures were achieved easily or with great effort, he had to contend with lesser stock on that evening than he will in tonight's better race. By the same criterion, a horse moving down in class should be given credit for having achieved his own figures in more formidable company than he faces tonight.

Therein lies a basic reason why animals on the preferred lists at minor tracks have all they can do to remain vertical in big-league competition. And why hotshot country-fair performers fail at raceways, losing to horses that would be no faster or more successful than they at the fairs. It is infinitely easier to beat one good horse than seven or eight. The cheaper the race, the less probable that more than one horse in it will be able to press a fit animal of superior quality. But as he ascends the scale of classes, that formerly superior animal must contend with more and more good horses in each race. He wins a B-1 race in 2:04, but cannot equal that speed after being rushed off his feet by the toughies in A-3. He has the courage, stamina and adaptability for the lower class but not for the higher. He has passed the limits of his present capabilities.

I therefore recommend that the handicapper make the following adjustments in his pace ratings:

1. If the pace rating is based on a race of lower class than tonight's, deduct 5 points.

2. If the pace rating is based on a race of higher class than tonight's, add 5 points.

Forgive me for repeating an earlier warning: It would be a mistake to think of these points as representing lengths or fifths of seconds. They simply are numbers that approximate the differences among horses. I shall show later that the approximations are mighty accurate, but I concede without argument that the individual handicapper may achieve bountiful results by adding or deducting three or four or seven points instead of five. Or he can do well by avoiding points altogether, preferring to act on the basis of a total impression and not wanting to get hung up with pen and paper. I suggest that the reader reserve judgment about these details until we have had a chance to cover the principles and techniques of handicapping more completely. Whoever understands those principles and adheres to them will manage nicely at his raceway, no matter what special handicapping gimmicks he devises for his own convenience.

Class, Time, Price, Purse

After making notes on the results of all races at Yonkers during 1968 and 1969, I have compiled a chart which compares New York classified and claiming races in terms of par times and purses. New York racegoers may find the tabulation helpful in sizing up horses that move into claimers from classified races, or vice versa. They may also use it to judge the prospects of out-of-town shippers, provided that they are able to evaluate the times of out-of-town races.

Players not in New York may use the chart to help them form opinions about New York horses, after seeing where each type of race fits into the overall scheme of things.

Words of caution: The charted times indicate the standard *differences* in speeds among various grades of races. These standard differences prevail in the long run, regardless of the time of year or the condition of the track. But one almost never finds a single evening on which every race drops into its proper time category. Differences in pace invariably produce atypical final times in a race or two. That some C races are faster than some B races does not alter the fact that a representative number of B races are faster than an equal number of C races—and by the margins given on the chart. The chart uses times more likely to occur at the height of the summer season when the footing is dry and fast. Winter times are considerably slower.

The listed purse schedule existed in 1969 and undoubtedly will change. But the internal relations should remain stable. The purse in an A-1 race is likely to remain twice as large as the purse in a B-2 race—because the earning capacities of 2:02 horses are traditionally twice those of 2:04 horses.

Class	Purse	Equivalent Claiming Price	Times Trot	Pace
FFA	$25,000	—	2:03–	2:00:3–
JFA	15,000	—	2:03:2	2:01
AA	10,000	—	2:04	2:01:4
A-1	7,500	—	2:04:3	2:02:2
A-2	6,250	—	—	2:03
A-3	5,250	$15,000	—	2:03:3
B-1	4,500	12,500	2:05:1	2:04
B-2	3,750	10,000	2:05:3	2:04:2
B-3	3,250	7,500	2:06	2:04:4
C-1	3,000	6,000	2:06:2	2:05:2
C-2	2,750	4,500	2:07	2:06
C-3	2,500	3,000	2:07:3+	2:06:3+

Track Class

A horse that performs well in Class B-2 at Yonkers can be expected to do as well in invitationals at Freehold or in conditioned races with $3,000 purses at Liberty Bell.

A horse that can win one of the $550 purses at Georgetown should be able to hold its own in $3,000 claiming races for $1,800 purses at Liberty Bell.

A horse that races for $1,000 purses at Detroit races for $2,500 purses in New York.

All the statements in the preceding three paragraphs were absolutely true when written. Each is certain to be wrong by the time it appears in print. Raceways increase or lower their purses rather frequently, depending on variations in the mutuel handle, and in state laws, and in agreements they make with horsemen. At times, Liberty Bell offers as much for overnight races of low and medium class as New York does. "Overnight," by the way, refers to the bread-and-butter events that are the bulk of all programs. Entries remain open until a day or two or three (usually three) before the race. Although not exactly overnight, the meaning is clear.

Not only does Liberty Bell pay as much, on occasion, as New York, but Brandywine sometimes takes advantage of its favorable tax position to pay as much or more than Liberty Bell. And the big Chicago tracks often pay cheap horses the highest purses available to them anywhere in the country, while remaining competitive in the purses they post for major events.

It stands to reason that Yonkers Raceway is the continent's top track in point of class. Its mutuel handle of almost $300 million a year permits it to survive the confiscatory New York tax laws and pay purses at a nightly rate from 25 to 50 percent higher than prevails in other leading centers of the sport. Why, then, should Washington Park, with an average nightly purse distribution of about $30,000 (as of 1969), ever pay higher purses in some categories than Yonkers does with its average nightly distribution of about $50,000?

Within certain severe limits, these discrepancies are a matter of management policy. Each raceway strives to construct the kind of purse schedule likely to attract the best possible stables, so that the races will draw the largest possible crowds of liberal spenders. Management's ability to do this depends in the first instance on the current popularity of its raceway. In this business as in all others, it takes money to make money: Although higher purses might mean plumper revenue, the raceway cannot offer higher purses without the revenue. Secondly, state law limits the percentage of the mutuel handle the raceway is allowed to retain for operating expenses, including purses. Additionally, maintenance costs, the wages of raceway employees and the demands of stockholders differ from place to place. What finally is available for purses also depends on contractual agreements with local arms of Harness Horsemen International, which represents owners, trainers and drivers in their bargaining with the corporations that conduct race meetings at the tracks. At most major raceways, these contracts guarantee purses amounting to about 40 percent of the track's share of the mutuel handle.

So far so good. But see how state laws affect the purses. The following table shows in rounded figures what various leading tracks handled at the mutuel windows on an average night during 1968, plus the percentage they were allowed by law to retain, plus what this left them to operate with, plus what they paid out in purses on an average night.

Track	Nightly Handle	Nightly Retention		Nightly Purses
Yonkers	$2,000,000+	5.7%	($118,000)	$46,270
Sportsman's Park	840,000	10.0	($ 84,000)	29,000
Liberty Bell	750,000	10.5	($ 80,000)	31,000
Brandywine	560,000	13.1	($ 73,000)	29,000

The differences in nightly distribution of purse money are anything but a true reflection of the differences in mutuel handle. Moreover, differences in the purses available for the overnight bread-and-butter races are even slighter than the summary suggests. Yonkers and Roosevelt pay enormous purses for feature races, a policy that rewards them at the box office and mutuel windows, but makes their overnights not much more lucrative than those at other major tracks.

On Saturday, March 29, 1969, to pick a humdrum example from an unspectacular time of year, the feature race at Roosevelt was the Adios Butler Cup, an invitational with a $25,000 purse. On the same night at Washington Park, the feature was the Gene Abbe, an invitational pace with a $12,000 purse. At Liberty Bell on that night, the feature was the Bowmans Tower, an invitational pace with a $20,000 purse.

At Roosevelt on that night, the eight other races offered purses of $2,600 (2), $2,750, $3,000, $3,250, $3,750, $5,500 and $7,500.

At Washington Park, nine supporting races had purses of $3,000 (2), $4,000 (2), $5,000, $5,800, $6,200, $6,600 and $7,000.

At Liberty Bell, purses in eight supporting races were $2,400, $3,400, $4,100, $4,400, $4,800, $5,000, and $5,500 (2).

On that particular Saturday, horses in nonfeature events competed for almost 50 percent more in purses at Chicago than at New York. And for $5,000 more at Philadelphia than at New York.

Washington Park reduced its purses almost immediately afterward, offering $2,600 to the same animals that had been racing for $4,000 a few days earlier. The example shows how fluid purse schedules may occasionally become, and how chary the player must be in using purses to measure the relative class of a race that occurred at a track other than his own.

When Ed Parker was racing secretary at Monticello, he provided that raceway's past-performance program with a tabulation of equiva-

THE CLASS FACTOR   211

lent purses. It showed the bettors that a $900 purse at Saratoga, for example, attracted horses of a class equal to those that competed for a $1,200 purse at Pompano Park or a $2,000 one at Roosevelt.

It was an heroic effort, but the chart required constant revision. Purse structures changed so rapidly and so unevenly that new editions of the chart became obsolete as soon as they appeared in print. I had hoped to resurrect Parker's idea for this book, but several weeks of effort convinced me not to. Apart from the certainty that the whole shooting match would be outdated by the time the book reached its reader, I found that it would tend to contradict itself even before it became outdated. For weeks, often months after a track revises its purse structure, the past-performance records of hundreds of horses include purse notations made both prior to and after the revision. Returning to the unusual reduction made at Washington Park early in 1969, horses that had been racing for $5,000 suddenly began racing for $4,000 or less, and the records showed it. Any tabulation of equivalent purses worth reading would defeat itself in confusion if it said that purses of $2,000 to $2,800 at Track "A" were equal to purses of $2,400 to $2,700 at Track "B" and purses of $3,000 to $4,000 at Track "C." Not only would that be confusing in itself, but footnotes would be needed to point out that *some* races with $2,700 purses at "A" were equal to *some* with $2,300 purses at "B" and *some* with $2,700 purses at "C." You can go crazy that way.

Rather than allow the subject of comparative track class to go entirely by the board, I have classified leading raceways in groups, according to the *ranges* of purses they paid on average nights during 1968 and 1969. These general relationships tend to remain constant for years. To indicate how greatly the purses for a specific *type* of race may vary within one group, or from group to group, I show in parentheses what certain tracks were offering pacers with $4,000 claiming tags at various times during that two-year period. I hope the reader will conclude that caution is necessary when attempting to handicap a shipper in terms of its earnings, or the values of the purses for which it has been contending.

On representative evenings during the surveyed period, the following tracks were paying total purses of more than $35,000: Hollywood Park ($2,500 for $4,000 pacers); Roosevelt Raceway ($2,750); Sportsman's Park ($2,600); and Yonkers ($2,750). Yonkers purses averaged about $50,000, placing that operation in a class of its own.

The following raceways offered average nightly purses of $30,000 or more: Brandywine ($2,000) and Liberty Bell ($2,400).

The following raceways distributed $20,000 or more per night in purses: Bay State, Freehold, Hazel Park ($1,800); Maywood Park ($2,500); Wolverine Raceway ($2,200).

The following raceways distributed from $10,000 to $20,000 a night: Atlantic City ($1,500); Aurora Downs; Balmoral ($1,000); Batavia Downs ($1,600); Bay Meadows ($1,400); Buffalo, Green Mountain Park, Laurel Raceway, The Meadows, Monticello, Northfield Park, Northville Downs ($1,200); Pocono Downs, Pompano Park ($900); Rockingham Park ($1,800); Rosecroft ($1,500); Saratoga Raceway ($900); Scioto Downs, Suffolk Downs ($1,800); and Vernon Downs ($1,500).

Conclusion: There is no sure way to compare the class of overnight races at tracks on different circuits, or to evaluate the class of a common or garden raceway animal when it ships into your territory. But if you are able to evaluate the animal's trainer and driver and have a line on the comparative speed of the tracks at which it has been racing, you may be able to use pace handicapping as a measure of its worth.

9

The Fitness Factor

CALL IT FORM, condition, fitness, sharpness. It is crucial to training, driving and handicapping. It is the readiness of a horse to perform well in a race.

The horse with a theoretical advantage in class is unable to prove it unless in adequate physical shape. Among horses of approximately equal quality, current form identifies the best prospects.

After the preliminary business of reading the top of the program page to see what kind of race it is, the handicapper's first step is to eliminate all horses whose recent records contain no signs of potential winning form. The animals that survive this process are the logical contenders, the candidates for further study. It is not compulsory to work this way, but it saves time. If the player seriously intends to handicap, rather than trust to luck, he might as well dispose immediately of horses whose current form disqualifies them.

Do off-form horses win harness races? Indeed they do. And many more races go to horses with unprepossessing recent records who turn out to be in much better form than the handicapper could possibly have guessed. But the percentages and probabilities of the sport remain overwhelmingly in favor of a handicapping method that limits play to supposedly sharp horses. For every race won by a relatively unfit, lucky horse, or by a horse in unpredictably good condition, at least six or seven are won by logical contenders. By no means all of these logical contenders win at short mutuel prices.

Form and Date

Before a trotter or pacer makes its first start of the new season, the trainer puts about 120 miles of hard training under its hide. But it is not yet as sharp as it will be after a race or two or five. The typical

Jimmy Cruise, a genius at winning with unsound horses, examines one of his orthopedic cases.

Standardbred does not come into its own until it has been taxed the extra seconds of speed which only competition can produce.

Having achieved winning condition, or something like it, a sound animal remains chipper for months. Its percentage of victories then reflects the intelligence with which its races have been chosen and the competence with which it has been driven. Unfortunately, almost no Standardbreds are that sound, and none is impervious to illness and injury. The typical raceway horse's record therefore is one of fluctuating ability. A talented trainer capitalizes on good form and, by resting the horse or putting it in easier races, minimizes the adverse effects of declining form.

Around the barn, they usually know whether a horse is in trim or not. A sharp Standardbred eats everything in sight, has uncomplicated bowel habits, is bright-eyed, glossy of coat, eager to work, and capable of top speed without gait problems, wind problems or subsequent distress. When it goes off its feed or becomes less cheerful, something is wrong. It may still be able to race, even win. But the outlook is ominous. Failure to diagnose and treat the difficulty may be the ruination of the horse. Often it needs nothing but a few weeks of rest.

Good trainers provide such rest. Others do not, blaming the animal for their own failures.

Some superb specimens of Standardbred conformation have been able to win nothing in competition, even after training impressively. The only valid proof of fitness is performance on the crowded race-way—how the horse responds when asked for speed, and where it finishes and in what kinds of fractional and final times.

I doubt that many harness-racing fans are fully aware that every race is in itself a central part of the horse's training routine. When racing at intervals of a week or so, many animals only jog between engagements. The exertions of frequent racing are enough to keep them in shape. Other horses go two or three hard miles on one morning between weekly races, but not at racing speed.

Hence, tonight's form is a product of last week's form. If the horse has been in the doldrums but is beginning to round into winning condition, it usually gives notice of this improvement by performing with new vigor in a race. If it is on the ragged edge after doing its very best for two or three weeks, it gives notice by performing dully in a race. Improvement or deterioration of Standardbred form is seldom abrupt. Except among ouchy, aged animals in the lower claiming races, sudden reversals of form are quite infrequent. By analyzing the latest races of a horse and observing its behavior during the prerace warm-ups, a discerning player learns enough about its current condition to make sensible decisions.

The first of several key elements is the date of the horse's latest race. When the season is in full swing, an absence from competition of more than two weeks is a black mark against a run-of-the-mill pacer. Trotting races being fewer, an ordinary horse of that gait may be forgiven a two-week absence on the theory that its people were unable to find a vacant spot in a suitable field during that period.

In considering date, it is a good idea to look through the records of all entered horses. How long have most of them been idle? If, as usual, most have raced within the last eight or ten days, you should be skeptical about an entrant that has not competed in more than two weeks. Unless its last race was impressive and its record includes victories after absences of such duration, you can assume that it was in drydock for repairs and will need tonight's race for exercise. Better horses usually do perfectly well after absences of two or three weeks, being able to maintain their sharpness in semiweekly training workouts.

"We don't sit around waiting for the ideal opportunity, the soft touch," says Del Miller about the training and racing of Standardbreds. "We race them. That's how we keep them in top shape. So if you see that one has been away during a week when it could have been racing, you know that there must have been a reason, and you have a right to wonder if the horse is fit."

Excuses

Even though the horse raced recently, it does not qualify as a contender unless it raced impressively. Yet some performances seem dull because of circumstances unrelated to form. The horse may actually be in excellent condition. Before eliminating an entrant on grounds of unreadiness, the handicapper scans its latest past-performance line for indications that its poor showing was excusable. Any of the following information in the past-performance line constitutes an excuse:

1. An off track—provided that the racing strip is dry and fast tonight.
2. A break in stride or other difficulty caused by faulty equipment.
3. A break in stride caused by interference.
4. A lapse of more than two weeks between the last and next-to-last races.
5. The horse's first recent start on this racing circuit, especially if it had been racing at a track of different size.
6. A race against stock of considerably higher class than the horse could have been expected to handle—provided that it returns to its own class tonight.
7. A substitute driver with a low winning percentage—provided that a top man drives tonight.
8. An unfavorable post position, an unusually slow early pace and driving tactics that left the horse hopelessly behind when the real racing began in the final stages.
9. An unusually fast early pace, plus driving tactics that left the horse exhausted in the stretch—provided that the horse is not an habitual puller or quitter.

When an animal's most recent performance is excusable on any of the foregoing grounds—or if the performance was neither good nor bad enough for confident decision—handicappers turn their attention to the next-to-latest race. I consider it wiser to do this in doubtful cases than to eliminate the horses outright. Be especially conservative about eliminating horses that finished in the money or within three lengths of the winner in their latest starts. Unless you are quite certain that such an animal was hauled to its paycheck behind a wind-screen, you should look at the previous race for positive signs.

Once in a while, good reason arises to excuse the next-to-last race. Handicappers then retreat to the third race back. But they do not often base their decisions on performances that took place more than a month earlier. Recent excuses or not, month-old form is unreliable.

Bad Signs

Where excuses are lacking, a horse should be eliminated for unsuitable current condition if:

1. Its final time was as much as three seconds slower than the final time registered by *any other starter* in a recent, representative performance.

2. It failed to hustle for the lead at some point in the race, possibly on the outside. (This is especially important at half-mile tracks.)

3. It lost ground in the stretch or was badly beaten without setting or pressing a fast early pace or without roughing it on the outside.

4. It was sucked along to a spuriously good finish after having shown little in its previous race or two.

5. It broke stride and has had similar trouble in another recent race.

6. It won or lost by a narrow margin for the third time in succession and now is moving up in class.

Stated as they are, those ideas sound like rules. But they are not. They are principles, and should be applied thoughtfully. For example, it is quite true that few aged raceway horses retain their sharpness after three exhausting stretch battles in close succession. Yet some animals benefit from effort of that intensity, especially at the beginning of the season. And a really good horse might cut the mustard six or eight times in a row. Rather than eliminate a horse because of its recent exertions, it is wise to consider its overall record, its overall quality, its age, and the kind of challenge it confronts tonight.

The same kind of reasoning holds for all other items on the list. Regard them as guides, not gospel. They all derive from the one fundamental principle that informs this chapter: The horse likely to deserve a bet tonight is one that went out there and did a little something in a recent race.

The Big Decision

Having eliminated some horses for good and sufficient reason, and having excused the latest performances of others, the handicapper should review his situation.

He now must deal with the latest races of some horses, and the next-to-latest of some others. If any of these races were on out-of-town tracks, or occurred weeks ago, should he press forward, handicapping the animals by guess and by gosh?

I hope not. Handicapping is less likely to jell unless each starter can be analyzed in terms of recent action at the same track or on the same racing circuit. Washington Park racegoers can get by with performance lines recorded at Sportsman's Park. Brandywine and Liberty Bell are companion tracks. So are Yonkers and Roosevelt, and Rockingham and Suffolk Downs.

But when the race is at Roosevelt and the past-performance line describes a happening at Freehold or Liberty Bell or Rosecroft, the racegoer should apply the brakes and take a few seconds for deliberation. If he is a typical fan, the kind who goes to the track at irregular intervals and relies entirely on program information, he probably should not touch a race of this sort unless:

1. The horse is a local one to begin with, has been racing steadily, and simply made the out-of-town trip for one or two starts.

2. The horse is from a topnotch stable and has a driver to match, signifying the kind of management that does not merely stumble around the country hoping to fall into a purse.

3. The player is careful to use the program's table of comparative track speeds, adjusting the half-mile and final times (as suggested on page 179) before accepting the out-of-town figures at face value.

If the horse is a young up-and-comer or is otherwise identifiable as having a touch of class, and most particularly if it has been racing well at home *and* abroad, the player may occasionally decide that its present form can be no better or worse than it was on the night of its last local race, a month or so ago. If this conclusion is a result of sober thought rather than wishful thinking, the chance may be worth taking. The better the class of the race, the less extreme the chance. But, as repeated perhaps too often in these pages, the safest course is to stick to races in which each starter's credentials are local and very recent.

Having decided to continue handicapping the race, the next step is to seek out positive signs of sharp, preferably improving form.

The Stretch Gain

In bygone years, the first half-mile was kind of an overture. The race took place in the homestretch. The time of the second half was predictably faster than that of the first half.

At mile tracks and ⅝-milers, most races still are cut that way. It also happens at half-milers, depending mainly on the battles of wits among drivers. But modern racing emphasizes early speed. I imagine that the first half-mile is the faster in at least half of the races at half-mile tracks.

With everybody going lickety-split for early position and the stretch drive often rewarding the animal that decelerates least, handicappers have mixed attitudes toward ground gained in the stretch. "He passed tired horses. It means nothing. Look at those fast early fractions," say one handicapper about a horse that finished third after gaining four lengths on the leader.

Or: "Why shouldn't he gain ground? He did nothing until the end, got lucky, found room and picked up a few yards. But they crawled the last quarter in thirty-three."

Debarking from the van at Goshen for Grand Circuit week.

We have already noticed that a sucked-along horse may well pick up a few lengths in the stretch, when the animals in front back up to him.

Stretch gains apparently should not be accepted uncritically. But I believe they should be viewed with respect. If the horse was in the race at all and the fractional and final times were good for the class, the stretch gain is a prime demonstration of strength.

Barring horses dragged to victory or a piece of the purse, the stretch gain therefore deserves extra credit in anyone's handicapping. On the other hand, a *loss* of ground in the stretch is an unpromising sign, unless excused by the horse's impressive exertions or bad racing luck in the earlier stages.

Under the point system I have been describing, players should add a point to the basic rating for every length gained in the stretch. If the horse led at the stretch call and won going away, it does no harm to add the full winning margin. If it led by a considerable distance at the stretch call and won eased up, losing some ground in the process, calculate the points on the basis of its lead at the stretch call.

If fractions of lengths are involved, credit each half-length or more as a point. A horse 2½ lengths behind at the stretch call is regarded as three lengths behind. If it wins by 1½ lengths, it earns five extra points for the gain of ground.

It probably goes without saying that these credits are awarded only to qualified contenders—horses whose recent efforts were good enough to warrant the pace ratings and class adjustments discussed earlier.

Roughing It

Most programs are quite conscientious about including the little degree symbol (°), which indicates that a horse traveled on the outside for a quarter mile, including most of a turn. Generally, the program places the symbol before or after the horse's racing position, to indicate the stage of the race at which it was parked.

The symbol indicates that the animal's performance was sturdier than the other figures might suggest. It traveled extra ground, either because its driver pulled out to fight for position or because he was flushed out by another driver and was parked there for the duration of the turn.

To be parked outside one horse on a complete turn is to travel about 16 feet farther than the inside horse does. This is true regardless of the size of the track. One might suppose that a horse would lose more ground racing outside on a turn at a mile track, because the turn is a quarter-mile long. Not so. At any track, a turn is a semicircle. To rough it on the outside is to travel a semicircle of about five feet greater radius than the semicircular path traversed by an inside horse. Five feet of radius adds about 16 feet to the circumference of any semicircle.

As an emblem of extra effort, the parked-out symbol adds considerable luster to a good past-performance line. It also may transform an apparently indifferent finish into a fully acceptable one. Some excellent handicappers credit a horse with a full second of additional speed for each parked-out symbol. They reason that the animal not only traveled at least two extra lengths but spent important energy getting to the outside and fighting for headway while there.

I think the reader should consider the following approach:

1. Accept any horse as fit if its latest, most relevant past-performance line contains the symbol.

2. At the very least, regard a parked-out symbol as an excuse for lengths lost in the stretch. Before eliminating a horse that lost ground in the stretch, see if parked-out symbols cancel the loss.

3. If apparent good form qualifies a horse as a contender, each parked-out symbol in the past-performance line is worth 5 points. The points should be added to the pace rating, as adjusted for class and stretch gain.

> *Example:*
> 1:06:2   7 8 7° 8° 7/8 3/4   2:10:4

The horse obviously is in sharp condition. It not only gained four lengths in the stretch but also roughed it for a half-mile. Its final time and the half-mile time of the race earn it a pace rating of 164 according to the procedure explained on page 178. Its stretch gain of four lengths is worth an additional 4, and the two parked-out symbols are worth 10. Its rating becomes 178.

If the horse had lost ground in the stretch, the two symbols would have excused the loss. Many examples of this kind of thing will arise later, when we handicap entire programs at leading tracks.

Form and Class

Like all animals, including man, Standardbreds are creatures of habit. They learn easily but forget slowly. When they acquire bad habits, the trainer cannot discuss the problems with them. He must undertake a program of re-education. It is not always easy.

Among bad habits is the losing habit. Having been trained from birth to respond as best they can to human direction, race horses sometimes carry the whole thing beyond reasonable limits. The colt that loses his first two or three races may be impressed enough by the raceway hullabaloo to try to repeat the performance the next time he finds himself in the same kind of uproar. He refuses to pass the horse in front of him.

This kind of psychological conditioning may be at work in the phenomenon that horsemen call "confidence." A seasoned raceway animal that loses repeatedly because it repeatedly is outclassed does not automatically win when dropped into the kind of company it should beat. It often needs a race or two in the lower class before recovering its supposed confidence and turning on its true speed.

This happens often enough to be a prominent factor in handicapping. A horse moving up in class after decisive victories is usually a better bet to win at the first asking in the new class than is a horse that backs up after five or six losses. Horsemen believe that successive triumphs "brave up" a Standardbred.

Confidence—if that is what it is—might as well be regarded as synonymous with fitness. It is a problem with some dropped-down horses and not with others. The best evaluation of the dropped-down horse is made in terms of its recent form and pace, with adjustment for the change in class. If you find that your figures too often put losers on top by overestimating the prospects of dropped-down animals, you might try withholding class credit from dropdowns until they have had a race in the new, low class. I have encountered little difficulty of that kind, but it is not unimaginable.

Qualifying Races

If the player is properly devoted to the principle that breaking horses deserve no bets, and that races full of breaking horses should be avoided, the qualifying race becomes an endurable problem.

As you know, horses race in qualifiers if they have been breaking stride or misbehaving behind the gate or swerving or finishing in truck-horse time, or if they have been absent from the local scene for a while.

The past-performance record contains strong clues as to why an animal's latest race was a qualifier. The break symbols or times or dates of its previous races tell the tale.

If the horse is a breaker, it is, by definition, out of form, regardless of the fact that it got through a qualifier in adequate time without breaking. The animal may hold together tonight and win at a price, but no law decrees that a handicapper should lose money by backing another horse in the race. If anything in the breaker's record hints that it might whip tonight's field, the handicapper should abstain from the race altogether.

A slow horse that finally qualifies for evening competition is also no riddle. Being slow, he hardly figures to become fast all of a sudden. The chances are enormous that his time in the qualifier was barely good enough to earn entry in tonight's race. Others in the field will have better figures and will attract the handicapper's attention.

If the horse has been unmannerly (which can be deduced if it has been neither a breaker nor slow nor absent, but went in a qualifying race or two before being readmitted to the fold), the handicapper can be fairly confident that its personality problems have been modified by training. It therefore can be dealt with as if it were any other horse. Does its record include a race good enough and recent enough for handicapping? If so, the player is in the clear. If not, the player must decide whether the horse might nevertheless be a real threat, in which case it is advisable to avoid the race.

On occasion, the qualifying race is itself fast enough to be used for handicapping purposes. At most tracks, horses race in times just about two seconds faster than their qualifying times. At other tracks, including those in New York, qualifying standards are more severe, and racing times may be only a second faster.

An extraordinarily dependable bet at any track is the nonbreaking animal that wins a qualifying race in faster time than its opponents have been recording in their best recent performances. This kind of opportunity bobs up several times a season, and should not be overlooked. If the horse has a top driver, it is as close to a cinch as one ever finds in this sport.

Darkened Form

If a horse is in condition to win but its recent past-performance lines look like those of an unfit animal, the audience is fooled, the odds inflate and somebody cashes a nice bet. Tearing up his losing tickets, gnashing his teeth and looking at the winner's record to see if he missed something, the handicapper concludes that he missed nothing. The horse's form had been darkened.

The next morning, the animal's trainer stands uneasily before the desk of the presiding judge and explains with all the sincerity at his command that the horse just suddenly woke up. "He hasn't been liking the track and I haven't been able to do a thing with him," says the trainer, shifting his weight from foot to foot, "but last week the groom moved him into an end stall and put a puppy in with him and he began doing better. I trained him on Wednesday and he was like a wild horse. Went in ten and change and could have gone all day. Damned near pulled my arms out of the socket. Never saw anything like it. . . ."

The judge looks at the trainer with the enthusiasm of an exterminator studying a roach. "Cashed a pretty good bet, did you?"

"Bet?" says the trainer.

"Bet," says the judge. "You and that pool hustler you work for, you didn't bet?"

"Well, sure," says the trainer. "We naturally bet a little when the horse begins doing good like he did. I mean, I don't know how much anybody else bet, but I had the man bet a little for me."

"A little?" asks the judge. "The odds drop to five to one in the last flash and you only bet a little?"

"Aw, you know how it is, Judge. You can't keep secrets around here. Must have been ninety people saw the horse train on Wednesday. Everybody and his brother must have sent it in last night."

"Strike two!" says the judge. "One more miraculous reversal of form and you wind up pumping gas somewhere."

"Thanks, Judge."

A favorite way to darken the form of a horse is to keep it out of competition for weeks, legging it up at a private training track. Then, after a lackadaisical performance in a qualifying race at a track which is lenient about such things, the stable cracks down. The crowd disregards the horse because it has been out of action.

Another method, often effective at smaller raceways, is to take the horse to a few country fairs, losing in poor company and returning to raceway competition with two or three horrible past-performance lines.

Other techniques:

1. At raceways where paddock supervision is lax or inexpert,

change the animal's equipment sufficiently to assure a losing race. For example, change the length of the hobbles or the weight of the shoes, or rig the nose band to hamper breathing.

2. Change the horse's feeding and watering routines, or work it too severely between races.

3. On the night of the race, warm it up in faster or slower time than is needed for a good performance.

4. Put an incompetent driver in the bike.

5. Make premature moves during the race, wasting the horse's energy.

The better the raceway, the less practical these methods become. Major-league paddock judges have complete records of every horse's normal equipment, check it carefully and demand a thorough explanation for the slightest change. Illogical driver assignments, though permitted on occasion, mark the trainer and the horse for continued scrutiny thereafter. Moreover, downright incompetent driving is punished almost as severely as fraudulent driving. Changes in training routines become subjects of gossip which echoes sooner or later in the front office.

Although numerous trainers and owners covet the tax-free proceeds of nice bets at good odds, they do not often try to build those odds by making a horse lose a race that it might win. Shenanigans of that kind not only invite the unwelcome attention of raceway officials but also defy common sense. After all, horses are not endlessly able to win. Trainers and owners tend to want the purse when they can get it.

The darkening of form becomes more practical when the horse is unable to win and, from the stable's point of view, might as well acquire an imposingly miserable past-performance line while getting some needed exercise. Perhaps the horse is returning to form after a layoff. Perhaps it is on the downgrade after several tough efforts and needs time to recover. If the horse cannot win, is it unethical for the stable to face that fact and let it lose?

I think so. Until such time as the rules permit horses to be barred from the betting on grounds that they are out for exercise, every animal that starts in a race does so with an implied guarantee that its stable will try to win. Its slim chances are then reflected in long odds. But if no effort is made to win or, indeed, every effort is made to lose badly, the stable perpetrates fraud on whoever is seduced into betting on the horse.

None of this contradicts the fact that the driver should deal intelligently and humanely with a horse that proves itself unable to win. It is foolish, wasteful and cruel to punish an animal that has nothing left in the stretch. It is equally brutal to demand a second big move from a horse that gave what little it had in a vain bid for the early lead. The average driver is sensible enough to excuse his hopelessly beaten horse from needless effort. But first, he gives the horse its opportunity to win, and he gives the audience its money's worth.

Where deliberately darkened form is concerned, the interests of the handicapper coincide, as usual, with those of the sport itself. The handicapper may have an advantage over other customers, sometimes interpreting pace figures, parked-out symbols and driver switches as evidence that a supposedly unfit horse is about to blossom. But it is not a wholesome advantage and it is not likely to be a lastingly profitable one at a track where the deliberate darkening of form is more than an occasional occurrence. If permitted to get away with such manipulation, betting horsemen are entirely capable of concealing form so well that no handicapper could find any sign of fitness in a winner's past-performance record.

When the crowd boos a surprise winner and curses the driver of the beaten favorite, it usually is wrong. But the indignant noise is a constructive influence. It keeps the judges and racing secretaries on their toes. It makes the raceway management suitably nervous. It bothers the honest horsemen, the majority, making them less tolerant than

Taking a sample for the pre-race blood test.

ever toward the incompetent training and driving that cause most upsets and the dishonest training and driving that cause a few.

Incidentally, a primary objective of prerace blood testing is to develop means of identifying a fit horse through analysis of its blood. This is not as fanciful an idea as it may seem. In fact, biochemists expect to acquire the necessary knowledge in a very few years. When they do, horses whose prerace tests betray them as unfit will be scratched from their races, and the sport's formfulness will take another giant step forward.

Doping

Many disabling afflictions of equine muscle, tendon, ligament and bone are painful inflammations associated with arthritic damage or plain wear and tear, or both. Certain anti-inflammatory chemicals, such as Butazolidin, relieve the painful symptoms, making potential winners of horses that might otherwise be too crippled to race. In recent years, state racing commissions have been under severe pressure to legalize the use of these medicines.

With less than complete candor, horsemen who press for the legalization of Bute argue that it does not make racers go faster than they should. It is not a pep pill, they say, but is more like an aspirin, relieving discomfort sufficiently to allow a horse to perform at its normal speed.

The truth is that no law forbids the use of anti-inflammatory agents as part of the legitimate medical care of an ouchy horse. In most cases, the medicine is an excellent supplement to more basic measures, of which the foremost is rest. Racing law simply forbids horses to race while active doses of the chemicals are still in their systems. This is humane. If the horse cannot race unless it is under the influence of Bute, the chances are that the exertions of racing will worsen the tissue damage which gave rise to inflammation in the first place.

The racegoer should remain alert. If Bute or anything like it becomes legal in his state, he should avoid the track until the past-performance records begin to include information about which horses have been dosed and which have not.

In justice to proponents of Bute and other anti-inflammation agents, I should point out that they now are asking for stringent controls, including compulsory notification of the betting public when the chemicals are used. This seems to promise that betting stables would be unable to make fortunes by using the medication when they wanted to win and withholding it when they wanted to lose. But it scarcely solves the problem likely to arouse the anxiety of humane societies—the well-being of the horse itself. Unless veterinary science can show that a suffering horse is better off training and racing under the influence of Bute than it would be if it were resting and getting good medical care, racing cannot justify a change in the rules governing medication.

So much for that. As for other kinds of doping, the National Association of State Racing Commissioners declares that the defense never catches up with the offense. There is a constant lag between the development of new drugs and the ability of raceway laboratories to detect them in the blood, urine or saliva of horses. Nevertheless, no present reason exists to regard doping as a serious problem.

The facts are that when the labs finally learn how to detect a new drug, they almost never find it in the blood, urine or saliva of a Standardbred. The explanation is obvious enough. Cheating horsemen do not know when the defense will catch up with the offense, and do not propose to be caught when it does. They rarely dope a sick or sore horse to make it win when it should be resting or losing. Such doping cases as are reported in the press almost invariably represent feats of daring by hoodlums, not horsemen.

Corking

A horse finishes second in its first engagement of the year, after matching strides with the winner all the way from the three-quarter pole. Its time surpasses its career record. A week later it goes again as an odds-on favorite and finishes fifth. A week later it goes at 2 to 1 and finishes sixth. By this time the owner should have shot the trainer. The horse has been asked for too much too early in the season. It was not ready to tiptoe a mile in good company. It has been corked. Gutted. It may round into winning condition in two months, but there is no certainty.

A horse forced to win or come close before achieving sharp condition suffers dreadfully. It stops eating. Its digestive apparatus knots up. It may be able to produce a second hard race before collapsing, or it may turn sour after the one prematurely hard effort.

Hence, if a horse in tonight's race has been out only twice this year and the first performance was considerably better than the second, the handicapper should beware. If it has been out three times and the first two were considerably better than the third, equal caution is indicated. The corked horse is a trap for the unwary. Far preferable is the animal that has not yet won but has been gathering strength and has begun to show it. Tonight could be the night!

Form Angles

In raceway lingo, an angle is something significant which may be overlooked by handicappers concerned with fundamental factors. One of the most familiar angles is actually basic to the selection methods of thousands of racegoers: They watch the tote board to see where the late money is going. I have already commented on that kind of play, suggesting that the reader stick with his own selections and not try to decide which horses are being backed by "smart money," or even which money is "smart."

Another angle finds players at half-mile tracks betting the favorite when it has a top driver and an inside post. This is handicapping to the extent that it conforms with the percentages of the sport—a favorite of that kind is quite likely to win. But the angle is nonhandicapping to the extent that the player has no way of knowing whether the animal deserves to be favorite, not having studied its record and that of the other horses.

Yet another angle depends on the phenomenon of Standardbred "confidence." Many New Yorkers automatically play horses that lost their last races while dropping in class. The theory is that such a horse, having regained its confidence, may do better in its second or third attempt in the lower class. It's a reasonable theory but of no use to readers of this book, who will be looking at the horse's latest lines to see whether it has begun to race vigorously. This is more effective than an attempt to psychoanalyze the animal.

Of all angles, I can recommend only two. First of these is the angle of the beaten favorite. If a horse qualifies in terms of form, pace, class, driver, etc., and happens also to have been beaten as the betting favorite in its race, it deserves extra respect. Beaten favorite or not, the horse would be eliminated unless the performance had been impressive, or unless the loss was excusable. But since the horse does qualify, and since it was so highly regarded last time, it becomes more attractive tonight. One reason for this is that the crowd occasionally underbets such a horse in its next start, having been disappointed by its loss. When it wins, it may well pay a few pennies more than it should. In the numerical handicapping procedure I recommend, a qualified beaten favorite gets 5 extra points.

A second potent angle derives from the traditional selection method known as "comparison handicapping." If Horse "A" beat "B" and "B" beat "C," the comparison handicapper assumes that "A" is better than "C." This is foolishness, because it overlooks the special circumstances of pace and driving tactics that might explain why previous races ended as they did, and why tonight's race might turn out quite differently. Comparison handicappers also tend to favor "A" over "C" if "A" finished ahead of the other in their last encounter. Here again, errors are inevitable unless thorough handicapping reveals that the pattern of the previous race might repeat itself tonight.

Because few readers of this book are likely to ignore the fundamentals of handicapping when they make their future raceway selections, they will find one kind of comparison handicapping useful. The angle becomes appropriate when fewer than 5 points separate the two top contenders in the race. That is, when all fit starters have been given pace ratings, adjusted for class, stretch gains, parked-out symbols, post position, driver and the beaten-favorite angle. If these final ratings leave two horses within 4 or fewer points of each other, check to see whether each is being rated on the basis of its latest race. If one or both is being handicapped in terms of a *previous* race, see whether they have faced each other in a *subsequent* race. If so, and if one performed more powerfully than the other on that occasion, give it an extra 5 points. This angle may change one selection for you in a month of racegoing. More often than not, it will change the selection for the better.

Because I have been dispensing the numerical rating procedure piecemeal, readers may be having trouble keeping track of it. I have done this deliberately, believing that the basic principles deserve emphasis over procedure. In Chapter 13, we review the procedure completely.

10

The Post-Position Factor

THE STARTING POSITION closest to the inside rail is a substantial advantage at half-mile tracks, where races usually begin only 200 feet from the first of four crucial turns. Leaving from that ideal position, the driver with a reasonably quick horse can be expected to enter the first turn on the lead or, at least, with nobody directly in front of him. Without losing an inch of ground on the turn, he adjusts his throttle to sap any horse that tries to overtake him. He cuts the earliest pace to his own pattern. Emerging from the turn onto the backstretch, he has the only horse that has contended for the lead without really being used. If he decides to let someone pass at that point, he remains comfortable in the second hole on the rail, awaiting developments. Having been guaranteed a pleasant trip for the hectic first quarter of the race, the pole horse need not always be best to win. Statistics prove it.

Even if the animal starts rather sluggishly, the inside position helps. Before the drivers of quicker ones can exploit their advantage, the turn arrives and the pole horse is tucked in, saving ground and getting into gear. With a middle or outside starting position, the slow-leaving horse must shuffle back to find a spot on the rail, lest it be parked for the entire first turn. In either eventuality, it enters the backstretch with problems. To a lesser extent, so does a quick horse with a middle or outside start. Unless it is clearly the best animal in the bunch, it may pay later for the exertion of capturing the lead before or during the first turn.

The advantage of the rail position and the difficulties of outside positions diminish as (a) distance increases between the starting point and the first turn and (b) distance increases between the head of the stretch and the finish line. At Sportsman's Park, a ⅝-mile track, the race begins 440 feet from the first turn and the homestretch is 902 feet long. At the beginning, a fast-leaving horse can use the straightaway to reach the rail and the lead without covering more than a foot of extra ground. At the end, a fast-finishing horse can overcome earlier obstacles to catch tiring leaders.

While the rail position is always better than the extreme outside at ⅝-mile and one-mile tracks, middle ramps such as 5 and 6 often produce higher percentages of winners than does the inside spot. The chief reason for this statistic is that the footing near the rail sometimes is deeper, damper and slower than in the middle lanes, from which moisture drains more readily. The statistics are more striking at large tracks simply because the inside posts at such ovals are not greatly superior even when the footing is hard and fast. A slight difference— even when the strip is pronounced "fast" or "good"—means an advantage to horses in the middle of the gate. At half-milers, on the other hand, these slight differences in footing seldom compensate for the advantages of the rail positions.

The Probabilities

The evaluation of post positions is one of the few phases of handicapping for which the player can arm himself with solid, proven probabilities. If one of every five horses that leaves from the pole

position at Yonkers Raceway wins its race, and if about half of all races there are won by horses from the three inside positions, the Yonkers racegoer has something substantial to work with. Because handicapping is inevitably an attempt to estimate probabilities, I would be intensely suspicious of a selection method that failed to take full advantage of what is known about the relative values of post positions.

Most racing fans seem to understand that positions 1 and 2 are advantageous and that 7 and 8 (8 and 9 at larger ovals) are bad news. The horse that performed well from an outside start is credited with extra sharpness, and attracts much play if it draws a more favorable position in its next race. A horse that accomplished little from an inside post is expected to perform even less virbrantly if shunted to the far outside for its next attempt.

Those principles are sound. Equally sound is the refusal of many good handicappers to touch a horse with an extreme outside post at a half-mile or ⅝-mile track unless they think that it is two seconds better than anything else in the field. Methods of measuring this detail vary. Some handicappers use intuition. Others use slide rules. All would be better off if they knew more precisely how each starting position affects performance at the individual raceway.

At every track in the world, the question can be answered with

Pacing down the long, wide stretch at Lexington's Red Mile.

statistics. At a few tracks in North America, adequate statistics are available. At other tracks, the statistics are inadequate. At some tracks, they seem to keep no statistics at all. No matter which track he patronizes, the serious handicapper has some homework to do before developing a clear picture of the post-position factor.

The necessary statistics would cover a two- or three-year period encompassing about 1,000 races. They would show how many horses started in each position, and how many horses won from each position. Dividing the number of starters by the number of winners would produce a percentage for each position. A comparison of the percentages would disclose the probable influence of each position on a typical race.

Some tracks publish statistics which show only the number of winners from each post position, without regard to the number of animals that actually raced. The figures give a reasonably accurate general impression but are useless beyond that. Certain experts have been known to spin elaborate theories from these misleading figures—adding the number of races held during the season and then computing the percentage of that total which was won from each position. The trouble with such figuring (and the reason that it would offend any bright high-school mathematics student) is that it gives meaningless results. For example, the outside post at many tracks is unoccupied in at least one-third of the races, since the fields are short of horses. But the kind of statistical mess now under discussion treats every position as if the same number of horses had performed in every race.

Illustration: At Northville Downs during 1967, 1968 and 1969, 282 winners left from the extreme inside and only 93 from berth 8. The supposition might be that the inside is three times as favorable as the outside at the Michigan raceway, but a handicapper could lose money if he made his selections accordingly. The fact is that only *1,030 horses left from post 8 during those three years, whereas 1,569 left from post 1!* In short, the inside produced twice as well as the outside, which is a considerable advantage but is not three times as good.

With help from the USTA, Harness Tracks of America and a scattering of raceway managements, I have been able to assemble quite dependable post-position percentages for some leading tracks. The figures under each post number show the percentage of horses that won when leaving in that particular lane. I have rounded the percentages because I am sure that each can vary upward or downward by a point or more without seriously affecting the basic differences

	1	2	3	4	5	6	7	8	9	10
Half-milers										
Buffalo	16	15	14	14	14	12	9	8	—	—
Maywood	15	15	13	16	16	13	10	7	—	—
Northville	18	15	15	15	13	10	9	9	—	—
Richelieu	17	15	15	15	15	11	9	6	—	—
Rockingham	19	17	15	15	13	11	7	6	—	—
Roosevelt	17	17	15	14	13	10	9	8	—	—
Suffolk Downs	17	15	16	16	14	9	9	6	—	—
Yonkers	20	18	15	14	13	9	8	7	—	—
⅝-milers										
Blue Bonnets	16	15	14	14	14	13	10	13	—	—
Hazel Park	13	14	13	13	16	13	10	9	9	—
Liberty Bell	15	15	14	15	15	11	8	6	—	—
The Meadows	13	14	14	13	16	12	10	9	—	—
Sportsman's	15	13	13	13	14	12	12	9	6	—
One-milers										
Bay Meadows	13	11	14	17	18	11	11	11	—	—
Hollywood	12	13	12	11	11	15	12	10	9	9

embodied in the chart. Among the causes of such fluctuations are weather, temporary changes in the texture and contour of the racing strip and the luck of the draw for post positions.

Using the Percentages

If the reader's favorite raceway is missing from the above table of post-position percentages, he should consider spending a few hours compiling his own statistics at a library, a newspaper office or the track itself. The track management probably has no idea of how many horses actually raced from each position during the past couple of seasons, but result charts contain the information.

Persons unable or unwilling to spend their time in that way can make effective use of general principles which I shall suggest a bit later. For them, and for everyone else, the problem of post-position comes in three parts:

1. Evaluating the horse's latest representative race in terms of the probable effect of the gate position from which it left.

2. Drawing conclusions about the probable effect of tonight's position.

3. Deciding whether tonight's driver compensates for a poor post position.

Reserving the third item for the next chapter, in which drivers are discussed, we are left with the fact that the best positions at some tracks are three times as good as the worst. And at other tracks the best are twice as good. At still others the differences are small.

Players who prefer to handicap mentally, without resort to numerical formulas, can probably go on from there, making mental allowances for the effects of one or another kind of starting position. I strongly believe, however, that greater ease and precision—and far better results—are obtainable with pen and paper.

The following tabulation is intended for use with the numerical handicapping procedure which we have been developing, step by step, in these pages. On it are point values for the tracks for which post-position percentages were given previously. Also on it are figures for use at tracks for which the player has no good statistics. The figures given for specific tracks are numerical reflections of the statistical differences among the various post positions. For example, at Holly-

	1	2	3	4	5	6	7	8	9	10
Half-milers	6	6	5	5	4	3	3	2	—	—
⅝-milers	8	7	7	6	7	6	5	4	3	—
Milers	6	7	7	7	7	7	6	5	4	—
Bay Meadows	6	5	7	8	9	5	5	5	—	—
Blue Bonnets	8	7	7	7	7	6	5	6	—	—
Buffalo	8	7	7	7	7	6	5	4	—	—
Hazel Park	6	7	6	6	8	6	5	4	4	—
Hollywood	8	8	8	7	7	10	8	7	6	6
Liberty Bell	8	8	7	8	8	6	4	3	—	—
Maywood	7	7	6	8	8	6	5	3	—	—
The Meadows	6	7	7	6	8	6	5	4	—	—
Northville	9	7	7	7	6	5	4	4	—	—
Richelieu	8	7	7	7	7	5	4	3	—	—
Rockingham	9	8	7	7	6	5	3	3	—	—
Roosevelt	9	9	7	7	6	5	4	4	—	—
Sportsman's	7	6	6	6	7	6	6	4	3	—
Suffolk Downs	8	7	8	8	7	5	5	3	—	—
Yonkers	10	9	8	7	6	5	4	3	—	—

wood, where the inside lane is one-third more productive than the extreme outside (12 percent winners as compared with 9 percent), the table preserves that relationship (8 points for position 1 and 6 points for position 9).

To develop such figures for his own track, the reader should begin with the proper percentages and then divide them by a factor of 2, 3 or 4—depending on which divisor produces fairly round answers in which the basic proportions remain intact.

Consult the tabulation briefly, and then see how the figures are used.

Assuming that the reader finds his local raceway on the list, he proceeds as follows:

1. To compensate for the effect of post position on the past performance, *deduct* the value of the post position from the pace rating.

2. To allow for the probable effect of tonight's post position, *add* its value to the rating.

Example:
Tonight's race is a C-1 pace at Yonkers. Last week the horse started in lane 8 in the same class of race. Tonight it draws position 2. Its past-performance line looks like this:

$$1:03 \quad 8 \ 6 \ 6 \ 6^0 \ 5/5 \ 3/2 \quad 2:06:2$$

The basic pace rating is 193 (see p. 178). No class adjustment is necessary because the horse has not been raised or lowered in class. Credits for roughing it on the outside plus gaining three lengths in the stretch increase the rating to 201 (see pp. 220 and 221). Deducting the value of last week's post position (3 points), and adding tonight's (9 points), makes the rating 207. If the horse had raced from post 2 last week and was exiled to 8 tonight, its rating would be 195—12 points less. In actual handicapping, as we shall see, these wide swings become a tremendous factor.

Readers whose own raceways are not included in the tabulation of post-position values can use the figures given for tracks of the appropriate sizes. I recommend, however, that they obtain whatever local post-position statistics are available, and modify the tabulated figures if necessary. Assuming that the local statistics, if any, list total winners in each starting position, but give no clue as to the number of horses that started, the handicapper should move cautiously. To reduce the distortions embodied in statistics of that kind, it is a good idea to increase the number of winners listed for the extreme outside post by

30 percent. And increase the number given for the next-to-outside post by 20 percent. If the adjusted totals seem greatly out of phase with the figures given on page 236 for tracks of the local raceway's size, proceed cautiously, experimenting with dry-run handicapping before risking much money. The effort will reward you.

The Two-Second Rule

I remarked that some good handicappers refuse to play a horse with an outside post position unless they think it is best in its field by at least two seconds. I do not know how all of them achieve this precise evaluation. I suspect that some merely guess at it. The numerical method I am trying to propound in this book seems to take ample care of the so-called two-second rule. If a horse leaving from the outside or next-to-outside at a typical half-miler or ⅝-miler does not rate at least 10 points the best in its race, I throw it out. I throw it out even if it has the highest rating in the field! The decision is not made, however, until the ratings have been adjusted to reflect the probable influences of drivers.

11

The Driver Factor

During 1968, more than 5,700 sulky drivers competed for $71 million in purses at North American raceways and fairs. Fewer than 200 of these drivers won more than $42 million of the purse money. It was a normal year.

Think about it. In a representative year of harness racing, 3.5 percent of the drivers romp off with 60 percent of the prizes. To accomplish this, the dominant minority wins virtually all the richest stakes races and captures much more than its arithmetical share of bread-and-butter dashes, six nights a week, all the year through, plus occasional afternoons.

At the typical raceway, six or seven drivers, perhaps one-tenth of the local roster, customarily take more than one-third of the races. Turnover is slow, the same men monopolizing the local winner's circle for years on end. To be a successful bettor, it is necessary to know who these local leaders are, and modify your handicapping figures accordingly. It also is necessary to know who the leading drivers are on other circuits.

To illustrate, in 1969 and for several previous years, the top drivers at Yonkers and Roosevelt were Carmine Abbatiello, John Chapman, anybody named Dancer, Lucien Fontaine, Billy Haughton, Del Insko and George Sholty. Intermittently, Bob Cherrix, Billy Myer, George Phalen or Jim Tallman would turn warm long enough to deserve top grades. Winning racegoers remained alert to these facts and interpreted them properly. But that was not enough. Every now and then, a Keith Waples, Bob Williams or Herve Filion would arrive in town with a good horse and catch the locals unaware. Wherever the handicapper may be located, he owes himself the protection of knowing the names and credentials of the best drivers on other circuits, so that he may profit from their invasions of his own bailiwick.

Driving Ability Defined

Before you have finished your second cup of coffee at a track kitchen, you surely will hear that certain drivers are overrated. They are not nearly as good as the public thinks. It's politics. And luck. Other drivers are much better but do not get the breaks. Take Joe Doakes. He has won only 6 percent of his starts this season and was not much more successful last year, but he actually is as sharp a horseman as you can find. He just does not have the stock. And he's not in The Clique, so he never gets a catch-drive behind somebody else's good horse. Give him a stable like Haughton's or Dancer's and he'd show them all what for.

It may be true. Perhaps we should sympathize with Doakes and root for him and form a Doakes fan club. But we had better not modify our handicapping procedures on that account. No profit comes from betting on a driver because of the feats he might achieve in a better world. Tonight's races take place in this world. Poor Doakes never seems to win unless he has much the best horse, or unless he benefits from somebody's else's bad racing luck.

In deciding who the best drivers are, the handicapper employs a cold-blooded definition of "best." For his purposes, the best drivers are those who win a high percentage of their starts—15 percent or more. Nothing else counts for much. It has been said that a hundred drivers could match Stanley Dancer's winning average (which often exceeds 30 percent), if they had access to horses like his and could afford to be as choosy as he about deciding when to drive and when to abstain. Let 'em say it. The handicapper needs only to know that Stanley Dancer gets home first with extraordinary consistency, multiplying the chances of any sharp horse he drives.

Billy Haughton believes that great drivers are born, not made. He speaks with authority and has no axe to grind. As of January 1, 1970, he had won more North American races (3,155) and more purse money ($14,417,719) than any other driver in the recorded history of harness racing. He could stop driving tomorrow and continue as a power in the sport. He is a fully accomplished horseman. He does it all. He has few equals as a judge of yearlings or as a trainer of colts. In the delicate arts of schooling, conditioning, hanging, balancing and driving a trotter, he rates at the very top, with Joe O'Brien, Ralph Baldwin, Del Cameron, Jimmy Cruise, Stanley Dancer, Frank Ervin, Clint Hodgins, Del Miller, Harry Pownall, Sanders Russell, John

Simpson and perhaps three or four others. As a handler of pacers, not more than thirty men rate as his peers.

Haughton declares that, while years of experience are indispensable, they produce greatness only in a driver endowed with a light touch, quick reflexes, unusually wide peripheral vision and a suitable mentality.

"Light hands are the basic requirement," he says. "This has absolutely nothing to do with how big a man is. I know little men who are heavy handed and will never make it to the top for that reason. I know heavy men with light hands.

"Heavy-handed men make hard-mouthed horses. Horses with hard mouths can't respond quickly to their drivers. A driver with that kind of horse loses a fraction of a second three or four times in a race. I have run into it myself in taking over horses that had been handled by heavy-handed drivers. Their mouths are tough and hard. They just don't respond as they should to my touch. It takes quite a while before I can get them to react properly. In the meantime, I lose races I should have won."

Light hands are most effective when associated with keen, experienced intelligence and cool emotions. Great drivers are smarter than others. And more composed. Their racing tactics resemble psychological warfare. They keep their opponents in a state of chronic anxiety, upstaging them at every opportunity, playing with them like cats with mice, provoking them to move prematurely or wait too long.

If a Haughton wants the "garden spot"—the choice position on the rail directly behind the leader—he often gets it by outwitting its occupant. He flushes the man out of there by storming up on the outside as if to steal the lead. Afraid of Haughton to begin with, and incapable of weighing all the alternatives in the split second available to him, the fish bites. He becomes impetuous. He takes out to reach the lead before Haughton can. As soon as he vacates the garden spot, Haughton eases into it, saving his horse on the turn while his victim's animal, parked out, loses its sting.

It happens over and over again. And then one night, as if Haughton wanted it that way, the sucker declines to be flushed out, whereupon Haughton makes an even truer believer of him by taking the lead at once and remaining there to the finish.

If a Haughton wants to leave the rail and travel overland, he frequently finds someone to run interference. This time the pigeon may be in front or behind. It does not matter. Feinting an outward move, Haughton induces the other to try to beat him to the front. As soon as the man takes the bait, Haughton moves directly behind him, under snug cover from the wind.*

Not many drivers combine the light touch with the eyes in the back of the head, the instant reflexes, the high intelligence and the years of constructive experience. Those who do are so obviously beneficial to fit horses that owners and trainers plead for their services.

The Catch-Drivers

The age of specialization has overtaken harness racing. Although that remarkable one-man band, the trainer-driver, remains prominent throughout the sport, his tribe diminishes. Many successful horsemen now concentrate on training, and drive scarcely at all. Some drive but leave the actual training to others. Some train and drive their best young stock, entrusting the rest to assistants. A horseman who does all his own training and driving probably has a small stable.

With horses deployed all over the map, emperors like Stanley Dancer, Billy Haughton and Del Insko do much of their training by long-distance telephone. Somebody else attends to the daily routines. The assistant who handles a local division of a big-time stable is legally accountable as its trainer and is named as such in the raceway program. Unless Haughton or Dancer or whoever heads the outfit has been driving a horse in its recent races, the inexperienced fan may have no clue that it is a Haughton or Dancer horse.

Many raceway programs clarify matters by naming the national head of the stable as well as the local trainer. The information is particularly helpful early in the season, when the probable class and readiness of a green three-year-old is more easily deduced from the name of its stable than from the names of its sire and dam. At any time of year, the fan appreciates knowing that the officially responsible trainer, Winky Mello, is actually minding the store for Billy Haughton, or that Jack LaBarge is Stanley Dancer's man, and Harold Brown stands in for Bob Farrington, and Yves Filion for brother Herve, and Wayne Burris for Vernon Dancer and so on.

Commuting from raceway to raceway in pursuit of the week's fattest prizes, and seldom roosting in one place for more than 72 hours at a time, the big operators take pains to guarantee competent drivers for their stock on nights when they are elsewhere. The various

---

* For a much more profound and comprehensive review of driving tactics than I can supply here, see Haughton's classic, "Driving the Race," in James C. Harrison's *Care and Training of the Trotter and Pacer.*

Dancers constantly fill in for each other. So do members of other raceway families such as the Farringtons, Camerons, Filions, Myers, Williamses, Nickellses and Popfingers. But catch-driving is more than a family convenience. It has become a source of substantial revenue for drivers who exel at it.

In New York, Carmine Abbatiello, Lucien Fontaine, John Chapman and Billy Myer frequently drive animals from top barns. So do George Sholty and Del Insko, who have glamorous strings of their own. Some insiders think that Sholty may be the best catch-driver in the business. Other authoritative observers harbor similar notions about Chapman, Abbatiello, Fontaine, Insko, Herve Filion, Bob Williams, Bud Gilmour and Billy Shuter. Also regarded highly are Gerry Bookmyer, Jim Larente, Tic Wilcutts, Jack Bailey, Waldo McIlmurray, Ted Taylor and George Phalen.

There are dozens of genuinely good ones. Some, like Abbatiello, Bookmyer and Fontaine, are uninterested in training horses. Others, like Filion and Chapman, are among the best trainers in the world. What they all have in common, aside from driving talent of the first order, is an uncanny ability to win with a strange horse. They take it on a warm-up tour and learn all they need to know.

During the past decade, dozens of trainers have been obliged to concede that expert training and expert driving are separate skills which do not necessarily coexist in the same person. So they employ catch-drivers. As they put it, "Five percent of something is better than 10 percent of nothing." The trainer's share of a purse is 5 percent, as is the driver's. A trainer-driver therefore collects 10 percent. But an Abbatiello or Bookmyer wins the race, whereas the horse's trainer might be unable to. No longer pretending that they can drive in fast company, numerous trainers now prosper on 5 percent, where they formerly suffered for want of the 10.

With trainers and drivers playing musical chairs in the sulky, alert handicappers make hay. If a horse displayed vigor when steered by an ordinary chauffeur last week, it should fly for Sholty tonight. If it won in a squeaker for Wilcutts last week, the switch to Doakes very probably means that not much should be expected tonight.

Universal Ratings

Most raceway programs summarize drivers' recent accomplishments numerically. Adjoining each name on the list is a three-digit figure which looks like a batting average. It also looks as if it might be the driver's percentage of winning starts, but it is not. Instead, it is an average computed in accordance with the Universal Driver Rating System, an ingenious statistical procedure which assumes that a victory is 80 percent more meritorious than a second-place finish and three times as good as coming in third. It charges the driver 9 points for every start and awards him 9 for each victory, 5 for each second and 3 for each third. With 3 wins, 3 seconds and 3 thirds in 9 attempts, the driver's UDR is .630. The rating is computed by adding the win credits ($3 \times 9 = 27$), and those for finishing second ($3 \times 5 = 15$), and those for finishing third ($3 \times 3 = 9$), and dividing the sum (51) by the debits for starts ($9 \times 9 = 81$).

Anything above .300 is considered quite good for a season's action, although many leading drivers do much better. Occasionally, the system leads into strange byways. For example, a driver with 10 wins (90 points), 24 seconds (120) and 30 thirds (90) in 100 starts (900) earns a UDR of .333—more appetizing than his miserable winning average of .100. Another driver with 20 wins (180), 18 seconds (90) and 10 thirds (30) in 100 starts (900) also rates a UDR of .333, although his winning average of .200 probably establishes him as one of the torrid drivers on the grounds and a more dependable bet than the other man.

Lacking other evidence, one surely would suppose that a driver who has been winning 20 percent of his starts has sharper horses or has been working wonders with inferior horses. The man who has been winning only 10 percent of his starts might actually be the superior driver, of course. Perhaps he gets money with impossible animals. But on whom does one bet? I should think that one bets on the man who, for whatever reason, has been winning consistently. Provided, of course, that his horse seems fit.

I recommend that handicappers be careful to note whether the decimals that accompany drivers' names are winning averages or UDR averages. If winning averages are missing, it is worthwhile to calculate them yourself.

It also is desirable to keep tabs on the leading drivers at the current . local meeting so that you will have something to go on when the horses move across town to the other raceway. The raceway program supplies driver statistics only for the meeting in progress. It is silent about what happened elsewhere on the same circuit during the same season. Players who know how the reinsmen have been doing in recent months are better equipped to evaluate their chances during the first week or so of a new meeting. As mentioned much earlier, the weekly *Horseman and Fair World* is helpful in this connection.

The Driver's Weight

Horsemen believe that the weight of the driver is inconsequential on dry tracks. If he sits properly and does not permit his weight to push the sulky shafts up or down, the horse gets there in time, whether the pilot is a midget or a mammoth. When tracks are muddy and the wheels plow deep furrows (which rarely happens at modern raceways), the lightweight driver is conceded a large advantage.

The effect of weight in muddy going has always been so obvious that nobody is surprised when occasional tests prove it. The theory that weight makes no difference on a fast track has also been tested but never, so far as I know, under conditions that would satisfy a scientist. Most arguments in behalf of the theory are based on common logic: Races do not begin from a standing start, but after the horses overcome inertia and reach competitive speed. If Standardbreds had to do this quickly, as Thoroughbreds do, a heavy load would be a detriment. But with plenty of space and time in which to get the wheels rolling, the initial effects of weight become imperceptible. Furthermore, once momentum is achieved, a properly seated driver who weighs 175 pounds causes hardly more drag on the wheels than a properly seated driver who weighs 125.

All that might be true under ideal circumstances. But it is difficult to believe that many drivers remain perfectly balanced over the sulky throughout every race. The heavier the driver and the farther he moves his backside, the greater the stress on the horse.

Clint Hodgins, unanimously regarded as one of the best drivers of all time, weighed between 195 and 200 pounds. A 250-pound Hollander named Willem Geersen won the 1960 International Trot at Roosevelt Raceway by taking Hairos II on the outside for the entire mile and one-quarter. Other large bulks win big races and small, wherever races are found. But the records of the sport imply quite insistently that little men have an overall advantage.

No conscious effort is made to recruit lightweights as drivers, yet they tend to win more than their quota of races. Of the ten top money-winners during 1968, the heaviest was Billy Myer at 160. The others were Haughton (150), Stanley Dancer (140), Del Insko (120), Fontaine (135), Herve Filion (145), Carmine Abbatiello (135),

Sholty (117), Bob Williams (140) and John Chapman (147). Among the ten drivers who won 180 or more races during that year, the heaviest were Gerry Bookmyer (170) and Keith Waples (165). Besides a few listed above as big money-winners, others who won more than 180 dashes were Don Busse (150), and Ronnie Feagan (135).

Pending scientific investigation, it can be assumed that lightness does more good than harm. Beyond that, it seems sensible to leave the issue in abeyance, where it was when we found it. Whether he be large or small, the only practical measure of a driver's ability remains his winning percentage. Except, of course, if it comes up muddy and Sholty has a sharp horse to drive. In those circumstances we should remember that betting opportunities arise when high winning percentage combines with low weight. Hurry to the window before all the tickets are gone.

Handicapping the Drivers

The attitude of this book is that the number of wins and the total purse money accumulated by a driver during a month, a season or a career are of no particular significance in handicapping a race. What counts is the winning average, the percentage of starts that result in victory. If the racegoer bets only on seemingly fit horses, preferring those whose drivers maintain satisfactory winning averages, he is as safe as he can be. If he learns how to decide when to bet on the third-best horse in the race, because of its winning driver, he will be no safer but he will have more fun.

Knotty problems crop up. For example, Don Busse. He races a large troop of inexpensive horses on the Chicago circuit, where insiders honor him as a superb trainer and an absolutely first-rate driver. His stock is so ordinary, and the competition so keen, that he seldom wins more than 12 percent of his year's starts. His UDR hovers in the humble neighborhood of .250. Yet he races so frequently and has such remarkable talent in the homestretch that he usually earns a place among the country's ten leading dash winners. In 1963, his 201 victories led the entire profession. His UDR was only .262, but he won about 16 percent of his 1,278 races—a high average for him.

In 1968, he raced 1,479 times, more than twice as often as most other trainer-drivers of comparable ability. His 232 wins were enough to place him fourth on the list of winners, behind Herve Filion, Lucien

Fontaine and Carmine Abbatiello. Once again, his winning average was about .160—uncharacteristically high. Far more often, he makes the annual list of big winners with an average like .120. It is hard to discount a man who wins that many races and is so highly regarded by his colleagues. But a line must be drawn. Filion, Fontaine and Abbatiello, who drive better horses and are every bit as competent as Busse, compile superior winning averages, while racing as often as Busse does. Indeed, Filion races more often than anybody, being obsessed with the idea that fewer than 400 triumphs a year is a personal disgrace.

What is a handicapper to do about a Busse, an Eddie Cobb, a Billy Myer, a Ben Webster—drivers who sometimes win lots of money or lots of races or both, but often end with unimpressive winning averages? Given a sharp horse, will not a Busse, Webster, Cobb or Myer compete on equal terms with anyone, regardless of winning averages? Does not the record prove it?

Tough questions. My answer, for what it may be worth, is that drivers who win fewer than 15 percent of their starts are risky betting propositions unless their horses stand out sharply. But a driver who consistently achieves a high seasonal or annual average is worth notice, *even when he is in a slump.* And any driver, including our bedraggled Joe Doakes, should be regarded as a winner during meetings that find him in a hot streak.

To be more detailed about it, I think that good handicappers are faithful to the following ideas:

1. *Drivers do not often win with unfit horses.* Unless a horse seems sharp and well situated, the handicapper should ignore it, no matter who the driver may be. To disregard this is to bet on drivers as if horses were not involved. This is more costly than the error of betting on horses as if drivers were not involved.

2. *By winning upward of 20 percent of their annual starts and leading local and/or national standings in that department year after year, a small minority of drivers are recognizable as likely winners whenever they turn up with fit horses.* This holds true even during periods in which the raceway program shows that such a driver has been winning a low percentage of his attempts. Top drivers do not remain losers for long. Even at 60 and 70 years of age, they continue to win a large fraction of their races, although they work less frequently. Most racegoers can identify the top drivers in their localities. A later section of this chapter will name them.

3. *At a typical raceway meeting, the dominant drivers are those who have been winning 15 percent or more of their races. If some have been achieving averages of 20, 25 or 30 percent, the handicapper should take that large difference into account.*

4. *Any driver, no matter how inconsistent his prior record, should be regarded as a potential winner if he has been getting home first with 15 percent of his horses at the current meeting, and if he goes with a sharp horse tonight.*

5. *No provisional driver is an acceptable bet unless he has been racing as frequently as others and is among the leading reinsmen at the meeting.* Provisional drivers are apprentices in the trade. Sooner or later the best of them begin winning, but consistency is not usually within their powers. A recent exception was Ronnie Dancer, Stanley's youthful son, who more than held his own at Liberty Bell with a string of dad's horses.

Players who do their handicapping mentally, distrusting arithmetical formulas, will get along if they confine their wagers to situations in which (a) the horse seems best and (b) the driver is either an authentic topnotcher or on a hot streak. Between two apparently equal horses, the one with the winning driver deserves support. If both drivers qualify, the player might consider making two bets—especially at half-mile tracks, where contention is so close.

This kind of handicapping requires the player to become a mental gymnast when a Del Miller or Joe O'Brien or Billy Haughton or the like turns up with a horse which, while apparently fit, is not as impressive as another horse whose driver has no special distinction. Sometimes the best horse wins. Sometimes the best driver wins. Sometimes the outcome is predictable. Certain theorists believe that the player should always take the best driver. Others think the best driver is the play at a half-miler but not on a longer oval. Still others think the race should be passed unless the best-looking horse goes with a winner in the sulky.

I have tested all these theories and have found profit in none of them. More precisely, there is profit in *all* of them, if the handicapper can determine which of them is applicable to the particular race. This puts him right back where he started, in the mental gymnasium.

I much prefer the numerical procedure that I have been piecing together at intervals throughout this book. In dealing with drivers, it awards the winning ones numerical credit for the contribution they make to Standardbred performance. The amount of credit is uniform, as if one top driver were as good as another. This is imprecise, but it is more practical than a procedure in which the handicapper tries to decide whether O'Brien is going to catch Marsh in the stretch. Or whether O'Brien and Marsh each deserve 18 points, whereas Doakes is entitled to 4 or 7. Determinations of that kind simply cannot be made. But the probability that a driver with a high winning percentage will move a fit horse is as substantial as any probability in racing. It is on probability that this handicapping method rests.

And it works. As the reader will see, the method sometimes indicates that a fit horse with a journeyman navigator is a better bet than another fit horse whose driver is an all-time great. In doing so, and in being right often enough to stave off the sheriff, the method eliminates the painful gyrations demanded by other approaches to handicapping.

I recommend the following:

1. *If the driver customarily is a national or local leader in terms of winning percentage (not less than 15, most years), add 10 points to the rating of his horse.* Needless to say, the horse qualifies as a contender and has been given a pace rating, modified to take account of class, form, post position and angles.

2. *If the driver is not an established national or local leader but has been winning 15 percent or more of his starts at the current meeting or during the current season, add 10 points to the horse's rating.*

3. *If the horse's driver in its key race (the race that qualified it as a contender) was the kind of driver specified in items 1 and 2 above, but tonight's driver is not, deduct 10 points from the rating.*

These recommendations cover all likely situations but two. The first occurs during the first days of a meeting, when mediocre drivers may be listed among the leaders in the program's tabulation. Obviously, a record of one victory in three starts hardly makes a top man of someone who has not previously set the world ablaze. If in doubt about a driver, the best procedure is to assume that his 15-percent record means nothing unless at least three victories are involved.

Another dilemma is that of the fan who patronizes one of our smaller raceways. What to do if a Billy Haughton turns up one night and accepts a couple of catch-drives while waiting to perform with one of his own champion Standardbreds? Unless the driving colony at the track includes national leaders, the handicapper probably should add 15 points to the rating of any fit horse driven by the invader.

The Consistent Ones

   The following U.S. and Canadian drivers usually win 15 percent or more of their annual starts—a statistic of great importance to the handicapper. Close followers of harness racing will notice that the names of many renowned drivers are missing, although some comparatively obscure ones are listed. The attempt here is not to imply that these are the sport's best drivers but to emphasize that they manage to win high percentages of their starts.

Carmine Abbatiello	Don Bromley	Sonny Dancer
Doug Ackerman	Bob Brown	Stanley Dancer
Jack Ackerman	Warren Cameron	Vernon Dancer
Bob Altizer	Bob Camper	Brent Davies
Jimmy Arthur	John Chapman	Jim Dennis
Earle Avery	Benoit Cote	Marcel Dostie
Jack Bailey	Leroy Copeland	Frank Ervin
Ralph Baldwin	Tom Crank	Bob Farrington
Howard Beissinger	Vern Crank	Brad Farrington
Hugh Bell	Jimmy Cruise	Richard Farrington
Gerry Bookmyer	Jim M. Curran	Bill Faucher
Chris Boring	Ross Curran	Ronnie Feagan
Earl Bowman	Harold Dancer	Marc Ferguson

Other Leaders

   The following drivers do not always win high percentages of their annual starts but often are listed among local or national leaders in terms of races won or purses earned. Included on the roster are some of the most promising of the younger reinsmen, along with many well-regarded veterans.

Angus Allen	Terry Buter	Herman Graham
Paul Battis	Del Cameron	Jerry Graham
Earl Beede	Charles Campbell	Tom Graham
Dave Begin	Bob Cherrix	Don Hall
Dolf Beitlich	Eddie Cobb	Warren Harp
Arthur Bier	Real Cormier	Fred Haslip
Ewell Binkley	Don Crisenbery	Ken Heeney
Johnny Blevins	Ronnie Dancer	Bill Herman
Tug Boyd	Bucky Day	Omar Hiteman
Tom Brinkerhoff	Leigh Fitch	John Holford
Harry Burright	Ed Gilman	Dave Howard
Don Busse		

Gilles Filion
Henri Filion
Herve Filion
Yves Filion
Harold Fisher
John Findley
Charles Fitzpatrick
Lucien Fontaine
William Fritz
Clint Galbraith
Glen Garnsey
Bud Gilmour
Eldon Harner
Levi Harner
Harry Harvey
Billy Haughton
Dick Hogan
Lou Huber, Jr.
Delbie Insko
Del Insko
Glen Kidwell
Charles King
Gilles LaChance

Jerry Landess
Jim Larente
Tom Lewis
Jim Macgregor
Duncan MacTavish
Del Manges
Joe Marsh, Jr.
Wally McIlmurray
Del Miller
Bruce Nickells
Wayne Nickells
Joe O'Brien
Freeman Parker
Howard Parker
John Patterson
John Patterson, Jr.
Dwayne Pletcher
Bill Pocza
Harry Pownall
Lou Rapone
Don Richards
Dick Richardson, Jr.
Gene Riegle

Sanders Russell
Ervin Samples
John Schroeder
Gene Sears
George Sholty
Billy Shuter
John Simpson
John Simpson, Jr.
Curly Smart
Clyde Snook
Jim Tallman
Ted Taylor
Ken Vander Schaaf
Keith Waples
Walter Warrington
Mac Weaver
Eddie Wheeler
Roger White
Tom Wilburn
Tic Wilcutts
Jack Williams
Bobby Williams
Alix Winger

Art Hult
Arlo Hurt
Ray Ireland
Bob Kane
Joe Lighthill
Alvin Lineweaver
Ray Lineweaver
Win Lineweaver
Ed Lohmeyer
Henry Lunsford
Ralph Mapes
Walter Marks
Bob Mars
Dennis May
Jim McGarty
Ken McNutt
Tom Merriman
Mel Miller
Vern Mitchell

Bob Mohr
Mike Novick, Jr.
Claude Paradis
Gay Parker
Marvin Parshall
Claude Pelletier
George Phalen
Mal Phillips
Dave Pinkney
Phil Pinkney
Wayne Plowman
Richard Putz
Ray Remmen
Floyd Roach
Jack Rohler
Gerald Sarama
Charles Sells
Joe Smallwood
Clark Smith

Elmer Smith
Phil Sowers
Alvin Stanke
Ben Steall
Bob Stiles
Abe Stolzfus
Hardd Story
Charles Sylvester
Frank Tagariello
Kevin Tisher
Jim Torre
Gene Vallandingham
Dave Vance
Rocco Vinci
Tom Wantz
Murray Waples
Elmore White
Frank Winkler
Greg Wright

The $2-Million Club

By winning $2 million in purses, a driver gains a permanent place in the history of harness racing. Until the 1960's, none but the greatest were able to do it. With year-round racing, enlarged purses and windfalls like sire stakes programs, the charmed circle has become accessible to horsemen whom the mantle of immortality would not fit without drastic alterations. A few older ones have entered the "club" by virtue of sheer endurance, having lasted long enough to amass the required career earnings. A few others have done it without displaying the consistency or versatility of greatness. Nevertheless, no mediocre driver has ever earned $2 million in purses, nor is any likely to in the foreseeable future. The horsemen discussed below are the members of the club still on the scene.

CARMINE ABBATIELLO
Born 5/23/36, New York, N.Y.
Weight: 135
Career earnings through 1969: $4,003,422
Career victories through 1969: 1,318

Brought to the track by his older brother Tony, a capable trainer-driver, this youngster went into high gear in 1959, with 52 wins in 222 starts at secondary raceways like Monticello and Free-hold. Was leading driver at both ovals before becoming a fixture on the tough Yonkers–Roosevelt circuit, where he promptly established himself as a superb catch-driver. Always in the running for national leadership in races won, he drives more than 1,000 times a year, yet manages to maintain a high winning average and a UDR above .300. Combines a hustling, aggressive style with extreme finesse. Knows exactly when to make his move. Wins or gets part of the purse with unpromising animals because of his remarkable ability to wake them up. Not enthusiastic about training, he threatens to unload his small public stable and become a full-time catch-driver. Early skepticism about his talents have long since vanished. The best trainers in the business use him when they can get him. He does as well with expensive colts and free-for-allers as with lesser stock. Horsemen think that his greatest years are yet to come.

EARLE AVERY
Born 2/24/94, Knowlesville, N.B.
Weight: 180
Career earnings: $3,199,025
Career victories: 1,196

In 1955, at the age of 61, the New Brunswick potato farmer became head trainer-driver for Norman Woolworth's important Clearview Farm. A colt specialist who wins about 20 percent of his starts, he has had world champions like Egyptian Princess, Meadow Skipper, Porterhouse and Muncy Hanover. In 1969, his Gun Runner was a prime prospect for the Hambletonian until disabled by illness. The 76-year-old marvel was driving about as well as ever that year, and gave no hint of slowing down. Loves to get out front early and stay there. Belying the notion that half-mile and ⅝-mile tracks are for youngsters, he led the driver standings at Atlantic City in 1968 and won big New York races in 1969.

RALPH BALDWIN
Born 2/25/16, Lloydminster, Sask.
Weight: 145
Career earnings: $4,048,067
Career victories: 1,013

The former head trainer for Castleton Farm has a poor year when he wins fewer than one-third of his starts. Has led the continent three times with UDR's of .610, .553 and .506. Twice led all Grand Circuit drivers. Rarely races more than 150 times a year, specializing as he does in quality animals like Speedy Scot, Dartmouth, Kentucky Bell, Scotch Jewel and Snow Speed. Began in 1933 as assistant to his father, a well-known Canadian horseman. An absolute master with high-grade two-year-olds, he is known as a perfectionist where gait and manners are concerned. If a Baldwin horse races, it is ready. And so is he—adjusting his tactics to the demands of the situation.

HOWARD BEISSINGER
Born 5/16/23, Hamilton, O.
Weight: 165
Career earnings: $3,292,907
Career victories: 1,191

This third-generation horseman has set world's records with Widower Creed, Right Time and Tarport Lib, and, in 1969, swept trotting's "Big Five" with Lindy's Pride. Has been leading driver at Hollywood, Sportsman's Park and Maywood. Almost invariably wins more than 20 percent of his annual starts, with a UDR in the neighborhood of .350. A calmly competent trainer, he is a master judge of pace who beats more spectacularly aggressive drivers by out-thinking them. Bettors sometimes criticize him for sitting still, but his record shows that there is more to this game than the flailing of arms.

HUGHIE BELL
Born 7/27/02, Delaware, O.
Weight: 125
Career earnings: $3,469,246
Career victories: 1,620

Doesn't compete much anymore, but retains most of the incredible strength, the pace-setting touch and the remarkable feeling for horses that made him an all-time great catch-driver. Was top winner at Roosevelt Raceway three times and at Yonkers four. Until he began easing off in 1965, was invariably among the top purse-earners of the year. Is thought to have won more than 1,000 races before the USTA established its modern record-keeping system in 1949.

NORMAN "CHRIS" BORING
Born 6/17/41, Indianapolis, Ind.
Weight: 135
Career earnings: $1,812,686
Career victories: 892

This son and grandson of harness horsemen had not yet reached the $2-million mark when this book was written. But nobody doubts that the kid will win many times that amount before he calls it a career. At 20, when most budding horsemen consider themselves fortunate to drive in a country fair, young Boring was leading driver at Sportsman's Park, an achievement he repeated two years later. In 1968, his UDR of .394 was seventh best in North America—he won almost 25 percent of his starts. Whether in raceway competition or on the Grand Circuit, the youngster consistently rates with the best. So far, his top horse has been True Duane, with whom he went in 1:56⅘ at Lexington.

HARRY BURRIGHT
Born 9/26/16, Oregon, Ill.
Weight: 180
Career earnings: $2,790,945
Career victories: 2,124

Like most other leading Standardbred horsemen, Burright comes from a harness-racing family. At one time, he and six other Burrights were active in the sport. In 1956, he and his brother Gene finished in a dead heat at Maywood Park, where Harry has been the driving champion four times. Has also topped the lists at Aurora, Washington Park, Sportsman's Park, Cahokia Downs and Kentucky Raceway. Since 1948, when his 129 victories led the nation, he has been among the top 25 in that category 13 times. Has also been among the leading purse winners eight times. In 1968, he became the seventh driver to record 2,000 victories since the USTA began keeping records of that kind. Strictly a raceway operative with bread-and-butter stock, he seldom has been able to win as much as 15 percent of his annual starts. Nevertheless, horsemen respect him as a dependable catch-driver whose notable aggressiveness combines with fantastic ability to keep a fading horse alive in the homestretch.

DON BUSSE
Born 6/6/18, Portage, Wis.
Weight: 150
Career earnings: $2,667,932
Career victories: 2,078

The dynamo of Kingston, Ill., shares credit with Stanley Dancer for proving that Standardbreds could be trained to tolerate "air." Their style of racing on the outside put an end to the Indian-file processions which formerly were routine. With better horses, Busse's record would be even more distinguished than it is. But mediocre stock is his bag, and his record places him among the greats. Son of horseman Hugo Busse, he came into his own in 1958, when only 18 drivers won more dashes than he. He has not been off the list since. In 1963, he led it. Trainers say that he has few equals at shoeing and rigging a horse. His racing style is simplicity itself: he takes the animal out and goes for broke. That he wins as often as he does is a tribute to his own gameness and the care with which he shapes cheap animals for raceway competition. His annual winning average seldom is impressive, making him a puzzlement for handicappers.

ADELBERT CAMERON
Born 6/9/20, Harvard, Mass.
Weight: 135
Career earnings: $3,135,545
Career victories: 1,102

This masterful handler of colts is the man whom the greatest Grand Circuit horsemen seek out when they need a catch-driver for an expensive trotter. Catch-drove Egyptian Candor and Speedy Streak to victory in Hambletonian, which he also won with Newport Dream. Took the Little Brown Jug with Forbes Chief and Tar Heel. Has uncanny ability to produce a horse's best on the day of its biggest race. Seldom makes more than 300 starts a year and does not always compile a high winning percentage but should never be taken lightly in a race involving high-grade Standardbreds. As trainer for the celebrated Newport Stock Farm, Del has won big stakes not only with Newport Dream but with Newport Star, Newport Judy, Major Newport, Newport Admiral, Newport Del, Newport Robbi, Newport Tarlet, Newport Chief and Newport Frisco. The son of a trainer-driver, he is the father of Warren and Gary, both good horsemen.

HOWARD R. "BOBBY" CAMPER
Born 8/8/29, Bowers Beach, Del.
Weight: 170
Career earnings: $2,253,791
Career victories: 731

This slick trainer and sound driver has never won more than 85 races in a year but has been among the 25 leading money-earners four times since 1952, when he began competing professionally. Among his big horses have been Active Don, Milford Hanover, Ritzy Hanover and Murdock Hanover. Has demonstrated that he can win consistently at major-league tracks but seems to prefer Monticello, with an occasional fling at bigger game elsewhere. Usually is good for first money in better than 15 percent of his starts.

JOHN CHAPMAN
Born 11/25/28, Toronto, Ont.
Weight: 147
Career earnings: $6,202,106
Career victories: 2,324

In 1949, his third year as a driver, this member of a celebrated Canadian racing family won 70 times, placing twelfth among
North American dash-winners. He has been among the top 20 ever
since, except during four years when a post as private trainer for the
exclusive Allwood Stable limited his activities. He also has been
among the 25 leading money-winners 12 times, and among the 25
Grand Circuit leaders 10 times. In an era of catch-drivers, he ranks
with the best. Leading reinsman at Batavia in 1957 and at Yonkers in
1963, he goes postward more than 1,000 times a year but invariably
wins more than 15 percent. Is a thoroughly versatile driver but may
be better than most New York stars at coming from off the pace to
win in the stretch.

BOB CHERRIX
Born 2/15/30, Snow Hill, Md.
Weight: 167
Career earnings: $2,740,594
Career victories: 943

Northern-trained horses perform better than others during the
first frigid weeks of the New York season. Anyone who did not know

this learned it in 1959 when young Bob Cherrix won seven of his first eight starts. He has been an early-season idol in Gotham ever since, often setting a remarkable pace with his winter-hardy stock. When the warm weather comes, his stable tends to cool off, but Cherrix is good for $250,000 in purse earnings during a typical year—especially since he does nicely in the lucrative New York Sire Stakes program. Horsemen respect his ability to leave quickly and get a good position on the first turn, a decisively important consideration at half-mile tracks. Has seldom produced a high percentage of winners, but some insiders think that he is getting sharper with the years and will become a frequent winner.

EDDIE COBB
Born 3/1/20, Whitesville, N.Y.
Weight: 190
Career earnings: $4,725,059
Career victories: 1,757

Although his annual winning average seldom is high, this sharp horseman has an intensely loyal following among New York racegoers, some of whom seem to think he can win whenever he feels like it. If the odds on his horse drop a point during the last five minutes of wagering, Cobbophiles stampede to the windows to get in on the supposed good thing. These incidents embarrass the man when he loses and are a greater embarrassment when he wins. No proof exists that he bets more shrewdly than other drivers do, but his fans are convinced of it, and he bears the cross. Since winning for the first time in 1938, he has demonstrated that he can get the job done with any kind of Standardbred on any kind of track. He has been leading driver at Maywood, Brandywine, Grandview, Hollywood and Suffolk Downs. He has been among the year's leading dash-winners nine times, money-winners 14 times, and Grand Circuit drivers eight times. His greatest horse was Adios Butler, a world champion. Other good ones have been Honest Story, Amortizor, Flaming Arrow, Honest Jimmie, Jerry the First, Jean Laird, Hodgen and Great Pleasure.

JIMMY CRUISE
Born 10/12/17, Shepherdsville, Ky.
Weight: 180
Career earnings: $4,501,920
Career victories: 1,571

On the farm, in the barn and on the track, this consummate horseman does more for a sore-legged Standardbred than any trainer-driver alive. His rehabilitation of ailing free-for-allers like Earl Laird, Mr. Budlong and Stormy Dream is legend in the industry. His consistently high winning average is a handicapper's delight. He has been leading driver at Hollywood Park (twice), Roosevelt Raceway (three times) and Santa Anita (twice). Nobody is better behind a trotting horse. He has been among the leading dash-winners 10 times, the leading money-winners five times, and the leading Grand Circuiteers five times. A patient driver, he spares his horse in every possible way, knowing just when to make his move. If he acts as if he can read horses' minds, it may be that he can: He was born and brought up in the game. His father, Hardy Cruise, was a topnotch trainer-driver.

HAROLD "SONNY" DANCER, Jr.
Born 10/5/35, Sharon, N.J.
Weight: 165
Career earnings: $2,842,867
Career victories: 838

Son of trainer-driver Harold R. Dancer, nephew of Stanley and Vernon and cousin of Ronnie, this highly capable member of the imperial clan has a nice touch with colts, maintains a consistently impressive winning percentage and is in demand as a catch-driver. During 1968, won $250,000 in purses for Stanley, catch-driving the likes of Cardigan Bay. Has won the Fox Stake with Golden Money Maker, the Betsy Ross with Ricci Reenie, a Bloomsburg Fair Stake with Ricci Reenie First, and has been driving champion at Monticello, Freehold and Roosevelt. Whether behind one of his own horses, or a relative's or a non-Dancer's, Sonny drives like a Dancer—aggressively. Regardless of the size of the track or the calibre of the competition, handicappers can depend on him to get the best from ready horses.

STANLEY DANCER
Born 7/25/27, Edinburg, N.J.
Weight: 140
Career earnings: $12,743,865
Career victories: 2,564

Nevele Pride was the fastest two-year-old, three-year-old, four-year-old and all-age trotting champion of all time. Noble Victory trotted the fastest race of all time. Su Mac Lad won more money than any other American trotter in history. Cardigan Bay was the richest pacer of all time. Stanley Dancer trained and drove them all. Usually drives in about 500 races a year, yet has not been worse than twenty-second on the annual list of leading dash-winners since 1950. Has topped the UDR list since 1962, and has been first, second or third on the money-winner list since 1960 (which was his eleventh successive year among the leaders in that department). In 1964, became the first driver to win purses of more than $1 million in one year.

Has been driving champion at Yonkers, Roosevelt and Liberty Bell four times each. Dominates the winner's circle—and grabs a huge slice of the prize money—in the New York Sire Stakes, meanwhile going like mad on the Grand Circuit with the expensive animals he buys for himself and his clients at yearling sales. No longer as obsessed with getting the early lead as he was during the early years when he showed the boys how to stay in front, he now is a better driver than ever. And after being thrust somewhat prematurely into the role of big-league trainer, he has become a superb handler of colts, trotters, what-have-you. Nobody has better stock or a more efficient staff of assistants or a better way with a horse. And he is not even in his prime yet.

VERNON DANCER
Born 8/3/23, Red Valley, N.J.
Weight: 142
Career earnings: $4,813,877
Career victories: 1,138

A dairy farmer who took up harness racing as a hobby because brother Stanley was so enthusiastic about it, Vernon Dancer drove his first winner in 1952. He has been a recognized topnotcher for more than a decade, maintaining a splendid winning average and earning a place among the 25 leading money-winners every year. Like Stanley, whose farm is across the way from his own in New Egypt, N.J., he has become a fully rounded horseman with a penchant for the Grand Circuit, sire stakes and the doings at Yonkers, Roosevelt and Liberty Bell. In effect, this requires him to operate three different kinds of Standardbred strings. He does it well, if not on so huge a scale as Stanley. Was driving champ at Roosevelt in 1966 and at Liberty Bell in 1967. Catch-drove Cardigan Bay to a 1:58:1 world record for aged pacers at Yonkers in 1964, beating the great Overtrick in the bargain. Likes to grab the rail early in the race, but is not likely to stay there too long unless he's on the lead. A clever tactician with a particular knack for holding a trotter together.

JIM DENNIS
Born 5/9/23, Rexburg, Idaho.
Weight: 165
Career earnings: $4,735,734
Career victories: 1,413

Son of Noah, nephew of Warren and brother of Ted, this Dennis drove his first professional race in 1948 at Santa Anita, and won. Inclined to wait a bit long before making his move, he excels in the homestretch and does his best work at mile and ⅝-mile ovals. A fierce competitor, he has topped all drivers at several Hollywood, Santa Anita and Washington Park meetings, and at Sportsman's Park. Has not been off the roster of 25 leading money-winners since 1957. Is good for at least 100 wins a year, plus the high average that inspires confidence. His best horse has been Adios Vic.

FRANK ERVIN
Born 8/12/04, Pekin, Ill.
Weight: 150
Career earnings: $4,264,996
Career victories: 1,194

Son and grandson of horsemen, this all-time-great trainer-driver has won two Hambletonians (Diller Hanover and Kerry Way) and three Little Brown Jugs (Good Time, Keystoner and Bret Hanover). He would have won a third Hambletonian in 1967 but was ill and put catch-driver Del Cameron behind his Speedy Streak. Ervin's 106 drives in 2:00 or less are an all-time record. He won 19 straight races with Sampson Hanover, 20 with Expresson, 22 with Yankee Hanover and 35 with Bret Hanover. He set 20 world's records with Scotland's Comet, Adios, Martha Doyle, Our Time, Good Time, Sampson Hanover, Old Blue Hen, Princess Rodney, Phantom Lady, Good Counsel, Yankee Lass, Record Mat and, of course, his beloved Bret, the fastest Standardbred in history.

Never one to drive as many as 300 races a year, Ervin concentrates on Grand Circuit competition. He lately has left much of the driving to his clever assistant, Art Hult.

BOB FARRINGTON
Born 7/15/29, Richwood, O.
Weight: 145
Career earnings: $4,780,520
Career victories: 2,520

In 1958, his fourth year as a driver, this phenomenal horseman made the top 25 among North American dash-winners. He has not been off the list since, and has led it six times. He has been driving champion at Brandywine, Sportsman's Park, Freehold, Hillsdale, Hollywood, Maywood, Washington Park and Roosevelt. His winning average and UDR are always high, although he races more than 1,000 times a year. He and his brothers, Dick and Brad, and their father, Louis, maintain a large troop. Their horses shuttle between raceway barns and the farm at Richwood, O., where they freshen up for more racing. Although Farrington believes in placing horses where they can cash checks, and does not hesitate to drop them in class, he loves to fool the experts by winning a purse and a bet with a supposedly outgunned animal. A smooth driver and a superior judge of pace, he tends to sit behind the early leaders, but can go the other way when the situation warrants. His best horses have been Grandpa Jim, Dancing David and Easy Prom, with most emphasis on the development of steady geldings for claimers and conditioned races. In recent years, however, Farrington has been investing in higher-grade stock and has done well in some Grand Circuit events.

HERVE FILION
Born 2/1/40, Angers, Que.
Weight: 142
Career earnings: $3,642,387
Career victories: 2,431

Being mortal, this Canadian undoubtedly has limitations. Nobody in harness racing has yet been able to discover what they are. His 407 wins in 1968 were an all-time record, but he was sure that he could surpass it. His ability to win with supposedly washed-up horses, his equal facility with high-grade ones and his fantastic gifts as a catch-driver would seem to make him the most important new trainer-driver in the business. He started with 29 victories in 1953—at age 13! One of eight racing sons of a racing father, he has been concentrating on U.S. raceways since 1965, winning driver championships at Brandywine, Liberty Bell, Suffolk Downs and Freehold. The big-timers began to take him seriously when he beat Cardigan Bay with Fly Fly Byrd, Romulus Hanover with Meadow Paige and Armbro Flight with All Aflame. Dancer and Haughton now accept him as their peer. He used to bet but gave it up. He can drive in any style but prefers to come from off the pace, believing that most horses race more gamely that way. If anyone ever wins 500 races in a year, it will be Filion. Meanwhile, handicappers have in him a most dependable friend.

CHARLEY FITZPATRICK
Born 6/13/26, Worcester, Mass.
Weight: 160
Career earnings: $2,105,267
Career victories: 743

He has never been especially active, has never made a national list of leading dash-winners or money-winners and has had only one really good horse—Speedy Pick. But Charley Fitzpatrick is a good horseman who produces a respectable winning average in most years. Three of his former assistants—Skip Lewis, Lloyd Davis and Bob Parkinson—now have successful public stables of their own. Most fans may be surprised to learn that Fitz has earned more than $2 million in purses. The information should alert them. Any time he turns up behind a sharp horse at a meeting in which he has been batting .150 or better, he can be relied on to leave promptly, find good position and retain some horse for the final stages. When he's right, he can beat anyone.

LUCIEN FONTAINE
Born 4/12/39, Pointe aux Trembles, Que.
Weight: 135
Career earnings: $4,158,797
Career victories: 1,209

After breaking in under Keith Waples in Canada, Loosh immigrated and became the protégé of Clint Hodgins, for whom he drove

Bye Bye Byrd, Elaine Rodney and other good ones. Primarily a catch-driver, Fontaine has some solid raceway stock in association with Steve Demas, the trainer. Has begun to try his hand on the Grand Circuit and, of course, does not overlook the New York Sire Stakes, for which he invariably has a couple of good candidates. Beginning in 1965, the youngster has been a regular among the continent's top dash-winners and money-winners. Has been driving champion at Yonkers, Monticello and Richelieu, and always is close to the top of the list at the two big New York raceways. Inclined to move early —a sound tactic at half-milers—Fontaine has a good pair of hands and a splendid sense of pace. During hot streaks, wins an enormous percentage of his starts—as in 1963 at Monticello, when he won 11 of his first 13. Usually ends the year at 15 percent or better.

WILLIAM "BUDDY" GILMOUR
Born 7/23/32, Lucan, Ont.
Weight: 145
Career earnings: $3,716,345
Career victories: 2,122

While still in his mid-twenties, this astute tactician established himself as a catch-driver with few peers, a perennial contender for national purse-winning and dash-winning honors, and a top man on the Yonkers-Roosevelt wheel. In 1967, New York suspended him after allegations that he had fallen into bad company. His fellow horsemen seemed to think that Gilmour may have made a few mistakes, but most continued to believe in the competitive pride and talent that had made him great. In 1969, largely as a result of urgings by horsemen, Gilmour was permitted to resume action at Brandywine Raceway. There and at Liberty Bell and in New England, he promptly demonstrated that he had not lost his driving touch. Wins a high percentage of his starts and gets the best from any kind of horse.

LEVI HARNER
Born 5/10/09, Keelersville, Pa.
Weight: 160
Career earnings: $2,737,898
Career victories: 2,116

Son of a fairgrounds sulky racer and father of Eldon Harner, who will pass the $2-million mark soon, Levi is one of the winningest drivers of all time. In a typical year, captures more than 20 percent of his races. Since 1949, has never had a UDR below .300, and has surpassed .400 several times. Does most of his racing in upstate New York. He and Eldon dominate the scene at Batavia and Buffalo, and grab some of that sire-stakes money, too. His best horse probably was Tar Boy, with which he won the 1960 International Encore in 1:59:1. As his extraordinary winning averages imply, he makes no mistakes in the sulky. Is a remarkable tactician with a sixth sense about when to hold the rail and when to take out.

BILLY HAUGHTON
Born 11/2/23, Gloversville, N.Y.
Weight: 150
Career earnings: $14,417,719
Career victories: 3,155

In 1969, Haughton became the first driver in USTA history to win 3,000 races and the first to achieve a career total of $14 million in purse winnings. Among the three leading money-winners every year since 1950, and tops in 12 of those years, Haughton typically wins 20 percent or more of his starts. With strong divisions in action at New York, Philadelphia and on the Grand Circuit, his stable is always there or thereabouts in competition for annual age and gait championships. In 1968, for example, Haughton had Laverne Hanover, the best two-year-old pacer; Rum Customer, the best three-year-old pacer; Flamboyant, the top four-year-old trotter; Carlisle, boss of aged trotters; plus miscellaneous champs and near-champs like Romulus Hanover, Bye and Large, That's Great, Nob Hill, Meadow Paige *et al.*

He has set world records with Quick Chief, Hillsota, Galophone, Faber Hanover, Belle Acton, Charming Barbara, Duke Rodney and Vicar Hanover. Whenever he chooses to remain in one place long enough to compete for the driving championship, he is a good bet to win it. Interestingly enough, he seldom pays as much money for yearlings as other big-timers do. He is notorious for making fortunes with bargain horses. Which proves that he knows a Standardbred when he sees it and knows exactly what to do with it after he gets it. As to driving, everyone agrees that he is as good as they come. With years of activity ahead of him, he can be expected to rewrite the record books time and again.

CLINT HODGINS
Born 6/18/07, Clandeboye, Ont.
Weight: 195
Career earnings: $5,076,928
Career victories: 1,597

Developer of the great mare, Proximity, with whom he set six world records at distances up to two miles, the large Canadian also has trained and driven such champions as Adios Butler, Prince Adios, Bye Bye Byrd and Elaine Rodney. From 1946 through 1963, was on every annual list of leading money-winners. Has been less active at raceways lately, but continues to win on the Grand Circuit. In his prime was considered a peerless developer and driver of stakes horses. Had a brilliant facility for keeping a good animal well within itself throughout a long season, bringing it to victory after victory without exhausting it. His racing tactics were in that same spirit. As if he had measured the distance to the wire, he timed his final sprint to win by inches.

BILL HUDSON
Born 7/14/15, Salisbury, Md.
Weight: 155
Career earnings: $1,991,020
Career victories: 714

A competent journeyman with an up-and-at-'em, pace-setting style, Hudson is well regarded on the Yonkers-Roosevelt wheel, where he has been active since 1951. His stock seldom amounts to much. Except as a catch-driver, he has never been associated with a top-flight horse. His winning average and UDR reflect this difficulty. On the other hand, his career earnings demonstrate that a seasoned professional need not be a star to get along in Fun City. With six or seven horses, each capable of earning around $10,000 a year in overnight events, plus catch-drives, plus occasional sire-stakes jackpots, a solid citizen like Hudson probably earns more at Yonkers-Roosevelt than he would on minor circuits.

DELMER INSKO
Born 7/10/31, Amboy, Minn.
Weight: 122
Career earnings: $8,207,775
Career victories: 2,473

Broke in with his horseman father at midwestern fairs in 1946 and installed himself on the annual list of leading dash-winners in 1957, for keeps. Usually rates among the top five in that department and is no lower on the list of leading money-winners. Since he began driving 1,500 times a year, in 1965, has had difficulty holding a 15-percent winning average, but is so obviously a great driver that handicappers don't fret. Keeps a large string on the Chicago circuit with younger brother Delbie, and another in New York with brother-in-law Arlo Nelson. Commutes between the two cities, but does not neglect the Grand Circuit or the New York Sire Stakes, in both of which his winnings are substantial. In his spare time, accepts catch-drives from outfits large and small.

A genius at finding cover for a horse that needs it and at provoking other drivers into beating themselves, Insko conforms to no driving pattern other than the one best calculated to suit the problems of the horse and the race. Is so adept at giving an animal its maximum chance that handicappers confidently write off any horse that gets another driver after racing poorly for Del. If it were fit, Insko would have moved it ahead a few lengths at some stage of the race.

Has topped the driver standings several times at Yonkers, Sportsman's Park and Maywood. Besides the great Overcall, has had champions like Henry T. Adios, Speedy Rodney. His greatness acknowledged throughout the industry, and his stable growing stronger with each year, Insko is permanently entrenched at the topmost level of big-league harness racing.

JOE MARSH, Jr.
Born 6/20/34, Curtice, O.
Weight: 125
Career earnings: $2,391,663
Career victories: 1,250

Started as a groom for his father in 1952, and began swinging on the big time in 1959, when his .316 UDR was twelfth highest on the continent. Wins at a 20-percent clip, racing about 600 times a year. Has topped the driver standings at Washington Park, Hazel Park, Wolverine and The Meadows, and is a consistent winner at Sportsman's Park and Hollywood. Few drivers in the world are quicker at leaving the gate and establishing themselves in a comfortable position. Also a fine judge of pace whose almost intuitive capacity for making the right move at the right time marks him as one of the very best of the younger drivers.

DELVIN MILLER
Born 7/5/13, Woodland, Cal.
Weight: 160
Career earnings: $4,995,623
Career victories: 1,582

The best horsemen in the business say that Del Miller is the best horseman in the business. Still a great driver, although he goes fewer than 200 competitive trips a year, he scores 20 percent of the time with his Grand Circuit colts and occasionally catch-drives Laverne Hanover (for example) to victory as a favor to his friend and business associate Billy Haughton. One of the nation's top breeders, whose phenomenal success in that phase of the sport began with the immortal Adios, Miller also is a peerless trainer and backstretch troubleshooter. Hundreds of horsemen have sought his counsel in the schooling or shoeing or rigging of horses, have been given it freely and have benefited. Stanley Dancer, with whom he always owns a horse or two, still remembers the encouragement Miller gave him when he was an unknown. Harrison Hoyt, the only amateur driver to win the Hambletonian, recalls how Miller, his rival that day, jollied him out of his prerace anxieties.

The first professional driver to become president of the Grand Circuit, Miller also runs The Meadows and formerly headed the Fox Valley Trotting Club, which conducts race meetings at Sportsman's Park. For a parallel in another sport, imagine someone managing and owning the baseball team, serving as a director of the league, holding the lease on the stadium, pitching 30 victories, hitting 58 home runs and batting .400 every year, instructing and inspiring other players and managers, and doing it all as easily and genially as if all-encompassing excellence were the most natural characteristic of mankind.

Until he cut back on his driving in 1963, Miller annually was at or near the top of the UDR, earnings, dash-winning and Grand Circuit lists. Has driven to 17 world's records and has taken at least 50 horses to their first 2:00 miles—an all-time mark. Has won only one Hambletonian (Lusty Song in 1950) but could have won again in 1953 if he had not insisted that the owners permit his assistant, Harry Harvey, to drive the victorious Helicopter. Has won only one Little Brown Jug (Dudley Hanover, 1950) but could have won with his great Tar Heel in 1951. Instead, he put Del Cameron behind Tar Heel and finished second with his other horse, Solicitor. He knew Tar Heel was the better animal, but felt duty-bound to drive the other, a more difficult animal to handle.

ALAN MYER
Born 6/9/26, Bridgeville, Del.
Weight: 185
Career earnings: $3,612,948
Career victories: 1,626

One of seven driving brothers whose father and grandfather also were in the sport, Myer gets lots of mileage from common livestock. Usually among the top 25 money-winners of the year, he seldom puts together an impressive annual UDR or winning average. His intermittent hot streaks in Philadelphia, New York and other eastern settings entitle him to close, respectful attention, however.

BILLY MYER
Born 5/19/16, Bridgeville, Del.
Weight: 160
Career earnings: $4,596,169
Career victories: 1,488

Long a popular catch-driver in New York, Myer took a great leap forward in 1965 and 1966 as Romeo Hanover's man in the bike. After parting company with Romeo's brain trust, Billy prospered even more, becoming the biggest money-winner (about $300,000) in New York's 1967 Sire Stakes series. Not celebrated for a high winning average, he turns warm for weeks on end, contending for leadership at Yonkers and Roosevelt alike. He is a good post man who not only leaves quickly but holds a horse together extremely well in the later stages. Handicappers should never take him for granted but should keep track of his winning average, giving him extra points when things begin breaking right and the percentage rises.

JOE O'BRIEN
Born 6/25/17, Alberton, P.E.I.
Weight: 140
Career earnings: $8,517,898
Career victories: 2,730

Second to none as a trainer and driver, the uncompromising O'Brien races from May through December and then withdraws to his California farm, offended by the notion that anyone would race a good horse more than 30 times a year just to pick up extra money. At Chicago and Hollywood, on the Grand Circuit and with occasional forays into New York, he does things exactly his own way. It works. He ends every year among the leaders in everything—purses and dashes won, UDR, Grand Circuit and winning average. Always wins more than 20 percent of his starts. Has taken numerous driving championships and has wòn about 115 races in 2:00 or less—surpassing all other drivers.

Among his great horses: Armbro Flight, Sunbelle, Shadow Wave, Fresh Yankee, Scott Frost, Governor Armbro, Adios Express, Sunnie Tar. His driving style is old-fashioned. Likes to sit under cover in that six hole on the rail until the stretch, and then come blasting home. This occasionally may cost him a race at a half-mile track, but not often. He has won every major event at Yonkers and Roosevelt. They call him "The Ice Man." I call him the handicapper's benefactor.

GEORGE PHALEN
Born 7/16/22, Plaistow, N.H.
Weight: 135
Career earnings: $3,779,355
Career victories: 1,308

This catch-driving specialist trains a modest string in New York but cashes most of his checks with other people's horses. Respected by horsemen and fans, he finds his quiet way onto the national list of leading money-winners in most years. Learned the trade from his late father, James, a prominent horseman in New England. George was co-owner of Adios Butler at the start of that champion's career, but unloaded his share after disagreements with his partner. His best trotter was Steamin' Demon, with whom he set a couple of world's records. Also had O'Brien Hanover, another world champion. Insiders say he is one of the keenest handlers of trotters in the country. Drives with considerable coolness, adapting his tactics to the special circumstances of the race and, above all, the widely varying talents of the inferior horses with which he sometimes gets stuck.

SANDERS RUSSELL
Born 4/26/00, Stevenson, Ala.
Weight: 137
Career earnings: $2,469,595
Career victories: 1,175

The headquarters of Sanders Russell's public stable are on an Alabama farm, exactly where his father established the business in

1903. The best Russell Standardbred of recent years has been A. C.'s Viking, winner of the 1962 Hambletonian and numerous other important stakes. He also brought out Fresh Yankee, Gratis Hanover and Junior Counsel—each a champion. Concentrating on Grand Circuit competition and rarely driving more than 300 times a year, even when much younger than he now is, Russell has long been acclaimed as a developer of colts. His best year was 1962, when he won one-third of his starts and more than $235,000 in prize money. In 1968, he started only 78 times, but won 21 races and $173,461. Insiders say that if he seems particularly alert in the sulky before the race, he has a live horse in front of him. He drives a trotter as well as anyone can, taking advantage of the slightest mistake by an opponent.

FRANK SAFFORD
Born 9/24/09, Keene, N.H.
Weight: 200
Career earnings: $2,517,095
Career victories: 1,629

He doesn't drive anymore, simply because he doesn't feel like it. Which is too bad because he was as good as they come. I include him here because he continues as a trainer around Philadelphia. Sends out fit horses with winning drivers.

GEORGE SHOLTY
Born 11/2/32, Logansport, Ind.
Weight: 117
Career earnings: $7,136,832
Career victories: 1,768

A consistent leader on the Grand Circuit and on the annual lists of money-winners and dash-winners, this energetic little man is in a slump when his winning average falls below 20. Has won driving championships at Hollywood, Yonkers, Roosevelt, Hazel Park, Wolverine, Northfield and Pompano. A great catch-driver, a great trainer, a great comfort to the beleaguered handicapping fan, he broke into the game under an uncle, and then worked for Tom Winn and Gene Sears. His own public stable includes larger numbers of high-grade animals every season, and he continues to cash in as a catch-driver, particularly with the horses of Billy Haughton. Among George's better stock have been Romeo Hanover, Royal Rick, Coffee Break, Bengazi Hanover, Truluck, Hammerin Hank, Shipshape Lobell. His fellow drivers rate him second to none as a tactician and as a marvel with fainthearted animals.

BILLY SHUTER
Born 8/7/28, Osgood, Ind.
Weight: 160
Career earnings: $2,104,602
Career victories. 974

Catch-driver deluxe, Billy probably has won more big Chicago purses in that role than any other navigator in the business. His admirers wish he would compete more frequently than he does, believing that he has the ability to go as far as he chooses. He lately has chosen to race not more than 350 times a year. His UDR always exceeds .300 and his typical winning percentage is above 20. Has won driving titles at Sportsman's Park (3), Maywood (2) and Lebanon. An aggressive driver with a great sense of pace, he is a smart opportunist who times his moves superbly. Gets extra yardage by whipping left-handed, which surprises horses. Handled the famous pacing brothers Stephen Smith and Irwin Paul. Also Song Cycle, Speedy Rodney, Princess Maud, Hi Lo's Solar.

JOHN SIMPSON, Sr.
Born 12/26/19, Chester, N.C.
Weight: 165
Career earnings: $4,716,326
Career victories: 1,465

Now that he is president and general manager of Hanover Shoe Farms, the gifted Simpson has entrusted the outfit's aristocratic racing stable to his son, Johnny, Jr., the family's third generation in the sport. Johnny, Sr., drives only rarely. In 1968, for example, he started 20 times, winning 11 and depositing checks for slightly less than $60,000. Until 1965, this great trainer-driver was always among the leaders in purse-earnings, and a big winner on the Grand Circuit. When the spirit moved him, he'd take a string to raceways and win driving championships, as he did at Roosevelt twice. An acknowledged master at bringing a horse to hand for the big races, he won the Hambletonian with Hickory Smoke and Ayres, the Jug with Noble Adios, Torpid and Bullet Hanover. Has set many world's records while going about 90 trips in 2:00 or better. His son, who broke in at 18 in 1961, has been carrying on with Simpsonian efficiency, winning more than 20 percent of his races.

T. WAYNE "CURLY" SMART
Born 8/29/04, Ostrander, O.
Weight: 175
Career earnings: $2,699,523
Career victories: 1,837

He used to win New York driving championships and occupy high places on all the national lists, although he seldom made more than 250 starts a year and was not fond of the raceway grind. He finally withdrew to Ohio where, as track superintendent of the Delaware Fair, site of the Little Brown Jug, he provided one of the fastest half-mile ovals in the world. Meanwhile, he trained and drove a few head and continued to elicit awe from other horsemen, all of whom agree that nobody has ever been Curly's superior in the sulky. Since 1948, his UDR has fallen below .400 only twice. He usually wins about 35 percent of his annual starts. At this writing he has disbanded his Ohio stable and has become consultant to Pompano Park, where he undoubtedly will show the best horsemen in the business a thing or two whenever he decides to take the reins. An immortal.

DICK THOMAS
Born 8/15/21, Omaha, Nebr.
Weight: 165
Career earnings: $2,317,998
Career victories: 724

Al Thomas was a famous horseman. His son Henry was among the greatest trainer-drivers of all. When Henry was training for Hanover Shoe back in the thirties, his own son, Dick, broke in around the barns. Years later, father and son tied for a Roosevelt Raceway driving championship. In recent seasons, Dick has been noted more as a developer and conditioner of high-class colts than as a raceway performer. Usually registers an indifferent UDR, is by no means a cinch to win 15 percent of his starts, but makes many a trip to the bank, thanks to his adeptness with good horses such as Fulla Napoleon and Ember Hanover, plus winners of New York Sire Stakes events.

EDDIE WHEELER
Born 1/24/32, Brooklyn, N.Y.
Weight: 130
Career earnings: $2,830,549
Career victories: 1,089

The aggressive little New Yorker is a substantial factor on the California and Liberty Bell–Brandywine circuits, winning 15 percent of his annual starts and showing a nice touch with trotters. Made the list of top money-winners for the first time in 1958, and has repeated in six subsequent years. Has won driving titles at Santa Anita, Hollywood and Brandywine. His best horses have been Duke Rodney, Big John, Gold Worthy and Kerry Pride.

JOHN "TIC" WILCUTTS
Born 11/23/19, Magnolia, Del.
Weight: 120
Career earnings: $2,901,653
Career victories: 1,258

Starting as an owner-trainer-driver in 1951, the enormously talented Wilcutts began leading the driver lists at Baltimore and Laurel in 1956. Became a national figure in 1961, when only two drivers won more races. His .355 UDR was eighth in the standings, and he rated among the top 13 in money won. Out with injuries in 1962, he resumed his victorious ways during the following year and now is entrenched among the Brandywine-Liberty Bell leaders. A resourceful catch-driver with an alert, brainy style, he is an asset to any kind of Standardbred. Can be depended on to win about 20 percent of his annual starts.

BOB WILLIAMS
Born 1/14/36, Grand Rapids, Mich.
Weight: 140
Career earnings: $2,939,834
Career victories: 1,029

Having followed brother Jack and their father into the business in 1954, this gifted youngster arrived at the top with a flourish in 1963, when he won more than 20 percent of his starts and was leading driver at Washington Park and Sportsman's Park. He now is among the biggest money-winners every year, while maintaining his high winning average. Misled by his masterfully patient tactics at one-mile and ⅝-mile tracks, some critics assumed that he would be out of his element at a half-miler. He proved otherwise when Jim Hackett, winner of the 1967 Little Brown Jug, entrusted Best Of All to him. All he did with the horse was win the National Pacing Derby and the Realization at Roosevelt Raceway. Equally adept with trottters, he once catch-drove Earl Laird to a world record.

On Their Way

At this writing, numerous drivers are approaching the $2-million mark. We have already listed the ones whose high winning percentages should commend them to the attention of handicappers. Several deserve additional notice, as do a few with low percentages but high ability. Their colleagues in the sport regard them as top professionals. Among them are:

DOUG ACKERMAN: A sound trainer and a good driving tactician who spends most of his time in California and Michigan.

JACK BAILEY: A good catch-driver who is a perennial sensation in upstate New York and has shown that he can win his share in Chicago.

GERRY BOOKMYER: His phenomenal catch-driving record around Windsor and Cleveland puts him on the national dash-winning and UDR lists. They say he can make it at the major raceways if he chooses.

WARREN CAMERON: Del's son has been driving champ at Brandywine, and in 1968 was the preferred catch-driver for Stanley Dancer's Hollywood division.

LEROY COPELAND: Brilliant young trainer-driver whose strong divisions of the Abraham Schultz stable are good for $250,000 a year at eastern raceways.

VERN CRANK: He and brother Tom are always factors in Pennsylvania, Maryland and Delaware.

BUCKY DAY: Biggest winner in New England, this popular catch-driver handles some woeful stock, which keeps his average down.

RON FEAGAN: Young Canadian is always in the running for national honors. Has shown in his forays in the United States that he can drive with anyone.

HENRI FILION: Unbelievable though it may seem, many horsemen think that Henri and kid brother Yves are potentially as good as the fantastic Herve.

DR. JOHN S. FINDLEY: The Canadian veterinarian is one of his country's foremost breeders, trainers and drivers. Seldom invades the United States, but wins more than 20 percent of the time against formidable opposition at home.

CLINT GALBRAITH: Canadian youngster is a consistent winner in upstate New York, takes back for nobody on his infrequent visits to Yonkers-Roosevelt, and is a factor in the New York Sire Stakes series.

GLEN GARNSEY: Head trainer-driver for the powerful Castleton Farm, where he is assisted by the brilliant Dick Baker, the son of 1,000-dash-winner Garland Garnsey is a smooth, strong reinsman who can win in any company.

ELDON HARNER: The great Levi's son will be heading toward his third million any day now. Spends most of his time in upper New York, with occasional excursions on the Grand Circuit. A top man.

GLEN KIDWELL: This fierce competitor is hard on his horses and on himself. Gives everything in every race and is invariably a force in the Chicago area.

GILLES LACHANCE: One of Canada's most frequent winners has begun to race in the eastern United States, where his enterprising, astute performances and good winning average mark him as a tremendous prospect.

GERRY BOOKMYER   BUCKY DAY   GLEN GARNSEY

JIM LARENTE: Former second trainer and regular driver for the powerful stable of Frank Safford, the nimble Canadian continues as a force on the Brandywine-Liberty Bell wheel. A superb catch-driver.

WALLY McILMURRAY: A regular in Michigan and California, this respected catch-driver can be depended on for a good annual average.

BRUCE NICKELLS: The former Del Cameron assistant is an aggressive driver who wins a high percentage of his starts and ranks among the top horsemen on the Chicago wheel.

DWAYNE PLETCHER: Another Chicago leader, this superior trainer usually has excellent stock. Wins enough races to take local driving championships, and scores a high average while doing it.

GENE RIEGLE: Second only to Curly Smart in the estimation of Ohio racegoers, this calm, resourceful driver sometimes wins 33 percent of his annual starts, and rarely falls below 20 percent. Has won driving titles in Chicago, and usually has something to offer in Grand Circuit competition.

ERVIN SAMPLES: Drove his first race at 41, in 1951, and has been recognized as an elderly prodigy ever since. Shuttles between Ohio and Chicago, winning better than one race in every five attempts. Remains formidable at any kind of raceway. His good hands and keen mentality would have made him an all-time great if he had started earlier.

JIM TALLMAN: The Pennsylvania youngster is one of the best prospects in New York racing. Manages to win about 15 percent of the time against the best in the business. With experience, his aggressive, opportunistic style may boost him into the headlines.

TED TAYLOR: A good man leaving the gate, and quick to exploit tactical advantages during a race, this Ohioan rates among the most dependable drivers on the Michigan circuit. Also does well at Pompano Park, where the opposition includes some of the foremost trainer-drivers in the game.

KEN VANDER SCHAAF: This kid has yet to win his first million, but has established himself as a star. Works wonders with cheap claimers in the Chicago area. One of the most astute trainers around, he rehabilitates horses by turning them loose on his farm. They reward him by winning at a phenomenal rate. His UDR is always at or near the top of the national list. It is not unusual for him to win 25 percent of his annual starts—sometimes hitting with as many as 4 out of 10 at a particular meeting.

KEITH WAPLES: Canada is cluttered with first-rate drivers, of whom at least six have been called the nation's best. Waples is one of them,

ERVIN SAMPLES   **KEN VANDER SCHAAF**

contending for the Canadian leadership in races won and money earned
—and winning either or both on occasion. When he travels south of
the border, he brings a really good horse with him, and never goes
home empty-handed. A poised, quick, thoroughly polished driver.

ROGER WHITE: Another of Canada's best, he invariably records a high
winning average when he races in the United States. Does nicely on
the Grand Circuit, too.

TOM WILBURN: The Mississippi breeder-owner-trainer-driver is a consistent winner in California and Pennsylvania, and has won driving
championships in Chicago. Can be depended on to take upward of 20
percent of his drives. Is one of the quickest of the good drivers, not
only reacting to situations but anticipating them.

12

The Warm-ups

THE PAPER WORK IS FINISHED. Having identified the top contenders, the player has made a tentative selection in every apparently beatable race. Comes now the final phase of handicapping. Before risking transactions with mutuel clerks, the player watches the horses warm up.

With special attention to his own choices, he checks the appearance and behavior of the animals during the two workouts (sometimes one, occasionally three), which they take at intervals of about forty-five minutes. He watches them jog the wrong way of the track before and after those warm-ups. He watches them in the post parade before the race itself. If still in doubt, he watches them score (sprint past the finish line) before the starter calls them to the mobile gate.

If he keeps his mind on his business, the player makes one or more of the following discoveries about each field of horses:

1. The top contender looks like an abject loser.

2. The top contender looks neither better nor worse than its rivals.

3. The top contender looks every inch a winner by comparison with the other horses in its race.

4. A green horse, or one that has been absent for weeks, or one with poor recent races, looks more like a winner than any of the other entrants in its race.

The observations described in items 1 and 4 require the player to revise his plans. In the first example, he turns his attention to his second choice in the race, unless, as a regular racegoer, he knows that the other animal always looks miserable before winning—a rare phenomenon, but not unheard of. In the fourth example, the player either passes the race entirely or checks the odds to see whether he should bet the top contender *and* the surprisingly fit-looking sleeper.

As often as not, the supposed noncontender is entered in a race previously written off as unplayable. Chances are that a more adventurous type of handicapper now changes his mind about the race and bets on the horse that caught his eye.

It can be seen that observation of the warm-ups enables a player to avoid losers and catch winners. This establishes warm-ups as important. But they are not nearly as important as the information contained in the past-performance records. A fan who knows his way through the records can register long-term profits without so much as looking at a warm-up. If he becomes interested in that final phase of handicapping, he probably can learn enough about it to spare himself one loser per week. And he may catch one winning sleeper every two or three weeks. These extra profits are not to be disdained, but they are unlikely to provide down payments for yachts.

Mountains of drivel have been published about warm-ups. Ill-informed gamblers have lost substantial fortunes by underestimating the significance of the program record and assuming that warm-ups were a source of miracles. I have seen such persons during and after their disasters. It is not a pleasant sight.

Let us agree, then, that a conscientious handicapper watches the warm-ups and helps himself by doing it. And that he helps himself most when he uses those prerace exercises as an opportunity to check on the appearance and deportment of his top choices, betting only on such of them as seem ready to race.

Looking 'Em Over

With exceptions too rare to alter the principle, a good horse looks the part. His stride is firmly powerful, his eye boldly alert, his coat lustrous with the glow of health. Cheap horses, being less sound, seldom present so grand an appearance. Hence the fan should expect less of them. The top contender in a cheap race need not look like Bret Hanover to justify a bet. He merely should look ready to race.

Here are the major checkpoints:

MANNERS. Most Standardbreds are docile, intensively schooled creatures that know what is expected of them and are willing to produce as much of it as they can. Beware of the fractious horse that fights the bit, flails its tail, flicks its ears, tosses its head, refuses to stay on gait and otherwise challenges its driver. If it is a green animal and/or one with a previous record as a breaker, it probably has not yet learned its trade. Perhaps it is a high-strung type, frightened by the sights, sounds and tensions of the raceway. Unless it calms down thoroughly before the end of its first workout, behaves perfectly during its next, and checks out well on all other points, it is a risky bet.

A seasoned animal that behaves badly and does not warm quickly to the spirit of the occasion has very likely gone sour. Sore, ailing or just plain unstrung by overwork, it communicates reluctance in the only language it has.

EYE. When it feels well, the Standardbred is interested in its surroundings. Its bright, dark eyes seem alert and ready for challenge. It scans the scene like radar. An ailing, unwilling or unready horse has a grim, uncomfortable, distracted—even tortured—look about the eye. In other cases, the eyes seem almost opaque, as if the animal had turned them off. When this unpromising sign combines with others and persists through the second workout or the post parade, it is time to revamp the handicapping figures.

COAT. If the horse is sound, fit, and well cared-for, its coat looks burnished, like fine furniture. In cheaper fields, with horses that are merely racing sound, comparatively dull coats are the rule and should not be regarded as deficits. On the other hand, when a horse turns up with a healthy coat in a race of that kind and happens also to be the top contender, its prospects improve. Notice how often the green three-year-old from the good barn has the only really good-looking coat in the whole field of C-3 animals, or nonwinners of two races, or the like.

Excessive, foaming sweat—washiness—often accompanies nervousness, pain and other causes of unreadiness. If the horse is not particularly fractious but simply looks uncomfortable and is washy besides, see how it looks at the beginning of its next warm-up. If necessary, check its appearance during the post parade. Obviously, horses sweat profusely while jogging back to the paddock after warming up. What counts is the amount of foam discernible on the flanks and between the rear legs before the actual warm-up begins. On a hot, humid night, all the horses may seem washy. On other nights, the washy ones are conspicuous. If they get over it before the race, no harm. Otherwise, be careful.

HEAD AND EARS. An eager Standardbred may move its head jauntily from side to side, leaning on the bit, asking to go faster than the driver wants. An unruly one shakes its head and shows other signs of distress. An ouchy one tends to turn its head toward the site of pain, sometimes with a bobbing motion on that side. Occasionally, the inclination of the head to one side means that the horse is having trouble striding on the other side and is trying its best to extend the leg farther. The strenuous warm-ups give an animal ample opportunity to work out the suspected soreness. If it still seems sore during its final prerace trip, and displays other unpromising signs, save your money.

When working or racing under pressure, a fit horse pricks its ears. Drooping ears signify exhaustion, lack of interest, defeat. Flicking ears are a sign of impatience and, with a swishing tail, are characteristic of unruly animals.

GAIT. A keyed-up horse can be forgiven a lapse from stride during the early stages of its first warm-up. But if the problem persists, it takes a brave sport to bet on the animal. Even while remaining flat on gait, a horse sometimes reveals problems by striding short on one side or another, as if favoring a foot or knee. Again, the horse may warm out of this. Be especially watchful as it takes the turns.

TACK. The leather should be clean. If it is not, somebody in the horse's entourage either does not know his business or does not care. Poorly cared-for horses are more than likely to be poorly trained, poorly conditioned and poorly driven.

DRIVER. The racing driver does not always take the horse on its warm-up trips. Whoever does should seem to have the animal under a stout hold to keep it from wasting its pent-up energy before the race. But if the driver has to lean straight back to restrain a pulling animal, and if this accompanies other forms of struggle and unruliness, the player should be wary. Pullers are not attractive bets.

At good raceways, the trainer or the veterinarian or the presiding judge declares a noticeably unfit horse out of its race before anyone can lose money on it. At all raceways, the tendency is to let the horse race if it seems even a bit ready. The player should be on his guard, but should not attempt to practice veterinary medicine from the grandstand. He seldom should amend his handicapping figures unless (a) he spots more than one bad sign during the warm-ups and (b) the combination of problems seems to persist. If the approach of post time finds him in doubt as to the significance of what he has seen, his best course is to pass the race entirely. After missing a few winners and more than a few losers that way, he will become sufficiently familiar with Standardbred appearance and behavior to make firmer decisions.

Clocking the Warm-ups

The horse shows unexpected signs of life during the warm-ups. The driver sends one of his cronies out of the paddock to bet. Some mutuel clerks make a small industry of such occurrences, retailing the information that So-and-so, who does the betting for Such-and-such Stable, has been shoving it in with both hands on the horse. Players haunt the windows in hope of scrounging inside tips of that kind. Nobody gets rich but the excitement resounds in the night.

How does the horse show the unexpected signs of life? By its appearance and deportment in the paddock and on the track. By working as rapidly as usual but with less effort and no urging. Or by working much more rapidly than usual in response to no more than the usual urging. And by returning to the paddock less winded than usual. And by cooling out more rapidly and being more eager for the next trip.

Hoping to share in the spoils when one horse perks up and another turns languid, certain hard-working handicappers have equipped themselves with stopwatches. Some hang eight or nine watches on a portable board—one watch for each horse in the race. They also keep voluminous notes on the fractional and final times in which each horse customarily warms up. If a horse has been going his final preparatory mile in 2:15 with the final quarter in :32, and now goes in 2:11 with the final quarter in :31, the clocker's nose twitches. As soon as he or his betting runner has bought the tickets, the word gets out and the odds begin to plummet.

It's enough to drive a betting horseman cuckoo. To promote maximum odds on their good things, betting horsemen take pains to foil the clockers. They take the horse for a fast trip in the afternoon and merely let it amble during the prerace exercises. If that doesn't suit the animal, they mix up the fractions—asking for speed during the second and third eighths of a mile but not in the first or fourth, and certainly not in the final quarter, to which clockers are so attentive.

Not many horsemen are so preoccupied with mutuel prices. Most could not care less than they do about the activities of clockers. They merely go about their business. In the normal course of events, they vary the warm-up routines sufficiently to upend the clocker's calculations. For example, a horse has been doing poorly in its races. The trainer decides to work it faster during tonight's warm-ups. The experiment fails, and the clocker who noticed the extra speed loses his shirt. Contrarily, a trainer may decide to work the horse more slowly than usual. And the experiment may enable the horse to race more swiftly than usual, again leaving the clocker with the wrong tickets.

Stanley Dancer seldom works a horse rapidly before its race. His warm-up times are so slow that they reveal nothing about the animal's fitness. Other drivers have adopted the same approach, having begun to concede that raceway horses work hard enough in their weekly competition and suffer when overworked betweentimes.

Another deterrent to profitable clocking of warm-ups is that the race driver sometimes takes the bike in one or both of the workouts, and sometimes does not. The trainer or assistant who handles the chores has his own influence on fractional and final warm-up times. Additionally, a switch in drivers may mean an entirely new approach to the horse's warm-ups. But one cannot tell in advance whether the particular driver will choose to work the particular horse swiftly or slowly. Experimental trial and error are fundamental to horsemanship.

The main rewards to clockers in return for their all-consuming efforts are the payoffs that befall them when some cheap old horse suddenly takes leave of its arthritic discomfort and proves it with an uncommonly swift, easy workout. If the trip was genuinely easy and did not gut the animal, it usually wins. Sometimes at a long price.

Such things occur perhaps once in two weeks. To recognize the opportunity and turn it to his own advantage, the clocker must be on the scene nightly, making laboriously detailed notes about every horse and every driver in every race, plus noting the effects of weather and footing. And operating stopwatches. And conferring with his partners, who keep charts of the actual races.

I have no doubt that some of these betting syndicates catch more winners than you or I can. But what a price to pay!

13

Handicapping Summarized

THE TIME HAS COME TO MOBILIZE the handicapping principles and procedures set forth in earlier chapters. We then shall be ready for a comprehensive demonstration in which we apply the techniques to programs at five major raceways.

As experienced racegoers may have noticed, and as others should be made aware, this book's approach to Standardbred handicapping is unconventional. I am convinced that traditional methods of making raceway selections are obsolete. Harness racing itself has changed radically. The handicapping ideas presented here are attuned to these changes, as well as to certain fundamental characteristics of the sport which, in my opinion, have not been properly analyzed in the past.

Our approach is unconventional in the following respects:

1. *It emphasizes current condition.*

Notwithstanding the remarkable steadiness and consistency of many Standardbreds, their physical condition fluctuates sufficiently to affect the outcome of all races. Recognition of improving or diminishing fitness is basic therefore to raceway handicapping. The prior achievements of the horse are secondary to its present class and form.

2. *It emphasizes pace, but without regard to the supposed racing styles of the animals.*

Experience shows that a good driver usually is able to modify the presumed style of a horse to suit the particular circumstances of the race. Even when this is not possible—as in the case of a rank "puller" —the animal's chances can be estimated by the kind of pace analysis recommended in these pages.

3. *It emphasizes the role of the driver.*

For excellent reasons, experts long have deplored the tendency of some fans to bet on drivers rather than on horses. The viewpoint of this book is that the best driver does not always need the best horse, and that good handicapping evaluates horse and driver as what they are—a team.

4. *It emphasizes the relationship of class and time.*

Although a good horse may defeat an inferior one in slower time than the lesser animal registers when beating its own kind, Standardbreds of such widely contrasting quality seldom engage each other in raceway competition. Raceway horses move up and down in class, but usually in small steps. Where the class difference between tonight's race and last week's is obscure, time analysis often provides dependable answers.

5. *It assumes that few fans attend the races nightly.*

Most bettors depend entirely on information contained in the past-performance records. Although nightly observation and the compilation of personal notes are immensely useful, the printed record offers enough information for profitable play.

To understand the bases of this approach, and to appreciate that harness racing is developing in such directions as to make the approach even more valid in the future, it is necessary to read the preceding chapters.

Here is a review of handicapping principles:

THE PLAYABLE RACE: A race is most suitable for play if all starters have performed recently at the present raceway or on the present circuit.

A race is less suitable for play if the current fitness or class of any starter is obscure. If one of the entrants has an impressive record but has been on the sidelines for a month or more, or has just arrived from another circuit with which the handicapper is not familiar, prudence suggests that the race be avoided. On the other hand, if the absentee or shipper has a poor record, one can count it a loser and proceed with the handicapping.

A race is unsuitable for play if the best horse has a tendency to break stride, or if other breakers in the field threaten to cause traffic problems.

A race is seldom suitable for play unless the racing strip is pronounced "fast" or "good" and the horses' recent records include representative performances on dry tracks. All contenders should be handicapped in terms of recent races on similar footing—either fast or good. It is as impractical to compare races on good tracks with races on fast tracks as to compare races on wet tracks with races on dry tracks.

IDENTIFYING THE CONTENDERS: If a horse seems fit (see pp. 213–230) and appears to enjoy a marked advantage in class (see pp. 181–212), it is an automatic play.

If a horse's latest outing was a qualifying race at the present track and it won in better time than its opponents have been achieving in their good recent races, it is an automatic play.

When a high-class three-year-old from a good barn faces cheap older stock, it is an automatic play—provided that it has a top driver.

In other races, the likely contenders are selected entirely on the basis of fitness displayed in recent races (see 213–230). Chronic losers and habitual breakers are never regarded as fit.

If a horse has been idle for more than two weeks and the rest of the field has been active during that period, the absentee usually is eliminated (see p. 215).

A horse is a contender if it raced vigorously in its latest start. The parked-out symbol denotes vigor. So does a gain of ground in the stretch after an earlier move or after setting or overcoming a fast early pace.

A horse that lost ground in the stretch without making a substantial earlier move is eliminated as unfit.

A horse that finished close to the winner and/or in good time without making any moves is eliminated as unfit, having been pulled along by faster horses. However, if the handicapper is doubtful on this score, he checks the horse's previous race and uses it for handicapping purposes if it contains signs of fitness. As a matter of routine, it usually is wise to toss out the latest race and use the previous race of any horse that finished third or better, or that finished within three lengths of the winner in its latest—even if it seemed to do little else.

If the latest race was excusably poor, use the previous race. Excuses include wet footing, an impossibly high class of competition, interference or accident, a poor driver or a poor post position combined with an unfavorable early pace (see pp. 216–217).

If the next-to-latest race proves unsuitable for handicapping, use the race immediately preceding. But no race that took place more than a month ago is relevant.

PACE: Among the fit horses that qualify as likely contenders, the best prospect is the animal able to finish in the fastest time after setting or overcoming the fastest early pace. All the fractional times of the horse's key race are pertinent. However, excellent results are attainable by evaluating the official half-mile time of the key race, plus the final time of the horse. In every case, "key race" refers to the recent race that qualified the horse as a contender.

CLASS: The horse deserves extra credit if its key race was in better company than it faces tonight. During the spring and early summer, an improving three-year-old can be granted ability to compete with better horses than it defeated in its last performance. All other horses moving up in class need superior pace figures or other advantages before being conceded the chance to do as well in the higher class as in their key races.

POST POSITION: The handicapper should estimate the effect of post position on the horse's performance in its key race, as well as the probable effect of tonight's post position (see pp. 236–237).

DRIVER: By consistently winning 15 percent or more of their annual starts, certain drivers have established their dependability (see pp. 246–249). During intermittent hot streaks which may endure for an entire meeting or an entire racing season, other drivers record winning percentages of 15 or higher, qualifying as dependable so long as they maintain the high averages. If the fit horse with the most impressive key race has a dependable driver and suffers no serious disadvantages of class or post position, it is a good bet.

CLOSE DECISIONS: If no horse stands out after the kinds of analyses suggested above, contenders may be differentiated from each other by giving credit to a horse whose key performance included an impressive gain of ground in the stretch, and/or a quarter-mile or more of racing on the outside.

A horse that lost its key race but performed well and was also the betting favorite is often an excellent prospect.

If one or more of the top contenders has been evaluated in terms of its next-to-last or some other performance prior to its latest, see whether it has faced any of the other contenders in a subsequent race. If so, give extra credit to the contender that raced most vigorously on that occasion.

Although the foregoing principles are few in number and easy to understand, difficulties arise when the player attempts to weigh one factor against another. I therefore recommend that readers experiment with the numerical rating method which I have mentioned at intervals throughout this book. The method does not replace handicapping judgment, but assists it, eliminating the usual confusions and producing firm figures on which the player can base his decisions.

The method is easiest, quickest and most effective when the handicapper takes a moment to draw a simple chart, as follows:

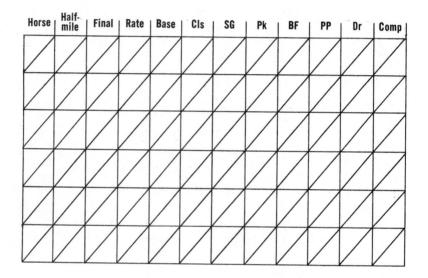

Horse	Half-mile	Final	Rate	Base	Cls	SG	Pk	BF	PP	Dr	Comp

Having found the fit contenders in a playable race, the handicapper lists their names in the first column.

Examining the past-performance line of each contender's key race —the race that qualified it as a contender—the handicapper writes the official half-mile time of the race in the top half of the divided box under the "Half-mile" heading. The horse's own final time in that key race is written in the top half of the adjoining box, under the "Final" heading. The lower half of each box is for the numerical rating assigned to each time notation.

Ratings may be computed by using the tabulation on page 179. Persons willing to do simple subtraction will find an alternative pace-rating method more convenient. As described on page 178, this other method eliminates the necessity of referring to a printed tabulation.

For example:

Half-mile	Final

1:01:2 / 19	2:03 / 17
1:01:4 / 17	2:02:3 / 19
1:02:1 / 15	2:03:4 / 13
1:01:1 / 20	2:02:2 / 20

Note that the *half-mile time* of the top horse, 1:01:2, earns a rating of 19, being one tick slower than 1:01:1, which earns a rating of 20 as the best half-mile time on the list. By the same procedure, the *final time* of the third horse on the list, 2:03:4, earns a rating of 13, being 1$\frac{2}{5}$ seconds slower than 2:02:2, the best final time on the list.

The basic pace ratings are computed by adding the ratings in the first two boxes. Hence, the top horse's basic rating is 36, identical with that of the second horse. The third horse's rating is 28. The bottom horse's rating is 40. The figures are written in the adjoining box.

If a horse's key race was in a class higher than that of tonight's race, add 5 points to the basic rating. If the key race was in a lower class, deduct 5 points. For example:

Base	Cls
36	36
36	36
28	33
40	35

Notice that the first two horses will compete tonight in the same class of race as in their recent key efforts. The bottom horse, which had the highest pace rating, no longer is the leading contender, a rise in class have reduced his rating. The third horse, dropping in class, has improved his rating.

In the column headed "SG," the handicapper should add a point for every length gained in the stretch of the key race. Count ½ length as a full length. Thus, a horse that trailed by 1½ lengths at the stretch call but won its race by 1½ lengths would be credited with a gain of 4 lengths, worth 4 points. See page 220 for the correct way to adjust the rating of a horse that led at both the stretch call and the finish.

The column headed "Pk" is for the credits earned by horses that raced on the outside in their key performances. For every parked-out symbol (°) in the past-performance line, add 5 points. In the rare event that a horse broke stride, yet raced well enough to qualify, add 5 points for the break—which usually will have been caused by interference.

If the horse was a beaten favorite in its key race, add 5 points to the rating and write the new sum in the column headed "BF."

Using the principles and point values explained on pages 231–238, adjust the rating to include the effect of post position on the key performance, plus the probable effect of tonight's post position. The adjusted rating goes in the column headed "PP."

If tonight's driver is a national or local leader (chances are that such a reinsman is listed on pages 250–287, add 10 points and put the new total under "Dr." Do the same if the driver is not a recognized leader but has been winning 15 percent or more of his races during the current season or at the current meeting—provided, of course, that the meeting has been in progress long enough to make such averages meaningful. Fewer than three victories would not be significant.

If tonight's driver is not a top man and does not have a winning percentage of 15 or better, but if the driver in the key race was a national or local leader or had the required average, deduct 10 points.

If the numbers in the "Dr" column reveal that one horse has a rating more than 5 points higher than that of any other contender, the top-rated horse is the play.

Should a margin of 5 or fewer points separate the top-rated contenders, and if the key race of any was a race other than its most recent, check the records to see if the top-rated horses met each other in a subsequent race. If so, award 5 points to the horse that performed most vigorously on that occasion, and put the new total under "Comp."

The horse with the highest final rating is the play, provided that it looks ready during its warm-ups. If not, go to the second horse.

At half-mile tracks, where contention usually is closest and most hectic, consider playing the two contenders with the highest ratings if:

1. The ratings are 3 or fewer points apart, and

2. The animal with the *lower* rating has a leading driver, and

3. The odds on both horses are high enough to return a profit on the double bet, should either horse win.

At other tracks, consider playing the two top contenders if the ratings differ by only 1 point and the horse with the lower rating has a leading driver.

At any track, if your choice is held at odds of 4 to 1 or higher during the final three minutes of wagering, consider betting it to win and place.

14

Liberty Bell, APRIL 12, 1969

THE TRACK IS FAST, the weather mild. The program is ideal for our purposes. It is full of down-to-earth problems that challenge the knowledge and self-discipline of the handicapper. It enables me to demonstrate some of the interesting successes and inevitable failures of the handicapping procedures recommended in this book.

Before tackling the first race, the reader should check the program's list of leading drivers:

Drivers	Starts	1st	2nd	3rd	UDR
RONNIE DANCER	95	23	25	15	.441
JIM LARENTE	145	43	18	15	.400
HERVE FILION	185	38	41	18	.361
VERNON DANCER	72	11	19	13	.360
VERN CRANK	105	20	18	21	.352
J. (Tic) WILCUTTS	67	13	13	7	.337
TOM LEWIS	83	15	17	3	.307
ELTON WHITE	53	7	5	16	.285
C. (Tug) BOYD	87	13	13	11	.275
WALTER MARKS	80	11	11	12	.264
BEN WEBSTER	60	7	7	11	.243
ALAN MYER	92	14	8	10	.237
DEL COTE	60	5	9	10	.222
JOE GREENE	120	13	15	13	.214
H. (Buck) GRAY	64	5	8	11	.205

Quite a roster. Ronnie and Vernon Dancer, Jim Larente, Herve Filion, Vern Crank, Tic Wilcutts, Tom Lewis, Tug Boyd and Alan Myer have all been winning at least 15 percent of their starts at Liberty Bell. When one of them takes the reins behind a contender, the horse deserves extra credit in anybody's handicapping.

Now turn back to page 236. It shows the relative values of the various post positions at this ⅝-mile raceway. The outside berth is no bargain. Neither is the seven slot.

BET THE BIG "E" EIGHTH AND NINTH RACES

LIBERTY BELL PARK

LADIES NIGHT
EVERY TUESDAY

OFFICIAL PAST PERFORMANCE PROGRAM

· THIRTEENTH NIGHT
SATURDAY, APRIL 12, 1969

←MORN. LINE

(1) PACE—1 MILE

Warming-Up Saddle Cloth
YELLOW

PURSE $2,400

ASK FOR HORSE BY PROGRAM NUMBER

First Half Daily Doubl

CLAIMING ALLOWANCE
Five-Year-Olds & Older To Be Claimed For $4,000, Four-Year-Ol
To Be Claimed For $5,000, Three-Year-Olds To Be Claimed F
$6,000. (Fillies & Mares Allowed 20%).

3

1 4800 Red

‡CONESTOGA LADY
br m, 7, by Harry Hill—Susie Song by Gay Song
A & R Stable, Clifton, N.J.
Trainer-B. Wagner
$17,902 — 4, 2:06³ Driver-BART WAGNER, 8-31-16 (135) BLUE-WHITE
1969 4 0 1 1 8.
(⅝)2:06³ 1968 28 2 3 4 4,0

3-25 LB⅝‡ 2900 gd 4800 clm cd mi 31¹1:03⁴1:35²2:07¹ 3 2 2 5 7⁵¼ 7⁷½ 2:08³ 3.50 (B.Wagner) BlytheAds.,MissArch,Bach.Debbi
3- 8 LB⅝‡ 2400 ft 4800 clm cd mi 31 1:03²1:35¹2:07¹ 2 2 4 1 1¹½ 3⁴½ 2:08 *1.20 (B.Wagner) MichelMir,Radnt.Vstr.,Cnstg.Lad
2-27 LB⅝‡ 2200 ft 4800 clm cd mi 30⁴1:04¹1:37¹2:08⁴ 4 3 4 1 1¹½ 2nk 2:08⁴ 5.60 (B.Wagner) Michl.Laird,Cnstg.Lady,MichlMir
1-30 YR‡ 2500 sy C3 cd mi 31²1:04²1:37³2:09³ 7 2° 1° 7° 8¹² 8dis 15.40 (B.Wagner) Evrgrn.Cindy,Printeena,Sentr.Gir
11-29 Fhld‡ 1800 gd 68nw4000 mi 31⁴1:04²1:36¹2:07³ 3 2° 3 6 5³½ 4¹¹½ 2:09⁴ 10.00 (B.Wagner) Arm.Dale,Cap.Daughter,G.Lil.Vol
11-21 Fhld‡ 1600 ft 68nw2000 cd mi 31⁴1:03²1:36¹2:09¹ 6 5° 2° 7 8⁶¼ 8¹⁷¾ 2:12⁴ 4.30 (B.Wagner) Blk.Pride,LaunchC.Lith,D.Parade
11-14 Fhld‡ 1800 ft 68nw2000 cd mi 31 1:04⁴1:36¹2:08¹ 5 x2 1 1 1³ 1¹² 2:08¹ 7.40 (B.Wagner) Cnstg.Lady,Lnch.C.Lith,Joaq.Jea

---

7/2

2 4000 Blue

BEN KWIK
b g, 5, by Flash Adios—Stockley Girl by Ernie Direct
Clifton & Gary C. Gray, Selbyville, Del.
Trainer-H. Gray
$2,824 — 3, 2:07² (⅝) Driver-H. (Buck) GRAY, 11-29-38 (145) TURQUOISE-WHITE-GOLD
(⅝)2:11 1969 4 1 1 1 1,5
1968 3 0 0 0

3-22 LB⅝ 2600 ft 4000 clm cd mi 30⁴1:03⁴1:35¹2:06² 6 6 6 5° 4³¾ 5³½ 2:07 9.30 (H.Gray) MyRight, AdiosBobo, RoyalBonus
3-11 LB⅝ 2400 gd 4000 clm cd mi 31⁴1:04¹1:36¹2:07⁴ 2 4 4 3 3²¾ 2²½ 2:08¹ 20.80 (H.Gray) VickGreer, BenKwik, AdiosBobo
3- 3 LB⅝ 2400 gd 4000 clm cd mi 32¹1:04¹1:37¹2:09¹ 4 6 6 5 4x⁴x3⁷½ 2:10³ 12.40 (H.Gray) WhatNext, Rabbit, BenKwik
2-20 LB⅝ 1500 gd 3000 clm cd mi 31³1:05 1:38 2:11 4 2° 1 1 1½ 1⁹ dh 2:11 5.50 (H.Gray) Don.Cmndr.dhBenKwik,ValleySam
2-14 LB⅝ gd Qua mi 32⁴1:04⁴1:38 2:11² 6 6 6 5 4⁴¼ 4¹½ 2:11³ N.B. (H.Gray) Mr.Hayes,BrightEntrprs.,Aft.Jac
3-27-68 LB⅝ 2900 ft nw4000 cd mi 31²1:04²1:34³2:05⁴ 8 8° 8 8 8²⁰¾8¹⁴¾ 2:08³ 151.10 (H.Gray) BeauButler,BrandyTm.B.,SeaWav
3-19-68 LB⅝ ft Qua mi 32¹1:04¹1:37 2:09¹ 6 6 6 7 7⁹¾ 6⁸ 2:10⁴ N.B. (H.Gray) MightyAndrea, Energy, BigFrost

---

9/2

3 4000 White

MICHEL MIR
b g, 9, by Famous Hanover—Miss Ilo by Chestertown
Peter Tilstra, Milford, N.J.
Trainer-F. Browne
$30,533 — 4, 2:05³ Driver-FRANK BROWNE, 4-29-30 (162) GREEN-WHITE
(⅝)2:07¹ 1969 9 1 0 1 2,1
2:05³ 1968 31 6 4 2 7,8

3-22 LB⅝ 2600 ft 4000 clm cd mi 30⁴1:03⁴1:35¹2:06² 5 5 5 6 7⁶½ 4²½ 2:06⁴ 7.90 (F.Browne) MyRight, AdiosBobo, RoyalBonus
3-14 LB⅝ 2400 ft 4000 clm cd mi 32 1:05²1:37³2:08⁴ 8 1 1 1 2¼ 4⁴¼ 2:09³ 7.30 (F.Browne) RoyalBonus,MissArch,Dolly'sAce
3- 8 LB⅝ 2400 ft 4000 clm cd mi 31 1:03²1:35¹2:07¹ 6 3° 1 2 2¹½ 1¹½ 2:07¹ 3.40 (F.Browne) MichelMir,Radnt.Vstr.,Cnstg.Lad
2-27 LB⅝ 2200 ft 4000 clm cd mi 30⁴1:04¹1:37¹2:08⁴ 1 5 5 5 3³¾ 3¹¾ 2:09 4.60 (F.Browne) Michl.Laird,Cnstg.Lady.Michl.Mi
2-20 LB⅝ 2000 gd 4000 clm cd mi 32 1:04¹1:37⁴2:10³ 4 1° 2 7 7⁶¾ 5⁷½ 2:12 6.10 (F.Browne) Symp.Belle,FrickaMac,RoyalBon
2-14 LB⅝ 5000 gd 68nw12500 Ec mi 31³1:03⁴1:35⁴2:05³ 9 4 4 4 7⁸¼ 7¹⁶½ 2:08⁴ 70.60 (C.LeCause) Release, BeauMartial, Leslie'sAc
2- 4 YR 2750 ft 4500 clm mi 32 1:05²1:37²2:09¹ 4 5 5 6 6⁶ 5⁵ 2:10² 28.80 (F.Browne) Ken.Dares,Spglr.Volo,Mt.Likeabl

---

5

4 4000 Green

CONEEDA
b g, 12, by Convivial—Austin Lass by New Derby
L. Pullen & Lord & Lady Stables, Inc., Short Hills, N.J.
Trainer-L. Pullen
$22,497 — 10, 2:10⁴ (⅝) Qua. Driver-LES PULLEN, 12-8-31 (167) DK. & LT. BROWN-GOLD
(⅝)2:08² 1969 4 2 0 0 2,0
Qua.(⅝)2:10⁴ 1968 24 0 4 4 4,4

3-26 LB⅝ 2300 ft 3000 clm cd mi 31³1:03³1:35⁴2:08² 1 5 6 4° 2⁵½ 1³ 2:08² 3.20 (L.Pullen) Coneeda, SkyClipper, OurJoe
3-10 LB⅝ 1900 ft 3000 clm cd mi 30⁴1:02³1:36¹2:10⁴ 8 2° 4° 6°xx8²²¾8dis 4.30 (L.Pullen) Tiny'sSparkle,SharonLu,Aft.Duke
2-24 LB⅝ 1700 gd 3000 clm cd mi 31⁴1:04⁴1:37 2:09⁴ 5 3 3 2 1½ 1nk 2:09⁴ 2.60 (L.Pullen) Coneeda,Gyp.HillHot,ScottCardin
2-15 LB⅝ 2000 gd 4000 clm cd mi 31¹1:02 1:35 2:07⁴ 5 2° 2°xx8 8x²⁰x8xdis 2.60 (L.Pullen) Frugal, HarryAdios, HiLo'sDeb
11-23 Fhld 1800 ft 4000 clm cd mi 30⁴1:03⁴1:36²2:07¹ 4 6 7 7 7¹³ 7dis 15.10 (M.Organ) DottieWick,DickByrd,Hon.Tp.Sct.
11- 4 LB⅝ 2000 ft 4000 clm cd mi 30 1:02¹1:33²2:05 7 5° 3° 7 8²²¾7dis 2:11¹ 6.60 (L.Pullen) MissLindaJo,LivingFaith,Deb.Ace
10-29 LB⅝ 2200 ft 68nw6000 cd mi 31²1:04 1:34²2:05⁴ 7 7 7 x8 8²⁰¾8dis 9.60 (L.Pullen) Kinleith, PhilW., FlashD.Adios

---

6

5 4000 Black

DILLON BYRD
b g, 7, by Poplar Byrd—Spitfire by Nibble Hanover
Sadie Zukofsky & Simon Berlin, Forest Hills, N.Y.
Trainer-B. Webster
$17,292 — 2, TT-2:03¹ (1) Driver-BEN WEBSTER, 11-8-39 (130) RED-WHITE-BLACK
1969 4 0 0 0 4
(⅝)2:06 1968 27 3 7 2 5,5

3-26 LB⅝ 2900 ft 4000 clm cd mi 31³1:04²1:35²2:07³ 4 7 7 6 6⁶ 4²½ 2:08 5.40 (B.Webster) RadiantVastar,Torpay,GoPeteGo
3-15 LB⅝ 2400 ft 4000 clm cd mi 30²1:05 1:36 2:07³ 8 2 2 4x 7¹⁸ 7²⁰½ 2:11³ 5.80 (B.Webster) Ammor'sSon,Wyn.Duke,RollonDrc
3- 5 LB⅝ 3100 ft 5000 clm mi 31¹1:03 1:34⁴2:05¹ 7 7 7 7 7⁶ 7¹²¼ 2:07³ 27.00 (G.Gilmour) Drct.Stone,CallMeLky.,Amaz.Han
2-19 LB⅝ 2400 sy nw6000 cd mi 33³1:06 1:38²2:10³ 3 2 3 3 3³¾ 4⁸½ 2:12¹ 6.70 (B.Webster) N.Z.So.Silver,TruaxHn.,SlupyTim
11-29 Fhld 2000 gd 3yr up cd mi 31 1:04 1:36²2:10² 2 4 4 4 4¹½ 1¹ 2:10² 3.30 (B.Webster) DillonByrd, SnuffySmith, AmosW
11-23 Fhld 1600 ft cd mi 30²1:01⁴1:35 2:06⁴ 3 6 6 4 4¹¾ 2¹½ 2:07 5.10 (B.Webster) Ioleen'sDiam.,Dlln.Byrd,Sym.Bell
11-16 Fhld 1800 ft 3yr up cd mi 31¹1:05¹1:37⁴2:09¹ 2 3 4 3 3² 1¹½ 2:09¹ 9.30 (B.Webster) DillonByrd,DaveyQue,Diam.Rush

---

12

6 6000 Yellow

SHALEE SUE
b m, 4, by Lehigh Hanover—Claire Abbe by Bert Abbe
Charles E. & Robert B. West, Birds Nest, Va.
Trainer-J. D. Dennis, Sr.
$3,387 — 3, 2:07² Driver-J. (Tic) WILCUTTS, 11-23-19 (120) BLUE-RED-WHITE
1969 10 0 1 2 1,0
2:07² 1968 19 2 5 2 3,3

3-28 LB⅝ 3000 ft nw6000 cd mi 31³1:04²1:34²2:05⁴ 8 8 8 5 4⁶ 6⁷ 2:07¹ 90.40 (J.DennisSr) Gd.L.Boy,Yola'sPrd.,M.Scrlt.Daw
3-17 LB⅝ 2900 ft nw5000 cd mi 31¹1:04²1:35³2:05⁴ 8 8 8 8 8⁶¾ 8¹³½ 2:08² 62.70 (J.Stafford) Emb.Irish,MabelAds.,Tam.BenJo
3-10 LB⅝ 2600 ft nw5000 cd mi 31¹1:03¹1:34 2:04² 8 8 8 8 8¹⁶¾8²³¼ 2:09 70.40 (J.DennisSr) Ging.Rod,Yola'sPrd.,DistantDrum
3- 6 LB⅝ 2600 ft nw5000 cd mi 31²1:04³1:35⁴2:07² 3 4 4 6 6⁸ 3³½ 2:08 8.00 (J.DennisSr) CocoaDean, BrerFox, ShaleeSue
2-28 LB⅝ 2200 ft nw4000 cd mi 32²1:06¹1:37 2:08⁴ 5 1 1 1 1¹¾ 4²½ 2:09¹ 7.20 (J.DennisSr) Exclnt.Scot,Chip.Dncr.,Mk.Dscvr
2-24 LB⅝ 2400 gd nw5000 cd mi 30³1:02¹1:34¹2:06² 2 5 6 8 7⁵½ 6⁸½ 2:08 31.00 (J.DennisSr) Cmd.Major,Emb.Irish,GingerRod
2-19 LB⅝ 2000 sy nw4000 cd mi 32 1:04²1:38¹2:11² 1 3 2 1 2½ 2¹⁵ 2:14² 7.80 (J.DennisSr) Escalate,ShaleeSue,DistantDrum

---

8

7 4000 Pink

MR. SMOOTHIE
b g, 6, by O'Brien Hal—Afton Gene by Volation
Mitchell Bonneville & Lynwood Duncan, Pocomoke City, Md.
Trainer-F. Abbott
$8,704 — 4, 2:06¹ Driver-FRANK ABBOTT, 10-30-36 (135) BLUE-BLACK
1969 1 0 0 0 1
LAST RACED IN 1967

3-25 LB⅝ 3600 gd nw6000 cd mi 31³1:04³1:35²2:06⁴ 4 5 4 4 4⁵½ 5¹⁰ 2:08⁴ 48.90 (F.Abbott) HighSass, BigStirk, BuckyBee
3- 4 LB⅝ ft Qua mi 32²1:04²1:38¹2:08⁴ 5 1 2 2 3¹ 4⁴½ 2:09³ N.B. (F.Abbott) PainterAbe,TupeloLou,SkyClipper
9-26-67 Fhld 1700 ft 67nw3750 mi 30¹1:02 1:34³2:07 4 5 5 6 2² 2² 2:07¹ 10.30 (J.Morrill) Wthy.Philip,M.Smoothie,Sar.Smi
9-16-67 Fhld 1700 sl 67nw3750 mi 33 1:06²1:39²2:12¹ 6 6 6 6 5³¾ 3⁴ 2:13 9.00 (Au.Thomas) Rec.Malone,FirstDark,M.Smoothi
9- 9-67 Fhld 1400 ft 4yr up cd mi 31¹1:03²1:34³2:05⁴ 5 4° B.E. dnf 7.20 (Au.Thomas) BillyBayama,FirstDark,AftonDill
8-28-67 Fhld 1200 ft 4yr up cd mi 31³1:04 1:36 2:07⁴ 6 8 8 6 6⁸½ 4¹½ 2:08 6.60 (Au.Thomas) SkipperChf.,RecordMalone,Magni
8-19-67 Fhld 2000 ft 67nw3750 mi 30¹1:02³1:36¹2:06³ 8 8 8 7 7⁴¾ 5³½ 2:07² 10.30 (Au.Thomas) GoldPtny.,Drmr.Lobell,BevanDrct

---

6

8 4000 Black-Yellow

AFTON DUKE
b g, 7, by Jug Chief—Afton Margaret by Jerry Patch
Frank A. Xhilone, Woodstown, N.J.
Trainer-N. Shoemaker, Jr.
$10,093 — 5, 2:04² (⅝) (P) Driver-NORTON SHOEMAKER, JR., 11-23-29 (175) WHITE-BLUE
(⅝)2:09² 1969 4 1 0 2 1,5
(⅝)2:06⁴ 1968 10 1 3 3 2,8

3-25 LB⅝ 2700 gd 3000 clm cd mi 31³1:03¹1:35 2:09² 2 1 1 1 1⁵½ 1² 2:09² 2.70(N.ShoemakerJr) AftonDuke,SharonLu,DonnaCmnd
3-10 LB⅝ 1900 ft 3000 clm cd mi 30⁴1:02³1:36¹2:10⁴ 7 1 1 1 1³½ 3¹ 2:11 2.40(N.ShoemakerJr) Tiny'sSparkle,SharonLu,Aft.Duke
2-21 LB⅝ 1500 gd 3000 clm cd mi 30³1:02⁴1:34³2:07⁴ 4 2° 2 2° 2½ 3²¾ 2:08¹ 5.60(N.ShoemakerJr) NewburyKey,TeenyBits.AftonDuk
2-15 LB⅝ 2000 gd 4000 clm cd mi 31¹1:02 1:35 2:07⁴ 8 5° 4° 6° 7⁸ 7dis 13.50(N.ShoemakerJr) Frugal, HarryAdios, HiLo'sDeb
5-24 AC⅝ 1300 ft 3200 clm cd mi 30⁴1:02²1:32²2:06¹ 8 7° 1° 1 1³½ 2² 2:06³ 12.70 (L.Rathbone) JerrimahHal,Aft.Duke,Nwpt.Buell
5-17 AC⅝ 1400 ft 3600 clm cd mi 30 1:00³1:32 2:04¹ 7 1° 1 1 1½ 6¹⁰¾ 2:06² 4.70 (L.Rathbone) Ral.VanB.,TomStrong,PutP.Ptny.
5-13 AC⅝ 1400 ft 3600 clm cd mi 29³1:00²1:32³2:06 7 1° 1 1 1⁴ 3⁶½ 2:07 *1.70 (L.Rathbone) TomStrong,BattleStatn.,AftonDuk

---

TRACKMAN: 1—2—3

(2) **PACE—1 MILE**

Warming-Up Saddle Cloth
GRAY

PURSE $2,400

ASK FOR HORSE BY PROGRAM NUMBER

Second Half Daily Double

CLAIMING ALLOWANCE

Five-Year-Olds & Older To Be Claimed For $4,000, Four-Year-Olds To Be Claimed For $5,000, Three-Year-Olds To Be Claimed For $6,000. (Fillies & Mares Allowed 20%).

7/2

1 — 4800 Red

MISS ARCH

br m, 5, by Aristocratic Boy—Arch's Miss by Arch Hanover — Trainer-W. Marks
Joseph Centini, Lebanon, Pa. — 1969 5 0 3 0 2,001
$6,103 — 4, 2:073 — Driver-WALTER MARKS, 1-19-31 (150) BROWN-WHITE — 2:073 1968 31 1 6 8 4,907
3-25 LB⅝ 2900 gd 4800 clm cd mi 3111:0341:3522:071 7 7 7 7 63¾ 22½ 2:073 5.60 (W.Marks) BlytheAds.,MissArch,Bach.Debbie
3-14 LB⅝ 2400 ft 4800 clm cd mi 32 1:0521:3732:084 1 4 4 4 31¼ 2hd 2:084 11.20 (W.Marks) RoyalBonus,MissArch,Dolly'sAce
3- 5 LB⅝ 3100 ft 6000 clm cd mi 3011:0311:3432:062 6 7 7 7° 63¼ 84 2:071 25.20 (W.Marks) FlosHal, AmyDares, Lofty
2-27 LB⅝ 2200 ft 4800z clm cd mi 3041:0411:3712:084 6 4° 1 2 21¾ 42½ 2:091 4.80 (A.Stoltzfus) Michl.Laird,Cnstg.Lady,MichlMir
2-19 LB⅝ 2000 sy 4800 clm cd mi 3341:0641:3912:122 4 6 6 5 610½28 2:14 18.00 (A.Stoltzfus) Fl.Forever,MissArch,Cmd.Paloma
11-25 Fhld 1800 gd cd mi 32 1:0521:3732:092 3 4 5 6 67 813 2:12 40.20 (W.Marks) CyCry,Keystn.Aloha,TruaxHonor
11-18 Fhld 1800 sl cd mi 3211:0641:4022:123 2 3 3 4° 58 619 2:162 5.00 (W.Marks) Hester'sTm.,BobbyMike,BlazeBoy

---

8

2 — 4800 Blue

ROYAL CHARMER

b m, 7, by Royal Blackstone—Sultra's Dream by Knight Dream — Traner-L. Pullen
Charles W. Camp, Dorchester, N.J. — 1969 0 0 0 0
$8,542 — 3, 2:07 — Driver-LES PULLEN, 12-8-31 (167) DK. & LT. BROWN-GOLD — LAST RACED IN 1967
3-26 LB⅝ ft Qua mi 3131:04 1:3622:094 4 3 3 1 1¾ 23 2:102 N.B. (L.Pullen) Ynk.Trgr.,Ryl.Chrmr.,Lonsme.Valy.
8-15-67 Fox 2000 ft nw2500 cd mi 3121:0441:3642:071 7 7 7 8 713 711 2:092 51.70 (A.Winger) S'cessDonna,Rck.N.Rye,T.Gogetter
8- 3-67 Fox 1300 ft nw2500 cd mi 3111:04 1:3532:07 5 3° 3 4 43¼ 86¾ 2:082 25.30 (J.Sprouse) Rebob, MasterGlenn, Coppermite
7-22-67 Fox 1200 ft nw2000 cd mi 3131:0441:3632:082 5 8 7 8° 85½ 811 2:104 9.30 (A.Winger) EbonyPk.,Comm.Moraka,FootSteps
7-18-67 Fox ft Qua mi 3221:05 1:3732:091 7 3 3 3 21½ 22¾ 2:094 N.B. (J.Sprouse) M.Chance,Ryl.Charmer,TopazPete
5- 2-67 Rock 1400 sy nw5000 cd mi 3231:0711:4122:143 2 4 4 5 53¾ 67¾ 2:161 6.30 (J.Sprouse) RovingGirl, BlackBlaze, PolkaPal
4-26-67 Rock 1400 ft nw5000 cd mi 3041:0321:3532:072 8 6 5 6 43¼ 55¼ 2:083 58.50 (J.Sprouse) Grnd.LillianVolo,BillyV.,IrishEddie

---

3

3 — 5000 White

TORPAY

b h, 4, by Torpid—Maxine's Rose by Cardinal Prince — Trainer-Her. Filion
Capital Hill Farms, Reg'd., Montreal, Que., Can. — 1969 2 0 1 0 917
$1,637 — 3, 2:071 (⅝) — Driver-HERVE FILION, 2-1-40 (142) RED-DK. BLUE-WHITE — (⅝)2:071 1968 23 5 2 3 1,637
3-26 LB⅝ 2900 ft 5000 clm cd mi 3131:0421:3522:073 2 2 3 3 32¼ 2ns 2:073 *2.70 (Her.Filion) RadiantVastar,Torpay,GoPeteGo
3-15 LB⅝ 2400 ft 5000 clm cd mi 3021:05 1:36 2:073 5 4 5 5 4x3 49¼ 2:092 5.80 (Her.Filion) Ammor'sSon,Wyn.Duke,RollonDrct.
8- 7 Lau⅝ 900 ft nw100 pr st cd mi 31 1:0331:3442:072 7 4 4 4° 43¼ 711¾ 2:094 15.60 (D.Filion) SincerelyYours, Titleist, Mr.Tell
8- 5 Lau⅝ 950 ft nw100 pr st cd mi 3021:0331:3432:071 6 8 9 7 64¾ 86½ 2:082 7.10 (D.Filion) Aft.Mike,Ioleen'sDiam.,Wdvll.Lad
8- 1 Lau⅝ 1000 ft 68nw2000 mi 2941:0311:3442:064 2 5 5 7 84¾ 84¼ 2:074 32.30 (D.Filion) P'cessTmhwk.,Capmarge,Har.Camp
7-29 Lau⅝ 900 ft nw100 pr st cd mi 3141:0521:3632:09 5ix4 4 3ex33¼ 7dis 2:162 *1.10 (D.Filion) Floodlight,Mr.Tell,HyCrestDirect
7-25 Lau⅝ 900 ft 68nw1750 mi 2921:0031:3332:053 2 3 3 3 41½ 66 2:064 3.40 (D.Filion) TheGimp,WoodvilleLad,Aft.Model

---

5

4 — 4000 Green

YANKEE DANDY N.

br g, 11, by Captain Adios—Heather Dillon by Dillon Hall — Trainer-M. Matheson, Jr.
Fair Acres Farm, Freehold, N.J. — (⅝)2:081 1969 3 1 0 0 1,000
$7,384 — None At Mile — Driver-CHARLES SMITH, JR., 1-31-37 (200) RED-WHITE — 1968 9 0 1 0 603
4- 8 LB⅝ ft Qua mi 3011:0121:3222:021 3 3 4 5 58¾ 618¼ 2:054 N.B. (M.MathesonJr) Adaptor, Carpathian, CircusTime
4- 1 LB⅝ ft Qua mi 3111:04 1:3622:091 8 5° 5 5 63½ 54¼ 2:10 N.B. (M.MathesonJr) BetterChoice,RitaSong,Mjstc.Beau
2-26 LB⅝ 2800 gd 5000 clm mi 3031:0231:3432:07 6 4° 4 8 815 8dis 6.50 (C.SmithJr) YankeeGuy, FlosHal, SeaBuoy
2-20 LB⅝ 2800 gd nw8000 cd mi 3131:0331:36 2:07 3 1 2 8 x8x12½8dis 2:143 6.80 (C.SmithJr) AdOSam,GarrisonPride,SpikeEd
2-14 LB⅝ 2000 gd 4000z clm cd mi 3121:0411:37 2:081 7 3 3 3 31¾ 11 2:081 *1.10 (R.Dancer) Y.DandyN.,KingKongN.,Mncy.Tune
2- 7 LB⅝ gd T-P Qua mi 32 1:0441:3712:092 6 1 1 1 12¼ 11 2:092 N.B. (R.Dancer) Ynk.DandyN.,TenGrd.N.,Gar.Pride
6- 3 Ashburton T.C. 24 yd hcp 2 Miles in 4:31 Unplaced (D.J.Townley) Maj.Bright,Norlight,DrydenSmoke

---

9/2

5 — 4800 Black

DOLLY'S ACE

b m, 5, by Meadow Ace—Forever Amber by Royal Napoleon — Trainer-R. Moffett
George R. Moffett, Chestertown, Md. — 1969 5 0 1 1 1,230
$4,966 — 4, 2:05 — Driver-J. (Tic) WILCUTTS, 11-23-19 (120) BLUE-RED-WHITE — 2:05 1968 28 3 1 3 4,966
3-25 LB⅝ 2900 gd 4800 clm cd mi 3111:0341:3522:071 2 4 4 1 1¼ 44 2:08 *1.90 (J.Larente) BlytheAds.,MissArch,Bach.Debbie
3-14 LB⅝ 2400 ft 4800 clm cd mi 32 1:0521:3732:084 2 3 3 2 1½ 33 2:092 *.90 (J.Larente) RoyalBonus,MissArch,Dolly'sAce
3- 5 LB⅝ 2400 ft 4800 clm cd mi 3031:0241:34 2:064 7 8 8 5 54¾ 2hd 2:064 6.90 (J.Larente) Sil.D.Truax,Dolly'sAce,RoyalBonus
2-25 LB⅝ 2200 ft 4800 clm cd mi 3121:0231:3512:071 2 4 4 4 32¼ 57½ 2:083 2.20 (J.Larente) IrishOaks, VickGreer, RoyalBonus
2-18 LB⅝ 2000 gd 4800 clm cd mi 3111:0331:3532:063 x6 7 7 6 65 711½ 2:084 2.50 (Her.Filion) Fly.KingN.,HoboBob,Andy'sEvrtt.
11- 4 LB⅝ 2000 ft 68nw4000 cd mi 3121:0321:3412:052 7 7 7 7° 75 814 2:081 12.50 (A.Galentine) Rita'sDrm.,SheDares,ChampRnbw.
10-28 LB⅝ 2200 ft 68nw6000 cd mi 3031:0321:3442:052 7 1° 1 1 11½ 611½ 2:073 24.50 (A.Galentine) SturdyGold, HiFiFrost, TinaLobell

---

6

6 — 4800 Yellow

LEILA'S STAR

b m, 7, by Farvel—Leila Lee by Dominion Grattan — Trainer-J. Larente
H. Birdman & M. Rounick, Philadelphia, Pa. — 1969 4 0 0 0
$19,510 — 6, 2:053 — Driver-JAMES LARENTE, 5-21-31 (160) BLUE-GOLD — 2:053 1968 38 2 6 5 9,455
3-21 LB⅝ 2600 ft 4800 clm cd mi 32 1:0411:3542:073 6 8 6 6° 85 65¾ 2:083 10.10 (J.Larente) Nwbry.Key,HoboBob,SandyWilkes
3-10 LB⅝ 2400 ft 4800z clm cd mi 3041:0241:3442:071 4 2 2 6 811 817½ 2:103 10.40 (E.Davis) RoyAbbe,Suz.Rocket,Symph.Belle
3- 1 LB⅝ 2800 ft 6000 clm cd mi 3211:0411:36 2:082 4 4 4 4 43¼ 63 2:09 16.80 (E.Davis) TimelyPrince,Qk.Lightng.,RedFlax
2-21 LB⅝ 2500 gd 6000 clm cd mi 31 1:05 1:3642:073 6 7 8 8 86¾ 76¼ 2:084 26.50 (E.Davis) LennyByrd, QuickLightining, Lofty
11-16 Har 600 ft 68nw3000 cd mi 3341:0531:3632:072 3 1 2 2 27 610¾ 2:093 2.80 (E.Davis) MaryJ.Marlw.,Tm.Prince,Tr.Storm
11- 9 Har 1000 sy Inv hcp mi 33 1:06 1:3742:093 4 2 2 3 x5x8 6dis 5.60 (E.Davis) TaxExempt,MaryJ.Mrlw.,BillyBoot
11- 2 Har 1000 ft Inv hcp mi 30 1:0111:3312:044 5 4 3 3° 32¼ 21½ 2:051 11.55 (E.Davis) Charnie, Leila'sStar, TheGimp

---

6

7 — 4000 Pink

MEADOW ADD

b g, 5, by Add Hanover—Sweet Georgette by Cannon Ball — Trainer-H. Kelley
Billy A. Williams, Hebron, Md. — (⅝)2:073 1969 10 4 2 1 2,703
$4,902 — 4, 2:061 (⅝) Qua. — Driver-BILLY WILLIAMS, 5-2-28 (155) DK. BROWN-TAN-GOLD — Qua.(⅝)2:061 1968 36 5 6 5 3,760
3-22 LB⅝ 2600 ft 4000 clm cd mi 3041:0341:3512:062 2 3 3 3 33½ 63½ 2:07 9.70 (B.Williams) MyRight, AdiosBobo, RoyalBonus
3-14 LB⅝ 2400 ft 4000 clm cd mi 32 1:0521:3732:084 6 7 6 6 65 68¼ 2:102 5.00 (B.Williams) RoyalBonus,MissArch,Dolly'sAce
3- 5 LB⅝ 3100 ft 5000 clm cd mi 3011:0311:3432:062 4 6 6 8 85½ 73 2:07 3.80 (B.Williams) FlosHal, AmyDares, Lofty
2-27 LB⅝ 2700 ft nw6000 cd mi 3131:04 1:3642:081 1 2 2 2 2¾ 2hd 2:081 *1.60 (B.Williams) RedBarbara,MeadowAdd,Homely
2-22 LB⅝ 2000 ft 4000 clm cd mi 3031:0141:3422:073 8 7 7 6 62½ 11 2:073 20.60 (B.Williams) MeadowAdd,JudgeDares,HoboBob
2-13 Grgtn 550 ft nw125 pr st cd mi 3231:06 1:3832:102 2 3 3 1 13 11 2:102 *1.45 (B.Williams) Mdw.Add,Qk.Rudagar,AftonMike
2- 6 Grgtn 550 ft nw125 pr st cd mi 3141:0431:3622:09 6 6 7 5 53 1nk 2:09 4.35 (B.Williams) Mdw.Add,QuickRudagar,Titleist

---

12

8 — 4000 Black-Yellow

ROLLON DIRECT

br g, 5, by Newport Mike—Sharon May Direct by Watson E. Direct — Trainer-H. Gray
Rowland D. Scott, Georgetown, Del. — 1969 5 0 0 1 388
$3,213 — 4, 2:061 (⅝) — Driver-H. (Buck) GRAY, 11-29-38 (145) TURQUOISE-WHITE-GOLD — (⅝)2:061 1968 21 2 2 2 2,824
3-26 LB⅝ 2900 ft 4000 clm cd mi 3131:0421:3522:073 8 6° 4° 4 55¼ 710½ 2:093 29.00 (H.Kelly) RadiantVastar,Torpay,GoPeteGo
3-15 LB⅝ 2400 ft 4000 clm cd mi 3021:05 1:36 2:073 2 3 4 3° 32 34¼ 2:082 24.40 (H.Gray) Ammor'sSon,Wyn.Duke,RollonDrct.
3- 4 LB⅝ 2400 ft 4000 clm cd mi 3231:0431:3742:092 3 5 6 7 63½ 76½ 2:103 18.20 (H.Gray) StoneyDale, Junibee, TeenyBits
2-22 LB⅝ 2000 ft 4000 clm cd mi 3031:0321:35 2:07 1 3 3 3 33¼ 69½ 2:084 17.10 (H.Gray) VerdugoRdny.,Cwn.R'bow,SeaOats
2-18 LB⅝ 2000 gd 4000 clm cd mi 3111:0331:3532:063 4 6 6 5 54¼ 58 2:081 53.20 (H.Gray) Fly.KingN.,HoboBob,Andy'sEvrtt.
10-18 Fhld 1500 ft 2600 clm cd mi 3121:03 1:3432:071 3 6 7 7 65¼ 613 2:094 9.20 (H.Gray) Aft.Henry,BusyB.Chris,Peg.A.Guy
10-10 Fhld 1500 ft 3650 clm cd mi 3141:0521:3742:09 3 x8 8 8 8x168dis 6.40 (H.Gray) Nona'sPride,SnowSwitch,NobleDan

---

TRACKMAN: 3—1—5

← MORN. LINE

(3) PACE — 1 MILE

Warming-Up Saddle Cloth WHITE

PURSE $4,000

ASK FOR HORSE BY PROGRAM NUMBER

Exacta Windows Now Open For Wagering On 4th Race

CLAIMING ALLOWANCE

Five-Year-Olds & Older To Be Claimed For $8,000, Four-Year-Olds To Be Claimed For $9,000, Three-Year-Olds To Be Claimed For $10,000. (Fillies & Mares Allowed 20%).

---

6 | **1** | 8000 | Red

CARPATHIAN

ch g, 11, by King Oro—Royal Conquest by Jack Potts
P. Damon Stable, Bethesda, Md.
$15,639 — 10, 2:031 — Driver-F. (Bill) CARROLL, 4-30-35 (185) GOLD-BROWN
Trainer-F. W. Carroll — (⅝)2:061 1969 7 1 1 1 3,05 — 2:031 1968 26 3 2 1 7,42

4- 8 LB⅝	ft Qua mi	3011:0121:3222:021	1 1 1 1 11½ 25	2:031	N.B.	(F.W.Carroll)	Adaptor, Carpathian, CircusTime
4- 2 LB⅝	4000 ft 8000 clm cd mi	3121:03 1:3532:051	7 8 5° 7° 712 8dis		38.60	(C.Fitzpatrick)	Shdy.Hymn.,NextKngt.,TonyStort
3-28 LB⅝	4000 ft 8000 clm cd mi	30 1:03 1:34 2:043	8 1° 1 4 55½ 710½	2:063	46.80	(C.Fitzpatrick)	SirDuane,NextKngt.,BrownieDares
3-21 LB⅝	4400 ft 8000z clm cd mi	3131:04 1:3412:043	8 8 8 5 65¼ 713½	2:071	10.00	(R.Dancer)	NextKngt.,SirDuane,Shdydl.Hymn
3-12 LB⅝	4000 ft 8000 clm cd mi	3031:02 1:3322:052	6 7 5 3° 32 41¾P3	2:053	2.10	(R.Dancer)	JoeyLad,NextKnight,†Carpathian
3- 4 LB⅝	4100 ft nw10000 cd mi	31 1:0231:35 2:054	3 4 1 1 11½ 43½	2:062	4.80	(R.Dancer)	JethroHan.,Aft.Speedy,EastBridge
2-22 LB⅝	3400 ft nw10000 cd mi	3111:0341:3612:064	2 2 1 1 1¼ 21½	2:07	*.90	(R.Dancer)	EdwardJ.,Carpathian,NextKnight

8 | **2** | 8000 | Blue

‡PRANCER HANOVER

b h, 6, by Torpid—Phoebemite by Volomite
Murray Fairthorne, Windsor, Ont., Can.
$26,155 — 5, 2:034 (⅝) — Driver-CHAS. FITZPATRICK, 6-13-26 (160) GREEN-WHITE-RED
Trainer-C. Fitzpatrick — 1969 4 0 0 0 25 — (⅝)2:034 1968 41 4 6 4 14,14

4- 8 LB⅝‡	ft Qua mi	3011:0121:3222:021	6 7 7 6 69½ 418	2:054	N.B.	(C.Fitzpatrick)	Adaptor, Carpathian, CircusTime
3- 7 BM1‡	1700 ft 6000 clm cd mi	3211:0311:3532:064	5 4 2 8 8ix23¾8dis		*1.80	(J.Williams)	MarsonHn.,Hobby.Chngr.,Sp.Fever
2-28 BM1‡	1900 sy 6000 clm cd mi	3211:0441:3712:094	4 6 6 7 76¾ 41½	2:10	10.10	(J.Williams)	MarsonHn.,GlenH.W.,Hobby.Chngr
2-21 BM1‡	2000 sy 6000 clm cd mi	3221:0431:3742:113	3 5 8 8 7x107x10	2:133	9.10	(J.Williams)	Armb.Champ,MarsonHn.,GlenH.W.
2-15 BM1‡	2000 sl 6000 clm cd mi	3121:02 1:3422:071	4 5 6 5 59 55¼	2:081	5.30	(J.Williams)	MarsonHn.,GlenH.W.,Mr.Budlong
12-21 Hol1‡	3000 ft 6000 clm cd mi	31 1:02 1:3332:033	6 1 1 1 2½ 52½	2:041	6.50	(T.Merriman)	OdetteAds.,Cunny.Phil.,Gon.Mark
12-16 Hol1‡	2700 gd 5000 clm cd mi	3011:0131:3322:043	9 10 8 7 89 74¼	2:052	10.30	(T.Merriman)	Cunny'sPhilip,JustlySo,Gon'sMark

3 | **3** | 8000 | White

SIR DUANE

b h, 7, by Duane Hanover—Roxburgh Carmen by Goose Bay
Barry Lashin, Albany, N.Y.
$65,048 — 4, 2:003 (⅝) — Driver-JAMES LARENTE, 5-21-31 (160) BLUE-GOLD
Trainer-A. Bier — (⅝)2:043 1969 12 4 1 1 7,46 — 2:05 1968 32 9 3 2 14,375

3-28 LB⅝	4000 ft 8000 clm cd mi	30 1:03 1:34 2:043	3 5 4 1° 11¾ 11	2:043	*1.80	(J.Wilcutts)	SirDuane,NextKngt.,BrownieDares
3-21 LB⅝	4400 ft 8000 clm cd mi	3131:04 1:3412:043	6 6 6 6° 54¼ 21	2:044	2.50	(J.Larente)	NextKngt.,SirDuane,Shdydl.Hymn
3-12 LB⅝	4000 ft 8000 clm cd mi	3031:02 1:3322:052	7 3° 3° 7° 76 64¾	2:061	*1.70	(A.Bier)	JoeyLad,NextKnight,†Carpathian
3- 5 LB⅝	3800 ft 7000 clm cd mi	3131:0341:3512:061	1 2 4 2 21 1½	2:061	*1.60	(A.Bier)	SirDuane,FargoHanvr.,NextKnight
2-20 LB⅝	3000 gd 6000 clm cd mi	3141:0441:3712:083	6 6 6 6 64 11½	2:083	*.90	(A.Bier)	SirDuane, FlosHal, CallMeLucky
2-15 LB⅝	2500 gd 6000 clm cd mi	3021:0131:3422:061	6 7 7 7 67¾ 32	2:063	5.10	(A.Bier)	LennyByrd, Lofty, SirDuane
2- 8 Aur	2000 ft w4000 cd mi	3041:0241:3522:074	2 4 4 4 43½ 41½	2:081	13.40	(A.Bier)	Biggs,SpikeR.L.,SizzlerHanover

5 | **4** | 8000 | Green

JOEY LAD

ch g, 7, by Gene Abbe—Dundee Lassie by The Widower
Michael A. Stolte, South Amboy, N.J.
$19,546 — 5, 2:06 (⅝) — Driver-FRANK BROWNE, 4-29-30 (162) GREEN-WHITE
Trainer-F. Browne — (⅝)2:052 1969 5 1 0 1 2,68 — (⅝)2:064 1968 30 4 3 4 8,55

3-22 LB⅝	4900 ft 10000 clm cd mi	31 1:02 1:33 2:032	6 7 7 7 75¼ 65	2:042	22.60	(F.Browne)	Chf.Saint,LordStacey,WinslowLady
3-12 LB⅝	4000 ft 8000 clm cd mi	3031:02 1:3322:052	3 2 2 2 1½ 11	2:052	12.30	(F.Browne)	JoeyLad,NextKnight,†Carpathian
3- 4 LB⅝	4100 ft nw10000 cd mi	31 1:0231:35 2:054	1 2 4 5 45¼ 55	2:064	13.80	(F.Browne)	JethroHan.,Aft.Speedy,EastBridge
2-24 LB⅝	4000 gd 8000 clm cd mi	3111:04 1:3432:063	2 4 4 4 45¼ 32¾	2:07	21.80	(F.Browne)	Efficient, Lyndhurst, JoeyLad
2-14 LB⅝	5000 gd 68nw12500 Ec mi	3111:0311:3622:073	7 10 10 10 98 87½	2:09	39.30	(C.Hand)	Std.Boy,Hap.Songster,LimelightN.
11-25 Fhld	2200 gd cd mi	3131:0511:3642:091	6 2° 2 2 21 2½	2:091	3.60	(E.Lohmeyer)	ElFaber,JoeyLad,CamdenPaloma
11-18 Fhld	2200 sl cd mi	3311:0821:4142:14	4 1 1 1 11 11½	2:14	4.60	(F.Browne)	JoeyLad, TabExpress, SandyLeo

6 | **5** | 8000 | Black

ADD FRISCO

b g, 10, by Add Hanover—Merry May by Real Frisco
David Harris, Trenton, N.J.
$45,382 — 9, 2:04 — Driver-MICHAEL GALE, 1-2-41 (175) GREEN-WHITE-GOLD
Trainer-M. Gale — 1969 5 0 0 0 992 — 2:04 1968 31 5 6 4 16,769

4- 2 LB⅝	4000 ft 8000 clm cd mi	3121:03 1:3532:051	3 5 6 6 63 68	2:064	8.90	(M.Gale)	Shdy.Hymn.,NextKngt.,TonyStort
3-21 LB⅝	4400 ft 8000 clm cd mi	3131:04 1:3412:043	7 7 7 8 76¼ 44	2:052	42.10	(M.Gale)	NextKngt.,SirDuane,Shdydl.Hymn
3-15 LB⅝	4000 ft 8000 clm cd mi	3111:0441:3612:062	5 6 7 7 54 45	2:072	9.20	(M.Gale)	EdwardJ.,Paramnt.Pick,TonyStort
3- 8 LB⅝	4000 ft 8000 clm cd mi	3021:0231:34 2:051	3 6 7 6 66¼ 43	2:054	18.50	(M.Gale)	ElbeeN., Automatic, YankeeGuy
3- 1 LB⅝	4000 ft 10000 clm cd mi	31 1:0311:35 2:051	6 6 7 6 77 718	2:084	41.70	(M.Gale)	Efficient,Hap.Songster,Prmnt.Pick
12-14 RR	3250 sy B3 mi	3141:06 1:3832:11	8 8 8 8 85¾ 84¼	2:12	12.80	(D.Wood)	MultiChief,Foresail,Scott'sTaffy
12- 7 RR	3000 ft B3 mi	3121:0231:3512:07	5 7 8 4° 33 21½	2:072	*1.20	(J.Chapman)	Kgt.Missn.,AddFrisco,Ptyhll.Mart

9/2 | **6** | 8000 | Yellow

PARAMOUNT PICK

b g, 10, by Gene Abbe—Fall Brook by Abbedale
Walter R. & George R. Moffett, Chestertown, Md.
$95,996 — 5, 2:002 (¾) — Driver-J. (Tic) WILCUTTS, 11-23-19 (120) BLUE-RED-WHITE
Trainer-R. Moffett — (⅝)2:082 1969 6 2 1 1 5,720 — (⅝)2:031 1968 29 8 5 8 24,618

3-29 LB⅝	4400 sy 10000 clm cd mi	3211:0541:38 2:103	4 1 2 3 42¼ 53½	2:111	3.30	(J.Murray)	EdwardJ.,Whirl.Lobell,LordStacy
3-15 LB⅝	4000 ft 8000 clm cd mi	3111:0441:3612:062	6 8 8 2° 2¼ 2hd	2:062	2.70	(J.Murray)	EdwardJ.,Paramnt.Pick,TonyStort
3- 7 LB⅝	4400 gd 10000 clm cd mi	3021:0321:3332:053	7 1 1 2 32 53¼	2:061	3.10	(J.Murray)	DianeFarvel, GoBye, PhilFrost
3- 1 LB⅝	4000 ft 10000 clm cd mi	31 1:0311:35 2:051	2 4 5 4° 32¼ 33¼	2:054	4.50	(J.Murray)	Efficient,Hap.Songster,Prmnt.Pick
2-19 LB⅝	3800 sy 10000 clm cd mi	3031:0421:3732:112	8 1° 1 1 11¼ 1½	2:112	2.20	(J.Murray)	Prmnt.Pk.,Medea'sCmnd.,Efficient
2-14 LB⅝	3800 gd 9000 clm cd mi	31 1:0441:3832:082	7 2 2 3 31½ 1ns	2:082	2.60	(Her.Filion)	Prmnt.Pick,DianeFarvel.PhilFrost
10-31 LB⅝	4500 ft 68w15000 mi	30 1:0121:3232:024	4 4 4 2 2¼ 87½	2:041	18.90	(A.Galentine)	StewartHn.,LewOregon,Lusc's.Lou

12 | **7** | 8000 | Pink

PHIL FROST

b g, 6, by Dale Frost—Meadow Ola by Direct Rhythm
C. A. W. Hurtubise, Jr., Haverford, Pa.
$32,099 — 5, 2:033 (⅝) — Driver-GENE DAISEY, 10-12-37 (170) BROWN-GOLD
Trainer-A. Iancale — 1969 6 0 0 2 1,876 — (⅝)2:033 1968 34 4 5 6 14,110

3-28 LB⅝	4000 ft 8000 clm cd mi	30 1:03 1:34 2:043	7 3 5 7 77¾ 810½	2:063	21.10	(G.Cameron)	SirDuane,NextKngt.,BrownieDares
3-21 LB⅝	4400 ft 8000 clm cd mi	3131:04 1:3412:043	3 2 3 1 1½ 57	2:06	4.50	(G.Daisey)	NextKngt.,SirDuane,Shdydl.Hymn
3-14 LB⅝	4400 ft 10000 clm cd mi	3111:0211:34 2:052	3 5 3 4 43 42½	2:054	12.40	(G.Daisey)	ChiefSaint, TopDollar, Efficient
3- 7 LB⅝	4400 gd 10000 clm cd mi	3021:0321:3332:053	1 4 4 3° 21¼ 32¼	2:06	8.10	(G.Daisey)	DianeFarvel, GoBye, PhilFrost
2-24 LB⅝	4000 gd 9000 clm cd mi	3111:04 1:3432:063	5 7 5 1 12 43¼	2:071	8.10	(G.Daisey)	Efficient, Lyndhurst, JoeyLad
2-14 LB⅝	3800 gd 9000 clm cd mi	31 1:0441:3832:082	6 6 6 4 41¾ 32	2:084	11.60	(G.Daisey)	Prmnt.Pick,DianeFarvel,PhilFrost
11- 4 LB⅝	3600 ft 8000 clm cd mi	2941:0131:3232:03	4 7 8 8 73½ 45¼	2:04	10.40	(W.Pocza)	Sun.B.Bye,Whirlw.Lobell,Car.Copy

7/2 | **8** | 8000 | Black-Yellow

SHADYDALE HYMN

b h, 6, by Airliner—Ruth Ann Song by Gay Song
Roland Lariviere & Son & P. Raymond, Hull, Que., Can.
$107,002 — 3, 2:004 — Driver-HERVE FILION, 2-1-40 (142) RED-DK. BLUE-WHITE
Trainer-Her. Filion — (⅝)2:051 1969 6 1 0 1 3,123 — 2:03 1968 27 2 2 4 12,546

4- 2 LB⅝	4000 ft 8000 clm cd mi	3121:03 1:3532:051	4 2 3 5 52¾ 11½	2:051	2.80	(Her.Filion)	Shdy.Hymn.,NextKngt.,TonyStort
3-28 LB⅝	4000 ft 8000 clm cd mi	30 1:03 1:34 2:043	5 7 7 8 89¼ 45½	2:053	3.90	(Her.Filion)	SirDuane,NextKngt.,BrownieDares
3-21 LB⅝	4400 ft 8000 clm cd mi	3131:04 1:3412:043	2 4 4 4 43¼ 32	2:05	*2.30	(Her.Filion)	NextKngt.,SirDuane,Shdydl.Hymn
3-14 LB⅝	6000 ft 68nw20000 Ec mi	3011:0141:3212:022	6 7 7 6 710¾7dis		8.70	(Her.Filion)	Ardrossan, Donora, RobinHill
3- 8 LB⅝	6000 ft 68nw20000 Ec mi	3021:0111:3232:03	7 4 4 6ix713½7dis		e*2.40	(Her.Filion)	MontageN.,LiberaceHanvr.,Donora
3- 1 LB⅝	5500 ft 68nw20000 Ec mi	3121:0321:3412:053	7 6 6 4 42½ 54½	2:062	e2.30	(Her.Filion)	Pad.Night,VoloTime,LiberaceHan.
2-25 LB⅝	gd Qua mi	3141:04 1:37 2:092	7 2 3 2 21¾ 22	2:094	N.B.	(Her.Filion)	Contin'tal,Shdy.Hymn,Aft.Empress

TRACKMAN: 3—8—6

(4) ←MORN. LINE

PACE—1 MILE

Warming-Up Saddle Cloth GREEN

PURSE $3,400

ASK FOR HORSE BY PROGRAM NUMBER

EXACTA WAGERING THIS RACE

THREE & FOUR-YEAR-OLDS NON-WINNERS OF $8,000 IN 1968-69 COMBINED EARNINGS. Also Eligible: Non-Winners of $10,000 in 1968-69 combined earnings that are non-winners of a race in last 6 starts.

7/2 — **1** — Red

MR. HENRY W.
blk h, 4, by Adios Oregon—Henrietta W. by McSpencer
M. Bonneville & L. Duncan, Marion & Pocomoke City, Md.
Trainer-F. Abbott
(⅝)2:062 1969 5 1 2 1 3,602
2:052 1968 11 7 1 1 3,543
$3,543 — 3, 2:052 Driver-FRANK ABBOTT, 10-30-36 (135) BLUE-BLACK

4- 1 LB⅝ 4100 ft nw10000 cd mi 3041:0311:3342:042 1 2 3 2 21 2nk 2:042 5.00 (F.Abbott) Lhgh.Exprs.,Mr.HenryW.,Cmd.Maj.
3-24 LB⅝ 3600 sy nw6000 cd mi 3021:0511:3642:084 4 2 2 3 32 2nk 2:084 8.30 (F.Abbott) GingerRod,Mr.HenryW.,Emb.Irish
3-17 LB⅝ 3300 ft nw6000 cd mi 2941:0221:33 2:05 6 6 4 3° 31 5½ 2:051 3.50 (F.Abbott) TabExpress,KeyEntrprs.,FastByrd
3- 8 LB⅝ 2400 ft nw4000 cd mi 30 1:02 1:3232:062 8 1 3 1 1¾ 1ns 2:062 *1.70 (F.Abbott) Mr.HenryW.,GideonS.,ChangeTime
3- 3 LB⅝ 2600 ft nw5000 cd mi 3111:0231:3312:043 4 4° 1 1 1¼ 32 2:05 3.60 (F.Abbott) Yola'sPrd.,GingerRod,Mr.HenryW.
9-28 Rock 1500 ft 68nw4000 mi 31 1:03 1:3342:052 4 3 3 3x 822 8dis 1.90 (Au.Thomas) MegByrd,Charmoore,HobokumJoe
9-20 Rock 1200 ft 68nw3000 mi 30 1:0141:3422:06 3 5 5 3° 31¾ 11 2:06 *1.70 (Au.Thomas) Mr.HenryW., WhizAdio, Chevette

---

8 — **2** — Blue

PACESETTER PICK
ch h, 4, by Hal Senator—Poplar Annabel by H. D. Hanover
Frank S. Grant, Woodbury, N.J.
Trainer-W. Marks
(⅝)2:04 1969 9 3 0 0 4,383
(⅝)2:061 1968 11 3 2 0 2,117
$2,117 — 3, 2:061 (⅝) Driver-WALTER MARKS, 1-19-31 (150) BROWN-WHITE

4- 7 LB⅝ 3400 ft nw8000 cd mi 3011:0241:3312:034 5 1 1 2 2¾ 5¾ 2:042 2.90 (W.Marks) M.Scrlt.Dawn,Cm.Astra,Emb.Irish
3-29 LB⅝ 4100 ft nw10000 cd mi 3111:0331:36 2:06 6 1° 1 1 2¼ 41 2:061 7.70 (W.Marks) DinnerDate,Spdy.Troy,Wnslw.Lady
3-20 LB⅝ 2900 ft nw5000 cd mi 2941:0231:3312:04 4 1 1 1 1¼ 1nk 2:04 1.90 (W.Marks) Pacesttr.Pk.,RuthD.Ace,Yola'sPrd.
3-15 LB⅝ 2400 ft nw4000 cd mi 3031:0231:3412:044 5 2 2 2 1¾ 14½ 2:044 8.20 (W.Marks) Pcsttr.Pick,GiantKiller,CocoaDean
3- 8 LB⅝ 2400 ft nw4000 cd mi 30 1:02 1:3232:062 1 4 1 5 68¼ 69¾ 2:081 3.30 (J.Larente) Mr.HenryW.,GideonS.,ChangeTime
3- 4 LB⅝ 2100 ft nw2500 mi 3221:03 1:35 2:07 5 4 2° 4 32¼ 1½ 2:07 9.80 (J.Larente) PacesetterPk.,AnchorW.,SolidMike
2-25 LB⅝ 1900 gd nw2500 cd mi 3311:0721:3912:103 4ixacc dnf 8.20(N.ShoemakerJr) AnchorW.,Houdini,LitoniaHanover

---

6 — **3** — White

INHERITANCE
br g, 4, by Brown Star—Bequeath by Dominion Grattan
Jo-Jo-Na Farms, Washington, D.C.
Trainer-A. Cameron
(⅝)2:032 1969 8 2 0 1 3,999
(1)2:053 1968 13 4 1 1 3,781
$3,781 — 3, 2:053 (1) Driver-J. (Tic) WILCUTTS, 11-23-19 (120) BLUE-RED-WHITE

4- 3 LB⅝ 3400 ft nw8000 cd mi 2941:0041:31 2:032 1 4 4 4 32¼ 1ns 2:032 23.90 (R.Myers) Inheritance,ChancyBrk.,CitationPk.
3-24 LB⅝ 3200 sy nw5000 cd mi 32 1:0621:38 2:101 5 3 3 5 44½ 14 2:101 16.00 (G.Daisey) Inheritance,KnightLeo,Cmd.Astra
3-17 LB⅝ 2900 ft nw5000 cd mi 3111:0421:3532:054 6 1° 1 1 1¼ 42 2:061 14.30 (J.Larente) Emb.Irish,MabelAds.,Tam.BenJoe
2-28 YR 2500 ft C3 mi 3041:0321:3532:073 3 5 5° 5° 54½ 67 2:092 5.40 (W.Myer) LidaLisa, Airbrush, ChiefBunny
2-24 YR 2750 ft C2 cd mi 3121:0441:3612:081 5 3 2° 4° 64¼ 86½ 2:094 4.30 (W.Myer) Chock.Roy,ColbyDares,StarDapple
2-13 YR 2750 ft C2 cd mi 3121:0331:3542:09 8 8 6° 6 45 43 P3 2:094 7.40 (L.Fontaine) Ads.Robbie,FlameBill,†Inheritance
1-18 YR 2750 gd C2 cd mi 3111:0341:3532:083 7 7 7 8 x7x7 713 2:114 37.30 (G.Regan) FlagPole, MovieStar, AdiosBobo

---

5/2 — **4** — Green

PRESTWICK
b c, 3, by Bye Bye Byrd—Presley Wick by Gene Abbe
Hardwood Stable, Freeport, N.Y.
Trainer-A. Winger
(⅝)2:024 1969 7 4 0 1 6,075
2:062 1968 11 2 4 0 1,450
$1,450 — 2, 2:062 Driver-AL WINGER, 12-18-21 (180) RED-WHITE-BLUE

4- 3 LB⅝ 6000 ft 68nw10000 Ec mi 32 1:0421:3342:033 3 4 4 4 43 54½ 2:042 e*1.70 (C.Fitzpatrick) Wejover, Adnev, KeyEnterprise
3-28 LB⅝ 6000 ft 68nw10000 Ec mi 3011:0031:3112:03 10 7 6 2° 2¼ 11 2:03 *.50 (W.Haughton) Prestwick,J.M.Rhythm,AnchorW.
3-22 P.Pk⅝ 5000 ft nw6500 cd mi 283 :5941:2942:00 3 5 5 3° 21 31¾ 2:002 N.B. (W.Haughton) ArmbroIrma, Tanner, Prestwick
3- 8 P.Pk⅝ 2500 sy nw6500 cd mi 2931:0131:3122:024 6 2° 1 x6 615 515¾ 2:06 e*.20 (W.Haughton) Armb.Irma,Rstc.Coast,Wntr.Frisco
3- 1 P.Pk⅝ 2500 ft nw6500 cd mi 2941:0241:3312:024 10 4 4 6 52¼ 1½ 2:024 e*1.30 (W.Haughton) Prestwick, Chataqua, ShadyTime
2-21 P.Pk⅝ 800 ft nw3000 cd mi 3141:0241:3432:042 7 4° 1 1 1½ 11½ 2:042 *.80 (W.Haughton) Prestwick, Jerry'sFirst, ButBut
2-12 P.Pk⅝ 800 ft nw3500 cd mi 32 1:04 1:3522:053 3 2° 1 1 1½ 12¼ 2:053 *.60 (W.Haughton) Prestwick,CaptainKnox,Swanlette

---

6 — **5** — Black

MISS SCARLET DAWN
b m, 4, by Scarlet Sam—Miss Keyman Braden by Keyman
John A. Murphy, Oriskany Falls, N.Y.
Trainer-Her. Filion
(⅝)2:034 1969 4 1 0 1 2,348
(¾)2:034 1968 19 6 4 3 5,510
$6,412 — 3, 2:034 (¾) Driver-HERVE FILION, 2-1-40 (142) RED-DK. BLUE-WHITE

4- 7 LB⅝ 3400 ft nw8000 cd mi 3011:0241:3312:034 3 5 5 4 42¼ 11 2:034 *2.80 (Her.Filion) M.Scrlt.Dawn,Cm.Astra,Emb.Irish
3-28 LB⅝ 3000 ft nw6000 cd mi 3131:0421:3422:054 6 7 7 7 58 33½ 2:062 15.90 (Her.Filion) Gd.L.Boy,Yola'sPrd.,M.Scrlt.Dawn
3-18 LB⅝ ft Qua mi 3021:0241:3542:073 5 3 4 3 44 45 2:083 N.B. (C.Poisson) Kystn.Dream,I'mABoot,KeyDemon
2- 2 BB⅝ 1800 gd nw6500 cd mi 3121:0421:3642:083 4 5 5 6 68¾ 47¼ 2:10 5.50 (Her.Filion) Ad.Watts,Mor.Dares,S.WinstonPk.
1-22 BB⅝ 1800 ft nw6500 cd mi 3221:0521:3712:073 7 4 4 3° 24 49 2:092 2.00 (Her.Filion) AdiosWatts,RebelL.Jill,Mor.Dares
12-15 BB⅝ 1800 gd nw10000 cd mi 3241:0541:40 2:121 6 3 3 3 31½ 34½ 2:13 *1.80 (Her.Filion) T.Mt.Babe,Ar.Hazard,M.Scr.Dwn.
12- 9 BB⅝ 1600 ft nw8000 cd mi 3121:0411:3542:081 5 5 5 5 31¾ 1½ 2:081 2.65 (Her.Filion) M.Scar.Dawn,Hon.Rnbw,,O.Jessie

---

9/2 — **6** — Yellow

GOOD LUCK BOY
b c, 3, by Good Time—Primrose Pearl by DeSota Hanover
Giuffrida Stable, Philadelphia, Pa.
Trainer-J. Larente
(⅝)2:054 1969 1 1 0 0 1,500
(¾)2:043 1968 15 3 4 0 5,406
$5,406 — 2, TT-2:011 (1) Driver-JAMES LARENTE, 5-21-31 (160) BLUE-GOLD

3-28 LB⅝ 3000 ft nw6000 cd mi 3131:0421:3422:054 3 4 3 2° 2¾ 1½ 2:054 *.80 (J.Larente) Gd.L.Boy,Yola'sPrd.,M.Scrlt.Dawn
10-18 LB⅝ 3000 ft 2yr C-G mi 2941:02 1:3212:021 3 1° 1 1 2¼ 74½ 2:03 1.80 (V.Dancer) BarberHn.,Pont'cHn.,OceanMouth
10- 9 LB⅝ 2000 ft 2yr C mi 3031:0111:3112:02 6 6 7 5° 54¾ 24 2:024 7.10 (J.Larente) Dwight, Gd.LuckBoy, RicciGreatA.
9-20 LB⅝ 4000 ft 2yr Lc mi 3021:0031:3012:003 5 2° 1 2 23¼ 45 2:013 3.80 (V.Dancer) SetShot,BakerLobell,Mizll.Mickey
9-13 LB⅝ 4000 ft 2yr Lc mi 3031:0141:3142:03 1 3 3 7 65¾ 4¾ 2:03 4.70 (S.Dancer) LordRgr.dhBarberHn.,Kystn.Treat
9- 7 VD¾ 1000 ft cd mi 2911:01 1:3222:032 4 4 3 3° 33¼ 2½ 2:033 2.60 (T.Smith) Frnd.Harhu,Gd.Lck.Boy,ZekeZam
8-31 VD¾ 1000 ft cd mi 284 :5941:3112:023 1 7 6° 6° 56 22¾ 2:031 3.00 (T.Smith) WillingJspr.,Gd.L.Boy,Frnd.Harhu

---

8 — **7** — Pink

CHIEF BUTLER
b h, 4, by Adios Butler—Marylin Chief by Chief Abbedale
Fermer Perry, Suffolk, Va.
Trainer-O. Mumford
1969 0 0 0 0
Qua.(⅝)2:031 1968 19 1 5 3 8,020
$20,251 — 2, 2:021 (⅝) Driver-CHAS. FITZPATRICK, 6-13-26 (160) GREEN-WHITE-RED

10-22 LB⅝‡ 2500 ft 68nw8000 cd mi 2931:0041:3212:031 6x 8 8 8 8dis 8dis 3.20 (A.Galentine) MightyAndrea,VoloTime,ChenDon
10-18 LB⅝‡ ft Qua mi 3121:0231:33 2:031 4 1 1 1 112 118¾ 2:031 N.B. (A.Galentine) Chf.Butler,CamdenBingen,Spdy.Val
10-15 LB⅝‡ ft T-P Qua mi 3041:0411:3512:062 5 x8 8 8 8dis 8dis N.B. (A.Allen) Jck.Flash,ChloeDirect,MellowMoon
10-10 LB⅝ 2200 ft 68nw6000 cd mi 2931:0031:31 2:023 7 2 1 1 11 73½ 2:031 5.40 (V.Crank) Mohawk,SteadyBoy,Tm.AndAgain
10- 1 LB⅝ 3500 ft 68nw8000 cd mi 3021:0121:3312:031 2 2 3 2 2¾ 41½ 2:032 *1.90 (V.Crank) BillyBoyK., RuthGold, Mohawk
9-20 LB⅝ 2200 ft 68nw6000 cd mi 2941:0031:32 2:021 1 3 3 3 33 21¾ 2:022 *.70 (V.Crank) Weasel,Chf.Butler,MiraculousStar
9-10 LB⅝ 2000 ft 68nw6000 mi 2941:03 1:3412:041 5 2 2 3 31½ 2¾ 2:041 *1.30 (V.Crank) DustyJ.Scott,Chf.Butler,Swt.Kngt.

---

12 — **8** — Black-Yellow

GINGER ROD
br m, 4, by Jackson Dale—Dixie Dimples by Eric Hanover
C. A. W. Hurtubise, Jr., Haverford, Pa.
Trainer-A. Iancale
(⅝)2:042 1969 7 3 1 1 5,310
2:072 1968 19 2 4 1 2,514
$2,514 — 3, 2:072 Driver-GENE DAISEY, 10-12-37 (170) BROWN-GOLD

4- 3 LB⅝ 3400 ft nw8000 cd mi 2941:0041:31 2:032 8 2° 1 3 42½ 45 2:042 8.50 (G.Cameron) Inheritance,ChancyBrk.,CitationPk.
3-24 LB⅝ 3600 sy nw6000 cd mi 3021:0511:3642:084 7 1° 1 1 1¾ 1nk 2:084 3.20 (J.Larente) GingerRod,Mr.HenryW.,Emb.Irish
3-10 LB⅝ 2600 ft nw5000 cd mi 3111:0321:34 2:042 3 1 1 1 1½ 13 2:042 2.80 (Her.Filion) Ging.Rod,Yola'sPrd.,DistantDrums
3- 3 LB⅝ 2600 ft nw5000 cd mi 3111:0231:3312:043 3 2 2 3 31¾ 22 2:05 *2.00 (Her.Filion) Yola'sPrd.,GingerRod,Mr.HenryW.
2-24 LB⅝ 2400 gd nw5000 cd mi 3031:0211:3412:062 7 1° 2 2 21¼ 31¼ 2:063 *1.60 (Her.Filion) Cmd.Major,Emb.Irish,GingerRod
2-19 LB⅝ 2000 sy nw4000 cd mi 32 1:0421:3812:112 x6x pulled up B.E. dnf *.70 (V.Crank) Escalate,ShaleeSue,DistantDrums
2-14 LB⅝ 2000 gd nw4000 cd mi 32 1:0441:36 2:072 7 1 1 1 1¼ 12 2:072 *1.50 (Her.Filion) GingerRod,Cmd.Astra,Dstnt.Drums

---

TRACKMAN: 4—1—6

←MORN. LINE

(5) PACE—1 MILE

Warming-Up Saddle Cloth
BLACK

PURSE $4,100

Exacta Windows Now Open For Wagering On 6th Rac

NON-WINNERS OF $10,000 IN 1968-69 COMBINED EARNINGS. Al
Eligible: Non-Winners of $12,500 in 1968-69 combined earnings th
are non-winners of a race in last 6 starts. Winners of 5 races in 19
ineligible.

ASK FOR HORSE BY PROGRAM NUMBER

3 — **1** — Red

JUANIT'S GLORY

b m, 5, by Ken Scot—Louise C. by Jerry The First — Trainer-W. Wilson
Samuel Hatch · Overton,Fayetteville,N.C. — (⅝)2:063 1969 7 2 0 1 4,0
$4,669 — 4, 2:03 (⅝) Driver-C. (Tug) BOYD, 1-25-36 (145) DK. BLUE-GOLD-LT. BLUE — (⅝)2:03 1968 22 5 0 3 4,6

3-29	LB⅝	3400 gd nw8000 cd mi	32	1:053	1:382	2:081	2	2	2	4	32	11	2:081	3.50	(J.Wilcutts)	Juanit'sGlory,Pr.Garry,Spc.Cdt.N.
3-25	LB⅝	4100 gd nw8000 cd mi	301	1:022	1:314	2:031	6	8	8	8	612¼	410½	2:051	12.10	(J.Wilcutts)	HalRuer, Crockett, CitationPick
3-18	LB⅝	3700 ft nw8000 cd mi	303	1:023	1:331	2:04	3	2	2	5	65¾	43½	2:043	13.70	(C.Boyd)	ValleySmsn.,Cm.Major,BabyMineA
3- 7	LB⅝	3400 gd nw8000 cd mi	313	1:04	1:344	2:054	5	7	7	5°	610¾	67½	2:071	9.70	(C.Boyd)	NewZ.South.Slvr,Bly.Dale,SpikeE.
2-26	LB⅝	3100 gd nw8000 cd mi	302	1:021	1:334	2:05	7	5°	1	3	34¾	37	2:062	5.60	(C.Boyd)	F.Adventure,Lnsm.Vlly.,Juan.Glor
2-20	LB⅝	2800 gd nw8000 cd mi	313	1:033	1:36	2:07	5	5	5	4°	64¾	614½	2:094	2.10	(C.Boyd)	AdOSam,GarrisonPride,SpikeEd
2-15	LB⅝	2800 gd nw8000 cd mi	304	1:03	1:35	2:063	1	5	1	2	2¾	11¼	2:063	5.70	(C.Boyd)	Juanit'sGlory, EdwardJ., AdOSam

6 — **2** — Blue

PRIDE'S POMP

b g, 6, by Greentree's Pride—Mountain Patsy by White Mountain Boy — Trainer-M. Martyniak
Ruth Furst, Ridgefield, N.J. — 1969 3 0 0 0 18
$24,739 — 5, 2:034 Driver-MICKY MARTYNIAK, 8-7-21 (165) TAN-BLUE — 2:034 1968 36 5 7 7 11,51

4- 4	LB⅝	ft Qua mi	311	1:04	1:354	2:07	5	5	5	5	43½	34¼	2:074	N.B.	(C.Fitzpatrick)	Shk.UpN.,SomersetA.,Pride'sPom
1-20	YR	3750 ft B2 cd mi	31	1:03	1:351	2:064	8	8	8	8°	84½	88¼	2:084	119.20	(T.Luchento)	Mzl.Rodney,Sh.Yankios,M.TripleE
1-13	YR	3750 ft B2 cd mi	303	1:03	1:34	2:061	5	8	3°	4°	52¼	62	2:063	24.40	(T.Luchento)	Admire, Adorato, IrishCam
1- 6	YR	3750 sy B2 cd mi	332	1:08	1:422	2:144	1	4	4°	3°	31¼	52	2:151	16.30	(T.Luchento)	MissionLad,Wildcat,Shdy.Yankios
12-14	RR	5000 sy A3-B1 hcp mi	31	1:03	1:353	2:071	2	5	5	7	78½	715	2:11	34.70	(T.Luchento)	Gd.Tm.Gene,FareT.Well,SchellHn.
12- 3	RR	3500 ft B1 mi	313	1:024	1:34	2:051	4	1	5°	4	42½	55½	2:062	33.10	(T.Luchento)	Exltd.Ruler,NiagaraBllt.dhAddieH
11-26	RR	3500 ft B1 mi	304	1:024	1:343	2:044	2	3	3	3°	42	66¼	2:062	11.60	(T.Luchento)	FareTheeWell,Raidal,DarrylM.Bee

12 — **3** — White

KAMMY'S KNIGHT

b g, 7, by Tar Heel—Kammy by Knight Dream — Trainer-P. Quaglietta
Dinny / Mrs. Dinny Tong, New York, N.Y. — 2:091 1969 1 1 0 0 1,50
$30,231 — 6, 2:042 (⅝) Driver-JAMES CURRAN, 5-11-29 (160) BLUE-YELLOW — (⅝)2:042 1968 24 3 2 5 7,42

3-31	RR	3000 ft C1 cd mi	333	1:061	1:372	2:091	2	1	1	1	11	11¾	2:091	9.50	(J.Curran)	Kmmy.Kngt.,Cop.Jacket,T.Premis
12- 9	RR	3000 ft C1 cd mi	311	1:054	1:382	2:111	4	5	7	7°	74¾	3hd	2:111	4.30	(J.Curran)	MikeScott,Trdr.Lloyd,Kam.Knight
11-28	RR	2700 sy C1 cd mi	314	1:062	1:383	2:104	8	8	5°	5°	53½	55	2:12	43.80	(R.Latzo)	WairauLord,Trdr.Lloyd,Coppr.Ads
11-18	RR	2700 gd C1 cd mi	31	1:05	1:361	2:082	2	4	2°	1°	11	12	2:082	*2.30	(J.Curran)	Kammy'sKngt.,Mk.Scott,KeyWhir
11- 7	LB⅝	2200 sy 68nw6000 cd mi	313	1:041	1:362	2:084	2	4	4	5	53	41¼	2:09	6.70	(R.Latzo)	DudleyAce,MissSantios,Har.McGe
11- 1	LB⅝	2200 ft 68nw6000 cd mi	294	1:012	1:321	2:034	2	4°	2	3	31½	37½	2:051	*2.80	(J.Curran)	IrishMay,Pillbox,Kammy'sKnight
10-25	LB⅝	2200 ft 68nw6000 cd mi	302	1:021	1:33	2:052	4	6	6	7	73½	41	2:053	4.50	(J.Curran)	Snead, EastmanHn.dhFrostDirect

6 — **4** — Green

RESURREXI

b m, 4, by Knight Dream—Bonney Maxine by Royal Napoleon — Trainer-C. Fitzpatrick
Chas. J. Fitzpatrick, Warwick Downs, R.I. — 1969 0 0 0 0
$9,411 — 3, 2:044 Driver-CHAS. FITZPATRICK, 6-13-26 (160) GREEN-WHITE-RED — 2:044 1968 23 7 1 3 9,41

10-24	RR	3000 ft C1 cd mi	313	1:043	1:361	2:064	7	1	1	1	11	11	2:064	2.90	(C.Fitzpatrick)	Resurrexi,ConfettiHan.,Ryl.Romar
10-16	YR	2750 ft C2 cd mi	302	1:012	1:333	2:044	6	1	2	1	12	11¾	2:044	*1.40	(L.Fontaine)	Resurrexi,Anita'sStar,Tracey'sGi
10-10	YR	2750 ft C2 cd mi	304	1:03	1:344	2:061	4	2	4	5	32	3½	2:062	3.00	(C.Fitzpatrick)	AdeleAdios,Unfm.P'cess,Resurrex
9-24	Fhld	3000 ft 68w6000 mi	311	1:033	1:343	2:053	8	8	8	8	84½	51½	2:054	41.50	(C.Fitzpatrick)	Lit.Hodge,Jim.Knight,Cl'retAndsn
9-16	Fhld	1600 ft cd mi	31	1:034	1:363	2:063	6	1°	1	1	1¾	1ns	2:063	1.80	(C.Fitzpatrick)	Resurrexi,Conestg.Way,Dk.Victor
9- 7	LB⅝	2000 ft 68nw6000 mi	31	1:031	1:351	2:054	2	4	4	7	85¾	53½	2:062	25.90	(C.Fitzpatrick)	CarbonCopy,Lky.Rocket,QuakerGa
8-28	Brdwn	3400 ft 68nw5500 cd mi	304	1:04	1:341	2:053	2	5	5	3°	47	88½	2:072	10.20	(C.Fitzpatrick)	Vesta'sDream, Apex, Jovolette

5 — **5** — Black

MISS GOLDEN BLADE

b m, 4, by Knight Time—Golden Blade by Gene Abbe — Trainer-W. Pocza
Robert Wilcox, Waynesfield, Ohio — (⅝)2:05 1969 10 1 4 1 1,90
$7,026 — 3, 2:062 (⅝) Driver-W. (Bill) POCZA, 1-8-26 (185) PURPLE-WHITE-RED — (⅝)2:062 1968 22 2 5 3 6,17

3-25	P.Pk⅝	1300 ft w5000 cd mi	302	1:03	1:34	2:05	1	3	4	1	11	1hd	2:05	*1.10	(W.Pocza)	M.Gldn.Blade,CoastLady,Suc.June
3-13	P.Pk⅝	1100 ft nw5500 cd mi	313	1:024	1:342	2:04	3	5	5	4°	31	45½	2:05	16.20	(W.Pocza)	PeppyTar,I'mTheJudge,Sentr.Glib
3- 6	P.Pk⅝	1200 ft 68nw10000 mi	311	1:042	1:344	2:053	6	4	5	6	64¾	32¼	2:061	7.80	(W.Pocza)	Sen.Glib,B.Majastic,M.Gldn.Blade
2-28	P.Pk⅝	1200 ft nw1000 cd mi	304	1:024	1:334	2:034	5	6	6	6	74	64¼	2:043	5.20	(W.Pocza)	Science, MelodyWarrior, Sen.Kno
2-22	P.Pk⅝	800 ft nw200 pr st cd mi	302	1:024	1:333	2:043	3	4	5	4°	31½	2ns	2:043	8.40	(W.Pocza)	BairdsAds.,M.Gld.Blade,B.Wheele
2-14	P.Pk⅝	900 ft nw4500 cd mi	304	1:03	1:351	2:054	4	2	3	3	2½	2½	2:054	10.60	(W.Pocza)	Sureshot,M.Gld.Blade,BayWheele
2- 6	P.Pk⅝	1100 ft nw5500 cd mi	303	1:041	1:341	2:052	3	2	2	1	11½	45	2:062	6.80	(W.Pocza)	GallantArmb.,MelodyFly,Scot.Pac

8 — **6** — Yellow

MIGHTY ANDREA

br m, 4, by Adios Senator—Follow Girl by Follow Up — Trainer-F. Browne
Mighty Acres, Inc., Toms River, N.J. — 1969 0 0 0 0
$9,484 — 3, 2:031 (⅝) Driver-FRANK BROWNE, 4-29-30 (162) GREEN-WHITE — (⅝)2:031 1968 24 6 0 2 9,4

4- 4	LB⅝	ft Qua mi	311	1:04	1:354	2:07	3	4	4	3°	31½	44½	2:074	N.B.	(F.Browne)	Shk.UpN.,SomersetA.,Pride'sPom
11- 6	LB⅝	3000 ft 68nw10000 cd mi	30	1:01	1:321	2:024	5	7	7	x8xx	820¾	821½	2:07	10.70	(J.Greene)	Tart.Sauce,B.ByeGene,LiberaceH
10-30	LB⅝	3000 ft 68nw10000 cd mi	314	1:031	1:342	2:052	5	6	6	5	64¼x	4x3¼P5	2:06	12.10	(J.Greene)	CallHerLady,ByeB.Gene,ChenDon
10-22	LB⅝	2500 ft 68nw8000 cd mi	293	1:004	1:321	2:031	4	6	6	6°	53	1ns	2:031	6.90	(J.Greene)	MightyAndrea,VoloTime,ChenDon
10-15	LB⅝	2500 ft 68nw8000 cd mi	301	1:01	1:311	2:013	1	5	5	5	55	41½	2:014	22.10	(J.Greene)	CallH.Lady,Sem.Gene,Ldy.Emeral
10- 4	LB⅝	3000 ft 68nw6000 cd mi	302	1:014	1:321	2:03	8	8	8x	8	815¾	8dis		31.60	(J.Greene)	VoloTime, LadyEmerald, Mr.Hoff
9-27	Fhld	6000 ft Stk mi	311	1:04	1:342	2:041	1	3	3	4	33	35¼	2:051	N.B.	(J.Greene)	GoOnBye,TrueEden,Mgty.Andrea

7/2 — **7** — Pink

MOONGLO HANOVER

b f, 3, by Gamecock—Moonlite Hanover by Adios — Trainer-F. Safford
Gray Brothers & Walter M. Reed, Jr., Ft. Fairfield, Me. — 1969 0 0 0 0
$9,935 — 2, 2:042 (⅝) Driver-J. (Tic) WILCUTTS, 11-23-19 (120) BLUE-RED-WHITE — (⅝)2:042 1968 7 4 1 1 9,9

6-28	Lau⅝	3571 ft 2yr F Stk mi	311	1:032	1:361	2:042	5	2	2	2	2¾	1¾	2:042	e*.90	(R.James)	MoongloHn.,SuppleYnk.,W.Thank
6-20	RcR	2500 ft 2yr Ec cd mi	331	1:052	1:354	2:073	9	4	2°	1	12	14	2:073	e*.50	(R.James)	MoongloHan.,Gd.Maxine,Min.J.D
6-11	Brdwn	10950 ft 2yr F Ec mi	312	1:041	1:373	2:084	6	2°	1	1	1½	11¼	2:084	*.65	(R.Myers)	MoongloHn.,Overwhelm,Parads.H
5-30	RcR	1500 gd 2yr Ec mi	321	1:062	1:381	2:091	5	5	4°	1°	12	16¾	2:091	6.20	(R.James)	Mnglo.Hn.,J.D.Solctr.,M.SnugHr
5-23	RcR	1500 sy 2yr Ec mi	32	1:081	1:403	2:141	2	7	7	7	76½	42¾	2:144	e2.60	(H.Tudor)	Minn.J.D.,J.D.Solicitor,EmmyHa
5-16	RcR	1500 ft 2yr F Ec mi	324	1:044	1:371	2:10	1	4	4	3°	63½	2nk	2:10	e*1.30	(H.Tudor)	JacquelynS.,MngloHn.,M.S.Hrbr.
5- 9	RcR	1500 ft 2yr Ec mi	33	1:07	1:391	2:093	6	7	7	6	68	34¾	2:103	e11.30	(H.Tudor)	LaverneHn.,Ben'sImp,MoongloHn

9/2 — **8** — Black-Yellow

THUNDER ROYAL

br h, 9, by Thunder On—Tyrone Queen by Jack High — Trainer-Her. Filion
G. Bartoli, H. Birdman, Capital Hill Farms, Reg'd., E. & J. Durkin, Kingston, Pa. — (⅝)2:051 1969 7 1 3 0 3,3
$16,614 — 8, 2:071 Driver-HERVE FILION, 2-1-40 (142) RED-DK. BLUE-WHITE — 2:071 1968 12 3 4 0 4,7

4- 1	LB⅝	3000 ft nw6000 cd mi	30	1:03	1:343	2:051	1	5	5	2°	2½	1¾	2:051	*1.70	(Her.Filion)	Thndr.Royal,IrishRuss,Rd.Ranger
3-22	LB⅝	3300 ft nw6000 cd mi	31	1:022	1:34	2:044	2	3	4	4	34¼	46¼	2:06	3.10	(Her.Filion)	Mdw.Spirit,Sp.CadetN.,SheDares
3-13	LB⅝	3400 ft nw8000 cd mi	304	1:023	1:322	2:042	3	4	5	5	55¼	62½	2:044	10.30	(Her.Filion)	Aft.Spdy.,AllenBeaver,Mdw.Spiri
3- 4	LB⅝	3400 ft nw8000 cd mi	313	1:021	1:344	2:061	8	6	6	5	43½x	7x6¼	2:072	8.80	(Her.Filion)	Grrsn.Prd.,Mdw.Spirit,AllenBea
2-26	LB⅝	2700 gd nw6000 cd mi	32	1:033	1:363	2:071	3	1	2	3	41½	21½	2:072	1.70	(Her.Filion)	Mr.Hayes, ThunderRoyal, BigSti
2-17	LB⅝	2400 ft nw6000 cd mi	31	1:031	1:353	2:06	1	3	3	3	32¼	21½	2:061	2.20	(Her.Filion)	Stdy.Strk.,Thndr.Royal,SturdyGe
1-26	BB⅝	1400 ft nw4000 cd mi	304	1:043	1:38	2:092	6	6	6	6	46	2hd	2:092	1.90	(Her.Filion)	EarthelMcKlyo,Thndr.Ryl.,Will.A

TRACKMAN: 1—7—8

←MORN LINE

(6) PACE—1 MILE

Warming-Up Saddle Cloth
BLUE

PURSE $5,500

ASK FOR HORSE BY PROGRAM NUMBER

EXACTA WAGERING THIS RACE

WINNERS IN EXCESS OF $15,000 IN 1968-69 COMBINED EARNINGS.

7/2 **1** Red

‡NEWPORT ROBBI b h, 6, by Tar Heel—Newport Judy by Adios — Newport Stock Farm, Pompano Beach, Fla. — Trainer-A. Cameron
(⅝)2:043 1969 2 1 0 0 2,500
$96,232 — 5, 2:002 Driver-GENE DAISEY, 10-12-37 (170) BROWN-GOLD 2:002 1968 35 6 6 7 36,521

4- 5 LB⅝‡ 5000 gd nw15000 cd mi 3111:0331:34 2:043 2 4 4 2 21 13 2:043 2.60 (Her.Filion) Npt.Robbi,Qk.Return,LibertyKngt.
3-28 LB⅝‡ 5000 ft nw15000 cd mi 3011:0221:3242:024 7 7 8 8 74¾ 65 2:034 4.70 (G.Cameron) EasterColleen,LewOre.,Steve'sPhil
11- 7 LB⅝‡ 4500 gd 68w15000 cd mi 3031:0321:3442:053 3 5 5 4° 43 66 2:064 4.00 (A.Cameron) LewOregon,XPertTime,Transpondr
11- 1 LB⅝‡ 4000 ft 68nw15000 cd mi 2911:01 1:3042:02 2 2 2 2 21½ 1½ 2:02 2.20 (A.Cameron) Nwpt.Robbie,LincHan.,CrownBlue
10-24 LB⅝‡ 4500 ft 68w15000 cd mi 3011:04 1:3422:032 5 6 7 6 65½ 64½ 2:041 5.40 (A.Cameron) JazzyCrain, GoOnBye, SchellHan.
10-17 LB⅝‡ 4500 ft 68w15000 cd mi 284 :5931:2922:003 4 3 4 4° 41½ 41 2:004 3.70 (A.Cameron) YourKiddin, LewOregon, GoOnBye
10-10 LB⅝‡ 4500 ft 68w15000 cd mi 30 1:0131:3312:024 7 8 6 6° 63½ 63½ 2:032 5.10 (A.Cameron) GoOnBye,StewartHan.,EffratHan.

6 **2** Blue

DIAMOND DALE br g, 7, by Meadow Ace—Coleen Sampson by Sampson Hanover — The Seymour Stable, DeKalb Junction, N.Y. — Trainer-F. Parks
(⅝)2:042 1969 3 1 0 0 3,090
$43,361 — 6, 2:021 (⅝) Driver-FRED PARKS, 12-9-06 (155) GOLD-BLACK (⅝)2:021 1968 31 5 1 2 14,610

4- 3 LB⅝ 5000 ft nw15000 cd mi 3011:0211:3142:023 6 7 7 8 74½ 51½ 2:024 6.40 (F.Parks) Rdr.Gamble,Bywd.Boy,FlaveHan.
3-21 LB⅝ 5500 ft nw15000 cd mi 3011:0221:3222:022 7 7 6 5° 52¾ 41½ 2:023 10.40 (Her.Filion) Cardnl.Bruce,Ad.Uniteus,Bywd.Boy
3-12 LB⅝ 4800 ft nw12500 cd mi 3041:0131:3322:042 6 3 4 6 64¾ 1hd 2:042 12.80 (F.Parks) Diam.Dale,JethroHn.,Region'sPrd.
11-11 LB⅝ 3500 gd 68nw12500 cd mi 3011:0111:34 2:05 5 7 7 6 54½ 46½ 2:061 4.30 (F.Parks) Hckry.Kngt.,DuaneLbll.,Key.Aloha
11- 1 LB⅝ 4000 ft 68nw15000 cd mi 2911:01 1:3042:02 1 3 3 3 33 4¾ 2:02 16.20 (F.Parks) Nwpt.Robbie,LincHan.,CrownBlue
10-22 LB⅝ 4000 ft 68nw15000 cd mi 2941:0131:3232:031 2 5 6 8 86 55 2:041 18.50 (F.Parks) PoconoHan.,W.Miss,Raid.Gamble
10-12 LB⅝ 4500 ft 68w15000 cd mi 3011:0231:3212:02 1 2 2 3 32½ 64¾ 2:024 7.10 (F.Parks) Trpt.Karen,Sen.Roan,M.Wynbl'gh.

3 **3** White

ROYAL GENE PICK b g, 6, by Gene Abbe—Colette Wick by Darn Flashy — Double L. Farms, Liverpool, N.Y. — Trainer-R. Dancer
(⅝)2:042 1969 5 1 0 2 3,880
$112,666 — 5, 1:583 (⅝) Driver-RONNIE DANCER, 5-31-49 (140) BLUE-GOLD (⅝)1:583 1968 28 8 6 3 51,127

4- 5 LB⅝ 5500 gd w15000 cd mi 3121:0421:3712:073 3 1 1 1 1½ 31¾ 2:074 *1.40 (R.Dancer) GloriaGray,CrownBlue,Roy.GenePk.
3-29 LB⅝ 5500 sy w15000 cd mi 31 1:0321:3442:073 7 3° 2° 3° 46½ 711¾ 2:094 9.70 (R.Dancer) M.Drm.Girl,Sen.Roan,Jer.Gauman
3-22 LB⅝ 6000 ft w15000 cd mi 2941:0211:3312:02 5 1 1 1 11½ 31¾ 2:021 2.40 (R.Dancer) Sen.Roan,QuickReturn,RoyalG.Pick
3-15 LB⅝ 5500 ft nw15000 cd mi 2911:0031:3132:013 6 3° 3 3 43 65¾ 2:023 7.30 (V.Dancer) M.Con.Ads.,StewartHn.,J.Gauman
3- 7 LB⅝ 5000 gd nw15000 cd mi 3031:0311:3342:042 3 1 1 1 11¾ 1½ 2:042 *1.10 (R.Dancer) RoyalG.Pk.,Steve'sPhil,Aft.Apollo
11-22 SD 44750 ft 67nw35000 mi 2911:0021:31 2:02 4 2 1 1 1nk 22 2:022 4.80 (S.Dancer) Jer.Gauman,RoyG.Pick,Dan.R.Gil
11-16 SD 6000 ft Inv hcp mi 2931:0031:3132:022 1 1 3 6 65 54¾ 2:032 7.40 (R.Dancer) Jer.Gauman,Edgwd.Crd.,C.K.Adios

4 **4** Green

QUICK RETURN b h, 4, by Bullet Hanover—Valentine Dream by Knight Dream — Gray Bros., E. Providence, R.I. & A. Parsons, London, Ont., Can. — Trainer-F. Safford
1969 2 0 2 0 2,750
$17,285 — 3, 2:01 (⅝) Driver-J. (Tic) WILCUTTS, 11-23-19 (120) BLUE-RED-WHITE (⅝)2:01 1968 23 6 4 5 17,285

4- 5 LB⅝ 5000 gd nw15000 cd mi 3111:0331:34 2:043 1 3 3 1 11 23 2:051 *.80 (J.Wilcutts) Npt.Robbi,Qk.Return,LibertyKngt.
3-22 LB⅝ 6000 ft w15000 cd mi 2941:0211:3312:02 4 5 5 5 42¾ 2nk 2:02 9.60 (J.Wilcutts) Sen.Roan,QuickReturn,RoyalG.Pick
9-25 Bloomsburg 10891 gd 3yr Stk, 2 dashes, Mile in 1:593 fin. 3rd—Mile in 2:052 fin. 2nd (H.Tudor)
9-14 LB⅝ 4500 ft 68w15000 cd mi 292 :5921:3042:011 6 7 7 7 74½ 66 2:022 14.10 (H.Tudor) LewOregon,Cardnl.Bruce,EffratHn.
9- 5 Brdwn 4700 ft 68w10000 mi 2921:02 1:3332:041 5 6 7 6° 42¾ 2hd 2:041 12.65 (R.James) LeaderPick,Qk.Return,Joam.Pony
8-31 Brdwn 4700 ft 68w9000 mi 3041:0241:3312:034 6 6 6 6 54¾ 43½ 2:042 6.60 (R.James) BerryBoy,SenatorRoan,Rdr.Gamble
8-21 Brdwn 4700 ft 68w8000 mi 3111:0141:33 2:031 1 2 2 2° 21 32½ 2:033 *1.55 (R.James) SenatorRoan, GoBye, QuickReturn

5 **5** Black

HICKORY KNIGHT b g, 6, by Knight Dream—Butterfly Hanover by Dean Hanover — Hickory Way Stables, Inc., St. James, N.Y. — Trainer-D. Sergi
(⅝)2:03 1969 4 2 0 1 6,225
$27,760 — 4, 2:03 (⅝) Driver-HERVE FILION, 2-1-40 (142) RED-DK. BLUE-WHITE (⅝)2:04 1968 14 5 2 1 12,735

4- 5 LB⅝ 5500 gd w15000 cd mi 3111:0411:3532:054 1 4 7 7 62 11 2:054 3.70 (Her.Filion) HickoryKngt.,Ibidem,EvergreenDot
3-29 LB⅝ 5500 sy w15000 cd mi 31 1:0321:3442:073 1 2 3 5 56¾ 54½ 2:082 11.50 (B.Webster) M.Drm.Girl,Sen.Roan,Jer.Gauman
3-21 LB⅝ 5500 ft nw15000 cd mi 3031:0211:3222:03 6 6 7 2° 21 12 2:03 2.70 (Her.Filion) Hckry.Knight,C.B.Sen.,Mtn.Creed
2-27 YR 3750 ft B2 cd mi 3141:0511:3642:071 4 5 6 5° 33 33 2:074 8.40 (C.Abbatiello) ToughTime,Northwood,Hckry.Kngt.
11-11 LB⅝ 3500 gd 68nw12500 cd mi 3011:0111:34 2:05 6 8 8 4° 42½ 12½ 2:05 7.30 (Her.Filion) Hckry.Kngt.,DuaneLbll.,Key.Aloha
11- 6 LB⅝ 3500 ft 68nw12500 cd mi 30 1:0121:32 2:02 8 4° 1 3 32 68 2:033 23.00 (G.Mahony) DustyJ.Scott,Michls.Edict,Qkr.Gal
10-30 LB⅝ 3500 ft 68nw12500 cd mi 3021:0211:3422:041 3 5 5 4° 41½ 2nk 2:041 7.40 (Her.Filion) DustyJ.Scott,Hick.Knight,Qkr.Gal

12 **6** Yellow

FAR HEEL b h, 6, by Tar Heel—Miss Farvel by Farvel — Carlton L. Williams, Baltimore, Md. — Trainer-C. Williams
1969 2 0 0 0 250
$33,125 — 4, 2:013 (⅝) Driver-W. (Bill) POCZA, 1-8-26 (185) PURPLE-WHITE-RED (⅝)2:013 1968 28 4 4 5 17,480

4- 5 LB⅝ 5000 gd nw15000 cd mi 3121:05 1:3612:072 8 2° 2 3 31¾ 53½ 2:08 6.30 (A.Myer) LewOregon,HistoricTime,Donora
3-22 LB⅝ 6000 ft w15000 cd mi 2941:0211:3312:02 1 4 4 2 31¾ 64½ 2:024 12.90 (A.Myer) Sen.Roan,QuickReturn,RoyalG.Pick
11-23 Fhld 6000 ft Pref-Inv mi 3111:0241:3312:03 1 4 4° 5° 65 68½ 2:043 3.60 (A.Myer) BonneFille,JetButler,Sthrn.Song
11-16 Fhld 10000 ft Inv mi 2921:0121:3212:022 7 4° 3° 4° 42½ 87 2:034 19.70 (A.Myer) DeputyHn.,BonneFille,Pep.R'nbow
11- 9 Fhld 7500 ft Pref-Inv mi 2941:0021:3032:014 2 4 4 3 22 2½ 2:014 1.80 (W.Pocza) BonneFille,FarHeelAirN.Zealand
11- 2 Fhld 7500 ft Pref-Inv mi 2931:0041:3122:012 2 3 3 4 42½ 32½ 2:014 14.80 (W.Pocza) PeppyR'nbow,Recnp.Jack,FarHeel
10-29 LB⅝ 4000 ft 68nw15000 cd mi 31 1:0231:3212:022 3 3 3 2° 32 56½ 2:033 *1.50 (W.Pocza) XPertTm.,Transpndr.,Wilson.Miss

8 **7** Pink

STEVE'S PHIL ro g, 9, by Philip Scott—Vale Crest by Mighty H. — Rose & Michael Lomoriello, Brooklyn, N.Y. — Trainer-V. Kachel
(⅝)2:08 1969 7 1 1 1 4,600
$40,549 — 8, 2:003 (⅝) Driver-VINSON KACHEL, 7-3-20 (165) BLACK-WHITE (⅝)2:003 1968 38 6 4 5 28,376

4- 5 LB⅝ 5000 sy nw15000 cd mi 3141:0411:3532:08 8 7 7 2° 21 14 2:08 8.20 (V.Kachel) Steve'sPhil,Jeeves,Sentr.BillyMac
3-28 LB⅝ 5000 ft nw15000 cd mi 3011:0221:3242:024 3 5 5 2° 2½ 33 2:032 3.70 (V.Kachel) EasterColleen,LewOre.,Steve'sPhil
3-21 LB⅝ 5500 ft nw15000 cd mi 3011:0221:3222:022 6 5° 1 1 2½ 72 2:024 6.30 (V.Kachel) Cardnl.Bruce,Ad.Uniteus,Bywd.Boy
3-14 LB⅝ 5000 ft nw15000 cd mi 3031:0231:34 2:051 4 2° 1 2 31¾ 52¾ 2:053 4.10 (V.Kachel) Transponder,Crdnl.Bruce,GoOnBye
3- 7 LB⅝ 5000 gd nw15000 cd mi 3031:0311:3342:042 7 7 7 4 43½ 2½ 2:042 18.70 (V.Kachel) RoyalG.Pk.,Steve'sPhil,Aft.Apollo
3- 1 LB⅝ 5000 ft w15000 cd mi 3031:0121:3222:021 7 8 5° 6° 67½ 69½ 2:04 20.60 (V.Kachel) StewartHan., BerryBoy, GoOnBye
2-15 LB⅝ 4500 gd w15000 cd mi 3111:04 1:3432:043 1 x7 7 7 719¼7dis 3.90 (J.Quinn) AftonDay,SenatorRoan,GoOnBye

8 **8** Black-Yellow

EASTER COLLEEN b m, 4, by Adios Senator—Easter Dream by Knight Dream — Herbert W. Scott, Perryman, Md. — Trainer-H. W. Scott
(⅝)2:024 1969 5 2 0 1 5,960
$10,370 — 3, 2:042 Driver-HERB SCOTT, 8-24-12 (170) RED-WHITE 2:042 1968 19 6 1 3 10,370

4- 5 LB⅝ 5500 gd w15000 cd mi 3111:0411:3532:054 3 5 2 2° 2½ 64¾ 2:063 5.40 (Herb.W.Scott) HickoryKngt.,Ibidem,EvergreenDot
3-28 LB⅝ 5000 ft nw15000 cd mi 3011:0221:3242:024 5 2 2 1 1½ 1ns 2:024 *3.20 (Herb.W.Scott) EasterColleen,LewOre.,Steve'sPhil
3-21 LB⅝ 5500 ft nw15000 cd mi 3021:0211:32 2:014 4 5 5 2° 2¾ 32 2:021 8.60 (Herb.W.Scott) BerryBoy,GoOnBye,EasterColleen
3-14 LB⅝ 5000 ft nw15000 cd mi 3021:0141:3212:023 4 7 7 7 66½ 44 2:032 3.70 (Herb.W.Scott) Bywd.Boy,Wilson'sMiss,BerryBoy
3- 5 LB⅝ 4800 ft nw12500 cd mi 30 1:0311:3532:052 5 6 6 2° 2½ 14 2:052 3.60 (Herb.W.Scott) EasterColleen,DocVan,PinkVelvet
9-27 LB⅝ 4500 ft 68nw12500 cd mi 3131:03 1:3312:041 3 4 4 5 44 63 2:044 11.30 (Herb.W.Scott) Miraculous,CrownBlue,LittleWillie
8-30 Brdwn 4000 ft 68nw8500 cd mi 32 1:0431:3422:053 1 1 1 1 1½ 1ns 2:053 3.65 (Herb.W.Scott) EasterClln.,Lusc.Lou,Mrylln.Han.

TRACKMAN: 3—1—4

MORN. LINE

(7) **PACE—1 MILE**
Warming-Up Saddle Cloth
RED

PURSE $20,000

ASK FOR HORSE BY PROGRAM NUMBER

"BIG E" WINDOWS NOW OPEN

THE PENNSBURY PACE

INVITATIONAL

8 — **1** — Red
AFTON DAY
blk h, 6, by Trooper Lee—Sybil K. M. by Guy Day — Trainer-O. Mumford
F. Perry, Suffolk. Va. & L. Midgett, Elizabeth City, N.C. — (5/8)2:012 1969 8 6 1 0 29,250
$23,317 — 4, 2:04 — Driver-JAMES LARENTE, 5-21-31 (160) BLUE-GOLD — 2:05 1968 31 3 7 8 15,392

4- 5 LB5/8	25000	gd	Inv	mi	2931:0121:3142:021	7	7	5	3°	33	42½	2:023	4.50	(J.Larente)	Lit.Jer.Way,Nard.Byrd,M.Con.Ads		
3-27 LB5/8	15000	ft	68nw20000 Ec	mi	29 1:00 1:3042:012	9	5	3	2°	1¼	13½	2:012	*.90	(J.Larente)	AftonDay, Ardrossan, RobinHill		
3-21 LB5/8	25000	ft	Inv	mi	2931:0121:3042:002	8	7	4	4°	33¾	22	2:004	14.70	(J.Larente)	MissCon.Ads.,AftonDay,Nard.Byrd		
3-14 LB5/8	6000	ft	68nw20000 Ec	mi	30 1:0141:34 2:031	1	3	1	1	1¾	14	2:031	*.50	(J.Larente)	AftonDay,Prd.OfHan.,FireawayN.		
3- 8 LB5/8	6000	ft	68nw20000 Ec	mi	3011:0031:33 2:022	5	6	1	1	1¼	12	2:022	*1.70	(J.Larente)	AftonDay,PrideOfHan.,FireawayN.		
3- 1 LB5/8	5500	ft	68nw20000 Ec	mi	3021:0041:3112:02	6	4°	1	1	1½	1hd	2:02	*1.50	(J.Larente)	AftonDay,FireawayN.,LibertyKngt.		
2-21 LB5/8	5000	gd	68nw20000 Ec	mi	3111:0321:3532:051	6	1	1	1	12½	14	2:051	2.60	(J.Larente)	AftonDay, RobinHill, VoloTime		

3 — **2** — Blue
RUM CUSTOMER
b h, 4, by Poplar Byrd—Custom Maid by Knight Dream — Trainer-A. Winger
Kennilworth Farms & Louis & Connie Mancuso, Deer Park, N.Y — 2:044 1969 1 1 0 0 7,500
$411,902 — 3, 1:56 (1) — Driver-AL WINGER, 12-18-21 (180) RED-WHITE-BLUE — (1)1:56 1968 24 15 4 3 355,618

4- 5 RR	15000	gd	Opn hcp	mi	30 1:0231:3422:044	6	2°	1	1	11	1¾	2:044	*.40	(J.Chapman)	RumCustmr.,HodgenSpcl.,DingleN.
10-26 RR	189018	ft	3yr Stk	mi	2931:01 1:3142:014	8	5°	4°	1°	1½	13	2:014	e*.90	(W.Haughton)	RumCustmr.,Trop.Song,IsolatorHn
10-19 LB5/8	35839	gd	3yr C Stk	mi	292 :5941:31 2:012	6	2°	2	4	41	31½	2:013	*.30	(W.Haughton)	F.Napoleon,Batman,RumCustomer
10-12 YR	150000	ft	3yr Stk	mi	292 :5911:3011:594	3	1	3	4	41	1¾	1:594	e*.30	(W.Haughton)	RumCustmr.,F.Napoleon,Pref.Time
10- 5 YR	25000	ft	3yr Stk	mi	29 :5941:30 2:003	9	5	2	1	1hd	11	2:003	e*.40	(W.Haughton)	RumCustmr.F.Napoleon,HollySand
9-19 Dela	41689	ft	3yr Stk	mi	281 :5841:3021:593	2	4	4	2°	11	13	1:593	*.20	(W.Haughton)	RumCust.,Gd.Tm.Kngt.,Crlss.Time
9-19 Dela	31267	ft	3yr Stk	mi	284 :5911:29 1:593	7	4°	2°	1	1½	13¼	1:593	*.50	(W.Haughton)	RumCustmr.,IsolatorHn.,Care.Time

12 — **3** — White
MOONDOWNER
ch g, 4, by Greentree Adios—Josedale Roselyn by Scotch Dillon — Trainer-W. Pocza
Polen Coalmont Farms, Hopedale, Ohio — (5/8)2:022 1969 2 1 1 0 5,500
$46,538 — 3, 1:594 (5/8) — Driver-W. (Bill) POCZA, 1-8-26 (185) PURPLE-WHITE-RED — (5/8)1:594 1968 30 7 9 1 43,783

3-29 P.Pk5/8	10000	ft	Stk	mi	31 1:0211:3212:022	1	1	1	1	1½	1½	2:022	*.50	(W.Pocza)	Moondowner,Mstr.Adios,JeffreyR.
3-15 P.Pk5/8	2000	ft	w7500	mi	2941:02 1:3232:014	5	2	2	2	2½	2½	2:014	2.40	(W.Pocza)	TraderNard.,Moondowner,Disband
11- 9 LB5/8	7500	sy	Pref hcp	mi	3041:05 1:36 2:073	4	1	1	2	21	23¼	2:081	*2.00	(W.Pocza)	BeauBtlr.,Moondowner,M.Drm.Girl
11- 2 LB5/8	7500	ft	Pref	mi	2941:0111:3022:013	3	2	1ix2x		68½	67¾P5	2:031	*2.00	(W.Pocza)	LadyEvrgrn.,Jer.Gauman,†So.Song
10-26 LB5/8	7500	ft	Pref	mi	3031:0241:3222:021	2	1	1	1	1¼	1¾	2:021	*2.70	(W.Pocza)	Moondowner,LadyEvrgrn.FourLeaf
10-19 LB5/8	7500	gd	Pref	mi	29 :5931:3022:004	5	4°	2	6	64¼	21½	2:01	15.80	(W.Pocza)	Gd.Tm.Boy,Moondowner,Silnt.Byrd
10-12 LB5/8	7500	ft	Pref	mi	293 :5921:2932:001	3	3	4	5	53	41¼	2:002	5.80	(W.Pocza)	S'thern.Song,FourLeaf,BeauButler

4 — **4** — Green
NARDIN'S BYRD
b h, 5, by Bye Bye Byrd—Miss Tempo by Good Time — Trainer-A. Winger
Trader Horn, Inc., North Bay Village, Fla. — 2:053 1969 5 1 3 1 34,250
$385,666 — 3, 1:59 — Driver-CHAS. FITZPATRICK, 6-13-26 (160) GREEN-WHITE-RED — (1)2:002 1968 11 4 6 0 110,803

4- 5 LB5/8	25000	gd	Inv	mi	2931:0121:3142:021	3	2	2	2	21½	21¾	2:022	*1.60	(W.Haughton)	Lit.Jer.Way,Nard.Byrd,M.Con.Ads.
3-29 RR	25000	sy	Inv	mi	30 1:0221:3422:053	4	1°	1	1	12	1hd	2:053	1.90	(W.Haughton)	Nard.Byrd,OrbiterN.,HodgenSpcl.
3-21 LB5/8	25000	ft	Inv	mi	2931:0121:3042:002	4	4	5	5	55	32	2:004	*1.10	(W.Haughton)	MissCon.Ads.,AftonDay,Nard.Byrd
3-14 WR5/8	15000	ft	Inv	mi	2921:0141:3242:033	3	1	1	1	1½	21	2:034	*.35	(W.Haughton)	PhilipBrian,Nardin'sByrd,Mr.Duke
3- 6 WR5/8	35000	ft	Inv	mi	291 :5941:3012:004	2	3	4	2°	2ns	22	2:011	*.80	(W.Haughton)	W.W.Smith,Nard.Byrd,PhilipBrian
7-13 Spk5/8	25000	ft	FFA	mi	2831:0111:3011:583	5	4	4	5	22	2¾	1:584	2.20	(D.Insko)	BestofAll,Nardin'sByrd,Tmly.Kngt
7- 6 Spk5/8	15000	ft	JFA	mi	29 1:00 1:3011:582	5	5	5	5	42	2nsdh	1:582	3.80	(W.Haughton)	BestofAll,Nard.ByrddhTrueDuane

2 — **5** — Black
ADAPTOR
br h, 6, by Dick Adios—Mirthful Lass by Dons Ayr — Trainer-R. Dancer
Irving Berkemever, New Milford, N.J. — 1969 5 3 1 0
$33,457 — None In USA — Driver-STANLEY DANCER, 7-25-27 (135) BLUE-GOLD

4- 8 LB5/8		ft	Qua	mi	3011:0121:3222:021	7	4°	2°	2	21½	15	2:021	N.B.	(S.Dancer)	Adaptor, Carpathian, CircusTime

THE INFORMATION BELOW WAS OBTAINED FROM THE VICTORIAN TROTTING BOARD, MELBOURNE, AUSTRALIA

3-14 Harold Park	1 Mile in 1:591 fin. 1st	(J.Hargreaves)	Adaptor,TwinkleHan.,VikingWater
1-31 Harold Park	1⅝ Miles in 3:374 fin. 2nd	(J.Hargreaves)	CockyRaider,Adaptor,CoraleOaks
1-18 Melbourne	1 Mile in 2:002 fin. 1st	(J.Hargreaves)	Adaptor,GoldenAlley,TaraMdw.
1-11 Melbourne	1¾ Miles in 3:46 fin. 5th	(J.Hargreaves)	GoldenAlley,CoraleOaks,FairDeed
1- 7 Bendigo	1⅝ Miles in 3:291 fin. 1st	(J.Hargreaves)	Adaptor, BonAdios, GarryRowan

6 — **6** — Yellow
MISS CONNA ADIOS
b m, 4, by Adios Senator—Americonna Direct by Watson E. Direct — Trainer-F. Milby
N. Franklin Milby, Cordova, Md. — (5/8)2:002 1969 5 4 0 1 30,50
$31,760 — 3, 2:01 (5/8) — Driver-TOM LEWIS, 8-20-09 (135) RED-WHITE-BLUE — (5/8)2:01 1968 30 15 5 4 30,864

4- 5 LB5/8	25000	gd	Inv	mi	2931:0121:3142:021	5	1	1	1	1½	31¾	2:022	1.70	(T.Lewis)	Lit.Jer.Way,Nard.Byrd,M.Con.Ads
3-29 LB5/8	20000	sy	Inv	mi	3131:04 1:36 2:073	5	1	1	1	12¼	12½	2:073	*.70	(T.Lewis)	MissCon.Ad.,Lit.Jer.Way,L.Evrgrn
3-21 LB5/8	25000	ft	Inv	mi	2931:0121:3042:002	2	1	1	1	13½	12	2:002	3.80	(T.Lewis)	MissCon.Ads.,AftonDay,Nard.Byrd
3-15 LB5/8	5500	ft	w15000 cd	mi	2911:0031:3132:013	5	1	1	1	1¾	1½	2:013	*1.10	(T.Lewis)	M.Con.Ads.,StewartHn.,J.Gauman
2-22 LB5/8	4500	ft	w15000 cd	mi	?041:0341:3332:023	5	1	1	1	11¾	11½	2:023	2.10	(T.Lewis)	M.Con.Ads.,GoOnBye,StewartHan.
9-28 LB5/8	8000	ft	3yr Inv	mi	29 1:01 1:3122:01	6	1	1	1	1½	21	2:011	4.50	(T.Lewis)	Batman,MissConnaAdios,Jaz.Crai
9-18 LB5/8	6000	ft	3yr Inv	mi	274 :5921:28 1:583	5	2°x6		6	613¾	310½	2:003	*1.60	(T.Lewis)	BeauButler,Skunk,MissCon.Adios

5 — **7** — Pink
LITTLE JERRY WAY
ch h, 4, by Jerry Way—Little Goody by Good Time — Trainer-Her. Filion
Eleanor M. French, Washington C.H., Ohio — (5/8)2:021 1969 2 1 1 0 17,50
$64,476 — 3, 1:584 (1) — Driver-HERVE FILION, 2-1-40 (142) RED-DK. BLUE-WHITE — (1)1:584 1968 29 12 8 5 53,38

4- 5 LB5/8	25000	gd	Inv	mi	2931:0121:3142:021	4	5	6	5	44½	1¾	2:021	12.10	(Her.Filion)	Lit.Jer.Way,Nard.Byrd,M.Con.Ads
3-29 LB5/8	20000	sy	Inv	mi	3131:04 1:36 2:073	6	5	5	4	43½	22½	2:08	8.80	(Her.Filion)	MissCon.Ad.,Lit.Jer.Way,L.Evrgrn
3-26 LB5/8		ft	Qua	mi	3111:0341:3622:082	8	2	2	2	12¼	11	2:082	N.B.	(Her.Filion)	LittleJ.Way,EllaH.Volo,CaseyDare
3-18 LB5/8		ft	Qua	mi	3121:0411:3442:054	2	1	1	1	11¾	13	2:054	N.B.	(Her.Filion)	LittleJerryWay,IowaTime,Aft.Cliff
12-21 Hol1	10000	ft	Inv	mi	3011:0141:3222:01	6	2	2	2	21½	21¼	2:011	3.80	(R.Buxton)	C.K.Adios,LittleJerryWay,FirstLe
12-14 Hol1	10000	ft	Inv	mi	2921:0031:3031:591	5	1	2	2	22	2nk	1:591	3.90	(R.Buxton)	C.K.Ads.,LittleJry.Way,DwyerHan
12-10 Hol1		ft	Qua	mi	3031:0211:3332:052	9	1	1	1	13	1¾	2:052	N.B.	(E.Wheeler)	Li'leJ.Way,St.ExpressN.,Amndmt.

TRACKMAN: 5—2—4

HOME OF THE $100,000 COLONIAL—SEPT. 13

MORN. LINE

(8) PACE—1 MILE

Warming-Up Saddle Cloth BROWN

PURSE $7,000

"BIG E" WAGERING THIS RACE

PREFERRED

ASK FOR HORSE BY PROGRAM NUMBER

---

4 — **1** Red

ADIOS UNITEUS
ch g, 5, by Adios—Amber Ann by Billy Direct
F. Perry, Suffolk, Va. & L. Midgett, Elizabeth City, N.C.
$14,557 — 4, 2:03 Driver-JAMES LARENTE, 5-21-31 (160) BLUE-GOLD
Trainer-O. Mumford
(⅝)2:022 1969 7 2 2 2 15,875
2:03 1968 14 3 2 4 8,138

4- 5 LB⅝ 7000 gd Pref mi 3011:0231:3322:04 2 6 5 4° 42½ 3hd 2:04 4.90 (J.Larente) Sen.Roan,Jer.Gauman,Ads.Uniteus
3-26 LB⅝ 17000 ft 68nw12500 Ec mi 2921:0041:3132:022 9 7 8 1° 1¾ 1hd 2:022 2.60 (J.Larente) Ads.Uniteus,Release,PreciousScot
3-21 LB⅝ 5500 ft nw15000 cd mi 3011:0221:3222:022 8 8 8 7° 63 21 2:023 12.00 (J.Larente) Cardnl.Bruce,Ad.Uniteus,Bywd.Boy
3-15 LB⅝ 6000 ft 68nw12500 Ec mi 3131:03 1:3322:05 1 3 3 4 3½ 2ns 2:05 *2.00 (J.Larente) LimelightN.,A.Uniteus,Cmd.Dctr.
3- 7 LB⅝ 6000 gd 68nw12500 Ec mi 3011:0121:3312:043 5 8 7 7° 72¾ 32 2:05 3.30 (J.Larente) Weasel, Release, AdiosUniteus
2-28 LB⅝ 5500 ft 68nw12500 Ec mi 2931:0141:3312:033 6 7 5 7 73½ 4½ 2:033 7.70 (J.Larente) Release, LimelightN., SteadyBoy
2-22 LB⅝ 5000 ft 68nw12500 Ec mi 3011:0241:3442:053 9 6 5 2° 2½ 1nk 2:053 *2.10 (J.Larente) AdiosUniteus,JohnPic,Duffy'sBet

---

5 — **2** Blue

JERRY GAUMAN
br h, 5, by Jerry Way—Black Gauman by Chris Scott
Neil J. Helfrich, Washington C. H., Ohio
$103,639 — 3, TT-1:592 (1) Driver-HERVE FILION, 2-1-40 (142) RED-DK. BLUE-WHITE
Trainer-Her. Filion
1969 4 0 1 2 3,070
2:02 1968 28 10 6 4 73,310

4- 5 LB⅝ 7000 gd Pref mi 3011:0231:3322:04 4 4 4 2° 2½ 2ns 2:04 3.80 (Her.Filion) Sen.Roan,Jer.Gauman,Ads.Uniteus
3-29 LB⅝ 5500 sy w15000 cd mi 31 1:0321:3442:073 8 8 8 4° 35½ 32½ 2:08 3.10 (Her.Filion) M.Drm.Girl,Sen.Roan,Jer.Gauman
3-21 LB⅝ 25000 ft Inv mi 2931:0121:3042:002 1 3 3 3° 44 79 2:021 6.90 (Her.Filion) MissCon.Ads.,AftonDay,Nard.Byrd
3-15 LB⅝ 5500 ft w15000 cd mi 2911:0031:3132:013 4 6 6 5 53¾ 32 2:02 3.70 (Her.Filion) M.Con.Ads.,StewartHn.,J.Gauman
12-21 GrR⅝ 4000 gd Inv hcp mi 3221:0641:3922:093 5 1° 1 1 1¾ 12½ 2:093 *1.00 (Her.Filion) J.Gauman,Arm.HardydhMr.Glphne.
12-14 WR⅝ 5000 ft Inv hcp mi 3021:02 1:34 2:054 4 1 2 2° 43 412 2:081 *.45 (R.Filion) WalvisBay,ByeTime,PedroWilson
12- 8 BB⅝ 5000 ft Pref hcp mi 3031:02 1:3342:042 4 2° 1 1 11 1½ 2:042 *.80 (Her.Filion) JerryGauman,LionCy,NesterAdios

---

3 — **3** White

HUMPHREY N.
b g, 8, by Morano—Dalene by Light Brigade
Lunar Stable, New Egypt, N.J.
$48,535 — None At Mile Driver-STANLEY DANCER, 7-25-27 (135) BLUE-GOLD
Trainer-R. Dancer
Qua.(⅝)2:04 1969 0 0 0 0
None At Mile 1968 25 9 2 5 33,142

4- 8 LB⅝ ft Qua mi 31 1:03 1:3412:04 6 5 4 2 21 12 2:04 N.B. (S.Dancer) Hmphry.N.,Doug'sChoice,ByeB.Ray
4- 4 LB⅝ ft Qua mi 3141:0441:36 2:074 7 x8 4° 4° 41½ 12 2:074 N.B. (S.Dancer) HumphreyN.,WiseGreek,GreggTass
12-31 Auckland 30 yard hcp 2 Miles in 4:091 Unplaced (W.E.Lowe) Cardnl.Grrsn.,Loy.Knight,Cud.Doon
12-27 Auckland 48 yard hcp 1⅝ Miles in 3:283 Unplaced (W.E.Lowe) Tobias, James, BeatTime
12-21 Rangiora 12 yard hcp 1¼ Miles in 2:362 fin. 2nd (W.E.Lowe) Chf.Command,Humph.N.,Lordship
11-23 Metropolitan 42 yard hcp 1⅝ Miles in 3:244 fin. 3rd (W.E.Lowe) LoyalKnight,GreatAdios,Humph.N.
11-19 Metropolitan 42 yard hcp 1⅝ Miles in 3:243 Unplaced (W.E.Lowe) GreatAds.,MilesGentry,ChiefCom.

---

20 — **4** Green

BERRY BOY
b g, 6, by Berrymite—Kit Volo by High Volo
Triple M. Stables, Wynnewood, Pa.
$47,603 — 5, 2:024 (⅝) Driver-JOE GREENE, 7-3-36 (165) WHITE-GREEN-BLACK
Trainer-J. Greene
(⅝)2:014 1969 12 1 1 1 6,077
(⅝)2:024 1968 29 6 4 6 24,636

4- 5 LB⅝ 7000 gd Pref mi 3011:0231:3322:04 7 3° 1 3 32 64 2:044 26.50 (C.Greene) Sen.Roan,Jer.Gauman,Ads.Uniteus
3-29 LB⅝ 5500 sy w15000 cd mi 31 1:0321:3442:073 4 1° 1 2 25½ 43½ 2:081 7.00 (J.Greene) M.Drm.Girl,Sen.Roan,Jer.Gauman
3-21 LB⅝ 5500 ft nw15000 cd mi 3021:0211:32 2:014 1 4 3 1 1¾ 12 2:014 2.70 (J.Greene) BerryBoy,GoOnBye,EasterColleen
3-14 LB⅝ 5000 ft nw15000 cd mi 3021:0141:3212:023 7 2° 1 2 22 31½ 2:024 5.20 (J.Greene) Bywd.Boy,Wilson'sMiss,BerryBoy
3- 7 LB⅝ 5000 gd nw15000 cd mi 3031:0311:3342:042 1 2 2 2 21¾ 53½ 2:05 1.50 (J.Greene) RoyalG.Pk.,Steve'sPhil,Aft.Apollo
3- 1 LB⅝ 5000 ft w15000 cd mi 3031:0121:3222:021 5 1 1 1 1½ 2hd 2:021 15.30 (J.Greene) StewartHan., BerryBoy, GoOnBye
2-15 LB⅝ 4500 gd w15000 cd mi 3111:04 1:3432:043 4 1 1 2 21½ 67¾ 2:06 9.60 (J.Greene) AftonDay,SenatorRoan,GoOnBye

---

6 — **5** Black

SENATOR ROAN
ro g, 5, by Adios Senator—Mountain Sue by White Mountain Boy
W. M. Camp, Jr. & B. E. Babb, Franklin & Courtland, Va.
$27,823 — 4, 2:02 (⅝) Driver-RICHARD CUSTIS, 9-30-19 (178) GRAY-BLUE
Trainer-V. Crank
(⅝)2:02 1969 7 2 2 1 10,295
(⅝)2:02 1968 24 8 5 5 22,357

4- 5 LB⅝ 7000 gd Pref mi 3011:0231:3322:04 3 7 7 6° 53 1ns 2:04 6.80 (V.Crank) Sen.Roan,Jer.Gauman,Ads.Uniteus
3-29 LB⅝ 5500 sy w15000 cd mi 31 1:0321:3442:073 3 4 4 1 15½ 22 2:08 *2.50 (V.Crank) M.Drm.Girl,Sen.Roan,Jer.Gauman
3-22 LB⅝ 6000 ft w15000 cd mi 2941:0211:3312:02 2 2 2 3 21½ 1nk 2:02 *1.40 (V.Crank) Sen.Roan,QuickReturn,RoyalG.Pick
3-15 LB⅝ 5500 ft w15000 cd mi 2911:0031:3132:013 1 2 2 2 2¾ 52¾ 2:02 4.10 (V.Crank) M.Con.Ads.,StewartHn.,J.Gauman
3- 8 LB⅝ 5500 ft w15000 cd mi 2941:0031:3112:024 7 2° 1 1 1¾ 3nk 2:024 3.00 (V.Crank) CrownBlue,StewartHn.,Sentr.Roan
2-22 LB⅝ 4500 ft w15000 cd mi 3041:0341:3332:023 4 6 6 5° 55½ 46¾ 2:034 *1.70 (V.Crank) M.Con.Ads.,GoOnBye,StewartHan.
2-15 LB⅝ 4500 gd w15000 cd mi 3111:04 1:3432:043 6 5 5 5 52¾ 21 2:044 2.80 (V.Crank) AftonDay,SenatorRoan,GoOnBye

---

7/2 — **6** Yellow

‡MISS DREAM GIRL
b m, 6, by Good Time—Dream Girl by Knight Dream
Gray Brothers, East Providence, R.I.
$43,574 — 5, 2:011 (⅝) Driver-J. (Tic) WILCUTTS, 11-23-19 (120) BLUE-RED-WHITE
Trainer-F. Safford
(⅝)2:073 1969 2 1 0 0 4,000
(⅝)2:011 1968 28 6 6 3 29,250

4- 5 LB⅝‡ 25000 gd Inv mi 2931:0121:3142:021 2 4 4 6 56½ 54½ 2:03 8.70 (J.Wilcutts) Lit.Jer.Way,Nard.Byrd,M.Con.Ads.
3-29 LB⅝‡ 5500 sy w15000 cd mi 31 1:0321:3442:073 6 7 7 8 89½ 12 2:073 9.40 (J.Wilcutts) M.Drm.Girl,Sen.Roan,Jer.Gauman
11- 9 LB⅝‡ 7500 sy Pref hcp mi 3041:05 1:36 2:073 2 5 5 6 67 33¾ 2:081 3.60 (Her.Filion) BeauBtlr.,Moondowner,M.Drm.Girl
11- 1 LB⅝‡ 6000 ft Pref mi 2941:0231:33 2:024 1 4 5 4° 42 21 2:03 *2.20 (J.Wlicutts) BeauButler,M.Drm.Girl,Ryl.G.Pick
10-25 LB⅝‡ 6000 ft Pref mi 2941:0041:3112:012 7 7 7 6 54¾ 1hd 2:012 10.00 (J.Wilcutts) MissDreamGirl, KingTar, CarlY.
10-18 LB⅝‡ 6000 ft Pref mi 30 1:0041:3142:013 1 4 6 6 43½ 1½ 2:013 7.30 (J.Wilcutts) M.Dm.Girl,Brth.Walter,Clandeboye
10-11 LB⅝‡ 6000 ft Pref mi 29 1:0111:32 2:011 1 4 4 5 6x4¾8dis 7.40 (J.Wilcutts) Ryl.G.Pick,Nevl.Holiday,J.M.Harry

---

5 — **7** Pink

LADY EVERGREEN
b m, 8, by Knight Dream—Miss Worthy Grapes by Worthy Boy
Walter M. Reed, Jr., Fort Fairfield, Maine
$97,313 — 7, 2:001 (⅝) Driver-DEL COTE, 12-12-36 (170) WHITE-RED
Trainer-F. Safford
1969 3 0 0 1 4,000
(⅝)2:001 1968 31 6 7 7 41,856

4- 5 LB⅝ 7000 gd Pref mi 3011:0231:3322:04 1 5 6 7 74½ 53½ 2:043 *2.10 (J.Wilcutts) Sen.Roan,Jer.Gauman,Ads.Uniteus
3-29 LB⅝ 20000 sy Inv mi 3131:04 1:36 2:073 3 3 3 3 32½ 32½ 2:08 7.50 (J.Wilcutts) MissCon.Ad.,Lit.Jer.Way,L.Evrgrn.
3-21 LB⅝ 25000 ft Inv mi 2931:0121:3042:002 5 5 7 7 76¾ 55½ 2:012 15.30 (J.Wilcutts) MissCon.Ads.,AftonDay,Nard.Byrd
11- 2 LB⅝ 7500 ft Pref mi 2941:0111:3022:013 2 4 4 3 21 1ns 2:013 3.70 (J.Wilcutts) LadyEvrgrn.,Jer.Gauman,†So.Song
10-26 LB⅝ 7500 ft Pref mi 3031:0241:3222:021 1 2 2 5 41½ 21¾ 2:022 3.60 (J.Wilcutts) Moondowner,LadyEvrgrn.FourLeaf
10-12 LB⅝ 7500 ft Pref mi 293 :5921:2932:001 6 7 7 7 63½ 51½ 2:002 5.60 (J.Wilcutts) S'thern.Song,FourLeaf,BeauButler
10- 5 LB⅝ 9000 ft Pref mi 2911:0121:3032:004 5 7 6 4° 31¾ 2½ 2:004 *2.50 (J.Wilcutts) Slnt.Byrd,LadyEvrgrn.,Sthrn.Song

---

8 — **8** Black-Yellow

MEADOW ELVA
br m, 5, by Thorpe Hanover—Julia Frost by Adios
Jane Falley Galt, Golf, Ill.
$258,914 — 4, 1:592 Driver-AL WINGER, 12-18-21 (180) RED-WHITE-BLUE
Trainer-A. Winger
1969 1 0 0 0
1:592 1968 27 10 4 3 98,712

4- 5 LB⅝ 25000 gd Inv mi 2931:0121:3142:021 6 6 7 7 79½ 612½ 2:043 12.40 (A.Winger) Lit.Jer.Way,Nard.Byrd,M.Con.Ads.
12-20 Hol1 75000 gd Inv 1⅛ 274 :5941:3122:153 6 2 2 2 22 34 2:161 11.50 (W.Haughton) Overcall, BestOfAll, MeadowElva
12-13 Hol1 25000 ft FA mi 2841:0021:3021:581 6 2 2 2 22 22½ 1:583 34.50 (W.Haughton) BestOfAll, MeadowElva, Overcall
11-29 May 20000 gd Lc cd mi 3021:03 1:3342:034 4 1 1 1 1¾ 12 2:034 *.70 (W.Haughton) MeadowElva,HonestStory,EdByrd
11-23 May 10000 ft Lc cd mi 29 1:0031:3112:014 3 2 3 1 1½ 13½ 2:014 *1.50 (J.Ackerman) Mdw.Elva,Rslnd.Beauty,Pep.Relco
11-16 May 7500 gd 68nw40000 mi 3011:0211:34 2:05 5 1 2 3 41½ 31½ 2:052 1.70 (C.Boring) Pep.Relco,RobinDundee,Mdw.Elva
11- 8 May 7500 ft 68nw40000 mi 2921:0131:3212:023 7 4 1 1 1¾ 12½ 2:023 *.40 (G.Sholty) Mdw.Elva, EdByrd, Mdw.Ruby

---

TRACKMAN: 3—6—1

(9) PACE—1 MILE

Warming-Up Saddle Cloth
ORANGE

PURSE $5,500

"BIG E" EXCHANGE THIS RAC

WINNERS IN EXCESS OF $15,000 IN 1968-69 COMBINE
EARNINGS.

←MORN. LINE

ASK FOR HORSE BY PROGRAM NUMBER

6
1 Red
SARALEE HANOVER
b f, 3, by Tar Heel—Sarong Hanover by Adios — Trainer-C. Champion
H.Soucie,J.Barnett,H.Alexander & Harrison-Shields Stable,Pittsburgh,Pa. 1969 0 0 0 0
$18,644 — 2, 2:034 (⅝) Driver-CECIL CHAMPION, 7-25-06 (150) RED-WHITE (⅝)2:034 1968 17 8 3 1 18,64
9-26 Lex1 8892 ft 2yr F Stk mi 292 :59 1:3011:592 9 5 5 5 65¾ 76¼ 2:013 36.70 (C.Champion) ScotchJewel,AdiolaHan.,Qn.Omah
9-26 Lex1 6669 ft 2yr F Stk mi 31 1:0211:34 2:022 6 7 7 7 76½ 56 2:033 3.60 (C.Champion) TigerLilyLobell,AdiolaHan.,Glynis
9- 6 PcD⅝ 11735 ft 2yr F Stk mi 2941:0221:3332:044 7 6° 2° 2° 2½ 31 2:05 2.60 (C.Champion) CafeAuLait,FiestaLbll.,SaraleeHn.
8-31 PcD⅝ 3000 ft 2yr Inv mi 3111:0321:3322:04 8 4 4 5 65 54 2:044 2.80 (C.Champion) TampaHn.,KarneeHn.,Fashn.Cloud
8-20 Carlisle 7585 ft 2yr F Ec, 2 dashes, Mile in 2:052 fin. 2nd—Mile in 2:062 fin. 4th (C.Champion)
8-12 Btva 18600 ft F Stk mi 30 1:0311:3432:06 9 3 3 3° 21 11¼ 2:06 *1.20 (C.Champion) SaraleeHn.,FiestaLobell,TampaHn
8- 5 Mea⅝ 9331 ft 2yr F Stk mi 3121:0211:3242:043 6 x7 7 7 75½ 2½ 2:043 *1.60 (C.Champion) OctaviaHn.,SaraleeHn.,AdiolaHn.

7/2
2 Blue
HISTORIC TIME
br c, 3, by Good Time—Queenly Lorraine by Worthy Boy — Trainer-L. Pullen
Thomas E. Graham, Upper Saddle River, N.J. 1969 1 0 1 0 1,25
$20,415 — 2, 2:06 (⅝) Driver-LES PULLEN, 12-8-31 (167) DK. & LT. BROWN-GOLD (⅝)2:06 1968 19 1 7 1 20,41
4- 5 LB⅝ 5000 gd nw15000 cd mi 3121:05 1:3612:072 6 8 8 6° 63½ 2nk 2:072 4.00 (L.Pullen) LewOregon,HistoricTime,Donora
10-25 LB⅝ 23826 ft 2yr C Stk mi 2931:0011:3042:02 4 5° 2° 2 21¼ 24½ 2:024 17.90 (L.Pullen) HammerinHank,Hist.Tm.,Barb.Hn.
10-14 YR 9500 ft 2yr Stk mi 3021:0221:3242:023 4 5 5° 4° 52 54 2:033 N.B. (L.Pullen) PennHan.,BergenHan.,BakerLobell
9-28 LB⅝ 13100 ft 2yr Lc mi 2911:0031:3122:021 6 5 5 3° 31¾ 2nk 2:021 49.00 (L.Pullen) BakerLbll.,Hist.Time,Mrksmn.Hn.
9-21 YR 50000 ft 2yr Stk mi 3011:01 1:3222:03 6 9 9 9° 87¼ 73½ 2:04 92.90 (L.Pullen) Ham.Hank,Tmprd.Ynk.,BergenHn.
9-13 LB⅝ 4000 ft 2yr Lc mi 3011:0111:3222:03 2 4 4 3 21½ 2½ 2:03 4.00 (L.Pullen) Mrksmn.Hn.,Hist.Time,PanicBttn.
9- 2 YR 25000 gd Stk mi 3021:0111:32 2:023 6 9 9 8 56¼ 45¾ 2:04 103.60 (L.Pullen) Hammer.Hank,PennHn.,BergenHn.

3
3 White
RELEASE
b g, 6, by Court Martial—Jubilant by Lucky Jack — Trainer-R. Dancer
Flicker Stable, Inc., Trenton, N.J. (⅝)2:033 1969 7 2 3 0 12,69
$11,806 — 5, 2:034 Driver-RONNIE DANCER, 5-31-49 (140) BLUE-GOLD 2:034 1968 27 6 2 2 11,32
4- 5 LB⅝ 5500 gd w15000 cd mi 3111:0411:3532:054 7 7 6 4° 3¾ 41¼ 2:06 3.40 (R.Dancer) HickoryKngt.,Ibidem,EvergreenDot
3-26 LB⅝ 17000 ft 68nw12500 Ec mi 2921:0041:3132:022 5 8° 7° 2° 2¾ 2hd 2:022 5.70 (R.Dancer) Ads.Uniteus,Release,PreciousScot
3-15 LB⅝ 6000 ft 68nw12500 Ec mi 3131:03 1:3322:05 4 6 6 5 5x2 84½ 2:054 2.10 (R.Dancer) LimelightN.,A.Uniteus,Cmd.Dctr.
3- 7 LB⅝ 6000 gd 68nw12500 Ec mi 3011:0121:3312:043 8 3° 3 3 31¼ 2hd 2:043 6.90 (R.Dancer) Weasel, Release, AdiosUniteus
2-28 LB⅝ 5500 ft 68nw12500 Ec mi 2931:0141:3312:033 2 5 6 4° 41¼ 1hd . 2:033 *3.00 (R.Dancer) Release, LimelightN., SteadyBoy
2-22 LB⅝ 5000 ft 68nw12500 Ec mi 2921:0041:3232:031 2 4 4 2° 2¼ 2hd 2:031 *2.00 (R.Dancer) LimelightN.,Release,HappySngstr.
2-14 LB⅝ 5000 gd 68nw12500 Ec mi 3131:0341:3542:053 1 1 1 1 11 11½ 2:053 *.50 (S.Dancer) Release, BeauMartial, Leslie'sAce

8
4 Green
MUNCY BOY
ch g, 5, by Muncy Hanover—Sonnet Hanover by Titan Hanover — Trainer-J. W. Carroll
Clearview Stables, New Canaan, Conn. 1969 1 0 0 0 40
$29,361 — 4, 2:034 Driver-J. WELDON CARROLL, 4-7-13 (185) SILVER-RED-BLUE 2:034 1968 29 3 6 4 15,89
4- 5 LB⅝ 5000 gd nw15000 cd mi 3121:05 1:3612:072 4 6 6 8 75 43½ 2:08 15.80 (J.W.Carroll) LewOregon,HistoricTime,Donora
11-18 RR 3250 sy B2 mi 3131:0431:3722:091 4 6 5 4° 42 3¾ 2:092 *2.10 (A.Abbatiello) Science, ThePremise, MuncyBoy
11-11 RR 3250 ft B2 mi 3131:0211:3342:06 2 2 3 4° 32 21¼ 2:061 *2.20 (E.Avery) CaseKey, MuncyBoy, NotableWick
11- 1 RR 3500 ft B2 cd mi 2921:0141:33 2:041 5 6 6 7° 41½ 2hd 2:041 6.70 (E.Avery) McByrd, MuncyBoy, GerardPick
10-21 RR 3750 ft B2 mi 3121:0231:3312:044 8 8 8 8 75¼ 52½ 2:052 10.10 (E.Avery) VistaAbbey, McByrd, SteadyBert
10-12 YR 3750 ft B2 cd mi 2941:0031:3112:031 1 2 2° 2° 2nk 5nk 2:031 *2.00 (E.Avery) AddieH.,Kystn.Ranger,StormProof
10- 4 YR 3750 ft B2 cd mi 3041:0241:3322:05 7 8 8 8° 84½ 42½ 2:053 11.70 (G.Phalen) ForeignPol.Stm.Proof,Kystn.Rngr.

5
5 Black
SEA ORBIT
b m, 5, by Good Time—Sea Foam by Ensign Hanover — Trainer-C. Fitzpatrick
L. P. Quinn & R. W. Gallagher, West Newton, Mass. 1969 0 0 0 0
$31,987 — 4, 2:011 (¾) Driver-CHAS. FITZPATRICK, 6-13-26 (160) GREEN-WHITE-RED (¾)2:011 1968 28 7 5 6 23,94
10- 3 LB⅝ 5500 ft 68w15000 cd mi 30 1:01 1:3132:013 6 7 7 5 63 89 2:032 28.30 (C.Fitzpatrick) M.Drm.Girl,Lusc.Lou,Cardnl.Bruce
9-21 LB⅝ 4500 ft 68w15000 cd mi 2941:03 1:3212:024 3 4 6 6 65½ 84¾ 2:033 3.90 (C.Fitzpatrick) StewartHn.,Elgnt.Wick,YourKiddi
8-24 VD¾ 2500 ft Inv mi 2921:0241:3232:02 2 2 2 3 32¼ 32 2:022 3.40 (A.Allen) EddieDell, SquirePick, SeaOrbit
8-17 VD¾ 2500 ft Inv mi 2811:0021:2932:004 6 2 2 3° 24½ 23 2:012 7.20 (A.Allen) AutumnFrost,SeaOrbit,EddieDell
8-10 VD¾ 4000 ft Inv mi 291 :5941:2942:01 3 3 4 5 51¾ 3¾ 2:011 7.70 (A.Allen) GoWorthy, Norndorf, SeaOrbit
8- 3 VD¾ 2500 ft Inv mi 281 :5921:3032:011 4 4 4 5 43¾ 1ns 2:011 7.30 (A.Allen) SeaOrbit, BlackSire, Northwood
7-27 VD¾ 2500 ft Inv mi 2831:0341:3442:052 7 1 2 2 1ns 2¾ 2:053 *1.80 (A.Allen) Frn.P.Adios,SeaOrbit,Niag.Bullet

9/2
6 Yellow
IBIDEM
ro g, 7, by White Mountain Boy—Miss Rip by Rip Hanover — Trainer-R. Hayter
Almert Stable, Pasadena, Calif. (⅝)2:093 1969 6 1 1 0 4,55
$50,266 — 5, 2:004 (⅝) Driver-A. (Ned) GALENTINE, 6-6-31 (145) MAROON-GREEN (⅝)2:013 1968 36 4 5 3 18,02
4- 5 LB⅝ 5500 gd w15000 cd mi 3111:0411:3532:054 2 3 1 1 1¼ 21 2:06 4.20 (V.Crank) HickoryKngt.,Ibidem,EvergreenDot
3-29 LB⅝ 5500 sy w15000 cd mi 3211:0441:3722:093 3 1 3 3 21¼ 12½ 2:093 3.70 (V.Crank) Ibidem, GloriaGray, CrownBlue
3-21 LB⅝ 5500 ft nw15000 cd mi 3011:0221:3222:022 5 3° 2 4 42 51½ 2:023 20.50 (V.Crank) Cardnl.Bruce,Ad.Uniteus,Bywd.Boy
3- 8 BM1 2500 ft nw15000 cd mi 3021:01 1:3212:032 6 4 1 4 42 68¼ 2:05 9.40 (J.Russell) MajorBreeze, Kabulo, Lornaway
3- 1 BM1 3000 ft nw12000 cd mi 3121:0221:3342:05 5 2 2 3 42¼ 53 2:053 15.20 (J.Russell) AdiosCarl,FastCraig,Scot.Design
2-22 BM1 4000 my nw10000 cd mi 3411:0611:38 2:08 6 6 6 6 63¾ 610¼ 2:10 14.50 (J.Russell) ExpressZ.,Armb.Insko,RedWave
12-21 Hol1 6500 ft 13000 clm cd mi 3031:0221:3242:022 8 1 1 1 1½ 44¼ 2:03 11.20 (J.Lighthill) Scotty'sColt,Mdw.Cobb,RupertH.

12
7 Pink
TAX EXEMPT
b h, 7, by Widower Creed—Wall Street by Nibble Hanover — Trainer-D. Legum
Midway Stable, Washington, D.C. 1969 4 0 0 0 30
$51,981 — 6, 2:023 Driver-DAVE LEGUM, 5-28-12 (175) WHITE-RED-BLUE 2:023 1968 37 12 4 3 15,07
4- 5 LB⅝ 5500 gd w15000 cd mi 3111:0411:3532:054 8 8 8 8 84¼ 88¼ 2:072 43.80 (D.Legum) HickoryKngt.,Ibidem,EvergreenDot
3-29 LB⅝ 5500 sy w15000 cd mi 3211:0441:3722:093 4 2° 2 2 31¾ 610¾ 2:113 6.70 (D.Legum) Ibidem, GloriaGray, CrownBlue
3-14 LB⅝ 6000 ft 68nw20000 Ec mi 3011:0141:3212:022 4 5 6 4 43¼ 57 2:034 22.90 (D.Legum) Ardrossan, Donora, RobinHill
3- 8 LB⅝ 6000 ft 68nw20000 Ec mi 3021:0111:3232:03 1 3 3 2 34¾ 614¼ 2:054 15.10 (D.Legum) MontageN.,LiberaceHanvr.,Donora
11- 9 Har 1000 sy Inv hcp mi 33 1:06 1:3742:093 5 1 1 1 1½ 1nk 2:093 2.60 (D.Legum) TaxExempt,MaryJ.Mrlw.,BillyBoot
11- 2 Har 1000 ft Inv hcp mi 30 1:0111:3312:044 6 2° 4° 7 67 59½ 2:064 2.95 (D.Legum) Charnie, Leila'sStar, TheGimp
10-26 Har 1000 ft Inv hcp mi 32 1:0221:3432:06 7 5° 5° 6° 67 59½ 2:08 8.10 (W.Manemon) Charnie,MaryJ.Marlw.,Frb.Special

8
8 Black-Yellow
TRANSPONDER
b g, 6, by Irish Hal—Hot Tip by Hot Feet — Trainer-F. Parks
The Seymour Stable, DeKalb Junction, N.Y. (⅝)2:051 1969 5 1 0 0 3,42
$48,261 — 5, 2:011 (⅝) Driver-FRED PARKS, 12-9-06 (155) GOLD-BLACK (⅝)2:011 1968 22 5 7 1 16,19
4- 5 LB⅝ 5500 gd w15000 cd mi 3121:0421:3712:073 4 4 4 5 63¾ 66¼ 2:084 8.90 (F.Parks) GloriaGray,CrownBlue,Roy.GenePk
3-29 LB⅝ 5500 sy w15000 cd mi 3211:0441:3722:093 7 4° 1 1 11¼ 711¾ 2:114 7.00 (F.Parks) Ibidem, GloriaGray, CrownBlue
3-22 LB⅝ 6000 ft w15000 cd mi 2941:0211:3312:02 6 6 6 7 74½ 43¾ 2:023 10.30 (Her.Filion) Sen.Roan,QuickReturn,RoyalG.Pick
3-14 LB⅝ 5000 ft nw15000 cd mi 3031:0231:34 2:051 5 3 3 3 21½ 1hd 2:051 5.30 (F.Parks) Transponder,Crdnl.Bruce,GoOnBye
3- 8 LB⅝ 5500 ft w15000 cd mi 2941:0031:3112:024 1 1 3 3 31½ 41¼ 2:03 8.00 (F.Parks) CrownBlue,StewartHn.,Sentr.Roan
11-11 LB⅝ 4000 gd 68nw15000 cd mi 3021:0231:3322:04 2 1 2 1 11½ 21 2:041 5.30 (F.Parks) LincHn.,Transponder,Wilson'sMiss
11- 7 LB⅝ 4500 gd 68w15000 cd mi 3031:0321:3442:053 8 1 1 1 11¾ 35 2:063 15.90 (F.Parks) LewOregon,XPertTime,Transpondr

DELIGHTFUL WAY—Scratched

TRACKMAN: 3—2—6

The First Race

A claiming pace for horses that are nondescript to begin with and, in the second place, have been idle too long. The most recent starter in this woeful bunch is Shalee Sue, roundly trounced 15 nights ago when she went at 90 to 1 in a conditioned race.

This race is absolutely unplayable for the rare bird who seeks long-range profits by picking as many winners and as few losers as possible. The current form of the horses is unknown. Rather than guess, the hard-boiled handicapper abstains.

On the other hand, few racegoers are so grimly dedicated. This race is, after all, the first half of the daily double. Many fans hate to detour the double, regardless of contrary advice offered by sourpusses like me. Let us assume, then, that I and a few other eccentrics avoid this race. Is there any way for others to make comparatively sensible selections?

In my opinion, the likeliest approach to this unlikely kind of situation is to look for the horses that have turned in acceptable performances most recently. One might also consider an animal whose high lifetime earnings suggested former class—especially if it had been recording an occasional good race. No such horse is in this particular field, however.

Let's now go down the list to see if we can find a comparatively recent, comparatively good performance.

Conestoga Lady can be eliminated for her poor effort of March 25. Ben Kwik raced well on March 22—three full weeks ago. If there is nothing more recent, I suppose he becomes a contender.

Michel Mir finished ahead of Ben Kwik three weeks ago, but apparently had been tucked against the rail all the way. Ben Kwik's race was much more vigorous.

Coneeda, an ancient breaker, paced beautifully 17 nights ago, roughing it on the outside for a quarter and then gaining more than eight lengths in the stretch to win going away. He moves up in class tonight (from a $3,000 claiming price to $4,000), but has the nearest thing to recent good form in the entire field.

Dillon Byrd has done nothing all year. His stretch gain of March 26 was no more impressive than Michel Mir's of March 22, bearing the earmarks of a sucked-along finish.

Shalee Sue, though dropping into a claimer after racing in livelier company, deserves no support. She has demonstrated no form at all.

Neither has Mr. Smoothie. As to Afton Duke, his pace-setting victory on March 25 was slow, even considering that the track was off. He has never been able to hold his speed to the finish after leaving from an outside post. And his driver is a provisional—a beginner.

The player looking for comparatively recent form in this race must surely go to Coneeda. To hedge, he might also buy a ducat on Ben Kwik. For purposes of the daily double, he might couple those two with whatever he finds promising in the second race.

RESULT: Afton Duke led to the head of the stretch and then folded, beating only Shalee Sue. Les Pullen snugged Coneeda against the wood in sixth position until the final turn, when he made a big move on the outside. Fourth by two lengths at the top of the stretch, he won by a length, going away. And paid $19.20. Conestoga Lady (5 to 1) was second and Ben Kwik (4.80 to 1) was third. The favorite, for some unaccountable reason, was Michel Mir (3 to 2). He finished fourth.

Although it evidently was possible to pick Coneeda by compromising a factor as vital as recent action, I must re-emphasize that a representative series of such selections inevitably must end in the red.

The Second Race

The second race is exactly the same as the first. It cannot be handicapped properly and I shall not try. Once again, the player who wants to have something going for him will be best advised to take the horse or horses whose latest performances were good and who have not been sidelined as long as others.

Miss Arch qualifies. As her record shows, she has never appreciated an off track, yet she did nicely enough on March 25, racing quite close to the leader at the stretch call and gaining thereafter. Do you suspect that she may simply have been pulled along in that race? She is not the type. Note how gamely she has performed in each of her last four outings. She may have lost her competitive sharpness while being unraced for 18 days, but the same unhappy possibility exists for any other horse in this field.

Royal Charmer is unacceptable, having done nothing since 1967 except go slowly in a qualifying heat. Torpay, on the other hand, is a logical contender. So is Rollon Direct, although he figures to get nothing from that outside post.

Yankee Dandy N. has been racing in qualifiers, miserably. Dolly's

Ace has been dying in the stretch. Leila's Star raced well—but it was more than three weeks ago. Meadow Add has been doing nothing.

Which seems to leave Torpay and Miss Arch. Especially Torpay.

RESULT: Filion got the lead with Torpay before the quarter pole but the animal went into a break at the half. In the ensuing melée, Yankee Dandy N., Rollon Direct, Royal Charmer and Meadow Add also broke, the latter two colliding. Torpay continued galloping for most of the journey, but still managed to finish third. Miss Arch, a lucky horse, won by five lengths, after avoiding all the scrimmages. She paid $7.20 as second favorite. The unfortunate Torpay went at slightly better than 8 to 5. The daily double paid $88.

The Third Race

Here are claiming pacers better than those in the first two races. Unimpressive recent form or inactivity eliminates Carpathian, Prancer Hanover, Joey Lad, Add Frisco and Phil Frost.

Sir Duane has been idle for 15 days, which some handicappers might regard as too long for a claiming racer. However, the horse has performed so well in his five latest races that it is impossible to overlook him. Had he been absent for three weeks, the attitude would be different. Note that he won on March 5 after an absence of two weeks.

Paramount Pick is another horse that performs well after a rest. On February 14, he won his first outing of the year, after being away for more than three months. His March 29 effort was on a sloppy track against a tougher field than he faces tonight. He definitely ranks as a contender here.

Shadydale Hymn, condemned to the outside post position, comes off a good victory only 10 nights ago. A contender.

One of these animals is so obvious a selection that no arithmetic is needed to recognize it. However, we shall now go through the process. The exercise will be helpful.

Using the pace-rating table on page 179, we rate the latest performances of Sir Duane and Shadydale Hymn. To get figures for Paramount Pick on a fast track, we use his race of March 15.

Sir Duane's half-mile time of 1:03 and final time of 2:04:3 earn him a basic rating of 202.

Paramount Pick (1:04:4 and 2:06:2) comes up with 184.

Shadydale Hymn gets 199.

Sir Duane earns 5 extra points for roughing it on the outside, and 10 for the red-hot Larente. I'd also be inclined to give him 2 for his lead at the stretch call. His final rating is 219.

Paramount Pick ends with 199, after adding 5 for the parked-out symbol and 10 for Wilcutts.

Shadydale Hymn gets 5 for the stretch gain and 10 for Filion, but loses 5 for the transfer from post-position 4 to the outside. His net is 209.

The play is Sir Duane.

RESULT: The horse went off at a measly 3 to 2 and finished third. Paramount Pick got the lead at the three-quarter pole and held it to the finish, paying $8.80. Prancer Hanover (16.50 to 1) took second. Sir Duane gained some ground in the stretch but remained in third place, where he had been for most of the final half. Absolutely the only lesson to be derived from this race is that you can't win 'em all.

The Fourth Race

This conditioned event looks like a gift for Prestwick, from the powerful stable of Billy Haughton. Alix Winger is listed as trainer, but happens to be Haughton's man in Philadelphia. The horse's two local races have been in early closers, one of which he won at odds-on. Competition of that kind is beyond anything else in tonight's field. Note, for example, that Inheritance, winner on April 3 of a race exactly like tonight's, was unable to beat C-3 stock at Yonkers only a few weeks earlier.

Prestwick is a representative sample of the up-and-coming three-year-old that lays over a cheap field. No more handicapping is necessary.

Fanciers of exacta wagering can wheel Prestwick with the other seven starters for $14. For $28, they can include the possibility that Haughton's pacer may finish second to one of the others. Or, for $12 they can speculate that he will finish 1–2 with Inheritance, Miss Scarlet Dawn or Good Luck Boy. Those three, as the reader should be able to demonstrate, are the animals with the best figures. After Prestwick, that is.

RESULT: Prestwick finished second to, of all things, Chief Butler. That one, making its first start of the year, raced on the outside for the first half-mile and still had enough left to charge from fifth to first in the stretch. The mutuel was only $22.20, suggesting that somebody bet heavily. The exacta paid $69.40.

The Fifth Race

So far I have recommended bets on two horses—Sir Duane and Prestwick. Both lost. Hardly an exhilarating start. But starts don't count in this pastime. All that counts is the condition of the bankroll at the end of the season. Or the month. Or the week. Or, if you insist, the night.

This fifth race strikes me as comparable to the fourth. The conditions are similar and one of the starters is a high-class three-year-old from a leading barn. I would be inclined to look no farther than Moonglo Hanover. No other horse in the field has her credentials. Her great trainer, Frank Safford, invariably sends out ready horses. No need to worry about the filly's lack of races this season.

RESULT: Eighth at the stretch call, Moonglo Hanover ate up the others in the final yards and won bravely. The payoff was $5.00. I'm still in the red.

The Sixth Race

Another exacta, this time with added complications. Six of the starters raced on off tracks in their last outings. Five of them can be evaluated in terms of fairly recent form on fast tracks, but Newport Robbi cannot. His only fast-track performance this year was indifferent. What to do?

The latest races of these horses do not lend themselves to handicapping comparison. Some were on an allegedly good track, one was in the slop. Note also that Newport Robbi beat Quick Return on April 5. Was Newport Robbi helped by the condition of the racing strip and by having Herve Filion in the bike? Will Quick Return enjoy tonight's fast footing and be able to reverse the order of the finish— especially now that Newport Robbi has Gene Daisey instead of Filion?

Except for the Newport Robbi problem, this looks like a nice race to handicap. So I shall do it, eliminating Newport Robbi on grounds that the switch from Filion cannot possibly help the horse.

The contenders are:

Diamond Dale. His last race is hard to analyze, but the March 21 outing earns him a rating of 211—including 5 for roughing it, 2 for gaining in the stretch and 4 for the improved post position. On the other hand, he loses 10 for the switch from Filion to Parks and 5 for the slight rise in class (from a race for nonwinners of $15,000 to a race for winners of more than that).

Quick Return. His March 22 race is worth 232 points. Note that the race was of a class identical with tonight's, although the purse was $500 higher. However, to the basic pace rating of 219, we add 3 for the stretch gain and 10 for the estimable Tic Wilcutts.

Hickory Knight. Going back to the March 21 performance, which earns a basic pace rating of 217, we deduct 5 for the slightly lower class of that race, while adding 3 for the stretch gain, 5 for roughing it on the outside, 2 for tonight's improved post position and 10 for Filion. The final figure is 232—identical with Quick Return's.

Steve's Phil. The March 28 race is worth 208, after subtracting 5 for the rise in class and 3 for the worsened post position, while adding 5 for the parked-out symbol.

It is impossible to separate Quick Return and Hickory Knight. Both should be bet.

Does everyone agree that Royal Gene Pick, Far Heel and Easter Colleen are noncontenders? Royal Gene Pick must be appraised in terms of his March 22 outing—his most recent on a fast track. He backed up in the stretch. Far Heel was in the same race and did the same thing. Easter Colleen won her last race on a fast strip (March 28) but was losing ground in the stretch.

RESULT: Quick Return and Hickory Knight went as co-favorites at 2.70 to 1. Safford's horse won it in the stretch when Wilcutts came all the way from seventh to defeat Newport Robbi by a length. Hickory Knight finished fourth. The $7.40 mutuel on Quick Return represented a profit of $3.40 on the two bets, and put my selections in the black for the evening. Anyone who bet the Quick Return–Hickory Knight exacta lost his money.

The Seventh Race

Here is the Pennsbury Pace, about which I had something to say on page 162. The program suggests that Adaptor, a Stanley Dancer import, will be the favorite. The program is right, but the bettors are wrong. In addition to being one of the world's foremost drivers, Dancer is one of its outstanding optimists and leading promotional experts. He is forever praising his own horses in statements to the press. Sometimes the horses deserve it, sometimes they do not. In this case, the horse has the physical appearance of a superstar but has not yet performed like one on American soil. The likelihood that it might need time to become accustomed to its new environment has not been mentioned by Dancer in his several optimistic interviews. A qualifying race in 2:02:1 does not guarantee victory over the likes of Rum Customer, who is fit as can be after a triumphant seasonal debut only seven days ago.

RESULT: Rum Customer paid $5.40. Adaptor raced gallantly at 6 to 5, but finished an exhausted fifth after going to the half in an incredible 58:4 and to the three-quarters call in 1:28:1.

The Eighth Race

Here is the first half of the "Big E," or twin exacta. All you have to do is pick this race's first two horses in exact order of finish, and then repeat the feat in the next race. Hard to do but fun to try.

Six of the eight starters in this race met each other on April 5. The track was slightly off, but not enough to make us dredge up earlier races for handicapping purposes.

We begin by eliminating Humphrey N., Miss Dream Girl, Lady Evergreen and Meadow Elva. In one fell swoop we have discarded the three highest-class animals in the race, plus another of Stanley Dancer's highly touted imports. The reason for eliminating Humphrey N. is simply that he has not yet done anything in the United States. Miss Dream Girl raced in top company last time out, but demonstrated nothing like winning form. And form, as I keep saying, is all important. Lady Evergreen has class but showed none of it on April 5. The same goes for Meadow Elva.

The contenders and their ratings:

Adios Uniteus. Like Jerry Gauman and Senator Roan, two other contenders against which he raced on April 5, this gelding earned a basic rating of 207 on that occasion. Its final rating is 224, including 2 for the stretch gain, 5 for roughing it on the outside and 10 for Jim Larente.

Jerry Gauman. His final rating is 223, after adding 1 for the stretch gain, 5 for roughing it and 10 for Filion.

Berry Boy. His April 5 basic rating was 203. He picks up 4 for the improved post position and 5 for roughing it. His final rating is 212.

Senator Roan. He won the April 5 race, but does not figure in this one. He earns 5 points for racing on the outside, 3 for the stretch gain and 1 for an improved post position. But the switch from Vern Crank to Dick Custis costs him 10, and his final rating is 206.

Adios Uniteus and Jerry Gauman are the picks. Because they are separated by only one point, I think both should be bet to win. Additionally, since Adios Uniteus is going off at better than 5 to 1, it would be worth betting on him to place, as well. Twin exacta customers should buy tickets on the same two animals.

RESULT: Adios Uniteus stalked Meadow Elva to the stretch, put her away and won by a neck over the onrushing Jerry Gauman. He paid $13.60 to win and $5.00 to place.

The Ninth Race

Two classy three-year-olds need to be evaluated before we can decide what to do about this race. Saralee Hanover was a factor among the two-year-old pacing fillies on the Grand Circuit during 1968, and now makes her 1969 bow. Historic Time picked up more than $1,000 per start during that same year, chasing the best juvenile male pacers. His race on April 5 was a mighty powerful one. He looks like a three-year-old on his way to bigger things than he faces tonight. Saralee Hanover is from a competent barn but inevitably will not be ready to perform at her best after having been idle for more than six months. Historic Time, however, should be at his best. He figures to lay over this field.

For the benefit of twin exacta players, let it be noted that Release earns an enormous rating for his March 26 performance. The only other contender is Ibidem (March 21), whose switch from Crank to Galentine costs him 10 points. Historic Time and Release certainly look like the coupling for the exacta, and in that order.

RESULT: Historic Time, the 8 to 5 favorite, beat Release by a neck. Saralee Hanover was third. The win mutuel was $5.20. The "Big E" paid $245.40.

A follower of this book's handicapping principles would have made ten bets, cashing six of them. A summary: Sir Duane (lost), Prestwick (lost), Moonglo Hanover ($5.00), Quick Return ($7.40), Hickory Knight (lost), Rum Customer ($5.40), Adios Uniteus ($13.60, $5.00), Jerry Gauman (lost), Historic Time ($5.20).

Official
Roosevelt Raceway
PROGRAM
and past performances

HIS SATURDAY:
$25,000
BYE BYE BYRD PACE

	1/4	1/2	3/4	FIN
Wsmnile Time	29-3	59:-	1:28:3	1:57:4

Bye Bye Byrd sets Roosevelt Raceway record for mile pace, Aug. 28, 1959.

9 RACES NIGHTLY THROUGH MAY 24

FOR GROUP PARTY NIGHT INFORMATION TELEPHONE
(212) 895-3277   (516) 746-6000

EXACTA
3rd, 5th, 7th and 9th Races

60c
(Tax included)

MORN. LINE

1 PACE-ONE MILE (1st HALF OF DAILY DOUBLE

SADDLE CLOTH—YELLOW

CLASS C-3—FILLIES & MARES—ALL AGES

PURSE $2,50

5

1 SPEEDY BARBARANNE

ch m, 5, by Jack Frost, Drafton Eloise by Eric Hanover (Tr.-I. Fertel
I. & G. Fertel & M. Berkowitz, N.Y. 1969 6 0 1 2 1,17
($5,808) 3, 2:06:2 REAL CORMIER (145) Blue-Orange MR 2:06:2 1968 26 1 3 5 3,095

3-24 RR	sy C-3 Cd	2500 m	31:4	1:04:4	1:38:4	2:12	5	1	1	1	1/2	2/ns	2:12	15.70(Dplse)JMMllie,SpdyBrbrne,Ht'leKt'i
3-15 RR	ft C-3 Cd	2500 m	31:4	1:04:3	1:36:2	2:07:4	1	4	4	6°	4/2½	5/4¾	2:09	11.40(NDplse)NveleBlaze,I.C.Paul,CurlyKid
3-4 LB(⅝)	ft Cd	2400 m	32:2	1:05	1:37:2	2:08	2	4	4	3	4/3¼	3/8	2:10:2	3.80(PMyr)PtrickWy,BllyEd,SpdyBrbrann
2-21 GR	ft Cd	500 m	31	1:04:3	1:37:3	2:08:3	4	5	5	5	5/3½	4/5	2:09:3	14.70(CTylr)MssnFrst,CBLnda,LdyPrfrmnc
2-13 GR	ft Cd	550 m	32:3	1:06	1:38:3	2:10:2	6	6	6	7	7/8½	5/9	2:12:1	8.75(PMyr)MdwAdd,QuickRdagr,AftnMike
2-7 GR	ft Cd	550 m	32:1	1:05:2	1:36	2:08:2	1	2	2	2	2/5	3/3	2:09	4.30(PM'r)AhmdB'Hsn,VckiSq're,SpdyB'r
12-11 RR	ft C-3 Cd	2500 m	31:3	1:04:3	1:38:3	2:11:1	5	7	6	6°	5/3¾	3/4¼	2:12:1	3.00(RCrmr)OC'sSndy,ClrsT'Hl,SpdyB'ann
11-27 RR	ft C-3 Cd	2500 m	31:1	1:04:1	1:37	2:09	2	4	4	3°	2/½	3/¾	2:09:1	5.00(JTllmn) GayBty,AnnJo,SpdyBrbrann

3

2 SALCOS APRIL

b m, 4, by Meadow Ace, Knight Joy by Knight Dream (Tr.-D. Insko)
Salco Stables, Bronx, N.Y. 1969 2 0 2 0 1,25
($4,647) 3, 2:09:1 DEL INSKO (120) Purple-Gold Stga 2:09:1 1968 10 1 0 0 1,23

4-9 RR	ft C-3 Cd	2500 m	32:1	1:04:1	1:36:2	2:08:2	1	2	2	1	1/2	2/½	2:08:3	2.10(DI'ko)Claire'sTrHl,Salco'sAprl,MssH
3-26 RR	ft C-3 Cd	2500 m	32	1:03:4	1:35:1	2:06:3	2	4	4	3	3/2	2/1¾	2:07	9.50(DI'ko)FairMdn,SlcosAprl,SstrFreehl
• 3-18 RR	ft qua	m	31	1:03	1:35:3	2:07:3	1	2	2	2°	2/1	4/4	2:08:3	N.B.(JChpmn)BllyKnght,KidDmino,Sprtac
• 3-15 RR‡	ft qua	m	33	1:06	1:39	2:11:3	4	x8	8x	8	8/dis	8/dis		N.B.(DI'ko)RouteTwoTwo,FstDrm,Sprtcus
• 2-4 YR	ft qua	m	33:3	1:07	1:39:1	2:11	3	5	5	3	3/12	5/16	2:14:4	N.B.(GMlnr)ChfBnny,MstrTmby,MssSildio
11-27 Fhld	ft Cd	1400 m	30:4	1:04	1:35:3	2:08:1	2	6	7	5	5/4¼	6/5¾	2:09:2	37.30(GMlnr)FlyBye,Liberator,CottonCandy
11-20Fhld	gd3-4yrCd	1300 m	31:1	1:02:1	1:35:1	2:08	4	6	6	6	6/13	5/24	2:12:4	14.40(GMlnr)HvenlyWay,FlyBye,DutchsSta
11-14 Fhld	ft Cd	1400 m	32	1:04:4	1:38	2:11	4	3	4	8	3/1¼	4/5	2:12	3.90(WMyer)JMJan,ChickPick,DutchsSta

5

3 SHINING HANOVER

b f, 3, by Tar Heel, Shy Hanover by Adios (Tr.-H. Dancer, Jr
William B. Weaver, III, Darien, Conn. 1969 0 0 0 0
(00.00) HAROLD DANCER, JR. (165) Yellow-Grey 1968 0 0 0 0

• 4-8 RR	ft qua	m	31:1	1:03:1	1:36	2:08:1	1	5	5	4°	6/9¼	4/8	2:10	N.B.(DncrJr)KystneGem,RomeoLbll,Oxfor
• 3-26 RR	ft qua	m	32	1:04:4	1:37:4	2:11:2	1	x7	7	7	7/dis	8/dis		N.B.(FJnes)Mastrtme,A'broInstep,Bubele

10

4 JIFFY JOY

ch f, 3, by Noble Dean, White Mountain Girl by Volomite (Tr.-D. Macedoni
Macedonio Stables, Ronkonkoma, N.Y. 1969 0 0 0 0
($245) DOMINIC MACEDONIO (145) Red-White 1968 5 0 1 0 24

• 4-8 RR	ft qua	m	31:1	1:03	1:36:2	2:09	4	4	4	3°	4/2¼	4/3½	2:09:3	N.B.(M'dno)ShdwRkt,SprmeBty,JfyJy byc
6-14 RR	ft 2yr	500 m	32	1:04:2	1:37:3	2:09:3	3	4	4	3	4/3½	4/9	2:11:4	N.B.(DMcdnio)Mrcie,ElenaBrmn,SevnVeil
6-6 RR	ft 2yr	500 m	31:2	1:04:4	1:36	2:07:2	6	4	4	4	4/7½	4/21	2:12:3	N.B.(Mcdnio)AdrasChpie,Sfrza,MzllesMck
5-30 RR	ft 2yr	500 m	32:1	1:05:1	1:38:4	2:11:2	4	1	2	1°	1/2	2/hd	2:11:2	N.B.(DMcdnio)Sforza,JffyJoy,KeystneMd
5-23 RR	ft 2yr	500 m	33:2	1:07:2	1:40:1	2:13:2	2	3	2°	2°	2/ns	6/3¼	2:14	N.B.(DMcdnio)MdwChld,MnicaHn,LeaGir
5-17 RR	ft 2yr	500 m	32:3	1:06:4	1:39:1	2:09:4	6	5	5	5	4/7½	4/10	2:12:1	N.B.(Mcdnio)H'mrnHnk,MdwTm,KystnMc

4

5 BUTTERCUP SMITH

b m, 4, by Stephan Smith, Butternut Marie by Butternut King (Tr.-J. Higgins) (St.-W. Popfinge
Galaxy Stables, Brooklyn, N.Y. 1969 2 0 0 0
($6,335) 3, 2:06 WILLIAM POPFINGER (168) Green-White YR 2:06 1968 25 3 6 6 6,32

4-3 RR	ft C-3 Cd	2500 m	31:1	1:04:1	1:36:3	2:08:2	3	5	5°	5°	4/3¾	7/3½	2:09:1	7.20(WPopfinger)SirEthan,QuickGirl,Salc
3-26 RR	ft C-3 Cd	2500 m	32	1:03:4	1:35:1	2:06:3	5	5	5°	5°	6/4½	7/6¼	2:08	2.90(WPfgr)FairMdn,SlcosAprl,SstrFrha
11-20 RR	ft C-3 Cd	2500 m	31:4	1:05:4	1:38:2	2:10:4	7	7	6	8°	7/4½	4/2	2:11:1	4.40(FPfngr)AnnL'Ad's,Clr'sT'H'l,PgyPtn
11-8 RR	ft C-2 Cd	2600 m	30:2	1:02:3	1:34:2	2:05:4	8	8	8	8	8/7	8/11	2:08:2	32.90(WPfngr)MrcleGlw,Anglta,AmsnsPgg
• 10-30 RR	ft qua	m	31:1	1:04	1:36:2	2:08:4	6	3°	3	1	1/1½	2/nk	2:08:4	N.B.(WPfgr)MssHrlm,BtrcpSmth,Emncpt
9-5 YR	ft C-3	2500 m	30:3	1:02:4	1:34:3	2:06	1	1	2	1	1/1	1/nk	2:06	•1.00(WPfngr)BttcpSmth,MssMlfrd,IrshO
8-29 YR	ft C-3 Cd	2500 m	29:3	1:02	1:33:2	2:05:2	6	8	8	8°	7/6¾	3/4	2:06:2	•2.10(WP'fgr) AntsStr,S'dleA'gro,B'cpSm
8-23 YR	ft C-3 Cd	2500 m	30:1	1:01:4	1:35:1	2:07	8	2°	1	1	1/1	4/1	2:07:1	11.40(WP'gr)S'nonGln,S'dleAlgro,I'shM'pt

8

6 RUTH T. DIRECT

b m, 4, by George Direct, Elizabeth Abbe by Happy Blackstone. (Tr.-F. Mule) (St.-W. Hudso
Christine Stables & Aaron & Iris Kraut, N.Y. 1969 0 0 0 0
($648) 2, 2:06:3 NORMAN DAUPLAISE (139) Brown-Gold-White 1968 4 0 0 1 40

• 4-8 RR	ft qua	m	32	1:03	1:35:3	2:08	3	1	1	1	1/½	2/ns	2:08	N.B.(Dplse)NrdnsB'Bye,RthTDrct,EbnJne
• 3-14 LB(⅝)	ft qua	m	32:4	1:05:3	1:37:2	2:09:3	1	2	2	5	5/2½	3/3½	2:10:2	N.B.(Cte)C'mnsSntr,VrgniaBOrgn,RthTDc
8-27 MR	ft C-3	800 m	31:3	1:06	1:38	2:10:3	2	1	1	1	1/½	7/4½	2:11:2	6.70(JCrrn)YnkeeFury,MissCrlU,J.M.Joh
8-20 MR	ft C-3	800 m	30:4	1:02:2	1:36:3	2:09:2	1	1	1	2	2/hd	6/5	2:10:2	5.30(JCrrn)AftnNick,J.M.John,DianaLob
• 8-13 MR	ft qua	m	31	1:03	1:35:2	2:08:2	6	1	1	5	6/7½	7/11	2:10:3	N.B.(JCrrn)Ovrtme,MgtyArnldH,SlvrStrm
• 7-17 RR	ft qua	m	31:4	1:04:3	1:35:4	2:07	4	1	1x	7x	7/dis	7/dis		N.B.(JCrrn)Myfair,SwngnBtlr,RedCmmtic
3-26 YR	ft 3yr Cd	2000 m	31:4	1:05:2	1:38:2	2:09:2	8	6	7	7°	4/3	3/5¾	2:10:4	10.30(GBtrwth)LrdsJwll,KnnyVle,RthTDrc
3-19 YR	ft 3yr Cd	2000 m	33	1:07	1:39:2	2:10:1	5	1	1	1	3/1	4/3½	2:11	3.40(GB'wrth)TrialLwyr,LordsJewl,BoyS

8

7 MAE FLIP

b m, 4, by Noble Dean, Challdale Colleen by Worthy Boy (Tr.-G. Procir
Ceeyar Corp., Brooklyn, N.Y. 1969 3 0 0 0
($2,782) 3, 2:04:4 GERALD PROCINO (170) Red-White-Black YR 2:04:4 1968 12 2 1 1 2,25

• 4-8 RR	ft qua	m	32	1:03	1:35:3	2:08	4	4	4	4°	4/2	6/3	2:08:3	N.B.(Prcno)N'dnsB'Bye,RthTDrct,EbnJn
2-6 YR	ft C-2 Cd	2750 m	31	1:04.2	1:36	2:07:2	7	7	7	6°	7/5	7/9	2:09:3	60.80(GPrcno)MissArlne,JMMillie,StdyNa
2-1 YR	gd C-2 Cd	2750 m	30:3	1:03:4	1:35:3	2:07:4	7	3°	2	3	7/5¾	8/16	2:11:4	25.10(GPrcno)BeautyGld,TrprtBlle,HerIri
1-24 YR	sy C-2 Cd	2750 m	31:1	1:05:2	1:36:3	2:10:2	7	x8	8	bkn hopple		DNF		12.50(LFntne)TrprtBelle,BtyGold,HerIrish
11-13 RR	ft C-2 Cd	2600 m	30:4	1:03:3	1:36:2	2:09:2	5	1°	2	2°	2/½	8/10	2:11:4	15.00(GWlls) AntsStr,Calsara,HrrysJnsin
10-30 RR	ft C-2 Cd	2600 m	30	1:02:3	1:35:1	2:07:3	1	2	1	1	1/1½	6/4½	2:08:3	•1.60(Shlty)BtnaWck,Cl're'sDrm,AftnPnd
10-17LB(⅝)	ft3yStk	20568m	29:4	1:00:4	1:31:2	2:01:3	3	1	3	5	7x/6½	7/dis		55.40(JLrnte)TtwdT'tie,ThpeMge,R'ciR'F
10-9 YR	ft C-2 Cd	2750 m	30:4	1:03:3	1:36	2:07:2	4	6	7	7	6/4¼	5/2¾	2:08	4.20(BMrgn)DhnHlly,AnitasStar,JuneMl

4

8 GAY LANDS

b m, 6, by Meadow Lands, Kristie Brewer by Direct Brewer (Tr.-F. Annunzia
Marion Annunziato, Plainview, N.Y. 1969 5 0 1 0 8
($10,614) 5, 2:05:4 CARMINE ABBATIELLO (135) Gold-Red YR 2:05:4 1968 18 2 2 2 4,7

4-2 RR	ft C-3 Cd	2500 m	30:2	1:04:1	1:36:1	2:09:1	5	8	7°	6°	5/2½	4/3	2:09:4	4.70(CAbt)Capmarge,FairWidow,JuneMl
3-24 RR	sy C-3 Cd	2500 m	31:4	1:04:4	1:38:4	2:12	3	2	2	2°	2/2	6/7¼	2:13:4	7.40(A'zto)JMMllie,SpdyBrbrne,Ht'ieKt
3-17 RR	ft C-3 Cd	2500 m	31:2	1:03:4	1:36	2:08:2	3	4	2°	2°	2/1	8/6	2:09:4	2.70(Fntne)TrcysGirl,ClresT'Heel,SntrsG
3-11 RR	ft C-3 Cd	2500 m	31:3	1:06:1	1:39:1	2:11:4	1	2	2	2	2/½	2/1½	2:12:1	2.60(LFntne)LadyThrne,GayLands,JneM
3-5 RR	ft C-3	2500 m	32:2	1:06:4	1:38:4	2:11	1	3	3	1°	1/1	6/4¾	2:12:1	•1.90(A'zto)F'Mdn,C'T'Hl,M'tJD-H'Kchi
12-6 RR	ft C-3 Cd	2500 m	31:3	1:04:3	1:37:4	2:11:3	4	4	4°°	1°	1/½	4/5¾	2:13	•.80(FAnnunziato)AnnJo,RitaSong,OurG
11-22 RR	ft C-3 Cd	2500 m	31:1	1:04	1:35:3	2:08:4	6	1°	1	1	1/1	2/nk	2:08:4	6.40(FAnzto) JMStfnie,GyLnds,S'dleA
11-13 RR	ft C-3 Cd	2500 m	32	1:04:4	1:37:1	2:11	4	4	4	5°	5/2¼	6/3¾	2:11:4	4.10(FA'zto)UnfrmPrncss,LckyGm,Ad's

FIRST RACE — 8:00 P.M.

2 PACE-ONE MILE (2nd HALF OF DAILY DOUBLE)

SADDLE CLOTH—GREY

CLASS C-2—FILLIES & MARES—ALL AGES **PURSE $2,750**

1

MAY CHAMP b m, 5, by Champ Adios, Maytime Thunder by Thunderbird (Tr.-K. McNutt)
Carlo Niccolai & F. Castellazzi, Yonkers, N.Y. RR 2:09:3 1969 1 1 0 0 1,250.
($2,711) 4, 2:05:2 (⅝) KENNETH McNUTT (185) Green-White-Black WR(⅝) 2:05:4 1968 18 5 1 7 2,711.

4-9 RR	ft C-3 Cd	2500	m	30:2	1:04:1	1:37	2:09:3	2	4	3°	2°	2/½	1/1	2:09:3	*2.40(KM'Ntt)MayChmp,SstrF'hall,JneMiss
* 4-1 RR	ft qua		m	32:1	1:05:1	1:37:2	2:09:4	6	7	6°	3°	3/2½	2/ns	2:09:4	N.B.(M'Ntt)DnsD'Dee,MayChmp,E'prorJns
* 3-22 RR	ft qua		m	31:4	1:04:4	1:37:2	2:09:4	2	4	4	3°	4/2½	4/5½	2:11	N.B.(M'Ntt)RteT'Two,DrmrLbll,N'prtLadN
12-2 WR(⅝)	ft Cd		m	30	1:05:3	1:37	2:08:4	5	2	2	1	1/1	6/2¼	2:09:1	*2.25(JWeiner) MaxBoy, Betcha, Badger
11-27 WR(⅝)	ft Cd		m	30:3	1:04:1	1:35:2	2:07	8	1	1	1	1/1¼	3/2¾	2:07:3	2.05(JWnr)BretJhnstn,HnstArch,MayChmp
11-22 WR(⅝)	ft Cd		m	29:4	1:04:1	1:36:3	2:08	7	2	2	1	2/hd	3/nk	2:08	8.45(JWnr)JhnyMisnr,Chmpndle,MayChmp
11-15 WR(⅝)	ft Cd		m	30:1	1:03:2	1:35:3	2:06:2	7	2	2	1	1/2	3/6½	2:07:3	3.05(JWnr)AuntieMame,NrthScty,MayCh'p
11-4 WR(⅝)	ft Cd		m	30:1	1:03:4	1:35:2	2:06:2	8	1	2	1	1/1¼	2/2dh	2:06:4	3.70(JWnr)JhnnyMisnr,GtyHal-MayCh'pdh

---

2

OUI OUI BYRD b f, 3, by Bye Bye Byrd, Oreo Hanover by Adios (Tr.-W. Burris) (St.-V. Dancer)
Alnoff Stable & Gargreve Stable, New York 1969 1 0 0 1 330.
($1,947) 2, 2:06:2 HAROLD DANCER, JR. (165) Yellow-Grey MR 2:06:2 1968 11 2 2 1 1,947.

4-9 RR	ft C-2 Cd	2750	m	32:3	1:06:2	1:38:1	2:09:4	8	5	3°	2	2/2½	3/4¼	2:10:4	8.80(SD'cr)MssGntry,TrdyDmnd,OuiO'Byrd
* 3-29 RR	ft qua		m	31	1:04:4	1:37	2:09	4	2	2	2	3/1½	3/3	2:09:4	N.B.(WBrrs)SlickAce,GarthHn,OuiOuiByrd
* 3-22 RR	ft qua		m	31	1:05	1:36:2	2:09	2	2	2	2	2/2	5/5¼	2:10	N.B.(Brrs)HrnllsAce,AdrsChppie,E'hrstQ'n
8-19 MR	ft 2yr Stk	10874	m	31:1	1:02:2	1:34:3	2:06:4	5	2	2	2°	3/1	7/4	2:07:4	4.00e(NrrsJr) WthThnks,Sforza,VickiKgt
8-14 MR	ft 2yr	1000	m	31:4	1:05:4	1:37:2	2:09:4	4	2	3	4	3/1½	2/¾	2:10	*.90(NrrsJr) Prmpter,OuiOuiByrd,Gngrbrd
8-5Mdws(⅝)	ft 2yrStk	9631	m	30:4	1:04	1:34:3	2:07	6	1	2	2	6/3½	6/4	2:07:4	9.20(NrrsJr)TgrLilyLbl,WdwTme,K'stneIrs
7-29 MR	ft 2yr Stk	9540	m	30:1	1:01:3	1:33:2	2:06	2	5	5°	6°	4/4	5/3¾	2:06:4	22.90(NrrsJr)WthThnks,QnOmha,FrndlyFlly
7-23 VD(¾)	ft 2y Stk	6316	m	30:3	1:01:2	1:32:3	2:04:1	5x	8	8	8	8/dis	8/dis	2:11:4	4.50(N'sJr)WthTh'ks,K'stneMdw,MyG'Wck

---

3

J. M. MILLIE b m, 7, by Adios Boy, Jean Gallon by Bill Gallon (Tr.-D. Insko)
Dante Di Camillo, Long Island City, N.Y. RR 2:12 1969 13 1 1 2 3,654.
($28,095) 5, 2:05:1 DEL INSKO (120) Purple-Gold RR 2:05:4 1968 35 3 5 4 12,364

4-9 RR	ft C-2 Cd	2750	m	32:3	1:06:2	1:38:1	2:09:4	7	8	7°	8°	7/8½	5/4¼	2:10:4	10.80(Insko)MssGntry,TrdyDmnd,OuiO'Byrd
3-24 RR	sy C-3 Cd	2500	m	31:4	1:04:4	1:38:4	2:12	6	6	6	5°	5/4¼	1/ns	2:12	3.20(Tgrlo)JMMlie,SpdyBrbrne,Ht'ieKt'ie
3-11 RR	ft C-3 Cd	2500	m	32	1:05:4	1:38:2	2:11:4	8	8	4°	4°	4/2½	3/1¾	2:12:1	2.90(DInsko)FairFlrt,Clr'sT'Heel,JMMillie
3-5 RR	ft C-3	2500	m	30	1:03	1:35:2	2:06:4	6	7	7°	6	3/2	3/1¾	2:07:1	5.00(DInsko)Calsara,LadyThrne,J.M.Millie
2-28 YR	ft C-3	2500	m	30:4	1:03:2	1:35:3	2:07:3	7	7	8	8°	8/6	4/5½	2:09	7.90(DInsko)LidaLisa,Airbrush,ChiefBunny
2-22 YR	ft C-2	2750	m	31	1:02:3	1:33:2	2:06:1	7	3°	2	7	7/20	8/26	2:12:3	13.50(DInsko)MrcleGlw,BckyBlle,SprsAway
2-14YR	ft C-2 Cd	2750	m	32:3	1:06:2	1:38:3	2:10:4	8	8	8°	7°	7/4¼	8/3¾	2:11:4	9.10(DI'ko)StdyNan,MrcleGlow,Anita'sStr
2-6 YR	ft C-2 Cd	2750	m	31	1:04:2	1:36	2:07:2	4	5	4°	3°	2/1	2/1½	2:07:4	3.60(DInsko)MissArlne,JMMillie,StdyNan

---

4

FAIR DANCER ch m, 5, by Amortizor, Musical Miss by Titan Hanover (Tr.-W. Dracksley) (St.-E. Cobb)
Hasty Chance Co., Lessee, Copiague, N.Y. 1969 2 0 0 0
($5,493) 4, 2:05:3 B. W. NORRIS (182) Blue-White RR 2:05:3 1968 14 5 3 1 5,269.

* 4-8 RR	ft qua		m	31:2	1:03:4	1:36:1	2:07:1	5	5	6	6°	3/3	3/2½	2:07:3	N.B.(ECobb)CamdnComet,CFAdio,FairDncr
4-4 RR	ft C-2 Cd	2750	m	32	1:03:4	1:35	2:06:2	7	7	7	8	8/16	8/dis		10.90(JGSmth)FairMdn,UncleRss,ChrsDncr
3-27 RR	ft C-1 Cd	3000	m	31:1	1:03	1:34:3	2:05:4	3	5	6	8	8/7	8/5¾	2:07:1	12.20(ECbb)Calsara,ValleyPrincss,Lind'sGirl
11-8 RR	ft C-1	2700	m	30:3	1:04	1:35:1	2:06:3	2	5	3°	2°	2/1	5/1½	2:07	*1.20(Cobb)DlhisDrm,MayBHvn,KeyWhirl
11-1 RR	ft C-2	2600	m	30:4	1:02	1:33:3	2:05:3	5	6	6°	5°	4/1½	1/3	2:05:3	4.20(ECobb)FairDancer,Angelita,LidaLisa
10-24 RR	ft C-3	2500	m	31:4	1:05	1:36:4	2:07:2	6	6	4°	2°	2/ns	1/¾	2:07:2	8.50(ECbb)FairDncr,RcktAdios,MrshllClls
10-4 Fhld	ft Cd	1600	m	31:2	1:03	1:32:4	2:08	6	8	7	6°	5/3½	1/ns	2:08	17.00(ECbb)FairDncr,JMDuchss,HoboDans
9-21 Fhld	ft Cd	1500	m	31:2	1:02	1:33	2:05:2	3	5	6	7	7/22	7/25	2:10:2	5.10(ECbb)Coldstream,InskoHn.,RomanJoe

---

5

CLAIRE'S DREAM b m, 6, by Knight Dream, Adios Claire by Adios (Tr.-J. Faraldo)
Annroc Stables, Brooklyn, N.Y. YR 2:08:4 1969 12 2 1 1 4,302.
($17,525) 5,2:06:1 JOE FARALDO (187) White-Green-Black YR 2:06:1 1968 32 4 5 5 9,978.

4-9 RR	ft C-2 Cd	2750	m	32:3	1:06:2	1:38:1	2:09:4	6	7	8	7	6/8	4/4¼	2:10:4	16.40(Frldo)MssGntry,TrdyDmnd,OuiO'Byrd
4-2 RR	ft C-2 Cd	2750	m	31:2	1:03:3	1:36	2:08:1	8	8	7	6	6/4	3/3¼	2:09	36.30(JFrldo)MssHoliday,AnitasStr,ClrsDrm
3-24 RR	sy C-2 Cd	2750	m	33	1:07:2	1:40:3	2:12	3	5	7	7	7/5½	7/7½	2:13:4	4.80(JFrldo)ClrtAndrsn,MssGntry,TrprtSsn
3-17 RR	ft C-2 Cd	2750	m	31	1:01:4	1:34:4	2:06:2	7	3	4	4	3/2	4/3¼	2:07:1	20.60(JFrldo)AftnFlsh,ClrtA'drsn,MssGntry
3-7 RR	ft C-2	2750	m	30:4	1:04:1	1:34:3	2:06:4	7	6	8	6	6/7¼	6/3	2:07:3	18.10(JFrldo)ChmpR'bow,ClbyDars,BaylrHn
3-3 YR	ft C-2	2750	m	31:2	1:05	1:36:4	2:08:4	5	2	3	3	3/1¼	1/ns	2:08:4	12.90(JFrldo)ClrsDrm,OttoHn,ChampR'bow
2-22 YR	ft C-2	2750	m	31	1:02:3	1:33:2	2:06:1	5	7	8	5	5/7½	4/2	2:06:4	17.80(JFrldo)MrcleGlow,BckyBlle,SprsAway
2-8 YR	ft C-3 Cd	2500	m	30:3	1:04:2	1:36:4	2:09:1	4	4	3°	2°	2/½	1/hd	2:09:1	3.40(JFrldo)Claire'sDrm,OurGem,JuneMiss

---

6

REBA WAVE ch f, 3, by Shadow Wave, Reba Sampson by Sampson Hanover (Tr.-W. Mello) (St.-W. Haughton)
Joan & Howard Mann, New Hope, Pa. PPk(⅝) 2:04:4 1969 9 2 3 2 1,448.
(00.00) WM. HAUGHTON (150) Green-White-Gold 1968 0 0 0 0

4-9 RR	ft C-2 Cd	2750	m	32:3	1:06:2	1:38:1	2:09:4	5	6	6°	5°x4x/7		x8x/dis		2.80(BStll)MissGntry,TrdyDmnd,OuiO'Byrd
3-25 PPk(⅝)	ft Cd	1500	m	30:2	1:01:3	1:32:4	2:04	3	4	3	3°	4/2¾	6/11	2:06:1	2.20(WHghtn)Rosewll,AerialDoug,J'dleS'Hl
3-8 PPk(⅝)	ft Cd	750	m	30:2	1:01:4	1:33:1	2:04:4	5	1	3	2	2/1	1/½	2:04:4	2.90(WHghtn)RebaWve,GldnBankr,HalsJay
3-1 PPk(⅝)	ft Cd	750	m	31	1:03:3	1:34	2:05:1	2	3	3	3	3/1¼	2/ns	2:05:1	6.00(WHghtn)DstyHeel,RebaWve,GldnBnkr
2-22 PPk(⅝)	ft Cd	750	m	33:1	1:04:4	1:35:4	2:06:3	6	7	6	5	5/3½	2/1¾	2:07	6.10(WH'htn)MdwAd's,RebaWve,M'ylouHn
2-15 PPk(⅝)	ft Cd	750	m	30:4	1:02:2	1:33:1	2:05:2	1	4	4	3	3/1¾	3/2½	2:06	3.30(WHghtn)GldnBtlr,MdwAd's,RebaWve
2-10 PPk(⅝)	ft Cd	700	m	31:1	1:04:1	1:36	2:07:3	3	2	2	1	1/6	1/6	2:07:3	2.10(WHghtn)RebaWve,Mr.Rlco,ByeB'Btty
2-3 PPk(⅝)	ft Cd	700	m	31:2	1:02:4	1:34:1	2:04:2	4	5	5	3°	3/3	2/5¾	2:05:3	3.30(WHghtn)Wejover,RebaWve,DustyHeel

---

7

DAHN HOLLY ro m, 6, by Capetown, Mighty Heather by Mighty H. (Tr.-J. Chapman)
Green River Stock Farm, Inc., Green River, Can. YR 2:07:2 1969 12 1 1 1 3,249.
($33,991) 4, 2:05:4 JOHN CHAPMAN (147) Green-White YR 2:06:2 1968 33 6 6 5 17,115.

4-2 RR	ft C-2 Cd	2750	m	31:2	1:03:3	1:36	2:08:1	3	5	6°	7°	7/4½	4/4¾	2:09:2	3.90(JChp'n)MssHoliday,AnitasStr,ClrsDrm
3-19 RR	ft C-2	2750	m	30:3	1:02:2	1:34:2	2:05:2	1	3	4	3	3/1½	4/4¾	2:06:2	6.00(JChapmn)OurGem,Calsara,DustyJean
3-12 RR	ft C-2 Cd	2750	m	31:4	1:05:1	1:37:4	2:09:3	4	4	3	4	4/2	5/2	2:10	6.30(DWd)SmmieStrng,CityBts,DllyD'Joey
3-6 RR	ft C-1 Cd	3000	m	30:3	1:02:4	1:34	2:05:1	4	6	6	6	6/5½	7/8½	2:07:1	9.80(JChp'n)ReneWck,MrcleGlw,YnkeShdw
3-1 YR	ft C-1 Cd	3000	m	32	1:05:1	1:36:3	2:09:2	7	7	7°	7°	7/3¼	6/2¾	2:10	9.20(CAbto)ChrgrAdios,MrcleGlow,KatyR
2-22 YR	ft C-1 Cd	3000	m	30:3	1:03:4	1:35:1	2:07	1	3	4	6°	4/2¾	3/2¼	2:07:3	3.30(JChpmn)StdyNan,ChrgrAd's,DhnHlly
2-14 YR	ft B-3 Cd	3250	m	31	1:04:2	1:35:4	2:07	8	8	8	8	8/11	8/12	2:09:4	82.70(Dplse)PrincssOmaha,GdCndy,Emulate
1-31 YR	ft B-3 Cd	3250	m	31	1:03:4	1:36:1	2:07:4	5	7	7°	8	8/6¼	7/9½	2:10	32.50(DWood)SilkySquire,MrAvery,Charnie

---

8

ELMHURST QUEEN b m, 4, by Tar Heel, Kirk's Queen by Hodgen (Tr.-J. Edmunds)
Elmhurst Stables, N. Babylon, N.Y. 1969 2 0 0 1 330.
($11,608) 2, 2:06 JACK RICHARDSON (145) Blue-Grey (qua) RR 2:08:2 1968 15 0 1 3 3,513.

4-9 RR	ft C-2 Cd	2750	m	32:3	1:06:2	1:38:1	2:09:4	4	1°	2	4°	5/7	6/6¾	2:11:2	31.50(Bente)MssGntry,TrdyDmnd,OuiO'Byrd
3-29 RR	sy C-2 Cd	2750	m	32	1:05:4	1:38:2	2:10:3	3	3	3	4	3/1¼	3/1¾	2:11	22.10(Edmnds)SprsAwy,WntwnPck,E'hrstQn
* 3-22 RR	ft qua		m	31	1:05	1:36:2	2:09	5	3	4	4	4/3	3/2¼	2:09:2	N.B.(Ed'nds)HrnlsAce,AdrsCh'pie,E'hrstQ'n
11-6 RR	ft C-2 Cd	2600	m	30:1	1:02:1	1:34:1	2:05:4	2	2	3	4°	7/6¾	7/10	2:08:1	3.20(JEdmds)JMMllie,ClrtAndrsn,HerIrish
10-29 RR	ft C-2 Cd	2600	m	31:3	1:04:3	1:35:4	2:07:3	4	5	2°	2°	2/1	3/2½	2:08:1	8.80(Edmnds) GrnR'Ally,Brdside,E'hrstQn
10-19 RR	sy C-2	2750	m	31	1:03	1:34:4	2:08	1	4	5	6°	7/4½	5/2¼	2:08:3	*1.90(Ed'nds)PrntoPck,Clr'sDrm,TrueChnce
10-10 YR	ft C-2 Cd	2750	m	30:4	1:03	1:34:4	2:06:1	7	7	8	8	7/4¾	5/2½	2:06:4	18.80(Edmnds) AdleAd's,UnfrmP'css,Rsrrexl
10-3 YR	ft C-2 Cd	2750	m	29:2	1:01:2	1:33:3	2:05:3	3	4	3°	2°	2/hd	6/4	2:06:3	5.80(Edmnds)BthnyHn,GrnR'Ally,TrcysGrl

---

Exacta Windows Open 5 Minutes Before This Race.

MORN. LINE

3 TROT-ONE MILE EXACTA

SADDLE CLOTH—WHITE

CLASS B-2

B'NAI B'RITH MASADA LODGE

PURSE $4,00

---

8 **1**

MAJOR BRYCE b g, 7, by Rapid Hanover, Lyncell by His Excellency (Tr.-K. McNut
Lucky G.M. Stable, Levittown, N.Y. 1969 1 0 0 0
($30,009) 5, 2:05:2 KENNETH McNUTT (185) Green-White-Black BR 2:06:3 1968 28 4 4 2 11,27
4-3 RR ft B-1/B-2 4000 m 31:1 1:03:3 1:36 2:07:3 1 4 5 6 7/7½ 7/16 2:11:3 20.20(M'Ntt)VctryCdt,DsrtPrnce,PnthrsF
11-15 Btva sy Inv 3500 m 32 1:05:4 1:38:2 2:10:3 2 5 5 4 4/2½ 6/16 2:13:3 10.40(KM'Ntt)Floradel,Scndalous,HghSm
11-9 Btva gd Inv 2300 m 31:2 1:04:2 1:36:4 2:08:4 8 3° 1° 2 3/2½ 6/8½ 2:10:3 7.25(KM'Nutt)CeeZam,RingoHn,Bonjule
11-4 Btva ft Inv 2300 m 30:4 1:04 1:37 2:08:4 5 4 4 4° 3/1½ 1/nk 2:08:4 3.00(KM'Ntt)MajrBryce,RingoHn,MissBr
10-26 Btva gd Inv 2000 m 31:4 1:05:2 1:38:1 2:10:1 1 1 1 1 1/1 1/1¼ 2:10:1 *.80(KM'Nt)MjrBrce,RylTny,Dmpsy'sVct
10-21 Btva ft Inv 2300 m 31:1 1:05:3 1:36 2:08:1 5 6 6 4° 3/1¼ 4/1 2:08:2 3.50(KM'Ntt)Scndlous,CeeZam,SngleCre
10-14 Btva ft Inv 2700 m 30:3 1:04:3 1:35:3 2:06:2 7 1° 1 2 2/1¼ 4/3½ 2:07 5.75(KM'Ntt)MyGlLbll,Scndalous,CeeZa
10-7 Btva ft Inv 2700 m 30:3 1:03:2 1:35:4 2:06:3 5 6 6 3° 2/1¼ 2/1¾ 2:07 11.00(KM'Ntt)TprtLou,MjrBryce,Scndalo

---

3 **2**

SPERANZA COLBY b m ,7, by Tag Me, Girly Colby by Colby Hanover (Tr.-F. Annunziat
M.Annunziato,H.Geyer&J.R.Eustic,N.Y. RR 2:07:3 1969 4 1 1 0 2,82
($35,466) 4, 2:06:3 LUCIEN FONTAINE (134) Green-White-Red RR 2:08 1968 26 2 8 6 13,35
4-10 RR sy B-2 4000 m 31:2 1:04:1 1:38:4 2:11:1 3 2 2 2 2/1 2/2 2:11:3 5.00(F'tne)PrnceHnry,SprnzaClby,MrclM
3-28 RR ft B-1/B-2 4000 m 31:2 1:04:1 1:35:4 2:07:3 5 5 5° 4° 5/2 4/2¼ 2:08:1 6.90(LFntne)PplrJmie,MrclMir,ChmpRch
3-19 RR ft C-1 3000 m 31:4 1:03:1 1:35:2 2:07:3 3 5 4° 1 1/2 1/1¾ 2:07:3 2.50(LFntne)SprnzaClby,VctrDke,BoyOB
3-12 RR ft B-1/B-2 4000 m 32 1:06:1 1:38:1 2:10:2 2 x8x 8 8 8/dis 8/dis 11.80(LF'tne)RdnysStr,HppyN'prt,NtveYn
12-13 RR ft B-2 3750 m 33 1:06:2 1:38:1 2:10:1 8 7 7° 6° 6/3¼ 4/1 2:10:2 11.30(FAnzto)Carmik,ShrpCat,NativeY'ke
12-6 RR ft B-2 3000 m 31:2 1:05:2 1:37:4 2:09:2 7 6 3°°2° 3/1¾ 4/2 2:10 11.30(FAnzto)SharpCat,Carmik,PartysOve
11-29 RR ft B-2 3000 m 31 1:02:3 1:34:2 2:06:3 3 4 4° 2° 2/1 2/¾ 2:06:4 3.20(FAnzto)PrtysOvr,SprnzaClbyNvlBlz
11-22 RR ft B-2 3000 m 30:3 1:03:3 1:35:2 2:07:3 6 8 8° 4° 4/2¼ 2/¾ 2:07:4 14.00(FAnzto) BgC'Boy,SpnzaClby,PrtysC

---

5 **3**

NOVEL BLAZE br m, 5, by Blaze Hanover, Novel Hanover by Star's Pride (Tr.-R. McPhillips) (St.-G. Sholt
Thomas King, Bronx, N.Y. 1969 0 0 0 0
($21,420) 4, 2:04:4 (⅝) GEORGE SHOLTY (117) Brown-Gold-White PPk(⅝) 2:04:4 1968 25 2 8 2 11,40
11-29 RR ft B-2 3000 m 31 1:02:3 1:34:2 2:06:3 6 6 6 4° 3/2½ 3/4¼ 2:07:3 2.30(Shlty)PrtysOvr,SprnzaClby,NvlBlze
11-22 RR ft B-2 3000 m 30:3 1:03:3 1:35:2 2:07:3 4 7 6ix 7ix 8/15 6/12 2:10:3 2.20(Shlty) BgC'Boy,SprnzaClby,PrtysC
11-14 RR ft B-2 3250 m 30:4 1:03:2 1:34:4 2:06:4 4 5 2° 2° 2/½ 4/1¼ 2:07:1 2.70(GShlty)BenBen,Gwendolyn,Endearir
11-7 RR gd B-2 Cd 3250 m 32:4 1:06:3 1:38 2:09:3 3 3 3 3 3/1¼ 1x/¾dq 2:09:3 2.50(WMyr)T'yEdn,NvlBlz bydq,PnysH'N
10-31 RR ft B-2 Cd 3500 m 31:3 1:04:2 1:35:2 2:07:3 6 6 4° 3° 3/1 5/4¾ 2:08:4 5.20(WMyr)UlysseMb,Endrng,PnnysHsNt
10-24 RR ft B-2 3750 m 30 1:02:3 1:33:2 2:04:2 7 7 8 7° 7/6½ 3/3¾ 2:05:1 8.80(Shlty) PnthrsFlght,PrtysOvr,NvlBl
10-9 YR ft B-2 Cd 3750 m 30:2 1:02 1:33:4 2:05:2 2 4 6° 5° 3/1 2/1½ 2:05:4 *2.90(BMrgn)Socraplato,NovlBlze,Vn'sFir
10-2 YR ft B-2 3750 m 30 1:02 1:34 2:05:3 5 5 8 4 3/1¼ 2/¾ 2:05:4 14.50(BMrgn)SwtCere,NvlBlaze,GoldnPrk

---

4 **4**

MARCEL MIR b g, 9, by Solon Hanover, Southern Melody by Phonograph (Tr.-R. Aro
Lon Frocione, Syracuse, N.Y. 1969 10 0 2 1 4,31
($71,422) 8, 2:04:4 RALPH ARONE (165) Orange-Grey YR 2:04:4 1968 36 2 5 6 14,30
4-10 RR sy B-2 4000 m 31:2 1:04:1 1:38:4 2:11:1 5 3° 4 4 4/2½ 3/2 2:11:3 4.50(RArne)PrnceHnry,SprnzaClby,Mrcl
3-28 RR ft B-1/B-2 4000 m 31:2 1:04:1 1:35:4 2:07:3 3 3 4 5 4/2 2/¾ 2:07:4 12.50(RArne)PplrJmie,MrclMir,ChmpRich
3-20 RR ft B-1/B-2 4000 m 30:2 1:02 1:34:3 2:06 3 2 3 3 3/1 5/1¼ 2:06:2 13.20(RArne)NtveYkee,PplrJmie,PnthrsF
3-6 RR ft B-1/B-2 4000 m 31:2 1:03:1 1:34:4 2:06 3 4 2° 1 3/1¼ 5/2¼ 2:06:2 17.70(RArne)HlnsAdns,RdnysStr,PnthrsF
2-27 YR ft B-1/B-2 4125 m 31:1 1:03:4 1:35:1 2:06:4 4 2° 3 4 4/2¼ 4/4½ 2:07:4 19.20(Frldo)NeonRdny,RdnysStr,PnthrsFl
2-20 YR gd B-1 4500 m 31:3 1:05:1 1:36:4 2:08:1 1 2 3 5 5/3 5/2¼ 2:08:4 8.40(JFrldo)DndyDate,HlnsAdns,RdnysS
2-6 YR ft AA/B-1 7500 m 30:3 1:04:2 1:35:4 2:07:1 1 2 3 3 3/1¼ 5/1¾ 2:07:3 23.60(JFrldo)PrlssYkee,RdnysStr,FrmYnk
1-30 YR sy A/B-1 6000 m 32:1 1:06:2 1:39 2:13:1 5 4 5 6 6/3¼ 2/hd 2:13:1 37.30(JFrldo)SweetCere,MarcelMir,Spect

---

5 **5**

VICTORY CAMP br g, 9, by Spencer Camp, Victorian by Victory Song (Tr.A. Burt
James Monett & John McCambridge, N.Y. 1969 0 0 0 0
($91,445) 6, 2:03:4 AL BURTON (157) White-Red MR 2:04 1968 26 3 1 1 9,3
4-11 RR ft wk m: ¼ - :32; ½ - 1:05:2; ¾ - 1:39; Mile - 2:12 with A.Burton driving.
12-3 RR ft C-1 2700 m 31:2 1:03:4 1:36:2 2:09 5 x7 7 7 7/dis 8/dis 5.30(Brtn)CrnshMan,P'hvnDoll,MlrseMm
11-26 RR ft C-1 2700 m 31:2 1:04:1 1:36:4 2:08:4 3 5 4° 2° 2x/ns x6x/2¾ 2:09:2 *2.00(ABrtn)NtveYnke,P'hvnDoll,ShrpSh
11-14 RR ft B-2 3250 m 30:4 1:03:2 1:34:4 2:06:4 3 4 7 7° 8/4 8/4¾ 2:08 12.40(ABrtn)BenBen,Gwendolyn,Endearin
10-31 RR ft B-2 Cd 3500 m 31:3 1:04:2 1:35:2 2:07:3 5 5 7 8 8x/4¾ x8x/7¾ 2:09:2 17.50(ABrtn)UlysseMb,Endring,PnnysH'N
10-24 RR ft B-2 3750 m 30 1:02:3 1:33:2 2:04:2 1 2 1° 4 4/4 6/5½ 2:05:4 4.90(ABrtn) PnthrsFlght,PrtysOvr,NvlB
10-16 YR ft B-2/C-1 3750 m 30 1:01:1 1:33:1 2:04 7 8 8 7 6/6½ 3/7½ 2:05:4 20.10(ABrtn)DchssRose,Terrell,VictryCam
10-9 YR ft B-2 Cd 3750 m 30:2 1:02 1:33:4 2:05:2 6 5° 2° 3° 8/4¾ 8/9½ 2:07:3 10.00(ABrtn)Socraplato,NvlBlze,Van'sFirs

---

12 **6**

SWEET CERE br m, 7, by Lawde Me, Silver Hope by Silver King (Tr.-Z. Cherrix) (St.-R. Cherr
Belle R. & Zadok Cherrix, III, Md. YR 2:09:2 1969 11 2 1 0 10,15
($31,053) 6, 2:05 ROBERT CHERRIX (167) Black-White YR 2:05 1968 29 6 6 2 15,4
4-11 RR ft A/B-1 5000 m 31 1:04:1 1:36 2:07 4 4 4 x6x 8/dis 8/dis 33.60(RChrrx)PplrJmie,FrmYnke,PnthrsF
4-3 RR ft B-1/B-2 4000 m 31:1 1:03:3 1:36 2:07:3 7 7 7 7° 6/5 6/4 2:08:3 32.20(RChrx)VctryCdt,DsrtPrnce,PnthrsF
3-27 RR ft B-1 4500 m 31 1:02:2 1:34 2:05:2 5 6 7 8 8/5¾ 8/8 2:07:2 43.20(ZChrx)DchssRse,FrmYnke,PnthrsFl
3-20 RR ft B-1/B-2 4000 m 30:2 1:02 1:34:3 2:06 8 8 8 7° 7/5½ 7/7¼ 2:07:4 30.10(ZChrx)NtveYkee,PplrJmie,PnthrsF
3-12 RR ft JFA/A 10000 m 30:3 1:01 1:33:4 2:05:2 3 5 8 8 8/20 8/dis 61.30(RChrrx)ArgoPort,Pomp,PrlessYanke
2-27YR ft JFA/A-1 10000m 31 1:05:1 1:37:1 2:08:4 1 3 3 4 4/2¼ 5/3¼ 2:09:3 11.50(RChrx)StyleStr,PrlssYnkee,JustJn
2-20 YR gd AA/A 8750 m 32:1 1:05:1 1:37:2 2:09:2 3 3 3 4 3/2 1/ns 2:09:2 13.80(RChrx)SwtCere,FrmYnkee,PrlssYnk
1-30 YR sy A/B-1 6000 m 32:1 1:06:2 1:39 2:13:1 6 1 1 1 1/1 1/hd 2:13:1 11.90(RChrrx)SweetCere,MarclMir,Specta

---

6 **7**

JOSEPPE b h, 7, by Flying Star, Abbey Emlen by My Son (Tr.-J. Firet
Joseph Firetti, Brooklyn, N.Y. PPk(⅝) 2:06 1969 10 3 1 1 3,2
($20,818) 6, 2:08 JOSEPH FIRETTI (140) Red-White-Gold Fhld 2:08 1968 22 6 1 1 5,6
4-9 RR ft C-1 3000 m 30:4 1:04 1:37 2:08:2 2 3 3 1° 1/1 1/1 2:08:2 6.30(JFiretti)Joseppe,Pridewood,BoyOB
4-2 RR ft C-1 3000 m 32 1:05:4 1:37:1 2:09:2 6 7 6° 7° 5x/2¼ 6/7¼ 2:11:1 9.50(JFiretti)BernardC,HickiHi,VctorDu
3-26 RR ft C-1 3000 m 30:4 1:03:3 1:36 2:08:2 3 5 5 5° 6/3¾ 2/1 2:08:3 19.60(JFrtti)VictoryCadet,Joseppe,BoyOB
3-3 PPk(⅝) ft Cd 1000 m 29:3 59:3 1:31:2 2:04:2 4 5 5 6 5/20 4/15 2:07:3 6.80(JFrtti)MdgsTmmy,ClearBrk,OneFif
2-14 PPk(⅝) ft Cd 800 m 31:2 1:02:4 1:35 2:06 6 7 7 5° 5/2¼ 1/½ 2:06 3.90(JFrtti)Joseppe,IndnJohn,CrystlLigh
2-3 PPk(⅝) ft Cd 1000 m 31 1:03:3 1:35:3 2:07 6 6 6 7 7/6 6/4¼ 2:07:4 10.50(JFrtti)TrueValley,SpclProduct,Majo
1-23 PPk(⅝) ft Cd 1000 m 33 1:05:3 1:36:4 2:07:3 5 6 6 6 6/5½ 6/3¾ 2:08:1 7.10(JFrtti)TownDmn,SpclProduct,Majo
1-14 PPk(⅝) ft Cd 1000 m 32:2 1:05:4 1:37 2:08 7 5 5 6 6/8½ 4/6½ 2:09:1 17.70(JFrtti)MdgsTmmy,VllyMd,Jsppe by

---

6 **8**

TERRELL br g, 9, by Newport Dream, Arpege by Hoot Mon (Tr.-F. Leightley) (St.-S. Lew
A. Borrelli & S. Lewis, N.Y. RR 2:10:1 1969 4 1 0 0 2,1
($71,422) 5, 2:04:2 JAMES TALLMAN (150) Wine-Grey-Yellow RR 2:04:4 1968 31 2 7 6 14,3
4-10 RR sy B-2 4000 m 31:2 1:04:1 1:38:4 2:11:1 6 6 6 6 6/3¾ 4/4½ 2:12:1 13.70(Tlmn)PrnceHnry,SprnzaClby,MrclM
3-28 RR ft B-1/B-2 4000 m 31:2 1:04:1 1:35:4 2:07:3 4 4 3° 2° 3/1 6/5½ 2:09 7.50(JTllmn)PplrJmie,MrclMir,ChmpRic
3-20 RR ft B-1/B-2 4000 m 30:2 1:02 1:34:3 2:06 2 6 7 8 6/3¼ 4/1¼ 2:06:2 4.20(Tlmn)NtveYkee,PplrJmie,PnthrsFl
3-11 RR ft C-1 3000 m 31:4 1:06 1:38:2 2:10:1 5 5 5° 5° 4/2¼ 1/¾ 2:10:1 3.90(CAbtlo)Terrell,HickiHi,PinehavenB
10-31 RR ft B-2 Cd 3500 m 31:3 1:04:2 1:35:2 2:07:3 7 7 6° 5° 5/2¼ 6/5¾ 2:09 19.80(HBsngr)UlysseMb,Endrng,PnysHsN
10-24 RR ft B-2 3750 m 30 1:02:3 1:33:2 2:04:2 4 4 5 6 5/5½ 7/7 2:06:1 3.50(Fntne) PnthrsFlght,PrtysOvr,NvlB
10-16 YR ft B-2/C-1 3750 m 30 1:01:1 1:33:1 2:04 6 6 6 4° 2/1 2/1 2:04:1 8.90(BWbstr)DchssRose,Terrell,VctryCa
10-9 YR ft B-2 Cd 3750 m 30:2 1:02 1:33:4 2:05:2 1 3 4 6 7/4¼ 7/5½ 2:06:3 3.10(BWbstr)Socraplato,NvlBlze,Vn'sFl

---

EXACTA WINDOWS OPEN FOR THIS RACE.

4

PACE-ONE MILE

SADDLE CLOTH—GREEN

EQUITABLE LIFE

CLASS A-2 **PURSE $6,500**

1

MONEY WISE
br h, 6, by Patrick Song, Victory Captain by Captain Eddie (Tr.-F. Leightley) (St.-S. Lewis)
Bantam Stock Farms, Huntington, N.Y. RR 2:03:2 1969 2 1 1 0 4,125.
($78,360) 3, 2:00 GEORGE SHOLTY (117) Brown-Gold-White Brdwn 2:02 1968 23 4 4 3 19,217.

4-11 RR ft A-3 5500 m 29:3 1:01:1 1:32:4 2:03:2 2 5 4° 2° 2/ns 1/hd 2:03:2 2.90(DInsko)MoneyWise,A'craig,BrwnSmke
4-5 RR gd A-3 5500 m 31:3 1:04:2 1:35:1 2:06:4 1 3 5 5 5/2 2/2 2:07:1 3.20(DInsko)MrJimT,MoneyWise,LmlghtN
11-13 RR ft A-3 4000 m 29:3 1:02 1:33:4 2:04:3 3 5 5 1 1/2 1/3 2:04:3 3.30(DInsko)MoneyWise,Chukkah,Spoiler
11-6 RR ft A-3 5000 m 29:2 1:01 1:32:2 2:03 7 7 7 6 7/4 6/3¾ 2:04 14.00(CF'ptrk) Eyreton,Spoiler,TrprtKaren
10-29RR ft Opt A-3 5000 m 29 1:01:3 1:32:4 2:03:3 1 2 2 3° 2/1 2/1½ 2:04 •1.80(DInsko)AC'sDndy,MnyWse,PrdeOfHn.
10-21 RR ft A-3 5250 m 30 1:01:4 1:32:1 2:03:1 7 7 7 7 7/5¼ 3/1¼ 2:03:2 7.40(DInsko)EvenBrk,YnkeMck,MoneyWise
10-14 YR ft A-3 5250 m 29:4 1:00:2 1:31 2:02:1 4 3° 1 2 1x/ns 7/11 2:05 4.50(DInsko)FrancisPAdios,Candios,A'craig
10-4 YR ft A-2 6250 m 30:1 1:00:3 1:31:2 2:02:4 7 1° 1 2 3/2 6/1 2:03:1 7.60(DInsko)AdiosMssge,Hopalng,HerLady

---

2

MIRACLE MAKER
b h, 4, by Miracle Knight, Tiny Volo Scott by Hollyrood Hermes (Tr.-Z. Cherrix) (Stable-R. Cherrix)
Harry W. Kelley, Ocean City, Md. RR 2:05:2 1969 3 1 2 0 6,375.
($30,355) 3, 2:03:4 ROBERT CHERRIX (167) Black-White YR 2:03:4 1968 9 1 3 3 15,241.

4-10 RR sy A-2 6500 m 31 1:02:3 1:34 2:06:2 3 6 6 3° 2/nk 2/ns 2:06:2 •1.10(RChrx)JC'seG'tree,MrcleMkr,HpeTme
4-4 RR ft A-2 6500 m 30:1 1:00:4 1:31:1 2:01:4 2 4 1 2 2/1 2/nk 2:01:4 3.70(RChrx)Mndian,MracleMkr,GneBGood
3-22 RR ft A-2 6250 m 31:1 1:02:3 1:34:1 2:05:2 2 3 4° 4° 5/2 1/ns 2:05:2 4.30(RChrx)MrcleMkr,GneBGd,NshbaL'me
9-19 YR ft A-2 6250 m 29:2 59:3 1:30:2 2:01:1 2 4 4 5 4/2½ 3/2¾ 2:01:4 •1.30(RChrx)TudrHn,LawDmnd,MrcleMkr
9-12 YR ft A-2 6250 m 30:2 1:02 1:32:3 2:03 8 7 7 8 7/4¾ 4/2¼ 2:03:3 8.00(RChrx)BradHn,LimelightN,MneyWise
7-6 Brdwn ft Inv 5500 m 29:3 59:2 1:30:3 2:00:3 2 3 4 3° 5/2¼ 4/5 2:01:3 •.80(RChrrx)StwrtHn,SchellHn,BulletStar
6-22AC(½) ft3y Stk 15300 m 28:1 59:3 1:28:4 1:59:4 1 2 1 1 1/nk 3/3¾ 2:00:3 2.40(Chrrx)FullaNpln,ByeA'Lrge,MrcleMkr
6-15 Brdwn ft Cd 4500 m 30:2 1:01:1 1:31 2:00:4 3 2 1 1 1/1¼ 2/nk 2:00:4 •.55(RChrrx)PpprsWay,MrcleMkr,HrlnLee

---

3

NEVELE ROMEO
b h, 4, by Lehigh Hanover, Romola Hanover by Tar Heel (Tr.-D. Insko)
A. Natelson, D. Kessler & J. Greck, N.Y. 1969 2 0 0 0 520.
($79,429) 3, 2:01:2 DEL INSKO (120) Purple-Gold RcR 2:01:2 1968 31 7 9 4 63,878.

4-10 RR sy A-2 6500 m 31 1:02:3 1:34 2:06:2 6 7 8 6° 5/3¾ 4/2¼ 2:07 12.00(DI'ko)JC'seG'tree,MrcleMkr,HpeTme
3-29 RR sy A-1/A-2 7500 m 29:3 1:01:1 1:34 2:07:3 3 5 5 8 8/8¼ 6/5¼ 2:08:4 •2.30(DInsko) Drambuie,NeveleWay,Clay
11-14 RR ft A-1/A-2 4500 m 29:2 59:4 1:31:1 2:02:2 3 2 4 4 3/3¼ 2/1 2:02:3 8.30(DInsko)FortNlsn,NvleRomeo,HollySnd
11-7 RR gd Opt A-2 4500 m 30:1 1:02:1 1:32:2 2:04:1 5 5 5 5 5/4 3/2¼ 2:04:3 8.70(WHdsn)AC'sDndy,Goodnff,NvleRomeo
10-29RR ftA-1-2 hcp 6500m 29:3 1:01 1:31:2 2:03:2 8 1° 3 4 4/2 6/4 2:04:2 4.30(DInsko)PneH'Tme,F'csPAd's,StvnFrst
10-19LB(½) gd 3yStk 35839m 29:2 59:4 1:31 2:01:2 4 7 7 3° 3/3¾ 8/6 2:02:3 15.60(HerFiln)FllaNpln,Batman,RumCustmr
9-19Dela ft 3yr Stk 31267 m 29:1 1:01:4 1:32 2:01:4 3 2 2 3 3x/½ 5/7¼ 2:03:1 6.80(SDncr)Ad'sWvrly,ByeB'Pt,GdT'Knght
9-11 LB(½) ft Inv 6000 m 30 1:00:1 1:30:1 2:01 1 2 2 ix4 4/19 5/23 2:05:3 •.90(RDncr)MissCnaAd's,ByeB'Pt,IsoltrHn

---

4

GOOD TIME GENE
b g, 7, by Gene Abbe, Good Time Princess by Good Time (Tr.-J. Liso) (St.-L. Copeland)
Abraham Schultz, Bal Harbour, Fla. RR 2:03:4 1969 14 2 1 1 10,774.
($61,399) 4, 2:02:2 (½) LEROY COPELAND (170) White-Green YR 2:04:3 1968 38 7 1 9 25,624.

4-10 RR sy A-2 6500 m 31 1:02:3 1:34 2:06:2 1 4 4° 4° 4/3¼ 5/5¼ 2:07:4 18.50(Tllmn)JC'seG'tree,MrcleMkr,HpeTme
3-29 RR sy A-1/A-2 7500 m 29:3 1:01:1 1:34 2:07:3 1 3 3 4 4/3¼ 4/4¼ 2:08:2 4.20(CAbtlo) Drambuie,NeveleWay,Clay
3-22 RR ft A-3 5250 m 29:4 1:02 1:32:4 2:03:4 8 1 1 1 1/1¼ 1/ns 2:03:4 7.80(CAbtlo)GoodT'Gne,HopeTime,MntgeN
3-15 RR ft Inv 12500 m 29:3 1:01:1 1:31:4 2:02:3 7 8 7 8 7/5¼ 8/7¼ 2:04:1 72.50(RRsh)W.W.Smith,OrbiterN.,Clay
3-8 RR ft Inv 10000 m 29:3 1:00:4 1:32:4 2:04:1 3 6 8 8° 8/3¼ 7/3¼ 2:05 43.50(RRsh)NZKmbrlyKid,Drmbuie,FrstLee
3-1 YR ft A-3 5250 m 29:4 1:02:1 1:33:2 2:05:3 3 5 5 5° 5/2 2/hd 2:05:3 4.70(CAbtlo)Bombrdr,GdT'Gene,DuaneAgn
2-21 YR ft A-3 5250 m 31:3 1:02:4 1:34 2:05:2 2 3 2 3 3/1¼ 5/1¼ 2:05:4 6.10(Cplnd)CardnlWay,StvnFrost,D'reAgn
2-14 YR ft A-2 6250 m 29:3 1:02 1:33:2 2:04:2 7 8 4°°8 8/8¼ 8/13 2:07:4 92.40(Tllmn)SmpsnKght,MstrDke,VoloTime

---

5

VOLO TIME
ro g, 5, by Right Time, Scottlana by Scottish Pence (Tr.-S. Demas)
B. Epstein, A. Epstein & M. Rappaport, N.Y. YR 2:05:2 1969 12 3 1 3 12,250.
($19,510) 4, 2:02:2 (½) LUCIEN FONTAINE (134) Green-White-Red LB(½) 2:02:2 1968 25 10 2 3 14,913.

3-27 RR ft A-2/A-3 6000 m 31:1 1:03:4 1:34:3 2:05:3 2 4 2° 1 1/3¼ 1/2¼ 2:05:3 6.70(LF'tne)VoloTme,A'craig,JCr'seG'tree
3-22 RR ft A-3 5250 m 29:4 1:02 1:32:4 2:03:4 3 5 5 5° 5/4¼ 4/2¼ 2:04:2 2.90(LF'tne)GoodT'Gne,HopeTime,MntgeN
3-14 LB(½) ft ec 6000 m 30 1:01:4 1:34 2:03:1 6 6 6 5 5/5¼ 4/5 2:04:1 19.10(RCrmr)AftnDay,PrideOfHn,FireawyN.
3-8 LB(½) ft ec 6000 m 30:1 1:00:3 1:33 2:02:2 2 5 6 5 5/5¼ 6/8¾ 2:04 7.70(RCrmr)AftnDay,PrideOfHn,FireawyN.
3-1 LB(½) ft ec 5500 m 31:2 1:03:2 1:34:1 2:05:3 1 2 4 3 3/1¼ 2/1 2:05:4 3.50(RCrmr)PddysKngt,VloTme,LibraceHn
2-21 LB(½) gd ec 5000 m 31:1 1:03:2 1:35:3 2:05:1 2 5 5 4° 4/3¾ 3/6¼ 2:06:2 2.60(RCrmr)AftonDay,RobinHill,VoloTime
2-14 YR ft A-2 6250 m 29:3 1:02 1:33:2 2:04:2 3 5 3° 1 1/1 3/1¼ 2:04:4 8.00(LFntne)SmpsnKght,MstrDke,VoloTme
2-7 YR ft A-2 6250 m 30:2 1:02:4 1:33:4 2:04:2 1 4 4° 5 4/1¾ 3/1¼ 2:04:4 15.40(Fntne)DngleN,NZKmbrlyKid,VoloTme

---

6

HOPE TIME
br h, 7, by Julep Time, Marlene Hope by Stanhope (Tr.-J. Chapman)
Bert V. James, Windsor, Ont. RR 2:08:1 1969 8 1 1 2 5,562.
($174,434) 4, 1:59:3 (½) JOHN CHAPMAN (147) Green-White HP(½) 2:00:3 1968 35 5 7 5 39,899.

4-10 RR sy A-2 6500 m 31 1:02:3 1:34 2:06:2 4 2 2 2 3/1¼ 3/1¾ 2:06:4 4.60(JC'mn)JC'seG'tree,MrcleMkr,HpeTme
3-29 RR sy A-3/B-1 5500 m 31 1:04:4 1:36:1 2:08:1 8 1° 1 1 1/1 1/2¼ 2:08:1 2.60(JC'mn)HpeTme,RoyalRmn,DxieTomby
3-22 RR ft A-3 5250 m 29:4 1:02 1:32:4 2:03:4 5 2 2 2 2/1¼ 2/ns 2:03:4 3.40(JChp'n)GoodT'Gne,HopeTme,MntgeN
3-13 RR ft Inv 12500 m 29:4 1:02:4 1:33:2 2:04:1 2 5 7 8 7/4¼ 7/6 2:05:3 40.70(JChpmn)HdgnSpcl,NvleWy,MzelRdny
3-8 RR ft A-2/A-3 6000 m 30:3 1:01:3 1:32:3 2:05:1 1 2 2 2 2/1 3/nk 2:05:1 •1.40(JChpmn)VldBet,AustS'Slvr,HopeTime
2-28 YR ft A-2 6250 m 30 1:02:1 1:33:2 2:05 5 4 4° 3° 4/1¼ 7/3¾ 2:05:4 20.50(MDky)J.C'G'tree,IdahoN.,CardinlWay
2-21YR ft A-2 6250 m 31:1 1:03:2 1:34:1 2:04:3 7 7 7 6 5/5¼ 6/5¼ 2:06 35.40(MDky)MstrDuke,NZK'brlyKid,IdahoN
2-15 YR ft A-1/A-2 6875 m 31:1 1:02:4 1:33:2 2:04:4 2 3 6 7 7/4 7/4¼ 2:05:4 14.40(MDoky)EscpdeLbll,RselndB'ty,NvleWy

---

7

AUST SOUTHERN SILVER
b g, 7, by Southern Brigade, Flaming Silver by Silver Peak (Tr.-R.Baker) St.-S.Dancer)
Thomas N. Siciliano, N.J. RR 2:06:3 1969 4 1 1 1 5,400.
($29,181) 6, 2:02 STANLEY DANCER (142) Blue-Gold Fhld 2:02 1968 21 8 5 1 27,771.

4-5 RR gd A-1/A-2 7500 m 31:2 1:02:3 1:34 2:06:1 1 2 3 3 3/1¼ 3/¼ 2:06:2 3.60e(SDncr)PblcAffr,Drmbuie,Ast.So.Silvr
3-22 Rock ft ec 7500 m 29:4 1:02:3 1:33:4 2:04 7 1° 1 1 2/2 6/7 2:05:2 1.80(SDncr)DrHrryC.,SmpsnCnsl,AndysSon
3-15 RR ft A-2/A-3 6000 m 30:3 1:03:2 1:36 2:06:3 8 1° 1 1 1/1 1/1 2:06:3 •1.10e(D'crJr)A'stS'Slvr,MntgeN,GneBGood
3-8 RR ft A-2/A-3 6000 m 30:3 1:01:3 1:32:3 2:05:1 5 6 6° 5° 5/3 2/hd 2:05:1 2.50e(DncrJr)VldBet,AustS'Slvr,HopeTime
10-29RR ftA-1-2 hcp 6500m 29:3 1:01 1:31:2 2:03:2 7 8 4° 3° 2/¼ 5/3¼ 2:04:1 9.30(SDncr)PneH'Tme,F'csPAd's,StvnFrst
10-5 YR ft A-1 7500 m 29:3 1:01 1:32 2:02:3 2 5 5° 7° 8/3¼ 6/2¾ 2:03:1 5.90(DncrJr)TradrNrdin,Goodnff,MrLcifer
9-28 YR ft A-2 6250 m 29:3 1:00:3 1:32 2:02:2 3 2 3 3 3/1¼ 1/hd 2:02:2 •1.00e(AMyr)AustSoSlvr,SpclDrm,MdwTrpt
9-20 YR ft A-2 6250 m 31 1:01 1:31:4 2:02:2 4 4 4° 2° 1/nk 2/hd 2:02:2 1.70(SDncr)ShreWill,AstSthrnSlvr,ZipTar

---

8

N. Z. KIMBERLY KID
b g, 6, by Goodland, Heathmount by Garrison Hanover (Tr.-B. DeFonce) (St.-C. Abbatiello)
Milbern Stable, Elmont, N.Y. RR 2:04:1 1969 15 4 2 0 17,811.
($8,876) N.R. CARMINE ABBATIELLO (135) Gold-Red (qua) RR 2:09:1 1968 14 1 2 2 2,565.

4-12 RR ft A-1 7500 m 29:3 1:01 1:30:4 2:02:1 2 4 4° 6° 8/6¾ 7/6¼ 2:03:3 6.00(CAbtlo)NiftyNelse,FirstLee,Peerswick
4-5 RR gd A-1/A-2 7500 m 31:2 1:02:3 1:34 2:06:1 3 5 6 7 4/2¾ 5/1 2:06:2 8.50(CAbtlo)PblcAffr,Drmbuie,Ast.So.Silvr
3-29 RR sy Inv 25000 m 30 1:02:2 1:34:2 2:05:3 5 6 6 7 6/6¼ 7/8 2:07:3 32.80(CAbtlo)NardnsByrd,OrbiterN,HdgnSpcl
3-22 RR ft Inv 25000 m 29:1 1:01 1:31:4 2:02 2 1 2 3 3/2¼ 10/8¼ 2:04:1 16.60(CAbtlo)OrbtrN.,HdgnSpcl,CardinlKing
3-13 RR ft Inv 12500 m 29:4 1:02:4 1:33:2 2:04:1 8 8 8° 7° 8/4¼ 4/3¼ 2:05 18.10(CAbt)HdgnSpecl,NveleWay,MazlRdny
3-8 RR ft Inv 10000 m 29:3 1:00:4 1:32:4 2:04:1 4 3 4 5 5/2¼ 1/1¼ 2:04:1 5.70(CAbt)NZKmbrlyKid,Drmbuie,FrstLee
3-1 YR ft A-1/A-2 7500 m 29:1 1:01:3 1:32:2 2:04:3 1 3 2° 1° 2/nk 5/2 2:05 •1.60(CAbto)SmpsnKngt,NvleWay,DngleN
2-21YR ft A-2 6250 m 31:1 1:03:2 1:34:1 2:04:3 4 2 2 2 2/nk 2/hd 2:04:3 •1.40(DncrJr)MstrDuke,NZK'rlyKid,IdahoN

Exacta Windows Open 5 Minutes Before This Race.

MORN. LINE

5 PACE-ONE MILE EXACTA

SADDLE CLOTH—BLACK

PLAINVIEW KIWANIS

CLAIMING $5,000—6-YEAR & UP
ALL HORSES ENTERED MAY BE CLAIMED FOR $5,000 PURSE $3,00

4 — 1 TOM THUMB b g, 7, by Chief Lenawee, The G Lady by Johnny Song (F. Daris
Frank Darish, Westbury, N.Y. YR 2:09 1969 9 2 2 4 5,01
($18,820) 3, 2:04:4 (⅝) FRANK DARISH (176) Red-Grey RR 2:09 1968 33 1 2 4 4,23

4-5 RR	sy clm alw	4000	m	31:3	1:06:1	1:38:3	2:10:3	1	4	5	5	6/3¾	1/½	2:10:3	6.50(Drsh)TomThmb,GrndPtch,S'phnyBll
3-24 RR	sy clm	4000	m	32	1:05:4	1:38:2	2:10:3	1	2	2	2°	2/nk	3/1½	2:11	4.60(FDrsh)MdwRch,CareerCnsl,TomThm
3-17 RR	ft clm	3000Z	m	31	1:04:4	1:36:3	2:08	7	8	8	8	7/4½	3/1	2:08:1	4.30(Plvne)LthrioLindsy,Pywckt,TomThm
3-10 RR	ft clm alw	3000	m	30:2	1:04	1:36:3	2:09	7	8	8	7°	6/4½	3/3½	2:10	4.20(Plvne)NowH'This,Pywckt,TomThumb
3-5 RR	ft clm alw	3000	m	31:2	1:04:2	1:36:2	2:08:3	6	5	5	3°	2/2	2/1	2:08:4	3.80(Plvne)FishermnBert,TomThmb,Matt
2-25 YR	ft clm	3000	m	32:1	1:06:3	1:38	2:09:4	4	2	2	3	3/1½	2/1½	2:10	3.70(Plvne)GrndPtch,TomThmb,G.T.Stevr
2-18 YR	ft clm alw	3000	m	31:1	1:04:2	1:36:4	2:09	7	7	6°	5°	5/2½	3/3½	2:09:4	25.20(Plvne)GayRbin,SeldmSafe,TomThum
1-28 YR	ft clm	4500	m	30:1	1:01:1	1:32:4	2:06	7	6•	6•	7°	8/11	8/11	2:08:3	15.40(Plvne)ForestMite,AvanteN,JMRegal

3 — 2 STORMY DREAM b g, 13, by Knight Dream, Madam Boussac by Volomite (Tr.-J. Cruis
Saul Finkelstein & Sidney Morgan, N.Y. RR 2:07:3 1969 6 1 3 0 3,62
($162,957) 6, 1:58:2 (1) JIMMY CRUISE (173) Green-Red YR 2:05:3 1968 10 2 0 3 4,27

4-7 RR	ft clm alw	5000	m	30:2	1:04	1:36	2:07:2	1	3	3	5	5/2½	2/¾	2:07:3	2.10(JCrse)Emnciptn,StrmyDrm,CopprJck
3-29 RR	gd clm	4000	m	30:3	1:02:4	1:36:1	2:08:2	1	4	4	2°	2/1	2/1	2:08:3	•1.20(JCrse)Emncptn,StrmyDrm,ScotHaye
3-22 RR	ft clm	4000	m	30:2	1:03	1:35:1	2:07:3	8	8	8	5	5/3½	1/1¾	2:07:3	6.20(JCr'se)StrmyDrm,MattB,CopperJcke
3-11 RR	ft clm	4000	m	31	1:04:2	1:38	2:12:3	5	7	7	4°	4/2	2/¾	2:12:4	2.60(JCrse)GrndPatch,StrmyDream,Matt
3-5 RR	ft C-2	2750	m	31:3	1:04:1	1:36:1	2:07:3	2	4	4	4	4/3	5/2¾	2:08:1	3.00(JCrse)HrrcneMd,B'h'ksDll,DllyD'Joe
2-24 YR	ft clm alw	3000	m	30:4	1:04:1	1:35:4	2:09:2	4	6	6°	6	7/3	4/1½	2:09:4	•1.80(JClhn)OurQuestn,PostRail,TomStron
9-3 YR	ft clm alw	5000	m	29:3	1:01:1	1:32	2:03:4	8	8	8	7	7/8½	5/6	2:05:2	7.10(JCrse)JMRegal,HiawathaHn,KllyGrn
8-27 YR	ft clm alw	5000	m	29:1	1:00:2	1:33:1	2:05:3	6	7	7	7	5/2½	1/1	2:05:3	2.80(Chpmn) StrmyDrm,CareLss,Speakea

8 — 3 WINSTADT br g, 9, by Volstadt, Lucy Truax by Donald Truax (Tr.-W. Maricond
Natale & Carmella Luchento, N.J. 1969 9 0 1 0 1,11
($53,610) 5, 2:02:1 (⅝) THOMAS LUCHENTO (170) Green-White Fhld 2:06 1968 34 2 5 7 10,85

4-4 RR	ft clm	5000	m	31:3	1:04:1	1:35:1	2:07	1	2	2	2	2/2	2/1½	2:07:2	38.50(TL'nto)Ad'sGrgeA.,Wnstdt,SpnglrVl
3-28 RR	ft clm	5000	m	30:3	1:03:4	1:35:4	2:08:4	7	7	6°	4°	4/1	6/2½	2:09:2	67.30(TLchnto)KnnyDars,I'MAGndr,FrstM
3-19 RR	ft clm	5000	m	31	1:04:1	1:35:2	2:07	8	8	8	8°	8/6	8/5¾	2:08:2	79.90(Lchnto)SpnglrVolo,JtDncr,LeglFrgh
3-8 RR	ft clm	5000	m	30:2	1:04:1	1:36:1	2:08:2	4	5	6°	7°	6/3	5/5½	2:09:3	29.20(TLchnto)FstGn,SpnglrVolo,OurQuest
2-28 YR	ft clm	4500	m	31	1:03	1:35:2	2:08	1	3	3	3°	4/1½	5/3	2:08:4	18.20(Lchnto)SpnglrVlo,AlbrtGne,MtnLkbl
2-19 YR	sy clm alw	4500	m	32	1:05:2	1:38:1	2:10:2	5	7	7°	6°	6/4½	7/6½	2:12	25.20(TLchnto)Gunkhr,FrstMite,GrntreeRe
2-12 YR	ft clm alw	6000	m	30:4	1:02:3	1:35	2:07:4	7	8	8	8	5/6½	5/6½	2:09:2	93.20(TLchnto)J.M.Regal,JetDncr,Goldville
2-5 YR	ft clm	6000	m	31:1	1:03:1	1:34:3	2:07:2	1	4	4°	5°	6/3½	6/3	2:08:1	17.90(TLchnto)Dukegan,JetDancer,Goldvil

8 — 4 JET DANCER b g, 7, by Jimmy Creed, Penny Pace by Meadow Pace (Tr.-G. Kovia
George W. Young, Jersey City, N.J. 1969 12 0 3 1 3,31
($11,024) 6, 2:06:2 GEORGE KOVIAN (150) Brown-Tan-Green Fhld 2:06:2 1968 19 1 1 4 2,14

4-4 RR	ft clm	5000	m	31:3	1:04:1	1:35:1	2:07	4	5	6	5	5/5	6/5½	2:08:2	13.40(GKvn)Ad'sGrgeA.,Winstdt,SpnglrVlo
3-27 RR	ft clm	6000	m	30:4	1:03:3	1:35:1	2:06:4	1	3	3°	2°	2/1	4/4½	2:08	8.00(GKvn)MastrGlenn,Judson,CopperAd
3-19 RR	ft clm	5000	m	31	1:04:1	1:35:2	2:07	6	7	7°	4°	3/1½	2/¾	2:07:1	28.70(GKvian)SpnglrVolo,JetDncr,LeglFrg
3-12 RR	ft clm	5000	m	30:4	1:03:1	1:35:2	2:08:1	2	5	5	7	8/7	5/3½	2:09	18.80(GKvian)ForstMte,HonrBoy,ChmpRch
3-4 YR	ft clm	6000	m	30:4	1:03:1	1:36	2:07:4	5	6ix	8	8	8/10	8/12	2:10:4	23.20(GKvian)GrrisnLght,JMRegl,CpprAd
2-26 YR	gd clm	6000	m	30:4	1:02:4	1:35:4	2:08:2	6	6	6	6	6/4½	4/2½	2:09	20.10(GKvn)XpertBud,Delhi'sDrm,JMRega
2-18 YR	ft clm	6000	m	31	1:03:1	1:35:4	2:08:4	3	5	6	5	7/2¾	7/1	2:09	7.90(GKvian)Speakeasy,Gldville,J.M.Rega
2-12 YR	ft clm alw	6000	m	30:4	1:02:3	1:35	2:07:4	3	6	6	5	3/3½	2/¾	2:08	4.30(GKv'n)J.M.Regal,JetDancer,Goldvill

5 — 5 HIAWATHA HANOVER br g, 7, by Sampson Hanover, Heath by Scotland (Tr.-R. Ras
Double C. Stable, New York, N.Y. RR 2:09 1969 7 2 0 1 3,49
($18,082) 3, 2:06:2 RUSSELL RASH (165) Red-Black-Silver RR 2:08:2 1968 22 3 4 0 6,83

3-31 RR	ft clm alw	5000	m	30:1	1:02:4	1:33:4	2:07:2	6	3	5	5	5/3	5/2½	2:07:4	12.70(RRash)HonorBoy,FastGun,WarrenD
3-26 RR	ft clm alw	5000	m	31:2	1:05:3	1:38	2:09:1	7	3	3	3	3/1½	3/1¾	2:09:3	24.50(RRsh)SlvryWvs,RealYnkee,HwathaHr
3-14 RR	ft clm	4000	m	31:3	1:05:2	1:37:4	2:09	1	1	1	1	1/1	1/2½	2:09	4.30(RRsh)HiawathaHn,R'mdeDve,F'mnB
3-4 YR	ft clm alw	4500	m	30:4	1:05	1:37:1	2:09:2	3	1	1	1	1/1	4/2	2:09:4	3.10(RRsh)GayRobin,DukesVictor,PostRa
2-26 YR	gd clm	4500	m	30:1	1:03:4	1:36:2	2:08:2	5	3	3	5	5/2¾	5/1½	2:08:4	19.80(RRsh)ForestMte,AmzingVle,GayRob
2-18 YR	ft clm alw	4500	m	31:1	1:05	1:36:2	2:09:1	4	1	1	2	1/1	1/¾	2:09:1	20.10(RRsh)H'thaHn,Inst'ctYts,ChmpRich
2-4 YR	ft clm alw	4500	m	32	1:05:2	1:37:2	2:09:1	8	1	1	3	4/3½	7/6½	2:10:4	13.30(RRsh)KnyDrs,SpnglrVlo,MtnLkeable
12-2 RR	ft C-2 Cd	2600	m	31:2	1:05:1	1:37:3	2:09:3	3	1	1	2	3/1	5/7	2:11:1	6.50(RRsh)CpeNwprt,WhtNxt,ChmpRichi

4 — 6 FOREST MITE b g, 9, by Florican, June Mite by Volomite (Tr.-J. Michael
J. & A. Stable, Bedford Hills, N.Y. YR 2:06 1969 11 4 2 1 7,56
($40,767) 6, 2:01:2 (⅝) CARMINE ABBATIELLO (135) Gold-Red Fhld 2:04 1968 31 9 3 3 13,67

4-4 RR	ft clm	5000	m	31:3	1:04:1	1:35:1	2:07	3	4	3°	6°	7/7	5/5½	2:08:2	2.90(CAbtlo)Ad'sGrgeA.,Winstdt,SpnglrV
3-28RR	ft clm	5000	m	30:3	1:03:4	1:35:4	2:08:4	4	3	2°	2°	2/nk	3/½	2:09	•1.80(CAbtlo)KnnyDares,I'MAGndr,FrstM
3-19 RR	ft clm	5000	m	31	1:04:1	1:35:2	2:07	3	1	1	2	4/2¾	6/3½	2:07:3	•.90(CAbt)SpnglrVolo,JetDncr,LegalFrgh
3-12 RR	ft clm	5000	m	30:4	1:03:1	1:35:2	2:08:1	3	3	3	2°	2/2	1/¾	2:08:1	•1.00(CAbt)ForestMte,HnorBoy,ChmpRch
3-3 YR	ft clm	4500	m	30:2	1:04:2	1:35:4	2:07:2	2	4	4°	2	2/1	2/¾	2:07:3	•1.20(CAbt)TmmysPrde,ForstMte,I'mAGn
2-26 YR	gd clm	4500	m	30:1	1:03:4	1:36:2	2:08:2	6	2	2	3	3/1	1/¾	2:08:2	3.90(CAbt)ForestMte,AmzingVle,GayRob
2-19 YR	sy clm alw	4500	m	32	1:05:2	1:38:1	2:10:2	2	2	2	2	2/1	2/1	2:10:3	•1.00(CAbtlo)Gnkhr,ForestMite,GrntreeRe
2-12 YR	ft clm alw	4500	m	31	1:03:4	1:37:2	2:10	3	1	1	1	1/½	1/nk	2:10	•1.10(CAbt)FrstMte,MntnLkable,ChstrMy

10 — 7 HONOR KEY br h, 8, by Keystoner, Nervolonor by His Honor (Tr.-J. Higgins) (St.-W. Popfinger)
W. Popfinger & S. Ransom, Jr., New York 1969 2 0 0 0
($39,703) 7, 2:03:2 WILLIAM POPFINGER (168) Green-White YR 2:03:2 1968 35 5 4 3 13,26

4-2 RR	ft clm alw	5000	m	31:2	1:03	1:34:2	2:06:2	7	8	8	7°°	6/3¾	8/8¾	2:08:2	27.20(WPfgr)AmazingVle,MattB,RealYnke
3-27 RR	ft clm	6000	m	30:4	1:03:3	1:35:1	2:06:4	6	6	6	6	6/3½	7/6½	2:08:3	31.40(WPfgr)MastrGlnn,Judson,CpperAdio
12-14 RR	sy clm alw	6000	m	33	1:06:2	1:39:4	2:13:2	7	1°	1	4	6/4½	7/21	2:18:3	18.00(WPfgr)DnAbbe,Jess'sG'son,VonDowr
12-9 RR	ft Opt B-3	3250	m	30:3	1:04:1	1:36:1	2:10	8	8	7°	8°	8/4½	8/7	2:11:4	15.10(DInsko)HurryOnN,Charlestn,Goldville
11-28 RR	sy B-3	3000	m	31:3	1:04:1	1:37:3	2:10:3	8	8	8	8	7/4½	5/6½	2:12:1	34.10(WPfgr)HrryOnN,MlesBrte,DrlosPrnc
11-20 RR	ft clm alw	6000	m	31	1:03:3	1:34:4	2:07	8	2°	1	6	8/18	8/dis		19.60(FPfgr)Chrlestn,MilesBrite,LeglFrgh
11-14 RR	ft clm alw	6000	m	30	1:01:2	1:33:2	2:06	6	6	6	6°	5/3½	4/2½	2:06:3	13.80(WPfngr)Chrlstn,MilesBrite,A'broDon
11-8 RR	ft clm alw	6000	m	30:3	1:03:4	1:35:1	2:06:3	5	6	5°	4°	4/1½	4/2¾	2:07:1	8.00(WPpfgr)LeroyHn,LglFrght,Charlesto

5 — 8 COPPER JACKET ch g, 6, by Darneau, Diann Liner by Mainliner (Tr.-S. Smit
R.A. & R. R. Williams, Massapequa, N.Y. 1969 8 0 1 2 1,86
($15,394) 3, 2:04:1 SAM SMITH (145) Brown-Beige RR 2:06 1968 15 3 1 1 5,13

4-7 RR	ft clm alw	5000	m	30:2	1:04	1:36	2:07:2	4	2	2	3	3/1	3/1	2:07:3	10.90(SSmth)Emnciptn,StrmyDrm,CpprJck
3-31 RR	ft C-1 Cd	3000	m	33:3	1:06:1	1:37:2	2:09:1	3	3	3	3	3/1	2/1¾	2:09:3	20.80(SSmth)KmmysKgt,CpprJckt,T'Prms
3-22 RR	ft clm	4000	m	30:2	1:03	1:35:1	2:07:3	1	1	1	1	1/hd	3/1¾	2:08	14.80(SSmith)StrmyDrm,MttB,CopprJcket
3-11 RR	ft clm	4000	m	31	1:04:2	1:38	2:12:3	3	5	5	5	5/2	4/2½	2:13:1	19.90(NDplse)GrndPtch,StrmyDream,Matt
3-4 YR	ft clm alw	4500	m	30:4	1:05	1:37:1	2:09:2	5	6	7	8	5/4	5/2	2:09:4	23.50(MPsy)GayRobin,DukesVictor,PostRa
2-26 YR	gd clm	4500	m	30:1	1:03:4	1:36:2	2:08:2	3	6	6	7	6/3¾	7/2½	2:09	35.30(Dplse)ForestMte,AmzngVle,GayRobi
2-19 YR	sy clm	3000Z	m	31:2	1:05:4	1:39:4	2:13:1	7	3	2°	5°	7/8½	7/18	2:17:2	22.50(JTllmn)GrndPtch,ChfMldy,ChstrMa
2-13 YR	ft clm alw	3000	m	32	1:05:1	1:37:1	2:09:4	4	4	6	7°	6/6½	5/5	2:11	6.90(JTllmn)OurQuestn,ShwsFlsh,ChfMld

EXACTA WINDOWS OPEN FOR THIS RACE.

6 PACE-ONE MILE

SADDLE CLOTH—BLUE

CLASS B-2

PURSE $4,000

1

FREDA'S PRIDE b m, 8, by Scotch Victor, East Star by Star's Pride (Tr.-D. Tovim)
Benjamin Fisher, Bronx, N.Y. YR 2:05:2 1969 12 5 2 1 11,209.
YR 2:04:3 1968 34 8 6 4 19,405
($37,813) 7, 2:04:3 CARMINE ABBATIELLO (135) Gold-Red

4-8 RR ft B-2 3750 m 30 1:02:4 1:35:3 2:05:2 5 1° 1 1 2/½ 2/1½ 2:05:4 •1.20(CAbt)PrncssOmaha,FrdasPrde,Kravat
3-28 RR ft B-2 3750 m 29:4 1:01:3 1:33:1 2:05:1 3 1 1 1 1/½ 2/hd 2:05:1 •1.60(CAtlo)AtmnBay,Frda'sPrde,T'tfll'trdr
3-14 RR ft B-2 3750 m 30:3 1:04 1:35:1 2:05:4 4 1 1 1 1/nk 1/½ 2:05:4 5.70(CAbt)FrdasPrde,RndzvsTrdr,RoylRmn
3-7 RR ft B-3 3250 m 31 1:04 1:35:2 2:06:4 7 2 2 3 3/1 1/1¾ 2:06:4 4.90(CAbt)Frda'sPride,SrniaRse,GoodCndy
3-1 YR ft clm alw 10000 m 30:1 1:03:1 1:34:4 2:05:4 5 6 4° 3 4/2¾ 3/2¼ 2:06:2 4.30(LFntne)TarDncr,LadRnbw,Frda'sPrde
2-22 YR ft B-2 Cd 3750 m 30:4 1:03:1 1:34:4 2:06:1 8 7 2° 3° 6/3¼ 8/7 2:08 12.30(C'mn)C'mnsC'dy,P'cssO'ha,S'dleS'Off
2-14 YR ft clm alw 10000 m 31:2 1:03:3 1:36:1 2:08:1 3 5 6° 4°°2/1 1/nk 2:08:1 4.70(DInsko)Freda'sPrde,KeyWhrl,Kinleith
2-6 YR ft clm alw 7500 m 30:2 1:02 1:33:3 2 05:2 3 2 2 1 1/1 1/¾ 2:05:2 •.80(CAbtlo)FrdsPride,MultiChf,MilesBrte

2

MIZELLES MICKEY b c, 3, by Hickory Smoke, Mizelle by Rodney (Tr.-W. Mello) (St.-W. Haughton)
Farmstead Acres, Glen Head, N.Y. RR 2:06:2 1969 1 1 0 0 1,625.
MR 2:05:2 1968 16 5 4 4 7,062.
($7,062) 2, 2:05:2 WM. HAUGHTON (150) Green-White-Gold

4-7 RR ft B-3 3250 m 31:2 1:02:4 1:35:1 2:06:2 1 1 1 1 1/2½ 1/2½ 2:06:2 •.60(AThms)MzlsMky,R'd'sTrdr,TrueStrm
10-9 LB(⅝) ft 2yr Cd 2000 m 30:3 1:01:1 1:31:1 2:02 8 8 8 8 6/5¾ 6/5¾ 2:03 18.30(JGrne)Dwght,GoodLckBy,RicciGreatA
10-1 LB(⅝) ft 2yrCd 5000 m 31 1:02:1 1:32:2 2:03:3 1 5 5 2° 2/nk 2/hd 2:03:3 2.70(JGrne)Go'gThru,MzllsMky,KyEntrprse
9-20 LB(⅝) ft 2yr Cd 4000 m 30:2 1:00:3 1:30:1 2:00:3 2 5 5 3° 3/4¼ 3/5 2:01:3 6.30(JGrne)SetShot,BakrLobll,MzllesMcky
9-13 LB(⅝) ft 2yr ec 4000 m 30:3 1:01:4 1:31:4 2:03 5 6 4 2° 3/2 5/4 2:03:4 10.50(JGrne)LrdRgr-BrbrHn(dh)KystnTreat
9-6 MR ft B-3 1500 m 30:3 1:02:3 1:34 2:05:2 2 6 6 3° 3/½ 1/1½ 2:05:2 •.80(Vghn)MzlsMcky,TmlyQte,Bbby'sChmp
8-30 MR ft C-1 1350 m 31 1:03:4 1:35:3 2:06:2 7 6 7 6° 2/hd 1/1½ 2:06:2 •.80(Hghtn) MzlsMky,TmeA'Agn,FrdieAd's
8-21 Carlisle ft 2yr Stk m 2 heats: 2:04:4 finished 2nd; 2:04:2 finished 3rd; N.B. with WHaughton driving. Race winner-AmerigoHanover

3

MR. TRIPLE E. b h, 6, by Shadow Wave, Alema Jay by Allmite (Tr.-M. Foley)
Frank Fullerton, Setauket, N.Y. YR 2:05 1969 9 1 1 1 4,087.
YR 2:04:2 1968 23 3 5 2 12,059.
($24,757) 5, 2:04:2 EUGENE MATTUCCI (170) Pink-Black

4-5 RR gd B-2 3750 m 29:1 1:01:2 1:33:3 2:06:1 5 6 5 5 5/3 2/1½ 2:06:2 37.10(EMttcci)Angelita,MrTrpleE,NgaraBllt
3-28 RR ft B-2 3750 m 29:4 1:01:3 1:33:1 2:05:1 4 6 8 7° 6/3¾ 6/2¼ 2:05:4 19.70(Mtt'ci)AtmnBay,F'da'sPrde,T'tfll'trdr
3-15 RR ft Opt B-2 3750 m 31 1:04:2 1:35:4 2:06:1 7 7 5° 4° 4/3 4/4½ 2:07:1 9.60(EMtci)BrdvwBbe,Wildcat,MiteDream
3-11 RR ft qua m 32:2 1:04:4 1:36:3 2:08:2 2 3 3 2 2/2 2/1 2:08:3 N B.(EMttcci)ReprveN.,MrTripleE,MyPeak
3-5 RR ft Opt B-1 4500 m 31 1:03:1 1:35 2:06:1 3 4 4 4° 4/2 6/4¼ 2:07:1 26.80(EMtci)SmrtMney,GrtCrdit,Jrry'sPluff
2-24 YR ft B-1 Cd 4500 m 30:3 1:03:2 1:35:2 2:06:4 3 5 6 6° 6/3 5/2¾ 2:07:2 4.40(Mttcci)MrHff,InContentn,SlckYnkee
2-12 YR ft B-1 Cd 4500 m 30:4 1:02:3 1:33:2 2:05:3 7 8 8 8 8/7¼ 7/6¼ 2:07:1 39.20(EMtci)JerrysPluff,BlckieAd's,MrHoff
2-6 YR ft B-2 Cd 3750 m 30:3 1:02:1 1:33:2 2:05 2 4 3° 1 1/1 1/½ 2:05 2.50(EMttcci)MrTrpleE,GlxyN,TuttaTryx

4

JERRYS PLUFF b g, 5, by Knight Dream, Princess Carol by Greentree Adios (Tr.-J. Cruise)
M. Robins & Carol Slavin Stable, Riverdale, N.Y. YR 2:05:3 1969 11 2 2 1 7,590.
YR 2:03 1968 31 5 2 5 16,310.
($27,770) 4, 2:03 JIMMY CRUISE (173) Green-Red

4-7 RR ft Opt B-1 4500 m 31:2 1:04 1:34:2 2:05:2 7 7 7° 8 8/7¼ 8/5 2:06:3 26.20(JCrse)WairauLrd,TrryFrbs,Ad'sMssge
3-20 RR ft B-1 4500 m 31:3 1:03:3 1:34:2 2:05:2 4 6 6 7 7/4¼ 7/4½ 2:06:3 8.10(JC'se)RbrtEdn,HighlndRdr,Q'rryRoad
3-10 RR ft B-1 4500 m 30:3 1:04:1 1:35:2 2:06:2 7 7 7° 6° 7/5 5/5½ 2:07:4 4.00(JCruise) Mindian,Alytor,AftonBullet
3-5 RR ft Opt B-1 4500 m 31 1:03:1 1:35 2:06:1 1 3 3 6 6/2¼ 3/1½ 2:06:3 •1.50(JCrse)SmrtMney,GrtCrdit,Jrry'sPluff
2-25 YR ft B-1 Cd 4500 m 30 1:00:4 1:33 2:05:1 4 6 6 4° 4/1 2/ns 2:05:1 3.20(NDplse)AftnBllt,JrrysPlff,BrwnSmke
2-17 YR ft B-1 Cd 4500 m 29:3 1:02 1:32:4 2:04:1 1 4x 5x 8° 7/8¼ 5/9½ 2:06:2 2.10(NDplse)MzlRdny,AftnBllt,SlickYnkee
2-12 YR ft B-1 Cd 4500 m 30:4 1:02:3 1:33:2 2:05:3 5 6 5° 5° 5/1¾ 1/nk 2:05:3 4.70(Dplse)JrrysPluff,BlckieAdios,MrHoff
2-5 YR ft B-1 Cd 4500 m 30:1 1:01:3 1:33:3 2:04:3 5 7 7• 6° 6/3 5/2¼ 2:05 3.10(JCrse)HghlndRdr,BlckieAd's,BywdBy

5

BOBBALOU b m, 4, by Devastor, Ermine Hanover by Knight Dream (Tr.-J. Chapman)
Green River Stock Farm, Inc., Green River, Canada 1969 1 0 0 0
YR 2:03:2 1968 20 3 4 4 10,903.
($15,327) 3, 2:03:2 JOHN CHAPMAN (147) Green-White

4-4 RR ft B-2 3750 m 30:1 1:02 1:32:4 2:04:3 2 5 7 8 8/4¾ 6/2¼ 2:05:1 6.60(JChapmn)RexPick,CaptainJay,Bengal
11-22 RR ft B-2 3250 m 31:2 1:04 1:35:4 2:06:2 6 2° 1 1 1/1 2/¾ 2:06:3 1.90(Chpmn)SmpleSmn,Bbbalou,MdwBrce
11-14 RR ft B-2 Cd 3250 m 31:1 1:03 1:34:1 2:05:3 4 1 3 4 4/1 2/¾ 2:05:4 •2.40(Chpmn)GrrdPck,Bobbalou,DnnyDuane
11-7 RR gd B-2 3250 m 31:4 1:04:1 1:35:2 2:06:1 2 2 2 4 4/2¾ 2/¾ 2:06:2 4.40(DBgn) GerardPick,Bobbalou,TheChffr
10-30 RR ft B-2 3500 m 30:3 1:02:3 1:34:2 2:05 5 6 6° ix5 4/8 3/6½ 2:06:3 4.30(Chpmn)TyrosHn,TheChauffeur,Bbalou
10-19 RR ft B 2 3750 m 30:3 1:02:3 1:33:3 2:04:3 4 5 5 5 6/4 3/2½ 2:05:1 8.30(DBegin)MrTrpleE,Sen.Brtn,Bobbalou
10-4 YR ft B-2 Cd 3750 m 30:4 1:02:4 1:33:2 2:05 4 5 5 5 5/2¼ 5/2¼ 2:05:3 13.30(DBgn)FrgnPlcy,StrmPrf,KystneRngr
9-26 YR ft B-3 3250 m 30:4 1:01:4 1:33:1 2:03:2 1 2 2 1 1/1 1/1½ 2:03:2 1.50(RChrrx)Bobblou,AftnFlsh,TwnC'Adios

6

ANGELITA br m, 7, by Garrison Hanover, Sweet Wren by Young Charles (Tr.-S. Demas)
Lucien Fontaine & Condurso's River Front Farm, N.Y. RR 2:06 1969 11 4 1 3 8,522.
RR 2:05:3 1968 30 3 7 2 10,152.
($30,460) 5, 2:04:3 LUCIEN FONTAINE (134) Green-White-Red

4-5 RR gd B-2 3750 m 29:1 1:01:2 1:33:3 2:06:1 1 5 4 4 4/2¼ 1/1½ 2:06:1 8.00(LFntne)Angelita,MrTrpleE,NgaraBllt
3-28 RR ft B-3 3250 m 30:3 1:02:3 1:34 2:06 4 4 3° 1 1/2½ 1/5 2:06 5.20(Fntne)Angelita,Thrpe'sKin,ToboRdny
3-19 RR ft Opt B-3 3250 m 31:2 1:02:2 1:33:2 2:05:4 2 1 1 2 2/1½ 7/1¼ 2:06:1 2.50(LFntne)ToboRdny,NevleGlfr,ThrpsKin
3-13 RR ft B-3 3250 m 30:3 1:01:4 1:33:2 2:06:2 8 3° 1 1 1/1 3/1¾ 2:06:4 10.50(LFntne)Sal'sMite,MilesBrite,Angelita
3-7 RR ft B-3 3250 m 31 1:04 1:35:2 2:06:4 3 3 3° 2° 2/¼ 5/3½ 2:07:3 10.40(LF'tne)FrdasPrde,SrniaRse,GoodCndy
2-28 YR ft C-1 Cd 3000 m 30:4 1:03:1 1:35:3 2:07:2 2 4 5° 1 1/3 1/2¼ 2:07:2 •1.70(LFntne)Angelita,HerIrish,RitasDream
2-15 YR ft C-1 Cd 3000 m 31 1:02:3 1:34:2 2:07 3 6 4° 4° 5/2 7/2 2:07:2 •1.60(LFntne)BthnyHn,KatyR.,SngngWater
2-7 YR ft C-1 Cd 3000 m 31:3 1:03:3 1:36:3 2:09:3 6 5° 5° 2° 1/nk 3/2¼ 2:10:1 •1.30(LFntne)Rita'sDrm,BethnyHn,Angelita

7

SEARUS BOY ch g, 6, by Flash Adios, Ednas Dawn by Jimmy Junior (Tr.-J. Liso) (Stable-L. Copeland)
Abraham Schultz, Bal Harbour, Fla. 1969 4 0 1 1 1,387.
YR 2:04:1 1968 27 4 7 7 13,431.
($20,175) 5, 2:04:1 LEROY COPELAND (170) White-Green

4-4 RR ft B-2 3750 m 30:1 1:02 1:32:4 2:04:3 1 4 5° 5° 6/3½ 8/5¾ 2:06 •2.10(JTllmn)RexPick,CaptainJay,Bengal
3-25 RR ft B-2 3750 m 31:2 1:03:4 1:35:4 2:08 7 2° 1 1 1/½ 7/3½ 2:08:4 3.10(Tllmn)AbbeG'Vlo,SilkySq're,RicksClt
3-18 RR ft B-2 3750 m 31:2 1:02:1 1:33:1 2:04:1 2 2 3 2 2/1 2/ns 2:04:1 5.90(Cplnd)Repr'veN,SearusBoy,Tctfll'trdr
3-10 RR ft Opt B-2 3750 m 31 1:04:1 1:35:1 2:06:3 3 3 4 2 2/1½ 3/3 2:07:2 30.00(RRsh)JhnCraig,MiteDream,SearusBoy
10-15 YR ft B-2 Cd 3750 m 30 1:03 1:33:4 2:05:1 8 4 4 3° 5/2 8/5 2:06:2 8.50(Wbstr) IrshCam,S'dleYnkios,TbyStar
10-7 YR ft B-2 Cd 3750 m 30:2 1:01:4 1:33:1 2:04 8 4 4 4 4/3¼ 4/nk 2:04 15.10(Wbtr) KgtMsn,TbyStr,S'rsBoy(by dq)
9-30 YR ft B 2 Cd 3750 m 29:2 1:00:3 1:33:1 2:04:3 6 4 4 5 5/5¼ 5/5¼ 2:06 2.50(BWbstr)SenatrBrtn,WellDone,Goliath
9-17 YR ft B-2 Cd 3750 m 30:1 1:02:4 1:33 2:03:4 4 5 5° 3° 2/1 2/¾ 2:04 •2.00(CAbtlo)SmpleSmn,SrsBoy,GreatCrdit

8

IN CONTENTION br g, 6, by The Intruder, Myrt Hanover by Nibble Hanover (Tr.-J. Richardson)
Delbert French, Worthington, Ohio 1969 12 0 1 0 3,314.
RR 2:03:2 1968 37 7 6 7 22,646.
($30,371) 5, 2:03:2 JACK RICHARDSON (145) Blue-Grey

4-3 RR ft Opt B-2 3750 m 30 1:01:2 1:33 2:04:1 4 5 5 5° 4/5 4/3¾ 2:05:1 7.80(JRichrdsn)RodKngt,SilkySquire,WJW
3-25 RR ft B-2 3750 m 31:2 1:03:4 1:35:4 2:08 4 6 6° 5° 6/2¾ 2x/1¼dq2:08:2 5.90(JR'sn)AbbeG'Vlo,SlkySq're,RcksClt
3-18 RR ft B-2 3750 m 31:2 1:02:1 1:33:1 2:04:1 6 6 6° 4° 4/3½ 5/5¼ 2:05:3 20.70(JR'sn)Repr'veN,SearusBoy,Tctfll'trdr
3-11 RR ft Opt B-1 4500 m 30:1 1:02:1 1:34:3 2:06:4 7 8 8 7 6/3¾ 8/9¾ 2:09:1 74.40(JRichdsn)Apt,RobtEden,Auchencraig
3-3 YR ft B-1 Cd 4500 m 30:2 1:02:4 1:33:3 2:04:4 3 5 5 4 5/2¼ 7/5¼ 2:06:1 10.70(JR'sn)Mnd'n,ChpmnsCndy,BrwnSmke
2-24 YR ft B-1 Cd 4500 m 30:3 1:03:2 1:35:2 2:06:4 1 2 2 3 3/1¼ 2/1¾ 2:07:1 9.50(JR'dsn)MrHoff,InContentn,SlckYnkee
2-17 YR ft B-1 Cd 4500 m 30 1:02:2 1:33:4 2:05 1 1 3 3 4/3½ 8/8¾ 2:07 3.70(JRichrdson)Alytor,Apt,BrownSmoke
2-3 YR gd B-1 Cd 4500 m 30 1:03:3 1:36:2 2:08:4 2 3 5 5 4/¾ 4/1½ 2:09:1 4.60(JRichdsn)Bmbardier,Alytor,TrrlLeeN

Exacta Windows Open 5 Minutes Before This Race.

7 PACE-ONE MILE EXACTA

MORN. LINE

SADDLE CLOTH—RED

CLASS B-3—CONDITIONED
A.E. $10,000 OPTIONAL CLAIMERS (ALL AGES)

PURSE $3,50

4 **1** **MASTER CLEAO** b g, 7, by Celestial, Cleao Gaillard by Gaillard
Lucien Fontaine, Yonkers, N.Y. (Tr.-S. Demas
($3,358) N.R. LUCIEN FONTAINE (134) Green-White-Red (qua) RR 2:06:2 1969 1 0 0 0
N.R. 1968 20 1 0 1 97
° 4-12 RR ft qua m 30:3 1:03:2 1:35 2:06:2 2 3 3 4 4/3½ 1/nk 2:06:2 N.B.(LFntne)MstrCleao,Oktwn,KnghtDuar
° 4-8 RR ft qua m 32:1 1:04:1 1:36:1 2:08:4 2 2 2 2° 2/nk 1/hd 2:08:4 N.B.(LFntne)MstrCleao,Rapid,DelH'Drear
3-31 RR ft C-1 Cd 3000 m 33:3 1:06:1 1:37:2 2:09:1 1 2 2° 2° 2x/1 x4/3¼dq2:10 *1.20(Fntne)KmmysKght,CpprJckt,T'Prms
° 3-18 RR ft qua m 31:1 1:03:3 1:35:1 2:07 6 6 4° 2° 2/½ 3/¾ 2:07:1 N.B.(LFntne)FlrneFrst,LrryTme,MstrClea
° 3-15 RR ft qua m 32:3 1:05:1 1:36:3 2:09 4 2 2 2 2/6 2/5 2:10:1 N.B.(LFntne)ByrdBtlr,MstrCleao,JhnnyRn
12-21 Auckland(NewZealand) approx. 1⅝ m (36 yd. hcp.) 3.29:2 finished unplaced; (DBeloe) Bewitched, WillieMac, Yakamo
12-7 Thames(NewZealand) 2 m 4:24:3 finished unplaced; (DBeloe) Drumore, Giggles, QuickKnock
12-3 Waikato(NewZealand) 2 m 4:22 finished unplaced; (DBeloe) Morris, HalfMoon, QuickKnock

3 **2** **RENDEZVOUS TRUDER** b h, 11, by The Intruder, Betty Astra by Peter Astra
Ray M. Garrity, Wash'gton C.H., O. (Tr.-A. Niles, Jr
($114,889) 4, 2:00:1 (1) ARCHIE NILES, JR. (162) White-Green YR 2:04:1 1969 9 0 2 0 2,72
1968 37 4 9 3 23,43
4-7 RR ft B-3 3250 m 31:2 1:02:4 1:35:1 2:06:2 7 2 3 2 2/2½ 2/2½ 2:07 11.70(NlsJr)MzllsMky,R'dzvsTrdr,TrueStrm
3-28 RR ft B-2 3750 m 29:4 1:01:3 1:33:1 2:05:1 6 2° 4 6 8/7½ 8/9 2:07:2 13.50(NlsJr)Aut'nBay,Frda'sPrde,Tctfll'trc
3-21 RR ft B-2 3750 m 30:3 1:02:1 1:33:1 2:03:3 7 7 7 7 6/5¾ 6/7 2:05:1 11.40(NlsJr)AdOSam,RedThrd,NiagaraBlle
3-14 RR ft B-2 3750 m 30:3 1:04 1:35:1 2:05:4 2 2 2 2° 2/nk 2/½ 2:06 4.30(NilsJr)FrdasPrde,RndzvsTrdr,RylRm
3-6 RR ft B-2 3750 m 31:2 1:04:1 1:34:3 2:05:4 7 7 7° 6° 6/4 5/2¾ 2:06:2 17.90(NlsJr)FirstAdvntre,TrriLeeN.,N'wood
2-27 YR ft B-2 Cd 3750 m 31:4 1:05:1 1:36:4 2:07:1 6 7 5° 4 4/4 4/5½ 2:08:2 29.70(GFldi)ToughTime,N'wood,HckryKngt
2-20 YR gd B-2 Cd 3750 m 30:4 1:02 1:34:4 2:06:2 4 6 6 6 6/2 5/1½ 2:06:3 15.10(GFldi)ToughTime,BlladeerN,ChfSain
2-15 YR ft B-2 Cd 3750 m 30:1 1:03 1:34:4 2:06:2 2 2 3 3 3/1 6/4½ 2:07:3 3.00(GFldi)ChpmnsCndy,AddieH,S'dleS'O

5 **3** **SANDY LEO** b g, 7, by Meadow Leo, Princess Yama by Brown Prince
P. A. Reich & Sons, Inc., Hicksville, N.Y. (Tr.-D. Tovin
($19,523) 6, 2:05:3 (⅝) RANDOLPH PERRY (115) Grey-Red-Black YR 2:05:4 1969 12 4 3 0 9,13
AC(⅝) 2:05:3 1968 30 5 4 4 8,53
3-26 RR ft Opt B-3 3250 m 30 1:02:2 1:34:1 2:05:4 6 7 7 6° 7/4 6/3¾ 2:06:3 6.50(RPrry)RexPick,WarilyN,GoodTmeLa
3-17 RR ft Opt B-3 3250 m 29:4 1:02:3 1:34 2:05:1 2 6 6 4° 3/4 2/4½ 2:06:2 2.80(RPerry)Adnev,SandyLeo,HelloByeBy
3-8 RR ft Opt B-2 3750 m 30:4 1:04:1 1:36 2:06 5 6 7 7 6/5 6/4¾ 2:07 7.80(RPrry)NtbleWck,B'vwBabe,ShdyS'Pa
2-28 YR ft clm 10000 m 30 1:02:3 1:34:1 2:05:4 3 5 5 4° 4/2½ 1/ns 2:05:4 2.20(RPrry)SandyLeo,KingYnkee,KeyWhir
2-22 YR ft clm alw 10000 m 30:2 1:02:3 1:33:3 2:05 8 8 6 5° 5/3½ 5/3 2:05:4 14.50(WMyer)B'vwBbe,LdRnbw,HrbyTryax
2-15 YR ft clm alw 7500 m 30 1:03 1:34:2 2:05:4 4 3 2° 2° 2/ns 1/¾ 2:05:4 2.30(JTllmn)SandyLeo,MultiChief,LeWhip
2-7 YR ft clm 6000 m 31:1 1:04:2 1:35:3 2:06:4 4 5 4° 3° 2/½ 1/1½ 2:06:4 *1.30(DInsko)SndyLeo,MghtyDvid,WrthGln
1-31 YR ft clm 7500 m 30:3 1:02:4 1:35 2:06:2 8 8 6° 6°x8/12 8/21 2:11:2 8.30(WMyr)TrueStm,KyWhrl,WstrnChnce

8 **4** **WE GOTTA BYRD** br h, 8, by Parker Byrd, Congressional Ann by Congressional
Milton Kaplan & Aaron Koren, New York, N.Y. (Tr.-L. Schwart
($28,137) 7, 2:00:2 (1) FRANK TAGARIELLO (150) Tan-Brown-White Hol(1) 2:00:2 1969 8 0 0 1 93
1968 19 2 1 1 5,84
° 4-8 RR ft qua m 31:2 1:02:4 1:34:2 2:06:4 2 3 2° 2° 2/1 4/2¼ 2:07:2 N.B.(FTagrllo)LBKing,Raidal,BlackTulipN
3-8 RR ft clm 10000 m 31:3 1:03:1 1:34:4 2:07 8 1 2 2 2/1½ 8/8¾ 2:09 40.40(JChpmn)KngYnkee,LdRnbw,MrnciCh
2-28 YR ft clm 10000 m 30 1:02:3 1:34:1 2:05:4 5 6° 6° 8° 8/9½ 8/15 2:09:2 27.90(JTllmn)SndyLeo,KingYnkee,KeyWhir
2-21 YR ft clm 10000 m 30:1 1:03 1:34:1 2:06:1 5 1 1 1 2/hd 5/3¾ 2:07 9.30(Tllmn)CntrlRnge,SpcialHn,KngYnkee
2-13 YR ft clm 12500 m 30:3 1:03:3 1:36 2:08:3 3 4 4° 3° 2/hd 8/5½ 2:09:4 4.40(JTllmn)LopezHn,HiDeeN,SomeDrean
2-4 YR ft B-2 Cd 3750 m 31 1:02:2 1:34:4 2:06:1 8 4° 2° 2° 5/2 8/7½ 2:08 14.00(CAbt)A'broHrvy,S'dleY'k's,PdroWils
1-28 YR ft B-2 Cd 3750 m 31:1 1:02:3 1:33:4 2:05 4 1 2 2 2/1 3/¾ 2:05:1 15.50(CAbt)LrryTme,S'dleYnks,WeGttaBrd
1-20 YR ft B-2 Cd 3750 m 31 1:03 1:35:1 2:06:4 5 1° 2 4 4/¾ 4/2¾ 2:07:2 16.20(Fntne)MzlRdny,S'dleY'kios,MrTrpleE

5 **5** **TEST OF TIME** b h, 5, by Good Time, Merrie Pride by Ensign Hanover
Tamarack Farms, Inc., Painesville, O. (Tr.-J. Chapmar
($30,156) 3, 2:03 JOHN CHAPMAN (147) Green-White YR 2:05 1969 5 0 1 1 1,88
1968 35 3 4 9 13,85
4-7 RR ft B-3 3250 m 31:2 1:02:4 1:35:1 2:06:2 8 4 4 7 7/5½ 4/3½ 2:07:1 7.40(C'mn)MzllsMcky,R'zvsTrdr,TrueStrm
3-31 RR ft B-3 3250 m 31 1:03 1:34:1 2:06 8 1 1 2 1/nk 2/¾ 2:06:1 42.00(JChpmn)Keravat,TstOfTme,WrthTim
3-22 RR ft B-3 Cd 3250 m 30:3 1:01:3 1:34 2:05 4 6 6 5 5/3 4/2¾ 2:05:3 17.80(JC'pmn)Klvrwdn,WrthTme,UnfrmAle
3-15 RR ft B-3 Cd 3250 m 31 1:03:4 1:35:3 2:06:3 3 4 4° 5° 7/4½ 5/5 2:07:4 2.90(JChpmn)WrthTme,Keravat,T'SndyMr
3-8 RR ft B-3 3250 m 31 1:03:2 1:34:4 2:06:2 6 4 5 6° 6/3 3/2½ 2:06:4 26.10(JChapman)Keravat,Adnev,TestOfTim
12-7 RR ft B-2 3250 m 32:3 1:05:2 1:35:4 2:06:3 8 8 8 8° 6/5½ 8/9 2:08:4 29.10(JChpmn)Hrvrd,JrrysPlff,MgtyMthild
11-29 RR ft B-2 3250 m 30:2 1:02:4 1:35:1 2:07:1 6 6 7 7 7/4½ 6/2¾ 2:07:4 13.50(Chpmn)Antnea,PtrW'Sltn,C'trVeeCe
11-19 RR ft B-3 Cd 3000 m 31:3 1:05:4 1:38:1 2:09:2 2 1 1 1 1/½ 1/2½ 2:09:2 *1.40(JChpmn)TstOfTme,ChrgrAd's,AFllyH

12 **6** **SNOW JOB** b h, 6, by Shadow Wave, Lottasnow by Direct Spangler
Morris Swarzman, New York, N.Y. (Tr.-P. Napol
($8,888) 5, 2:05:1 PETER NAPOLI (190) Blue-Gold-White YR 2:05:1 1969 1 0 0 0
1968 15 3 2 3 7,27
4-7 RR ft B-3 3250 m 31:2 1:02:4 1:35:1 2:06:2 5 3° 2 4 6/4½ 8/14 2:09:4 24.90(WMyr)MzlsMky,R'dzvsTrdr,TrueStrn
11-18 RR sy B-3 3000 m 32:1 1:05:1 1:36:2 2:09 2 1 2 1 1/ns 7/8 2:11 10.70(AGrfla)GneMjsty,DffysBet,Automati
11-11 RR ft Opt B-3 3000 m 31:1 1:02:4 1:34:3 2:06:1 6 1° 3° 2° 2/1 3/2 2:06:3 6.30(WMyr)JsiesGrndsn,GneMjsty,SnwJob
11-4 RR ft B-3 Cd 3000 m 30:1 1:02:2 1:33:3 2:05 3 4 2° 1° 2/ns 8/6 2:06:2 10.20(AGrfla)QnsCdet,TstOfTme,Automatic
10-26 RR ft B-3 Cd 3250 m 31:2 1:03:2 1:34:3 2:06:1 2 3 3 4 3/1 4/3 2:07 13.70(AGrfla)D'neAg'n,CmltAd's,WrnMByr
10-17 YR ft B-3 Cd 3250 m 30:3 1:01:3 1:33:1 2:04:4 2 4 6° 5° 5/3 5/4 2:05:4 *1.90(AGrfla)SomeDrm,LnweeSpcl,FargoH
10-9 YR ft B-3 Cd 3250 m 31:4 1:04:2 1:35:2 2:07:1 3 1 2° 2° 2/ns 3/1 2:07:2 3.70(AGrfola) Bmbrdier,MrWxford,SnwJo
10-1 YR ft B-3 Cd 3250 m 30:4 1:02:3 1:32:4 2:04:1 2 2 3 3° 3/2½ 2/2 2:04:3 8.60(AGrfla)SlickYnkee,SnwJob,TagWrthy

5 **7** **RAIDAL** b g, 7, by Alcoran, Cissy Raider by Carl Raider
Leon Machiz, Great Neck, N.Y. (Tr.-W. Dracksley) (St.-E. Cobb
($15,964) 6, 2:03:4 EDWARD COBB (193) Blue-White RR 2:03:4 1969 5 0 0 0 59
1968 29 8 1 3 10,71
° 4-8 RR ft qua m 31:2 1:02:4 1:34:2 2:06:4 4 1 6 6 6/3 2/1½ 2:07:1 N.B.(ECobb)LBKing,Raidal,BlackTulipN
2-3 YR gd B-2 Cd 3750 m 31 1:04:2 1:37 2:10:1 6 6 7 6 5/2½ 5/3½ 2:11 13.10(ECobb)BalladeerN.,ChipPick,GoBye
1-25 YR ft B-2 Cd 3750 m 29:3 1:00:2 1:33:1 2:06 4 7 7 6 7/3 5/6½ 2:07:3 11.50(ECobb)JMWin,KildareDan,GoBye
1-18 YR gd B-1 Cd 4500 m 31:3 1:04:3 1:37 2:08:3 7 8 8 8 8/7¾ 8/9¾ 2:11 52.10(ECbb)NZKmberlyKd,GrardPck,LckyA
1-10 YR ft B-1 Cd 4500 m 31 1:03:1 1:34:1 2:05 4 4 5 6 6/4½ 7/6¾ 2:06:3 8.60(Cobb)WairauLrd,DuaneAgn,RllyGdN
1-3 YR ft B-1 4500 m 31:3 1:04:1 1:36:2 2:08 6 6 6 7 7/3½ 5/3½ 2:08:4 23.30(ECobb)SntrBrtn,RllyGdN,B'viewBbe
12-10 RR ft B-1 4500 m 31:2 1:04 1:35:1 2:06:1 2 2 2 4 6/4 5/4½ 2:07:1 8.50(ECobb)VoloTime,DelightflWay,Goliat
12-2 RR ft B-1 3500 m 30:4 1:02:3 1:33:2 2:05:1 1 2 4 6 6/1½ 4/1 2:05:2 3.10(ECobb)SlckYnkee,DngleN,SntrBurton

8 **8** **KING YANKEE** b h, 10, by Sampson Hanover, Adios Linda by Adios
Galaxy Stables, Inc., Brooklyn, N.Y. (Tr.-J. Higgins) (St.-W. Popfinger
($41,525) 2, 2:02:3 (1) B-3 WILLIAM POPFINGER (168) Green-White YR 2:06:2 1969 11 2 2 1 6,66
YR 2:05:3 1968 22 5 1 2 11,52
4-4 RR ft clm alw 10000 m 32 1:04:1 1:35:2 2:06:4 7 7 7 7° 7/5½ 7/4½ 2:07:3 18.20(WPfgr)BobAgain,TwnkleO,LadRnbow
3-28 RR ft clm 10000 m 30:3 1:02 1:34 2:06:1 1 3 4 3 3/1 2/hd 2:06:1 9.50(WPfgr)BobAgain,KngYkee,MrTmblnc
3-21 RR ft clm 10000 m 29:4 1:01:1 1:32:1 2:03:2 1 2 2 2 2/6 5/7½ 2:05:1 7.90(WPfngr) W.J.W.,GalaxyN,BobAgair
3-14 RR ft clm 10000 m 31:3 1:04:2 1:36 2:08 2 2 3 3° 3/1½ 5/3¼ 2:08:4 3.60(WPfngr)Admire,BobAgain,DodgeTim
3-8 RR ft clm 10000 m 31:3 1:03:1 1:34:4 2:07 1 4 4° 4° 3/2½ 1/¾ 2:07 *2.40(WMyr)KingYnkee,LadRnbw,MrnciCh
2-28 YR ft clm 10000 m 30 1:02:3 1:34:1 2:05:4 2 2 2 3 3/1½ 2/ns 2:05:4 9.60(M'Ntt)SandyLeo,KingYnkee,KeyWhi
2-21 YR ft clm 10000 m 30:1 1:03 1:34:1 2:06:1 4 6 7 5 5/3½ 3/2 2:06:3 11.60(FPfgr)CntrlRnge,,SpcialHn,KngYnke
$10,000 2-14 YR ft clm alw 10000 m 31:2 1:03:3 1:36:1 2:08:1 5 7 7°°2° 5/2¾ 6/2¾ 2:09 10.90(Fntne)Frda'sPride,KeyWhirl,Kinleith

EXACTA WINDOWS OPEN FOR THIS RACE.

8 PACE-ONE MILE

SADDLE CLOTH—BROWN

CLASS B-1—CONDITIONED **PURSE $4,500**

A.E. $15,000 OPTIONAL CLAIMERS (ALL AGES)

1

ABBE GENE VOLO b h, 7, by Gene Abbe, Tess Volo by True Volo (Tr.-G. Regan)
Edgewater Stables, Edgewater, N.J. RR 2:08 1969 3 1 1 0 3,360.
($69,600) 5, 2:00:2 WILLIAM MYER (165) Blue-Red 1968 7 0 0 0 900.
4-8 RR ft B-1 4500 m 31 1:02.4 1:36:2 2:06:3 3 4 4° 2° 2/1½ 2/¾ 2:06:4 •1.50(WMyr)Chp'nsCndy,A'beG'Vlo,SlyYnke
4-1 RR ft B-1 4500 m 30:2 1:02:4 1:34:3 2:05:3 8 2° 2 2° 2/1½ 4/1¼ 2:06 •3.30(WMyr)BlckieAd's,C'mnsCndy,MdwTpt
3-25 RR ft B-2 3750 m 31:2 1:03:4 1:35:4 2:08 5 7 5° 3° 4/1¾ 1/1¼ 2:08 6.20(WMyr)AbbeG'Vlo,SilkySq're,RicksClt
° 3-18 RR ft qua m 30:1 1:03:2 1:35:2 2:06:3 2 4 4 5 5/3½ 3/2½ 2:07:1 N.B.(WMyr)MstrJ'N,M'trChpsN,AbbeGVlo
6-25 RR gd Opt B-1 4400 m 30:1 1:01:3 1:32 2:03:3 3 5 5° 5° 6/4 8/6¼ 2:05 3.50(WMyer) MtCrd,GneMjsty,S'hvnBmbr
6-18 RR ft A-3 5000 m 30:3 1:01:3 1:32 2:02:2 7 8 8 8 6/8¾ 6/9½ 2:04:4 13.50(WMyer) HiDeeN,TrprtBll,ScotchDuke
5-25 MR ft FFA 4000 m 29:3 1:01:2 1:32:3 2:03 6 1° 1 3 4/3¼ 6/15 2:06:2 4.40(GGlmr)PaulTAce,NvleHldy,CshBattle
5-18 MR gd FFA 4000 m 31:4 1:04:1 1:35:2 2:05:2 6 6 5° 5be5/2½ 6/8¾ 2:07:3 •2.10(GGlmr)NveleHldy,JayDrct,CshBattle

---

2

TORO CREST b h, 6, by Duane Hanover, Takeoff Time by Good Time (Tr.-F. Darish)
Mr. & Mrs. Anthony Tavolacci, Yonkers, N.Y. 1969 4 0 0 0 780.
($42,781) 5, 2:02:3 LUCIEN FONTAINE (134) Green-White-Red YR 2:02:3 1968 26 5 4 2 16,035.
4-10 RR sy Opt B-1 4500 m 32 1:05.2 1:37 2:09:1 5 5 5 5° 5/3½ 4/2½ 2:09:4 8.60(Dl'ko)HghlndRdr,AceHill,JsdleGoLcky
4-3 RR ft A-3 5250 m 30 1:01:4 1:32 2:03:1 2 3 3 6 8/4¾ 8/10 2:05:3 33.10(Drsh)JC'seG'tree,KmysAOkly,Achncrg
3-27 RR ft A-2/A-3 6000 m 31:1 1:03:4 1:34:3 2:05:3 1 3 4 6 6/6½ 7/6½ 2:07 18.00(FDrsh)VoloTme,A'ncraig,JCr'seG'tree
3-20 RR ft A-3 5250 m 31:4 1:03:1 1:33:1 2:03:3 1 2 3 4 4/2¾ 4/7½ 2:05:2 12.00(FDarish)Mindian,TarportBill,LuckyA.
10-11 YR ft A-2 6250 m 29:2 1:00:2 1:31:3 2:02:1 6 7 8° 8 7/5¼ 7/7¾ 2:04:1 5.30(Fntne)Ad'sM'ge,N'twnC'mdr,MtyDrs
9-19 YR ft A-2 6250 m 29:2 59:3 1:30:2 2:01:1 8 3° 1° 2° 2/1 7/6½ 2:02:3 17.50(LFntne)TudrHn,LawDmnd,MrcleMkr
9-10 YR ft A-3 5250 m 30:3 1:01 1:31:3 2:02:3 1 1 1 1 1/½ 1/1½ 2:02:3 •1.30(LFntne)ToroCrst,Chkkah,CherryShade
9-3 YR ft A-3 5250 m 29:2 59:4 1:30:1 2:01:2 4 1 1 1 1/hd 3/nk 2:01:2 5.70(LFntne)LmightN,StyleFshn,ToroCrest

---

3

DONORA b m, 4, by Adios Don, Marcy Hanover by Tar Heel (Tr.-W. Burris) (St.-V. Dancer)
Fury Stable & Fiesta Farm, N.Y., N.Y. 1969 5 0 1 2 4,020.
($30,014) 3, 2:02:4 DEL INSKO (120) Purple-Gold YR 2:02:4 1968 21 5 2 6 17,039.
4-5 LB(⅝) gd Cd 5000 m 31:2 1:05 1:36:1 2:07:2 2 4 4 2° 2/1 3/3¼ 2:08 2.30(VDncr)LewOrgn,HistoricTime,Donora
3-27 LB(⅝) ft ec 15000 m 29 1:00 1:30:4 2:01:2 1 3 4 5 7/4¼ 4/4 2:02:1 11.40(VDncr)AftonDay,Ardrossan,RobinHill
3-21 LB(⅝) ft Cd 5500 m 30:1 1:02:2 1:32:2 2:02:2 1 2 5 6 7/3½ 6/1½ 2:02:3 •2.90(VDncr)CrdnlBrce,Ad'sUnteus,B'wdBoy
3-14 LB(⅝) ft ec 6000 m 30:1 1:01:4 1:32:1 2:02:2 3 2 2 3 3/1¼ 2/3½ 2:03 2.30(VDancer)Ardrossan,Donora,RobinHill
3-8 LB(⅝) ft ec 6000 m 30:2 1:01:1 1:32:3 2:03 8 8 8 7 5/7 3/3¼ 2:03:3 7.10(VDncr)MontageN,LiberaceHn,Donora
12-5 RR ft B-1 3500 m 31:1 1:05 1:36:4 2:09 2 1 1 1 1/½ 2/nk 2:09 •1.40(VDncr)GerardPick,Donora,TigerPaws
11-29 RR ft B-1 3500 m 30:3 1:02:3 1:34:3 2:06:3 7 1° 2 4 4/½ 2/ns 2:06:3 4.80(VDncr)SmrtMoney,Donora,Northwood
11-22 RR ft Opt B-1 3500 m 30 1:01:3 1:34:1 2:05:3 6 2 4 6 5/2½ 4/1¼ 2:05:4 3.40(VDncr)TwoDmnd,MzlleSmky,GrrdPick

---

4

ARMBRO HARVEY b g, 5, by Capetown, Tarport Rhythm by Direct Rhythm (Tr.-K. McNutt)
Ronald Bestine, Cheektowaga, N.Y. YR 2:06 1969 12 7 0 0 11,575.
($11,537) 3, 2:04:2 (⅝) KENNETH McNUTT (185) Green-White-Black GrR(⅝) 2:06:3 1968 24 2 6 3 5,936.
4-10 RR sy Opt B-2 4000 m 32:4 1:06:1 1:39:2 2:11:4 1 1 1 1 1/½ 1/nk 2:11:4 4.60(KM'Ntt)A'broHrvy,GrtCrdt,Knigt&Dy
3-31 RR ft Opt B-1 4500 m 31:4 1:03:4 1:34:3 2:06:2 8 8 8 8 8/5 8/3¼ 2:07:1 46.30(M'Ntt)AdiosMssge,SlyYnkee,LrryTme
3-24 RR sy B-1 4500 m 30:2 1:02:1 1:34:1 2:07:3 4 6 6 4° 4/7 5/6½ 2:09:1 4.20(KM'Ntt)PnthrHn,DixieT'boy,TrryFrbs
3-15 RR ft B-1 4500 m 30 1:01:4 1:33 2:04:2 6 7 8 8 7/6½ 5/4¾ 2:05:3 14.10(RRsh)JhnCraig,TrryForbs,SlickYankee
3-1 Btva gd hcp 3000 m 30:3 1:04:3 1:36:3 2:08:4 4 4 4 2° 2/nk 1/1¼ 2:08:4 •1.30(M'Ntt)A'broHrvy,VlleyVwFlme,Jupitr
2-25 YR ft B-1 Cd 4500 m 30 1:00:4 1:33 2:05:1 3 5 5° x8 8/14 8/16 2:09 6.30(KM'Ntt)AftnBllt,JrrysPlff,Br'nSmoke
2-17 YR ft B-1 Cd 4500 m 29:3 1:02 1:32:4 2:04:1 8 8 6° 3° 3/5 6/11 2:06:4 5.60(KM'Ntt)MzlRdny,AftnBllt,SlckYnkee
2-4 YR ft B-2 Cd 3750 m 31 1:02:2 1:34:4 2:06:1 1 5 5 5° 3/1 1/½ 2:06:1 •.70(M'Nt)A'broHrvy,S'dleY'kios,PdroWlsn

---

5

ALYTOR b g,7,by Torrid, Aly's Lady by Alemite (Tr.-A. Abbatiello)
Hay-Day Stable, Farmingdale, N.Y. YR 2:05 1969 13 2 3 1 8,670.
($49,826) 4, 2:03:3 CARMINE ABBATIELLO (135) Gold-Red YR 2:04:1 1968 24 2 3 2 8,954.
4-7 RR ft Opt B-1 4500 m 31:2 1:04 1:34:2 2:05:2 6 6 4° 4° 4/2½ 6/3½ 2:06:2 23.00(AAbt)WairauLrd,TrryFrbs,Ad'sMssge
3-31 RR ft B-2 3750 m 30:4 1:02:4 1:33:4 2:05 1 2 2 1 1/1 1/1¾ 2:05 •1.20(CAbbatllo)Alytor,GlenVale,NobleFlip
3-24 RR sy Opt B-2 3750 m 32 1:05:3 1:38:2 2:09:4 2 2 2 3 3/1 3/2 2:10:1 •1.50(AAbt)ShdySdePat,LiberaceHn,Alytor
3-17 RR ft Opt B-1 4500 m 31 1:04 1:35:2 2:06 6 6 7 7 7/3½ 7/5 2:07 17.60(AAbt)Auchencrg,BriansWy,BlckieAd's
3-10 RR ft B-1 4500 m 30:3 1:04:1 1:35:2 2:06:2 5 2 2 3 2/1 2/½ 2:06:3 12.60(AAbbtllo)Mindian,Alytor,AftonBullet
3-4 YR ft B-1 Cd 4500 m 30 1:02 1:32:1 2:05:1 7 7 7° 7 6/7½ 6/3½ 2:06 13.60(AAbt)S'dleYnk's,BeauMdw,TrryFrbes
2-25 YR ft B-1 Cd 4500 m 30 1:00:4 1:33 2:05:1 6 1 2 1° 2/ns 6/5 2:06:2 •2.20(CAbtlo)AftnBllt,JrysPlff,BrwnSmoke
2-17 YR ft B-1 Cd 4500 m 30 1:02:2 1:33:4 2:05 4 2° 1 1 1/1½ 1/1 2:05 •1.60(CAbbatiello)Alytor,Apt,BrownSmoke

---

6

HIGHLAND RAIDER b g, 9, by Morano, Tradition by Nelson Derby (Tr.-W. Dracksley) (St.-E. Cobb)
Helm Wind Farm, Inc., Mineola, N.Y. YR 2:04:3 1969 12 4 1 2 11,385.
($49,577) 6, 2:01 (⅝) A-3 EDWARD COBB (193) Blue-White RR 2:04:3 1968 35 4 6 4 15,685.
4-10 RR sy Opt B-1 4500 m 32 1:05:2 1:37 2:09:1 7 7 7 7 6/4¼ 1/nk 2:09:1 22.10(ECbb)HghlndRdr,AceHll,JsdleGoLcky
4-3 RR ft B-1 4500 m 30:2 1:02:2 1:33:2 2:04 1 3 4 5 6/2½ 4/3¼ 2:04:4 3.80(ECbb)BrwnSmke,SntoTm,JsdleG'Lcky
3-27 RR ft B-1 4500 m 29:4 1:01:1 1:32:3 2:04:1 x3 7 7 8 8/7 8/6 2:05:3 4.30(ECobb)AdOSam,ReprieveN.,Mr.Hoff
3-20 RR ft B-1 4500 m 31:3 1:03:3 1:34:2 2:05:2 5 2 3 3 3/2½ 2/¾ 2:05:3 2.90(ECbb)RbrtEdn,HghlndRdr,Q'rryRoad
3-13 RR ft B-1 4500 m 30:2 1:01:2 1:31:4 2:04:1 2 3 4 6° 6/6 3/1¼ 2:04:3 8.50(ECbb)FrstA'vntre,NtbleWck,H'lndRdr
3-7 RR ft Opt B-1 4500 m 30:4 1:01:4 1:33:3 2:05 4 4 4 4 3/2 4/¾ 2:05:1 3.50(ECbb)Chp'nsCndy,PnthrHn,BrwnSmke
2-5 YR ft B-1 Cd 4500 m 30:1 1:01:3 1:33:3 2:04:3 4 3 3 5 5/3 1/1 2:04:3 9.00(ECbb)HghlndRdr,BlckieAd's,BywdBoy
$15,000 1-30 YR sy B-2 Cd 3750 m 31 1:04:2 1:37:1 2:10:2 1 4 4° 3° 1/nk 1/¾ 2:10:2 •1.90(ECbb)HighlndRaidr,MldyFlsh,NbleFlp

---

7

ROYAL ROMAN br h, 4, by Royal Bill, Homestretch Ellen by McEllen (Tr.-F. Mule) (St.-W. Hudson)
Sally Farms, Jackson Heights, N.Y. RR 2:04:3 1969 7 3 2 1 9,950.
($12,770) 3, 2:04:3 NORMAN DAUPLAISE (139) Brown-Gold-White Fhld 2:04:3 1968 28 5 7 5 11,482.
4-11 Rock ft ec 7500 m 30:1 1:02:1 1:33:3 2:04:1 8 3° 4° 3° 5/2¼ 7/4½ 2:05 14.10(NDplse)WldctLbll,StwrtHn,DrHarryC
4-5 RR gd B-1 4500 m 32:3 1:04 1:35 2:07 4 6 5 2 2/1 2/½ 2:07:1 3.20(NDplse)NtbleWck,RylRmn,FireawayN
3-29 RR sy A-3/B-1 5500 m 31 1:04:4 1:36:1 2:08:1 1 3 2° 2° 2/1 2/2½ 2:08:4 •1.60(Dplse)HpeTme,RoyalRomn,DxieTmby
3-21 Rock gd ec 7500 m 31 1:01:3 1:33:3 2:05 3 3° 1° 1 1/1¼ 1/½ 2:05 7.20(Dplse)RoylRmn,StwrtHn,ForeverBold
3-14 RR ft B-2 3750 m 30:3 1:04 1:35:1 2:05:4 6 7 5° 3° 3/1¼ 3/½ 2:06 •1.30(Dplse)FrdasPrde,RndzvsTrdr,RylRmn
3-5 RR ft B-3 Cd 3250 m 31:1 1:02:4 1:33:2 2:04:3 4 6 6 4° 3/1 1/2¼ 2:04:3 •1.10(Dplse)RoylRomn,CnfttiHn,RedThread
2-26 YR gd B-3 Cd 3250 m 30:3 1:05 1:35:3 2:07:2 4 5 5 5° 5/2½ 1/1 2:07:2 6.90(NDplse)RylRomn,FrgnPolicy,TwnkleO.
12-11 RR ft Opt B-3 3250 m 30:3 1:03 1:35:3 2:06 2 5 6 6° 5/2½ 2/1¼ 2:06:1 9.30(WHdsn)AttrnyN,RylRomn,HbbyH'Bllt

---

8

GOLIATH b h, 6, by Sampson Hanover, Way Dream by Adios (Tr.-M. Tolson)
Rallye Stable, Inc. & Leo Glickberg, N.Y. 1969 14 0 1 0 5,671.
($39,975) 3, 2:02:1 JOHN CHAPMAN (147) Green-White YR 2:04:3 1968 12 2 1 4 7,215.
4-8 RR ft B-1 4500 m 31 1:02:4 1:36:2 2:06:3 2 3 3 5 5/4 4/2¾ 2:07:1 15.30(JChp'n)Chp'nsCndy,A'beG'Vlo,SlyYnke
3-31 RR ft Opt B-1 4500 m 31:4 1:03:4 1:34:3 2:06:2 2 4 6 7 7/3½ 5/2¼dh 2:07 10.60(Dplse)AdiosMssge,SlyYnkee,LrryTme
3-24 RR sy B-1 4500 m 30:2 1:02:1 1:34:1 2:07:3 1 4 5 7 8/12 4/5¾ 2:09 8.80(JTllmn)PnthrHn,DxieT'Boy,TrryFrbes
3-15 RR ft B-1 4500 m 30 1:01:4 1:33 2:04:2 2 1 2 2° 2/2 6/5½ 2:05:4 6.90(JTllmn)JhnCraig,TrryForbs,SlckYnke
3-7 RR ft Opt B-1 4500 m 30:4 1:01:4 1:33:3 2:05 6 6 7 6 5/3¼ 5/2½ 2:05:3 11.50(JChp'n)Chp'nsC'dy,PnthrHn,Br'nSmke
2-28 YR ft A-3 5250 m 30:4 1:04 1:35 2:05:4 5 6 7 7 7/6½ 7/6¾ 2:07:3 12.80(JChpmn)J.D.Exprss,MzlRdny,LuckyA.
2-21 YR ft A-3 5250 m 29:4 1:02:1 1:33:2 2:05 1 3 3 2° 3/1½ 6/3¾ 2:06 •1.30(JChpmn)ValidBet,Bmbrdr,PantherHn
2-13 YR ft A-3 5250 m 30:1 1:03:1 1:34:3 2:06:3 4 3 3° 2° 2/1 4/¾ 2:06:4 5.40(JTllmn)Drmbuie,ExaltedRuler,Forshy

SCRATCHED—MR. HOFF (7) A.E.—ROYAL ROMAN—*races in P.P. of scratched horse.*

MORN. LINE

9 PACE-ONE MILE EXACTA

SADDLE CLOTH—ORANGE

CLAIMING $4,000—6-YEAR & UP
ALL HORSES ENTERED MAY BE CLAIMED FOR $4,000 PURSE $2,75

12 **1**

PRONTITO

b h, 7, by Sampson Hanover, Cassin Hanover by Hoot Mon (Tr.-J. Firett
J. Firetti & H. Green, N.Y. 1969 11 0 0 1 4
($8,774) 3, 2:05 JOSEPH FIRETTI (140) Red-White-Gold PPk(⅝) 2:05:1 1968 21 2 1 2 1,6

4-8 RR	ft clm alw	3000	m	30:2	1:04	1:35:4	2:08:3	6	8	8	8	7/3½	4/1½	2:09	37.00(JFrtti)Lachaglen,ScotHayes,Bargel
3-29 RR	ft clm	4000	m	31	1:02:4	1:34:2	2:07:4	8	8	8	8°	7/8½	7/4¾	2:09	51.00(Frtti)FlyngBts,CpeNpt,R'mdeDve-ShrGns
3-6 PPk(⅝)	ft Cd	750	m	30:1	1:04:1	1:35	2:08:1	1	3	3	3°	3/1¾	4/nk	2:08:1	*2.20(JFrtti)PopsAd's,Lawmstr,ChrokeeR
2-26 PPk(⅝)	ft Cd	750	m	31:1	1:04:1	1:35:2	2:06:4	5	7	7°	5°	4/1½	3/4¼	2:07:3	18.50(JFrti)StdyRhythm,T'GryTycn,Prntit
2-19 PPk(⅝)	ft Cd	850	m	31:1	1:04:4	1:36:3	2:07:4	1	2	4	2x	7/8¼	7/14	2:10:4	4.90(Frtti)PsntPrnce,HalToThee,BlueSis
2-12 PPk(⅝)	ft Cd	850	m	31	1:04:2	1:36:1	2:08	7	7	7	6°	5/3¾	8/4	2:08:4	5.70(Frti)PrncssStrng,AbbePCnsl,BlueSis
2-5 PPk(⅝)	ft Cd	750	m	30:3	1:03:4	1:35:3	2:07:2	5	5	6	7	7/5¾	5/6	2:08:3	30.90(JFrtti)MddaGldie,SirT'Gallnt,BnMr
1-30 PPk(⅝)	ft Cd	700	m	31:2	1:03:3	1:34:2	2:04:4	3	7	7	7	8/11	8/18	2:08:2	27.30(JFrtti)LieutMrdle,SrT'Glnt,CntataH

3 **2**

TORMAX

b h, 9, by Torrid, Maxine's Rose by Cardinal Prince (Tr.-S. Train
AMF Farms, Inc. & A. & F. Delia, N.Y. RR 2:06:3 1969 4 2 0 0 2,76
($39,407) 3, 2:00:2 (¾) LUCIEN FONTAINE (134) Green-White-Red 1968 4 0 0 0 4

4-9 RR	ft clm	3000	m	31:3	1:03:3	1:34:4	2:06:3	4	2	1	1	1/3	1/2¾	2:06:3	*1.50(LFntne)Tormax,BenCaseyN,VonDow
3-29 RR	ft clm	4000	m	31	1:02:4	1:34:2	2:07:4	3	4	3°	1	1/1	5/3¼	2:08:3	*1.30(F'tne)FlyngBts,CpeNpt,R'mdeDve-ShrGns
3-18 RR	ft clm	3000	m	30:3	1:03:3	1:35:2	2:07:1	7	3	3	1°	1/1	1/1	2:07:1	12.70(Fntne)Tormax,Emncpation,CountD'r
3-11 RR	ft clm	4000	m	31	1:04:2	1:38	2:12:3	1	3	3	3	3/1	5/2¼	2:13:1	4.90(LFntne)GrndPtch,StrmyDream,Matt
11-25 RR	ft C-1 Cd	2700	m	30:3	1:03:2	1:36	2:08:2	7	1	1	1	1/1	4/3¾	2:09:2	9.40(LF'tne)SpceCdtN,KnnyDares,SfldSc
11-2 RR	ft B-3	3000	m	29:3	1:00:2	1:32:3	2:04:3	5	6	6°	8°	8/7¼	7/10	2:07	19.40(STrna)GoodT'Lss,MissnLad,AftnFls
10-21 RR	ft Opt B-3	3250	m	30:4	1:02:1	1:33	2:05	4	1	1	1	1/1	4/3¼	2:05:4	55.50(STrna)SrC'Pck,GdT'Lss,BuenoTmpo
10-2 YR	ft B-2 Cd	3750	m	29:4	1:01:2	1:33:2	2:04:3	1	3	5	7	6/3¾	7/5¾	2:06	44.90(STrna)PrdeOfHn,SntoTom,TheP'ms

6 **3**

SANTOS JOHN

b g ,8, by Santo Eden, Miss Honoretta by His Honor (Tr.-L. Grass
J. Ettinger & Alexander Sharkey, Jr., N.J. RR 2:07:2 1969 10 3 0 0 4,65
($23,020) 3, 2:06:2 JOSEPH GRASSO (162) White-Brown-Gold Fhld 2:07:2 1968 30 3 2 4 5,81

4-9 RR	ft clm	3000	m	31:3	1:03:3	1:34:4	2:06:3	8	8	8	8	7/9	5/7	2:08:1	8.50(JGrsso)Tormax,BenCaseyN,VonDowe
3-31 RR	ft clm alw	3000	m	31:3	1:04:3	1:37:3	2:09:2	5	4	4	4	4/2	1/¾	2:09:2	*2.10(JGrsso)SntsJohn,BenCasyN.,WhsCal
3-19 RR	ft clm alw	3000	m	30:2	1:02:1	1:35	2:07:2	1	4	4	4°	3/2	1/1¼	2:07:2	5.90(JGrsso)SntsJohn,Invoke,AftnPandor
3-13 RR	ft clm alw	3000	m	30:4	1:03:3	1:36:2	2:09:4	6	8	8	8	8/5¾	4/¾	2:10	23.90(JGrsso)MrJ'Cstle,SctHays,AftnPndr
3-7 RR	ft clm alw	3000	m	31:3	1:05:3	1:38:1	2:10:4	6	2	2	2°	3/1¼	5/4	2:11:4	17.10(JGrsso)MrJCstle,S'ftBttle,AftnPnd
3-3 YR	ft clm alw	3000	m	31:1	1:04:4	1:37	2:10	4	5	6	6	5/2½	5/2½	2:10:3	18.60(Grsso)GrndPtch,AftnPndra,MrJ'Cst
2-25 YR	ft clm	3000	m	31:1	1:04:4	1:37:1	2:10	3	2	2	3	3/1	1/ns	2:10	19.40(JGrsso)SntsJhn,RckS'Kay,SwiftBtt
2-19 YR	sy clm	3000	m	31:2	1:05:4	1:39:4	2:13:1	5	7	6	6	6/5¼	5/5¼	2:14:1	16.30(NDplse)GrndPtch,ChfMldy,ChstrMa

4 **4**

ALBERT GENE

bg, 13, by Gene Abbe, Betty Heekin by Guy Abbey (Tr.-F. Mule) (St.-W. Hudso
Frank Mule & Cono G. D'Elia, N.Y. 1969 8 0 2 1 2,25
($122,861) 6, 2:02:1 CARMINE ABBATIELLO (135) Gold-Red 1968 11 0 2 2 2,86

4-8 RR	ft clm alw	3000	m	30:2	1:04	1:35:4	2:08:3	2	1	1	1	1/½	5/2	2:09	*2.00(RRash)Lachaglen,ScotHayes,Bargel
3-29 RR	gd clm	4000	m	30:3	1:02:4	1:36:1	2:08:2	3	5	5	4°	4/2¼	6/3	2:09	10.40(RRash)Emncptn,StrmyDrm,SctHaye
3-22 RR	ft clm	4000	m	30:2	1:03	1:35:1	2:07:3	5	6	6	4°	4/2¼	4/2¼	2:08:1	3.20(RRash)StrmyDrm,MattB,CopprJcke
3-12 RR	ft clm	5000	m	30:4	1:03:1	1:35:2	2:08:1	7	8	8	8°	7/7	6/4¾	2:09:2	13.80(RRsh)ForestMte,HonrBoy,ChmpRch
3-5 RR	ft clm	5000	m	31	1:03:2	1:35:2	2:07:1	7	7	6	3°	5/5	4/6½	2:08:4	*2.50(RRsh)HlloByeBye,ChmpRchie,Exmo
2-28 YR	ft clm	4500	m	31	1:03	1:35:2	2:08	6	7	8°	7°	5/2¼	2/¾	2:08:1	2.80(RRsh)SpnglrVlo,AlbrtGne,MtnLkabl
2-20 YR	gd clm	4500	m	32	1:04:4	1:38	2:09:1	5	4	4	3°	2/½	3/1½	2:09:3	*2.10(RRsh)MntnLkeable,HghLw,AlbrtGer
2-15 YR	ft clm	4500	m	30:1	1:02	1:34:3	2:07:1	2	4	4	4	4/2½	2/3½	2:08	4.70(LDvs)AvanteN,AlbertGene,RealYnke

6 **5**

KNIGHT STREAK

br g, 8, by Knight Dream, Up High by Follow Up (Tr.-R. Kruege
Stefano Liuzzi, Lake Ronkonkoma, N.Y. RR 2:08:1 1969 2 1 0 0 1,45
($24,165) 2, 2:04:3 (1) ROLAND KRUEGER (165) Blue-White RR 2:07:3 1968 11 1 0 2 1,75

4-3 RR	ft clm alw	3000	m	30:3	1:04:4	1:36:3	2:08:1	5	1	1	1	1/1	1/4	2:08:1	4.60(RKrgr)KngtStrk,Ad'sSlvr,MskdPain
3-25 RR	gd clm	3000	m	30:1	1:05:1	1:36:4	2:09:3	6	2	1	1	1/1	4/1	2:09:4	26.80(RKrgr)LthrioLindsy,RedFlngn,HalD
* 3-15 RR	ft qua		m	31:3	1:05:1	1:36:3	2:07:4	1	2	3	3	3/4	5/6	2:09:1	N.B.(RKrgr)MrJimT,EvenBreak,TenGrnd
12-10 RR	ft clm alw	3000	m	31:4	1:05:1	1:38:4	2:11	7	8	8	8°	8/9	5/13	2:14	80.50(RFlmme)Jacana,ShellyHvn,HrvaCm
11-28 RR	gd clm alw	3000	m	30:4	1:03:2	1:35:3	2:08:1	6	7	7	7	7/7½	6/9¾	2:10:3	59.50(RFlmme)AmzngVle,HrmlouBrd,Clvr
11-19 RR	ft clm alw	3000	m	31:4	1:06:1	1:39	2:11:2	2	5	5	6	6/6	6/11	2:14:1	55.00(Flmme)DllyR'bow,Jacna,HrmlouByr
11-6 RR	ft clm alw	3000	m	31	1:02:3	1:35:1	2:06:4	5	7	7	8	7/4¾	7/9¼	2:09	28.90(RFlmme)VinAbbe,AdiosAgain,Jacar
* 10-23 RR	ft qua		m	31:1	1:03:2	1:35:3	2:08:1	5	1	1	2	2/3	3/3	2:09	N.B.(RFlme)MrrieKm,WtrmllTgr,KgtStrk

8 **6**

LEGAL FREIGHT

b g, 12, by Vonian Chief, Brown Bunny by Attorney (Tr.-R. Burgholze
Primrose Stables, Oscawanna, N.Y. YR 2:09:2 1969 9 1 1 2 3,27
($109,959) 7, 2:02:2 ROBERT BURGHOLZER (165) Gold-White-Black MR 2:06:2 1968 24 3 6 6 7,75

4-7 RR	ft clm alw	5000	m	30:2	1:04	1:36	2:07:2	2	4	4°	2°	2/½	4/1¾	2:07:4	12.10(RBrghzr)Emncptn,StmyDrm,CpprJc
3-28 RR	ft clm	5000	m	30:3	1:03:4	1:35:4	2:08:4	6	1°	1	1	1/nk	7/2¼	2:09:2	25.40(RB'lzer)KnnyDars,I'MAGndr,FrstMi
3-19 RR	ft clm	5000	m	31	1:04:1	1:35:2	2:07	2	2	2	5	5/3¼	3/2	2:07:2	9.60(RBrghlzr)SpnglrVlo,JetDncr,LglFrg
3-5 RR	ft clm	5000	m	31	1:03:2	1:35:2	2:07:1	6	3°	2°	6°	6/6½	7/8½	2:09:1	4.80(Dplse)HlloByeBye,ChmpRchie,Exmo
2-27 YR	ft clm	6000	m	30:4	1:02:4	1:34:3	2:06:2	5	3	3	3°	3/1½	4/1¾	2:06:4	5.50(Dplse)MrWxfrd,SixThrteen,KnnyDre
2-18 YR	ft clm	6000	m	31	1:03:1	1:35:4	2:08:4	1	2	2	2°	2/nk	6/1	2:09	3.10(LFntne)Speakeasy,Goldville,JMRega
2-8 YR	ft clm	6000	m	30:3	1:02:3	1:34	2:06:3	1	3	4	3°	2/1	2/1½	2:07	*1.80(LFntne)ChnWhskrs,LglFrght,FastGu
1-30 YR	sy clm	6000	m	31:1	1:04:2	1:37:2	2:09:3	5	fog	1	fog	fog	3/2¾	2:10:1	2.90(Fntne)MdwR'ch,GdGrttnA,LgalFrgh

4 **7**

BEN CASEY N.

b g, 9, by Historic Crown, Purple Trust by Unproven (Tr.-G. Rega
Phyllis Fredericks & Blanche Kanrich, N.Y. 1969 7 0 2 1 1,73
($14,078) 8, 2:04:1 (1) WILLIAM MYER (165) Blue-Red Lex(1) 2:04:1 1968 28 5 3 2 7,10

4-9 RR	ft clm	3000Z	m	31:3	1:03:3	1:34:4	2:06:3	3	1	2	2	2/3	2/2¾	2:07:1	2.60(RRash)Tormax,BenCaseyN,VonDowe
3-31 RR	ft clm alw	3000	m	31:3	1:04:3	1:37:3	2:09:2	6	1	2	1°	1/1	2/¾	2:09:3	2.90(RRsh)SantsJhn,BnCasyN.,WhosCalll
* 3-26 RR	ft qua		m	31	1:04:2	1:37:2	2:10:1	4	4	4	4	3/2	2/1	2:10:2	N.B.(RRsh)GuyAdios,BenCseyN,FncyG'rg
2-18YR	ft clm	4500	m	30:3	1:02:4	1:35:4	2:08	5	7	8	8	8/11	8/17	2:12:2	5.70(RRsh)AmzngVale,WarChnt,Honorabl
2-5 YR	ft clm	4500	m	30:2	1:01:2	1:34	2:07	6	2	2	2	3/3	3/3	2:07:3	2.90(RRsh)HBLind,JMRegal,BenCaseyN.
1-30 YR	sy clm	6000	m	31:1	1:04:2	1:37:2	2:09:3	8	fog	8	fog	fog	5/3½	2:10:2	20.20(RRsh)MdwRoach,GdGrttnA,LgalFrg
1-23 YR	sy clm	7500	m	31:2	1:05:3	1:38:2	2:11:4	8	3°	2	5	7/9½	7/18	2:16:2	16.10(RRash)JssiesG'son,ArlieFrst,MlsBrt
1-13 YR	ft clm	7500	m	30:4	1:03:1	1:35:1	2:07:3	5	6	3°	4	5/4¾	6/4½	2:08:3	6.60(Rsh) MrnciChf,TmysPrde,JsiesGrnd

5 **8**

LACHAGLEN

b g, 12, by Lawn Raider, Louise Lynette by Louis Direct (Tr.-S. Moisey
H. Brenner & F. Martone, Rosedale, N.Y. RR 2:08:3 1969 4 2 0 0 2,34
($10,759) 11, 2:06:2 HAROLD DANCER, JR. (165) Yellow-Grey Fhld 2:06:2 1968 26 7 2 4 5,25

4-8 RR	ft clm alw	3000	m	30:2	1:04	1:35:4	2:08:3	8	5	5°	4°	3/½	1/½	2:08:3	6.40(Dncr,J.)Lachaglen,ScotHayes,Barge
3-29 LB(⅝)	gd clm	4000	m	31:1	1:03:4	1:35:2	2:07:1	6	1°	1	3	5/3¼	5/4	2:08	3.70(Grne)BlytheAd's,MssArch,BchlrsD'b
3-13 LB(⅝)	ft clm	3000	m	32	1:04:4	1:36:1	2:09:1	1	2	1	1	1/3¼	1/4½	2:09:1	*1.50(HrFln)Lachagln,MrrlyAnne,HoustnH
3-1 LB(⅝)	ft clm	4000	m	31	1:02:4	1:35:1	2:08:1	3ix	7	7	7	7/15	6/10	2:10:1	8.00(RHwrd)HiL'Deb,HrryAd's,DnnaCmn
* 2-19 LB(⅝)	gd qua		m	32:4	1:05:1	1:38:2	2:10:1	4	1	1	1	1/1¾	1/2½	2:10:1	N.B.(RHwrd)Lachagln,GypsyH'Hat,Houdi
11-23 Fhld	ft clm	4000	m	30:4	1:03:4	1:36:2	2:07:1	2x	8	8	8	8/dis	8/dis		10.30(M'Gee)DttieWck,DckByrd,HnyT'Scte
* 11-15 Fhld	ft qua		m	31:3	1:03.4	1:36:4	2:08:2	4	5°	5	5	5/20	5/23	2:13	N.B.(M'Gee)SpceCdetN,Oaktwn,PutP'Ptr
11-13 Fhld	gd Cd	2500	m	32:3	1:06:2	1:37:1	2:09:1	3x	5°	3°	8	8/10	8/23	2:13:4	5.80(VKac)SilkySquire,BllyDuane,HghSa

EXACTA WINDOWS OPEN FOR THIS RACE

15

Roosevelt Raceway, APRIL 17, 1969

WEATHER BALMY, TRACK FAST. The leading drivers are Carmine Abbatiello, John Chapman, Leroy Copeland, Sonny and Stanley Dancer, Lucien Fontaine, Billy Haughton, Del Insko, Billy Myer, George Phalen. Statistical studies reveal (see p. 236) that the two inside post positions at this famous half-miler are somewhat more than twice as favorable as the two outside ones.

The First Race

Speedy Barbaranne has been away too long. Salcos April had no excuse on April 9. Shining Hanover is unraced and has had trouble qualifying. Jiffy Joy has not done anything yet this year. The same goes for Ruth T. Direct. Mae Flip has been idle.

The contenders:

Buttercup Smith. A basic rating of 173, plus 10 for roughing it a half-mile, minus 1 for the change in post position. Final rating is 182.

Gay Lands. Basic rating of 170, plus 10 for roughing it and 10 for Abbatiello, less 2 for the change in post position. Final rating of 188. This is insufficient to overcome the disadvantage of the outside start (see p. 238). The one and only play in the race is Buttercup Smith.

RESULT: Ruth T. Direct (8 to 5) was on top by two lengths when they entered the stretch. Gay Lands was second, having broken stride earlier and having also traveled outside for a quarter. Both tired enough for Popfinger to fly past, winning by daylight over Salcos April (6 to 5 favorite). Buttercup Smith paid $12.80 to win and $4.60 for the place.

The Second Race

Neither Fair Dancer, Claire's Dream nor Reba Wave has developed any form this year. Elmhurst Queen is scratched. The contenders:

May Champ. Basic rating of 171, plus 10 for roughing it a half-mile, plus 2 for the stretch gain, minus 5 for the rise in class from C-3 to tonight's C-2. The final rating is 178.

Oui Oui Byrd. Basic rating is 154, plus 5 for roughing it, 5 for the improved post position, 10 for Sonny Dancer. Total is 174.

J. M. Millie. Basic rating of 154, plus 10 for roughing it, 5 for the stretch gain, 3 for the better post position and 10 for Del Insko. Final rating is 182.

Dahn Holly. Basic rating of 175, plus 10 for roughing it and 10 for John Chapman, less 3 for the poor post position. Total is 192, which is 10 points the best in the field—enough to overcome the disadvantage of leaving from the outside.

RESULT: May Champ (favored at 9 to 5) held the lead until the stretch, with Oui Oui Byrd (3 to 1) hot on her trail. When they tired, J. M. Millie (6.60 to 1) came along but Dahn Holly came even more vigorously, having had a pleasant trip in the fifth hole. Dahn Holly paid an elegant $26.60 to win, $10.20 for the place. Daily double lovers will be enchanted to learn that the double paid $174.40.

The Third Race

A trot. Major Bryce, Novel Blaze and Victory Camp show nothing good and recent. Sweet Cere, on the downgrade since February, might be forgiven for breaking on April 11 and might, therefore, be given a rating for the April 3 effort, but it would be a waste of time. A glance at her figures shows that she does not compare with others in this field. Terrell also is a contender, technically, but would not earn a high enough figure for his March 28 race to overcome the outside start.

The contenders are Speranza Colby, Marcel Mir and Joseppe. Instead of using the pace-rating table on page 179, let me develop basic ratings for the three contenders by the alternative method, which many players may find preferable.

For Speranza Colby and Marcel Mir, we use the March 28 figures, achieved on a fast track. For Joseppe, we obviously take the April 9 figures.

	Half	Final	Basic
Speranza Colby	1:04:1 [19]	2:08:1 [18]	37
Marcel Mir	1:04:1 [19]	2:07:4 [20]	39
Joseppe	1:04　[20]	2:08:2 [17]	37

Note that these basic ratings are computed by crediting 20 points to the fastest time in each column. The other times get a point less for each fifth of a second by which they fail to match the best figure. The credits then are added. The arithmetical differences among the basic ratings are the same as would be produced by the pace-rating table. In short, Marcel Mir's basic rating is two points better than those of the other contenders, no matter which of our computation methods you use.

Let us now look for the extra credits.

Speranza Colby gets 10 for roughing it, 5 for dropping in class and 10 for Lucien Fontaine. Deduct 3 for the post position. Total: 59.

Marcel Mir gets 5 for roughing it and another 5 for the drop in class. His total is 49.

Joseppe picks up 5 for roughing it, but loses 5 for the bad post position and another 5 for moving up in class. His total becomes 32.

RESULT: Speranza Colby, favored slightly over 2 to 1, overtook Marcel Mir (2.40 to 1) as the horses entered the stretch. She extended her lead to about ¾ of a length before passing under the finish wire. She paid $6.20. And we seem to have picked the winning exacta, 2–4, which paid a miserable $16.60.

The Fourth Race

Because people are always teasing me about my wide-ranging definition of "the unplayable race," I have been leaning over backward to concede that not everybody needs to be as rigid as I am about passing some races. But I simply must draw the line here. There is no way on earth of really handicapping the field. As Exhibit A, consider Nevele Romeo, a good horse at three, and as yet untested on a fast track during 1969. If the horse had been assigned tonight to an inferior driver, excuses might be found for eliminating it and handicapping the other starters off their fast-track form. But Insko has Nevele Romeo, and the race cannot (in my unyielding opinion) be handicapped well enough to justify a bet.

RESULT: The favored Miracle Maker won with authority, paying $4.20. Nevele Romeo finished dead last. This may make me seem silly, but it does not mean that the race was suitable for a bet.

The Fifth Race

Some interesting problems here. Tom Thumb, claimed for $3,000 a month ago, has raced well in the slop with a $4,000 price tag and now moves up to $5,000 company. To get any sort of line on his fast-track form, we have to go all the way back to March 17, when his performance may not have been quite as good as it looks.

A glance at the record of Stormy Dream relieves the quandary. That one's race on April 7 was doubtful for handicapping purposes but was certainly good enough to justify use of the March 22 race, its next previous outing on a fast track. The figures make Stormy Dream a clear choice here (including due credit for the presence of the great Jimmy Cruise. Cruise has not been winning here lately, but, as explained in our chapter on drivers, horsemen of this quality always deserve extra points).

As you will see if you work out the ratings, Forest Mite ranks second to Stormy Dream. The other contenders are Winstadt and Honor Key. And, of course, Tom Thumb.

RESULT: Tom Thumb beat the favored Stormy Dream (7 to 5) in the stretch. Winstadt was third, Forest Mite fourth. Tom Thumb paid $12.80, indicating strong support in face of his boosts in class and his failure to approach Stormy Dream's performances on fast tracks. The exacta was worth $31.

The Sixth Race

Mizelles Mickey is a good example of the rising three-year-old matched against older animals of lesser quality. He dwarfs the field.

RESULT: He won going away, paying $3.20.

The Seventh Race

This program was made to order for a manual of handicapping instruction. Here now is an example of the horse that wins a qualifying race in better time than its opponents have been recording in their own good, recent efforts.

Look at Master Cleao. His 2:06:2 in a qualifier five days ago is better than any of the other horses have managed in good, recent performances. See for yourself. Go through the records. Identify the contenders. Compare their key races with Master Cleao's. He is an automatic play.

RESULT: He paid $8.40. The favorite, Rendezvous Truder (2.30 to 1), got nothing.

The Eighth Race

Here comes another beautiful example for you.

The first problem is Donora, invading New York after a nice race over an off track at Liberty Bell. Her recent fast-track form at the Philadelphia raceway has been only moderate. Liberty Bell is *at least* two seconds faster than Roosevelt. Even crediting Donora with good form in any of those March races (which would be stretching things slightly), her figures would be no better than those of other animals in tonight's field. It seems safe enough to write her off as a noncontender.

Toro Crest also is out, for lack of good recent form on a fast surface. Likewise Armbro Harvey and Goliath. Highland Raider came to life in the slop on April 10. To find a presentable performance of his on dry footing, we have to go back to March 20, when his figures were below par for this field.

The contenders:

Abbe Gene Volo. The basic rating is 192, plus 1 for the stretch gain, 10 for roughing it, 2 for the better post position, 10 for Billy Myer (who is in one of his periodic warm streaks) and 5 for being a beaten favorite. Total is 220.

Alytor. Basic rating of 188, plus 10 for roughing it, 1 for an improved position at the gate and 10 for Carmine Abbatiello. Final rating of 209.

Royal Roman. That was some kind of race six nights ago at Rockingham Park. This animal shuttles back and forth between New York and New Hampshire with no loss of form. For the best available line on his pace, we should use the April 11 race at Rockingham. The disadvantage of computing a rating from that particular out-of-town performance is not as great as that of using the outdated March 14 race, which was Royal's next previous effort on fast footing. If Rock were not a half-miler, or if Royal Roman were not at home on both tracks, the New Hampshire pace rating might be less trustworthy.

To rate the horse, we check the table of comparative track speeds in the program. Roosevelt is rated at 2:05, Rockingham at 2:05:4. This means that the half-mile time of a Rockingham race should be lowered by two-fifths of a second, and the horse's final time by four-fifths.

Royal Roman's basic rating is a dazzling 210; plus 15 for traveling on the outside for at least three-fourths of the race, 5 for dropping in class tonight and a point for moving from the outside at Rockingham to tonight's post here (see p. 236). The total is 231, more than enough to make this horse the play, poor post position notwithstanding.

RESULT: Abbe Gene Volo, favored at 2 to 1, and Alytor (6 to 1), cooked each other in a speed duel during the third quarter of the race. Royal Roman circled the field on the last turn, coming from last to first in the stretch, and winning by a length. The second-fastest finisher was Highland Raider, and Donora was third in a good effort. Royal Roman paid $15.20 to win and $8.20 to place, mighty fine numbers for a horse that stood out as clearly as this.

The Ninth Race

Nothing approaches Tormax in this group. Which is why he goes as an odds-on favorite. Alas, he folds up on the turn for home and finishes sixth. The winner is Knight Streak, in 2:06:2—faster than the gelding has traveled in years.

It has been an instructive program. Our handicapping principles turned up eleven plays, of which nine were successful. Be assured that this is an abnormally high batting average. There will be nights on which you will be unable to do anything right.

To recapitulate: Buttercup Smith ($12.80, $4.60), Dahn Holly ($26.60, $10.20), Speranza Colby ($6.20), Stormy Dream (lost), Mizelles Mickey ($3.20), Master Cleao ($8.40), Royal Roman ($15.20, $8.20), Tormax (lost).

I hope that the reader has begun to find the procedures simple. Contenders are selected on the basis of recent good form. They are assigned pace ratings by one of the methods described earlier. The pace ratings then are modified to reflect stretch gains, racing on the outside, drivers, changes in class and post position and the angles mentioned on pages 229–230.

16

Sportsman's Park, JUNE 11, 1969

A WARM CLOUDY NIGHT. Track fast. Post positions 1 through 7 are about equal. Some of the world's best drivers are on hand, including greats like Joe O'Brien and Howard Beissinger, who have been unable to win much at the meeting. The program includes each driver's performance statistics in the individual horse's record, a nice convenience for the handicapper.

The First Race

A claiming affair for cheap trotters. Prince Randolph drops sharply in claiming price but is unacceptable as a contender. Why? Because he lost in the stretch after having everything his own way in the earlier stages.

Knotty Pine has not done anything in more than a year. Kemosa made a game showing two weeks ago and may be a contender. But Intruder's Margie and Winning Song are not. Neither is Speedy Mark, unraced since April.

County Land, idle for three weeks, should be eliminated. Prince Elby also is out, not having done a thing locally or recently. Roy's Boy broke badly nine nights ago, three weeks after a good effort at Washington Park. The only possible choices here are Kemosa (idle for two weeks in a field that includes four more recently active animals) and Roy's Boy, who is stuck with the outside berth and went into a gallop in his first effort at this track.

My advice is to pass. Daily double addicts might couple Kemosa and Roy's Boy with whatever they find in the second race.

RESULT: Kemosa (5 to 1) did absolutely zero, finishing seventh. Roy's Boy (6 to 1) raced on the outside for the first half-mile until reaching second place and managed to retain that spot to

ONE MILE TROT

1st RACE

Purse $2,400

(FIRST HALF OF DAILY DOUBLE)

Claiming. Claiming price $3,500. 3-year-olds and up.

PLEASE ASK FOR HORSE BY PROGRAM NUMBER

2:08 (Was1, '68) ($16,927) Driver-Trainer—DON BUSSE (49-4-6-6—.190) Gray-Red

9-2 1 Prince Randolph ⊗ B. g (1964), by Paul D.—Do Tone, by R. E. Mc. 1969 10 1 2 0 $2,244
Owner, Mrs. Gilbert W. Busse, Randolph, Wis. 1968 35 4 4 2 $6,650

Jun 2-694Spk⅝ 1 :31 1:04 1:35 2:062ft 5 3 1 11¼ 1nk 53½ BusseD1 5000 2:07⅕ Smart Son Eyre Yell Capri Key
May20-694Spk⅝ 1 :31 1:0141:3422:053ft 8¼ 1 3 53½ 55 65¼ BusseD3 6000 2:06⅗ Cr'wnS'ng OldRanger BraveN'wp't
May14-696Was1 1 :3131:03 1:3612:064ft 15 1 1 2h 4½ 43¼ BusseD7 6000 2:07⅖ MyIrishQu'n S'cr'tS'ss'n D'n'sTide
May 6-691Was1 1 :31 1:0241:3632:064ft 5½ 1 1 1nk 11 22¼ BusseD5 3000 2:07⅕ EyreYell Pr'ceR'nd'h Int'd'r'sM'gie
Apr17-691Was1 1 :3321:0721:4032:11 gd 13 1 1 11¼ 12 2¾ BusseD5 2500 2:11⅕ H'z'rlOaks Pr'ceR'd'lph Br'th'rR't
Feb24-691Was1 1 :3031:03 1:3812:103ft 6 3 3 43½ 62 77¼ BusseDa2 2000 2:12 Florsong DeanYankee FinalSpring

($57,202) Driver-Trainer—ALVIN STANKE (13-4-3-1—.462) Gold-Purple

8-1 2 Knotty Pine B. g (1959), by Scotch Valley—Rose Mite, by Volomite. 1969 2 0 0 0 $35
Owner, R. P. & Lavena S. Hoffmann; Northville, Mich. 1968 11 0 2 1 $1,700

Jun 6-69 Spk⅝ 1 :31 1:0141:34 2:06 ft N.B. 8 7 713 515 513 StankeA9 Qua 2:08⅗ Brazenboy Deam'n'J.W'y K'yExpr's
Jan27-69 PmP⅝ 1 :3221:05 1:3542:073ft 6¼ x8 8 8P'd up. dnf.StankeA3 1500 Dolbedoe LittleRodn'y Kickap'oLou
Jan22-69 PmP⅝ 1 :3231:0611:3722:082ft 5¾ 6 6 5 x89¼ 59¾ StankeA5 2000 2:10⅕ BairnCloud PeteDoyle Mr.Betters
Sep10-681Was1 1 1/16 :34 1:0822:1612:24 sl 5¼ 1 3 57¼ 716 8di. DaultonL2 3000 ElvaPride CarlaAnnLou MelodyHal
Apr 8-681Was1 1 :32 1:03 1:3712:083ft 7¾ 9' 9 97½ 54 22¼ DaultonL7 3500 2:09 HisGrace KnottyPine ToughStuff
Mar28-681Was1 1 :3131:0241:3612:08 ft 9¾ 9 9 85½ 65 65½ HoltG9 3500 2:09⅕ SanJ'nFr'ht CoalS'ng C'rlaAnnL'u

2:06⅘ (Was1, '68) ($15,282) Driver-Trainer—MAYO PRIEBE JR. (1-0-0-1—.333) Blue-Gold

6-1 3 Kemosa ⊗ B. m (1960), by Early Key—Tonyette, by (unproven). 1969 11 0 0 5 $1,319
Owner, Mayo Priebe, Jr., Marengo, Ill. 1968 36 6 5 2 $5,489

May28-691Spk⅝ 1 :3031:05 1:36 2:07 ft 19 6 40 66 55½ 33½ PriebeMJr5 3500 2:07⅘ SmartSon HughieCastle Kemosa
May 7-693Was1 1⅛ :32 1:05 2:0942:252ft 3½ 3 2 45½ 59 314 EdenT1 c2500 2:28⅕ JohnColby CollectFreight Kemosa
Apr28-691Was1 1 :3311:0631:4122:131sy 5 7 7 75½ 54 32½ MeyocksD2 3000 2:13⅘ JohnColby CollectFreight Kemosa
Apr15-691Was1 1 :3221:0421:3722:091gd 5¼ 7 7 97½ 88½ 89¼ DeJuliusL1 3000 2:11 HiramsSon EyreYell Brucie
Apr 2-697Was1 1 :32 1:0431:3712:091gd 18 8 70 77 44½ 33 DeJuliusL2 3000 2:09⅘ Queen'sNotion HiramsSon Kemosa
Mar17-691Was1 1 :3131:0431:3812:104ft 20 6 50 54 77 77 DeJuliusL4 3000 2:12⅕ Florsong HughieCastle RedCastle

2:07⅗ (Was1, '68) ($15,736) Driver—HARRY BURRIGHT. Trainer, C. Gordon (43-5-3-6—.202) Blue-Gold

8-1 4 Intruder's Margie B. m (1961), by The Intruder—Barbara Reed, by Wayward. 1969 13 2 0 3 $2,638
Owner, Robert Dunn, Franksville, Wis. 1968 32 6 4 6 $9,750

May28-691Spk⅝ 1 :3031:05 1:36 2:07 ft 22 1 1 31½ 44½ 53¾ BurrightH9 3500 2:07⅘ SmartSon HughieCastle Kemosa
May 6-691Was1 1 :31 1:0241:3632:064ft 6¼ 6 6 62½ 32 33¾ BurrightH4 3000 2:07⅗ EyreYell Pr'ceR'nd'h Int'd'r'sM'gie
Apr22-691Was1 1 :32 1:0541:3932:094ft 5½ 1 2 22 24 45¼ BurrightH6 3000 2:10⅘ HazearlOaks MarleneMir Florsong
Apr 7-691Was1 1 :3241:0511:39 2:093ft 9¾ 1 3 31 83½ 76¼ BurrightH1 3500 2:10⅘ Kitsarn Zeke Oaks Mike G.
Mar24-693Was1 1 :3311:08 1:4322:141sy 14 4 7 811 810 817 BurrightH6 4800 2:17⅗ ZekeOaks D'kT'wnStr'tt'r V'lleyAir
Mar10-693Was1 1 :3121:0521:3832:093ft 6¾ 6 60 53½ 55½ 53¾†BurrightH6 4800 2:10⅖ D'tchDill'rd Qu'n'sNotion GinnyL'd

2:07⅖ (Was1, '68) ($46,568) Driver—TOMMY RYAN. Trainer, K. Bartlett (6-0-0-0—.000) Gold-Silver-Black

12-1 5 Winning Song Br. g (1959), by Victory Song—Winsome Lucy, by Scotland. 1969 10 1 1 2 $3,912
Owner, Tommy Ryan, Morton Grove, Ill. 1968 25 2 3 1 $2,590

May28-691Spk⅝ 1 :3031:05 1:36 2:07 ft 9½ 4 5 78 811 78 RyanT3 3500 2:08⅗ SmartSon HughieCastle Kemosa
May13-696Was1 1 :3131:0311:3642:072ft 7¾ 5 50 41½ 67 512 RyanT3 nw400068 2:09⅘ SilverSh'rt'ge Sh'ld'nH'v'r D'nR'ph
May 6-696Was1 1 :3011:03 1:35 2:061ft 11 4 4 44½ 68 56¼ RyanT3 nw400068 2:07⅖ MyIrishQ'n K'ly'sM'l MyB'rn'sCh'f
May 1-691Was1 1 :3231:0411:3642:081ft 5½ 2 1 32 34½ 27 RyanT2 nw400068 2:09⅗ Haz'rlO'ks Winn'gS'ng Ex'c'tiveP'k
Apr28-697Was1 1 :33 1:0441:3822:11 sy 11 5 5 611 614 714 RyanT8 nw400068 2:13⅘ D'v'da'sB'y Sc'chPixie MissMcN'ra
Apr18-693Was1 1 :3331:0611:39 2:103sy 6 3 3x 612 512 414 RyanT1 nw400068 2:13⅖ ZekeOaks Dean'sTide GiroPesky

2:05⅖ (Hol1, '68) ($9,709) Driver-Trainer—HAM ADAMS (2-0-0-0—.000) Maroon-Gray

7-2 6 Speedy Mark Br. g (1962), by Speedster—Victorian, by Victory Song. 1969 5 1 2 0 $2,617
Owner, A. H. Adams, Jacksonville, Fla. 1968 11 3 2 1 $4,873

Apr 2-695Was1 1 :3111:0231:35 2:053gd 7¾ 4 30 2½ 1½ 53½ AdamsH2 nw600068 2:06⅖ Pr'c'sR'd'lph M'htyPop'l'r FullSp'd
Mar25-698Was1 1 :3241:08 1:4132:123sy 7¾ 1 1 21 33½ 23 AdamsH6 nw600068 2:13⅕ Tr'v'rHan'r Sp'dyMark SunnyPride
Feb26-69 B.M1 1 :3241:0511:40 2:103gd8-5 ▲2 1 1 11½ 2h AdamsH7 4500 2:10⅗ Glid'nH'v'r Sp'dyMark Bl'zeR'dn'y
Jan 8-69 B.M1 1 :3311:05 1:3542:07 ft 4 2 4 3 42 42½ AdamsH3 nw500068 2:07⅗ Dyn'micVict'y C.J'sH'ws D'keLiner
Jan 3-69 B.M1 1 :3231:0431:3732:083ft 3¼ 3 2 3 41¾ 1¾ AdamsH1 nw500068 2:08⅗ SpeedyMark FairVale DukeLiner
Dec23-68 Hol1 1 :32 1:0431:3632:064ft 2½ ▲5 2 2 12 2no AdamsH6 4000 2:06⅘ LadyMaryD. SpeedyMark VicArden

2:08 (Spk⅝, '68) ($23,674) Driver—JOE MARSH JR. Trainer, L. Kraman (51-8-8-7—.290) Gray-Blue-Red

10-1 7 County Land ⊗ Br. g (1961), by Isolandia—Countess Lee, by Leelike. 1969 12 2 2 1 $3,033
Owner, Brian Monieson & Martin Smith; Chicago, Ill. 1968 27 7 2 8 $11,430

May22-691Spk⅝ 1 :3131:0441:3632:081ft 32 20 2 31¼ 53¾ 95½ VallandinghamG6 3500 2:09⅖ Capri Key Blaze Rodney Eyre Yell
May12-691Was1 1 :3111:0211:36 2:073ft 17 4 5 85¼ 811 712 VallandinghamG3 3500 2:10 BombBlast Hir'msSon H'zearlOaks
Apr29-691Was1 1 :3121:0321:3622:09 ft 4¾ 40 60 78 815 818 VallandinghamG6 3500 2:12⅗ HiramsSon GinnyLad Mistaleen
Apr 7-691Was1 1 :3241:0511:39 2:093ft 6½ 40 20 2nk 96½ 917 VallandinghamG9 4000 2:13 Kitsarn Zeke Oaks Mike G.
Mar31-696Was1 1 :3241:04 1:3632:074ft 5¾ 3 3 42½ 34¼ 34¼ VallandinghamG1 4000 2:08⅗ Fr'nchGuy Wid'wMillie CountyL'nd
Mar19-697Was1 1 :3211:0341:3522:054ft 23 2 2 21¼ 21½ 22½ VallandinghamG4 4000 2:06⅖ ActiveMike CountyLand DanOakie

2:08⅖ (Nor, '68) ($8,872) Driver-Trainer—TOM MERRIMAN (24-2-5-1—.213) White-Maroon

8-1 8 Prince Elby ⊗ B. g (1962), by Elby Hanover—Mary Ruth, by Volation. 1969 17 1 0 1 $2,919
Owner, Robert Kalish, Southfield, Mich. 1968 26 5 7 5 $6,029

Jun 2-694Spk⅝ 1 :31 1:04 1:35 2:062ft 21 5 5 63½ 64 64 MerrimanT7 5000 2:07⅕ Smart Son Eyre Yell Capri Key
May17-69 Det 1 :3121:04 1:3732:104gd 13 6 7 8 62¼ 62¼ MerrimanT2 5000 2:11⅕ SpeedyNibble D.J'sAnnie LordD'le
May 7-69 Det 1 :3241:0631:3842:111ft 9¾ x8 8 8 84½ 43† NilesH7 c4000 2:11⅘ C'rlaAnnLou J'hnExpr's B'nieC'lby
†Dead heat.
Apr29-69 Det 1 :33 1:0531:3732:093ft 6¼ 70 60 7 78½ 69¾ NilesH1 4000 2:11⅖ Hava'sPrince DaringDude LizaG'n
Apr24-69 Det 1 :3141:0641:3932:122gd 10 7 7 7 73¼ 41¾ NilesH6 4000 2:12⅗ H'va'sP'nce C'rlaAnnL'u Ch'lieH'se
Apr19-69 Det 1 :33 1:0611:39 2:103gd 9¾ 20 1 2 32¾ 46½ NilesH6 5000 2:11⅘ Sp'dyNibble DevedaGirl ChrisD'r's

2:05⅗ (Hol1, '68) ($25,831) Driver-Trainer—JIM CURRAN (33-8-6-4—.384) Gray-Gold

5-1 9 Roy's Boy ⊗ B. g (1959), by Way Yonder—Lou Reynolds, by Dick Reynolds. 1969 11 3 1 1 $5,164
Owner, G. Lewis, D. Garmel, Jo Curran; Detroit, Jackson, Mich. 1968 20 4 4 2 $8,993

Jun 2-694Spk⅝ 1 :31 1:04 1:35 2:062ft 4½ 7x 7 98x 98½ 89 CurranJ2 5000 2:08⅕ Smart Son Eyre Yell Capri Key
May12-691Was1 1 :3111:0211:36 2:073ft 9¾ 60 30 32½ 34½ 44¾ CurranJ9 4000 2:08⅗ BombBlast Hir'msSon H'zearlOaks
Apr30-697Was1 1 :31 1:03 1:3612:062ft 5 4 5 63½ 98 98¼ CurranJ1 5000 2:08 Cr'wnS'ng OurProsp't Hist'yM'k'r
Apr24-691Was1 1 :3041:0211:3622:07 ft 7 8 8 84½ 56½ 36½ CurranJ4 5000 2:08⅖ ZekeOaks CrownSong Roy'sBoy
Mar19-697Was1 1 :3211:0341:3522:054ft 3¼ 8 5x 88½ 815 815 CurranJ9 5500 2:08⅘ ActiveMike CountyLand DanOakie
Mar12-691Was1 1 :3131:0411:3712:08 ft 4½ 1 1 11 11½ 11¼ CurranJ9 5000 2:08 Roy's Boy Dilemma Dan Oakie

Trackman's Selections—6 1 9

ONE MILE PACE

2nd RACE

Purse $2,600

(SECOND HALF OF DAILY DOUBLE)

Claiming. Claiming price $4,000. 3-year-olds and up. Emma C., So Fiann in for $4,800; rest for $4,000.

PLEASE ASK FOR HORSE BY PROGRAM NUMBER

2:06⅗ (V.D¾, '68) ($20,313) Driver-Trainer—CHARLES McDERMOTT (33-1-4-4—.138) Red-White-Blue

Scotch Note B. g (1961), by Sharp Note—Above All, by Scotland. 1969 10 1 0 0 $1,554
Owner, Arthur D. & Helen E. Kniffen; Homer, N. Y. 1968 36 8 2 6 $6,401

8-1 **1**
May30-69²Spk⅝ 1 :32⁴1:06³1:37³2:08²ft 11 1 2 1¼ 1¼ 1nk McDermottC⁷ 3500 2:08⅖ ScotchNote EyreNavarch E.F.C'lby
May19-69¹⁰Spk⅝ 1 :30¹1:01³1:33²2:06²ft 46 9 9 7⁸ 7⁶ 5¾ McDermottC⁹ 4000 2:07 RedEblis PhilDorw'd Emaj'n'sP'de
May13-69⁷Was¹ 1 :31⁴1:03²1:36⁴2:07 ft 62 7 7 6³ 3¼ 6½ McDermottC⁶ 5000 2:08⅕ LouieH. Laurinda SatinGrattan
May 2-69¹Was¹ 1 :30 1:01¹1:34²2:04⁴ft 29 5⁰ 1 2½ 7¹¹ 7¹⁸ McDermottC⁹ 5000 2:08⅖ SirTruGallant Renard MissFed'rski
Apr21-69⁸Was¹ 1 :30 1:02¹1:35⁴2:07¹ft 23 8 8⁰ 8⁵ 8⁵ 7¼ TallmanT⁶ 5000 2:08⅕ LoBeGo B'neyBl'kstone Diplo'tTrip
Apr 9-69¹⁰Was¹ 1 :31¹1:04⁴1:37 2:07³ft 12 4 5 5¾ 4½ 4⁴ TallmanT¹ 5000 2:08⅘ V'sityKnight Sh'ft'rH'll Rick'sR'y'l

2:09⅗ (F.P¹, '68) ($2,610) Driver—WILLIAM ROSEBOOM. Trainer, C. Weber (24-1-3-1—.125) Gold-Purple

Emma C. B. f (1965), by Brooks Hanover—Princess First, by Bay Prince. 1969 8 2 2 0 $2,400
Owner, Silas Schmidtgall, Fairbury, Ill. 1968 21 4 5 2 $1,925

8-1 **2**
May28-69⁴Spk⅝ 1 :29³1:01¹1:32¹2:03³ft 27 9 8 7⁷½ 5⁶½ 7¹⁶ RoseboomW⁹ n3R 2:06⅘ Pancho ChiefRed RangerRichard
May16-69³Was¹ 1 :30⁴1:02²1:33⁴2:05 ft 9½ 7 7 6⁴½ 5⁶½ 6¹³ RoseboomW⁷ nw3000⁶⁸ 2:07⅗ M'rioH'n'v'r Andy'sD'n D'tyG.H'yes
May 1-69⁶Was¹ 1 :31 1:02¹1:35²2:06¹ft 32 9 9 6⁴ 2¹½ 2⁴ RoseboomW⁹ nw3000⁶⁸ 2:07 F'lshieR'th EmmaC. ByeByeSt'rl'g
Apr19-69¹⁰Was¹ 1 :30⁴1:03 1:35³2:06¹ft 34 7 7 8⁵½ 4² 6⁹¾ RoseboomW⁸ nw3000⁶⁸ 2:08⅕ Pleasem CrispChief ShiawayAdios
Apr 9-69³Was¹ 1 :31 1:04³1:37⁴2:07²ft 8½ 1 2 2¹½ 2³ 2⁵½ RoseboomW⁵ nw3000⁶⁸ 2:08⅗ Drummondville EmmaC. AdiosRunt
Mar28-69⁷Was¹ 1 :30³1:03²1:36³2:06¹ft 11 5 5 5⁴½ 4⁶ 7⁹½ RoseboomW² nw3000⁶⁸ 2:08⅕ Fr'tyTime Dr'm'dv'le St'teExp'sN.

2:06⅗ (PmP⅝, '69) ($3,217) Driver—HAROLD FISHER. Trainer, D. Guerrettaz (16-3-4-3—.389) Green-Gold

So Fiann Ch. f (1965), by Knox Hanover—Louise Lenawee, by Chief Lenawee. 1969 14 1 2 2 $2,005
Owner, Sandra Fisher, Adrian, Mich. 1968 27 2 8 4 $3,217

6-1 **3**
May26-69¹⁰Spk⅝ 1 :31²1:02⁴1:34 2:05¹ft 5¾ 3 4 4²½ 3²½ 5⁴½ GuerrettazD⁴ 4800 2:06⅕ ShawnHill PhyllisC.Sc't PrebleCh'f
May16-69⁶Was¹ 1 :31¹1:00⁴1:32¹2:04¹ft 16 5 6 6⁹ 5⁸ 4⁹ FisherH⁷ 4800 2:06 RichAdios GlennH.W. ChiefSmile
May 9-69³Was¹ 1 :32¹1:04 1:38 2:10¹sy 20 8 9 7³½ 3⁴½ 4⁴¾ FisherH⁹ 4800 2:11⅕ Sh'ft'rH'll B'blingBr'ke H'nry'sC'sh
May 2-69³Was¹ 1 :31²1:05 1:37⁴2:07⁴ft 5½ 2 2 2¹ 2²½ 3⁸ FisherH¹ 4800 2:09⅘ RedEblis ChiefReveler SoFiann
Mar26-69 PmP⅝ 1 :31¹1:03⁴1:33⁴2:05²sy 16 4 5 5 4³ 5⁴ FisherH² Cond 2:06⅕ ChiefFarvel CounselB. Outerail
Mar19-69 PmP⅝ 1 :29³1:03¹1:33¹2:03⁴ft 7½ 4 4 2 2¹½ 6⁸¼ FisherH² Cond 2:05⅘ Gall'tArmbro Ch'fF'rv'l M'mieQu'n

2:07⅘ (B.R, '69) ($1,187) Driver-Trainer—ROBERT WILLIAMS (44-12-10-1—.407) Purple-White

Doctor Kildare Br. g (1962), by Last Scott—Blue Jet, by Van Derby. 1969 7 1 0 0 $425
Owner, P. Jensen & A. T. Silverstein; Pontiac, Detroit, Mich. 1968 16 1 4 1 $359

7-2 **4**
May27-69²Spk⅝ 1 :30²1:03²1:35²2:06⁴ft 6-5 ▲3⁰ 10 1¼ 2¾ 7³¼ SlyzuikG⁵ c3000 2:07⅖ PerryWin SilverDella WiggleWick
May13-69 B.R 1 :33 1:05³1:37²2:07⁴ft 2¾ 5 6 8 8¹¹ 7¹⁵ WetzelJ³ nw3500⁶⁸⁶⁹ 2:10⅘ They'reOff Edw'rdSp'nc'r J'y'usL'd
May 7-69 B.R 1 :31¹1:04¹1:37 2:07⁴ft 6-5 ▲2 2 2 2¾ 1¼ WetzelJ² Cond 2:07⅘ D't'rKild're R'd'g'rFl'me M'd'w're
Apr30-69 B.R 1 :34 1:07³1:40⁴2:13²gdN.B. 2 2 2 2² 2²¼ WetzelJ⁴ Qua 2:13⅘ Eblis'sReEcho D't'rKild'e Tr'p'sG'y
Jan25-69 Lithgow, Australia—Finished 5 in a 1 mile race in 2:10⅘, (S. Bond).
Jan23-69 Parramatta, Australia—Finished 7 in an about 1¾ miles race in 3:37⅖, (S. Bond).

2:05⅕ (Was¹, '68) ($34,106) Driver-Trainer—GENE VALLANDINGHAM (24-0-1-3—.065) Red-White-Blue

Hi Buster ⊗ Br. g (1962), by Flashy Jamie—Kay Barnes, by Zeb Barnes. 1969 14 2 0 0 $4,575
Owner, Alan Riseman, Los Angeles, Calif. 1968 35 4 5 5 $14,061

6-1 **5**
May31-69³Spk⅝ 1 :30¹1:01³1:32⁴2:04¹ft 13 3 4 8⁵½ 7⁵½ 5⁵¼ VallandinghamG¹ 5000 2:05⅕ SportAdio Colvin'sLad O.B'sAdm'l
May22-69⁴Spk⅝ 1 :31¹1:04 1:35³2:06³ft 12 6 6 7³¼ 7³½ 6³ VallandinghamG⁵ 5000 2:07⅕ FlamingParker CityCom'd C'nieL.
May12-69⁷Was¹ 5½f :28³1:00¹ 1:23⁴ft 13 4 5 5⁴½ 2nk 1¹ VallandinghamG⁵ 4500 1:23⅘ Hi Buster Whizmor Bonanza Bill
May 2-69¹Was¹ 1 :30 1:01¹1:34²2:04⁴ft 8½ 1 2 4²x 9²⁴ 8di. VallandinghamG⁶ 5000 SirTruGallant Renard MissFed'rski
Apr25-69¹⁰Was¹ 1 :31²1:02³1:34⁴2:06¹ft 16 3 4 5²½ix8²⁰ 7²¹ VallandinghamG² 5000 2:10⅖ Mich'lB. B'kieGr't'n M'sM'hy'sW'y
Apr15-69⁹Was¹ 1 :31³1:03⁴1:36⁴2:06⁴gd 12 1 3 4²½ 6⁴¼ 7⁷½ VallandinghamG⁴ 5000 2:08⅖ PiuteBuckley MichaelB. Brightest

2:03 (Hol¹, '68) ($62,071) Driver-Trainer—LLOYD DAULTON (17-2-1-1—.170) Gold-Blue

Shawn Hill ⊗ Br. g (1959), by Aralac—Merbrooke, by Brookdale. Owner, 1969 8 2 3 0 $5,773
L. Daulton & Kai Rothenborg; Nancy, Ky.; Los Angeles, Calif. 1968 40 11 9 5 $15,945

4-1 **6**
May26-69¹⁰Spk⅝ 1 :31²1:02⁴1:34 2:05¹ft 9-5 ▲1⁰ 1 1¼ 1¼ 1² DaultonL⁵ 4000 2:05⅕ ShawnHill PhyllisC.Sc't PrebleCh'f
May14-69¹⁰Was¹ 1 :31 1:02³1:36¹2:07 ft 6-5 ▲3⁰ 3 2h 1² 2½ DaultonL⁸ 4000 2:07⅕ MissLuella ShawnHill FriscoCross
May 3-69¹Was¹ 1 :31³1:02¹1:35²2:05²ft 3¾ 2 2 2h 3³½ 2⁶ DaultonL⁶ 4000 2:06⅗ Laurinda Shawn Hill Active Ruth
Apr21-69¹⁰Was¹ 1 :30²1:02¹1:34³2:06⁴ft 10 6 6 6¹⁰ 4⁷½ 2²¾ DaultonL⁸ 4000 2:07⅖ JayArN. ShawnHill MissFedorski
Apr11-69⁷Was¹ 1 :30⁴1:02¹1:35²2:06⁴ft 6¼ 3⁰x8⁰ 9¹⁷ 9²⁴ 9²⁵ BerryD⁷ 4000 2:11⅘ Athl'eR'n'lds Gl'nnPrimr'e LoBeGo
Apr 3-69¹⁰Was¹ 1 :30²1:02¹1:34⁴2:06 ft 2½ ▲7 6⁰ 6⁴ 6⁵ 4⁴½ DaultonL¹ 4000 2:07 C'nnieL. R'thAnnAbbe Del'y'dF'm's

2:07⅖ (Spk⅝, '68) ($10,761) Driver-Trainer—JACK BELTZ (3-1-0-0—.333) White-Blue

Alwyn Yates Br. g (1963), by Don Adios—Alabam, by Brookdale. 1969 12 3 2 2 $6,986
Owner, Jack Beltz, DeLeon Springs, Fla. 1968 25 2 8 1 $6,665

10-1 **7**
May30-69²Spk⅝ 1 :32⁴1:06³1:37³2:08²ft 4¾ 2 3 5³½ 5³ 5² BeltzJ⁴ 3500 2:08⅖ ScotchNote EyreNavarch E.F.C'lby
May12-69⁷Was¹ 5½f :28³1:00¹ 1:23⁴ft 3¼ ▲7 6⁰ 8⁶½ 7³ 4⁴½ BeltzJ³ 4000 1:24⅘ Hi Buster Whizmor Bonanza Bill
May 5-69⁴Was¹ 5½f :28 :59² 1:23¹ft 4¼ 2 3 4⁴½ 4²½ 3nk†BeltzJ⁶ 4000 1:23⅕ Whizmor AlwynYates BonanzaBill
†Placed second through disqualification.
Apr26-69³Was¹ 5½f :27⁴ :59⁴ 1:24¹ft 4¾ 2 2 2¹x 6¹³ 6⁹ BeltzJ⁹ 4000 1:26 B'zaB'l Em'j'n'sP'de M'sB'k'yeL'd
Apr19-69³Was¹ 5½f :29 1:00³ 1:24²ft 2 ▲5 5 5³½ 3²½ 3½ BeltzJ⁴ 4000 1:24⅗ L'dyB'rdJ'y C'ny'sPh'p Alw'nY'tes
Apr12-69³Was¹ 5½f :28⁴1:00² 1:23²ft 4¼ 2 3 2⁴ 1¹ 1⁶ BeltzJ¹ 3000 1:23⅖ AlwynYates BonanzaBill CraftyBill

($1,469) Driver-Trainer—ROBERT FARRINGTON (68-17-8-7—.350) Red-Gray

Tough Trot B. g (1959), by Lawnrock—Medomeara, by Medoro. 1969 3 0 2 1 $646
Owner, Robert Farrington, Richwood, Ohio. 1968 30 0 1 4 $241

6-1 **8**
May31-69¹Spk⅝ 1 :29³1:02³1:34 2:05²ft 2½ 4⁰ 4 2nk 2¹ 3¹¼ DennisJ⁸ c3000 2:05⅗ FunnyMan DominionK. ToughTrot
May19-69 B.R 1 :32²1:05¹1:40²2:13⁴sl 6-5 ▲6 5 6 6³¾ 2no†HodginsJ⁴ nw1000⁶⁸⁶⁹ 2:13⅘ OurGirlChance GuySail'r ToughTr't
†Dead heat.
May 8-69 B.R 1 :32⁴1:06³1:40 2:13³sy 4-5 ▲1⁰ 1 1 1¹ 2¾ WetzelJ⁵ nw1500⁶⁸⁶⁹ 2:13⅘ Nifty'sJudge ToughTrot TooSweet
Apr30-69 B.R 1 :32¹1:05 1:38³2:11²gdN.B. 2 2 2 2¹¼ 3³¾ WetzelJ² Qua 2:12⅕ EdwardSpencer Lois'Dr'm T'ghTr't
Dec27-68 Bankstown, New Zealand—Finished 6 in a 1½ miles race in 3:27, (H. Redmile).

2:09⅕ (Mea⅝, '68) ($27,439) Driver—HARRY BURRIGHT. Trainer, A. Shuter (43-5-3-6—.202) Blue-Gold

Orphan Whitney B. g (1956), by H. D. Hanover—Highland Peggy, by Scotland. 1969 2 0 0 0 $100
Owner, Ancil L. Shuter, Bedford, Ky. 1968 28 4 1 4 $2,291

20-1 **9**
May26-69¹Spk⅝ 1 :30⁴1:02²1:34³2:06¹ft 64 2 3 4⁹ 6¹¹ 5¹⁴ BurrightH⁸ 2500 2:09 Pal'rC'shC'ban R'thmAid Ch'kM'rs
May 8-69⁴Was¹ 1 :32²1:05⁴1:39⁴2:12¹sy 17 6 5 5⁷x 7²⁰ 6²¹ PaisleyW¹ 2500 2:16⅖ BrioSc'tt Painter'sCh'ce Van'sCh'f
Aug 2-68 Mea⅝ 1 :30²1:04 1:35⁴2:08²ft 6-5 ▲x7x7 7 7 7di. WilburnT⁴ 1250 LocalAdeline D'n'ldB'rn's R'xR'n'd
Jly 29-68 Mea⅝ 1 :32 1:06 1:38 2:10¹ft 3 5 5 7 7⁴½ 6³¾ WilburnT⁵ 1500 2:11 Lynnh'rstV'lo H'th'rD'min'n T'yP'r
Jly 20-68 Mea⅝ 1 :31²1:04²1:38¹2:10¹ft 4½ 8 6 4 4²½ 1²¼ WilburnT⁸ 1250 2:10⅕ OrphanWhitn'y B'dyP'rd'e R'y'lJ'y
Jly 15-68 Mea⅝ 1 :31 1:04¹1:36 2:09²ft 2¾ 6 6 5 4⁷½ 1¾ WilburnT⁵ 1250 2:09⅗ Orph'nWhitn'y M'rc'sP'k Imp'leT'd

Trackman's Selections—4 6 8

ONE MILE PACE

3rd RACE

Purse $2,200

Conditioned. Colts and geldings. Illinois bred. Maidens. Races for $750 or less not considered.

PLEASE ASK FOR HORSE BY PROGRAM NUMBER

8-1 — 1
(——) Driver-Trainer—SONNY GRAHAM (6-1-0-0—.167) White-Blue
Roman Empire B. g (1963), by Empire Hanover—Holly Colleen, by Peter Colleen. 1969 1 M 0 0 (——)
Owner, Richard A. & Beverly L. Kozlowski; Royal Oak, Mich. 1968 0 M 0 0 (——)
Jun 4-692Spk⅝ 1 :3111:0341:35 2:062gd 31 8 8 911 812 68 GrahamS8 Mdn 2:08 Edg'w'dBr't Ch'p'ld've S'rch'rW've
May26-69 Spk⅝ 1 :3241:0511:3822:091ft N.B. 5 5 44 44¼ 32¼ GrahamS1 Qua 2:09⅗ AirV'nt're D'miT'sse R'm'nEmpire
May13-69 Lex1 1 :3241:03 1:35 2:071ft N.B. 8 4 4 41¼ 3½ GrahamS6 Qua 2:07⅕ L'taBr'kie K'yst'neG'l R'm'nE'pire

6-1 — 2
(——) Driver-Trainer—DON BUSSE (49-4-6-6—.190) Gray-Red
Jack Knight B. c (1965), by Knight Pilot—Victory Jacky, by Bristle Hanover. 1969 1 M 0 0 (——)
Owner, Ray Gillilan, Palos Verdes Penninsula, Calif. 1968 0 M 0 0 (——)
Jun 2-693Spk⅝ 1 :30 1:02 1:3312:052ft 47 9 8 75½ 55 66¼ GillilanRJ8 4800 2:06⅗ VoloPurdue CrispChief Headstart
May20-69 Spk⅝ 1 :3221:0511:37 2:082ft N.B. 70 70 811 88 74½ GillilanRJ7 Qua 2:09⅘ ElvisH'v'r M'rieKiwi D'minic'sPick
May 6-69 Was1 1 :3021:03 1:3712:094ft N.B. 7 40 34 55 46½ GillilanRJ8 Qua 2:11⅕ AmlinAdios B.Beck'r P'interDirect

5-1 — 3
2:08⅗ (Was1, '69) ($1,148) Driver—NELSON WILLIS. Trainer, C. Willis (14-1-3-1—.214) Maroon-Gray-White
Tug Way B. g (1963), by Direct Way—Mission Girl, by Congressional. 1969 3 0 0 0 $426
Owner, F. Yanagidate & A. S. Miller; Chicago, Elmwood Park, Ill. 1968 0 0 0 0 (——)
Jun 4-694Spk⅝ 1 :3121:0531:38 2:09 gd 4¼ 2 2 31½ 2½ 54 WillisC1 Mdn 2:09⅘ DemiTasse IrishDuane TheFooler
May21-694Spk⅝ 1 :3121:0431:3742:10 sy 14 7 7 65 46 43 WillisC9 Mdn 2:10⅗ D'dyA'dyTh'r R'd'sSh'd'w Ch'lD've
May 8-692Was1 1 :3021:0341:38 2:094sy 11 3 5 73½ 65½ 55¼ WillisC2 nw2000 2:10⅘ C'syMcKlyo Br'kn'llCh't'h K'g'sF'll
May 2-69 Was1 1 :31 1:04 1:3742:083ft N.B. 2 2 21½ 11½ 13 WillisC3 Qua 2:08⅗ TugWay TeddyLincoln DanReed
Jly 17-67 Spk⅝ 1 :3021:0411:3522:073ft 15 6 6 76 43½ 54½ WillisC4 nw2000 2:08⅖ M'ncy'sQ'nk T'py'sP'de Mir'cleD'ke
Jly 5-67 Spk⅝ 1 :3021:04 1:3522:061ft 39 9 9 65 56 66 WillisC9 nw2000 2:07⅖ WidowGay JayAdioway ChiefSun

10-1 — 4
(——) Driver—HAROLD FISHER. Trainer, D. Guerrettaz (16-3-4-3—.389) Green-Gold
Mr. Vincent B. g (1965), by Waylay—Jessie Reed, by Darnley. 1969 0 M 0 0 (——)
Owner, Richard J. Abraham, Adrian, Mich. 1968 0 M 0 0 (——)
May31-69 Spk⅝ 1 :3031:0221:3422:044ft N.B. 8 8 716 719 716 FisherH7 Qua 2:08 Cupid'sArrow J.S.M. FreightTr'k'r

10-1 — 5
2:08⅗ (Was1, '68) ($408) Driver—ROBERT WILLIAMS. Trainer, F. Bettis (44-12-10-1—.407) Purple-White
Speedy Dennis B. g (1963), by Chief Strong—Success Honoretta, by His Honor. 1969 3 M 0 0 $130
Owner, E. Siena, Chicago, Ill. 1968 5 M 0 0 $408
May21-694Spk⅝ 1 :3121:0431:3742:10 sy 21 6 6 810 818 920 WilliamsR3 Mdn 2:14 D'dyA'dyTh'r R'd'sSh'd'w Ch'lD've
May 6-693Was1 1 :3011:0421:3732:073ft 25 5 5 66 58 58¼ BettisF5 nw1000 2:09⅕ Sh'ry'sTime G'ldenD'ze Stripe'sse
Apr29-693Was1 1 :3121:0211:3432:064ft 21 6 7 78½ 714 821 BettisF5 nw1000 2:11 King'sFull B'k'rM'rsh Reid'sSh'd'w
Nov20-687May 1 :31 1:0321:3632:091ft 35 6 6 84½ 63½ 65½ BettisF6 nw2500 2:10⅖ TheG'tW'ln't AdiosP'le Sh'y'sK'ht
Nov14-681May 1 :3221:0611:4042:15 sy 3¾ 30 2 21 1h 58½ BettisF6 nw1000 2:16⅘ Adios Runt Western's Sheri Akers
Nov 7-687May 1 :3321:0641:3942:111gd 47 4 4 31½ 21½ 42½ BettisF7 nw2500 2:11⅗ PaulE.Dixon Flo'sTime Lydia'sGirl

5-1 — 6
2:11 gd (Sandwich, '69) ($947) Driver—JOE O'BRIEN. Trainer, J. Baier (46-5-8-5—.242) Gold-White
King Selka B. g (1966), by Selka's King—Harvabrook, by Harvere. 1969 2 0 0 0 $146
Owner, J. Baier & K. E. Wiedrick; Elgin, Ill. 1968 11 2 3 3 $947
May25-69 Sand 1 :35 1:1021:43 2:141gdN.B. 5 40 2 2½ 23 JamesK1 st210 2:14⅘ PrairieByrd KingSelka G'r'ldineK'g
May25-69 Sand 1 :3321:0721:40 2:11 gdN.B. 3 10 1 1h 1no JamesK1 st210 2:11 KingSelka PrairieByrd G'r'ldineK'g
Sep 1-68 Mendota—Finished 2-2 in two non-wagering races in 2:11⅘ and 2:09⅕, good (W. Carney).
Jly 28-68 Cambridge—Finished 3-3 in two non-wagering races in 2:07 and 2:09, good (K. James).
Jly 7-68 Aledo—Won two non-wagering races in 2:13 and 2:13, good (K. James).
Jun23-68 Mend 1 :34 1:08 1:4322:16 gdN.B. 4 4 2 1no 2no JamesK3 st201 2:16 L.B.Crystal KingSelka Ev'n'gPl's're

3-1 — 7
2:09⅘ (Was1, '69) (——) Driver-Trainer—DELBERT G. INSKO (24-3-0-5—.194) Purple-Gold
G. T. Winter B. g (1966), by Winter Time—Erleta, by Wilmington. 1969 2 M 0 1 $394
Owner, Brown & Chevelle Farms; Viola, Aledo, Ill. 1968 4 M 0 0 (——)
May31-69 Spk⅝ 1 :3031:0221:3422:044ft N.B. 5 5 56 57 45½ InskoDG8 Qua 2:06 Cupid'sArrow J.S.M. FreightTr'k'r
May28-6910Spk⅝ 1 :35 1:08 1:3922:103ft 18 50 1 43 46 32½ InskoDG7 Mdn 2:11⅕ TimmieWin J. S. M. G.T.Winter
May16-692Was1 1 :31 1:0441:3642:072ft 6½ 8 7 58½ 58½ 514 InskoDG4 nw1000 2:10⅕ Jet Bro Regal An Amlin Adios
Apr30-69 Was1 1 :32 1:0531:3832:094ft N.B. 1 1 11½ 12 11½ FrancisL3 Qua 2:09⅘ G.T.Winter RushOn Slick
Jun16-68 Morris 1 :34 1:0821:4112:131gdN.B. 6 6 6 6 6di. BusseD6 st145 Front'rBruce L'dyTrip D'zleQueen
Jun16-68 Morris 1 :3321:09 1:43 2:141gdN.B. 6 6 6 622 6di. BusseD6 st145 FrontierBruce LadyTrip T'scoByrd

8-1 — 8
(——) Driver-Trainer—WENCE MacDONALD (9-0-2-2—.198) White-Blue
Torpedo Pat Ch. g (1966), by Torpedo Hanover—Patty Byrd, by Poplar Byrd. 1969 5 M 0 0 $240
Owner, Wenceslas MacDonald, Indianapolis, Ind. 1968 0 M 0 0 (——)
Jun 6-692Spk⅝ 1 :3111:0421:3632:081ft 60 20 1 52½ 88x 77½ MacDonaldW9 n2R 2:09⅘ Fr'kD'zl'w'y Silv'rTr'fic Dill'rD'll'r
Jun 2-69 Spk⅝ 1 :2941:0211:33 2:051ft N.B. 4 4 48½ 46½ 47½ MacDonaldW1 Qua 2:06⅘ Stately SierraBilly DiamondJoeN.
May28-6910Spk⅝ 1 :35 1:08 1:3922:103ft 47 3 4 54 59 55 MacDonaldW1 Mdn 2:11⅗ TimmieWin J. S. M. G.T.Winter
May19-692Spk⅝ 1 :32 1:0611:3942:102ft 52 5 5 84 96 95½ MacDonaldW3 Mdn 2:11⅗ Out O Miway Sherry'sTime Mitar
May13-691Was1 1 :3111:0431:3712:081ft 28 3 5 46 47½ 55½ MacDonaldW3 nw1000 2:09⅘ DillerDean DanReed SampsonTime
May 1-692Was1 1 :3041:0321:35 2:051ft 9¾ 7 8 811 715 719 MacDonaldW5 nw1000 2:09 Ch'ryB'mb K'yst'eExpr's D'naR'b'a

10-1 — 9
2:11⅘ (Elkhorn, '68) ($425) Driver-Trainer—STANLEY BANKS (23-4-3-0—.246) White-Purple
New Rule Ch. g (1966), by Newport—Miss Fuzzy, by H. D. Hanover. 1969 4 0 0 0 $318
Ow., Banks, Peterman-J. Langley; P'l's Hts., P'k F'r'st, O'k P'k., Ill. 1968 9 2 1 0 $425
Jun 4-692Spk⅝ 1 :3111:0341:35 2:062gd 39 7 7 89 914 919 BanksS7 Mdn 2:10⅕ Edg'w'dBr't Ch'p'ld've S'rch'rW've
May21-694Spk⅝ 1 :3121:0431:3742:10 sy 12 20 4 53½ 59 511 BanksS5 Mdn 2:12⅕ D'dyA'dyTh'r R'd'sSh'd'w Ch'lD've
May 8-693Was1 1 :3231:0741:4212:131sy 17 6 6 53½ 45 43½ BanksS5 nw1000 2:13⅘ ChanceyBeau All Go FourStarFrost
Apr29-693Was1 1 :3121:0211:3432:064ft 7¾ 3 5 46½ 512 616 BanksS3 nw1000 2:10 King'sFull B'k'rM'rsh Reid'sSh'd'w
Sep 2-68 Elkhorn—Finished 2-1 in two non-wagering races in 2:13⅖ and 2:11⅘, good (S. Banks).
Aug27-68 Spk⅝ 1 :32 1:0331:3542:072ft N.B. 1 2 23 47½ 413 BanksS6 Qua 2:10 Lo'sKing KingeryExpr's Sn'pyP'nce

Trackman's Selections—7 6 3

ONE MILE TROT — **4th RACE** — **Purse $2,500**

Conditioned. 3-, 4- and 5-year-olds. Non-winners of $1,250 1st money twice in last 10 starts.
Non-winners of $20,000 in 1968-1969 combined.

PLEASE ASK FOR HORSE BY PROGRAM NUMBER

8-1 — 1
2:07⅕ (Spk⅝, '69) ($2,845) Driver-Trainer—WILLIAM KLOPP (2-1-0-1—.667) Green-Gray
Amoca Br. g (1964), by Demon Van—Secoma, by Chestertown. Owner, Wm. G. Klopp, Batavia, Ill.
1969 2 1 0 1 $1,488
1968 11 6 2 3 $2,845

Jun 2-691Spk⅝ 1 :3041:06 1:3522:071ft 2¼ 1 1 1² 1½ 1½ KloppW5 n3R 2:07⅕ Amoca SpeedA Plenty MuchoPride
May26-693Spk⅝ 1 :3111:0331:3422:05 ft 6¼ 2 2 3½ 3¾ 3⁵ KloppW3 n3R 2:06 BakerStreet SheerSpeed Amoca
Nov25-684May 1 :3041:0411:3712:09 ft 3-5 *4 4⁰ 1h 1¹ 1¾ KloppW1 nw300068 2:09 Amoca MelodyHal FullofFun
Nov15-683May 1 :3131:0341:3622:091gd 3¾ 2⁰ 2⁰ 3¼ 2¼ 2½ KloppW7 nw400068 2:09⅖ HappyNewport Amoca TheFullb'ck
Nov 7-683May 1 :32 1:0411:3732:102gd 6¾ 7⁰ 5⁰ 3¹ 2¾ 1h KloppW7 nw300068 2:10⅖ Amoca JollyDuke SeaKing
Oct23-68 May 1 :3211:0421:3712:101ft N.B.6 6 6⁷ 3¼ 3¼ KloppW6 Qua 2:10⅗ Linden LadyBerry Amoca

12-1 — 2
2:03⅖ (Lex1, '68) ($9,646) Driver-Trainer—FRANK TODD (12-1-1-1—.157) Blue-White
Special Product Br. h (1964), by Something Special—Satin Hanover, by Dean Hanover. Owner, Hawley Todd, Miamiville, Ohio.
1969 14 2 2 2 $3,764
1968 26 3 4 2 $3,892

Jun 4-693Spk⅝ 1 :3111:0231:3442:063gd 13 5⁰ 4x 6⁵½ 5⁴½x5⁵½ ToddF8 nw12502-10 2:07⅘ Cr'ftyL'b'll BigG'meP'k P'p'l'rFr't
May27-696Spk⅝ 1 :3011:0111:3242:033ft 27 8⁰ 9x 8¹⁸ 8²²x9di. ToddF8 nw12502-8 G'lie'sR'thm W'ttaAm'ss'n F'llSp'd
May15-69 Det 1 :3231:0511:3732:093ft 4¼ 2⁰ 1 1 1¹ 1² ToddFSr4 nw65006869 2:09⅗ Spec'lPr'd't RhythmV'lo H'hl'dP'k
May 8-69 Det 1 :3041:0431:35 2:071ft 4 4 4⁰ 3 3⁵½xx6²¹ ToddFSr2 nw65006869 2:11⅘ Oak Grove Mainlander Deveda Girl
May 1-69 Det 1 :3211:0331:3622:081ft 5 1 1 1 1¾ 3½ ToddFSr5 nw65006869 2:08⅕ M'nl'nd'r Kit'sTr'x Spec'lProduct
Apr21-69 Det 1 :3241:0531:39 2:113gd 4¾ 2⁰ 1 1 1¹ 1¹ ToddFSr8 Cond 2:11⅗ SpecialProduct R'ndyD. ScotchD'g

7-2 — 3
2:05⅕ (Spk⅝, '69) ($6,417) Driver-Trainer—JOE MARSH JR. (51-8-8-7—.290) Gray-Blue-Red
Portfolio ⊗ B. c (1966), by Porterhouse—Proxiecan, by Florican. Owner, Koehler Brothers; Findlay, Ohio.
1969 1 1 0 0 $1,250
1968 16 12 1 0 $6,417

Jun 3-693Spk⅝ 1 :31 1:03 1:3432:051ft 1 *4⁰ 1 1¼ 1½ 1½ MarshJJr9 nw12502-8 2:05⅕ Portfolio Dean'sTide DawnR'dolph
May26-69 Spk⅝ 1 :3221:0421:3632:072ft N.B. 1 1 1² 1²½ 1³½ MarshJJr4 Qua 2:07⅖ Portfolio VolcanicDan WoodU.
Sep19-68 Dela 1 :3041:0311:36 2:064ft 9½ 1 1 2 4⁷½xx6¹⁷ MarshJJr6 st2660 2:10⅕ HassieBlaze MedalFrost Richey
Sep19-68 Dela 1 :3211:0631:3832:092ft 6-5 *2 2 3 x3⁵ 5¹⁶†MarshJJr6 st2660 2:12⅘ MedalFrost HassieBlaze Richey
†Disqualified and placed sixth.
Sep 9-68 Montpelier—Won one non-wagering race in 2:15, sloppy (C. Sylvester).
Sep 2-68 Wauseon—Won two non-wagering races in 2:13⅘ and 2:14, fast (C. Sylvester).

5-1 — 4
2:03⅖ (Hol1, '68) ($13,059) Driver—JOE O'BRIEN. Trainer, F. Redden (46-5-8-5—.242) Gold-White
Crafty Lobell ⊗ Br. g (1964), by Hickory Smoke—Cita Mac, by His Excellency. Owner, B. N. Redden, Mayfield, Ky.
1969 13 4 2 1 $8,018
1968 27 3 2 5 $9,001

Jun 4-693Spk⅝ 1 :3111:0231:3442:063gd 9-5 *2 3 3²½ 2h 1½ O'BrienJ1 nw12502-10 2:06⅗ Cr'ftyL'b'll BigG'meP'k P'p'l'rFr't
May28-695Spk⅝ 1 :3041:0331:34 2:041ft 9¼ 4 4 6⁴½ 5⁴½ 4⁴½ O'BrienJ2 nw15008 2:05⅕ SaraRodney DillyVic GaleForce
May22-695Spk⅝ 1 :3031:0141:3342:05 ft 8 4⁰ 4⁰ 7⁵½ 8⁶ 7⁶½ O'BrienJ7 nw15008 2:06⅖ Frisco Lad Gale Force Cambev
Mar 7-69 B.M1 1 :3141:0421:3532:053ft 12 6 6 6 6⁴ 6⁴¾ WilliamsR4 Cond 2:06⅗ DynamicVict'ry Tr'v'rH'n'v'r L'rS'n
Mar 4-69 B.M1 1 :3311:06 1:3732:072ft 5¾ 1 2 2 2¹ 4³½ ReddenF6 15400 2:08⅕ G'ytideTheGr't Dy'micV'y P'eK'm
Feb28-69 B.M1 1 :33 1:0741:41 2:11 sy 12 2 3 2 2¹ 5³½†RichmondR3 w60006869 2:11⅘ G'ytideTheGr't Tr'v'rH'n'v'r B'rM'n

8-1 — 5
2:05 (Lex1, '68) ($12,149) Driver-Trainer—SONNY GRAHAM (5-1-0-0—.200) White-Blue
Poinciana Br. f (1966), by Hickory Smoke—Pixie Hanover, by Hoot Mon. Owner, Laura F. Griffin, Brimfield, Ill.
1969 4 0 1 0 $340
1968 23 7 7 2 $12,149

Jun 5-693Spk⅝ 1 :3131:0221:3332:051ft 5¼ 9x 9 8¹⁹ 7¹⁶ 7¹⁴ GrahamS4 n4R 2:08 Bilmar ForestFlower Lindy'sLady
May28-693Spk⅝ 1 :3121:0321:3342:04 ft 3½ 4 4 4⁴½ 4⁶ 5⁷ GrahamS4 nw12502-10 2:05⅖ MarkRod Pop'l'rFr't BelleGalop'ne
May16-69 Lex1 1 :3041:0131:3442:034ft 9 3 4 4 4² 5⁴½ GrahamS2 w3000 2:04⅗ MarlynVan K'nt'ckyAdmir'l Q'sM'e
May 9-69 Lex1 1 :3221:0611:4022:113sl 8-5 *4⁰ 4⁰ 4 2¹ 2nk GrahamS6 w3000 2:11⅗ Nancy'sDarnley Poinciana TitusG.
Oct 1-68 Lex1 1 :2941:0121:3312:022ft 62 12x12 13 13 13di. GrahamS9 st5075 Parula SheerSpeed Brocade
Sep25-68 Lex1 1 :29 1:00 1:3242:022ft 54x10 10 10x 10 10di. GrahamS7 st7564 SparklingMolly SheerSpeed Parula

6-1 — 6
2:05⅕ (Spk⅝, '69) ($1,249) Driver-Trainer—ERNEST MILLER (6-1-1-0—.259) Black-Gold-Gray
Bilmar B. g (1964), by Newport Mascot—Marimar, by Willglow. Owner, Wm. R. Marquis, Waunakee, Wis.
1969 14 4 4 1 $3,971
1968 14 2 4 2 $1,169

Jun 5-693Spk⅝ 1 :3131:0221:3332:051ft 5¼ 4⁰ 2⁰ 1³ 1¼ 1¹ MillerE8 n4R 2:05⅕ Bilmar ForestFlower Lindy'sLady
May29-691Spk⅝ 1 :3111:02 1:3322:051ft 3 3⁰ 2⁰ 2½ 2¾ 2½ MillerE4 n3R 2:05⅖ JetBold Bilmar Forest Flower
May22-693Spk⅝ 1 :3121:0531:3732:08 ft 4¼ 7x 9 9⁶ 7⁸½ 7¹⁰ MillerE3 n4R 2:10 Silv'rSh't'ge A.C'sPr'c's P'p'l'rFr't
May 2-69 Nfld 1 :3031:02 1:3332:053ft 32 3 3 5 7³¾ 7²½ MillerE1 in4000 2:06⅕ SilverGh'st GuyY'tes G'ySaintPat
Apr28-69 Nfld 1 :3131:0311:3642:092ft 6¼ 1 1 1 1¼ 1² MillerE5 nw40006869 2:09⅖ Bilmar Sabetha CelticSaber
Apr23-69 Nfld 1 :3311:0731:4212:164sy 4¼ x7 7 7 7²² 6di. MillerE6 nw40006869 JackDan'l B'dyS'nders HiL'ndEm'y

5-1 — 7
2:04⅘ (Hol1, '68) ($7,263) Driver-Trainer—JIM DENNIS (55-3-7-12—.198) Green-White
Popular Freight B. g (1965), by Florlis—Freight Pride, by Star's Pride. Owner, A. B. C. Stables, Inc., New York, N. Y.
1969 3 0 1 2 $1,225
1968 26 3 2 4 $7,263

Jun 4-693Spk⅝ 1 :3111:0231:3442:063gd 2½ 3⁰ 1 1¼ 1h 3²½ DennisJ7 nw12502-10 2:07⅕ Cr'ftyL'b'll BigG'meP'k P'p'l'rFr't
May28-693Spk⅝ 1 :3121:0321:3342:04 ft 2¼ *1 2 3¼ 2¹ 2¹ DennisJ6 nw12502-10 2:04⅕ MarkRod Pop'l'rFr't BelleGalop'ne
May22-693Spk⅝ 1 :3121:0531:3732:08 ft 3¼ 2 2 3¹ 3² 3¹ DennisJ9 n4R 2:08⅕ Silv'rSh't'ge A.C'sPr'c's P'p'l'rFr't
Dec 9-68 Hol1 1 :3141:0241:3412:044ft 5½ 1 2 3 2² 2³ DennisJ5 nw700068 2:05⅕ Dyn'micV't'ry P'p'l'rFr'ght D'keL'r
Dec 2-68 Hol1 1 :3021:0331:3632:063ft 7½ 2 3 3 3²½ 3nk CorleyP1 nw650068 2:06⅗ MightyP'p'l'r Sp'c'lPr'd't P'p'l'rF't
Nov25-68 Hol1 1 :30 1:0111:3342:043ft 9½ 2 3 1 1½ 4¹½†DennisJ1 nw650068 2:04⅘ MightyP'p'l'r Sp'c'lPr'd't P'p'l'rF't

8-1 — 8
2:05 (Lex1, '69) ($11,149) Driver—GLEN KIDWELL. Trainer, R. Tripp (17-6-2-0—.418) Blue-Gold
Flying Trip ⊗ B. g (1965), by Lee Frost—Roxburgh Marcia, by Farcry. Owner, Clarence A. Tripp, Poplar Grove, Ill.
1969 5 2 1 0 $1,700
1968 43 10 5 15 $11,149

May28-695Spk⅝ 1 :3041:0331:34 2:041ft 11 9x 9 8¹² 7¹⁷x7¹⁴ KidwellG6 nw15008 2:07 SaraRodney DillyVic GaleForce
May21-693Spk⅝ 1 :3131:04 1:3712:084sy 6¾ 2 2 1nk 1² 1² KidwellG8 nw12502-10 2:08⅘ FlyingTrip FancyFrost Pat'sDee
May 9-69 Lex1 1 :32 1:0341:3622:071sl 11 x7 7 5 4²¼ 6³ ArtmanR3 w3000 2:07⅘ Queen'sMissile GaySam MarlynVan
May 3-69 Lex1 1 :3041:0121:34 2:05 ft 8-5 *1 1 1 1¹ 1² ArtmanR3 Cond 2:05 FlyingTrip IowaGirl UncoAlice
Apr26-69 Lex1 1 :3141:0441:3622:064ft 4 1 1 1 1¹ 2¹½ TrippR4 Cond 2:07 Qu'n'sMis'le Fly'gTrip Sp'dF'rmula
Dec 7-688May 1 :3031:0321:3522:071ft 51 3 3 3³ 4³½ 4³ TrippR6 w600068 2:07⅘ HappyN'p'rt TommyD'rw'd KatieS.

8-1 — 9
2:18⅗ gd (Cambridge, '68) ($5,328) Driver-Trainer—DON BUSSE (49-4-6-6—.190) Gray-Red
Dawn Randolph Br. f (1966), by Spencer Camp—Clever Charl, by Clever Hanover. Owner, Mrs. Gilbert W. Busse, Randolph, Wis.
1969 8 0 1 4 $2,788
1968 23 7 5 2 $5,328

Jun 3-693Spk⅝ 1 :31 1:03 1:3432:051ft 24 9 7⁰ 5³ 3⁴½ 3² BusseD7 nw12502-8 2:05⅗ Portfolio Dean'sTide DawnR'dolph
May21-693Spk⅝ 1 :3131:04 1:3712:084sy 10 5 5 5³ 6⁶½ 7¹⁰ BusseD2 nw12502-10 2:10⅘ FlyingTrip FancyFrost Pat'sDee
May13-696Was1 1 :3131:0311:3642:072ft 3½ 8 8 6³½ 3³ 3⁵½ BusseD2 nw400068 2:08⅗ SilverSh'rt'ge Sh'ld'nH'v'r D'nR'ph
May 6-696Was1 1 :3011:03 1:35 2:061ft 13 5⁰x8 8⁹½ 4⁷ 4⁴¾ BusseD5 nw400068 2:07⅕ MylrishQ'n K'ly'sM'l MyB'rn'sCh'f
Apr21-693Was1 1 :32 1:0531:3812:084ft 6¾ 8 8⁰ 5²½x8²² 8²³ BusseD8 nw300068 2:13⅗ Fly'gDr'm L'ckyB'tch SilverSh't'ge
Apr 3-693Was1 1 :3141:0431:37 2:08 ft 5¾ 8 8 8⁹ 6⁹ 3⁵½ BusseD6 nw4000 2:09⅕ My IrishQ'n ColbyL'r DawnR'nd'lph

Trackman's Selections—3 4 7 **Scratched—SAMMY TIDE.**

ONE MILE PACE

5th RACE

Purse $2,400

KIM MARTELL PURSE

Conditioned. 3-, 4- and 5-year-olds. Non-winners of 3 races that are non-winners since May 15. Races for $750 or less not considered.

PLEASE ASK FOR HORSE BY PROGRAM NUMBER

1 (6-1) ($6,517) Driver-Trainer—GARY WILCOX (16-0-2-1—.090) Red-White

Undecided ⊗ Ch. m (1964), by Adios Paul—Virginia Key, by Keyman. Owner, Robert H. Thatcher, Russiaville, Ind.
1969 1 0 0 0 $162
1968 17 0 5 4 $4,060

Jun 2-696Spk⅝ 1 :3241:0621:3742:081ft 10 2 3 3½ 63¼ 42¾†WilcoxG3 fmnw12502-8 2:08⅘ J'tt'gBye Dutch'sExpr's G'dG'lW'k
†Dead heat.
Oct14-688Was1 1 :31 1:0141:3432:051ft 5 10 2 21½ 11½ 2no WilcoxG4 fmnw400068 2:05⅕ Count'sCash Und'cid'd G'dSel'ct'n
Oct 2-687Was1 1 :3011:0311:36 2:044ft 9 6 6 76 43½ 33¾ WilcoxG3 nw400068 2:05⅗ B'tleshipN. HiS'gleSt'r Undecided
Sep25-684Was1 1 :3131:0321:3412:052ft 2½ 4 3 21 11 22 WilcoxG5 nw300068 2:05⅘ GoinDirect Undecided BlackBeard
Sep17-685Was1 1 :3241:03 1:3432:05 gd 2¾ 3 3 22 21½ 21¾ WilcoxG3 nw300068 2:05⅖ HalryGene Undecided VarsityKni't
Sep11-685Was1 1 :3041:0131:3322:034ft 11 30 20 32 54 57½ WilcoxG4 nw300068 2:05⅖ Karen'sFilly Kimpam Dolly'sC'ndy

2 (6-1) 2:10 (LouD, '68) ($1,591) Driver—ROBERT WILLIAMS. Trainer, F. Bettis (44-12-10-1—.407) Purple-White

‡Wildwood Brown B. c (1966), by Noble Hanover—Wildwood Queen, by Jayzoff Council. Owner, Est. of Dave L. Brown, Chattanooga, Tenn.
1969 4 0 0 0 $240
1968 19 1 7 4 $1,591

May31-6910Spk⅝ 1 :31 1:0241:3442:05 sy 24 7 7 53 715 69¾ WilliamsR8 n4R 2:07 Ed'ew'dB'tch H'byH'eL'pe S'tD'c'r
May19-694Spk⅝ 1 :3031:0321:3412:043ft 20 3 3 31½ 32½ 58½ FarringtonR3 n2R 2:06⅖ GabrielAnderson King'sFull Frozen
May13-693Was1 1 :3011:0311:3512:05 ft 19 8 8 77 77 613 FarringtonR8 nw1000 2:07⅗ Torn'doPick Edgew'dBrett RushOn
May 5-692Was1 1 :3021:0131:3222:061ft 5 4 4 412 511 57½ FarringtonR1 nw1000 2:07⅘ AndyC'sh D'ndyAndyTh'r GonaWin
Sep18-68 Lawrenceburg—Finished 3-4 in two non-wagering races in 2:11⅖ and 2:10, good (C. Bettis).
Sep13-68 LouD 1 :32 1:0441:38 2:10 ft9-5 4 4 3 1½ 11½ BettisC1 Cond 2:10 W'dw'dBr'n Ind'nAbbe Wil'wlmp'h

3 (12-1) 2:08⅗ (Henry, '68) ($2,812) Driver-Trainer—JOHN SEARLE (17-0-2-1—.085) Green-Gold

Pedro Adios Ch. g (1964), by Adios Express—Victory Honey, by Bristle Hanover. Owner, Mort Enos, Eureka, Ill.
1969 0 0 0 0 (——)
1968 24 6 6 3 $2,486

May23-69 Spk⅝ 1 :3211:05 1:3842:102ft N.B. 20 1 1½ 2h 2no SearleJ7 Qua 2:10⅖ Sc'rch'rW've P'droAd's C'rdin'lFl'h
Dec16-685Aur 1 :32 1:0541:3842:112ft 8¾ 5 7 52½ 62½ 51½ RevardF3 nw350068 2:11⅘ AdiosPole MyronScott Aquarius
Dec11-689Aur 1 :3111:0411:3832:123ft 10 6 6 41½ 2h 31 RevardF6 nw250068 2:12⅘ Aquarius Skinan Pedro Adios
Dec 6-688May 1 :31 1:04 1:3532:074ft 28 5 50 21 32 44¼ RevardF6 nw3000 2:08⅘ Chataqua SharonByrd AdiosRunt
Nov29-6810May 1 :3121:0431:3722:084gd 15 1 1 1h 13 35¼ RevardF1 nw300068 2:09⅘ Emulate MadAdmiral PedroAdios
Nov20-687May 1 :31 1:0321:3632:091ft 3½ 5 5 53½ 43 42½ SearleJ1 nw2500 2:09⅗ TheG'tW'ln't AdiosP'le Sh'y'sK'ht

4 (6-1) 2:11 (Aur, '68) ($900) Driver-Trainer—NELSON WILLIS (14-1-3-1—.214) Maroon-Gray-White

Cumberland ⊗ B. g (1965), by Diller Hanover—Chaperone, by Protector. Owner, D. R. Van Witzenburg, Chicago Ridge, Ill.
1969 15 1 1 6 $3,372
1968 3 2 0 0 $900

May15-698Was1 1 :3111:0341:3612:053ft 38 7 7 63½ 33¼ 35¾ WillisN8 nw300068 2:06⅘ BrickRang'r WellToDo Cumberl'nd
May 3-692Was1 1 :2931:0021:3322:044ft 33 7 7 85½ 55 31½ WillisN4 nw300068 2:05⅕ TomsChoice AdiosW'yne Cumberl'd
Apr21-697Was1 1 :31 1:0411:3632:064ft 28 6 7 811 615 616 WillisN2 nw300068 2:10 O Boy L.B.Crystal Hick'ryStardust
Apr 9-693Was1 1 :31 1:0431:3742:072ft 5¾ 4 5 54½ 48x 624 WillisN2 nw300068 2:12⅕ Drummondville EmmaC. AdiosRunt
Apr 1-697Was1 1 :3231:0541:38 2:103sy 5½ 4 20 35 37½ 38½ WillisN3 nw300068 2:12⅖ M'l'dyCruis'r Ch'ceGr't'n C'mb'rl'd
Mar24-699Was1 1 :3241:0841:4242:15 sy 7 8 40 55 55 56 WillisN9 nw3000 2:16⅕ FirstImpr's'n Pr'bleC'f D'sC'tC'sh

5 (8-1) 2:08⅗ (Was1, '69) ($722) Driver—HARRY BURRIGHT. Trainer, R. Shepardson (43-5-3-6—.202) Blue-Gold

Birdie's Captain B. g (1966), by Dazzleway—Birdie McKlyo, by Walter McKlyo. Owner, Lillian E. Shepardson, Sycamore, Ill.
1969 7 1 1 0 $1,986
1968 10 M 2 0 $722

Jun 2-6910Spk⅝ 1 :3041:02 1:3232:034ft 32 6 6 63½ 54 516 BurrightH3 n2R 2:07 JetBro ByeByeRoger SecretW'tch
May19-694Spk⅝ 1 :3031:0321:3412:043ft 6¾ 4 4 43½ 43 610 BurrightH1 n2R 2:06⅗ GabrielAnderson King'sFull Frozen
May12-696Was1 1 :2911:0031:3422:053ft 11 5 5 52½ 34 68¾ BurrightH1 n2R 2:07⅖ TimelyLeg'd Maj'ticD't'y S'v'rF're
May 5-697Was1 1 :2931:0021:3312:052ft 51 8 8 811 54 23½ BurrightH8 nw2000 2:06⅕ ArgoTime B'die'sC'p'n Fr'kD'zl'w'y
Apr26-6910Was1 1 :3211:0311:3512:06 ft 23 4 5 67 76½ 818 BurrightH3 nw300068 2:09⅗ FrostyTime EasternTime Tension
Apr17-696Was1 1 :2941:0221:3432:052gd 29 3 3 32 32½ 48 BurrightH4 nw2000 2:07 Andy'sW'rthy BrickRanger JoeB'rd

6 (8-1) 2:09⅗ (Newton, '68) ($3,887) Driver-Trainer—DON BUSSE (49-4-6-6—.190) Gray-Red

L. B. Crystal B. g (1966), by Crystal Byrd—Queen of Clubs, by Don Adios. Owner, Lyle B. Cobb, Sun Prairie, Wis.
1969 9 1 1 1 $2,862
1968 27 9 4 4 $3,887

May28-694Spk⅝ 1 :2931:0111:3212:033ft 10 7 9 915 718 512 BusseD2 n3R 2:06 Pancho ChiefRed RangerRichard
May16-693Was1 1 :3041:0221:3342:05 ft 7½ 9 9 913 819 821 BusseD5 nw300068 2:09⅕ M'rioH'n'v'r Andy'sD'n D'tyG.H'yes
May 2-696Was1 1 :2931:0211:3342:041ft 8¾ 8 9 86½x9 9di. BusseD2 nw300068 KnoxPatch Doubled ShiawayAdios
Apr21-697Was1 1 :31 1:0411:3632:064ft 27 9 90 76½ 56½ 22½ BusseD8 nw300068 2:07⅖ O Boy L.B.Crystal Hick'ryStardust
Apr11-695Was1 1 :32 1:05 1:37 2:081ft 7½ 8 70 54 31 32½ BusseD7 nw300068 2:08⅘ WindyCole AdiosWayne L.B.Crystal
Mar28-694Was1 1 :3041:0531:3912:09 ft 11 5 70 42 63½ 64½ BusseD4 nw4000 2:10 Sh'w'yAd's M'ck'gDr'm Kn'xRev'w

7 (7-2) 2:07⅗ (Was1, '69) (——) Driver-Trainer—WENCE MacDONALD (9-0-2-2—.198) White-Blue

Ranger Richard Ch. g (1966), by Ranger Hanover—Adimite, by Don Adios. Owner, Wenceslas MacDonald, Indianapolis, Ind.
1969 5 2 0 2 $2,916
1968 0 M 0 0 (——)

May28-694Spk⅝ 1 :2931:0111:3212:033ft 9 4 4 44 32½ 3nk MacDonaldW1 n3R 2:03⅗ Pancho ChiefRed RangerRichard
Apr22-697Was1 1 :3011:0211:3632:073ft 3½ 4 5 64 32 11 MacDonaldW4 nw2000 2:07⅗ Rang'rR'h'rd C'rd'lB'b D'ch'sExp's
Apr15-694Was1 1 :3141:05 1:3822:09 gd 6½ 4 4 32½ 33 1h MacDonaldW4 nw1000 2:09 R'g'rR'h'd B'k'rM'sh D'dyA'dyTh'r
Apr 2-693Was1 1 :3121:0331:3712:073gd 35 8 8 64 42½ 34¾ MacDonaldW9 nw1000 2:08⅗ L'tleP'ter A'liner'sCh'f R'gerRich'd
Mar25-694Was1 1 :3221:0831:4322:144sy 20 6 7 53 33 44½ MacDonaldW8 nw1000 2:15⅘ WellToDo AllGo Airliner'sChief
Mar14-69 Was1 1 :31 1:0431:4012:11 ft N.B. 6 6 64½ 43½ 24½ MacDonaldW5 Qua 2:12 D'ndyAndyTh'r R'ng'rRich'd T'pG'e

8 (8-1) 2:07 (Was1, '69) ($4,603) Driver-Trainer—KEN JAMES (6-1-0-0—.167) Brown-Tan

Precious Hour B. f (1965), by Rush Hour—Hi Lo's Duchess, by Hollyrood Hermes. Owner, Allen R. Wilson, Erie, Ill.
1969 15 1 2 1 $3,160
1968 34 2 7 7 $3,404

Jun 2-697Spk⅝ 1 :3031:0521:36 2:07 ft 38 4 5 53 54½ 55 JamesK8 nw12502-6 2:08 FieldDiam'd RolaC'st'r Id'na'sF'th
May22-696Spk⅝ 1 :30 1:0141:34 2:04 ft110 9 70 52½ 74½ 79½ JamesK9 nw14002L 2:06 TarportCoulter StarJim BethExp's
May14-697Was1 1 :3011:0041:3312:052ft 4¾ 20 2 32 87 814 JamesK7 nw300068 2:08⅕ D'tch'ssExpr'ss Libby Is'b'llaH'v'r
Apr29-698Was1 1 :3111:0341:3432:051ft 32 5 5 64½ 55½ 69½ JamesK1 nw400068 2:07⅕ OBoy Pleasem Idona'sFaith
Apr18-691Was1 1 :32 1:05 1:3722:084sy 34 8 8 818 7 7di. JamesK9 nw400068 SantaDee Mr.Relco Qu'n'sRingl'd'r
Apr 4-699Was1 1 :3041:0241:3522:06 sy 28 5 9 917 925 9di. JamesK3 nw400068 F'sh'nCh'f Gr'mpyGabe Id'na'sF'th

9 (5-1) 2:06⅖ (Columbus, '68) ($5,052) Driver-Trainer—LOU HUBER JR. (2-0-0-1—.167) Maroon-White-Gold

Color Guard B. c (1966), by Good Time—Flying Colors, by Scottish Pence. Owner, R. D. & H. A. Ricketts; Houston, Texas.
1969 1 0 0 0 $125
1968 17 4 3 2 $5,052

Jun 3-695Spk⅝ 1 :3111:0331:3532:051ft 10 6 6 64 56 58 HuberLJr5 n4R 2:06⅘ StarJim ArgoTime GameAdios
Oct 1-68 Lex1 1 :294 :5941:3022:01 ft 6¾ 20 2 4 57 56 HuberLJr4 st1770 2:02⅕ TarportCoulter DukeDuane Cherico
Sep25-68 Lex1 1 :30 1:01 1:3222:031gd 5 3 4 4 45 35 HuberLJr2 st1387 2:04⅕ TarportCoulter DukeDuane C'l'rG'd
Sep11-68 H.P⅝ 1 :3041:04 1:3522:08 gd 2½ 6 6 6 64 53½ HuberLJr4 Cond 2:08⅗ SandyKnox PatColby WinterFrisco
Sep 2-68 Ind1 1 :291 :5941:3332:034gdN.B. 30 10 6 88 911 HuberLJr2 st7981 2:06 Sh'w'yL'd Lightn'gW've S'lidStart
Sep 2-68 Ind1 1 :3031:0321:35 2:06 gdN.B. 8 8 8 86 2nk HuberLJr10 st7981 2:06 BrownBred ColorGuard OceanM'th

Trackman's Selections—7 9 2

ONE MILE TROT

6th RACE

Purse $3,100

STOCK YARDS KIWANIS CLUB

Conditioned. 3-year-olds and up. Non-winners of $1,550 1st money twice in last 8 starts. Claiming races not considered.

PLEASE ASK FOR HORSE BY PROGRAM NUMBER

2:01⅘ (Hol1, '68) ($66,089) Driver-Trainer—ROBERT FARRINGTON (68-17-8-7—.350) Red-Gray

5-1 **1 Crown Song** Br. g (1959), by Darnley—Victory Rose, by Victory Song. 1969 18 5 6 3 $14,645
Ow., Farrington Sta., Inc.-Galanga; Richw'd, New Philadelphia, O. 1968 29 5 5 3 $9,182

Jun 4-695Spk⅝ 1 :30 1:02 1:3342:052gd 4¾ 4 4 3¹¼ 1½ x2nk Farring'nR3 nw15502-8 2:05⅖ VolcanicDan CrownSong PollyAnn
May27-694Spk⅝ 1 :31 1:0321:3632:06 ft 7-5 ▲1 2 2h 2¹ 2² FarringtonR9 9000 2:06⅖ A.C'sV'ct'y Cr'wnSong Wh'lw'dW'k
May20-694Spk⅝ 1 :31 1:0141:3422:053ft 2 ▲40 1 1nk 1¹ 1¾ FarringtonR9 8000 2:05⅗ Cr'wnS'ng OldRanger BraveN'wp't
May13-698Was1 1 :3131:04 1:3542:064ft 1 ▲1 1 1¾ 1³ 1¾ FarringtonR7 7500 2:06⅘ Cr'wnS'ng L'dyM'ryD. B'lleG'ph'e
Apr30-697Was1 1 :31 1:03 1:3612:062ft 2¾ 30 1 1nk 1²½ 1²½ FarringtonR8 7000 2:06⅗ Cr'wnS'ng OurProsp't Hist'yM'k'r
Apr24-691Was1 1 :3041:0211:3622:07 ft 2 2 3 5²½ 2² 2¹ FarringtonR6 7000 2:07⅕ ZekeOaks CrownSong Roy'sBoy

2:05⅖ gd (Spk⅝, '69) ($108,390) Driver-Trainer—JIM CURRAN (33-8-6-4—.384) Gray-Gold

9-2 **2 Volcanic Dan** B. g (1960), by Poplar Volcanic—Rose Chung, by Chungking. 1969 1 1 0 0 $1,550
Owner, John J. Curran, Jackson, Mich. 1968 0 0 0 0 (——)

Jun 4-695Spk⅝ 1 :30 1:02 1:3342:052gd 3¼ ▲5 6 5³ 2½ 1nk CurranJ2 nw15502-8 2:05⅖ VolcanicDan CrownSong PollyAnn
May26-69 Spk⅝ 1 :3221:0421:3632:072ft N.B. 20 2 2² 2²½ 2³½ CurranJ7 Qua 2:08⅕ Portfolio Volcanic Dan Wood U.
Oct20-67 L.B⅝ 1 :30 1:01 1:3042:013ft 33 7 8 8 8⁸ 8³¾ CurranJo5 in10000 2:02⅘ L'kyLindy P'rl'ssY'nkee JesR.Hoot
Oct14-67 L.B⅝ 1 :2931:0121:3132:012ft 25 40 1 3 3²¼ 7⁶½ DolbeeJ5 in10000 2:02⅗ SpeedyPlay Fr'shY'nkee P'rl'sY'k'e
Oct 6-67 L.B⅝ 1 :30 1:0041:3212:014ft 6½ 20 1 1 2¾ 6⁷½ CurranJo2 in12000 2:03⅕ SpeedyPlay ValidSam JesR.Hoot
Sep23-67 Was1 1 :3021:0021:3222:011ft 7-5 ▲40 10 11 1½ 3²¾ DolbeeJ5 in10000 2:01⅘ Gr'ndpaJim D'nF'ber V'lcanicDan

2:02⅖ (Hol1, '68) ($76,995) Driver-Trainer—RUSSELL VALLES KEY (11-0-1-0—.051) Green-White

10-1 **3 Prince Kam ⊗** Br. g (1961), by Prince Victor—Volo Kam, by Nibble Hanover. 1969 14 1 0 1 $2,418
Owner, Golden West Stable, Los Angeles, Calif. 1968 48 4 8 12 $29,159

Jun 4-695Spk⅝ 1 :30 1:02 1:3342:052gd 15 8 8 7⁶½ 5⁵½ 4⁵¼ VallesKeyR9 nw15502-8 2:06⅖ VolcanicDan CrownSong PollyAnn
May28-695Spk⅝ 1 :3041:0331:34 2:041ft 26 7 7 3² 4²½ 5⁵¼ VallesKeyR7 nw15008 2:05⅖ SaraRodney DillyVic GaleForce
May23-694Spk⅝ 1 :3121:0341:35 2:051ft 47 8 8 8⁵½ 5⁴ 6⁵ VallesKeyR7 w1550 2:06⅕ My IrishQ'n R's'd'leSt'r L'mb'rS'n
May16-695Was1 1 :30 :5941:3042:024ft 40 40 1 3³½ 9⁹ 9¹⁴ VallesKeyR6 nw1000068 2:05⅗ Meteore II. Rhythm Duke Farlen
May 9-695Was1 1 :32 1:0331:3732:081sy 20 7 7 8⁹ 5⁸½ 6⁸¼ FalknerJ3 nw1000068 2:09⅘ R'sed'leSt'r AllAm'ric'n J'nieBrook
May 2-695Was1 1 :2941:00 1:3142:031ft 9 1 3 4¹¼ 4²½ 6⁵¼ CurranJ4 nw1000068 2:04⅕ R's'd'leSt'r AllAm'ric'n D'nW.D'l'r

2:06⅖ (Hol1, '68) ($11,216) Driver-Trainer—DESMOND O'DONOHOE (6-0-0-0—.000) Green-White

12-1 **4 Lady Mary D.** B. m (1963), by Sigma Nu—Lady Seattle, by Seattle Dean. 1969 15 0 3 0 $2,407
Owner, Desmond O'Donohoe, Arcadia, Calif 1968 46 6 5 5 $8,368

Jun 5-696Spk⅝ 1 :30 1:0211:3342:041ft 45 3 4 5³x 8²⁴ 8²³ O'DonohoeD7 nw15508 2:08⅘ GaleForce A.C'sVict'ry OhioSpecial
May13-698Was1 1 :3131:04 1:3542:064ft 12 3 4 4² 2³ 2¾ O'DonohoeD1 6000 2:07 Cr'wnS'ng L'dyM'ryD. B'lleG'ph'e
May 5-696Was1 1 :3021:0221:3412:062ft 16 3 4 6³ 6²½ 2¹ O'DonohoeD1 3500 2:06⅗ B'leGal'ph'ne L'dyM'yD. H'rk'yW'y
Apr23-694Was1 1 :31 1:0321:37 2:082ft 18 30 50 5³½ 6⁵½ 7⁴¼ O'DonohoeD7 3500 2:09⅖ CapriK'y MyB'rnesCh'f B'leG'l'ph'e
Apr10-69 F.P1 1 :3121:0511:3532:083ft 7¾ 2 3x 7 7¹⁷ 7di. O'DonohoeD1 Cond ScotchAudie OhioPaul Highl'nD'na
Apr 3-69 F.P1 1 :3121:03 1:34 2:064ft 11 1 1 2 2³ 5¹¹ O'DonohoeD2 Cond 2:09 ScotchEcho Zingiber OhioPaul

2:05 (Spk⅝, '69) ($34,136) Driver-Trainer—AUBREY PETTY (15-6-0-1—.422) Maroon-Black

6-1 **5 Frisco Lad ⊗** B. g (1959), by Potomac Lad—Rhea Frisco, by Promoter. 1969 12 5 0 2 $11,741
Owner, Aubrey L. Petty, Mason, Tenn. 1968 13 4 2 2 $8,898

Jun 4-695Spk⅝ 1 :30 1:02 1:3342:052gd 3½ 2 3 2nkx6⁶ 5⁵½ PettyA1 nw15502-8 2:06⅖ VolcanicDan CrownSong PollyAnn
May22-695Spk⅝ 1 :3031:0141:3342:05 ft 8½ 7 7 2¹ 2nk 1no PettyA6 nw15008 2:05 Frisco Lad Gale Force Cambev
May15-697Was1 1 :3111:0211:3422:051ft 9 1 2 1no 3²½ 5⁴¾ PettyA7 12500 2:06⅕ Pr'c'sR'd'ph Kelly'sM'l Mi'tyPop'r
May 8-691Was1 1 :3131:0441:3942:094sy 2 ▲1 1 1¹½ 1²½ 1³¾ PettyA7 7500 2:09⅘ FriscoLad LocalS'mpson ZekeOaks
Apr30-699Was1 1 :3211:0341:37 2:063ft 12 4 5 6²½ 6⁶½ 6⁶ PettyA3 9000 2:07⅘ Fort'eT'll'r Rhy'mDuke FullSpeed
Apr22-695Was1 1 :3111:0331:3642:061ft 8½ 20 1 2h 4³½ 7⁵¾ PettyA8 9000 2:07⅖ RhythmDuke FullSpeed OldRanger

2:02⅘ (Spk⅝, '68) ($34,967) Driver-Trainer—JIM DENNIS (55-3-7-12—.198) Green-White

2-1 **6 Chancey Guy** B. g (1963), by Jean Laird—Edna Naylor, by Mr. Chips. 1969 5 0 1 1 $2,340
Owner, Victor & Morris Zeinfeld; Maywood, Lincolnwood, Ill. 1968 29 5 5 5 $27,182

Jun 2-699Spk⅝ 1 :2811:0211:3222:03 ft 2¾ 5 4 4²½ 4¹½ 3² DennisJ4 hp7000 2:03⅖ Met're II. G'ytideTheGr't Ch'yGuy
May27-699Spk⅝ 1 :3041:0341:34 2:034ft 2¾ 6 6 5³ 3³½x6⁸¼ DennisJ7 in6000 2:05⅖ G'ytideTheGr't HuckFinn M't're II.
May20-699Spk⅝ 1 :2941:0231:34 2:034ft 5¾ 3 3 3¹¼ 4¹ 2h DennisJ2 in6000 2:03⅘ G'ytideT'eGr't Ch'n'yG'y S'yF'rt'e
May16-695Was1 1 :30 :5941:3042:024ft 2½ 2 5 1² 1½ 6³¾ DennisJ1 nw1000068 2:03⅘ Meteore II. Rhythm Duke Farlen
May 9-697Was1 1 :31 1:0331:3532:064sy 32 6 6 8⁷½ 6¹⁰ 6⁸¾ RussellJ2 hp10000 2:08⅗ R'lSp'd G'ytideTheGr't S'nyF'rt'ne
Dec19-68 Hol1 1 :3021:0131:3342:023ft 3e▲3 3 3 3⁴ 3nk DennisJ4 in6500 2:02⅗ DarnFaber B'le'sDemon Ch'nc'yG'y

2:02 (L.B⅝, '68) ($15,285) Driver-Trainer—BRUCE NICKELLS (38-6-7-7—.322) White-Purple

6-1 **7 Cambev** B. g (1964), by Mr. Saunders—Minuet, by Star's Pride. 1969 2 1 0 1 $1,922
Owner, W. P. Cameron, Washington, Pa. 1968 20 6 2 3 $10,256

May29-695Spk⅝ 1 :3041:0331:3422:042ft 6-5 ▲3 3 2²½ 2nk 1³½ Far'ngtonR7 nw15002-8 2:04⅖ Cambev LadyTheresa ScotchRod'y
May22-695Spk⅝ 1 :3031:0141:3342:05 ft 5½ 3 3 5³½ 4¹½ 3h NickellsB2 nw15008 2:05 Frisco Lad Gale Force Cambev
Nov 9-68 L.B⅝ 1 :3011:0321:36 2:084gd 2 ▲ix7 7 7 7¹³ 5⁷½ ParkerG2 nw1250068 2:10⅕ Cl'thinaH'v'r M'sB'kyP'k Sp'kySue
Oct26-68 L.B⅝ 1 :3031:0221:3332:04 ft 4 5 5 2 2½ 1⁴½ ParkerG4 nw1000068 2:04 Cambev Goddard LanaHanover
Oct19-68 L.B⅝ 1 :3021:0111:3342:062gd 4 x6xx8 8 8 8di. ParkerG5 nw1000068 C.C.Org'n L'dySc'ndal LanaH'n'v'r
Oct12-68 L.B⅝ 1 :3011:0141:3242:03 ft 3½ 4 4 4 4²½ 5⁶ ParkerG3 nw1000068 2:04⅕ OurRainbow JimmyT. Specialist

2:06⅖ (Was1, '68) ($5,382) Driver-Trainer—JOE MARSH JR. (51-8-8-7—.290) Gray-Blue-Red

8-1 **8 Midnight Ronnie** Blk. g (1964), by Addup—Neva June Forbes, by Ronnie Forbes. 1969 0 0 0 0 (——)
Owner, Lyle Menchhofer, Celina, Ohio. 1968 26 10 4 2 $4,665

Nov 1-684May 1 :3041:0241:3542:073ft 3 4 4 3¾ 1nk 1³ SamplesE4 nw650068 2:07⅗ MidnightR'nie S'nyPride Fly'gTrip
Oct22-686May 1 :31 1:0331:36 2:081gd 2½ ▲x7 7 7¹² 7⁹½ 6⁹½ KnoxR2 nw400068 2:10⅕ Mimar Vesta'sP'p'l'r M'l'dyDyn'te
Oct10-683Was1 1 :3041:0211:3612:07 ft 2½ 7 8 8⁵½ 5⁷ 4⁷½ SamplesE5 nw400068 2:08⅗ Vesta'sPopular Mimar MissM'st'n
Sep16-684Was1 1 :31 1:02 1:33 2:04 ft 9-5 ▲50 1 1¾ 1¹½x6⁵ MarshJJr8 nw400068 2:05 HistoryMak'r OurPr'sp'ct Sm'rtS'n
Sep 2-683Was1 1 :3211:0311:3432:062ft 3¼ 40 20 11 1²½ 1¾ MarshJJr4 nw300068 2:06⅖ Midni'tRonnie ArestaGal EyreYell
Aug14-68 Celina—Finished 4-5 in two non-wagering races in 2:08 and 2:10⅕, fast (T. Penrod).

2:04⅗ (LouD, '68) ($24,687) Driver—WILLIAM ROSEBOOM. Trainer, R. Buckey (24-1-3-1—.125) Gold-Purple

10-1 **9 Watta Amosson** B. m (1959), by Seattle Dean—Watta Key, by Long Key. 1969 12 1 1 2 $3,455
Owner, R. D. Buckey & Gerald Hayes; Caldwell, Ohio. 1968 22 8 4 1 $9,386

Jun 4-695Spk⅝ 1 :30 1:02 1:3342:052gd 6¾ 6 5 4¹½ix7⁶ 6¹³ Roseb'mW6 nw15502-8 2:08 VolcanicDan CrownSong PollyAnn
May27-696Spk⅝ 1 :3011:0111:3242:033ft 9¼ 9 8 6⁶½ 4²½ 2² Roseb'mW9 nw12502-8 2:04 G'lie'sR'thm W'ttaAm'ss'n F'llSp'd
May 2-695Was1 1 :2941:00 1:3142:031ft 22 5 7 7⁴½ 7⁷ 7⁷¼ R'seboomW5 nw1000068 2:04⅗ R's'd'leSt'r AllAm'ric'n D'nW.D'l'r
Apr26-692Was1 1 :3111:0241:34 2:052ft 15 10 2 3¹ 4² 6⁵ R'seboomW8 nw1000068 2:06⅖ JanieBrook Farlen AllAmerican
Apr16-695Was1 1 :30 1:0031:34 2:052ft 33 8 8 8⁴ 5¹ 4¹½ Ros'boomW4 nw1000068 2:05⅘ MarengoDate Farlen FancyFrost
Apr 7-697Was1 1 :3041:0231:3442:053ft 8¼ 1 2 3² 7⁴ 7⁷¼ RoseboomW4 nw1000068 2:07⅕ Met're II. MarengoDate GuyYates

Trackman's Selections—6 2 1

ONE MILE PACE — **7th RACE** — **Purse $2,500**

Conditioned. 3- and 4-year-olds. Non-winners of $1,250 1st money in last 8 starts. For non-winners of $12,000 in 1968.

PLEASE ASK FOR HORSE BY PROGRAM NUMBER

12-1 — 1
2:03⅘ (Hol1, '68) ($8,386) Driver-Trainer—ROBERT WILLIAMS (44-12-10-1—.407) Purple-White
Profast ⊗
Ch. c (1965), by Prospectus—Fast Action, by Florican. 1969 6 1 0 1 $1,364
Owner, Bars Enterprises, Deerfield, Ill. 1968 27 3 5 5 $8,386
May31-694Spk⅝ 1:3021:0241:33 2:024ft 21 5 5 5⅜x920 9di. WilliamsR3 nw12502-8 PressAgent Jereo TimeClock
May 9-69 Det 1:3111:0341:3642:092gd 2½ 4 4 2 21 6²½ MerrimanT1 Cond 2:09⅘ CheerfulLady DoubleG.B'ttle Relco
Apr22-69 Det 1:3231:0641:4022:144sl 6-5 ▲10 1 1 1½x 711 WilliamsR7 Cond 2:17 HotC'rgo PamMcDon'd Ch'rfulL'dy
Apr16-69 Det 1:32 1:03 1:3442:061gd 22 7 7 7 6³¾ 6⁵¾ WilliamsR6 Cond 2:07⅕ St'rfliteSue Tim'lyG'se B'gin'rsL'k
Mar28-69 Det 1:36 1:1321:50 2:26 hy9-5 ▲10 1 1 1h 11 WilliamsR5 Cond 2:26 Profast PeacefulDale Smashette
Mar21-69 Det 1:3131:0511:3812:104gd8-5 6 7 7 63 3²¼ WilliamsR6 Cond 2:11⅕ MidnightJohnnie JonboySt'r Prof't

10-1 — 2
2:08⅗ (May, '68) ($5,785) Driver-Trainer—WAYNE SHORT (13-1-1-1—.145) Purple-White
Heather Chance
B. c (1965), by Chance Play—Widow Ann, by The Widower. 1969 6 0 1 0 $1,005
Owner, E. & A. Berlin; Cudahy, Wis. 1968 13 3 1 3 $4,830
Jun 4-696Spk⅝ 1:3131:0411:3532:063gd 16 5 5 5³½ 6³½ 6³½ ShortW1 nw12506 2:07⅕ Armbro Id'l Win'gC'st'l G'b'lAnd'n
May26-696Spk⅝ 1:2941:0141:33 2:031ft 6¾ 3 4 4⁴¼ 5⁵¼ 4⁷½ ShortW6 nw12508 2:04⅘ Galahad Hark Way Farmont
May19-695Spk⅝ 1:3131:0341:3512:054ft 18 10 2 22 4²½ 2¹½ ShortW7 nw12508 2:06⅕ BrownThistle H'th'rChance H'kW'y
May10-695Was1 1:31 1:0321:3522:073gd 41 2 4 2nk 1½ 5¹¼ ShortW5 nw400068 2:07⅘ GypsyGoose RacerWave Jean'sTea
Apr18-691Was1 1:32 1:05 1:3722:084sy 7½ 4 4 718 8 8di. BurrightH2 nw400068 SantaDee Mr.Relco Qu'n'sRingl'd'r
Apr10-699Was1 1:31 1:0121:33 2:042ft 22 3 3 410 717 819 BurrightH2 nw600068 2:08⅕ Chuck's Cousin Zeke Zam Lan Dow

7-2 — 3
2:09⅗ (Was1, '69) ($8,188) Driver—ROBERT FARRINGTON. Trainer, L. Fagan (68-17-8-7—.350) Red-Gray
Hark Way
B. c (1965), by Don Adios—Pearl Reed, by Waylay. 1969 10 0 1 4 $2,748
Owner, Don E. Fagan, Rushville, Ill. 1968 15 1 4 3 $4,363
Jun 4-696Spk⅝ 1:3131:0411:3532:063gd 4¾ 8 8 76 7⁴½ 7⁵½ FarringtonR3 nw12506 2:07⅗ Armbro Id'l Win'gC'st'l G'b'lAnd'n
May26-696Spk⅝ 1:2941:0141:33 2:031ft 3¾ 2 1 2¹½ 2¹½ 24 FarringtonR4 nw12508 2:04 Galahad Hark Way Farmont
May19-695Spk⅝ 1:3131:0341:3512:054ft 6 3 3 4³½ 3²½ 3²½ FarringtonR3 nw12508 2:06⅖ BrownThistle H'th'rChance H'kW'y
May13-699Was1 1:3011:0131:3342:041ft 35 7 7 7⁶½ 5⁵½ 5²½ FarringtonR9 nw400068 2:04⅘ R. Frisco Wyn O Boy Billy Frisco
May 3-695Was1 1:3021:0031:3222:031ft 6¾ 5 50 76 6⁶½ 5⁸¾ FarringtonR2 nw400068 2:05 Mock'gDr'm B'lyFrisco C'sdraDay
Apr24-695Was1 1:2941:0041:3312:041ft 18 3 5 5²½ 6⁵½ 710 MeyocksD1 nw500068 2:06⅕ BerthaParker Bock FashionChief

15-1 — 4
2:07⅗ (Was1, '69) ($3,346) Driver-Trainer—JOHN SEARLE (17-0-2-1—.085) Green-Gold
Varsity Signal ⊗
B. c (1965), by Adios Cleo—Meadow Mist, by King's Counsel. 1969 18 2 2 1 $4,776
Owner, Bernie Roberts, Juneau, Wis. 1968 15 3 6 3 $3,346
Jun 5-695Spk⅝ 1:3011:0331:3522:05 ft 16 5 5 4²½ 56 412 SearleJ4 nw14002L 2:07⅖ Ballock FlyingDutchman BeeRoyal
May22-699Spk⅝ 1:3041:0241:3412:041ft 89 8 8 7⁶½ 75 6⁵¾ SearleJ7 nw14002L 2:05⅗ ArgoTime OBoy FreddyThistle
May15-699Was1 1:3031:0131:3232:03 ft 57 7 8 8⁶½ 612 617 SearleJ5 nw600068 2:06⅖ Wee Herb Bock Mr. Lake County
May 7-698Was1 1:3031:0221:3532:07 sy 12 7 7 76 710 816 SearleJ2 nw400068 2:10⅕ KnoxPatch ChiefG.Direct Pleasem
Apr25-692Was1 1:2831:0121:3312:043ft 12 5 6 3²½ 35 2⁶½ SearleJ1 nw400068 2:06 T'ghieDir't V'sitySig'l S'teE'p'sN.
Apr17-699Was1 1:32 1:0431:3622:054gd 76 8 8 8⁶½ 89 814 SearleJ6 nw600068 2:08⅗ Darl'g'sVaper WeeHerb B'rb'nW'y

6-1 — 5
2:06⅖ (ScD⅝, '68) ($2,764) Driver-Trainer—JIM DOLBEE (6-2-1-1—.481) Green-White
Bo Bo Ranger ⊗
B. g (1966), by Ranger Hanover—Baroness Byrd, by Poplar Byrd. 1969 1 1 0 0 $1,200
Owner, J. Dolbee, J. McCann; Calumet City, Ill.; J'ks'n, Mich. 1968 11 2 1 5 $2,764
Jun 4-6910Spk⅝ 1:3041:0421:3532:064sy8-5 ▲5 40 21 1h 11 DolbeeJ1 n3R 2:06⅘ BoBoR'g'r D'z'leR.B'ke Br'kn'lCh'h
Sep20-685Was1 1:3131:0341:3622:054ft 5½ 5 5 5⁵½ 43 3³¾ DolbeeJ7 nw3000 2:06⅗ EasyJim HiddenMagic BoBoRang'r
Sep10-683Was1 1:3231:0811:42 2:13 sl 9-5 ▲10 1 1¹¼ 1²½ 1¹½ DolbeeJ6 nw2000 2:13 BoBoRanger CecilT. Raincoat
Aug30-683Spk⅝ 1:3121:0311:3432:043ft 8 7 7 513 49 38 DolbeeJ2 n2R 2:06⅕ Peak Time Cecelia Bo Bo Ranger
Aug23-6811Spk⅝ 1:3011:0331:3522:063ft 6½ 9 9 9⁶½ 7⁶½ 6⁵½ DolbeeJ7 n2R 2:07⅘ HotDeck Sp'dBoyPick Lydia'sGirl
Aug13-684Spk⅝ 1:3111:0741:3912:09 ft 3½ 1 1 32 32 3¹½ MinniearE4 n2R 2:09⅘ ArmbroJudd Bl'ckBeard BoBoR'g'r

6-1 — 6
2:04⅗ (Lex1, '69) ($7,356) Driver—GLEN KIDWELL. Trainer, R. Tripp (17-6-2-0—.418) Blue-Gold
Lady Trip
B. f (1966), by Crystal Byrd—Lady Belrock, by Beaver Hal. 1969 5 1 2 0 $1,725
Owner, Raymond G. Tripp, Poplar Grove, Ill. 1968 26 9 5 5 $7,356
Jun 4-696Spk⅝ 1:3131:0411:3532:063gd 4¾ 6 6 64 53 5²½ KidwellG5 nw12506 2:07⅕ Armbro Id'l Win'gC'st'l G'b'lAnd'n
May28-696Spk⅝ 1:3041:0311:3422:044ft 2½ 2 3 3¹½ 21 2½ KidwellG5 nw12508 2:05 JohnL.P'due LadyTrip RyanM'rsha
May19-696Spk⅝ 1:3031:0231:3322:04 ft 5¾ 7 7 65 4¹½ 2¹½ KidwellG6 fmnw12508 2:04⅕ PoplarCo'kie LadyTrip G'rry'sFirst
May 6-69 Lex1 1:3031:0131:34 2:043ft 8¾ 4 5 7 1½ 1¹½ TrippR1 w4000 2:04⅗ LadyTrip ShadowWin TrotwoodP'l
Apr25-69 Lex1 1:2931:0111:3242:032ft 10 5 6 6 7³¾ 7⁷½ TrippR2 Cond 2:04⅘ MeadowLeaf DellaStar S'cc'ssJ'ne
Sep 4-68 Sandwich—Won two non-wagering races in 2:11⅗ and 2:12, good (R. Tripp).

6-1 — 7
2:03⅖ (Hol1, '68) ($10,755) Driver-Trainer—JIM DENNIS (55-3-7-12—.198) Green-White
Sports Arena
Blk. c (1965), by Greentree Adios—Keystone Lass, by Keystoner. 1969 3 0 0 1 $625
Ow., Jean A. Massall & Beverly A. Paris; Arcadia, Yorbalinda, Calif. 1968 24 4 7 4 $10,755
Jun 4-696Spk⅝ 1:3131:0411:3532:063gd 7½ 10 2 3¹½ 3¹½ 4¹½ DennisJ8 nw12506 2:07 Armbro Id'l Win'gC'st'l G'b'lAnd'n
May28-696Spk⅝ 1:3041:0311:3422:044ft 2 ▲3 4 42x 611 5⁹¾ DennisJ2 nw12508 2:06⅘ JohnL.P'due LadyTrip RyanM'rsha
May19-698Spk⅝ 1:3111:0341:3512:053ft 6½ 10 2 2¹½ 3¹½ 3¹½ DennisJ7 nw12508 2:06 E.M.Tr'v'l J'hnL.P'due Sp'tsAr'na
Dec23-68 Hol1 1:3031:0331:3432:041ft 6½ 4 4 2 2²½ 2½ DennisJ2 Cond 2:04⅕ ScottishD'sign Sp'rtsAr'na D'mB'r
Dec17-68 Hol1 1:30 1:0111:3312:024ft 9¾ 40 2 1 9⁹½ 918 DennisJ9 Cond 2:06⅕ DarkRival MazelRodney AdiosCarl
Dec 4-68 Hol1 1:3021:01 1:3212:032ft 9-5 1 3 3 3⁴½ 1¹¼ DennisJ5 Cond 2:03⅖ SportsArena Arl'neD'r's Mr.EdD't

5-1 — 8
2:02⅕ (Lex1, '68) ($10,171) Driver-Trainer—JOE O'BRIEN (46-5-8-5—.242) Gold-White
Speedy Wave
B. c (1965), by Shadow Wave—Diana Mite, by Volomite. 1969 2 0 0 0 (——)
Owner, Frederick & Thomas Rimbey; Darlington, Pa. 1968 20 6 1 0 $6,382
Jun 5-69 Spk⅝ 1:32 1:0411:3332:044ft N.B. 40 10 18 110 19 O'BrienJ6 Qua 2:04⅘ SpeedyW've TimmieWin S'cc'sK'tie
May28-696Spk⅝ 1:3041:0311:3422:044ft 8 x9 9 921 924 9di. O'BrienJ8 nw12508 JohnL.P'due LadyTrip RyanM'rsha
May19-695Spk⅝ 1:3131:0341:3512:054ft 2½ ▲8x 8 825 825 8di. DennisJ5 nw12508 BrownThistle H'th'rChance H'kW'y
Dec21-68 Hol1 1:30 1:0041:3242:034ft 2 ▲7 7 6 5⁴½ 1¾ O'BrienJ7 nw750068 2:03⅘ SpeedyWave JoeParker P'r'tiPride
Dec17-68 Hol1 1:30 1:0111:3312:024ft 5½ 6 7 7 5⁴½ 4⁵½ O'BrienJ3 nw750068 2:03⅘ DarkRival MazelRodney AdiosCarl
Dec 9-68 Hol1 1:3011:0141:3322:032ft 3½ 5 1 1 12 12 O'BrienJ9 nw500068 2:03⅖ SpeedyWave PorotiPride TopBid

5-1 — 9
2:04⅗ (PmP⅝, '68) ($6,479) Driver-Trainer—HOWARD BEISSINGER (23-1-4-2—.169) Blue-White
Kip Hanover
Br. c (1965), by Tar Heel—Kaola Hanover, by Titan Hanover. 1969 2 0 0 0 $125
Owner, Lindy Farms, Inc., Lindenhurst, N. Y. 1968 8 2 1 1 $2,358
May30-695Spk⅝ 1:3041:0121:3142:031ft 8½ 30 1 22 3³½ 5⁴¾ BeissingerH9 nw12508 2:04⅕ Mr. Jack Roswell Quick Prom
May21-696Spk⅝ 1:3141:0541:3922:11 sy 2¾ ▲1 1 2¹½x818 8di. BeissingerH2 nw12508 TruH'n'v'r TipT'pT'per G'dGirlW'k
Jun15-683Spk⅝ 1:3041:0221:3412:05 ft 6¾ 20 1 1¹x 712 7⁷¼ Beissing'rH9 nw13002-8 2:06⅖ Qu'nColby C'lvin'sL'ss Ar'brolnsk
Jun 7-684Spk⅝ 1:3041:04 1:3522:043ft 2¼ ▲5 5 4¹¾ 3¼ 3²¼ Beis'gerH3 nw12002-68 2:05 TimeCl'ck B'tifulH'n'v'r KipH'n'v'r
May31-685Spk⅝ 1:30 1:0241:3412:052ft 4-5 ▲20 2 2½x 5⁷¼ 74 BeissingerH6 nw13008 2:06⅕ RyanM'rsha F'llSover'n Mich'lJ'hr
May23-686Spk⅝ 1:2931:02 1:3432:044ft 4½ 80 8 2¾ 13 14 BeissingerH9 nw10008 2:04⅘ KipH'v'r IrishByeBye Jef'ryW'st'n

Trackman's Selections—3 8 9

ONE MILE PACE **8th RACE** **Purse $3,800**

Claiming. Claiming price $7,500. 3-year-olds and up. Gerry's First in for $9,000; rest for $7,500.

PLEASE ASK FOR HORSE BY PROGRAM NUMBER

1 9-2
2:04⅖ (May, '68) ($28,252) Driver—JOE MARSH JR. Trainer, K. Bartlett (51-8-8-7—.290) Gray-Blue-Red
Helanja ⊗ Br. g (1958), by Express Direct—Harvest, by Peter McElwyn. 1969 4 0 1 0 $950
Owner, Tommy Ryan, Morton Grove, Ill. 1968 45 7 9 8 $15,468
Jun 4-698Spk⅝ 1 :3031:0311:3442:054sy 4 5 6 65 53 2½ MarshJJr2 7500 2:06 Gerry'sFirst Helanja DannyRip
May28-69 Spk⅝ 1 :3031:0331:3512:083ft N.B. 2 3 31 21 12¼ RyanT1 Qua 2:08⅗ Helanja Dallas Direct Headstart
Mar29-698Was1 1 :3111:0241:34 2:041ft 24 20 3 63 96½ 88¼ RyanT3 9000 2:05⅘ R'digoAd'sBill S'feR't'n P'l'kiSilv'r
Mar20-695Was1 1 :3031:0341:3812:09 sy 30 5 5 74¼ 911 917 RyanT2 14000 2:12⅖ MightyG.E. Scotty'sColt Galahad
Mar12-695Was1 1 :3031:03 1:3522:05 ft 21 5 6 76½ 711 712 RyanT6 14000 2:07⅖ MightyG.E. RioDean Fairm'deChief
Dec 2-685May 1 :3111:0321:3632:072gd6-5 *1 1 1h 1h 21¼ BanksS5 10000 2:07⅘ RioDean Helanja MidnightBrownie

2 9-2
2:04 (Was1, '69) ($14,139) Driver-Trainer—CHARLES McDERMOTT (33-1-4-4—.138) Red-White-Blue
Fascinating Dream ⊗ B. g (1962), by Demon's Dream—Miss Steffan, by Hayfield Direct. 1969 14 4 2 2 $12,148
Ow., McDermott & Steinberg; Chicago Heights, Lincolnwood., Ill. 1968 17 5 2 2 $7,384
Jun 4-698Spk⅝ 1 :3031:0311:3442:054sy 3½ 4x 40 21¼ 42 53¼ McDermottC6 7500 2:06⅗ Gerry'sFirst Helanja DannyRip
May21-697Spk⅝ 1 :3231:0421:3722:092sy 3½ 50 2 1hx 34 34 McDermottC7 7500 2:10⅕ TidalGale OrbitMan F'scin't'gDr'm
May17-6910Was1 1 :3241:0611:3942:104sy 4⅗ 2 1 1½ 1½ 2h McDermottC2 7000 2:10⅘ Sp'k'gD'm'd F'c't'gD'm SirTruG'l't
May 9-6910Was1 1 :3121:0321:3622:092sy 2 *4 3 2nk 11¼ 1¾ McDermottC2 6000 2:09⅖ F'scin't'gDr'm SirTruG'l't X.P'tB't
May 3-6910Was1 1 :3111:0211:3422:06 ft7-5 *6 6 31½ 2h 2h McDermottC5 6000 2:06 X.P'rtB'rt F'scin't'gDr'm D'sD'nl'y
Apr25-698Was1 1 :3021:0021:3242:04 ft 2⅗ *7 7 85 42½ 43¼ McDermottC4 8000 2:04⅘ Lo'sKing JustlySo BattleLine

3 15-1
2:10⅖ (B.M1, '68) ($16,909) Driver-Trainer—JACK WILLIAMS (19-3-3-3—.298) Red-White
Famous Cyrus ⊗ B. g (1963), by Famous Hanover—Jane Averill, by Averill. 1969 1 0 0 0 (—)
Owner, J. Williams & C. Meyers; Solana Beach, Escondido, Calif. 1968 2 0 0 0 (—)
Jun 2-698Spk⅝ 1 :2931:0211:3242:044ft 40 9 9ix714 711 611 WilliamsJ9 7000 2:07 RichAdios C'rd'lPaul Midn'tBr'nie
Jly 17-688Spk⅝ 1 :291 :5941:3042:012ft 21 7 7 711 915 916 WilliamsJ7 nw10008 2:04⅗ AprilLad SirWinst'nP'k Sc't'sPl'to
Jly 9-687Spk⅝ 1 :3131:04 1:35 2:061ft 5¾ 7 7 67 67½ 76 WilliamsJ5 nw10008 2:07⅖ RupertH. West'n'sJody NellieK'lie
Jly 2-68 Spk⅝ 1 :3231:0511:3612:082ft N.B. 1 1 12½ 1½ 32 WilliamsJ4 Qua 2:08⅘ Katy's Bert IronEye FamousCyrus
Sep19-67 Pom 1 :31 1:03 1:3432:063ft 35 6 7 7 712 723 ShortW4 nw75006 7 2:11⅕ BoyTrust NuJean MountainLusty
Sep14-67 Hol1 1 :3011:0141:3222:011ft 83 8 8 8 920 9di. WilliamsJ6 nw75006 7 Assault Caramba PressAgent

4 6-1
2:05⅗ (Spk⅝, '69) ($8,967) Driver-Trainer—GEORGE HARDIE (17-3-1-2—.248) Black-Gold
Chief Sun B. g (1964), by Mighty Sun—Milady Hanover, by Adios. 1969 5 1 0 0 $1,700
Owner, George G. Hardie, Warwick, R. I. 1968 22 3 2 4 $4,680
Jun 3-696Spk⅝ 1 :2931:0131:3242:032ft 25 9 80 97 97½ 87¼ HardieG9 10000 2:05 MajorMah'ne ConMan Dick'sSister
May24-696Spk⅝ 1 :2931:0241:3412:052ft 9¾ 9 8 76 43 11 HardieG7 6000 2:05⅖ ChiefSun CardinalPaul Sorrowful
May13-699Was1 1 :3011:0131:3342:041ft 73 8 8 87¼ 99¼ 87¼ HardieG7 nw400068 2:05⅗ R. Frisco Wyn O Boy Billy Frisco
May 3-695Was1 1 :3021:0031:3222:031ft 48 8 8 89 711 713 HardieG9 nw400068 2:05⅘ Mock'gDr'm B'lyFrisco C'sdraDay
Apr24-695Was1 1 :2941:0041:3312:041ft 91 7 7 99 911 917 HardieG9 nw500068 2:07⅗ BerthaParker Bock FashionChief
Oct22-68 Hol1 1 :30 1:0111:3242:013ft 45 6 7 6 812 814 HardieG5 nw550068 2:04⅖ ChiefCrazyLegs Hal'sGuy Kimpam

5 8-1
2:04⅕ (Was1, '69) ($10,731) Driver-Trainer—DON BUSSE (49-4-6-6—.190) Gray-Red
Rich Adios ⊗ B. g (1964), by Noble Adios—Shadow Haven, by Eddie Havens. 1969 13 6 2 0 $10,075
Owner, Robert R. Petersen, Elmhurst, Ill. 1968 40 7 6 3 $9,506
Jun 2-698Spk⅝ 1 :2931:0211:3242:044ft 6⅗ 6 60 21¼ 1½ 1¾ BusseD3 6000 2:04⅘ RichAdios C'rd'lPaul Midn'tBr'nie
May24-694Spk⅝ 1 :3131:0441:3432:052ft 4½ 20 30 43½ 822 919 McDermottC6 c5000 2:09⅕ Whizmor Louie H. Brightest
May16-696Was1 1 :3111:0041:3212:041ft 3-2 *1 2 21½ 11 11 BusseD4 c4000 2:04⅕ RichAdios GlennH.W. ChiefSmile
May 9-694Was1 1 :31 1:0331:37 2:074sy 3½ 7x 9 9 9 9di. BusseD7 5000 JayArN. Brightest MillieByrd
May 2-6910Was1 1 :3041:0121:34 2:05 ft 2½ *20 10 1nk 2nk 21½ BusseD6 5000 2:05⅗ Brightest RichAdios ConnieL.
Apr24-6910Was1 1 :3141:04 1:3522:063ft 6-5 *50 1 1nk 12 12½ BusseD2 4000 2:06⅗ RichAdios RudyCounsel ActiveRuth

6 3-1
2:03⅗ (PmP⅝, '69) ($14,081) Driver—ALVIN STANKE. Trainer, D. Frizzell (13-4-3-1—.462) Gold-Purple
Gerry's First ⊗ B. m (1964), by Norris Hanover—Reed's Keepsake, by Don Adios. 1969 20 7 4 6 $8,935
Owner, R. P. & Lavena S. Hoffmann; Northville, Mich. 1968 18 2 2 1 $3,359
Jun 4-698Spk⅝ 1 :3031:0311:3442:054sy 5½ 1 2 31½ 31½ 1½ StankeA9 9000 2:05⅘ Gerry'sFirst Helanja DannyRip
May26-695Spk⅝ 1 :3041:0211:33 2:043ft 3½ 1 2 31 31 1nk StankeA7 nw12508 2:04⅗ Gerry'sFirst Kimpam Skinan
May19-696Spk⅝ 1 :3031:0231:3322:04 ft 4⅗ 3 4 53½ 31½ 32¼ StankeA2 fmnw12508 2:04⅗ PoplarCo'kie LadyTrip G'rry'sFirst
May10-69 Nfld 1 :3211:05 1:3712:082sy 4½ x8x 8 8 8 8di. StankeA3 w75006869 Butch'sTime HalryAbbe Sc'mpDir't
May 2-69 Nfld 1 :32 1:04 1:3522:064ft 6 2 3 3 41¾ 3¾ StankeA5 Cond 2:07 SatanTass GoGoRoy'ltime G'ry'sF't
Apr26-69 Nfld 1 :3021:0231:34 2:05 ft 9¾ 6 6 7 76¼ 46 StankeA4 w75006869 2:06⅕ FreckleFace V'l'yV'wFl'e P't'rK.S't

7 8-1
2:02⅘ (Hol1, '68) ($61,145) Driver-Trainer—RUSSELL VALLES KEY (11-0-1-0—.051) Green-White
Joe Parker ⊗ Ch. g (1963), by Airliner—Spring Weather, by Norris Hanover. 1969 15 1 5 0 $4,414
Owner, Golden West Stables, Los Angeles, Calif. 1968 10 1 3 2 $3,976
Jun 3-696Spk⅝ 1 :2931:0131:3242:032ft 13 3 3 32¼ 22 42¼ VallesKeyR3 10000 2:04 MajorMah'ne ConMan Dick'sSister
May26-698Spk⅝ 1 :31 1:0541:3622:054ft 7¼ 3 3 32 33 54¼ VallesKeyR2 nw12508 2:06⅗ Ballock ChiefG.Dir'ct Gu'stSpeaker
May16-698Was1 1 :31 1:0141:3332:031ft 79 10 2 32 25 48¼ VallesKeyR9 12000 2:05 Instantly Major Pip Rupert H.
May10-695Was1 1 :31 1:0321:3522:073gd 11 4 8 84¼ 52 41 FalknerJ2 nw400068 2:07⅘ GypsyGoose RacerWave Jean'sTea
Apr22-699Was1 1 :3021:0221:3532:06 ft 42 1 2 2nk 2⅗ 41¼ FalknerJ7 nw400068 2:06⅖ Gr'mpyGabe B'rtStone M'ck'gDr'm
Apr15-695Was1 1 :3121:0221:3432:05 gd 38 40 20 2½ 44¼ 89 FalknerJ2 nw300068 2:06⅘ FashionChief ZekeZam Chataqua

8 10-1
2:03⅘ (Hol1, '68) ($3,844) Driver-Trainer—DEL CRONK (7-0-0-1—.048) Green-Gray
Pride of Egypt Br. g (1961), by Johnny Globe—Egyptian Rose, by Light Brigade. 1969 11 0 0 1 $329
Owner, Menlo Stable, El Monte, Calif. 1968 12 1 1 1 $3,376
Jun 2-697Spk⅝ 1 :3031:0521:36 2:07 ft 58 1 1 1½ 32½ 67 CronkD3 nw12502-6 2:08⅗ FieldDiam'd RolaC'st'r Id'na'sF'th
Mar 6-69 B.M1 1 :30 1:03 1:3532:06 ft 30 3 4 7 813 820 CronkD2 nw375068 2:10 ChoiceP'nter Mock'gDr'm B'bC'lith
Feb26-69 B.M1 1 :3141:0421:38 2:091gd 38 3 4 4x 818 819 CronkD3 nw350068 2:13 QuintoAdios Command Chicory
Feb19-69 B.M1 1 :3121:0321:3612:073gd 37 2 3 7 714 723 CronkD3 nw35006869 2:12⅕ Voison Chicory SaintEstepheA.
Feb 7-69 B.M1 1 :3111:0221:3512:071ft 27 1 3 8 814 716 CronkD6 Cond 2:10⅖ ArgoPat SaintEstepheA. Chicory
Feb 4-69 B.M1 1 :3231:0511:3612:084ft 15 3 3 4 67 57¼ CronkD2 nw5000 2:10⅕ Linc'lnL'ndBr'k HiLoHill BillFrisco

9 12-1
2:06⅘ (Btva, '68) ($8,543) Driver—ROBERT WILLIAMS. Trainer, F. Bettis (44-12-10-1—.407) Purple-White
Claude F. B. h (1964), by Spanish Abbey—Ruth Brainerd, by Wayne Scott. 1969 1 0 0 0 (—)
Owner, Est. of Dave L. Brown, Chattanooga, Tenn. 1968 35 5 5 3 $5,373
Jun 4-698Spk⅝ 1 :3031:0311:3442:054sy 43 8ix8 87 89 76½ WilliamsR4 7500 2:07⅕ Gerry'sFirst Helanja DannyRip
Nov29-68 Btva 1 :3131:05 1:37 2:102sl 18 5 6 6 64½ 43¾ FullerC5 Cond 2:11⅕ WhiteCr'sc't Ch'st'rCol's'l Gil'reC'f
Nov22-68 Btva 1 :3131:0541:3722:09 sl 15 8 8 8 610 510 FullerC7 Cond 2:11⅕ Gilm'reCh'f N'rdin'sFury DinoMin'r
Nov15-68 Btva 1 :3131:0421:38 2:12 sy 5¾ 30 2 2 21 22 FullerC6 Cond 2:12⅘ LuckyLarry ClaudeF. HiLuzelta
Nov 6-68 Btva 1 :3131:05 1:3812:094sy 6 5 5 6 53¾ 34¾ FullerC4 Cond 2:10⅘ CombatCh'f Y'nkeeSher'f Cl'udeF.
Oct24-68 Btva 1 :3211:0521:3812:103sy 6 20 2 2 21½ 58¼ FullerC4 Cond 2:12⅕ SomeStep BigRedGrat'n Gen's'eSis

Trackman's Selections—6 1 2

ONE MILE TROT | # 9th RACE | **Purse $6,000**

THE HARLAN DEAN

INVITATIONAL. 3-year-olds and up.

PLEASE ASK FOR HORSE BY PROGRAM NUMBER

1 (6-1) 2:02⅗ (PmP⅝, '68) ($53,018) Driver-Trainer—GENE SEARS (19-4-2-4—.339) White-Brown
Gale Force
B. h (1964), by Galophone—Mary Dear, by Rodney. 1969 5 1 1 1 $3,022
Ow., Sears, Gangloff-Downham; Pomp'no B'h, Fla.; Log'nsp't, Ind. 1968 41 9 7 7 $41,527
Jun 5-696Spk⅝ 1:30 1:0211:3342:041ft 1 •2 3 2¼ 1½ 11 SearsG1 nw15508 2:04⅕ GaleForce A.C'sVict'ry OhioSpecial
May28-695Spk⅝ 1:3041:0331:34 2:041ft7-5 •6 6 5¾ 32 3½ SearsG4 nw15008 2:04⅘ SaraRodney DillyVic GaleForce
May22-695Spk⅝ 1:3031:0141:3342:05 ft 5¼ 8 8 4¼ 3½ 2no SearsG8 nw15008 2:05 Frisco Lad Gale Force Cambev
Jan17-69 PmP⅝ 1:3111:0121:3242:041ft 2¼ •5 5 5 5¼ 59 GassP3 pr2500 2:06 SteaminMissile MissB'kyP'k B'eQ'n
Jan10-69 PmP⅝ 1:32 1:0421:3512:054gd7-5 •4 4 4 42 41 SearsG3 pr2500 2:06 BelleQueen MissB'kyP'k St'minM'e
Dec27-68 PmP⅝ 1:3021:0311:3412:051ft8-5 3 4 3 21 1½ SearsG6 hp2500 2:05⅕ GaleForce BelleQueen Mudge'sT'y

2 (9-2) 1:59⅗ (Hol1, '68) ($92,321) Driver—JOE O'BRIEN. Trainer, F. Redden (46-5-8-5—.242) Gold-White
Huck Finn
Blk. g (1961), by Faber Hanover—Mary Main, by Main Scott. 1969 2 0 1 0 $2,060
Owner, B. N. Redden, Mayfield, Ky. 1968 28 9 4 5 $41,605
Jun 2-699Spk⅝ 1:2811:0211:3222:03 ft 2¼ 4ix5 56 5¾ 5⁸½†ReddenF3 hp7000 2:04⅘ Met're II. G'ytideTheGr't Ch'yGuy
†Placed fourth through disqualification.
May27-699Spk⅝ 1:3041:0341:34 2:034ft 5¼ 2 2 2¼ 22 2¾ O'BrienJ2 in6000 2:04 G'ytideTheGr't HuckFinn M't're II.
Nov15-68 Hol1 1:31 1:0211:36 2:07 sy 4½ x6 6 6 513 517 WilliamsR4 in10000 2:10⅗ BarMan Bri'tChance Gov'rArmbro
Nov 8-68 Hol1 1:2911:0021:31 2:002ft 6¾ 6 6 6 6⁸¾ 4²¼†WilliamsR5 in10000 2:00⅘ LumberSon Bri'tChance HuckFinn
†Placed third through disqualification.
Nov 1-68 Hol1 1:2931:0021:3032:00 ft 7 4 1'1 2½ 6²¼ WilliamsR2 in10000 2:00⅖ Gov'rArmbro Bri'tCh'ce L'mb'rS'n

3 (8-1) 2:02⅖ (L.B⅝, '68) ($33,155) Driver—DWAYNE PLETCHER. Trainer, K. Bartlett (37-3-6-2—.189) White-Black
Our Rainbow ⊗
B. h (1963), by Star's Pride—Our Treat, by Rodney. 1969 2 0 0 0 $350
Ow., Ryan, M.-B. Morrison-Datone; M'rt'n Gr've, Sk'kie, Ill.; Atl'ta, Ga. 1968 15 6 4 3 $14,485
Jun 2-699Spk⅝ 1:2811:0211:3222:03 ft 19 2 1 1¼ 1h 4⁵¼†RyanT2 hp7000 2:04⅕ Met're II. G'ytideTheGr't Ch'yGuy
†Disqualified and placed fifth for interference.
May27-699Spk⅝ 1:3041:0341:34 2:034ft 27 5 5 32 6⁵¼ 7⁸¼ RyanT1 in6000 2:05⅖ G'ytideTheGr't HuckFinn M't're II.
Nov30-685May 1:3131:0311:35 2:063ft 5 1 1 1½ 1hx 2nk RyanT6 pr7500 2:06⅗ LilRodney OurRainbow DanW.Dil'r
Nov14-685May 1:3131:0311:3632:104sy 6¾ 20 10 1¼ 11 1¾ RyanT5 hp5000 2:10⅘ Our Rainbow Dan W. Diller Ira
Nov 7-685May 1:3031:0121:3332:054gd 3¾ 10 1 1¼ 1nk 4²¼ RyanT2 pr5000 2:06⅖ CrazyOtto AllAm'rican Fl'x'y'sB'be

4 (3-1) 2:01⅕ (Was1, '68) ($46,016) Driver-Trainer—JOE MARSH JR. (51-8-8-7—.290) Gray-Blue-Red
Propensity ⊗
Blk. g (1963), by Jamie—Profit, by Protector. 1969 8 2 1 1 $13,280
Owner, George & Ronald Oldfield, Tecumseh, Mich. 1968 24 6 3 2 $34,445
May24-699Spk⅝ 1:30 1:0121:31 2:021ft 14 1 1 1½x 914 914 MarshJJr6 fa25000 2:05 Fr'shY'kee BrightCh'nce RealSp'd
May16-697Was1 1:292 :5941:3132:021ft 2¼ 20 1 11 1no 2nk MarshJJr6 hp10000 2:02⅕ SonnyFort'ne Pr'p'sity Pr'v'nFr'ht
May 9-697Was1 1:31 1:0331:3532:064sy 2 •x9 9 9 9 9di. MarshJJr9 hp10000 R'ISp'd G'ytideTheGr't S'nyF'rt'ne
May 2-697Was1 1:292 :5931:3242:023ft9-5 •40 1 1¼ 1½ 1¾ MarshJJr7 hp10000 2:02⅗ Propensity SonnyFort'ne Cr'zyOtto
Apr25-697Was1 1:2921:0011:33 2:031ft7-5 •30 1x 7 7 7di. MarshJJr7 hp10000 CrazyOtto Met'reII. W'rthyC'lt'wn
Apr18-697Was1 1:3141:0341:36 2:062sy 5¼ 1 1 1¾ 1¼ 11 MarshJJr6 hp10000 2:06⅖ Propensity Meteore II. S'nyF'rt'ne

5 (6-1) 2:00⅘ (Hol1, '68) ($144,462) Driver-Trainer—JACK WILLIAMS (19-3-3-3—.298) Red-White
Lumber Son
B. g (1962), by Lumber Boy—Lumber Along, by Rodney. 1969 8 2 0 3 $6,680
Owner, Ed P. Schafer, Bradbury, Calif. 1968 32 4 6 9 $38,940
Jun 6-693Spk⅝ 1:3011:0141:3332:043ft 3-2 •20 2 2¼ 11 11 WilliamsJ8 w1550 2:04⅗ L'b'rS'n Pr'c'ssR'd'lph My IrishQ'n
May27-699Spk⅝ 1:3041:0341:34 2:034ft 7½ 7x 7 7⁵¼ 7⁶½ 5⁷¼ WilliamsJ6 in6000 2:05⅕ G'ytideTheGr't HuckFinn M't're II.
May23-694Spk⅝ 1:3121:0341:35 2:051ft 4¼ 3 4 4³½ 4²½ 3³¼ WilliamsJ1 w1550 2:05⅘ My IrishQ'n R's'd'leSt'r L'mb'rS'n
Mar 7-69 B.M1 1:3141:0421:3532:053ft 7½ 2 3 3 3¹½ 3¹¼ WilliamsJ5 Cond 2:05⅘ Dy'micVict'y Tr'v'rH'n'v'r L'b'rS'n
Feb28-69 B.M1 1:33 1:0741:41 2:11 sy 12 1 2 3 31 6³¼†WilliamsJ6 w60006869 2:11⅘ G'ytideTheG't Tr'v'rH'n'v'r B'rM'n
†Placed fifth through disqualification.

6 (5-1) 2:03⅕ (Was1, '69) ($24,628) Driver—ROBERT WILLIAMS. Trainer, M. Caponetto (44-12-10-1—.407) Purple-White
Rosedale Star ⊗
Br. m (1961), by Newport Mascot—Jean Armour, by Victory Song. 1969 8 3 1 0 $9,438
Owner, Rosedale Stable, Chicago, Ill. 1968 25 3 1 3 $10,491
May30-693Spk⅝ 1:3031:02 1:3342:043ft 2¾ 1 1 1¼ 1½ 1no WilliamsR1 w1550 2:04⅗ RosedaleSt'r G'ld'nW'l My Ir'hQ'n
May23-694Spk⅝ 1:3121:0341:35 2:051ft 2¼ 4 1 1¼ 1no 2¾ WilliamsR2 w1550 2:05⅖ My IrishQ'n R's'd'leSt'r L'mb'rS'n
May 9-695Was1 1:32 1:0331:3732:081sy 3¾ 30 1 1¼ 14 15 WilliamsR8 nw1000068 2:08⅕ R'sed'leSt'r AllAm'ric'n J'nieBrook
May 2-695Was1 1:2941:00 1:3142:031ft 12 6 10 1h 12 1¼ WilliamsR6 nw1000068 2:03⅕ R's'd'leSt'r AllAm'ric'n D'nW.D'l'r
Apr26-692Was1 1:3111:0241:34 2:052ft 6¼ 7 60 64x 9 9di. WelchW6 nw1000068 JanieBrook Farlen AllAmerican
Apr12-695Was1 1:3041:0231:3412:05 ft 5¼ 4 4 4²½ 4¹½ 4⁴¼ FarringtonR2 nw800068 2:05⅘ PhyllisDiller RhythmD'ke FriscoL'd

7 (7-2) 2:01⅗ (Atl⅝, '68) ($167,909) Driver-Trainer—ROBERT FARRINGTON (68-17-8-7—.350) Red-Gray
Meteore II. ⊗
Ch. g (1956), by Ri—Guepiere II., by Simoun M. Owner, Farrington 1969 15 3 4 1 $18,940
Stables, Inc. & Arnold Cattle Co., Inc.; Richw'd, Ohio; Gen'seo, Ill. 1968 41 7 4 3 $35,525
Jun 2-699Spk⅝ 1:2811:0211:3222:03 ft 2¾ 3 3 2¼ 2h 11 FarringtonR1 hp7000 2:03 Met're II. G'ytideTheGr't Ch'yGuy
May27-699Spk⅝ 1:3041:0341:34 2:034ft 3¾ 4 4 64 4⁴½x3¹¾ FarringtonR4 in6000 2:04⅕ G'ytideTheGr't HuckFinn M't're II.
May20-699Spk⅝ 1:2941:0231:34 2:034ft 3¼ 4 4 42 3½ 4½ FarringtonR6 in6000 2:04 G'ytideT'eGr't Ch'n'yG'y S'yF'rt'e
May16-695Was1 1:30 :5941:3042:024ft 2 •30 3 5⁴½ 53 12 Farringt'nR4 nw1000068 2:02⅘ Meteore II. Rhythm Duke Farlen
May 9-697Was1 1:31 1:0331:3532:064sy 7½ 7 8x 77 8 8di. FarringtonR3 hp10000 R'ISp'd G'ytideTheGr't S'nyF'rt'ne
May 2-697Was1 1:292 :5931:3242:023ft 4 5 5 3²½ 54 55 FarringtonR4 hp10000 2:03⅗ Propensity SonnyFort'ne Cr'zyOtto

Trackman's Selections—4 7 2

Thursday Is Quinella Night

The Quinella is held every Thursday on the ninth and tenth races. You select the first two horses in the race. If either one of your picks finishes first and the other second you win. When buying tickets, give the lower number first, e.g.: 1-2, 3-4, 5-6, 7-8, etc. Play any number of combinations. You may wheel a horse. Any time your selections finish 1-2 or 2-1 you're a winner.

ONE MILE PACE **10th RACE** **Purse $2,600**

Claiming. Claiming price $4,000. 3-year-olds and up. Rock Springs Bob, Phyllis C. Scott in for $4,800; rest for $4,000.

PLEASE ASK FOR HORSE BY PROGRAM NUMBER

2:03⅘ (Spk⅝, '68) ($29,200) Driver-Trainer—TOM MERRIMAN (24-2-5-1—.213) White-Maroon
1 **W. D.'s Orphan** Br. g (1964), by W. D. Direct—Ella Counsel, by King's Counsel. 1969 5 1 0 0 $1,303
Owner, Robert C. Kalish, Southfield, Mich. 1968 15 4 1 3 $12,428
May30-692Spk⅝ 1 :3241:0631:3732:082ft 2½ ⁴8 70 42½ 31½ 41½ MerrimanT8 3500 2:08⅘ ScotchNote EyreNavarch E.F.C'lby
May17-69 Det 1 :3131:07 1:4042:132gd 2½ ⁴4 4 2 2½ 52¼ MerrimanT2 3000 2:13⅗ MissEllenSue RogerL. TheCruiser
May 9-69 Det 1 :3221:0721:4112:132gd 1 ⁴2 2 2 1h 11 MerrimanT1 3000 2:13⅖ W.D'sOrph'n L'ckyD'min'n J'myD'o
Apr30-69 Det 1 :3211:0631:3912:10 ft 3-2 ⁴4 4 4 31 54 MerrimanT2 5000 2:10⅗ AdiosDan MightyKnox SomeAbbe
Apr24-69 Det 1 :32 1:0631:3812:094gd 4-5 ⁴6 6 7 42 44½ MerrimanT4 4000 2:10⅗ PrinceLeo Fr'nt'rM'rsh'll D'ncer
Jly 30-689Spk⅝ 1 :3011:0221:3212:02 ft 4½ 8 70 66 46 36 MerrimanT6 10200 2:03⅕ HankTheD'r W'thyH'rN. W.D'sOr'n

2:09⅖ (Was1, '69) ($360) Driver-Trainer—AUBREY PETTY (15-6-0-1—.422) Maroon-Black
2 **Rock Springs Bob** Br. g (1965), by Brooks Hanover—Eastertide, by Harvere. 1969 10 2 0 0 $3,353
Owner, Aubrey L. Petty, Mason, Tenn. 1968 3 M 1 1 $360
May28-692Spk⅝ 1 :3031:03 1:3342:05 ft 8½ 8 8 64 76½ 77 PettyA5 4800 2:06⅖ RudyCouns'l ArmbroHusky AirQu'n
May12-692Was1 1 :3041:0231:3442:061ft 12 8 8 76½ 65 75 PettyA6 4800 2:07⅕ RedEblis B'rn'yBl'kst'ne PaulaG'in
May 3-694Was1 1 :3031:0111:3342:051ft 12 8 8 74¼ 63½ 56¼ PettyA6 6000 2:06⅖ M'sM'phy'sW'y A'nieV'lo P'teB'k'y
Apr24-6910Was1 1 :3141:04 1:3522:063ft 10 9 9 912 810 55¼†PettyA8 4800 2:07⅗ RichAdios RudyCounsel ActiveRuth
†Dead heat.
Apr16-697Was1 1 :3021:0131:33 2:042ft 62 7 7 88¼ 69 66 PettyA6 nw300068 2:05⅗ St'teExpr'sN. E'st'rnTime D'nyRip
Apr 4-697Was1 1 :3141:0411:38 2:092sy 8¾ 1 4 53½ 51½ 67¼ PettyA6 n3R 2:10⅘ ScottishGrattan Folger C'nselBelle

2:02⅕ (Hol1, '68) ($42,095) Driver-Trainer—JOE MARSH JR. (51-8-8-7—.290) Gray-Blue-Red
3 **Jonboy Star** Blk. g (1956), by U. Scott—Solar, by Josedale Grattan. 1969 15 3 3 0 $5,266
Owner, Walter & Ruth Petersen; Lexington, Mich. 1968 38 8 1 4 $10,810
May23-692Spk⅝ 1 :3111:05 1:3642:081ft 8-5 ⁴2 2 12½ 14 1h MarshJJr8 3500 2:08⅕ Jonb'ySt'r Vict'ryBrig'de Ch'fR't'n
May14-698Was1 1 :3131:0341:37 2:081ft 6-5 ⁴1 2 2½ 1½x 920 MarshJJr6 3500 2:12⅕ Eddie'sM'yS'ng Ch'fR't'n S'raB'th
May 1-6910Was1 1 :30 1:01 1:3342:062ft 2¾ 5 6 65 32 13 MarshJJr1 3500 2:06⅗ JonboyStar DonRobin HighCasteN.
Apr22-694Was1 1 :3021:0311:3532:062ft 6-5 ⁴3 2 21½ 23 56½ MarshJJr4 3500 2:07⅘ Laurinda HighCasteN. Sundowner
Apr 9-691Was1 1 :3041:0231:3512:062ft 6-5 ⁴2 3 21½ 2½ 2no MarshJJr3 3500 2:06⅖ JayBroom JonboyStar ChiefSmile
Mar29-69 Det 1 :3221:08 1:42 2:134gd 2½ ⁴2 1 1 1½ 1h PetersenW3 3500 2:13⅘ JonboySt'r AndyAt'm S'n't'rH'ds'n

2:04⅖ (Spk⅝, '69) ($68,170) Driver-Trainer—ROBERT FARRINGTON (68-17-8-7—.350) Red-Gray
4 **Barney Blackstone** ⊗ Ch. g (1956), by Royal Blackstone—Opal Kirk, by Frank Jackson. 1969 7 2 2 2 $4,988
Ow., Ar'ld C'tle Co., Inc., F'ingt'n St'bles, Inc., G'seo, Ill., R'w'd, O. 1968 38 5 1 2 $6,743
May31-692Spk⅝ 1 :2911:0121:3242:043ft 2½ ⁴6 6 59 3h 1nk FarringtonR4 4000 2:04⅖ Bar'yB'stone MadAd'l E'j'n'sP'de
May21-695Spk⅝ 1 :3221:0641:3932:111sy 1 ⁴5 5 21 1½ 13 FarringtonR3 4000 2:11⅕ B'n'yBl'kst'e P'lm'rY'tes MissL'lla
May12-692Was1 1 :3041:0231:3442:061ft 2½ ⁴7 7 55 53½ 2nk FarringtonR5 4000 2:06⅕ RedEblis B'rn'yBl'kst'ne PaulaG'in
May 1-697Was1 1 :30 1:0021:32 2:043ft 6¾ 9 9 912 814 814 FarringtonR8· 5000 2:07⅖ Rainmak'r JayArN. Sp'rklingStone
Apr21-698Was1 1 :30 1:0211:3542:071ft 2½ 6 7 74½ 64¼ 21¼ FarringtonR4 5000 2:07⅖ LoBeGo B'neyBl'kstone Diplo'tTrip
Apr 7-698Was1 1 :3211:0421:3612:07 ft 2 ⁴6 60 63 41 3h FarringtonRi5 5000 2:07 Brightest MichaelB. B'n'yBl'kst'ne

2:04⅗ (Hol1, '68) ($15,252) Driver-Trainer—JACQUES GRENIER (20-1-2-0—.106) Red-White
5 **Pipe of Peace** B. h (1962), by Morris Eden—Grattan Dillon, by Dillon Hall. 1969 3 0 0 1 $120
Owner, M & A Stable, Chicago, Ill. 1968 12 1 1 2 $3,132
May31-693Spk⅝ 1 :3011:0131:3242:041ft 28 9 9 96½ 65 710 GrenierJ9 5000 2:06⅕ SportAdio Colvin'sLad O.B'sAdm'l
May19-697Spk⅝ 1 :3141:0421:3712:082ft 12 1 1 1½ 96 912 GrenierJ7 7000 2:10⅘ OldBl'e M'st'rR'dw'd W'rn'sJef'rey
Jan18-699BmlP 1 :3111:0421:3712:091ft 7 10 1 2no 2no 32¼ ShortW7 nw400068 2:09⅘ Darl'g'sVap'r H'styP'ce PipeofP'e
Dec18-68 Hol1 1 :30 1:0021:3142:023ft 23 30 2 3 10121025 GrenierM7 7000 2:07⅖ KingGene OrbitMan AprilLad
Dec13-68 Hol1 1 :2911:0011:3232:024ft 31 2 4 6 43 94½ GrenierM5 8000 2:03⅗ RupertH. PulaskiSilver SafeReturn
Nov30-68 Hol1 1 :2931:0141:3312:023ft 14 9 9 7 810 510 GrenierJ8 10000 2:04⅖ SafeReturn KnoxAway VernonAdi's

2:06 (Was1, '68) ($13,362) Driver—NELSON WILLIS. Trainer, C. Willis (14-1-3-1—.214) Maroon-Gray-White
6 **Eyre Navarch** ⊗ B. g (1964), by Sister's Son—Tactful Rosa, by Tactful Guy. 1969 17 0 4 2 $4,038
Owner, Glen Eyre Farm, Glasgow, Ky. 1968 28 3 3 4 $7,296
May30-692Spk⅝ 1 :3241:0631:3732:082ft 7½ 40 1 32 42½ 2nk WillisC3 3500 2:08⅖ ScotchNote EyreNavarch E.F.C'lby
May15-694Was1 1 :3041:0211:3542:071ft 7½ 8 8 83½ 61½ 32¼ WillisC6 3500 2:07⅗ HighT'sel RuthAnnAb'e EyreNav'h
May 7-696Was1 1 :3241:05 1:38 2:101sy 6¾ 5 5 43 54½ 23¼ WillisC1 3500 2:11 EllimacN. EyreNavarch D'min'nL'd
Apr29-692Was1 1 :3111:0411:3632:073ft 6½ 1 2 41½ 42½ 32 WillisC4 3500 2:08 G.G.P'rk'r Domin'nLad EyreN'v'rch
Apr16-696Was1 1⅟₁₆ :3131:0432:07 2:312ft 10 5 5 57½ixAcc. dnf.WillisC8 3500 Joan'sGirl JimmieTarw'y AlB'rsB'y
Apr 8-697Was1 1 :3131:0331:35 2:061ft 13 1 4 34 44½ 44½†WillisC8 3500 2:07 G'rgeAdios Whizm'r Eddie'sM'yS'g

2:05⅖ (Was1, '68) ($7,722) Driver-Trainer—JOHNNY BLEVINS (15-0-1-0—.037) White-Blue-Black
7 **Goin Direct** B. g (1964), by Direct Spangler—Rosa Pence, by Scottish Pence. 1969 6 0 0 0 $130
Owner, Ella M. & Joe W. Goins; Thorntown, Ind. 1968 21 2 2 1 $3,052
Jun 5-69 Spk⅝ 1 :32 1:0411:3332:044ft N.B. 5 4 612 414 411 BlevinsJ9 Qua 2:07 SpeedyW've TimmieWin S'cc'sK'tie
Jun 2-69 Spk⅝ 1 :3211:0541:3642:091ft N.B. 6 6 65½ 75½ 63½ BlevinsJ5 Qua 2:09⅘ Sh'dyd'leS'th Athl'neR'yn'ds S'lC'f
May23-69 Spk⅝ 1 :3241:0621:3932:093ft N.B. 1 1 11½ 32 45½ BlevinsJ3 Qua 2:10⅗ ArmbroJeff TheFooler LittleP'nt'r
Feb12-698BmlP 1 :3231:07 1:3842:103ft 9½ 4 30x612 818 8di. WillisN4 nw200068 AdiosCool HighTassel L'tleF'xAbbe
Feb 6-696BmlP 1 :3241:07 1:3922:104ft 25 7 7 76 67 68½ WillisN8 nw300068 2:12⅘ RosedaleEil'n V'loHon'r M'sFed'ski
Jan29-699BmlP 1 :3311:0831:4312:174sy 21 Fog.6 Fog.517 510 WillisN4 nw300068 2:19⅘ R'sed'leEil'n FreeCh'ce TrueH'rb'r

2:04⅘ (Lex1, '68) ($25,342) Driver-Trainer—JAMES CRANE (9-0-5-2—.383) Silver-Red
8 **Perry Win** B. g (1961), by Sky Raider—Wid I Win, by The Widower. 1969 3 1 0 0 $1,160
Ow., Richard & Norman Goguen; Glendale, Calif.; Lynnfield, Mass. 1968 38 5 4 5 $6,804
May27-692Spk⅝ 1 :3021:0321:3522:064ft 7½ 6 6 63½ 51½ 1½ O'BrienJ4 3000 2:06⅘ PerryWin SilverDella WiggleWick
Jan 8-69 B.M1 1 :3341:0821:39 2:101ft 6½ 6 6 6 75½ 77½ BerryD6 3000 2:11⅗ BrownJet WhangaEarl Jan'sPride
Jan 3-69 B.M1 1 :3341:0541:3622:072ft 5 4 6 6 68 56 CraneJ3 3000 2:08⅗ GlennH.W. GoldMite Jan'sPride
Dec23-68 Hol1 1 :3111:04 1:3642:064ft 11 6 8 7 78½ 54½ CraneJ4 3500 2:07⅖ ArmbroHusky AdioSquare Shotgun
Dec19-68 Hol1 1 :3021:0141:35 2:061ft 8¾ 5 7 7 64¼ 21¼ CraneJ2 3000 2:06⅕ ShawnHill PerryWin Fr'ghtPartner
Dec13-68 Hol1 1 :2931:0211:3412:044ft 11 7 9 9 97¼ 67 CraneJ5 3500 2:06 Lavina ConnieL. CardinalPaul

2:06 (Hol1, '68) ($39,619) Driver-Trainer—JAY RUSSELL (1-0-1-0—.556) Gold-Maroon
9 **Phyllis C. Scott** Blk. m (1960), by Callie G.—Abbie Gratt, by Grattan McKinney. 1969 3 0 1 0 $890
Owner, J. T. & Evelyn L. Russell; Huntsville, Ala. 1968 30 3 5 5 $7,228
May26-6910Spk⅝ 1 :3121:0241:34 2:051ft 10 5 5 53½ 43 22 RussellJ3 4800 2:05⅗ ShawnHill PhyllisC.Sc't PrebleCh'f
May16-6910Was1 1 :3011:0121:3432:063ft 14 3 6 62½ 62½ 44¾ RussellJ1 3500 2:07⅗ Gl'nPrimrose ArtBerry Ens'nPul'r
May 7-696Was1 1 :3241:05 1:38 2:101sy 14 7 7 74¾ 78 610 RussellJ4 3500 2:12⅕ EllimacN. EyreNavarch D'min'nL'd
Dec 2-68 Hol1 1 :3221:05 1:3512:06 ft 2¾ ⁴3 6 9 810 88¾ RussellJ2 3600 2:07⅖ PerryWin HappyHal TaylorCreek
Nov27-68 Hol1 1 :31 1:0211:3342:044ft 6¾ 60 2 1 11½ 57 RussellJ8 4200 2:06⅕ ConnieL. CardinalPaul S'mmitRoad
Nov20-68 Hol1 1 :33 1:0511:3622:06 ft 3 5 4 4 32½ 12½ RussellJ4 3600 2:06 PhyllisC.Sc't Vict'ryBrig'de H'sB'y

Trackman's Selections—4 9 2

the finish, despite breaking in the stretch. He paid $6.00 for place. The winner at 9 to 5 was Speedy Mark. The crowd counted on him retaining some of his former class, and was right.

The Second Race

The most recently raced horses in this field are Hi Buster and Tough Trot, neither of which is acceptable as a contender. Hi Buster raced dully and Tough Trot, a real cheapie from Buffalo Raceway, has been winless in 33 starts.

Scotch Note won by a hair against a lesser field and, like any other horse that backs up in the stretch without an excuse for doing so, is promptly eliminated. Emma C. is out of form. So Fiann is dull. Doctor Kildare showed plenty of hustle on May 27, and may be a contender if nothing better turns up.

Shawn Hill is a definite contender after his powerful effort of May 26. Alwyn Yates did nothing in its last. Neither did Orphan Whitney. Let's rate Doctor Kildare and Shawn Hill, the only possible contenders:

Doctor Kildare. His basic figure is 186. Add 10 for roughing it, 10 for the brilliant Bobby Williams and 5 for being a beaten favorite in the key race. Deduct 5 for the rise in class and 1 for the slight change in post position. The total is 205.

Shawn Hill. The basic rating here is 200, plus 5 for roughing it and 2 for the stretch gain, less 1 for the changed post position. The total is 206.

As uged on page 301, the margin of a single point between horses indicates that both should be bet. The more so when the horse with the slightly lower rating is to be driven by a topnotcher such as Williams.

RESULT: Williams lurked a length or so behind the leading Hi Buster until the stretch, when he took over and won. Shawn Hill, an 8 to 5 favorite, raced on the outside for a half-mile, then broke and finished seventh. Doctor Kildare paid $11.60 to win and a fat $6.20 to place.

The Third Race

This undertaking for Illinois-bred maidens cannot be handicapped. If you doubt this, try to handicap it yourself. The ultimate winner was Tug Way, who paid $13.40. The favorite was King Selka, who finished third.

The Fourth Race

This trot is another example of the race made to order for an improving three-year-old from a good barn. The colt in question is Portfolio, handled by the eminent Joe Marsh. Winner of 12 out of 16 at two and a romping victor only eight nights ago against animals similar to tonight's, the horse stands out. Raw figures make Bilmar a prospect, which I mention only because it finished second, paying $7.20. Portfolio paid $4.40 for the win.

The Fifth Race

The only animal in this group that comes close to qualifying as a contender is Ranger Richard. Note that Pedro Adios was in a qualifier, not a regular race, and that it happened almost three weeks ago. Ranger Richard wins tonight without any fuss, paying $5.80. Pedro Adios, a 27 to 1 shot, finishes second, paying $14.60. Which proves nothing, but is interesting.

The Sixth Race

Our usual handicapping procedures do not apply here, but there is a way out. The name is Chancey Guy. Let me explain.

Five of the starters trotted against each other on June 4, when the track was off. The strong winner on that occasion, Volcanic Dan, has not competed for a purse on a fast surface since 1967. To make head or tail of this race, we would have to compare animals in terms of performances at Sportsman's Park when the footing was "good." What would we do then about Chancey Guy and Cambev?

I see no reason to pass the race, however. Note that Chancey Guy has been racing in handicaps and invitationals. In his last four outings, facing some of the best second-flight stock in the country, he has been well supported in the betting. He is in tonight's conditioned race because his trainer, Jim Dennis, spotted the opportunity in the condition book. Being winless recently, the horse is eligible to take on this soft field. He surely is worth a bet.

RESULT: Prince Kam won, paying $37.60. Chancey Guy, the 6 to 5 favorite, was gaining on him at the end but failed by a half-length.

The Seventh Race

You are going to love this one.

Profast, Heather Chance, Hark Way and Varsity Signal can be dismissed on grounds of form. No need to wonder about Hark Way, who has come close without showing any of the desired extra zip.

Bo Bo Ranger's only race this year was a victory in the slop. If he were the kind of up-and-coming three-year-old we like, we'd make him an automatic play. But there is no hint of glamor in his background. And some of the other starters in this field are hardly the cheap stock which our pet three-year-olds victimize. Bo Bo can be written off as the type of three-year-old likely to encounter misery when he faces older animals of quality equal to his own.

If you disagree, believing that the youngster's good race of June 4 plus his breeding and barn entitle him to high marks, you must either bet on him or pass the race. His recent form on a fast track cannot be evaluated clearly, or rated by our methods. I suggest that he, not the race, be passed.

Lady Trip's effort of June 4 would disqualify her if it had not been on an off track. Her May 28 race makes her a contender, although she by no means is the type of winning three-year-old that becomes an automatic play.

For a line on the fast-track form of Sports Arena, we must go back to May 19. His last was on an off track, and he broke stride (uncharacteristically) on May 28.

Speedy Wave has been terrible in both his local races. His fleet performance in a qualifier would make him an automatic play (see p. 223), were it not for the presence here of Kip Hanover. Kip's latest good race, on May 30, was faster than Speedy's qualifier. Out goes Speedy. But Kip Hanover is a definite contender. Let us now rate them:

Lady Trip. The basic rating for the May 28 performance is 199. Deducting a point for the new, less favorable post but adding 10 for her topnotch driver, Kidwell, the final figure is 208.

Sports Arena. The basic rating for the May 19 trip is 191. Add 5 for roughing it and 10 for Jim Dennis, a national leader whose local record must soon improve. The total is 206.

Kip Hanover. The well-bred stablemate of Lindy's Pride earned a basic figure of 212 on May 30. Add 5 for his quarter-mile of racing on the outside, plus 10 for the slick Beissinger, another national leader on a local losing streak. The total is 227, which makes the horse a standout selection, regardless of its unfavorable post position.

RESULT: Beissinger was third on the outside by the time they reached the quarter pole. He was on the lead at the half and remained there, paying an incredible $25.40 to win and $9.60 to place. Speedy Wave, favored at slightly better than 9 to 5, raced well to finish third, a length behind Sports Arena.

The Eighth Race

This is a fascinating example of the results achieved by insisting on recent good form over a fast track, plus the advantages of recognizing the parked-out symbol as an emblem of vigor.

Helanja has no recent fast-track form and can be eliminated. Fascinating Dream has raced in slop so often that he probably will be unable to cope with fast footing. He's out. So is Famous Cyrus, who has shown nothing since 1967.

Chief Sun's last race would be awful, were it not for the fact that he was out there roughing it. This makes him a contender. His vigorous win on May 24 may comfort such readers as hate to qualify him off that June 3 performance.

Rich Adios is an obvious contender off his latest race. So is Gerry's First, using the May 26 effort on a fast track. Joe Parker looks dangerous, dropping in class after two fair races. But he simply has not done anything on this oval that pronounces him fit to win. To insist on recent *good* form, regardless of class, is to miss some winners. But it keeps us off a lot of losers.

Pride of Egypt and Claude F. have offered nothing and can be tossed out. The contenders and their ratings:

Chief Sun. That not-so-horrible race of June 3 earned a basic rating of 207. Add 5 for roughing it, 5 for dropping in class, 3 for the improved post position and 10 for George Hardie's current record of three wins (which represent considerably better than 15 percent of his starts). The total is 230.

Rich Adios. The basic rating is 205, plus 5 for roughing it, 1 for the stretch gain and 1 for the improved post. Deduct 5 for the rise in class. The total is 207.

Gerry's First. The May 26 performance earned a basic rating of 206. Note that the mare is entitled to no credit for the apparent drop in class. This claimer is of higher quality than the conditioned race in which she performed on May 26. As is stated at the top of the program page, Gerry's First is entered to be claimed for $9,000, just as she was on June 4. Note that, although she had won the conditioned race at odds of 3½ to 1, her odds rose when she went with a $9,000 claiming tag in her next outing. The player needs no file of result charts or old programs to see that 5 points should be deducted for a rise in class. The stretch gain earns 3 (see p. 220), and the hot Alvin Stanke means an extra 10. Total is 214.

Chief Sun is the overwhelming choice. Even if we had used his May 24 victory for handicapping purposes, he would have rated as best.

RESULT: Helanja was favored at 2.20 to 1 and finished third. Chief Sun came from fifth in the stretch to win by almost a length, paying $27.80 and $10.20. Gerry's First was second and Rich Adios was fourth. Prices like Chief Sun's and, in the previous race, Kip Hanover's, amaze me. May amazement never end.

The Ninth Race

Here is an invitational trot, hard to handicap.

Gale Force is scratched. Huck Finn, interfered with in his June 2 race, when he was heavily bet, was catching the winner on May 27, and can be accepted as a contender off that strong debut.

Our Rainbow is not in good form. Propensity, a galloper, has been idle since May 24. That is not a good sign, since the June 2 handicap (see Huck Finn's record) was made to order for him. Out he goes.

Lumber Son is moving far up in class, but must be rated after that last good race. Rosedale Star can be dismissed, after losing ground in the stretch against an inferior field.

Rating the contenders:

Huck Finn. The May 27 race produces a basic rating of 201. Add 1 for the small gain in the stretch, plus 10 for the great Joe O'Brien. The total is 212.

Lumber Son. The basic rating is 208. Subtract 5 for the rise in class. Add 5 for roughing it, 3 for the improved post position and 10 for Jack Williams. The total is 221.

Meteore II. The basic rating is 214, plus 1 for the stretch gain, less 1 for the post position, plus 10 for Bob Farrington. Final rating is 224, making this French horse the play.

RESULT: This time the crowd outsmarts us. Huck Finn, the 8 to 5 favorite, caught Our Rainbow at the wire and won by a neck. Meteore II was an undistinguished fourth at better than 7 to 2. Note that Huck Finn would have been our choice if we had rated his June 2 race, regarding the interference break as worth 5 points, as a parked-out symbol is. I am reluctant to rate such a race, however, unless the horse recovers sufficiently from the interference to gain on the leaders.

The Tenth Race

Barney Blackstone seems to lay over this field of cheap pacers. Nothing else is even close. He wins, paying $4.00.

Another rewarding program. Adhering as closely as we could to our few simple principles of handicapping, we were able to make selections in all but two of the races. We found reason to recommend purchase of 12 tickets, of which nine paid off: Doctor Kildare ($11.60, $6.20), Shawn Hill (lost), Portfolio ($4.40), Ranger Richard ($5.80), Chancey Guy (lost), Kip Hanover ($25.40, 9.60), Chief Sun ($27.80, 10.20), Meteore II (lost), Barney Blackstone ($4.00).

17

Yonkers Raceway, JUNE 25, 1969

TRACK FAST. EVENING WARM. The percentage drivers are Carmine Abbatiello, John Chapman, Lucien Fontaine, Del Insko, the John Pattersons (father and son), George Phalen, Frank Popfinger, Dick Thomas. As indicated on page 236, the post positions deteriorate in direct ratio to their distance from the inside rail.

The First Race

We begin by discarding Cornish Man, Sharp Volo and Trinidad Hanover, each of which comes off an indifferent performance in a qualifying race. Hicki Hi gets the gate for a poor showing last out. Marked Pick can be eliminated on the grounds that its rating will not possibly be high enough to compensate for the outside post (see p. 238).

The contenders and their ratings:

Novel Blaze. As nearly as can be deduced from the record, this mare did nothing but stay on gait in her last two races. But on each occasion she advanced slightly through the short Yonkers stretch, finishing close to the winner. At half-milers, performances of this kind are neither bad enough to establish an animal as a probable loser nor good enough to serve as a basis for handicapping. As suggested on page 216, the player should use the May 28 race, on the theory that (a) it more truly reflects the animal's ability and (b) the two more recent efforts do not represent a loss of form.

The May 28 race gets a basic rating of 194. Add 2 for the stretch gain, 2 for the improved post position, 5 for roughing it and 10 for Phalen. Deduct 5 for the slight rise in class. The final figure is 208.

Atlantic Frost. This one's brief local record suggests that it will beat lots of trotters whenever it contrives to remain flat on gait. The

YONKERS

THE BEST IN HARNESS RACING

COMING FEATURE EVENTS

FRIDAY, JUNE 27

THE MEADOW SKIPPER PACE $35,000
3-year-olds

FRIDAY, JULY 11

THE HUDSON TROT $35,000
Filly Triple Crown Event - 3-year-olds

SATURDAY, JULY 12

THE SU MAC LAD TROT $25,000
3-year-olds — one mile

LATE CLOSING 3-YEAR-OLD SERIES CONTINUES
SATURDAY — EST. $107,500

 3rd, 5th, 7th and 9th Races

MORN. LINE

1 TROT-ONE MILE

(1st HALF OF DAILY DOUBL

SADDLE CLOTH—GREEN

CLASS C-1

PURSE $3,00

6 — 1 CORNISH MAN

b h, 4, by Diller Hanover, Cornish Hen by Scotland (Tr.-M. Proman)
Don & Richard Julich, N.J. & S. Perlmutter, N.Y. — 1969 9 0 2 1 2,64
($10,287) 3, 2:08:3 — FRANK TAGARIELLO (150) — Tan-Brown-White — RR 2:08:3 1968 24 7 7 2 9,84

* 6-17 YR	ft qua		m	31:4	1:02:2	1:34:2	2:06:1	4	5	5	5	5/5	6/6	2:07:4	N.B.(FTgrlo)PeerlssYnkee,GallntD'ly,Spd
6-11 YR	ft C-1	3000	m	32	1:05:1	1:36:3	2:08:2	3	3	3x	8	8/16	8/18	2:12:4	10.20(Tgrllo)MrkdPick,HickiHi,NovelBlaze
* 6-3 YR	gd qua		m	32:2	1:04:3	1:36:2	2:08:3	1	3	3	4°	3/10	3/7	2:10:1	N.B.(Dplse)FneShot,MarkdPck,CornshMa
3-4 YR	ft C-1/C-2	3000	m	31:3	1:04	1:36:4	2:08:2	7	7	7	8	7/6½	5/6	2:10	6.50(Fntne)SmDrlngtn,PnhvnBoy,BoyOBc
2-19 YR	sy B-2/C-1	3375	m	32	1:05:2	1:38:2	2:12:1	2	4	4	4°	4x/1¼	x5x/¾	2:12:2	9.70(Tgrlo)NtveYnkee,NeonRdny,Gwndoly
2-13 YR	ft B-1/B-2	4250	m	31:2	1:03:3	1:36:2	2:09:4	3	4	4	5°	6/2	6/3¼	2:10:2	8.40(Fntne)HelensAdnis,Crmik,TddlrsWn
2-5 YR	ft B-2	3750	m	31:3	1:03:1	1:36:1	2:08:1	5	6	6	7x	8/15	8/dis		3.50(LFntne)Carmik,NeonRdny,HlnsAdni
1-29 YR	gd B-2/C-1	3750	m	31:1	1:03:3	1:36	2:09:1	8	4°	2°	3°	5/1¾	6/5	2:10:2	5.30(Fntne)TddlrsWndy,MssHln,DsrtPrnc

5 — 2 NOVEL BLAZE

br m, 5, by Blaze Hanover, Novel Hanover by Star's Pride (Tr.-T. Kin
Thomas King, Bronx, N.Y. — YR 2:06:3 1969 7 1 0 3 2,99
($21,420) 4, 2:04:4 (5/8) — GEORGE PHALEN (135) — Blue-White — PPk(5/8) 2:04:4 1968 25 2 8 2 11,40

6-18 YR	ft C-1	3000	m	31:2	1:04	1:35:3	2:07:4	2	3	3	4	4/3	4/2¼	2:08:2	3.40(WMyr)StrCrest,PinhvnBoy,SylvstrB
6-11 YR	ft C-1	3000	m	32	1:05:1	1:36:3	2:08:2	8	6	6	4	3/3	3/1½	2:08:4	7.80(GPhln)MarkdPick,HickiHi,NovelBlaz
5-28 YR	ft C-1/C-2	2875	m	31	1:02:3	1:34:2	2:06:3	4	6	6	6°	5/2	1/hd	2:06:3	3.30(Phln)NvlBlze,RseD'Anjou,LoneT'Ace
5-12 RR	ft B-2	4000	m	32:1	1:05	1:36:3	2:08:1	x1	8	8	8	7/22	7/dis		•1.60(GPhln)TerrellNativeYnkee,SweetCer
5-1 RR	ft B-2	4000	m	31:1	1:02:4	1:34:4	2:06:1	2	6	7	8°	6/6	3/1½	2:06:3	•1.50(GShlty)BernardC,Terrell,NovelBlaze
4-24 RR	gd B-2	4000	m	32:1	1:05:2	1:36:2	2:08:1	2	4	2°	2°	2/nk	3/¾	2:08:2	•2.10(CAbt)CalebsStar,MarcelMir,NovlBlz
4-17 RR	ft B-2	4000	m	31:2	1:05:2	1:36:1	2:07:2	x3	8	8	7	6/5½	6/5¼	2:08:3	4.00(GShlty)SprnzaClby,MrclMir,MjrBry
11-29 RR	ft B-2	3000	m	31	1:02:3	1:34:2	2:06:3	6	6	6	4°	3/2½	3/4¼	2:07:3	2.30(Shlty)PrtysOvr,SprnzaClby,NvlBlze

4 — 3 SHARP VOLO (NY)

b g, 4, by Sharpshooter, Kitty S. Volo by True Volo (Tr.-F. Popfinger)
R. Brunette & E. Pagano, N. Y. — 1969 0 0 0 0
($38,490) 3, 2:05:3 — FRANK POPFINGER (160) — Blue-Gold — MR 2:05:3 1968 17 2 7 2 34,56

* 6-3 YR	gd qua		m	32:2	1:04:3	1:36:2	2:08:3	2	2	2	3	6/13	7/14	2:11:4	N.B.(FPfngr)FneShot,MrkdPick,CornshM
11-5 RR	ft 3yr Stk	70000	m	31:3	1:03:4	1:36:3	2:06:4	6	5	3	3	3/19	4/dis		N.B.(ABrtn)FneShot,GallntD'ley,WrldBea
10-16YR	ft 3yrStk	71250	m	32:2	1:04	1,35:1	2:06	5	4	4x	4	4/17	4/dis		6.20(Brtn)FneSht(barred)GlntDly,TwgsB
10-1 VD(3/4)	ft3yrStk	7475	m	30:3	1:01:3	1:31:3	2:02:3	x4x	5	5	5	5/dis	5/dis		10.60(ABrtn)FineShot,MghtyStrds,TwgsB
9-24 YR	ft C-1	3000	m	30:3	1:02	1:33:4	2:05	7	7	7°	6°	7/6½	7/8¾	2:07:1	7.40(ABrtn) SwtCere,BenBen,TddlrsWin
9-9 Btva	ft 3yr Stk	16500	m	31	1:04:4	1:35:4	2:06:1	5	5	5	4	3/9	3/11	2:08:3	N.B.(ABrtn)FneShot,MgtyStrdes,ShrpVo
8-28Syr(1)	ft 3yrStk	23400	m	31	1:01:3	1:33	2:04:1	3	11	10	10	10/dis	10/dis		N.B.(ABrtn)FneShot,MtyStrdes,StchlT'P
8-28Syr(1)	ft 3yrStk	23400	m	31	1:03	1:35	2:06	4	3	3°	2°	2/ns	3/¾	2:06:1	N.B.(ABrtn)FineShot,Oneoakey,SharpVol

10 — 4 TRINIDAD HANOVER

b h, 5, by Stars Pride, Trinket Hanover by Dean Hanover (Tr.-J. Callahan)
Charles H. Schroeder, Cold Spring, N.Y. — (qua) YR 2:10:1 1969 2 0 0 0 15
($3,255) 4, 2:04:2 (5/8) — JAMES CALLAHAN (160) — Purple-Gold — AC(5/8) 2:04:2 1968 11 4 1 1 3,25

* 6-17 YR	ft qua		m	31:4	1:02:2	1:34:2	2:06:1	3	4	4	4	4/4	4/3	2:07	N.B.(Cllhn)PeerlssYnkee,GallntDooly,Spd
6-11 YR	ft C-1	3000	m	32	1:05:1	1:36:3	2:08:2	5	2	1x	5	5/6½	5/3¾	2:09:2	9.10(Cllhn)MarkdPick,HickiHi,NovelBlaze
* 6-3 YR	gd qua		m	32:2	1:04:2	1:37:2	2:10:1	1	1	1	1	1/3	1/3½	2:10:1	N.B.(JClhn)TrndadHn,Voltaire,R'medeGll
5-28 YR	ft C-1/C-2	2875	m	31	1:02:3	1:34:2	2:06:3	5	7	7	7	x7/4	7/4	2:07:3	25.70(Cllhn)NvlBlze,RseD'Anjou,LoneT'Ac
9-6 PcD(5/8)	ft Cd	5000	m	30:2	1:02:1	1:33:4	2:05:1	7	1	1	1	1x/1	4/5½	2:06:1	19.60(GFldi)BrbnCndy,StvnRchrd,SpnkySu
9-4 PcD(5/8)	ft Cd	2000	m	31:1	1:03:1	1:34:3	2:05:3	7	3°	1	1	2/½	3/1¾dq	2:05:4	5.60(GFoldi)LadraHn,LastBoy,Cinderella
* 8-24 VD(3/4)	ft qua		m	30:2	1:02:2	1:34:2	2:05:4	6	1	1	1	1/1½	1/3	2:05:4	N.B.(GLrlee)TrnddHn,CygaBllt,RjhsRdny
8-19 VD(3/4)	ft Cd	1500	m	29:1	1:01:1	1:32:4	2:04	7	8	7	x7x	7/18	7/dis	2:09:4	5.80(Lrlee)NteClub,BrghtNwprt,SmrtSar

3 — 5 ATLANTIC FROST

blk h, 5, by Worthy Frost, Anna McElwyn by A.G.K. (Tr.-J. Patterson, S
John Patterson, Dalton, Ga. — YR 2:06:1 1969 3 2 0 0 2,62
($1,659) 4, 2:08:1 — JOHN PATTERSON SR. (165) — Tan-Blue — Fayetteville 2:08:1 1968 15 9 4 2 1,65

6-17 YR	ft C-2	2750	m	32	1:03:3	1:35:1	2:06:1	6	3	3	2°	1/1	1/1¾	2:06:1	*2.40(P'snSr)A'l'tcFrst,Joe'sADlly,T'DvlP
6-9 YR	ft C-2	2750	m	31:2	1:03:2	1:35	2:07:2	8	8	5x	8	8x/15	8/24	2:13:2	5.60(JPtrsnJr)StrCrst,LnT'Ace,T'DvlsPdr
5-26 YR	ft C-3	2500	m	30:1	1:03:3	1:35:3	2:07:3	2	1	1	2	2/1	1/hd	2:07:3	3.40(PtrsnSr)AtlntcFrst,BlxiHn,W'dyLgt
9-20 Law	ft Cd	450	m	2 heats: 2:11:2 finished 1st; 2:12:3 finished 1st with E.Martin driving.											
9-13 Fayetteville	ft Cd	450	m	2 heats: 2:08:1 finished 1st; 2:08:3 finished 1st with E.Martin driving.											
9-2 FtInd	gd Cd	300	m	2 heats: 2:14 finished 2nd; 2:17 finished 2nd with E.Martin driving.											
8-22 Lewisburg	ft Cd	600	m	2 heats: 2:14 finished 1st; 2:10:1 finished 1st with E.Martin driving.											
8-1 Hopkinsvlle	hy Cd	300	m				2:14:4	.	.	.	.	.	1		(EMrtn)AtlntcFrst,HnrsSpcl,CnslBllr

5 — 6 NEON RODNEY (NY)

br m, 4, by Duke Rodney, Neon Hanover by Star's Pride (Tr.-B.DeFonc
Hi-Ho Stables, Bridgeport, Conn. — YR 2:06:4 1969 14 1 3 1 5,52
($79,501) 3, 2:06:3 — CARMINE ABBATIELLO (135) — Gold-Red — YR 2:06:3 1968 17 5 0 4 62,70

6-18 YR	ft C-1	3000	m	31:2	1:04	1:35:3	2:07:4	5	x7	7	7	7/12	7/13	2:11	3.20(CAbtllo)StrCrst,PnhvnBoy,SylvstrBo
6-4 YR	ft C-1/C-2	2875	m	31	1:03:3	1:35:3	2:06:4	4	5	3°	2°	2/1	2/1	2:07	3.60(CAbtlo)RseD'Anjou,NeonRdny,StrCr
5-22 RR	ft C-1/C-2	3000	m	31:2	1:03:4	1:35:2	2:06:4	3	4	4°	2°	2/1	3/1½	2:07:1	•1.60(CAblo) HickiHi,RoseD'Anju,NeonRd
5-12 RR	ft B-2	4000	m	32:1	1:05	1:36:3	2:08:1	7	4	6	6	6/7	6/11	2:11	46.90(BD'Fnce)Terrell,NtiveYnke,SweetCe
* 5-3 RR	ft qua		m	31:4	1:04	1:36:2	2:08:4	6	3°	2	2	3/2	3/3½	2:09:3	N.B.(CAbto)RdnysStr,S'dleMeg,NeonRdn
* 4-26 RR	ft qua		m	33	1:05:2	1:37:1	2:09:1	6	3	4	4	4/7	5/6½	2:10:4	N.B.(CAbt)VctryCmp,WndyLgtning,Sp'bn
4-10 RR	sy B-2	4000	m	31:2	1:04:1	1:38:4	2:11:1	4	x7	x7	7	7/dis	7/dis		•1.50(CAbt)PrnceHnry,SprnzaClby,MrclM
3-28 RR	ft B-1/B-2	4000	m	31:2	1:04:1	1:35:4	2:07:3	7x	7x	7	8	8/8½	8/11	2:10:2	5.50(CAbtlo)PplrJmie,MrclMir,ChmpRich

8 — 7 HICKI HI (NY)

b h, 7, by Bill Hickey, Titia Mite by Titan Hanover (Tr.-A. Burto
Pequot Farms Inc., Woodmere, N.Y. — RR 2:06:4 1969 20 1 3 1 5,41
($109,328) 4, 2:05:1 (3/4) — JOHN CHAPMAN (147) — Green-White — YR 2:07 1968 28 2 1 7 10,28

6-18 YR	ft C-1	3000	m	31:2	1:04	1:35:3	2:07:4	6	6	6	6	6/6	6/4½	2:08:4	20.70(Roe)StarCrest,PnhvnBoy,SylvstrBoy
6-11 YR	ft C-1	3000	m	32	1:05:1	1:36:3	2:08:2	1	1	2	1	1/1	2/nk	2:08:2	2.30(DncrJr)MrkdPick,HickiHi,NovelBlaz
5-28 YR	ft C-1/C-2	2875	m	31	1:02:3	1:34:2	2:06:3	6	3	4	5	6/2	6/2¾	2:07:1	10.50(ABrtn)NvlBlze,RseD'Anjou,LoneT'A
5-22 RR	ft C-1/C-2	3000	m	31:2	1:03:4	1:35:2	2:06:4	4	2	2	3	3/2	1/ns	2:06:4	3.70(ABrtn) HickiHi,RoseD'Anju,NeonRd
5-15 RR	ft C-1/C-2	3000	m	31	1:02:2	1:34:4	2:07:2	8	4°°	4°	6	5/3¼	7/7¼	2:09:1	6.50(LF'tne)TonyEdn,RseD'Anjou,OlvrBy
5-8 RR	ft C-1	3000	m	30:2	1:04:2	1:36:1	2:08:1	2	x5	3°	2°	2/½	5/4¼	2:09:2	3.00(ABrtn)LloydsEmbssy,MssHeln,TnyE
4-30 RR	ft C-1	3250	m	30:1	1:02:1	1:34:2	2:07:1	6	7	7	5°°	6/3½	5/3¼	2:07:4	9.20(ABrtn)VctrDuke,H'awayPddn,Spdw
4-23 RR	ft C-1	3000	m	29:4	1:02:4	1:35:3	2:08:1	5	7	7	6°	6/2¾	4/1½	2:08:3	8.20(ABurtn)BernardC,Boman,VictorDuk

6 — 8 MARKED PICK

b h, 5, by Famous Hanover, Merrie Magic by Rodney (Tr.-J. Tallma
County Stables, New Rochelle, N.Y. — LB(5/8) 2:07:3 1969 9 2 3 1 5,43
($2,692) 4, 2:03 (3/4) — JAMES TALLMAN (150) — Wine-Grey-Yellow — VD(3/4) 2:03 1968 18 3 4 2 2,49

6-11 YR	ft C-1	3000	m	32	1:05:1	1:36:3	2:08:2	6	4	4	2	2/1	1/nk	2:08:2	23.90(Tllmn)MarkdPick,HickiHi,NovelBlaz
* 6-3 YR	gd qua		m	32:2	1:04:3	1:36:2	2:08:3	4	6	4°	2	2/8	2/6	2:10	N.B.(Tllmn)FineShot,MarkdPck,CornshM
5-19 RR	ft B-2	4000	m	30:2	1:03:1	1:35:1	2:07	3	6x	7x	8	8/dis	8/dis		3.30(Tllmn) Terrl,LloydsEmbssy,AdiosPr
5-1 LB(5/8)	ft Cd	3300	m	30	1:01:3	1:33	2:04:1	1	4	4x	x8	8/dis	8/dis		*.80(PTllmn)Infallble,JillArden,TenGallo
4-17 LB(5/8)	ft Cd	3000	m	29:4	1:02	1:33:3	2:04:3	3	3°	2	3	3/2	2/1	2:04:4	2.30(PTlmn)RckyRvonah,MrkrPck,Kmbri
4-3 LB(5/8)	ft Cd	3000	m	30:1	1:02:4	1:33:4	2:05:3	6	2	3	3	3/2½	2/hd	2:05:3	4.20(PTllmn)RckyRvonah,MrkdPck,Spho
3-26 LB(5/8)	ft Cd	2900	m	32:1	1:04:1	1:36:1	2:07:3	1	1	1	1	1/2	1/5	2:07:3	*1.00(PTl'n)MrkdPck,CpeP'Bndios,E'grnF
3-17 LB(5/8)	ft Cd	2600	m	31:1	1:05	1:35:4	2:06:3	7	4°	4°	4°	4/3¼	3/2½	2:07	2.50(PTllmn)CmdnGndlier,OneKd,MrkdF

FIRST RACE—8:00 P.M. D.D. WINDOWS CLOSE 7:50 P.M.

MORN. LINE

2 PACE-ONE MILE (2nd HALF OF DAILY DOUBLE)

SADDLE CLOTH—GREY

CLASS C-3 — CONDITIONED — 3-YEAR & UP — FILLIES & MARES PURSE $2,500

---

5 **1**

ADELE ADIOS b m, 4, by Don Adios, Keep On Smiling by Red Steve (Tr.-A. Abbatiello)
Color Craft Inc., & Al-Cliff Stables Inc., N.Y., N.Y. 1969 6 0 0 2 797.
($6,457) 3, 2:06:1 ANTHONY ABBATIELLO (164) Gold-Red YR 2:06:1 1968 31 3 6 6 6,457.
° 6-17 YR ft qua m 31:1 1:03:1 1:34:3 2:05:2 2 7 8° 8° 8/6½ 8/11 2:07:4 N.B.(AAbtlo)MzileSmky,QrryRoad,LeroyHn
° 6-10 YR ft qua m 32 1:04 1:36:3 2:08:3 4 3 3 3 3/1½ 3/4 2:09:3 N.B.(AAbtlo)BenCasyN.,ArtExbt,AdeleAd's
2-14 YR ft C-3 Cd 2500 m 30:4 1:02:4 1:35:4 2:08:4 1 4 4 5° 4/2 6/5½ 2:10:1 2.90(AAbt)SssxDlght,ShnyStkngs,GrdL'Vlo
2-6 YR ft C-2 Cd 2750 m 31 1:04:2 1:36 2:07:2 6 1 1 2 3/1½ 6/3½ 2:08.1 10.30(AAbtlo)MissArlne,JMMillie,StdyNan
1-24 YR sy C-2 Cd 2750 m 31:1 1:05:2 1:36:3 2:10:2 6 7 6° 5° 5/7½ 7/10 2:13 16.10(AAbtlo)TrprtBelle,BtyGold,HerIrish
1-16 YR ft C-2 Cd 2750 m 31:1 1:02:4 1:35:3 2:08:3 6 7 7 7° 8/2¾ 5/2 2:09 2.50(AAbt)AftnP'dra,L'wdLdy,BlckiesPrde
1-9 YR ft C-2 Cd 2750 m 30:4 1:03:3 1:35:3 2:07:2 7 8 8 5° 2/nk 3/3½ 2:08:1 21.00(AAbtlo)Y'keS'dw,H'rysJnsna,AdleAd's
1-3 YR ft C-2 Cd 2750 m 30:4 1:03 1:35:2 2:06:2 1 4 4 4° 3/3 3/5 2:07:3 4.50(AAbtlo)CrcleAmy,RneCrptr,AdleAd's

---

6 **2**

‡MADGE CARLITH b m, 5, by Diller Hanover, Sweet Madalean by Scotland (Tr.-M. Deutsch)
J. Fernandes, Sy Finkelstein & M. Deutsch Leb 2:07:2 1969 7 1 0 0 616.
($2,485) 4, 2:07:4 (1) MICHAEL DEUTSCH (175) Yellow-Grey Lat(1) 2:07:4 1968 26 5 3 2 2,455.
° 6-17 YR‡ ft qua m 30:3 1:03 1:35 2:08 3 4 4° 2 2/1½ 2/½ 2:08:1 N.B.(Dtsch)E'gwdMrcl,MdgeCrlth,JMEmpr
* 6-10 YR‡ ft qua m 32 1:03:3 1:35:4 2:07:4 7 6 4 4 3/8¼ 2/8 2:09:4 N.B.(Dtsch)RoylTrck,MadgeCrlth,PTEndur
5-22 Leb‡ ft Cd 800 m 31:3 1:05:1 1:37 2:09:1 8 8 3°x7 8/dis 8/dis 6.50(Kirk)WardnLeo,LindaAnnQ'k,IrshKtty
5-15 Leb‡ ft Cd 800 m 31:2 1:03:1 1:35:1 2:07:2 2 3° 1° 1 1/1½ 1/4 2:07:2 1.90(HKirk)MadgeCarlth,McLizzy,MisterQ
5-6 Leb‡ ft Cd 800 m 33:1 1:06:2 1:38 2:09 2 3 1° 1° 2x/½ x3x2/¼dq2:09:2 2.40(Kirk)MrRoyalty,RoylKim,RudyAdams
4-28 Leb‡ gd Cd 800 m 31:4 1:03:4 1:37 2:09 4 6 6 7° 7/11 4/5¼ 2:10 6.70(Kirk)ShdyBoy,GldysLind,LndaAnnQ'k
4-24 Leb‡ ft Cd 800 m 31:3 1:05:4 1:38:2 2:09:2 6 7 7 7 7/14 6/7¾ 2:11 8.40(Krk)FrghtTrns,GrndMdgVlo,BrwnRngr
4-16 Leb‡ ft Cd 600 m 32:2 1:04 1:37:3 2:09:4 8 4° 5 6 7/8½ 4/5¾ 2:11 3.80(Kik)RudyAdms,CrdSprit,M'StrmyNght

---

3 **3**

DEENA b f, 3, by Sampson Hanover, Adrienne by Direct Way (Tr.-W. Betts)
William C. Betts, Franklin Lakes, N.J. MR 2:06:4 1969 4 2 0 0 1,100.
($1,364) FRANK TAGARIELLO (150) Tan-Brown-White (qua) Fhld 2:07:3 1968 4 0 0 1 1,364.
6-9 MR ft Cd 2000 m 30:2 1:01:4 1:33 2:04:1 1 2 4 7 7/4¼ 6/4 2:05:1 2.70(Betts)LoneRanger,Rapaco,A'someBoy
5-31PcD(⅝) ft 3yStk 21406m 29:3 1:00:2 1:31:1 2:02 10 7 1° 4° 7/8 8/9¾ 2:03:4 28.10(WmsII)WthThnks,SpleYkee,TptBrdie
5-26 MR ft Cd 1400 m 31:3 1:02:1 1:33:2 2:06:4 6 3 3x 5 5/5½ 1/ns 2:06:4 13.80(WBtts)Deena,DringDnna,AwesmeBoy
5-20MR ft3yr mdn Cd 800 m 31:2 1:04:1 1:38:3 2:11:3 2 1 1 1 1/4 1/5 2:11:3 *.50(WBetts) Deena, Gambrie, SmartLad
5-10 Gosh gd mat m 30:4 1:05:1 1:36:4 2:09:4 2 3 2 1° 1/3 1/6½ 2:09:4 N.B.(WBetts)Deena,Holly'sGal,LeaGirl
10-16LB(⅝) ft2yStk 21295m 29:2 59:4 1:30:3 2:01:2 5x10 10 10 10/11 5/9¾ 2:03:1 23.80(JLrnte)ShadowMir,QnOmaha,Glynis
10-7 LB(⅝) ft 2y Cd 2500 m 30:4 1:01:4 1:33:2 2:05:1 5 3° 4° 3° 4/2¾ 3/4½ 2:06 2.80(HFilion)GypsyGold,SevenVeils,Deena
9-24 Bloomsburg gd 2yr Stk 9050 m 2 heats: 2:04:2 finished 7th; 2:05:3 finished 7th with W. C. Betts driving.

---

8 **4**

‡ROWENA ch m, 5, by Jack Flanagan, Sheila Rhap by Rhapsody (Tr.-J. Tallman)
Donald & Diana Iogrossi & E. Riggi, N.Y. (qua) RR 2:08 1969 3 0 0 0 125.
($4,819) 4, 2:06:4 JAMES TALLMAN (150) Wine-Grey-Yellow Stga 2:06:4 1968 26 3 1 3 2,822.
6-12 YR‡ ft C-3 Cd 2500 m 30:2 1:02 1:33 2:05 5 3x 6x 8 8/13 8/13 2:08:1 9.00(Tllmn)Ant'sStr,K'stnMdw,TrdyDmnd
6-4 YR‡ ft clm alw 4000 m 30:4 1:04 1:35:1 2:06:1 4 6 7 8 7/3½ 5/4¼ 2:07:1 16.30(Tllmn)MjrBlck,WarChnt,StrmyDream
5-21 RR‡ ft C-2 Cd 2750 m 31:3 1:04:1 1:36 2:06:4 7 2° 1 3 3/1½ 7/5½ 2:08:1 6.00(Tllmn)HTEmly,OuiO'Byrd,K'stneMdw
* 5-10 RR‡ ft qua m 29:3 1:01:4 1:35 2:08 4 4 4 3 3/2 1/hd 2:08 N.B.(JTallman)Rowena,Adioax,TomTar
10-26 Stga gd Cd 1200 m 29:3 1:02:4 1:35:2 2:07:4 6 7 7 7 7 6/3½ 2:09:2 21.20(WAdams)NewDrm,BoAdyn,StoneChief
10-15 Stga ft Cd 1000 m 31 1:03:3 1:35:1 2:06:4 7 5 5 4 4 3/3½ 2:07:2 13.30(WAdams)ScotchStony,Ramble,Rowena
10-1 Stga ft Cd 800 m 30 1:01:2 1:33:2 2:06:4 3 5 5 4 4 1/1½ 2:06:4 2.90(WAdms)Rowna,MldyPte,HppyLndings
9-24 Stga ft Cd 1000 m 30:1 1:02:1 1:34:2 2:06:2 5 8 8 8 8 7/7¼ 2:07:4 5.30(WAdams)SponDilly,Ramble,LouArden

---

6 **5**

ELMHURST QUEEN b m, 4, by Tar Heel, Kirk's Queen by Hodgen (Tr.-J. Edmunds)
Elmhurst Stables, N. Babylon, N.Y. 1969 5 0 0 2 660.
($11,608) 2, 2:06 JOHN PATTERSON, JR. (125) Brown-Tan (qua) RR 2:08:2 1968 15 0 1 3 3,513.
6-12 YR ft C-3 Cd 2500 m 30:2 1:02 1:33 2:05 7 7 7 6 6/4¼ 7/6¼ 2:06:2 24.00(Edmds)Ant'sStr,K'stnMdw,TrdyDmnd
5-21 RR ft C-2 Cd 2750 m 31:3 1:04:1 1:36 2:06:4 6 8 8 8 8/dis 8dis 15.40(Edm'ds)HTEmly,OuiO'Byrd,K'stneMdw
5-7 RR ft C-2 Cd 2750 m 31:1 1:03:3 1:34:4 2:06:2 1 4 3° 1 1/1 3/2¼ 2:07 30.80(JEd'ds)CfeAuLait,HTEmly,ElmhrstQn
4-9 RR ft C-2 Cd 2750 m 32:3 1:06:2 1:38:1 2:09:4 4 1° 2 4° 5/7 6/6¾ 2:11:2 31.50(Bente)MssGntry,TrdyDmnd,OuiO'Byrd
3-29 RR sy C-2 Cd 2750 m 32 1:05:4 1:38:2 2:10:3 3 3 3 4 3/1¼ 3/1¾ 2:11 22.10(Edmnds)SprsAwy,WntwnPck,E'hrstQn
° 3-22 RR ft qua m 31 1:05 1:36:2 2:09 5 3 4 4 4/3 3/2¼ 2:09:2 N.B.(Ed'nds)HrnlsAce,AdrsCh'pie,E'hrstQ'n
11-6 RR ft C-2 Cd 2600 m 30:1 1:02:1 1:34:1 2:05:4 2 2 3 4° 7/6¾ 7/10 2:08:1 3.20(JEdmds)JMMllie,ClrtAndrsn,HerIrish
10-29 RR ft C-2 Cd 2600 m 31:3 1:04:3 1:35:4 2:07:3 4 5 2° 2° 2/1 3/2½ 2:08:1 8.80(Edmnds) GrnR'Ally,Brdside,E'hrstQn

---

4 **6**

YANKEE HOBO blk f, 3, by Hobo Ruble, Ambitous G. by Mighty Storm (Tr.-J. Patterson, Sr.)
John H. Land Builders, Inc., Tampa, Fla. 1969 1 0 0 0 200.
($1,600) 2, 2:07 JOHN PATTERSON SR. (165) Tan-Blue Lewisburg 2:07 1968 14 8 4 0 1,600.
6-11 YR ft C-3 Cd 2500 m 30:4 1:02:2 1:34:3 2:05:4 1 2 4 5 5/3¼ 4/3½ 2:06:3 7.30(JP'snSr)TrcysGrl,Clr'sDrm,BstBrwstr
* 6-3 YR ft qua m 33:2 1:07 1:39:4 2:12:1 2 1 2 3 3/3 3/1¾ 2:12:3 N.B.(PtrsnSr)Adonis,RebelJoe,YankeeHobo
9-18 Law gd Cd 450 m 2 heats: 2:11:2 finished 1st; 2:10 finished 1st; N.B. with E. Martin driving.
9-11 Fayetville ft Cd 450 m 2 heats: 2:11:4 finished 1st; 2:09:4 finished 1st; N.B. with E. Martin driving.
9-2Fountain Inn gd Cd 300 m 2 heats: 2:13:3 finished 2nd; 2:13:1 finished 1st; N.B. with E. Martin driving.
8-22 Lewisburg ft Cd 600 m 2 heats: 2:09:1 finished 2nd; 2:07 finished 1st; N.B. with E. Martin driving.
7-31Hpknsvll ft2yr ec 1070m 2 heats: 2:13 finished 4th; 2:14:2 finished 1st; N.B. with E. Martin driving.
7-25 LouD gd Cd 500 m 31:2 1:04:2 1:36:3 2:09:1 1 2 2 2 2/1¼ 2/½ 2:09:1 3.10(Mrtn)JstlyH'r,YnkeeHobo,LckyPrncss

---

9/2 **7**

TRUDY DIAMOND ch m, 5, by Add Hanover, Theda Hanover by Billy Direct (Tr.-J. Chapman)
Vineyard Stables, Inc., New York, N.Y. 1969 7 0 1 1 1,324.
($4,725) 4, 2:07:2 JOHN CHAPMAN (147) Green-White Fox 2:07:2 1968 46 8 3 5 4,600.
6-12 YR ft C-3 Cd 2500 m 30:2 1:02 1:33 2:05 3 4 1° 3 3/1¼ 3/1 2:05:1 11.20(Chpmn)Ant'sStr,K'stnMdw,TrdyDmnd
6-5 YR ft C-3 Cd 2500 m 32 1:03:4 1:35:3 2:06:4 2 3 2 3 3/3½ 4/2¾ 2:07:2 14.80(PtrsnJr)SnyCst,PgyR'bw,ShnyStckngs
5-21 RR ft C-2 Cd 2750 m 31:3 1:04:1 1:36 2:06:4 5 6 6 6° 6/4¼ 6/3¾ 2:07:4 27.40(Chpmn)HTEmly,OuiO'Byrd,K'stneMdw
5-7 RR ft C-2 Cd 2750 m 31:1 1:03:3 1:34:4 2:06:2 2 5 6ix 6 6/7 6/6 2:08 35.40(Chp'n)CfeAuLait,HTEmly,ElmhrstQ'n
4-29 RR ft C-2 2750 m 32:1 1:05:2 1:37:3 2:08:2 5 6 4° 2° 3/1¼ 5/6 2:09:4 30.10(JChpmn)Sforza,WrthyPlay,OuiO'Byrd
4-22 RR sy C-2 Cd 2750 m 31 1:05:1 1:37:4 2:10 3 5 5° 7° 7/7½ 7/6 2:11:3 14.80(DW'od)OC'sSndy,Claire'sT'Heel,Sfrza
4-9 RR ft C-2 Cd 2750 m 32:3 1:06:2 1:38:1 2:09:4 1 3 1 3 3/6½ 2/4 2:10:4 12.90(Chp'n)MssGntry,TrdyDmnd,OuiO'Byrd
* 3-29 RR ft qua m 31:2 1:04:2 1:36:2 2:08 5 4 4 4° 4/2 4/3 2:08:4 N.B.(JC'mn)RteTwoTwo,FrwrdStr,OldCney

---

12 **8**

MISS DEBATER b m, 5, by Queens Adios, Vera Volo by Congressional (Tr.-T. Gay) (St.-C. Ernst)
Wm. G. Mulligan, Mt. Vernon, N.Y. 1969 3 0 0 0 220.
($10,026) 3, 2:05 CARL ERNST (190) Red-Grey LB(⅝) 2:05:1 1968 28 2 3 4 5,651.
6-12 YR ft C-3 Cd 2500 m 30:2 1:02 1:33 2:05 8 8 8 7 7/4¾ 6/5¼ 2:06:1 20.20(Ernst)Ant'sStr,K'stnMdw,TrdyDmnd
6-5 YR ft C-2 Cd 2750 m 31:2 1:04:3 1:35:4 2:07 4 6 6° 5° 5/2 4/4¼ 2:08:1 23.00(Ernst)DxieOrgn,MryBGlln,CoastLady
5-29 YR ft C-2 Cd 2750 m 29:4 1:00:4 1:32:3 2:05:4 6 7 7 7 7/2¾ 4/1½ 2:06:1 26.20(Ernst)CoastLdy,ClairesT'Heel,Sonsie
10-16 YR ft C-2 Cd 2750 m 31:2 1:02:1 1:34:1 2:05:2 7 5° 4° 7° 7/6 5/3¼dh 2:06:1 34.90(CErnst)MayBHvn,ShrnW,SnwyVlntne
10-10 YR ft C-2 Cd 2750 m 30:4 1:03 1:34:4 2:06:1 6 6 7 7 4/3½ 4/2½ 2:06:4 25.60(Ernst) AdeleAd's,UnfrmP'css,Rsrrexi
10-3 YR ft C-2 Cd 2750 m 30:4 1:02:3 1:33:3 2:04:2 4 6 7° 5x 8/15 8/dis 6.50(E'mds)ExtraS'tzie,StrOfGld,U'fmP'css
9-25 YR ft C-2 Cd 2750 m 30:4 1:02:4 1:33:4 2:04:3 2 2 2 3 2/1 2/1½ 2:05 8.00(Ernst)Frda'sPrde,MssDbtr,Cl're'sDrm
9-18 YR ft C-2 Cd 2750 m 30:2 1:01:3 1:32:3 2:04:2 4 2° 1 2 3/1 6/3¾ 2:05:1 12.00(Ernst) F'rneFst,GrnR'Ally,ExtraS'zie

---

EXACTA WINDOWS OPEN 10 MINUTES BEFORE THIS RACE

MORN. LINE

3 TROT-ONE MILE

SADDLE CLOTH—WHITE

The Gramercy Boys Club

CLASS B-2 PURSE $3,750

THIS IS AN **EXACTA** RACE

5

1 BEAU DILLER
b h, 5, by Diller Hanover, Agatha Hanover by Dean Hanover (Tr.-H. Klein)
Irving & Blanche Altman, Great Neck, N.Y.
($43,899) 4, 2:05 SAM SMITH (145) Brown-Beige RR 2:05 1969 10 0 0 4 3,240. 1968 33 6 5 5 25,708.
6-12 YR ft B-1/B-2 4125 m 32 1:03:2 1:34:4 2:05:3 3 5 6 6°x8x/9 x8x/17 2:09:4 33.00(Smth)FineSht,PrinceHnry,PplrJamie
6-5 YR ft B-1 4500 m 31 1:03 1:35 2:06 3 3 3 5 5/2½ 6/3¾ 2:06:4 28.90(Smith)ArgoDuke,KandyKim,Terrell
5-29 YR ft B-1 Cd 4500 m 31:2 1:03:3 1:35:1 2:05:3 1 2 2 2 2/1 3/3 2:06:2 27.20(SSmth)RdnysStr,ArgoDke,BeauDiller
5-20 RR ft B-1/B-2 4500 m 30:1 1:02:2 1:34:2 2:05:3 8 4° 3° 5° 4/3¼ 6/6½ 2:07:1 40.50(SSmth) SprnzaClby,UlyssMab,BrnrdC
5-13 RR ft B-1 4500 m 32 1:05:1 1:36:4 2:07 2 1 1 3 3/2 4/4½ 2:08:1 4.70(WMyr) SxG'chmp,FrmYnk,SprnzClby
5-5 RR ft B-1/B-2 4500 m 31:2 1:03:2 1:35:4 2:07:2 5 1 2 2 2/½ 3/½ 2:07:3 2.30(WMyr)AngloPck,SprnzaClby,BeauDllr
4-25 RR ft B-1 4500 m 31:4 1:04:2 1:36:4 2:08:1 2 2 3 2° 2/nk 4/1¼ 2:08:3 6.50(WMyr)AngloPck,PnthrsFlgt,Sp'zaClby
1-24YR syA/B-1hcp 6000m 31:1 1:04:2 1:37 2:10:1 4 5 6 6 5/3 3/1½ 2:10:3 10.70(RCsts)PrlssYnkee,JstJmie,BeauDllr

5

2 ADIOS PROOF
br h, 7, by Adios Harry, Proof Positive by Darnley (Tr.-M. Tolson) (St.-C. Abbatiello)
John & Fred Calitri, New Canaan, Conn.
($40,880) 6, 2:05 CARMINE ABBATIELLO (135) Gold-Red RR 2:05 1969 5 0 0 1 1,267. 1968 30 5 5 3 14,529.
6-18 YR ft B-2 3750 m 32:4 1:04 1:36:2 2:09 7 x6x 6 6 6x/15x6x/dis 19.70(NDplse)TnyEdn,VctryCdt,GldnCarlene
6-11 YR ft B-2 3750 m 31:1 1:03:3 1:35:2 2:06:3 3 4 4 5 4/3 4/4 2:07:3 10.50(CAbbtllo)RseD'Anju,TnyEdn,GldnCrln
6-4 YR ft B-2 3750 m 31:4 1:03:3 1:34:4 2:06:1 2 4 4 5° 4/4 4/3 2:07 4.20(CAbtlo)BeauBrmml,BrnrdC,NtveYnkee
5-28 YR ft B-2 3750 m 30:3 1:03 1:34:2 2:05:3 7 6 6 6 5x/6 x5x/6½ 2:07 3.00(CAbto)VctrDke,NtveYnkee,NovaStar
5-19 RR ft B-2 4000 m 30:2 1:03:1 1:35:1 2:07 1 5 5 5 5/4 3/1½ 2:07:2 4.70(CAblo) Terrll,LLoydsEmbssy,AdiosPrf
9-4 YR ft B-1 4500 m 30 1:02:3 1:35:2 2:06:2 8 8 8 8 8/3½ 7/5 2:07:2 18.80(CAbtlo)L'rie'sMon,Rdny'sStr,Vn'sFrst
• 8-27 YR ft qua m 32:3 1:04:3 1:34:4 2:05:2 3 4 4 4 4/11 4/9 2:07:2 N.B.(CAbt)SpdyPlay,Ablephone,NovelBlaze
8-21 YR ft B-1 4500 m 30:2 1:02:3 1:34:2 2:05:3 4x 8 8x 8 8/dis 8/dis 7.10(CAbtlo) TimeSng,Terrell,Laurie'sMon

8

3 PARTYS OVER (NY)
br m, 4, by Sharpshooter, Precious Rodney by Rodney (Tr.-W. White) (St.-R. Thomas)
F.O.F. Farm, Inc., Greenwich, Conn.
($67,692) 3, 2:05:2 RICHARD THOMAS (165) Gold-Black YR 2:05:2 1969 2 0 0 0 187. 1968 22 7 3 3 36,745.
• 6-20 MR ft qua m 32:1 1:04:2 1:36:3 2:09:1 5 4 5° 4 4/4½ 3/4 2:10 N.B.(CFlmng)DeiedRetrn,ChfCloud,PrtysOvr
6-18 YR ft B-2 3750 m 32:4 1:04 1:36:2 2:09 2 x7 5 5 5/7 5/10 2:11:2 7.30(RThms)TnyEdn,VctryCdt,GldnCarlne
• 6-13 MR ft qua m 33:1 1:05 1:37:2 2:09:4 7 4 4 3 3/3 3/3 2:10:2 N.B.(CFlmng)SgrisDuke,ElmiraHn,PrtysOvr
• 6-10 YR ft qua m 31:2 1:03 1:34:2 2:05:4 3 5 6x 6 6/23 6/22 2:11:2 N.B.(WWhte)ErlLrd,FairlneHn,LlydsEmbsy
6-4 YR ft B-2 3750 m 31:4 1:03:3 1:34:4 2:06:1 3 2 2 4 x6x/6½x7/17 2:10:1 6.70(RThms)BeauBrmml,BrnrdC,NtveY'kee
• 5-27 YR ft qua m 32:3 1:04 1:35:3 2:07:2 3 2 2 2 2/1½ 2/2½ 2:07:4 N.B.(RThms)Scrplto,PrtysOvr,ChrmetteHn
12-13 RR ft B-2 3750 m 33 1:06:2 1:38:1 2:10:1 5ix 8 8 8° 8x/4 x8x/9½ 2:12:2 3.20(RThms)Carmik,ShrpCat,NativeYnkee
12-6 RR ft B-2 3000 m 31:2 1:05:2 1:37:4 2:09:2 4 5 6° 5° 2/1½ 3/¾ 2:09:3 2.90(RThms)SharpCat,Carmik,PartysOver

12

4 SPEEDY C.
b g, 6, by Speedster, Countess Song by Victory Song (Tr.-G. Procino)
Harry & Joyce Goodman, New York, N.Y.
($14,060) 4, 2:04:2 (⅝) GERALD PROCINO (170) Red-White-Black YR 2:05:2 1969 3 0 0 0 1968 30 3 1 6 7,605.
• 6-17 YR ft qua m 31:4 1:02:2 1:34:2 2:06:1 5 3 3 6 6/7 3/3 2:07 N.B.(Prcno)PrlssYnkee,GallntDooly,SpdyC
• 6-10 YR ft qua m 31:2 1:03 1:34:2 2:05:4 1 1 1 4 4/13 4/10 2:08:2 N.B.(Prcno)ErlLrd,FrlneHn,LloydsEmbssy
• 6-3 YR gd qua m 32:2 1:04:3 1:36:2 2:08:3 5 x8x 7 7 7/13 6/12 2:11:2 N.B.(Prcno)FineShot,MrkdPck,CornshMan
• 5-3 RR ft qua m 31:4 1:04 1:36:2 2:08:4 3 x7 pulled up DNF N.B.(Prcno)RdnysStr,S'daleMeg,NeonRdny
• 4-29 RR ft qua m 32:2 1:04:1 1:35:4 2:08:3 3 x6° 5° 4 4/9 3/5½ 2:10 N.B.(JChp'n)WndyL'ting,S'dleMeg,SpdyC.
• 4-26 RR ft qua m 33 1:05:2 1:37:1 2:09:1 4 x7 6x 7 7/22 7/21 2:14:1 N.B.(DInsko)VctyCmp,WndyL'ting,Spllbnd
• 4-23 RR ft qua m 33:2 1:07:1 1:39:3 2:11:3 5 x5° 1x 5 5/dis 5x/dis N.B.(GProcino)BiloxiHn,DocBlack,Tuscany
4-9 RR ft C-1 3000 m 30:4 1:04 1:37 2.08:2 5 x8x 8 x8 8/dis 8/dis 4.50(SDancer)Joseppe,Pridewood,BoyOBoy

4

5 NATIVE YANKEE
b m, 5, by Hickory Pride, Yankee Duchess by Duke of Lullwater (Tr.-A. Niles, Jr.)
L. Bruno, Paul Turtzo, Wm. Parente, N. Y.
($22,843) 4, 2:05:3 ARCHIE NILES, JR. (162) White-Green RR 2:06 1969 19 2 3 4 9,749. Stga 2:05:3 1968 31 5 3 7 16,621.
6-18 YR ft B-2 3750 m 32:4 1:04 1:36:2 2:09 6 2° 2° 3° 3/1 4/2½ 2:09:3 4.10(Niles,Jr)TnyEdn,VctryCdt,GldnCrlene
6-11 YR ft B-2 3750 m 31:1 1:03:3 1:35:2 2:06:3 6 x6x 8 8 8/20 8/21 2:12 9.10(ANlesJr)RseD'Anju,TnyEdn,GldnCrlne
6-4 YR ft B-2 3750 m 31:4 1:03:3 1:34:4 2:06:1 1 1 1 3 3/2½ 3/2½ 2:06:4 2.90(NlsJr)BeauBrmml,BrnrdC,NtveYnkee
5-28 YR ft B-2 3750 m 30:3 1:03 1:34:2 2:05:3 1 3 3 3 3/3½ 2/2½ 2:06:1 2.20(ANlsJr)VctrDke,NtveYnkee,NovaStar
5-19 RR ft B-2 4000 m 30:2 1:03:1 1:35:1 2:07 7 2 2 4 4/3 4/1½ 2:07:2 8.60(NilesJr) Terrl,LloydsEmbssy,AdiosPrf
5-12 RR ft B-2 4000 m 32:1 1:05 1:36:3 2:08:1 2 2 2 3 3/1½ 2/1½ 2:08:3 4.70(NlsJr)Terrell,NativeYnkee,SweetCere
5-1 RR ft B-2 4000 m 31:1 1:02:4 1:34:4 2:06:1 7 8 8° 7° 7/8½ 6/8¼ 2:08:1 13.80(GFoldi)BernardC,Terrell,NovelBlaze
4-11 RR ft A/B 1 5000 m 31 1:04:1 1:36 2:07 6 7 7 7 7/9 7/15 2:10:3 27.90(GFldi)PplrJmie,FirmYnke,PnthrsFlgt

3

6 STAR CREST
b m, 4, by Caleb, East Star by Star's Pride (Tr.-G. Phalen)
Murray Tobin & George Phalen, N.Y.
($2,215) 3, 2:06 (⅝) GEORGE PHALEN (135) Blue-White YR 2:07:2 1969 4 2 1 1 3,907. VD(⅝) 2:06 1968 17 2 4 2 2,215.
6-18 YR ft C-1 3000 m 31:2 1:04 1:35:3 2:07:4 1 1 1 1 1/ns 1/¾ 2:07:4 *1.80(Phln)StarCrest,PnhvnBoy,SylvstrBoy
6-9 YR ft C-2 2750 m 31:2 1:03:2 1:35 2:07:2 5 1 1 1 1/1 1/¾ 2:07:2 2.80(Phln)StrCrst,LneT'Ace,T'DvlsPrdnr
6-4 YR ft C-1/C-2 2875 m 31 1:03:3 1:35:3 2:06:4 3 2 2 4 3/2 3/2 2:07:1 5.10(GPhln)RseD'Anjou,NeonRdny,StrCrst
5-17 RR ft C-2 2750 m 31:2 1:03:3 1:35:3 2:08 4 2 3 2 4/1 2/1½ 2:08:2 N.B.(GPhln)Hndmdn,StarCrest,PeteSidney
10-28 LB(⅝) ft Cd 1600 m 31:1 1:03:1 1:35:2 2:07:3 8 4° 4 3 7x/6¾ 8/dis 3.50(AMyr)DngrousLck,AftnMssile,Brntwd
10-21 LB(⅝) ft Cd 1600 m 30:4 1:03:1 1:34 2:06:1 8 3 4 2° 2/½ 2/ns 2:06:1 2.30(GPhln)MssAlma,StarCrest,AftnMissle
10-16 LB(⅝) ft Cd 2000 m 30 1:00:4 1:32:2 2:04:1 3 5 5 3 3/3¼ 3/3½ 2:04:4 *1.60(AMyr)Kimbarillo,Brntwood,StarCrest
10-4 LB(⅝) ft Cd 1000 m 31:1 1:03:1 1:35:1 2:06:4 3 1 2 3 3/2½ 3/¾ 2:06:4 N.B.(AMyr)BetYBoots,MssBobS,StarCrest

6

7 VICTORY CADET
br h, 7, by Victory Song, Sugar Candy by Scotland (Tr.-B. DeFonce)
Gertrude & Benjamin Schaffer, Kings Point, N.Y.
($73,199) 2, 2:04:1 (1) JOHN PATTERSON SR. (165) Tan-Blue RR 2:07:3 1969 10 2 1 0 5,604. RR 2:07:3 1968 26 2 2 3 6,416.
6-18 YR ft B-2 3750 m 32:4 1:04 1:36:2 2:09 3 3 3 2 2/1 2/1 2:09:1 9.60(PttrsnSr)TnyEdn,VctryCdt,GldnCrlene
6-11 YR ft B-2 3750 m 31:1 1:03:3 1:35:2 2:06:3 4 5 5° 4° 5/4 5/4½ 2:07:4 22.20(HDncrJr)RsD'Anju,TnyEdn,GldnCrln
5-28 YR ft B-2 3750 m 30:3 1:03 1:34:2 2:05:3 2 4 4 4 4/4½ 4/4½ 2:06:3 9.10(HDncrJr)VctrDke,NtveYnkee,NovaStar
5-12 RR ft B-2 4000 m 32:1 1:05 1:36:3 2:08:1 6 6 5° 5 5/4 5/4½ 2:09:1 12.20(DncrJr)Terrell,NativeYnke,SweetCere
5-2 RR ft A/B-1 5000 m 30:4 1:03:4 1:35:2 2:06:4 2 5 6 5 5/2½ 8/3½ 2:07:3 21.50(DncrJr)PrnceHnry,SpdyNte,PplrJmie
4-18 RR sy B-1 4500 m 31:1 1:03:1 1:36 2:07:2 2 x7 6 6 6/22 6/21 2:12:4 7.10(DncrJr)Dayan,AngeloPck,HppyNwprt
4-3 RR ft B-1/B-2 4000 m 31:1 1:03:3 1:36 2:07:3 2 5 4° 4 2/1½ 1/½ 2:07:3 8.80(DcrJr)VctryCdt,DsrtPrnce,PnthrsFlgt
3-26 RR ft C-1 3000 m 30:4 1:03:3 1:36 2:08:2 2 4 4° 4° 4/2¼ 1/1 2:08:2 6.90(DncrJr)VictryCadet,Joseppe,BoyOBoy

5

8 GALLANT DOOLEY (NY)
b g, 4, by Bernie Hanover, Rosa Gallon by Bill Gallon (Tr.-W. Mello) (St.-W. Haughton)
Farmstead Acres, Glen Head, N.Y.
($83,472) 3, 2:05 (⅝) JOHN CHAPMAN (147) Green-White VD(⅝) 2:05 1969 0 0 0 0 1968 21 4 5 4 52,963.
• 6-17 YR ft qua m 31:4 1:02:2 1:34:2 2:06:1 6 2° 1 1 1/1 2/3 2:07 N.B.(Fntne)PrlessYnkee,GallntDooly,SpdyC
12-6 RR ft B-2 3000 m 31:2 1:05:2 1:37:4 2:09:2 6 7x 8 8 8/19 6/17 2:13:3 *1.30(DInsko)SharpCat,Carmik,PartysOver
11-27RR ftB-1/B-2 3250 m 30:4 1:03 1:35:3 2:06:2 1 3 3 1 1/½ 2/¾ 2:06:3 *.60(Hghtn)BeauDiller,GllntD'ley,MrclMir
11-18 RR gd C-1 2700 m 30:3 1:02:2 1:35 2:07:3 7 4 2° 2° 1/1 1/4¾ 2:07:3 *1.80(Hghtn)GllntDooly,NtveY'kee,P'hvnDoll
11-5 RR ft 3yr Stk 70000 m 31:3 1:03:4 1:36:3 2:06:4 2 1 1 1 1/1 2/¾ 2:07 N.B.(Hghtn) FineShot,GllntD'ley,WrldB'ter
10-28 RR ft C-1 2700 m 30:3 1:02:1 1:33:2 2:05:3 3 4 4° 2° 1/1 2/3 2:05:4 2.00(Hghtn)TinyEden,GllntDooly,Matabeth
10-16YR ft 3yrStk 71250 m 32:2 1:04 1:35:1 2:06 3 1 1 1 2/hd 2/1½ 2:06:1 1.40(H'tn)FneSht(barred),GllntDly,TwgsBy
10-8 YR ft C-2 2750 m 31 1:02:2 1:35 2:06:4 5 1 1 1 1/½ 1/1½ 2:06:4 *1.60(Hghtn)GllntDly,MlrseMamie,HickiHi

EXACTA WINDOWS OPEN FOR THIS RACE.

4 PACE-ONE MILE

MORN. LINE

SADDLE CLOTH— YELLOW

The Brooklyn Chapter of the Big E. Incorporated
CLASS C-1 — CONDITIONED — 3-YEAR & UP — FILLIES & MARES PURSE $3,000

4 **1** **SHANNON GALLON** br m, 5, by Bill Gallon, Lorena Hanover by Dean Hanover (Tr.-J. Faraldo)
Norman Forman, New York, N.Y. YR 2:06:3 1969 13 2 0 0 3,957.
($18,299) 3, 2:05:2 CARMINE ABBATIELLO (135) Gold-Red YR 2:07 1968 37 5 5 7 11,912.
6-18 YR ft C-2 Cd 2750 m 31:4 1:04:1 1:35:1 2:06:3 1 2 1 1 1/hd 1/1¼ 2:06:3 2.50(CAbtllo)ShnonGlln,WrthyPly,DxeOrgn
6-5 YR ft C-2 Cd 2750 m 31:2 1:04:3 1:35:4 2:07 8 8 8° 7° 7/3¼ 6/3¼ 2:07:4 25.80(CAbto)DxieOrgn,MryBGlln,CoastLdy
5-21 RR ft C-2 Cd 2750 m 31:3 1:04:1 1:36 2:06:4 1 1 2 5 5/3¾ 4/2¼ 2:07:2 17.30(JFrldo)HTEmly,OuiO'Byrd,K'stneMdw
5-1 RR ft C-2 Cd 2750 m 31:1 1:04 1:34:4 2:06 7 4 5 6 6/6½ 6/6¾ 2:07:3 35.20(JFrldo)B'cupSmth,JMMllie,RebaWave
4-24 RR gd C-2 Cd 2750 m 31:4 1:06:1 1:38:2 2:09:4 3 4 6 7 6/3 4/2½ 2:10:2 15.70(Frldo)BttrcpSmth,DstyJean,MayCh'p
4-10 RR sy C-2 Cd 2750 m 32:3 1:06:2 1:38:3 2:10:3 3 5 6 8° 8x/13 8/15 2:14:3 23.90(JFrldo)M'brookJhn,SirEthan,Ovrtime
4-3 RR ft C-2 Cd 2750 m 31 1:04:2 1:35:2 2:06:4 1 3 5 6 6/3 5/3¾ 2:07:4 6.00(JFraldo)Sonsie,StoutFella,OC'sSandy
3-24 RR sy C-1 3000 m 32:3 1:04:3 1:36:3 2:08:4 3 5 5 8 8/13 7/16 2:12:4 24.70(JFarldo)OurGem,SixThirteen,HerIrish

5 **2** **LIDA LISA** b m, 4, by Hickory Smoke, Lida Hanover by Bill Gallon (Tr.-D. Tovim)
Beurose Stable, Inc., Jersey City, N.J. RR 2:05:3 1969 19 4 1 0 7,654.
($6,688) 3, 2:06:2 LUCIEN FONTAINE (134) Green-White-Red YR 2:06:2 1968 18 5 0 2 6,688.
6-20 YR ft C-1 Cd 3000 m 30:4 1:03:2 1:35:1 2:06:2 2 ix5 6 4° 5/7 5/8 2:08:3 8.60(Fntne)KathysLassie,ElesGlory,Sforza
6-13 YR gd C-1 Cd 3000 m 31 1:02:3 1:34:1 2:06:3 4 1° 1 1 1/½ 1/nk 2:06:3 12.10(Fntne)LidaLisa,FairMdn,ReneCrpntr
6-6 YR ft C-1 3000 m 31:1 1:03 1:34:2 2:05:4 1 2 2 2° 3/1¼ 4/3 2:06:3 3.10(Fntne) SharonW,ElesGlry,FltSteward
5-30 YR ft C-1 Cd 3000 m 30:4 1:03:1 1:34:3 2:05:2 3 4 4° 4° 5/2 4/2½ 2:06 4.70(CAbt)CfeAuL't,HrrcnMaid-LttlMthr^dh
5-21 RR ft C-1 Cd 3000 m 30:3 1:02:4 1:33:4 2:04:4 1 3 4 4° 5x/2 7/8½ 2:06:4 2.60(JTllmn)BthnyHn,BttrcpSmth,OurGem
5-9 RR gd C-1 Cd 3000 m 30:2 1:04:4 1:36:2 2:07:4 7 6 4° 3° 3/1¼ 5/1¼ 2:08:1 29.90(JTllmn)LckyBen,BuckshotHn,Mohawk
5-1 RR ft C-1 Cd 3000 m 30:2 1:03:1 1:34:2 2:05:3 3 5 2° 1° 1/2 1/nk 2:05:3 10.40(LFontne)LidaLisa,KatyR,BethanyHn.
4-22 RR sy C-1 Cd 3000 m 30:4 1:04 1:34:4 2:06:4 2 3 4 5 3/3½ 5/5½ 2:08:1 14.10(CAbt)Glynis,NebachsDrm,FairMaiden

8 **3** **CHARGER ADIOS** b m, 5, by Adios Senator, Mighty Snubby by Mighty H. (Tr.-F. Darish)
J. E. Whitney, B. Mazzeo, Oyster Bay, N.Y. RR 2:06:1 1969 14 2 3 1 5,877.
($24,352) 4, 2:04:3 FRANK DARISH (176) Red-Grey YR 2:04:3 1968 34 6 3 6 16,857.
* 6-17 YR ft qua m 31:1 1:03:1 1:34:3 2:05:2 6 1° 3 6 7/6 5/5 2:06:2 N.B.(Drsh)MzelleSmoky,QuarryRd,LeroyHn
4-18 RR sy B-3 Cd 3500 m 30:4 1:02:4 1:34:3 2:08 8 1° 3 4 5/2¾ 8/2½ 2:08:3 47.30(FDrsh)LawDmnd,WrthTime,FxysGuy
4-8 RR ft B-3 Cd 3250 m 31 1:04 1:35:3 2:06:1 7 6 6x 8 8/13 8/16 2:10 9.70(CAbto)BstCh'ce,WrnMByrd,WrthTme
4-2 RR ft B-3 Cd 3250 m 30:2 1:02 1:34:4 2:07:2 6 3° 3 3 2/1 7/6½ 2:09 3.10(CAbt)PrfctPrde,FxysGuy,SwngrKnght
3-25 RR ft B-3 Cd 3250 m 31:1 1:03:1 1:35:2 2:06:2 4 2 3 2° 3/2½ 2/2 2:06:4 2.20(Fntne)RdKgt,ChrgrAd's,SlnsBoy-HDDmd^dh
3-20 RR ft B-3 3250 m 30:3 1:02:4 1:33:2 2:04:3 8 1 2 3 3/1¼ 6/2½ 2:05:1 11.50(CAbtlo)ConfttiHn,CircleAmy,CptnJay
3-13 RR ft C-1 3000 m 30:2 1:02:3 1:34:3 2:06:1 5 6 5° 5° 3/1 1/nk 2:06:1 *1.60(CAbt)ChrgrAd's,MrcleGlow,MssArlne
3-6 RR ft C-1 Cd 3000 m 30:3 1:02:4 1:34 2:05:1 8 5 5 5° 5/3 4/4¼ 2:06:1 14.90(FDrsh)ReneeWck,MrcleGlw,YnkeShdw

3 **4** **GOOD TIME LASS** b m, 7, by Good Time, Mist of Scotland by Scotland (Tr.-J. Chapman)
Al Bragin & Aaron Kipnes, Fair Lawn, N.J. 1969 9 0 1 2 2,080.
($48,346) 4, 2:04 JOHN CHAPMAN (147) Green-White YR 2:04:2 1968 27 4 7 2 11,863.
6-19 YR ft C-1 Cd 3000 m 30:3 1:02 1:32:4 2:03:4 2 5 5 6° 4/2 2/¾ 2:04 10.50(Chpmn)NbchsDrm,GdT'Lss,RneCrpntr
6-12 YR ft C-1 Cd 3000 m 30:2 1:02:2 1:33 2:04:2 2 4 5 5° 6/2¼ 6/3½ 2:05:1 4.30(Chpmn)B'cupSmth,Nbch'sDrm,ShrnW
6-5 YR ft C-1 Cd 3000 m 30:2 1:01:4 1:34 2:05 8 8 8 5 5/5 3/4 2:05:4 30.30(WMyr) AftnFlsh,FlrneFrst,GdTimeLss
5-21 RR ft C-1 Cd 3000 m 30:3 1:02:4 1:33:4 2:04:4 3 5 6° 6° 6/3 5/2½ 2:05:2 6.70(Chpmn)BthnyHn,BttrcpSmth,OurGem
5-1 RR ft C-1 Cd 3000 m 30:2 1:03:1 1:34:2 2:05:3 5 6 4° 3° 2/2 5/1½ 2:06 6.80(JChapmn)LidaLisa,KatyR,BethanyHn
4-22 RR sy B-3 3500 m 31:4 1:05:2 1:37:2 2:08:4 8 8 8 8 8/8½ 8/9¼ 2:11 48.70(DWood)Forsail,UnfrmAlee,BlueHrseA
4-12 RR ft B-3 3500 m 30:2 1:03 1:34:2 2:04:2 2 4 4 4 4/3½ 4/4½ 2:05:3 4.80(JChapmn)BoySan,TenGrandN,Foresail
4-3 RR ft B-3 3250 m 30:2 1:03 1:34:2 2:05:4 6 7 7 7° 6/5½ 6/4½ 2:06:4 3.80(JChpmn)Foresail,SpdyPce,DelHi'sBoy

4 **5** **KATHY'S LASSIE** b m, 4, by Solicitor, Princess Kathy by Good Time (Tr.-R. Walker)
Fred Goldhirsch, Kings Point, N.Y. YR 2:06:2 1969 9 1 0 2 2,755.
($14,308) 3, 2:03:4 DEL INSKO (120) Purple-Gold YR 2:03:4 1968 21 3 4 6 10,142.
6-20 YR ft C-1 Cd 3000 m 30:4 1:03:2 1:35:1 2:06:2 4 2 2 1° 1/1 1/3 2:06:2 7.20(Chpmn)KathysLassie,ElesGlory,Sforza
6-13 YR gd C-1 Cd 3000 m 31 1:02:3 1:34:1 2:06:3 6 6 6 5 5/2 4/1 2:06:4 *3.00(Chpmn)LidaLisa,FairMdn,ReneCrpntr
6-6 YR ft B-3 Cd 3250 m 30:2 1:02:1 1:34:1 2:04:4 8 5 6 7 7/4 6/4¾ 2:06 46.00(Walker)MissGentry,BethnyHnr,AddieH
5-30 YR ft B-3 Cd 3250 m 30:1 1:03:1 1:35:1 2:05:4 5 5 6 7° 7/4½ 6/5¼ 2:07 8.00(Wlkr)BethnyHn,MssGentry,ConfttiHn
5-21 RR ft B-3 3500 m 30:3 1:01:3 1:33:2 2:03:3 5 3 5 4 4/4¼ 5/4¾ 2:04:3 2.80(C'pmn) RomeoLbll,StdyBert,MiteDrm
5-14 RR ft B-3 Cd 3500 m 30:3 1:02:2 1:33:4 2:05:1 7 4 4 6° 6/3 3/1½ 2:05:3 15.00(Chpmn) CldWllSntr,SctsTfy,KthysLse
5-8 RR ft Opt B-3 3500 m 31:1 1:03:2 1:34:3 2:05:1 1 2 1 2 2/1 3/4 2:06:1 4.00(Ch'pn)BlzrdHn,HydroMjstc,KthysLssie
4-30 RR ft B-2 Cd 4000 m 30:4 1:03:3 1:34:2 2:05 6 1 3 4 4/1½ 7/8 2:07 31.90(RWlkr)Ed'sLady,AmerigoHn,Mr.Hoff

8 **6** **CONFETTI HANOVER** b m, 5, by Bullet Hanover, Connie Hanover by Volomite (Tr.-W. Burris) (St.-V. Dancer)
Calvin Sergent & J. Marucci, N.J. RR 2:04:3 1969 15 1 1 1 4,289.
($24,103) 4, 2:05:1 WILLIAM MYER (165) Blue-Red RR 2:05:1 1968 30 4 4 6 12,363.
6-19 YR ft C-1 Cd 3000 m 30:3 1:02 1:32:4 2:03:4 1 4 4 5 6/3¾ 6/5½ 2:05:1 3.00(SDncr)NbchsDrm,GdT'Lass,RneCrpntr
6-13 YR ft B-3 Cd 3250 m 30:1 1:01:3 1:32 2:03:2 8 8 8 7° 7/3½ 6/3 2:04:2 29.90(SDncr)TtseHn,CafeA'Lait,SprmeByrd
6-6 YR ft B-3 Cd 3250 m 30:2 1:02:1 1:34:1 2:04:4 3 4 4° 2° 2/½ 4/3 2:05:3 18.00(VDncr)MissGentry,BethnyHnr,AddieH
5-30 YR ft B-3 Cd 3250 m 30:1 1:03:1 1:35:1 2:05:4 2 3 3 4 4/2½ 3/3 2:06:2 18.60(VDncr)BthanyHn,MssGntry,CnfttiHn
5-24 RR ft B-3 Cd 3500 m 30:4 1:03:2 1:34:2 2:05:1 6 6 5° 4° 4/1½ 6/2¾ 2:05:4 5.10(GShlty)StrmyGrge,Brdside,MinnieBird
5-16 RR ft B-3 Cd 3500 m 30:3 1:02:3 1:33:4 2:04:3 6 2 2 4 4/2¼ 5/3½ 2:05:2 15.40(Fntne) EsprsoDgrn,WrthTme,MsGntry
5-10 RR ft B-3 Cd 3500 m 31:3 1:04:1 1:35:2 2:06:1 1 2 2 3 5/2¼ 6/4¼ 2:07:1 5.60(VDncr)Bobbaolu,GrrdPick,B'manLbll
4-30 RR ft B-3 Cd 3500 m 30:2 1:03 1:33:2 2:04:2 5 1° 3 4 4/3 4/4 2:05:2 13.80(Dancer,Jr)Glynis,Adour,UniformAlee

8 **7** **SHARON W.** b m, 4, by Shadow Wave, Classy Freight by Solicitor (Tr.-G. Phalen)
J., W., & R. Groeneveld & G. Phalen, N.Y. YR 2:05:4 1969 5 2 0 1 3,235.
($7,773) 3, 2:05:3 GEORGE PHALEN (135) Blue-White RR 2:05:3 1968 26 2 3 2 7,648.
6-19 YR ft C-1 Cd 3000 m 30:3 1:02 1:32:4 2:03:4 8 8 8 7x 8/dis 8/dis 9.70(Phln)NbchsDrm,GdT'Lss,RneCrpntr
6-12 YR ft C-1 Cd 3000 m 30:2 1:02:2 1:33 2:04:2 3 2 3 4 3/1½ 3/1¾ 2:04:4 2.60(Phln)B'cupSmith,Nbch'sDrm,ShrnW
6-6 YR ft C-1 3000 m 31:1 1:03 1:34:2 2:05:4 8 1 1 1 1/1 1/1½ 2:05:4 27.20(Phln) SharonW,ElesGlory,FleetStwrd
5-23 RR ft C-1 Cd 3000 m 30:3 1:01:1 1:32 2:03:3 6 6 6 7 7/5¾ 6/8¼ 2:05:2 29.50(GPhaln) HalPick,StoutFella,HTBreak
5-14 RR ft C-2 Cd 2750 m 31:1 1:02:2 1:35 2:07:2 7 5 5 5 5/3 1/hd 2:07:2 15.40(Phaln) SharnW,ClairsTarHeel,Calsara
11-15 RR ft C-1 Cd 2700 m 30:4 1:02:4 1:35 2:06:3 1 3 3 4 4/1¾ 6/1½ 2:07 17.20(Phln)MayBHvn,MrcleGlw,YnkeeShdw
11-6 RR ft C-1 Cd 2700 m 30:4 1:02:1 1:33:4 2:05:2 4 6 6 6° 6/4½ 5/3½ 2:06:1 15.80(Phln)WeeBttns,H'cneMaid,YnkeShdw
11-1 RR ft C-1 2700 m 30:3 1:02:1 1:33:4 2:05:1 3 1 1 1 2/nk 6/3½ 2:06 5.60(Phalen)ConfettiHn,FrdsPrde,DhnHlly

15 **8** **SPEEDY PACE** br m, 6, by Meadow Pace, Dazzling Rose by Dazzleway (Tr.-I. Fertel)
Alvin, Ira & Ann & Gerald Fertel & A. Goodman, N.Y. YR 2:08:2 1969 14 1 1 0 3,522.
($19,830) 5, 2:04:1 GEORGE FOLDI (165) White-Green MR 2:04:1 1968 29 7 4 1 11,890.
6-20 YR ft C-1 Cd 3000 m 30:4 1:03:2 1:35:1 2:06:2 6 ix4° 5 5 6/7¼ 6/8 2:08:3 45.40(Foldi)KathysLassie,ElesGlory,Sforza
6-13 YR gd C-1 Cd 3000 m 31 1:02:3 1:34:1 2:06:3 5 7 7 8 7/7 8/4½ 2:07:4 13.00(Dplse)LidaLisa,FairMdn,ReneCrpntr
6-6 YR ft B-3 Cd 3250 m 30:2 1:02:1 1:34:1 2:04:4 7 8 8 8 8/8 8/9¾ 2:07:1 47.90(Foldi)MissGentry,BethnyHnr,AddieH
*5-27 YR ft qua m 29:4 1:02 1:34:3 2:04:4 1 4 4 5 5/3½ 5/4 2:05:4 N.B.(Dplse)MzelRdny,LmelghtN,ByeByeBrt
4-21 RR ft Opt B-3 3500 m 30 1:02:1 1:33:3 2:04:4 6 7 7 7 7/6¼ 7/3½ 2:05:3 3.10(GFldi)TerriLeeN,GrndJuror,Slne'sBoy
4-12 RR ft B-3 3500 m 30:2 1:03 1:34:2 2:04:2 8 7 7 7 7/7½ 5/5¾ 2:05:4 21.80(GFoldi) BoySan,TenGrandN,Foresail
4-3 RR ft B-3 3250 m 30:2 1:03 1:34:2 2:05:4 2 3 3 3° 2/1 2/hd 2:05:4 4.10(NDplse)Foresail,SpdyPace,DelHi'sBoy
* 3-29 RR ft qua m 30:4 1:03:2 1:35:3 2:08:1 6 5 5° 4 4/4 3/1 2:08:2 N.B.(NDplse)DrmrLbll,PhlpT'Grt,SpdyPace

SCRATCHED—SCOTTS TAFFY (5). A.E.—KATHY'S LASSIE—races in P.P. of scratched horse.

MORN. LINE

5 PACE-ONE MILE EXACTA

SADDLE CLOTH—BLACK

CLAIMING ALLOWANCE FOR AGE & SEX — The Hadar Group of Hadassah

ALL HORSES ENTERED MAY BE CLAIMED FOR INDICATED PRICES — PURSE $3,250

5-YR.-OLDS & UP $7,500; 4-YR.-OLDS $10,000; 3-YR.-OLDS $12,000; FOR FILLIES & MARES ADD $1,750.

---

1 — Morn. Line 5 — $10,000

FROSTY SCOTT blk g, 4, by Prospectus, Miss Maryann B. by Hoot Mon (Tr.-G. Regan)
Hap A. Galfunt & Stuart Stillman, N.Y. — YR 2:07:4 1969 10 2 1 1 4,174.
($2,612) 3, 2:09 LUCIEN FONTAINE (134) Green-White-Red — Mendota 2:09 1968 18 4 2 5 2,612.

6-16 YR ft C-2 Cd 2750 m 30:1 1:01:4 1:33:1 2:05:1 4 5 5° 4° 4/1½ 2/1½ 2:05:2 6.40(Shlty)AvaJava,FrostyScott,TimeOff
° 6-10 YR ft qua m 30:4 1:02:2 1:35:1 2:07:1 6 4° 2 7 7/5¼ 4/3 2:07:4 N.B.(GRgn)MovieStar,LopezHn,BnnieT'Boy
4-1 RR ft C-1 Cd 3000 m 31:4 1:05:1 1:36:4 2:07:4 7 7 7 6 6/3½ 5/3¼ 2:08:2 37.00(GPhln)BbyB'dha,HstrsTme,C'strV'Cee
3-26 RR ft C-1 Cd 3000 m 31 1:03:2 1:34:2 2:05:4 4 6 7 6° 6/11 5/11 2:08:3 30.70(GPhln)EstesMnbr,WarPnter,GlmrBoy
3-14 RR ft C-1 Cd 3000 m 30:2 1:03:1 1:34:4 2:07:2 2 4 4° 3° 3/1¼ 7/2½ 2:08 7.50(GPhln)ChestrV'Cee,WarPntr,FlyrPick
2-17 YR ft C-2 Cd 2750 m 30:1 1:01:4 1:34:3 2:07:4 3 5 4° 1° 1/½ 1/2½ 2:07:4 3.30(GPhln)FrstySctt,Ch'ytteRoy,FltStwrd
2-4 YR ft C-2 Cd 2750 m 31:3 1:03:3 1:35:3 2:08:3 8 8 8° 5* 7/4½ 5/1¼ 2:08:4 14.20(GPhln)ClbyDares,J.M.Eagle,Sprtcus
1-28 YR ft C-3 Cd 2500 m 31:4 1:05 1:37:1 2:08:3 3 4 3° 2° 2/½ 1/nk 2:08:3 *2.80(GPhln)FrstySctt,Ad'sForry,MrrisWyn

---

2 — Morn. Line 3 — $7,500

IMP br g, 6, by Iroquois Pick, Midwest Polly by Widower Cyrus (Tr.-J. Tallman)
Marvin & Thelma Collin & Elsa Colletti, Flushing, N.Y. — YR 2:06:1 1969 18 2 4 1 8,432.
($10,659) 5, 2:03:3 JAMES TALLMAN (150) Wine-Grey-Yellow — Stga 2:03:3 1968 20 5 2 2 4,543.

6-14 YR ft clm 6000 m 30 1:02 1:34 2:04:3 4 5 5 4° 2/1 2/¾ 2:04:4 2.90(JTallman)VanRebeck,IMP,TomThumb
6-4 YR ft clm alw 6000 m 31 1:02:2 1:34:2 2:06 4 5 6 7 6/3 2/hd 2:06 3.70(JTallman) EasyJay, IMP, OC'sSandy
5-27 YR ft clm 6000 m 30:3 1:02:2 1:34 2:06:1 4 5 5° 3 3/2 1/¾ 2:06:1 4.00(JTllmn)IMP,MstrGlenn,CentralRange
5-20 RR ft clm 6000 m 31:2 1:04:2 1:35:1 2:06:2 7 1 1 1 fog 4/5 2:07:3 9.70(JTllmn)MorenciChf,DnnieM,VanRbeck
5-10 RR ft clm alw 7500 m 30:3 1:02 1:33:3 2:05:2 8 6 6 6° 5/4¾ 4/5¼ 2:06:3 30.80(JTllmn)PrbleTime,BeckerHn,LeroyHn
4-26 RR ft clm 7500 m 30:1 1:01:4 1:33:4 2:06:1 8 8 8 8 8/3¾ 8/4¼ 2:07:1 13.40(JTllmn)MrWexfrd,LeroyHn,SandyLeo
4-19 RR ft clm alw 7500 m 30:3 1:02:1 1:33:3 2:05:2 5 7 8 8 7/4½ 4/2 2:05:4 6.10(JTllmn)Rapid,GeminiDream,Sal'sMite
4-12 RR ft clm 7500 m 30:3 1:03 1:34 2:06 6 6 6° 5° 5/2½ 2/ns 2:06 25.40(JTallmn)JMRegal,IMP,GarrisonLight

---

3 — Morn. Line 6 — $7,500

COUNCIL DARES br g, 10, by Meadow Gene, Council's Maid by Chief Counsel (Tr.-G. Phalen)
Doris & John Wallrabe, Brooklyn, N.Y. — YR 2:06:4 1969 10 1 1 1 3,849.
($70,910) 5, 2:04:1 GEORGE PHALEN (135) Blue-White — RR 2:07:3 1968 38 2 12 4 17,147.

6-18 YR ft clm alw 7500 m 29:2 1:01:2 1:32:1 2:04 8 3 3 4 4/5½ 5/3¼ 2:04:4 61.40(Phln)B'viewBabe,SnowJob,KnoxEnsgn
6-5 YR ft Clm 7500 m 29:2 1:01 1:32:2 2:04:1 6 7 8° 7° 7/6 8/8¼ 2:06:1 18.20(Phln) YktyYakN,MghtyDavid,TopTrnd
5-31 YR ft clm alw 7500 m 29:2 1:01 1:33:2 2:04:2 6 6 4 5 6/3½ 3/3 2:05:1 29.30(GPhln)GrtCrdt,ElesGlry,CnclDares
5-24 RR ft clm alw 7500 m 31 1:02:2 1:34 2:05:1 5 5 5 6° 6/3¼ 5/6¼ 2:06:4 12.70(GPhln)MrWexford,AvaJava,KeyWhirl
* 5-17 RR ft qua m 31:1 1:03 1:34:4 2:06:4 8 4 4 4 4/3 2/1½ 2:07:1 N.B.(GPhln)DrmMjr,CnclDares,JhnnyGold
* 5-13 RR ft qua m 31:3 1:04:2 1:36:2 2:08:3 3 5 4° 5° 5/3 5/2½ 2:09:1 N.B.(GPhln)JackFrostA,Honorable,Ballock
2-22 YR ft clm alw 7500 m 29:3 1:02:3 1:34:4 2:06:4 2 3 2° 2 2/nk 1/hd 2:06:4 3.90(GPhln)CnclDares,ThrpsKin,DrumMjr
2-15 YR ft clm alw 7500 m 30 1:03 1:34:2 2:05:4 1 2 3 4 4/1 4/1¾ 2:06:1 8.90(AMyer) SandyLeo,MultiChief,LeWhip

---

4 — Morn. Line 4 — $7,500

RAPID b g, 9, by Rapid Hanover, Grandview Hattie by Gem Hanover (Tr.-R. Kurtz)
Richard Kurtz & Marvin Manheimer, N.Y. — RR 2:05 1969 20 2 2 2 7,711.
($56,620) 7, 2:02 JOHN CHAPMAN (147) Green-White — YR 2:04:2 1968 31 4 3 1 11,144.

6-11 YR ft clm 10000 m 29:3 1:00:4 1:32:1 2:03:1 7 6 6 5° 4/5 6/11 2:06 4.90(CAbto)Wldcat,BeckerHn,TimidMorris
5-29 YR ft clm 10000 m 30:2 1:01:2 1:32:2 2:03:4 1 4 4° 5° 6/2¾ 5/8¾ 2:05:4 3.80(LFntne)OrthoAce,SmrtMoney,Wildcat
5-20 RR ft Opt B-3 3500 m 31:3 1:04:1 1:35:3 2:05:4 6 fog 3 fog fog 4/N.R. N.R. 3.50(Chpmn)Heriot,OrthoAce,UniformAlee
5-12 RR ft Opt B-3 3500 m 29:1 1:03:3 1:35:3 2:07:3 3 4 5° 3°°4/2 2/nk 2:07:3 *1.50(JChpmn)TerriLeeN,Rapid,SmrtMoney
5-3 RR ft clm 10000 m 30 1:01:4 1:34:2 2:05 8 8 8° 1° 1/2 1/1¼ 2:05 20.50(JChpmn)Rapid,Mr.Tmblino,VanRebck
4-26 RR ft clm alw 10000 m 30:1 1:01:2 1:32:1 2:04:2 1 4 5 4 3/2½ 3/1¾ 2:04:4 5.80(JChpmn)LadRainbw,TrueStorm,Rapid
4-19 RR ft clm alw 7500 m 30:3 1:02:1 1:33:3 2:05:2 2 2 1 2 1/½ 1/1¼ 2:05:2 3.20(LFntne)Rapid,GeminiDream,Sal'sMite
4-12 RR ft B-3 3500 m 30:2 1:03 1:34:2 2:04:2 4 6 6 6 6/7 7/7¾ 2:06:1 8.50(JM'Dnld)BoySan,TenGrandN,Foresail

---

5 — Morn. Line 8 — $7,500

TOP TREND b g, 6, by Darn Flashy, Fontana by McI Win (Tr.-J. Kelley Jr.)
M. DeMarco, A. Zaccarello & M. Rogers, N. Y. — RR 2:05:4 1969 14 1 2 1 4,277.
($6,565) 4, 2:04:3 (⅝) JEFFERSON KELLEY, JR. (192) Red-Black — YR 2:05:2 1968 8 1 2 1 3,319

6-12 YR ft clm alw 7500 m 30:2 1:02:4 1:33:4 2:05:1 5 6 4° 4° 4/1¾ 4/1¾ 2:05:3 8.30(HerFlion)SandyLeo,Morant,SirC'Pick
6-5 YR ft clm 7500 m 29:2 1:01 1:32:2 2:04:1 1 3 3 3 3/4½ 3/4¾ 2:05:2 10:20(CAbtlo) YktyYkN,MightyDvd,TpTrend
5-31 YR ft clm alw 7500 m 30:1 1:01:2 1:32:1 2:04:2 2 4 5 5 5/3¾ 4/3¼ 2:05:1 11.70(CAblo)SalsMite,DplomaTme,JMRegal
5-17 RR ft clm alw 7500 m 30:2 1:02:3 1:34:3 2:06 8 8 7° 7 7/9 6/12 2:08:4 15.00(CAbtlo)GrtCrdt,AvaJava,CpprAdios
5-9 RR gd B-3 Cd 3500 m 29:2 1:02 1:34:2 2:06 7 3 3 8° 8/8¼ 7/9½ 2:08:1 37.60(Fntne)AdrsC'pie,St'yGrge,E'psoD'grn
4-28 RR ft Opt B-3 3500 m 30:1 1:02:1 1:33:4 2:05 1 4 2° 2 3/3½ 7/8¾ 2:07:1 8.40(FPfgr)Raidal,GoodOne,WorthTime
4-14 RR ft C-2 2750 m 30:1 1:02:1 1:34 2:05:4 2 4 1 1 1/nk 1/2½ 2:05:4 *2.00(GShlty)TpTrnd,DllyDllyJoey,GrndFlyr
3-31 RR ft C-2 Cd 2750 m 30:4 1:04 1:36:4 2:08:4 3 1 2 5 5/3 4/3¼ 2:09:3 2.70(FTgrlo)ArlieFrst,GzrkDm,BrdysChnce

---

6 — Morn. Line 4 — $7,500

ABBEY CRAIN b g, 9, by Ichabod Crain, Betty Heekin by Guy Abbey (Tr.-J. McDonald) (St.-W. Wathen, Jr.)
Matt-T. Ltd., Pound Ridge, N.Y. — YR 2:06:3 1969 8 1 2 0 3,454.
($60,622) 5, 2:03:4 CARMINE ABBATIELLO (135) Gold-Red — RR 2:04:2 1968 28 2 4 4 8,201.

6-16 YR ft clm 6000 m 30:2 1:03:4 1:35:2 2:06:3 4 6 3° 1 1/3 1/3½ 2:06:3 *1.20(CAbbtllo)AbbyCrn,DrmMajor,SfldSctt
6-6 YR ft clm 6000 m 30:4 1:01:4 1:33:3 2:05:2 2 5 5° 1° 1/nk 2/hd 2:05:2 4.90(Chpmn)KnxEnsgn,AbbyCrn,CptnMssie
5-28 Brdwn ft clm 6000 m 30:4 1:05:2 1:37:1 2:07:3 7 8 7° 6° 7/6¾ 6/7¼ 2:09:2 16.20(WthnJr)FlgtAppeal,SpceAge,TonyStrt
5-21 Brdwn ft Cd 2800 m 30:4 1:04 1:35:4 2:05:3 4 2 2 3 3/2 2/3½ 2:06:1 55.40(WthnJr)PcsttrPck,AbbyCrn,CWChpmn
5-13 Brdwn ft clm 6000 m 30:3 1:02:2 1:34 2:05:3 2 4 5 6 6/4½ 4/3¼ 2:06:2 41.95(JM'Dnld)TonyStrt,HoboBob,RitaGalln
5-6 LB(⅝) ft Cd 4100 m 30:3 1:03:1 1:34:1 2:04 3 4 4 5 6/6¼ 4/7 2:05:2 61.90(JM'Dnld)SmrstA,BckeysFrst,StrdyGld
5-1 LB(⅝) ft Cd 3700 m 28:4 1:02:1 1:33:2 2:04 4 4 4 5 5/5½ 6/6¼ 2:05:1 75.60(JM'Dnld)Ambit,FabrayHn,CWChpmn
4-19 LB(⅝) ft Cd 4100 m 31:3 1:03 1:34:3 2:05:1 3 3 5 7 8/8 7/8¼ 2:06:4 21.90(JM'Dnld)SnMrco,ShkeUpN,AdsM'Grth

---

7 — Morn. Line 12 — $7,500

GUY ADIOS b g, 9, by Adios Boy, Knightland by Scotland (Tr.-J. Callahan)
Lorelei Stable, New York, N.Y. — (qua) RR 2:10:1 1969 7 0 1 0 1,360.
($54,903) 5, 2:03:4 JAMES CALLAHAN (160) Purple-Gold — 1968 22 0 3 5 3,798.

6-12 YR ft clm alw 7500 m 30:2 1:02:4 1:33:4 2:05:1 1 4 6 7 7/4¾ 5/1¾ 2:05:3 16.50(Callahan)SandyLeo,Morant,SirC'Pick
5-31 YR ft clm alw 7500 m 30:1 1:01:2 1:32:1 2:04:2 6 8 8° 7 7/4¾ 6/4¼ 2:05:2 46.70(Cllhn)SalsMite,DplomaTime,JMRegal
5-24 RR ft clm alw 7500 m 31 1:02:2 1:34 2:05:1 4 4 4 5 5/3½ 4/3¾ 2:06:1 15.20(JCllhn)MrWxford,AvaJava,KeyWhirl
5-17 RR ft clm alw 7500 m 30:2 1:02:3 1:34:3 2:06 1 4 5 3° 2x/2 7/12 2:08:4 5.50(JCllhn)GrtCrdt,AvaJava,CopperAdios
5-5 RR ft C-2 Cd 2750 m 31:4 1:03:1 1:34:3 2:05:3 1 3 5 5 4/4 2/3½ 2:06:2 4.00(JCllhn)DllyDllyJoey,GuyAd's,GrndFlyr
4-14 RR ft C-1 3000 m 30:4 1:02:1 1:33:3 2:04:2 8 8 8 5 5/4 4/6½ 2:06 68.80(PKszgi)NoseyMite,RodAdios,HonrBoy
* 3-26 RR ft qua m 31 1:04:2 1:37:2 2:10:1 3 2 2 1° 1/1 1/1 2:10:1 N.B.(PKszgi)GyAd's,BnCseyN,FncyGeorgie
1-25 YR gd clm 6000 m 31:2 1:03:4 1:36:4 2:09:3 2 5x 7 7 x8/10 8/21 2:14:4 19.60(GFoldi)LeroyHn,SlvrD'Traux,JetDncr

---

8 — Morn. Line 8 — $7,500

LORD STACEY b g, 6, by Sampson Hanover, Candee by Tar Heel (Tr.-L. Pullen)
Lord &Lady Stables, Inc., Short Hills, N.J. — LB(⅝) 2:04:2 1969 15 2 1 3 7,351.
($42,914) 4, 2:02:2 (⅝) MICHAEL ORGAN (173) Brown-Gold — LB(⅝) 2:03 1968 31 3 6 3 14,181.

6-14 AC(⅝) sl Cd 1500 m 32:4 1:07:4 1:39:3 2:13 7 4 5 2° 1/2½ 1/2 2:13 5.10(DKys)LrdStacy,BlytheVctr,W'wndLbll
6-7 AC(⅝) ft Cd 1500 m 30:1 1:02 1:33 2:04:3 7 2° 1 1 1/1 4/1¾ 2:05 11.40(MSimn)SargentBill,Buster,SteadyBoy
5-12 AC(⅝) ft clm Cd 8000 m 31 1:03:1 1:34:2 2:06:2 8 3 3 5 6/3 4/8¼ 2:08 5.50(LPullen)SenatorR.,FlorArt,SpikeEd
5-3 LB(⅝) ft clm Cd 8000 m 30 1:01:3 1:31:3 2:02:2 7 6 6 5° 6/8¾ 5/10 2:04:2 18.30(LPlln)DrctStone,DrctMaq.,SpaceAge
4-28LB(⅝) ft clm Cd10000 m 30:1 1:01:4 1:32:3 2:03 2 4 5 5 5/5½ 7/9¼ 2:04:4 14.80(LPlln)Sagamon,JetAttack,BlytheDale
4-23LB(⅝) ft clmCd 10000 m 31 1:03:4 1:35:2 2:05:3 5 3 3 4 4/3¼ 3/3½ 2:06:1 7.00(LPlln)BlytheDle,RainTime,LordStacy
4-16LB(⅝) gd clmCd 10000m 31 1:04:3 1:34:4 2:06:1 1 3 4 4 4/3½ 5/7¼ 2:07:3 7.20(LPlln)Hap.Songstr,BlytheDle,EdwrdJ.
4-9 LB(⅝) ft clm Cd 10000 m 30:4 1:02:1 1:33:1 2:04 3 6 6 7 8/8½ 8/8¾ 2:05:3 5.00(MSmn)RainTime,EdwardJ.,JetAttack

EXACTA WINDOWS OPEN FOR THIS RACE

6 PACE - ONE MILE

SADDLE CLOTH— BLUE

The Greenwich

CLASS A-3 PURSE $5,250

1

RICCI REENIE FIRST b m, 4, by Tar Heel, Ricci Reenie by Santo Eden (Tr.-H. Dancer, Jr.)
Ricci Farms, Inc., Long Branch, N.J. YR 2:04:1 1969 11 1 3 1 7,807.
($56,241) 3, 2:02 JOHN CHAPMAN (147) Green-White YR 2:02 1968 19 3 3 3 25,217.
6-18 YR ft A-3 5250 m 30:2 1:01:3 1:33 2:03 1 3 5 6 7/3¼ 5/3½ 2:03:4 7.00(HDncrJr)BobbyEd,PrideO'Hn,Alytor
6-7 YR ft B-1 Cd 4500 m 30:3 1:01 1:32:3 2:04:1 2 3 4 4 3/1 1/¾ 2:04:1 *1.50(HDncrJr)RcciRneFrst,StrmPrf,Bobalu
5-30 Stga ft Inv 6000 m 30:3 1:01 1:30:2 2:00:1 5 5 5 5 5 5/9¼ 2:02 12.50(DBrmly)PneHllTme,FrncsTLry,Chck'n
5-23 RR ft B-1 4500 m 31:1 1:02:1 1:33 2:02:4 7 1 2 2° 2/1 4/3¾ 2:03:4 7.10(ECbb) BadMoe,BalladeerN,TigerPaws
5-17 RR ft B-1 4500 m 29:4 1:02:2 1:32:4 2:03:4 4 7 3°°1° 1/1 2/¾ 2:04 4.10(DncrJr) TrprtBll,RcciRniFrst,TigrPws
5-10 RR ft Opt B-1 4500 m 30:1 1:03:3 1:34:2 2:05 3 4 4° 2° 2/hd 4/1¾ 2:05:2 2.80(DncrJr)RexPick,StdyBrave,TarprtBill
5-5 RR ft B-1 4500 m 29:4 1:00:2 1:32:4 2:04:2 3 6 7° 7 7/5 3/¾ 2:04:3 5.90(DncrJr)Donora,SlyYankee,RicciR'First
4-24 RR gd Opt B-1 4500 m 30 1:02:2 1:33:3 2:04:3 3 4 3° 2° 2/1 6/5½ 2:05:4 4.70(DncrJr)MizellesMickey,Alytor,Donora

2

‡BROWN SMOKE br h, 5, by Brown Star, Red Amber by Red Prince (Tr.-G. Regan)
M.J.Fischer & K.N.Diamond, lessees, Wash., D.C. RR 2:04 1969 23 2 6 8 18,806.
($39,354) 3, 2:03 WILLIAM MYER (165) Blue-Red Brdwn 2:04:1 1968 32 2 4 3 11,644.
6-17 YR‡ ft A-3 5250 m 29:3 1:02 1:32:1 2:02:4 2 4 4° 4° 5/1 2/1½ 2:03 3.80(WMyr)TigrPaws,BrwnSmke,TorpidVic
6-10 YR‡ ft A-3 5250 m 30:2 1:02 1:32:2 2:02:3 4 5 5° 3° 2/nk 2/½ 2:02:4 14.00(WMyr)BadMoe,BrownSmke,PocnoHn
6-3 YR‡ ft A-3 5250 m 29:4 1:00:3 1:32:1 2:05 4 5 4 3° 3/3 5/1 2:05:1 *1.80(DInsko)TrprtBll,NshbaLttlm,ExltdRlr
5-24RR‡ ft A-2/A-3 6000 m 29:3 1:02:1 1:33:2 2:03:3 6 7 3° 2° 3/1½ 3/3½ 2:04:2 7.10(WMyr)TwoDmnd,H'IndRdr,BrwnSmke
5-19RR‡ ft A-2/A-3 6000 m 29:3 1:00:3 1:31:4 2:02 6 7 7 7° 7/4½ 3/2½ 2:02:3 14.30(GShlty)NvleRmeo,MrLcifr,BrwnSmke
5-14 RR‡ ftA-1/A-2 7500 m 30 1:02:1 1:33:2 2:03:1 3 4 4° 2° 3/1½ 6/3¾ 2:04:1 19.60(WMyr) KngOmha,AustS'Slvr,NvleRmo
5-9 RR‡ gd Opt A-3 5500 m 29 1:01 1:32:1 2:05:2 5 6 4° 3° 2/1 1/1¾ 2:05:2 3.70(WMyr)BrwnSmke,BobbyEd,MrrsHart
5-2 RR‡ ft A-3 5500 m 31:1 1:03 1:33:3 2:04:4 6 7 6° 6° 5/2¾ 2x/hd 2:04:4 *1.70(GShlty)Option,BrwnSmke,MrrisHart

3

TORPID VIC b h, 4, by Torpid, Cerise by Tar Heel (Tr.-T. Gay) (St.-C. Ernst)
C. Ernst & F. O. Rinker, Jr. Bloomsburg, Pa. 1969 4 0 0 1 1,630.
($40,422) 3, 2:02 CARL ERNST (190) Red-Grey YR 2:02 1968 29 4 6 3 28,694.
6-17 YR ft A-3 5250 m 29:3 1:02 1:32:1 2:02:4 4 1 1 1 1/ns 3/1¾ 2:03:1 *1.70(Ernst)TigrPaws,BrwnSmke,TorpdVic
6-12 YR ft A-2 6250 m 30:4 1:02:4 1:32:1 2:03 8 8 7 7° 7/3½ 6/2½ 2:03:3 25.90(Ernst)Rcnp'sJack,Dg'sChce,AC'sDndy
6-5 YR ft A-2 6250 m 29:4 1:00:2 1:29:4 2:00:3 3 4 4 4 4/3¼ 4/4¼ 2:01:3 7.70(Ernst) ChrisTime,ACDandy,RcnpJack
5-28 YR ft A-2 6250 m 30:4 1:02:3 1:34:1 2:02:4 6 6 6 4° 4/6 4/6¾ 2:04:2 28.40(Ernst)Rhyl,CardnalGarrsn,FrostyDrm
10-17 YR ft A-2 6250 m 29:3 1:00:1 1:30:4 2:01:3 7 7 7 5 4/3 3/¾ 2:01:4 39.80(CErnst)Mr.JimT.,WiseGuyN.,TrpdVic
10-5 YR ft A-1 7500 m 29:3 1:01 1:32 2:02:3 5 8 8 3° 3/1 8/3½ 2:03:2 33.90(CErnst)TrdrNrdin,Goodnuff,MrLcifer
9-28 YR ft A-1 7500 m 30:3 1:01:4 1:31:4 2:01:2 4 5 5 5 5/5 4/4½ 2:02:2 16.20(CErnst)ShoreWill,Goodnuff,Ironworks
9-21 YR ft A-1 7500 m 29:3 1:01:2 1:31:1 2:01:2 8 8 8 8° 8/4½ 8/5½ 2:02:4 61.80(CErnst)TropicSong,Prswick,Goodnuff

4

PRIDE OF HANOVER br g, 8, by H. D. Hanover, Eddys Lass by Nelson Eddy (Tr.-R. Baker) (St.-S. Dancer)
R. Hess, B. Murphy & S. Dancer, N.J. RR 2:04:1 1969 14 2 4 2 12,516.
($21,649) 7, 2:03 JOHN PATTERSON SR. (165) Tan-Blue YR 2:03 1968 27 9 2 6 19,795.
6-18 YR ft A-3 5250 m 30:2 1:01:3 1:33 2:03 6 6 6° 5° 2/1 2/2 2:03:2 6.10(WMyer)BobbyEd,PrideO'Hn,Alytor
6-10 YR ft A-3 5250 m 30:2 1:02 1:32:2 2:03:3 2 1 2 4 5/2¾ 5/3½ 2:03:2 3.10(HDncrJr)BadMoe,BrwnSmke,PcnoHn
6-2 YR ft A-3 5250 m 30:1 1:01 1:32 2:02:3 3 2 2 3 3/2 2/¾ 2:02:4 4.90(VDncr)KystneRngr,PrdeOfHn,RylRmn
5-26 YR ft A-3 5250 m 29:3 1:00:4 1:32:3 2:03:3 6 4° 4° 2° 2/½ 3/½ 2:03:4 *3.10(SDncr)DxieTmboy,T'prtBill,PrdeO'Hn
5-14 RR ft Opt B-1 4500 m 30:2 1:01:3 1:33:1 2:04:1 2 1 1 1 1/1 1/nk 2:04:1 7.10(DncrJr) PrdO'Hn,SctshFslier,AftnBllt
4-25 LB(⅝) ft Cd 5500 m 30:4 1:04 1:34:2 2:03:3 2 4 4 2° 2/½ 7/5½ 2:04:3 4.40(RDncr)ThdreDmnd,PcnoHn,JMFlash
4-11 LB(⅝) ft Cd 5000 m 31 1:03 1:34:1 2:03:3 5 6 5 3° 3/1 5/5½ 2:04:3 *2.80(RDncr)AftnSpdy,LttleWllie,Bee'sChf
4-5 LB(⅝) sy Cd 5000 m 31:4 1:04:1 1:35:3 2:08 3 5 4 5° 4/3 4/4½ 2:08:4 2.80(RDncr)StevesPhil,Jeeves,SntrBllyMac

5

CHARMING DEMON b m, 5, by Demon Rum, Secret Charm by Long Key (Tr.-P. Schell)
Paul Schell & Herbert McPhee, Pa. LB(⅝) 2:03:1 1969 11 2 4 1 24,113.
($19,632) 4, 2:05:1 LUCIEN FONTAINE (134) Green-White-Red Brdwn 2:05:1 1968 26 3 3 5 10,519.
6-18 YR ft A-3 5250 m 30:2 1:01:3 1:33 2:03 2 4 3° 2° 4/2 6/3¾ 2:03:4 4.80(Fontne)BobbyEd,PrideO'Hn,Ayltor
6-9 YR ft Ic 25000 m 29:1 1:01:1 1:33:1 2:03:2 4 8 7 7 5/3 2/1½ 2:03:4 65.80(WMyr)ChrmngDmnbydq,LcsLou,Mdan
6-2 YR ft Ic 12500 m 29:3 1:02 1:33:2 2:04:4 1 3 3 3 4/2 2/1¼ 2:05:1 6.60(Fntne)BwtchdN,ChrmngDemn,Chukkh
5-26 YR ft Ic 10000 m 32:1 1:04:3 1:36 2:05:4 5 2 2 3 3/1 2/1½ 2:06:1 23.00(Fntne)Disbnd,ChrmngDemn,QuickieHn
5-19 AC(⅝) ft Cd 2500 m 29:4 1:02 1:31:1 2:02:1 4 2 3 3 3/3½ 4/3 2:02:4 4.50(GD'sy)ThdreDmnd,SetShot,VctryAd's
5-10 LB(⅝) ft Cd 6600 m 30 1:01:2 1:31:1 2:00:4 6 ix7 7 7 7/dis 7/dis 2:09:1 22.60(AStltzfs)NwprtRbbie,Trnspndr,C'boye
4-30 LB(⅝) ft Cd 5200 m 30 1:03 1:33:3 2:03:1 3 2 2 3 4/1¾ 1/½ 2:03:1 3.50(Stltzfs)ChrmngDmn,MelStr,ThndrRyl
4-23 LB(⅝) ft Cd 5500 m 29:4 1:01 1:31:4 2:02:2 3 7 7 6 5/7¼ 3/5½ 2:03:2 5.60(HrFiln)Ardrssn,BeauMrtl,ChrmngDmn

6

DONORA b m, 4, by Adios Don, Marcy Hanover by Tar Heel (Tr.-W. Burris) (St.-V. Dancer)
Fury Stable & Fiesta Farm, N.Y., N.Y. RR 2:04 1969 14 2 2 4 13,500.
($30,014) 3, 2:02:4 DEL INSKO (120) Purple-Gold YR 2:02:4 1968 21 5 2 6 17,039.
6-18 YR ft A-3 5250 m 30:2 1:01:3 1:33 2:03 3 5 4° 4 6/3 7/3¾ 2:03:4 3.70(DInsko)BobbyEd,PrideO'Hn,Alytor
6-9 YR ft Ic 25000 m 29:1 1:01:1 1:33:1 2:03:2 1 4 5° 4° 3/2 8/5¾ 2:04:4 4.60(VDncer)ChrmngDemn,LucisLou,Midian
6-2 YR ft Ic 12500 m 30:1 1:01:2 1:32 2:03 7 7 6° 6° 6/2¼ 2/¾ 2:03:1 37.20(VDncer) Disband,Donora,NotableWick
5-26 YR ft Ic 10000 m 30:4 1:03:1 1:34 2:04:3 4 4 3° 2° 3/1 7/2½ 2:05:1 3.90(VDncr)BlkTulpN,TrprtKren,S'dleCarol
5-20 RR ft Opt A-3 5500 m 30:2 1:02:2 1:33:3 2:04 1 2 2 3 2/1 1/nk 2:04 4.00(VDncr) Donora,MontageN,BlckieAdios
5-13 RR ft A-3 5500 m 30:1 1:01 1:32:1 2:03:3 5 7 6° 5° 4/2½ 5/1¾ 2:04 5.40(DInsko) LsciusLu,ChrryShde,BnneFlle
5-5 RR ft B-1 4500 m 29:4 1:00:2 1:32:4 2:04:2 4 3 3 4° 4/2 1/½ 2:04:2 *1.40(VDncr)Donora,SlyYankee,RicciR'First
4-24 RR gd Opt B-1 4500 m 30 1:02:2 1:33:3 2:04:3 4 5 5° 5 5/3 3/3¼ 2:05:2 3.30(JCruise)MzellesMickey,Alytor,Donora

7

ALYTOR b g,7,by Torrid, Aly's Lady by Alemite (Tr.-A. Abbatiello)
Hay-Day Stable, Farmingdale, N.Y. YR 2:03:4 1969 22 3 5 5 16,005.
($49,826) 4, 2:03:3 CARMINE ABBATIELLO (135) Gold-Red YR 2:04:1 1968 24 2 3 2 8,954.
6-18 YR ft A-3 5250 m 30:2 1:01:3 1:33 2:03 7 7 7 7° 5/2 3/3½ 2:03:4 14.10(CAbbtllo)BobbyEd,PrideO'Hn,Alytor
6-11 YR ft B-1 Cd 4500 m 30:1 1:01:2 1:32:1 2:03:4 7 7 7° 6° 5/2¾ 1/¾ 2:03:4 14.20(AAbbtllo)Alytr,ChrryShde,WrthyJimy
6-5 YR ft B-1 Cd 4500 m 30:3 1:02:2 1:34:1 2:05 5 7 7° 6° 4/3½ 3/1¼ 2:05:1 6.50(CAbbtllo)Eyreton,WorthyJimy,Alytor
5-28 YR ft B-1 Cd 4500 m 30 1:01:4 1:31:4 2:02:3 1 2 2 3 2/1½ 2/1¾ 2:03 9.10(FTgrlo)DougsChoice,Alytor,PocanoHn
5-16 RR ft B-1 4500 m 30:1 1:02 1:33:1 2:04:3 2 4 5 5 5/4 3/2 2:05:1 6.20(CAbtlo)HootfireHan,Ed'sLady,Alytor
5-9 RR gd B-1 Cd 4500 m 30:1 1:02:4 1:34:4 2:06 5 2 1 1 1/1 4/1 2:06:1 *1.60(CAbtlo)Apt,WorthyJimmy,BrainsWay
5-3 RR ft B-1 4500 m 30 1:02 1:32:4 2:03:4 7 1 1 4 3/1 3/2 2:04:1 5.00(CAbt)AbbeGneVolo,TarportBill,Alytor
4-24 RR gd Opt B-1 4500 m 30 1:02:2 1:33:3 2:04:3 2 3 4 4° 4/1½ 2/1¾ 2:05 9.10(CAbtlo)MizellesMickey,Alytor,Donora

8

VALID BET br m, 6, by Noble Dean, Betty Genesee by Yankee Hanover (Tr.-R. Burgholzer)
Merit Stables, Jamaica, N.Y. RR 2:02:4 1969 18 3 0 0 10,107.
($24,845) 5, 2:02:3 NORMAN DAUPLAISE (139) Brown-Gold-White YR 2:02:3 1968 21 2 1 3 6,710.
6-18 YR ft A-3 5250 m 30:2 1:01:3 1:33 2:03 8 8 8 8 8/4¾ 8/5¾ 2:04:1 63.70(Dauplaise)BobbyEd,PrideO'Hn,Alytor
6-9 YR ft A-3 5250 m 30:1 1:02 1:32 2:02:2 3 5x 8 8 8/dis 8/dis 31.90(Chpmn)MdllnLbll,ScttshFslr,SchllHn
6-2 YR ft Ic 12500 m 29:3 1:02 1:33:2 2:04:4 6 7 7° 4° 3/1 6/4¼ 2:05:4 27.90(Chpmn)BwtchdN,ChrmngDemn,Chkkh
5-26 YR ft Ic 10000 m 29:2 1:00:1 1:32 2:03 3 1 1 2 5/7½ 5/12 2:05:4 17.50(C'pmn)LusciousLou,BwtchdN,Mindian
5-16 RR ft A-3 5500 m 30:2 1:01:1 1:32:2 2:03:4 4 1° 1 3 4/3½ 7/8¾ 2:06 9.70(Brghlzr)AbbeG'Vlo,ExltdRlr,DxieT'by
5-6 RR ft Opt A-3 5500 m 30 59:4 1:30:4 2:02:1 3 1 1 1 1/2 6/4½ 2:03:1 2.80(Chp'n)NtbleWck,BlkieAd's,LsciousLou
4-30 RR ft A-2/A-3 6000 m 31 1:01:3 1:31:2 2:02:4 7 7 2° 2 3/4 6/6 2:04:1 5.70(GShlty)PnthrHn,NvleRmeo,ChrryShde
4-23 RR ft A-2/A-3 6000 m 30:2 1:01 1:32 2:03:3 8 4 1 1°1x/1½ 8/dis 12.30(CAbtlo)BeauMdw,RylRoman,RobrtEden

EXACTA WINDOWS OPEN 10 MINUTES BEFORE THIS RACE

MORN. LINE

7 PACE-ONE MILE

SADDLE CLOTH—RED

The Garfield Lions Club

CLASS C-2 —CONDITIONED — 3-YR. & UP PURSE $2,750

FILLIES & MARES

THIS IS AN EXACTA RACE

3

1 LITTLE MOTHER

br m, 4, by Right Time, Darn Cool by Darnley (Tr.-W. Mello) (St.-W. Haughtc
Barbara Katz, Lido Beach, N.Y. 1969 6 0 1 0 79
($36,870) 2, 2:05:2 CARMINE ABBATIELLO (135) Gold-Red Brdwn 2:05:2 1968 22 1 6 2 17,1(

6-13 YR	gd C-1 Cd	3000	m 31	1:02:3	1:34:1	2:06:3	7	8	8°	7°	8/7¼	6/3¼	2:07:2	12.50(Shlty)LidaLisa,FairMdn,ReneCrpntr
6-6 YR	ft C-1	3000	m 31:1	1:03	1:34:2	2:05:4	3	4°	3°	7°	7/3¾	8/4¾	2:07	2.10(Haghtn)SharonW,ElesGlory,FltStwa
5-30 YR	ft C-1 Cd	3000	m 30:4	1:03:1	1:34:3	2:05:2	7	1°	2	3	4/1½	2/1½dh	2:05:4	11.60(H'tn)CfeAuL't,HrrcnMaid-LttlMthr
5-16 RR	ft C-1 Cd	3000	m 30:3	1:03:1	1:33:4	2:05:3	3	5	5	5	5/5	4/2¼	2:06:1	3.30(WHghtn)Mstrtme,MrkTme,HrryO'B
5-8 RR	ft C-1 Cd	3000	m 31:3	1:04	1:34:2	2:05:1	8	8	8	8	7/10	7/7¼	2:07	6.90(GShlty)F'rMdn,R'dsT'Heel,HrryO'B
4-30 RR	ft B-3 Cd	3500	m 30:2	1:03	1:33:2	2:04:2	4	5	7	6	6/4¼	7/5¾	2:05:4	12.30(WHaughtn)Glynis,Adour,UniformAle
10-17LB(⅝)	ft3yStk	20568	m 29:1	1:00	1:30:3	1:59:2	5	7	7	7	7/10	7/16	2:02:3	32.30(WHghtn)SnnieTar,TrprtKrn,Q'kieHr
10-10 YR	ft B-3 Cd	3250	m 30:1	1:01:2	1:32:3	2:03:4	5	3	2°	3°	5/3¾	6/6	2:05:1	*1.20(CAbtlo) KthysLssie,M'rseJsie,ElsGl

6

2 CALSARA

br m, 6, by Caleb, Lida Hanover by Bill Gallon (Tr.-D. Tovin
Beurose Stable, Inc., Jersey City, N.J. RR 2:05:4 1969 13 2 1 1 3,90
($23,931) 5, 2:05:3 LUCIEN FONTAINE (134) Green-White-Red YR 2:05:3 1968 28 5 4 6 11,75

6-12 YR	ft C-2 Cd	2750	m 30:4	1:02:1	1:34:2	2:06:2	6	1°	2	4	4/2	7/5¼	2:07:4	11.00(HDncrJr)FntblsWve,T'prtSusn,Katy
5-14 RR	ft C-2 Cd	2750	m 31:1	1:02:2	1:35	2:07:2	8	2°	2	3	3/1¼	3/¾	2:07:3	10.00(Fntne) SharnW,ClairsTarHeel,Calsa
5-7 RR	ft C-2 Cd	2750	m 31:1	1:03:3	1:34:4	2:05:4	8	8	8ix	8	8/12	8/12	2:09:2	7.90(LFntne)CfeAuL't,HTEmly,ElmhrstQ
4-24 RR	gd C-1 Cd	3000	m 30:3	1:03:2	1:34:2	2:06:3	5	1°	1	3	2/5	6/4	2:07:3	9.30(LFntne)RapidQn,BthanyHn,AftonFl
4-15 RR	ft C-1 Cd	3000	m 29:4	1:01:3	1:33:3	2:05	3	3°	2	5	6/3	7/8	2:07	4.60(JChp'n)BlckTulipN,KatyR,ClrtAndrs
4-9 RR	ft C-1 Cd	3000	m 30:3	1:02:3	1:34	2:06:2	8	2°	1	2	3/2¼	6/6¼	2:07:4	10.70(Fntne)VllyPrncss,Nbch'sDrm,HerIrsh
3-27 RR	ft C-1 Cd	3000	m 31:1	1:03	1:34:3	2:05:4	4	1	1	1	1/1	1/ns	2:05:4	3.70(LFntne)Clsara,ValleyPrncss,Lind'sG
3-19 RR	ft C-2	2750	m 30:3	1:02:2	1:34:2	2:05:2	5	2°	1	2	2/hd	2/2	2:05:4	2.70(CAbbatllo)OurGem,Calsara,DustyJe

8

3 CLAIRE'S TAR HEEL

b m, 4, by Tar Heel, Adios Claire by Adios (Tr.-J. Farald
Annroc Stables, Brooklyn, N.Y. RR 2:08:2 1969 14 1 7 0 6,56
($5,476) JOE FARALDO (170) White-Green-Black (qua) RR 2:06:4 1968 24 0 7 4 5,30

6-12 YR	ft C-2 Cd	2750	m 30:4	1:02:1	1:34:2	2:06:2	1	3	4°	2°	2/½	4/2¾	2:07	4.60(Frldo)FntblousWve,T'prtSusan,Katy
5-29 YR	ft C-2 Cd	2750	m 29:4	1:00:4	1:32:3	2:05:4	5	6	6	4°	2/½	2/¾	2:06	5.70(Frldo)CoastLdy,ClairesT'Heel,Sonsie
5-14 RR	ftC-2 Cd	2750	m 31:1	1:02:2	1:35	2:07:2	1	3	4	4°	4/1½	2/hd	2:07:2	9.10(Frldo) SharnW,ClairesTarHeel,Calsa
4-30 RR	ft C-2 Cd	2750	m 31:2	1:04	1:35:3	2:06:3	1	2	4	6	5/2¼	4/½	2:06:4	6.60(JFrldo)StoutFlla,DtchTme,StSailLb
4-22 RR	sy C-2 Cd	2750	m 31	1:05:1	1:37:4	2:10	6	3	3	3	2/2	2/¾	2:10:1	17.10(JFrldo)OC'sSndy,Claire'sT'Heel,Sfor
4-9 RR	ft C-3 Cd	2500	m 32:1	1:04:1	1:36:2	2:08:2	3	5	5	4°	3/3¼	1/½	2:08:2	7.70(JFrldo)ClairesTrHl,Slco'sAprl,MssH
4-2 RR	ft C-3 Cd	2500	m 30:2	1:04:1	1:36:1	2:09:1	7	1°	2	1	1/nk	5/3¼	2:10	5.70(JFrldo)Capmarge,FairWidow,JuneM
3-25 RR	gd C-3 Cd	2500	m 31	1:03	1:35:2	2:09:1	2	5	4°	2	2/1	2/ns	2:09:1	2.30(JFrldo)ChiefBunny,ClrsT'Heel,Salco

4

4 TARPORT SUSAN

b m, 7, by Thorpe Hanover, Dagsworthy Lady by Adios (Tr.-J. Webber
D.L. & J. Stable, Inc., Bayside, N.Y. 1969 13 0 1 1 1,22
($45,989) 6, 2:03:3 JAMES TALLMAN (150) Wine-Grey-Yellow YR 2:03:3 1968 27 4 0 3 8,9

6-12 YR	ft C-2 Cd	2750	m 30:4	1:02:1	1:34:2	2:06:2	4	6	6°	3°	3/1	2/hd	2:06:2	4.90(Tllmn)FntblousWve,T'prtSusan,Katy
* 6-3 YR	gd qua		m 31:1	1:02:4	1:35:2	2:08:1	3	1°	1	1	1/nk	2/ns	2:08:1	N.B.(Chp'n)NbchsDrm,TrprtSusn,KllyKn
4-9 RR	ft C-2 Cd	2750	m 32:3	1:06:2	1:38:1	2:09:4	3	4	5	6°	8/10	7/7¼	2:11:3	3.90(ECbb)MssGntry,TrdyDmnd,OuiO'Byr
3-24 RR	sy C-2 Cd	2750	m 33	1:07:2	1:40:3	2:12	4	6	5°	4°	4/2	3/4	2:13	3.40(C'pmn)ClrtAndrsn,MssGntry,TrprtS
3-11 RR	ft C-2 Cd	2750	m 31:1	1:05:2	1:37	2:09:2	2	3	4	5	6/4¼	7/7¼	2:11:1	27.00(Rl'nato)LindsGirl,AftnFlsh,AdiosGlv
3-5 RR	ft C-1	3000	m 31	1:03:3	1:34:4	2:06:3	6	7	7	7°	7/7¼	8/5¼	2:07:4	43.20(Rl'nto)A'broInstnt,FrwrdStr,HonrB
2-28 YR	ft C-1 Cd	3000	m 30:4	1:03:1	1:35:3	2:07:2	1	2	2	3°	4/3	5/5¾	2:08:3	9.10(Rl'nto)Angelita,HerIrish,RitasDream
2-21 YR	ft B-3	3250	m 30:3	1:02:2	1:34	2:05:4	3	5	6°	8°	8/7¼	8/11	2:08:3	32.80(Rl'dto)Sal'sMte,GoodCndy,BthanyH

5

5 ‡ANITAS STAR

br m, 6, by Walter McKlyo, Princess Dares by Dudley Hanover (Tr.-A. Niles, J
Julie Brown, Ft. Lauderdale, Fla. YR 2:05 1969 11 1 1 2 3,10
($24,148) 3, 2:04:1 (⅝) ARCHIE NILES, JR. (162) White-Green YR 2:05:2 1968 31 3 3 4 7,08

6-12 YR‡	ft C-3 Cd	2500	m 30:2	1:02	1:33	2:05	2	1	2	1	1/nk	1/¾	2:05	6.50(NlsJr)Ant'sStr,K'stnMdw,TrdyDmnd
* 6-3 YR‡	gd qua		m 31:1	1:02	1:36	2:08:3	2	2	2	3	6/4	5/5¾	2:10	N.B.(Fldi)TracysGirl,OzrkDom,GenrlBroo
* 5-27 YR	ft qua		m 31:2	1:02:3	1:35	2:07:2	3	1	1	1	2/nk	2/2¼	2:08	N.B.(GFoldi)AvanteN.,AnitasStar,ByePas
* 5-21 RR	ft qua		m 31:3	1:03:3	1:36	2:09:2	4	1	1	1	1/hd	2/½	2:09:3	N.B.(Fldi)PinkPoppy,AnitasStar,HerasBo
4-15 RR	ft C-2 Cd	2750	m 30:2	1:02:4	1:34:1	2:06:4	8	1	2	4	4/2	4/1½	2:07:1	17.90(NlsJr)S'phnyBlle,LdyThrne,MissyVn
4-2 RR	ft C-2 Cd	2750	m 31:2	1:03:3	1:36	2:08:1	4	1	2	3	2/1½	2/2¼	2:08:4	24.60(NlsJr)MssHoliday,AntasStr,ClairsDr
3-17 RR	ft C-2 Cd	2750	m 31	1:01:4	1:34:4	2:06:2	4	4	1	5	6/5¼	7/14	2:10	9.60(NlsJr)AftnFlsh,ClrtAndrsn,MissGnt
3-7 RR	ft C-2	2750	m 30:1	1:02:3	1:34:3	2:06:4	4	5	6	6	4/2¼	3/4¼	2:08	19.90(NlsJr)Frmamnt,WntwnPick,AnitasS

8

6 OUR GEM

b m, 9, by Sampson Hanover, Tru Sis by Dean Hanover (Tr.-J. Berube
Betty & Arthur Rubin, Ridgewood, N.J. RR 2:05:2 1969 17 4 1 1 7,01
($28,482) 4, 2:03:1 (1) JEAN BERUBE (160) Orange-White YR 2:06:2 1968 27 3 8 3 7,65

6-12 YR	ft C-1 Cd	3000	m 30:2	1:02:2	1:33	2:04:2	7	8	8	7°	7/5¼	7/5¼	2:05:3	20.70(HerFln)B'cpSmth,Nbch'sDrm,ShrnW
6-5 YR	ft C-1 Cd	3000	m 30:2	1:01:4	1:34	2:05	5	7	7	7	7/6	5/5½	2:06:1	3.70(HerFln) AftnFlsh,FlrneFrst,GdTmeL
5-21 RR	ft C-1 Cd	3000	m 30:3	1:02:4	1:33:4	2:04:4	4	6	3°	2°	2/½	3/1½	2:05:1	18.20(LFnte)BthnyHn,BttrcpSmth,OurGem
5-14 RR	ft C-1 Cd	3000	m 30:3	1:02:3	1:33:4	2:05:3	6	7	4°	6°	7/5¼	8/6	2:07	8.90(Fntn) MnneBrd,ClrtAndsn,B'cupSm
4-28 RR	ft Opt B-3	3500	m 30	1:02:1	1:33:4	2:05	4	7	8	8	7/7	6/5¾	2:06:2	14.80(LFntne)Raidal,GoodOne,WorthTime
4-10 RR	sy Opt B-3	3500	m 31:2	1:04:2	1:37:2	2:10	3	6	6°°	6°	8x/10	8/10	2:12:3	*.90(LF'tne)BrbraBrmn,SrniaRse,NplnAd
4-1 RR	ft B-3	3250	m 30:1	1:02	1:33:3	2:05:2	6	3°	1°	2	3/2¼	5/6¾	2:07:1	2.70(LF'tne)K'gtA'Day,WstrnC'nce,TenG
3-24 RR	sy C-1	3000	m 32:3	1:04:3	1:36:3	2:08:4	7	4	3°	2	2/1½	1/2	2:08:4	2.10(LFntne)OurGem,SixThirteen,HerIrish

10

7 LINDS GIRL

blk m, 7, by Peter Lind, Princess Chief by Chief Abbedale (Tr.-D. Insk
Ruby's Sterling Farm Stables, Morgantown, W.Va. RR 2:05:4 1969 17 3 2 1 6,59
($40,608) 3, 2:02:2 (⅝) DEL INSKO (120) Purple-Gold 1968 14 0 1 1 1,52

6-12 YR	ft C-2 Cd	2750	m 30:4	1:02:1	1:34:2	2:06:2	3	5	5	8	8x/5	x8x/7	2:08:1	7.20(DInsko)FntbiousWve,T'prtSusan,Katy
5-29 YR	ft C-2 Cd	2750	m 29:4	1:00:4	1:32:3	2:05:4	7	2	3	2	3/1	5/1½	2:06:1	4.80(DInsko)CoastLdy,ClairseT'Heel,Sons
5-22 RR	ft C-1 Cd	3000	m 30:1	1:01:2	1:34:3	2:06:3	7	3	3	4	4/3¼	5/3	2:07:2	13.20(DIsko) MddlbrkJohn,DahnHolly,Mor
5-14 RR	ft C-1 Cd	3000	m 30:3	1:02:3	1:33:4	2:05:3	3	1	2	3	4/2	7/4¼	2:06:3	8.10(DIsko) MneBrd,ClrtAndsn,B'cupSm
4-29 RR	ft C-1 Cd	3000	m 30:4	1:01:2	1:33	2:04	1	3	3	4	5/2¾	4/6	2:05:2	4.60(DI'sko)MssGntry,FairMaidn,MssHli
4-15 RR	ft C-1 Cd	3000	m 29:4	1:01:3	1:33:3	2:05	6	1	1	2	3/2	8/9½	2:07:2	5.60(DInsko)BlckTulipN,KatyR,ClrtAndrs
3-27 RR	ft C-1 Cd	3000	m 31:1	1:03	1:34:3	2:05:4	7	4	4	4	3/1	3/¾	2:06	5.70(DInsko)Calsara,VlleyPrncss,Lind'sGi
3-19 RR	ft C-1	3000	m 31:3	1:03:1	1:33:4	2:05:4	2	2	4	4	2/1	1/1	2:05:4	26.40(DI'sko)LindsGirl,KatyR.,YnkeeShad

9/2

8 KATY R.

b m, 5, by Hadley Hanover, Lepal by Mr. Volo Morris (Tr.-W. Drucksley) (St.-R. Rash)
Louis & Mary Theodore, Jackson Heights, N.Y. 1969 21 0 6 2 6,69
($10,616) 4, 2:04:4 (⅝) JOHN CHAPMAN (147) Green-White LB(⅝) 2:04:4 1968 32 8 5 2 9,54

6-12 YR	ft C-2 Cd	2750	m 30:4	1:02:1	1:34:2	2:06:2	8	4°	1	1	1/½	3/2¼	2:07	*2.30(Hghtn)FntblousWve,T'prtSusn,Katy
5-30 YR	ft C-1 Cd	3000	m 30:4	1:03:1	1:34:3	2:05:2	8	8	7°	7	6/2¼	6/2¾	2:06	30.80(Rsh)CfeAuL't,HrrcnMaid-LttlMothr
5-21 RR	ft C-1 Cd	3000	m 30:3	1:02:4	1:33:4	2:04:4	6	7	7	7	7ix/3	8/11	2:07:2	7.10(Rash)BthnyHn,BttrcupSmth,OurGem
5-9 RR	gd C-1 Cd	3000	m 30:2	1:04:4	1:36:2	2:07:4	5	5	7	6°	6/2¾	6/1¾	2:08:2	16.10(RRash)LckyBen,BuckshotHn,Mohaw
5-1 RR	ft C-1 Cd	3000	m 30:2	1:03:1	1:34:2	2:05:3	6	7	7	7°	6/3¾	2/nk	2:05:3	14.30(RRash)LidaLisa,KatyR,BethanyHn.
4-24 RR	gd C-1 Cd	3000	m 30:3	1:03:2	1:34:2	2:06:3	1	3	3	2°	3/5	8/5¾	2:08	2.70(RRsh)RapidQueen,BthanyHn,AftnFl
4-15 RR	ft C-1 Cd	3000	m 29:4	1:01:3	1:33:3	2:05	4	5	5°	4°	4/2	2/¾	2:05:1	11.40(RRsh)BlckTulipN,KatyR,ClartAndrs
4-2 RR	ft C-1 Cd	3000	m 31:3	1:04:1	1:36	2:07	3	4	4°	4°	4/2	4x/3¼dq2:08		*1.30(F'tne)M'yBHvn,ClrtA'dsn,F'tbl'sW

EXACTA WINDOWS OPEN FOR THIS RACE.

MORN. LINE

8 PACE-ONE MILE

SADDLE CLOTH—BROWN

The Fort Lee Rotary Club

CLASS B-2 — CONDITIONED — 4-YEAR & UP **PURSE $3,750**

---

6 **1**

HERIOT br g, 9, by Indictment, Lillana by Kingcobra (Tr.-D. Insko)
Green Hornet Racing Stable, Inc., (Lessee), Ohio RR 2:05:4 1969 4 1 1 0 2,687.
($31,658) 6, 2:02:3 DEL INSKO (120) Purple-Gold YR 2:05:1 1968 16 3 2 0 6,910.
6-18 YR ft B-2 Cd 3750 m 31:2 1:03 1:33:4 2:05 2 4 2° 2° 2/½ 6/1¾ 2:05:2 10.40(DI'ko)BrnsWay,TwnkleO,DelHi'sBoy
6-10 YR ft B-2 Cd 3750 m 30:4 1:02:2 1:33:1 2:04:1 8 8 6° 5° 6/2¼ 6/4¼ 2:05:1 11.70(DI'ko)IdahoN,TwnkleO,NiagaraBullet
6-3 YR ft B-2 Cd 3750 m 30:4 1:02:2 1:34:1 2:06:1 1 1 1 1 1/1 2/nk 2:06:1 3.40(DInsko)Ambit,Heriot,IdahoN
5-20 RR ft Opt B-3 3500 m 31:3 1:04:1 1:35:3 2:05:4 5 fog 1 fog fog 1/N.R. 2:05:4 18.60(DInsko)Heriot,OrthoAce,UniformAlee
* 5-10 RR ft qua m 31:3 1:03:1 1:34:4 2:07 3 2 2 2 2/1 1/ns 2:07 N.B.(DInsko)Heriot,RodAdiox,XPertBud
7-5 RR ft B-3 Cd 3300 m 31:1 1:03:1 1:35:1 2:06 3 3° 8 brkn hpple DNF 8.40(DInsko)OmegaGld,HDDmnd,MdwColn
6-21 RR ft B-3 Cd 3200 m 29:3 1:00:4 1:33 2:04:2 4 6 6 7 7/6¾ 6/5½ 2:06 5.50(Insko) MdwBruce,AbbyCrn,StrmyDrm
6-12 RR sy B-3 3200 m 31:2 1:03 1:35:3 2:07 7 2° 1° 3 5/4½ 8/8 2:09 20.90(WMyr)QrryRoad,SldmSafe,BconFlash

---

3 **2**

TWINKLE O. br g, 5, by Yankee Byrd, Victory Captain by Captain Eddie (Tr.-F. Mule)
Frank Giugliano & Jos. Pagano, Elmont, N.Y. RR 2:04:2 1969 20 3 5 2 11,955.
($20,078) 4, 2:04:2 LUCIEN FONTAINE (134) Green-White-Red May 2:04:2 1968 42 10 6 6 16,940.
6-18 YR ft B-2 Cd 3750 m 31:2 1:03 1:33:4 2:05 5 1 1 1 1/½ 2/nk 2:05 3.10(Fntne)BrnsWay,TwnkleO,DelHi'sBoy
6-10 YR ft B-2 Cd 3750 m 30:4 1:02:2 1:33:1 2:04:1 6 2° 1 1 1/1 2/1¼ 2:04:2 3.50(CAbbtllo)IdahoN,TwnkleO,NigaraBllet
6-2 YR ft B-2 Cd 3750 m 30:1 1:01:2 1:32:3 2:03:2 7 7 7 8° 8/9¾ 8/6¾ 2:05 3.50(LFntne)ToroCrest,FireawayN,JMWin
5-22 RR ft B-2 4000 m 30:4 1:02:2 1:33:1 2:04 5 6 4° 4° 3/1½ 3/2¼ 2:04:3 3.10(LFontaine)Antinea,Raidal,TwinkleO
5-12 RR ft Opt B-2 4000 m 31:2 1:03:3 1:34:2 2:06 2 2 2° 2° 3/hd 1/nk 2:06 3.10(DncrJr)TwnkleO,ByeB'Gene,BoySan
5-3 RR ft B-3 Cd 3500 m 31 1:03:1 1:33:4 2:04:2 2 4 1° 1 1/2½ 1/3½ 2:04:2 *2.00(LFntne)TwinkleO.,GoldH.,AdiosRobbie
4-26 RR ft clm alw 10000 m 30:1 1:01:2 1:32:1 2:04:2 2 5 4° 5° 6/5 4/2¾ 2:05 4.50(DIn'ko)LadRainbow,TrueStorm,Rapid
4-19 RR ft clm alw 10000 m 31 1:02:3 1:33:4 2:05 4 6 6 7° 7/6¾ 7/5½ 2:06:1 5.60(JChp'n)SmrtMony,Forshy,B'viewBabe

---

8 **3**

ROD KNIGHT b g, 5, by Knight Time, Ann MacPherson by Paul MacPherson (Tr.-W. Dracksley) (St.-R. Rash)
R. Snitofsky & N. Eisler, Bayside, N.Y. RR 2:04:1 1969 13 2 0 6 6,587.
($16,300) 3, 2:03:3 (⅝) FRANK TAGARIELLO (150) Tan-Brown-White YR 2:05 1968 27 3 4 5 10,548.
6-19 YR ft B-2 Cd 3750 m 30:2 1:01:1 1:31:2 2:03:1 5 3° 3 3 3/1½ 3/2¼ 2:03:4 17.80(Fntne)SilkySquire,SlyYnkee,RodKngt
6-11 YR ft B-2 3750 m 29:3 1:03 1:34:1 2:05:1 7 8 6° 6° 6/2 5/2¼ 2:05:4 9.00(Fntne)DelHi'sBoy,BrnsWay,PdroW'sn
6-4 YR ft B-2 Cd 3750 m 30:1 1:02 1:34 2:05:1 4 1 2 3 5/1½ 3/¾ 2:05:2 5.50(Steall)BrinsWay,MurryCrze,RodKnght
5-26 YR ft B-2 Cd 3750 m 29:3 1:00:1 1:31:4 2:03:1 3 2 3 5 5/4 3/3¼ 2:04 25.00(Rsh)LghtSilk,PreciousScot,RodKnght
5-12 RR ft Opt B-2 4000 m 31:2 1:03:3 1:34:2 2:06 4 1 1 3 1/hd 5/2¼ 2:06:3 3.60(Tallman)TwnkleO,ByeB'Gene,BoySan
5-5 RR ft B-2 4000 m 30:1 1:02:2 1:33:3 2:04:4 7 7 7 7 7/3¾ 3/1 2:05 13.50(CAbto)AfntBllt,WeeBttns,RodKnght
4-28 RR ft B-2 4000 m 30:1 1:02:1 1:33:2 2:04:4 8 8 6° 7° 6/3¾ 7/3 2:05:2 39.60(DcrJr)TmprdYkee,Sh'strng-AftnBllt dh
4-21 RR ft B-2 4000 m 30:3 1:01:2 1:32:4 2:04 5 2 2 2 2/1½ 3/4½ 2:05:1 21.80(LCplnd)BadMoe,RicksColt,RodKnight

---

6 **4**

HOOTFIRE HANOVER b h, 4, by Hickory Smoke, Hoot Lassie by Hoot Mon (Tr.-W. Mello) (St.-W. Haughton)
Ruderman Stables & Farms, Inc., N.Y. RR 2:04:3 1969 10 1 0 0 4,304.
($22,304) 3, 2:03:1 JOHN CHAPMAN (147) Green-White RR 2:03:1 1968 19 5 1 3 21,530.
6-19 YR ft B-2 Cd 3750 m 30:2 1:01:1 1:31:2 2:03:1 6 7 7° 6 6/4 5/3½ 2:04 7.70(Hghtn)SilkySquire,SlyYnkee,RodKngt
6-12 YR ft B-2 Cd 3750 m 30 1:02:3 1:33:2 2:04 1 2 3 5 5/3½ 5/2¾ 2:04:3 3.00(Hghtn)CldW'Sntor,ByeB'Gene,T'outN
6-6 YR ft B-1 4500 m 30:2 1:02:2 1:32:3 2:03:1 1 3 4 5 5/3½ 7/4¼ 2:04:2 8.20(Hghtn)TgrPaws,BoySan,BssmanLobell
5-30 YR ft B-1 4500 m 29:1 1:00 1:31 2:02:1 2 2 3 2° 2/1½ 5/3½ 2:03 3.90(Hghtn)MedllionLbll,TigrPaws,Release
5-24 RR ft A-2/A-3 6000 m 29:3 1:02:1 1:33:2 2:03:3 4 2 4 6 6/2½ 5/4 2:04:3 13.70(Hghtn)TwoDmnd,H'IndRdr,BrwnSmke
5-16 RR ft B-1 4500 m 30:1 1:02 1:33:1 2:04:3 4 5 4° 2° 2/1 1/¾ 2:04:3 3.50(WHghtn)HootfireHn,Ed'sLady,Alytor
5-9 RR gd Opt A-3 5500 m 29 1:01 1:32:1 2:05:2 3 5 6° 4° 4/1¾ 6/3 2:06:1 3.40(JChpmn)BrwnSmke,BbbyEd,MrrsHart
5-2 RR ft A-3 5500 m 31:1 1:03 1:33:3 2:04:4 3 4 4° 5 3/2 4/1 2:05 2.70(WHghtn)Option,BrwnSmke,MrrisHart

---

6 **5**

TRYOUT N. b g, 8, by Hal Tryax, Amiable by Dillon Hall (Tr.-Y. Filion) (St.-Her. Filion)
John Ross Williams, Dallas, Pa. Brdwn 2:06:3 1969 12 1 3 4 5,342.
($12,414) 7, 2:06 NORMAN DAUPLAISE (139) Brown-Gold-White SD 2:06 1968 26 4 3 4 7,602.
6-12 YR ft B-2 Cd 3750 m 30 1:02:3 1:33:2 2:04 7 1° 2 3 3/1 3/2½ 2:04:3 21:90(HerFln)CldW'Sntr,ByeB'Gene,T'outN
6-4 Brdwn ft Cd 2500 m 30:2 1:03:1 1:36 2:06:3 5 1 1 1 1/1 1/1 2:06:3 3.30(HerFln)TryoutN,Cldstrm,CpePineSctn
5-30 Brdwn ft Cd 2800 m 31 1:02:1 1:35 2:06 3 3° 1 1 1/½ 4/½ 2:06 *1.65(HerFln)BnitaWck,BrwnieDres,Resrrxi
5-23 Brdwn ft Cd 2800 m 31:4 1:06 1:36:3 2:07:2 1 2 3 1° 1/1 1/nk dq 2:07:2 6.40(Knwls)TomctRwrd,GoodMxne,GngrRd
5-17 Brdwn ft Cd 2800 m 30:2 1:02 1:34:1 2:04:4 7 1° 2° 2 4/4 6/10 2:06:4 7.45(HrFln)T'Footmn,Frmamnt,CmdnMajr
5-12 Brdwn ft Cd 2800 m 30 1:02 1:34:3 2:06 4 2° 2° 2° 2/½ 3/1¼ 2:06:1 3.05(Knwls)Tableau,GeorgnaGlry,TryoutN
5-3 LB(⅝) ft Cd 4500 m 29:3 1:02:1 1:32 2:03 2 3 4 2° 2/1 3/1½ 2:03:1 *2.10(HerFln)ChncyBrook,SctshFuslr,Try'tN
4-26 LB(⅝) ft Cd 3700 m 29:1 1:01:3 1:32:2 2:02:4 2 3 3 2° 2/¼ 2/1dh 2:03 *2.00(HrFln)BerryBttle,Try'tN-CitatnPck dh

---

5 **6**

BYE BYE GENE b h, 4, by Bye Bye Byrd, Fantan Wick by Gene Abbe (Tr.-R. Kurtz)
Marvin Manheimer, New York, N.Y. 1969 8 0 3 0 3,594.
($19,484) 3, 2:01:2 (⅝) JAMES TALLMAN (150) Wine-Grey-Yellow LB(⅝) 2:01:2 1968 31 3 8 6 15,108.
6-19 YR ft B-2 Cd 3750 m 30:2 1:01:1 1:31:2 2:03:1 2 4 2° 2° 2/1 6/3½ 2:04 *.60(CAbbtllo)SlkySqure,SlyYnkee,RdKngt
6-12 YR ft B-2 Cd 3750 m 30 1:02:3 1:33:2 2:04 2 5 1 1 1/½ 2/¾ 2:04:1 *1.70(Tllmn)CldW'Sntor,ByeB'Gene,T'outN
5-31 YR ft B-2 Cd 3750 m 30:2 1:00:3 1:31:1 2:02 2 4 3° 1 1/2½ 2/hd 2:02 9.50(Tllmn)Bbblu,B'B'Gene,EsprssoDigaren
5-19 RR ft B-2 4000 m 32 1:03:2 1:34 2:05:3 1 3 4 4 4/3 4/1½ 2:06 *2.00(JCrse)WeeBttns,Bobbalou,SearusBoy
5-12 RR ft Opt B-2 4000 m 31:2 1:03:3 1:34:2 2:06 7 3° 3 5 4/1¼ 2/nk 2:06 7.90(JCruise)TwnkleO,ByeB'Gene,BoySan
5-3 LB(⅝) ft Cd 5500 m 28:4 1:00:4 1:31:2 2:01:1 7 7 7 7 7/4¾ 6/4¾ 2:02:1 14.50(JWlcts)A'zngPck,CrwnBlue,LtleWllie
4-23 LB(⅝) gd Cd 5200 m 30:3 1:04:1 1:36 2:06:1 1 4 4 4 4/1¾ 6/6 2:07:2 6.20(CByd)HalRuer,Disband,ScttshFusilier
4-15 LB(⅝) ft Cd 5000 m 30:3 1:03:3 1:34:3 2:04:3 2 4 5 7 7/4¼ 4/1½ 2:04:4 3.20(HerFiln)CBSentr,RgnsPride,CloveVlly

---

5 **7**

NIAGARA BULLET b h, 6, by Bullet Hanover, Voleen by Volomite (Tr.-R. Bolton) (St.-L. Copeland)
Abraham Schultz, Bal Harbour, Fla. RR 2:04 1969 22 2 3 5 11,170.
($63,267) 3, 2:02:4 JOHN PATTERSON SR. (165) Tan-Blue Fox 2:04:1 1968 20 6 3 5 15,087.
6-17 YR ft B-2 Cd 3750 m 31:1 1:02:4 1:34:2 2:04 4 5 4 3° 3/1 2/¾ 2:04:1 3.10(Tllmn)IonesDrm,NiagaraBullt,IdahoN
6-10 YR ft B-2 Cd 3750 m 30:4 1:02:2 1:33:1 2:04:1 3 6 4° 3° 4/1 3/1¼ 2:04:2 *1.70(Tllmn)IdahoN,TwnkleO,NiagaraBullet
6-3 YR ft B-1 Cd 4500 m 30:4 1:02:1 1:33:1 2:04:3 1 2 3 3 3/1 5/1¼ 2:04:4 30.00(LCpl'd)PcnHn,Hplng,LightSlk-TCpy dh
5-28 YR ft B-1 Cd 4500 m 30 1:01:4 1:31:4 2:02:3 6 8 8 8 6/4 4/3¼ 2:03:2 60.70(Tllmn)DougsChoice,Alytor,PoconoHn
5-17 RR ft B-1 4500 m 29:4 1:02:2 1:32:4 2:03:4 3 6 4 5 5/5 4/4½ 2:04:4 4.70(CAblo) TrprtBill,RcciRniFrst,TigrPws
5-9 RR gd B-1 Cd 4500 m 30:1 1:02:4 1:34:4 2:06 1 3 3° 2° 3/1 5/1¼ 2:06:2 4.70(RChrrx)Apt,WrthyJimmy,BriansWay
4-29 RR ft Opt B-1 4500 m 30:3 1:01:1 1:32:1 2:03:3 2 6 6 4° 5/2½ 6/4 2:04:3 6.70(DInsko)AceHill,Y'rKddn,NewZS'Silvr
4-22 RR sy Opt B-1 4500 m 30:3 1:02:2 1:34:2 2:07 7 7 7 6° 4/2¾ 3/1½ 2:07:2 5.10(CAbt)ExltdRlr,FireawyN,NiagaraBllt

---

6 **8**

SLY YANKEE br h,9, by Tar Heel, Sue Adios by Adios (Tr.-R. Baker) (St.-S. Dancer)
Irving Berkemeyer, New Milford, N.J. 1969 16 0 6 2 9,209.
($239,717) 3, 1:59:3 (1) WILLIAM MYER (165) Blue-Red AC(⅝) 2:01 1968 28 5 3 5 19,770.
6-19 YR ft B-2 Cd 3750 m 30:2 1:01:1 1:31:2 2:03:1 7 6 6 5° 4/2½ 2x/½ 2:03:2 8.50(SDncr)SilkySquire,SlyYnkee,RodKngt
6-12 YR ft B-2 Cd 3750 m 30 1:02:3 1:33:2 2:04 4 6 8° 6° 6/4 4/2½ 2:04:3 6.50(VDncr)CldW'Sntr,ByeB'Gene,T'outN
6-4 YR ft B-2 Cd 3750 m 30:1 1:02 1:34:1 2:04:3 8 8 8 6° 7/4¼ 7/4¼ 2:05:3 6.10(HDncrJr)BeauMartl,DelHi'sBy,SntTm
5-27 YR ft B-2 Cd 3750 m 30:2 1:02:1 1:33:3 2:05 3 6 6° 5° 4/1¾ 2/1¼ 2:05:1 2.70(VDncr)TopCopy,SlyYnkee,DelHi'sBoy
5-16 RR ft B-1 4500 m 30:1 1:02 1:33:1 2:04:3 6 7 7° 7° 6/5 4/2½ 2:05:2 5.80(WMyer)HootfireHn,Ed'sLady,Alytor
5-5 RR ft B-1 4500 m 29:4 1:00:2 1:32:4 2:04:2 5 7 6° 5° 6/3½ 2/½ 2:04:3 5.90(WHghtn)Donora,SlyYnkee,RicciR'Frst
4-24 RR gd Opt B-1 4500 m 30 1:02:2 1:33:3 2:04:3 7 8 6° 6° 6/3½ 5/4½ 2:05:3 15.20(WMyr)MizellesMickey,Alytor,Donora
4-15 RR ft Opt B-1 4500 m 29:4 1:01:2 1:32:1 2:04 1 3 1 2 2/ns 2/hd 2:04 2.60(DncrJr)DixieTmby,SlyYkee,TrryFrbes

---

EXACTA WINDOWS OPEN 10 MINUTES BEFORE THIS RACE

MORN. LINE

9 PACE - ONE MILE — EXACTA

SADDLE CLOTH— ORANGE

CLAIMING $6,000 — 5-YEAR & UP
ALL HORSES ENTERED MAY BE CLAIMED FOR $6,000

The Technicon Corporation
PURSE $3,000

---

5 **1**

DRUM MAJOR b g, 6, by Duane Hanover, Helen Grayson by Scottish Pence (Tr.-J. Chapman)
M. & F. Gerber & J. & H. Heit, N.J. — RR 2:06:4 1969 18 1 3 4 6,536.
($22,228) 5, 2:05 — JOHN CHAPMAN (147) — Green-White — YR 2:05 1968 22 3 3 2 7,301.

6-16 YR	ft	clm	6000	m 30:2	1:03:4	1:35:2	2:06:3	6	7	5°	3°	2/3	2/3½	2:07:2	3.10(Chpmn)AbbyCran,DrmMjor,SfldScott
6-4 YR	ft	clm alw	6000	m 31	1:02:2	1:34:2	2:06	6	1°	2	3°	5/2½	5/1¼	2:06:2	5.40(EWilliams)EasyJay,IMP,OC'sSandy
5-22 RR	ft	clm alw	6000	m 31	1:03:2	1:36	2:06:2	3	4	5	6	5/2¼	4/2	2:06:4	3.50(EWllms)PplrDrct,GrsnLght,TmysPrde
• 5-17 RR	ft	dr qua		m 31:1	1:03	1:34:4	2:06:4	2	3	3	3	3/2½	1/1½	2:06:4	N.B.(EWllms)DrmMjr,CncilDres,JhnnyGold
• 5-13 RR	ft	dr qua		m 31:1	1:03:1	1:35:4	2:07:3	5	1°	2	2°	2/ns	1/2	2:07:3	N.B.(EWms)DrmMjr,SddnSquall,TrdiosCmt
5-10 RR	ft	clm alw	7500	m 30:3	1:02	1:33:3	2:05:2	5	7	7°	7°	7/6¾	5/7¾	2:07:1	3.70(JChpmn)PrbleTime,BeckrHn,LeroyHn
4-25 RR	ft	clm	6000	m 31	1:02:4	1:34:4	2:06:4	8	6	5°	2°	1/ns	1/¾	2:06:4	3.50(JChp'n)DrmMjr,CpprAd's,Jess'sG'dson
4-15 RR	ft	clm	6000	m 30:4	1:03:3	1:34:2	2:05:3	8	8	7°	6°	6/3¾	2/¾	2:05:4	9.50(CAbt)HrbyTryax,DrmMajr,Ad'sGrgeA

6 **2**

SEAFIELD SCOTT b g, 10, by U. Scott, Jennifer by Dillon Hall (Tr.-S. Werner)
Millbrook Enterprises, Inc., Munsey Park, N.Y. — 1969 21 0 5 4 4,668.
($43,585) 7, 2:03:2 (⅝) — SACHER WERNER (155) — Blue-Gold — RR 2:06:1 1968 29 6 3 7 17,905.

6-16 YR	ft	clm	6000	m 30:2	1:03:4	1:35:2	2:06:3	3	1	2°	2°	3/3¼	3/4¼	2:07:3	12.80(Cmrn)AbbyCrain,DrmMajor,SfldScott
6-6 YR	ft	clm	6000	m 30:4	1:01:4	1:33:3	2:05:2	5	2	3	5°	5/3	4/3¾	2:06:2	6.80(RCmrn)KnxEnsgn,AbbyCrn,CptnMssie
5-28 YR	ft	clm alw	6000	m 30	1:02:3	1:34:2	2:06:2	2	1°	1	1	1/½	5/2¾	2:07	4.80(Wrnr)GrrsnLght,CMCrtrght,KnxEnsgn
5-22 RR	ft	clm alw	6000	m 31	1:03:2	1:36	2:06:2	4	1	1	1	1/ns	5/3½	2:07:1	7.10(Wrnr)PplrDirct,GrrsnLght,TmysPride
5-16 RR	ft	clm alw	6000	m 30:4	1:03	1:35:2	2:08:1	8	5°	1°	1	1/½	3/1	2:08:2	14.10(SWrnr)TomThmb,AvnChrlie,S'fldSctt
5-9 RR	gd	clm alw	6000	m 32	1:04:4	1:36:4	2:09:4	2	2	3	3°	4/1¾	2/ns	2:09:4	3.50(SWrnr)GrndPtch,S'fldSctt,MrnciChf
5-2 RR	ft	clm	6000	m 31	1:03:2	1:34:2	2:07:1	2	1	2	3	3/2½	2/¾	2:07:2	7.50(SWrnr)GrndPtch,S'fldSctt,WrthGlnn
4-23 RR	ft	clm	6000	m 31:2	1:04:1	1:36:1	2:08	5	1	1	1	1/¾	2/1¾	2:08:2	4.30(CAbt)GrrisnLght,SeafldSctt,HonrBoy

5 **3**

MADAMS B. GALLON br g, 10, by Bill Gallon, Madam Pearl by Long Key (Tr.-S. Demas)
Strides Farm, Gansvoort, N.Y. — YR 2:06:2 1969 11 3 3 1 6,975.
($17,849) 6, 2:03:3 (⅝) — LUCIEN FONTAINE (134) — Green-White-Red — PcD(⅝) 2:03:3 1965 Raced on trot in '68 & '69

6-3 YR	ft	clm alw	5000	m 31	1:02:2	1:34:2	2:06:2	5	1°	1	1	1/nk	1/nk	2:06:2	2.40(Fntne)MdmsBGlln,AlbrtGne,WckdDrm
5-24 RR	ft	clm alw	5000	m 30	1:02:3	1:33:4	2:05:4	3	6	6	5°	6/2	2/2¾	2:06:2	2.90(LFntne)BaywdCsh,MdmsBGlln,PstRail
5-17 RR	ft	clm	5000	m 30:4	1:04	1:35:3	2:07	4	5	2°	1°	2/nk	2/nk	2:07	2.90(Fntn) WckdDrm,MdmsBGlln,BywdCsh
5-12 RR	ft	clm alw	5000	m 30:4	1:03:2	1:36	2:08:4	3	5	7	7	5/3½	2/ns	2:08:4	3.50(JChp'n)DnnieM,MdmsBGlln,ShdyMaid
5-3 RR	ft	clm alw	5000	m 30:3	1:03:1	1:35:2	2:06:2	4	5	5	5	4/4	3/3½	2:07:1	2.50(LFntne)Morant,ICPaul,MadmsBGalln
• 4-29 RR	ft	qua		m 31:1	1:03:1	1:35:1	2:07:4	3	4°	4	6	7/5½	3/hd	2:07:4	N.B.(Dplse)WayOnTp,AttrnyN,MdmsBGlln
• 4-26 RR	ft	qua		m 31:1	1:04	1:35:2	2:08	7	5	5	5°	4x/2	3x/3dq	2:08:4	N.B.(F'tne)GrndFlyr,BnCsyN,No.ByNrthwst
3-20 RR	ft	C-1	3000	m 30:2	1:02:1	1:33:3	2:05	2	3	3°	3	3/3	4/3¼	2:05:4	3.90(LF'tne)SmmieStrng,B'dside,MarkTme

3 **4**

ALBERT GENE bg, 13, by Gene Abbe, Betty Heekin by Guy Abbey (Tr.-F. Mule)
Frank Mule & Cono G. D'Elia, N.Y. — YR 2:04:3 1969 15 2 4 1 6,758.
($122,861) 6, 2:02:1 — FRANK TAGARIELLO (150) — Tan-Brown-White — 1968 11 0 2 2 2,862.

6-17 YR	ft	clm	5000	m 30	1:01:2	1:33:2	2:04:3	1	4	4	1°	1/1	1/1¼	2:04:3	4.30(Tgrllo)AlbrtGene,CpprJckt,R'mdeDve
6-3 YR	ft	clm alw	5000	m 31	1:02:2	1:34:2	2:06:2	4	7	7°	6°	3/1¾	2/nk	2:06:2	12.10(Tgrllo)MdmsBGlln,AlbrtGne,WckdDrm
5-24 RR	ft	clm alw	5000	m 30	1:02:3	1:33:4	2:05:4	2	3	4	6	5/2	4/3	2:06:3	6.40(FTgrllo)BaywdCsh,MdmsBGlln,PstRail
5-17 RR	ft	clm	5000	m 31	1:04:4	1:36:4	2:08:1	8	8	8	8	8/3½	7/2½	2:08:4	10.10(Shlty) FastGun,AmmrsSon,SpnglrVolo
5-9 RR	gd	clm alw	4000	m 30:3	1:04	1:36	2:08:1	2	3	4	6	6/3¼	2/hd	2:08:1	3.10(DncrJr)Tormax,AlbrtGne,LegalFrght
4-28 RR	ft	clm alw	4000	m 31	1:03:2	1:34:2	2:06:1	3	4	5	5°	4/2	1/¾	2:06:1	3.10(CAbto)AlbretGene,Tormax,ShwsFlash
4-17 RR	ft	clm	4000	m 30:2	1:02:3	1:35	2:06:2	4	7	7°	5°	5/2¼	5/2¼	2:06:4	4.50(CAbtlo)KngtStrk,SntsJohn,Lachaglen
4-8 RR	ft	clm alw	3000	m 30:2	1:04	1:35:4	2:08:3	2	1	1	1	1/½	5/2	2:09	•2.00(RRash)Lachaglen,ScotHayes,BargeIn

4 **5**

CAPTAIN MISSIE ch g, 10, by Captain Eddie, My Darling Missie by Baron Lee (Tr.-Y. Filion) (St.-Her. Filion)
Fernand Potvin, Ontario, Canada — VD(¾) 2:04:2 1969 20 6 2 3 5,660.
($30,701) 9, 2:05:3 — NORMAN DAUPLAISE (139) Brown-Gold-White — MR 2:05:3 1968 36 12 0 5 12,051.

6-18 YR	ft	clm alw	6000	m 30:4	1:02	1:34:4	2:06	2	4	3°	1°	1/½	3/½	2:06:1	•.70(HrFln)MgtyAmgo,F'tblsWve,CptnMse
6-6 YR	ft	clm	6000	m 30:4	1:01:4	1:33:3	2:05:2	8	3°	2°	2°	2/nk	3/¾	2:05:3	12.30(YFln)KnxEnsgn,AbbyCrn,CptnMissie
5-31 YR	ft	clm alw	7500	m 29:2	1:01	1:33:2	2:04:2	8	7	6	6	7/5	6/5¾	2:05:4	18.30(YFilion)GrtCrdt,ElesGlry,CnclDares
5-21 VD(¾)	ft	Cd	1500	m 28:4	1:00:3	1:32:2	2:04:2	7	4	1	2	2/¾	1/1½	2:04:2	7.20(YFln)CptnMssie,Chrmoore,MrksmnHn
5-17 VD(¾)	sy	Cd	1500	m 31	1:04:2	1:36	2:07:4	1	5	5	5°	5/1	2/hd	2:07:4	15.40(YFln)Dwght,CptnMissie,FrrsdeMridle
5-10 VD(¾)	hy	Inv	2000	m 29:1	1:01:4	1:33:4	2:06:2	5	7	7	7	7/21	7/22	2:10:4	22.30(YFln)RockyMite,Saracen,LbanonPride
5-3 VD(¾)	ft	Cd	1500	m 30	1:03	1:34:2	2:05	7	2	2	2	2/2	1/¾	2:05	3.60(YFln)CptnMissie,Bootemp,SterlinMir
4-26 GM(⅝)	ft	Cd	1200	m 30:3	1:02:2	1:34:3	2:06:2	5	5	5	3	3/3	1/2	2:06:2	4.50(YFln)CptMssi,ChckyttDc,RkSprngsKy

6 **6**

COPPER JACKET ch g, 6, by Darneau, Diann Liner by Mainliner (Tr.-S. Smith)
R.A. & R. R. Williams, Massapequa, N.Y. — YR 2:05:3 1969 15 2 2 3 5,804.
($15,394) 3, 2:04:1 — SAM SMITH (145) — Brown-Beige — RR 2:06 1968 15 3 1 1 5,136.

6-17 YR	ft	clm	5000	m 30	1:01:2	1:33:2	2:04:3	8	8	8	7	5/3¼	2/1¼	2:04:4	14.70(Smth)AlbrtGene,CpprJckt,R'mdeDave
6-10 YR	ft	clm alw	5000	m 30:4	1:02:3	1:33:1	2:05:3	3	4	5	5°	4/1	1/½	2:05:3	15.50(Smth)CpprJckt,LglFrght,S'topsBest
5-26 YR	ft	clm	4000	m 30:4	1:04:2	1:35:4	2:07:3	5	6	6	4	4/1½	1/hd	2:07:3	6.30(SSmth)CprJackt,FlyngBts,MdwRoach
5-17 RR	ft	clm	5000	m 30:4	1:04	1:35:3	2:07	5	6	7	8	7/5¼	5/1	2:07:1	28.90(SSmth) WkdDrm,MdmsBGln,B'wdCsh
5-9 RR	gd	clm alw	4000	m 30:3	1:04	1:36	2:08:1	6	1°	1	1	3/1½	8/5¼	2:09:2	14.20(SSmith)Tormax,AlbrtGne,LglFreight
4-28 RR	ft	clm alw	4000	m 30:2	1:03:3	1:35:3	2:08:1	7	1	2	3	3/1	3/1¾	2:08:3	12.70(SSmth)LeglFrght,MajrBlck,CpprJckt
4-17 RR	ft	clm	5000	m 31:2	1:05	1:37:2	2:08:2	8	6	6°	6°	7/3	5/2¼	2:09	23.10(SSmth)TomThmb,StrmyDrm,Winstdt
4-7 RR	ft	clm alw	5000	m 30:2	1:04	1:36	2:07:2	4	2	2	3	3/1	3/1	2:07:3	10.90(SSmth)Emnciptn,StrmyDrm,CpprJckt

10 **7**

MASTER GLENN (NY) b h, 6, by Amscot, Lovely Song by Uncle Scott (Tr.-J. Kelley, Jr.)
Morton Rogers, Bronx, N.Y. & The S. Stable — RR 2:06:4 1969 13 1 2 1 4,257.
($20,874) 5, 2:05:4 — JEFFERSON KELLEY, JR. (192) — Red-Black — Rock 2:05:4 1968 40 4 5 9 11,520.

6-6 YR	ft	clm	6000	m 30:4	1:01:4	1:33:3	2:05:2	7	1	1	3	4/2¾	7/4¾	2:06:3	10.60(LFntne)KnxEnsgn,AbbyCrn,CptnMssie
5-27 YR	ft	clm	6000	m 30:3	1:02:2	1:34	2:06:1	2	1	1	1	1/½	2/¾	2:06:2	4.30(CAbtlo)IMP,MsterGlenn,CentralRnge
5-13 RR	ft	clm alw	6000	m 31:1	1:02:2	1:34	2:06:4	3	2	3°	1	1/½	6/4¾	2:08	•2.50(CAbtlo) KnoxEnsign,Morant,Dukegan
5-2 RR	ft	clm	6000	m 31	1:03:2	1:34:2	2:07:1	7	7	6°	6°	5/3½	7/2¾	2:08	8.80(Shlty)GrndPtch,SeafldSctt,WrthGlnn
4-14 RR	ft	C-1	3000	m 30:4	1:02:1	1:33:3	2:04:2	7	7	7°	4°	4/3½	5/11	2:07	4.90(CAbt)NoseyMite,RodAdios,HonorBoy
3-27 RR	ft	clm	6000	m 30:4	1:03:3	1:35:1	2:06:4	7	1	1	1	1/1	1/½	2:06:4	4.40(CAbt)MastrGlenn,Judson,CopprAdios
3-17 RR	ft	clm	7500	m 30:3	1:02	1:33:4	2:06	2	3	3	5ix	acc.	DNF		27.10(FTgrllo)Gunkhr,ArlieFrost,GrrsnLght
2-20 YR	gd	clm	7500	m 31	1:04:1	1:36	2:08:1	8	1°	1	2	1x/ns	x8x/19	2:12:4	9.90(Dl'sko)LeroyHn,LnaweeSpcl,OzrkDom

10 **8**

GARRISON LIGHT b h, 7, by Garrison Hanover, Bonny Brigade by Light Brigade (Tr.-R. Kurtz)
Paul Ciavardini, Mt. Kisco, N.Y. — YR 2:06:2 1969 17 4 2 5 10,423.
($17,506) 6, 2:05:2 (⅝) — CARMINE ABBATIELLO (135) — Gold-Red — AC(⅝) 2:05:2 1968 31 2 4 6 6,921.

6-18 YR	ft	clm alw	6000	m 30:4	1:02	1:34:4	2:06	3	5	5°	3°	2/½	4/½	2:06:1	6.70(CAblo)MgtyAmgo,F'tblsWve,CptnMse
6-9 YR	ft	clm alw	6000	m 30:2	1:01:3	1:33:4	2:06	1	2	3	2°	2/½	3/1	2:06:1	•1.50(Chpmn)VctryMnrs,MgtyAmgo,G'snLgt
5-28 YR	ft	clm alw	6000	m 30	1:02:3	1:34:2	2:06:2	8	5	5°	4°	4/2	1/1½	2:06:2	21.30(C'pmn)GrsnLght,CMCrtrght,KnxEnsgn
5-22 RR	ft	clm alw	6000	m 31	1:03:2	1:36	2:06:2	1	2	3	4	4/1¼	2/1½	2:06:4	5.30(C'pmn)PplrDirct,GrrsnLght,TmysPrde
5-15 RR	ft	clm	7500	m 29	59:4	1:31:4	2:04:3	4	5	6	6°	5/8½	7/7	2:06:1	6.70(JChp'n)H'smeHrry,MrW'frd,DdgeTme
5-3 RR	ft	clm alw	7500	m 30:4	1:03:3	1:34:4	2:05:3	3	4	4	3°	6/3¼	3/4	2:06:3	5.40(LFntne)JMRegal,Hlldian,GarrisnLght
4-23 RR	ft	clm	6000	m 31:2	1:04:1	1:36:1	2:08	1	2	3	3	3/1	1/1¾	2:08	2.70(DcrJr)GrrisnLght,SeafldSctt,HnrBoy
4-12 RR	ft	clm	7500	m 30:3	1:03	1:34	2:06	3	4	4°	3°	3/2	3/1¼	2:06:1	7.50(DInsko)JMRegal,IMP,GarrisonLight

EXACTA WINDOWS OPEN FOR THIS RACE.

June 17 basic rating was 191, plus 5 for racing on the outside, 2 for the stretch vigor, 1 for the improved post position and 10 for Patterson, less 5 for the rise in class. Final rating is 204.

Neon Rodney. This breaker put together five nongalloping efforts before relapsing on June 18. We had better forgive her and rate the June 4 race. If she turns out to have a big figure, we can decide whether to bet on her or pass the race. The basic rating for June 4 was 187. Add 10 for roughing it, 10 more for Abbatiello, and deduct 2 for the worsened post position and 5 for the rise in class. Final rating is 200.

Novel Blaze's four-point margin over Atlantic Frost makes her the selection.

RESULT: Atlantic Frost was an overwhelming favorite at 3 to 5 but finished last by a half-block after galloping at the half. Novel Blaze roughed it for a half-mile before catching Neon Rodney, who faded to sixth. Leading Marked Pick by a neck at the top of the stretch, the mare held that lead to the wire, paying a handsome $12.00 and $4.80.

I believe that this race bears close review. It was not easy to recognize Novel Blaze as a contender. Neither was it immediately obvious that her May 28 race was the key one in her recent record. The principles that led to the selection are simple enough, but their application is not automatic. By studying this example, the reader will prepare himself for similar situations that arise dozens of times each season.

The Second Race

See if you can find the classy three-year-old that has a lock on this C-3 pace. If you picked Yankee Hobo you are forgiven, but you are wrong. True, the filly won 8 out of 14 as a two-year-old, and comes from the substantial barn of John Patterson, Sr. But she has been strictly a country fair performer until now. On June 11, she muffed her attempt to beat C-3 pacers here. Now look at Deena. Most especially, look at her energetic effort of May 31 at Pocono Downs against some of the best pacers of her age and sex. How do we know it was a high-class race? For one thing, look at the size of the purse. Also, if you subscribe to the trade papers you will recognize the names of With Thanks, Supple Yankee and Tarport Birdie, leading fillies. Deena's June 9 race was nothing much as a performance but it was against better stock than is classified as C-3 here. Deena over-shadows this field.

RESULT: As odds-on favorite at 4 to 5, Deena won with great aplomb. Interestingly enough, Yankee Hobo was second. For those interested in daily doubles, the payoff on Novel Blaze and Deena was $30.80, which is thin soup for picking the winners of two successive races. Deena's own mutuel price was $3.60.

The Third Race

This trot requires a more adventurous spirit than mine. Adios Proof, Partys Over and Speedy C. are all gallopers, especially the latter two, which are making careers of racing in qualifiers. With three breakers leaving so close to the rail, and with Beau Diller, the inside horse, coming off a galloping display of his own, I'll pass.

People who play exactas are fond of the long chance. They will want to know how to cope with this race. Passing is not their style. For their sake, but with no enthusiasm, I shall try to pretend that the race is playable.

Beau Diller's June 5 performance brands him a noncontender, even if one excuses his demonstration of June 12. Gallant Dooley also is dismissed, having performed only in a qualifier this season.

The likeliest prospects and their ratings:

Native Yankee. The basic rating is 172, plus 15 for roughing it and 1 for the improved post position. Total is 188.

Star Crest. Basic rating is 181. Deductions for the rise in class and the worsened post position cancel the 10 points of credit for Phalen. Add 1 for the stretch gain. Total is 182.

Victory Cadet. The June 18 performance was the kind that we talked about in connection with Novel Blaze, winner of the first race. Neither downright bad nor powerfully good, it suggests that we use the June 11 race, for which the basic rating is 183. Add 10 for rough-ing it and 10 because of driver Patterson, but deduct 3 for the poor post position. Final figure is 200—more than the 10-point margin that is necessary before a horse is acceptable in one of the two outside post positions at a half-mile track.

RESULT: Speedy C. stayed flat for a change and won, paying $50.40. Native Yankee finished second, for an exacta payoff of $358.40. Victory Cadet went off at 22 to 1 and performed like 200 to 1, beating only Adios Proof.

The Fourth Race

We can save time and trouble here. It hardly requires searching study to see that Good Time Lass will have by far the highest
rating in this field. Her final and fractional figures from the June 19
race, plus credit for roughing it, plus the presence of John Chapman,
add up to a standout selection.

RESULT: She won, paying $5.20.

The Fifth Race

We can write off Council Dares for a lusterless showing last
week and Guy Adios, winless in two years. We also eliminate Lord
Stacey, whose adjustment to a half-mile oval will not be helped by
his extreme outside post position. This leaves us with six possible
contenders:

Frosty Scott. Basic rating of 204, less 5 for the rise in class from
C-2 to a $10,000 claiming price (see 206). Add 10 for roughing,
1 for the slight stretch gain, 10 for Fontaine and 3 for the better gate
position. Total is 223.

Imp. Basic rating is 206, less 5 for moving from a $6,000 claiming
price to $7,500 (read the conditions of the race at the top of the
program page). Add 5 for roughing it, 10 for Jim Tallman and 2 for
the better position. Total is 218. Is anybody wondering why Jim
Tallman increases a horse's rating by 10 points? True, he is not winning 15 percent of his starts at the current meeting. But, as shown on
page 251, he qualifies as one of the topnotchers whose winning percentages seldom remain below par for long.

Rapid. We have to think twice before deciding whether to rate
this horse. He has been idle for two weeks, in a field full of horses
more recently active. His best listed performances have always come
after briefer rests. His decline in class from a $10,000 claiming price
to $7,500 may be a sign of trouble. Or it may mean an effort to re-
peat the strong victory of April 19. If you prefer to leave him out,
you get no argument from me. But I'll rate him. The basic rating is
206, plus 5 for roughing it, 5 more for the drop in class, 3 for the
improved post position and 10 for Chapman. Total is 229.

Top Trend. The deduction of 10 points for the switch from Herve
Filion to Jefferson Kelley eliminates this horse.

Abbey Crain. Basic rating of 188 with deductions for class rise and post position mean that this one will not have a rating high enough for play.

The play is Rapid. Exacta fans will play him and Frosty Scott.

RESULT: Frosty Scott won, paying $10. Imp, the 9 to 5 favorite, was second. Rapid (4 to 1) came along fast in the stretch for third. The exacta paid $35, and would have been won by players who felt that Rapid had been away too long for this field.

The Sixth Race

Ricci Reenie First was dull on June 18, and goes out. So does Torpid Vic, for backing up after having had things his own way. And so does Valid Bet for showing nothing.

Rating the contenders:

Brown Smoke. Basic rating of 215, plus 10 for roughing it. Billy Myer is in one of his losing spells, having finished first with fewer than 9 percent of his charges at the meeting. No extra points for the driver. Total is 225.

Pride of Hanover. Basic rating of 215, plus 10 for roughing it, 2 for the better position and 10 for Patterson. Total is 237.

Charming Demon. No need to expend time on this one. Where Pride of Hanover got a better rating off the same race, and now improves its post position, Fontaine's horse gets a worse post position and will have a total figure 7 points below the others.

Donora. Same is true of this one as of Charming Demon.

Alytor. Coming from the same June 18 race as the preceding three horses, this one does not have a high enough rating to compensate for the poor post position.

The play is Pride of Hanover.

RESULT: Wrong again. Torpid Vic led all the way as 6 to 5 favorite. Alytor (11 to 1) was second, Brown Smoke (2 to 1) was third. Pride of Hanover managed to finish ahead of Valid Bet (68 to 1) and Charming Demon (18 to 1).

The Seventh Race

Five of these pacers competed against each other on June 12. One of them, Linds Girl, broke stride that night and had little sting on her previous start. Much the best rating among the others will go to Tarport Susan, enabling us to eliminate Calsara, Claire's Tar Heel and Katy R. Rating the contenders:

Little Mother. Her last outing was on an off track, so we go to the race of June 6, for which the basic rating is 190. Adding 15 for her brave effort on the outside, plus 5 for the drop to class C-2, plus 2 for the inside post, plus 10 for Abbatiello, the total becomes 222.

Tarport Susan. Base rating is 197. Add 10 for roughing it, 1 for the stretch gain and 10 for Tallman. Total is 218.

Anita's Star. Base rating of 205, plus 1 for the stretch gain, less 3 for the worsened post and 5 for the rise in class. Total is 198.

Our Gem. Base rating of 200. Add 5 for the drop in class, 5 more for roughing it and 1 for the improved post. Deduct 10 for the switch from Herve Filion to Jean Berube. Total is 201.

The play is Little Mother.

RESULT: A strong favorite at less than 9 to 5, she ate up Tarport Susan in the stretch and won, paying $5.40. Tarport Susan was second choice at 2.20 to 1. Exacta customers who handicapped the race our way got $18.20.

The Eighth Race

Eliminate Twinkle O. for backing up and Sly Yankee for being winless in 16 successive starts. Rating the others:

Heriot. Basic rating of 198, plus 10 for racing on the outside, 1 for the slightly better post and 10 for Del Insko. Total is 219.

Rod Knight. Basic rating of 215, plus 5 for roughing it and 2 for the better post. Deduct 10 for the switch from Fontaine. Final rating becomes 212.

Hootfire Hanover. Basic rating of 214. Add 5 for roughing it, 2 for the better position and 10 for Chapman. Total is 231.

Tryout N. No point in bothering with this, considering the slower times and the driver switch.

Bye Bye Gene. Basic rating of 214. Add 10 for roughing it over half a mile, 10 for Tallman and 5 for being a beaten favorite. Deduct 4 for the new post position. Total is 235.

Niagara Bullet. Will not get enough points to be a play from this post position.

The play is Bye Bye Gene.

RESULT: The 2 to 1 favorite, Twinkle O., had a slight lead at the head of the stretch, but Bye Bye Gene came blazing up in time to win by a neck. The mutuel was $7.80. Heriot, a surprising 10 to 1, finished third.

The Ninth Race

Toss out Madams B. Gallon for absenteeism, Master Glenn for poor form and Seafield Scott for being a chronic loser. Garrison Light is scratched.

Rate the contenders:

Drum Major. Basic rating is 184. Add 10 for roughing it, 5 for the better post position and 10 for Chapman. Total is 209.

Albert Gene. Basic rating is 210. The rise in class cancels the credit for roughing it. Deduct 3 for the changed post position. Total is 207.

Captain Missie. Basic rating is 199. The switch from Herve Filion cancels the credit for racing on the outside. Add 5 for being a beaten favorite, but deduct 3 for the worsened post. Final rating is 201.

Copper Jacket. Might have been pulled along on June 17, but finished close enough to deserve a rating. Use the June 10 race, for which the basic rating was 199. The rise in class nullifies the credit for roughing it. Deduct 3 for the change in post position. but add 2 for the stretch gain. Final rating is 198.

Drum Major is the play. Albert Gene rates within three points of the top one and would also be played if he had a leading driver.

RESULT: Old Sacher Werner got Seafield Scott on the lead at the beginning and kept him there all the way, beating the favored Drum Major (2 to 1) by a nose. Seafield paid $15.80 for winning his first race in 22. The exacta paid $54.60. Albert Gene, who would have been the other half of the exactas played by persons using our rating system, finishes fourth. Madams B. Gallon was third.

Our handicapping pointed out 11 plays in eight races. Of these, six were successful: Novel Blaze ($12.00, $4.00), Deena ($3.60), Good Time Lass ($5.20), Rapid (lost for both win and place), Pride of Hanover (lost for win and place), Little Mother ($5.40), Bye Bye Gene ($7.80), and Drum Major (lost).

HOLLYWOOD PARK
OFFICIAL PROGRAM

with past performances

50¢

Sales Tax Included

ONE MILE PACE 1st RACE (1st half Nightly Double) PURSE $1,800

CONDITIONED. (Cd-1). FIVE-YEAR-OLDS AND UNDER THAT HAVE NEVER WON $500 FIRST MONEY.

ASK FOR HORSE BY PROGRAM NUMBER

1 — On To Fame — 30-1

No Record, '69 Driver-Trainer—LEO LA COSTE Red-White-Green

On To Fame B. f, 3, by Newport Mike—Hazel Hal M. 1969 18 0 4 2 $1,904

Owner, Linden Creek Farms, Inc., Canonsburg, Pa. 1968 8 1 2 2 $924

Oct23-69^{5}Hol 1 :30⅗1:02⅗1:33⅗2:04⅘ft 39 3 5 4^{5} 3^{6} 5^{11} LaC'teL^{1} Cd-1 2:06⅗ FrontierSue Blazit BullHill

Oct20-69 Hol 1 :31⅘1:03 1:35 2:05⅘ft 2 4 4^{3} $4^{4½}$ $4^{4½}$ LaC'steL^{1} Qua 2:06⅘ Galiss Amphion StarEast

Oct13-69^{2}Hol 1 :30⅗1:01⅗1:32⅘2:03⅗ft 50 x8 8 8^{13} 10^{14} 10dis LaC'teL^{1} Cd-1 Ancestor PeterG'se UncleSm'ge

Aug13-69 Dytn 1 : gd 3 H'k'maH^{4} 3-Yr 2:11⅕ Emb'syTar K'st'eR'm'o OnToF'e

Aug13-69 Dytn 1 : gd 4 H'k'maH^{4} 3-Yr 2:10⅕ Emb'syTar Rita'sRip J'nib'eH'v'r

Aug11-69 Wash 1 : 2:08 gd 6 H'lkemaH^{9} Stk JayThorpe J'myAcres PertArden

2 — Copper Green Tree — 15-1

2:08⅕, F.P, '69 Driver—JOE LIGHTHILL. Trainer, C. Marcotte Green-White-Gold

Copper Green Tree B. g, 4, by Greentree Adios—Hot Penny. 1969 17 2 2 0 $1,681

Owner, Clarence Marcotte, Chino, Calif. 1968 0 0 0 0 ——

Oct27-69^{3}Hol 1 :32⅗1:02⅘1:33⅗2:03 ft 24 4 4 4^{5} 4^{5} 4^{9} L'hth'lJ^{2} Cd-1 2:04⅘ Sist'rBr'ks Pet'rG'se ArmbroK'g

Oct23-69^{4}Hol 1 :30⅗1:02⅗1:33⅘2:04⅗ft 45 3 3 $4^{4½}$ 4^{4} $2^{3½}$ L'hth'lJ^{1} Cd-1 2:05 RosieF'v'l C'p'rGr'nT'e AzosH'er

Oct13-69^{2}Hol 1 :30⅗1:01⅗1:32⅘2:03⅗ft 78 7 7 7^{13} 7^{10} 9^{16} L'hth'lJ^{7} Cd-1 2:06⅗ Ancestor PeterG'se UncleSm'ge

Sep30-69^{4}Hol 1 :30⅗1:02⅕1:35⅕2:05⅘ft 32 6 6 8^{10} 6^{12} 5^{14} BerryD^{3} Cd-1 2:08⅘ TrueJ'lie LoriFl'id'n D'taByeBye

Sep16-69^{1}Pom 1 :32⅗1:06⅗1:38 2:10⅗ft 13 8 8 8^{16} 8^{25} 7dis M'c'teC^{7} Cond Sh's'd'll Fl'rD Am'r L'dyJ'nPr'se

Jly 17-69 Mea 1 :31⅕1:06⅗1:37⅗2:08 ft 39 7 7 7 $7^{8½}$ 7^{12} AdamsC^{3} Cond 2:10⅗ TheG'bl'r A'tM'b'v'n B'h'miaW'r

3 — Status — 6-1

No Record, '69 Driver-Trainer—MARC GRENIER Red and White

Status Br. g, 5, by Morano—Tradition. 1969 8 0 2 1 $1,440

Owner, M. & A. Stable, Inc., Chicago, Ill. 1968 3 0 0 0 ——

Oct27-69^{3}Hol 1 :32⅗1:02⅘1:33⅗2:03 ft 21 x9 8 $7^{9½}$ 7^{9} 6^{15} Gr'n'rM^{3} Cd-1 2:06 Sist'rBr'ks Pet'rG'se ArmbroK'g

Oct10-69^{3}Hol 1 :31⅗1:03 1:34⅘2:05 ft 20 4 6 4^{3} $2^{1½}$ 7^{3} Gren'rM^{6} Cd-1 2:05⅗ TopG'ne Blaz'gRed Sc'ch'rWave

Oct 1-69^{2}Hol 1 :31⅗1:04⅕1:34⅗2:05 ft 3¾ 1 1 $1^{2½}$ 1^{2} $2^{¾}$ Gren'rM^{4} Cd-1 2:05 DiamantePhil Status MisterRex

Aug25-69^{3}Spk 1 :30⅕1:02⅗1:35⅕2:06 ft 5½ 4 4 4 $4^{3½}$ $4^{1¾}$ GrenierJ^{2} Mdn 2:06⅗ Idle'sVict'r Q'n'sTrav'r G'dEn'ty

Aug14-69^{3}Spk 1 :30⅗1:04⅗1:34⅗2:04⅗ft 8½ 2 2 3^{2} $3^{2½}$ 3^{7} †GrenierJ^{4} Mdn 2:05⅘† DH JB'ch'rlke HailT'rt'n Status

Aug 4-69 Spk 1 :30 1:03⅕1:34⅗2:05⅗ft 11 9 9 6^{7} 6^{6} $7^{6¾}$ Gren'rM^{7} Mdn 2:07 Mercury AdiosStr'ng S'rc'rWave

4 — Peter Goose — 9-5

2:09, Lyndn, '69 Driver-Trainer—JAMES DENNIS Green and White

Peter Goose B. g, 4, by Truabbe Jr.—Lucinda Goose. 1969 15 4 6 2 $2,910

Owner, Edward Towers, Ladner, B.C. 1968 3 0 1 1 $566

Oct27-69^{3}Hol 1 :32⅗1:02⅘1:33⅗2:03 ft 2¼ 2 3 $3^{2½}$ 3^{2} $2^{3½}$ DennisJ^{4} Cd-1 2:03⅘ Sist'rBr'ks Pet'rG'se ArmbroK'g

Oct20-69^{1}Hol 1 :30⅗1:02⅗1:34 2:04⅕ft 1 ▲ 10 2 2^{2} $2^{1½}$ 2^{2} DennisJ^{8} Cd-1 2:04⅗ BigTime Pet'rGoose Bew'gG'ldie

Oct13-69^{2}Hol 1 :30⅗1:01⅗1:32⅘2:03⅗ft 7-5 ▲ 1 2 2^{2} 4^{3} $2^{½}$ DennisJ^{6} Cd-1 2:03⅗ Ancestor PeterG'se UncleSm'ge

Oct 7-69^{4}Hol 1 :30 1:01⅗1:33⅕2:04⅗ft 2¾ ▲ 2 3 1^{3} $1^{2½}$ $2^{½}$ DennisJ^{2} Cd-1 2:04⅘ IrishJ.W. Pet'rGoose Fl'rD Am'r

Sep30-69^{3}Hol 1 :31⅗1:02⅘1:33⅗2:04⅗ft 8½ 4^{0} 1 $3^{1½}$ 3^{4} $5^{3½}$ DennisJ^{7} Cd-1 2:05⅗ W'hyMed'l DuMeans ValsPl'yb'y

Aug13-69Lyndn 1 : 2:09 ft 1 TowersT^{5} FFA 2:09 PeterG'se Sc'tishR'e L'mb'rD'me

5 — Princess Ellen — 10-1

No Record, '69 Driver—TOM WILBURN. Trainer, Al Bahouth Gold and Green

Princess Ellen Blk. m, 4, by Dillon Prince—Widow Ellen. 1969 20 0 2 3 $649

Owner, Alfred E. Bahouth, Los Angeles, Calif. 1968 23 1 2 1 $783

Oct20-69^{1}Hol 1 :30⅗1:02⅗1:34 2:04⅕ft 14 3 4 5^{7} 7^{10} 9^{14} Wilb'nT^{2} Cd-1 2:06⅘ BigTime Pet'rGoose Bew'gG'ldie

Oct 3-69^{1}Hol 1 :31 1:02⅘1:34⅗2:06 ft 3½ 4 5 5^{6} 5^{6} $7^{5¾}$ Wilb'nT^{9} Cd-1 2:07⅗ Bomb'rL'rd GoldWater BigTime

Sep25-69 Hol 1 :30 1:01 1:32⅘2:03⅗ft 3 3 3^{4} 3^{4} 2^{6} Baho'thA^{5} Qua 2:04⅗ SatanT's Pr'c'sEl'n Gov'rn'rTass

Sep19-69 Hol 1 :32 1:05⅘1:37 2:08 ft 4 4 4^{5} $4^{3½}$ 2^{1} B'houthA^{6} Qua 2:08⅕ D'm'tePhil P'c'ssEll'n R'cyC't'ss

Aug29-69 ScD 1 :30⅕1:06 1:38⅕2:11⅗ft x6 5 4 4^{8} 4^{6} Baho'thA^{3} Qua 2:12⅗ PattyB.L'g EnglishH'l Paci'cSue

Aug26-69 ScD 1 :31 1:03⅗1:36⅗2:08⅘ft 2 3 3^{0} 3^{2} 5^{6} Baho'thA^{5} Qua 2:10 Q'kMission OhiosJose Sup'rPilot

6 — Pacing Bear — 7-2

2:07⅕, LouD, '69 Driver-Trainer—HOWARD GILL Rose and Grey

Pacing Bear B. g, 5, by Direct Spangler—Miss Golden Belle. 1969 15 2 3 0 $1,031

Owner, Howard E. Gill, Prospect, Ky. 1968 0 0 0 0 ——

Oct27-69 Hol 1 :31⅗1:03 1:34 2:03⅘ft 4^{0} 3 3^{4} 3^{4} $2^{4¾}$ GillH^{9} Qua 2:04⅘ RicoBay PacingBear Sist'rDares

Oct23-69 Hol 1 :31⅗1:03 1:36⅗2:08⅕ft 1 1 $1^{½}$ 1^{2} 1^{2} GillH^{2} Qua 2:08⅕ PacingBear GlennH.W. Hastuki

Oct14-69^{2}Hol 1 :30⅗1:01⅕1:33⅗2:04⅘ft 21 2^{0} 2^{0} 2^{1} 9^{14}x9^{22} GillH^{5} Cd-1 2:10⅗ Y'keeM'd'm Tex'sFr't Fl'rDAm'r

Oct 9-69 Hol 1 :31⅘1:05⅗1:36⅘2:07 ft 2 3 $3^{1½}$ 2^{2} 4^{h} GillH^{3} Qua 2:07 J'hnnyR'no Farout S'mps'nFrisco

Oct 6-69 Hol 1 :32⅗1:05 1:37 2:07⅗ft 3^{0} 1 $1^{½}$ 1^{2} 3^{1} GillH^{5} Qua 2:07⅗ Poppy SilverRecord PacingBear

Sep30-69^{4}Hol 1 :30⅗1:02⅕1:35⅕2:05⅘ft 8-5 2 3 3^{3} 3^{6}x 4^{13} GillH^{4} Cd-1 2:08⅗ TrueJ'lie LoriFl'id'n D'taByeBye

7 — ‡Sister Dares — 8-1

2:09⅘, Pain, '69 Driver-Trainer—GERALD LONGO Green and Black

‡Sister Dares Br. m, 4, by Libbys Boy—Fast Rhythm. 1969 10 2 0 2 $765

Owner, Gerald Longo, Nicholas & Martha Sack, Fullerton, Calif. 1968 5 0 0 0 $45

Oct27-69 Hol 1 :31⅗1:03 1:34 2:03⅘ft 2 2 2^{2} 2^{2} $3^{6¾}$ LongoG^{4} Qua 2:05⅕ RicoBay PacingBear Sist'rDares

Oct20-69 Hol 1 :31⅘1:03 1:35 2:05⅘ft 1 3 $2^{1½}$ 2^{2} $5^{7½}$ LongoG^{2} Qua 2:07⅗ Galiss Amphion StarEast

Oct13-69 Hol 1 :31 1:02⅘1:35 2:06⅗ft 1 1 1^{1} $2^{½}$ $5^{4½}$ LongoG^{2} Qua 2:07⅗ KeyClip'r P't'rP'rkins L'ckyJohn

Oct 9-69 Hol 1 :30 1:02⅗1:35⅗2:07⅗ft 1 1 1^{2} 1^{2} 1^{1} LongoG^{4} Qua 2:07⅗ Sis'rD'res M'd'wH'th'r M'G'eT'ss

Sep27-69^{1}Hol 1 :32⅕1:04⅕1:35⅗2:06⅘ft 12 7x10 10 10dis 10dis LongoG^{7} Cd-1 Gr'dEnt'grity BigT'g Fr'styW'l'n

Sep 4-69 Nfld 1 :32⅗1:04⅗1:37 2:08⅗ft 3¼ x8x 8 8 8dis 8dis LongoG^{6} Cond Th'ftyM'n'y LawH'n'r ClayT'ship

8 — Ruby Stormcloud — 8-1

2:08⅗, Carmi, Ill. Driver-Trainer—RAY RICHMOND White and Purple

Ruby Stormcloud B. m, 4, by Storm Cloud—Gitana. Owner, 1969 28 6 5 8 $1,834

Ray C. Richmond, Stephen Grollneck, Los Angeles, Calif. 1968 12 2 1 3 $785

Oct27-69 Hol 1 :32⅕1:04⅗1:36⅗2:07⅗ft 1 1 $1^{½}$ 1^{2} $1^{½}$ Rich'ndR^{2} Qua 2:07⅗ R'bySt'cl'd R'y'sSh'ck Sp'dyP'ch

Aug14-69 Carmi Finished 2-1 in 2:10⅘, 2:08⅗ (R.Brinkley) Aug20-69 Anna Finished 3-3 in 2:16, 2:15 (R.Brinkley)

Jly 30-69 Hopk Finished 1-1 in 2:13, 2:15 (R.Brinkley) Aug12-69 Carmi Finished 1-1 in 2:12⅗, 2:11⅖ (R.Brinkley)

Jly 23-69 Frfld Finished 6-6 in 2:10, 2:09⅕ (R.Brinkley). Jly 24-69 Frfld Finished 3-3 in2:11⅘, 2:11⅕ (R.Brinkley)

Jly 12-69 Aud 1 :31 1:06⅘1:40 2:11⅗ft 3½ 1^{0} 1 1 1^{1} 1^{nk} Br'kleyE^{4} Cond 2:11⅗ R'bySt'cl'd KahokaKey J'ferCry

Jly 7-69 Aud 1 :32⅕1:05⅗1:36⅗2:09⅕ft 8¼ 3 4 4^{0} 3^{3} $3^{2½}$ Br'kl'yE^{5} Cond 2:09⅗ KayP'due JeniferCry R'bySt'cl'd

9 — Frosty Woollen — 15-1

2:10⅖, F.P, '69 Driver-Trainer—RODNEY JUNGQUIST White and Purple

Frosty Woollen B. h, 5, by Kim Frost—Desilu Woollen. 1969 36 2 8 4 $3,171

Owner, D. Jungquist & E. Mantha, Seattle, Wash. 1968 0 0 0 0 ——

Oct23-69^{4}Hol 1 :30⅗1:02⅗1:33⅗2:04⅗ft 34 7 7 7^{9} 8^{11} 10^{14} J'gq'stR^{8} Cd-1 2:07 RosieF'v'l C'p'rGr'nT'e AzosH'er

Oct13-69^{2}Hol 1 :30⅗1:01⅗1:32⅘2:03⅗ft 23 6 6 6^{9} 5^{5} 5^{7} J'gq'stR^{9} Cd-1 2:04⅗ Ancestor PeterG'se UncleSm'ge

Sep30-69^{3}Hol 1 :31⅗1:02⅘1:33⅗2:04⅗ft 15 1^{0} 2 $4^{3½}$ 4^{5} 6^{6} J'gq'stR^{6} Cd-1 2:05⅘ W'hyMed'l DuMeans ValsPl'yb'y

Sep27-69^{1}Hol 1 :32⅕1:04⅕1:35⅗2:06⅘ft 9 1 3 2^{2} $2^{½}$ $3^{½}$ J'gq'stR^{2} Cd-1 2:07 Gr'dEnt'grity BigT'g Fr'styW'l'n

Sep24-69^{1}Pom 1 :32⅗1:06 1:39 2:10⅗ft 4½ 1^{0} 1 1^{h} $3^{2½}$ $6^{6¾}$ J'gq'stR^{4} Cond 2:12 TopGene Shesadoll EmmasJoy

Sep18-69^{2}Pom 1 :32⅕1:07⅗1:41 2:13 ft 6¾ 4 4 $5^{4½}$ 3^{4} $2^{1½}$ J'gq'stR^{7} Cond 2:13⅗ WeeCanD Fr'styW'll'n J'rryGene

10 — Bewitching Goldie — 9-2

2:08, Med, '69 Driver-Trainer—ROBERT FARRINGTON Red and Grey

Bewitching Goldie B. m, 4, by Meadow Gold—Amossons Princess. Owner, 1969 12 5 2 1 $1,313

R.L., R.E. Farrington & Farrington Stables, Richwood, Ohio. 1968 20 8 1 3 $1,077

Oct27-69^{3}Hol 1 :32⅗1:02⅘1:33⅗2:03 ft 13 7 6 $6^{7½}$ $6^{8½}$ $5^{9¼}$ F'gtonR^{6} Cd-1 2:04⅘ Sist'rBr'ks Pet'rG'se ArmbroK'g

Oct20-69^{1}Hol 1 :30⅗1:02⅗1:34 2:04⅕ft 7¾ 4 5 $6^{7½}$ 3^{4} 3^{5} F'gtonR^{5} Cd-1 2:05⅕ BigTime Pet'rGoose Bew'gG'ldie

Oct13-69^{2}Hol 1 :30⅗1:01⅗1:32⅘2:03⅗ft 5 9 10 10^{16} 8^{11} 7^{10} F'g'nR^{10} Cd-1 2:05 Ancestor PeterG'se UncleSm'ge

Sep30-69^{3}Hol 1 :31⅗1:02⅘1:33⅗2:04⅗ft 2-3 ▲ 2 3 1^{1} 1^{3} $4^{2½}$ F'gtonR^{4} Cd-1 2:05⅕ W'hyMed'l DuMeans ValsPl'yb'y

Sep24-69^{2}Hol 1 :30⅗1:03 1:34⅗2:03⅘ft 3 ix9 9 9^{12} 8^{14} 8^{14} F'gt'nR^{10} Cond 2:07⅗ Marish Mr.Jazz PatchieGold

Aug27-69 ScD 1 :29⅘1:02 1:34⅕2:04⅗ft 3-5 ▲ 4 4 4^{0} 3^{3} $2^{4¼}$ F'gt'nRi^{3} Cond 2:05⅕ AgileP'k B'w'ch'gG'die Sh'l'eC'd

Declared—Rico Bay. ‡RACING WITHOUT HOPPLES.

HEAD NUMBER COLOR: BLACK—WHITE NUMBER

ONE MILE PACE 2nd RACE (2nd half Nightly Double) PURSE $1,800

CONDITIONED. (Cd-1). THREE-YEAR-OLDS AND UPWARD, HORSES THAT HAVE STARTED TEN OR MORE TIMES IN 1969 AND ARE NON-WINNERS OF $3,000 IN 1969. ALSO ELIGIBLE: HORSES THAT HAVE NEVER WON $3,000.

ASK FOR HORSE BY PROGRAM NUMBER

---

1 — 8-1

2:04⅕, Lex, '69 — Driver-Trainer—J. H. WEBB — Maroon and Cream

Blazit — B. h, 7, by Blaze Hanover—Victory Mite. — 1969 18 5 4 3 $2,589

Owner, Nacy H. Stone Jr. & M. C. Webb, Sharpsburg, Ky. — 1968 RACED AS TROTTER

Oct23-69 5Hol	1 :30⅘ 1:02⅗ 1:33⅗ 2:04⅗ ft	13	2 2 3^{2} 2^{3} $2^{2\frac{1}{2}}$	W'bbJH 2	Cd-1	2:05	FrontierSue Blazit BullHill
Oct13-69 4Hol	1 :30⅘ 1:01⅗ 1:33⅗ 2:03⅗ ft	67	10 10 10^{14} 10^{17} 10^{16}	W'bJH 10	Cd-2	2:06⅗	SisByrd SilverSing DirectSue
Oct 7-69 5Hol	1 :29⅘ 1:01⅗ 1:32⅕ 2:02⅘ ft	43	6 6 $7^{7\frac{1}{2}}$ 7^{7} $8^{7\frac{1}{4}}$	WebbJH 8	Cd-1	2:04⅕	DuMeans ArmbroJ'k Sh'dowRed
Sep26-69 4Hol	1 :30 1:00⅘ 1:32⅘ 2:02⅘ ft	7	8 8 9^{8} 9^{10} 7^{11}	WebbJH 5	Cd-3	2:05⅗	P'triciaL'se OurN'ncy Mis'leTrip
Sep 1-69 LouD	1 :30⅗ 1:02⅗ 1:33⅘ 2:07⅗ ft	3½	3^{0} 3 2 3^{5} 2^{h}	WebbJ 4	Cond	2:07⅗	J'tlysL'kyL'dy Bl'zit H'm'rW'thy
Aug22-69 LouD	1 :31⅗ 1:04⅘ 1:37 2:08⅗ ft	4	6 6 6^{0} $6^{3\frac{1}{2}}$ $7^{4\frac{3}{4}}$	WebbJ 6	Cond	2:09⅗	NobleSam SunnyDelite ChiefLaw

---

2 — 20-1

2:10⅘sl, B.M, '69 — Driver—LEO LA COSTE. Trainer, John Dick — Red-White-Green

Wee Johnny D. — B. g, 7, by Sigma Nu—Jean Manners. — 1969 17 1 0 2 $1,305

Owner, John Dick, Chino, Calif. — 1968 53 3 8 6 $6,953

Oct28-69 6Hol	1 :30⅗ 1:01⅗ 1:33 2:03⅗ ft	20	2^{0} 2 $3^{2\frac{1}{2}}$ $4^{3\frac{1}{2}}$ $7^{7\frac{1}{4}}$	LaC'steL 4	4000	2:05	A'roH'sky T'nM'rt'l Midn'tBr'ie
Oct17-69 3Hol	1 :30 1:01⅗ 1:33⅗ 2:03⅗ ft	19	3 3 $5^{4\frac{1}{2}}$ $6^{7\frac{1}{2}}$ $6^{5\frac{3}{4}}$	BaileyW 3	Cd-1	2:04⅗	T'x'sFr'ht R'y'lR'kHal R'sieF'v'l
Oct 7-69 4Hol	1 :30 1:01⅗ 1:33⅕ 2:04⅗ ft	11	6 7 5^{8} 6^{9} $9^{8\frac{1}{4}}$	JacobsC 8	Cd-1	2:06⅕	IrishJ.W. Pet'rGoose Fl'rDAm'r
Oct 2-69 Hol	1 :30⅘ 1:03 1:34 2:05 ft		2^{0} 1 2^{3} 2^{3} $2^{1\frac{1}{2}}$	JacobsC 5	Qua	2:05⅗	B'w'ch'gAd's WeeJ'yD. L'dP'b'y
Sep 6-69 Fhld	1 :30⅗ 1:02 1:35 2:07⅕ ft	5½	2 3 2ix 8dis 8dis	C'b'lCJr 2	Cond		Y'keeB'l't Br'ndaDr'm W.D.B'r'n
Sep 2-69 Nfld	1 :31⅗ 1:04⅗ 1:37⅘ 2:10⅘ gd	18	3^{0} 4^{0} 8 8^{21} 8dis	C'b'lCJr 5	Cond		AdaD'nise Din'hSt'm H'plest'h'r

---

3 — 5-1

No Record, '69 — Driver-Trainer—GEORGE HARDIE — Black and Gold

Sampson Frisco — Br. h, 9, by Sampson Hanover—Margy Frisco. — 1969 12 0 0 0 $760

Owner, George G. Hardie & Milton Aronowitz Jr., Warwick, R.I. — 1968 17 2 1 0 $2,610

Oct17-69 3Hol	1 :30 1:01⅗ 1:33⅗ 2:03⅗ ft	2¾ ▲	5 5 4^{4} 4^{5}x 9^{13}	HardieG 1	Cd-1	2:06⅕	T'x'sFr'ht R'y'lR'kHal R'sieF'v'l
Oct13-69 4Hol	1 :30⅘ 1:01⅗ 1:33⅗ 2:03⅗ ft	5½	7 8 8^{11} $6^{9\frac{1}{2}}$ $5^{5\frac{1}{2}}$	HardieG 5	Cd-2	2:04⅗	SisByrd SilverSing DirectSue
Oct 9-69 Hol	1 :31⅘ 1:05⅗ 1:36⅘ 2:07 ft		6 4^{0} $4^{2\frac{1}{2}}$ $3^{2\frac{1}{2}}$ 3^{h}	HardieG 6	Qua	2:07	J'hnnyR'no Farout S'mps'nFrisco
Oct 6-69 Hol	1 :31⅕ 1:04 1:36⅗ 2:07⅗ ft		6 5^{0} 2^{2} 1½ 1¾	HardieG 8	Qua	2:07⅗	S'ps'nFr'co A'rCh'fB. L'yJ'nP'se
Oct 2-69 9Hol	1 :31⅗ 1:02⅕ 1:33⅕ 2:03⅕ ft	3¼	6 6 $5^{3\frac{1}{2}}$ 6^{10}x9^{19}	H'rdieG 2	Cd-1	2:07⅕	Hick'yD'l's FreeH'th'r B'nieL'k't
Sep23-69 3Hol	1 :31 1:02⅕ 1:33⅕ 2:03⅘ ft	9	2 3 $4^{2\frac{1}{2}}$ 3^{3}xx5^{5}	HardieG 7	Cd-1	2:04⅘	S'tEst'heA. S'k'yBl'ze D'ndP'c's

---

4 — 9-2

No Record, '69 — Driver-Trainer—DOUG ACKERMAN — Blue and Grey

‡Beppi — B. m, 8, by Duane Hanover—Erlaway. — 1969 21 0 1 0 $2,814

Owner, United Stock Farm, Leonard, Mich. — 1968 29 4 2 5 $7,509

Oct27-69 9Hol	1 1/16 :29⅗ 1:01 1:33 2:10⅘ ft	20	9 9 8^{15} 8^{15} 8^{14}	Ac'm'nD 7	Cd-2	2:13⅗	Sp'nishCh'f Del'noKid H'pyOtto
Oct22-69 3Hol	1 :30⅕ 1:01⅕ 1:32 2:02⅘ ft	8¾	7 7 7^{16} 7^{17} 7^{11}	Ac'm'nD 4	Cd-2	2:05	WorthyByrd MaiTai DirectHome
Oct16-69 9Hol	1 :29 :59 1:30⅗ 2:01 ft	7	9 9 9^{16}x9^{19} 9dis	Ac'r'nD 7	Cd-1		BeagleBoy MiMargarita MaiTai
Oct 7-69 5Hol	1 :29⅘ 1:01⅗ 1:32⅕ 2:02⅘ ft	22	8 8 8^{10} 8^{8} 4^{2}	Ac'm'nD 5	Cd-1	2:03⅕	DuMeans ArmbroJ'k Sh'dowRed
Oct 2-69 4Hol	1 :29⅘ 1:00⅗ 1:33⅗ 2:03⅕ ft	51	7 8 6^{8} 6^{9} $4^{5\frac{3}{4}}$	Ac'm'nD 6	Cd-1	2:04⅕	SpanishChief DirectSue TopBid
Sep24-69 5Hol	1 :30 1:01⅗ 1:33⅘ 2:03 ft	30	7 7 8^{12} $5^{6\frac{1}{2}}$ $8^{7\frac{3}{4}}$	Ac'm'nD 2	Cd-1	2:04⅗	FrontierSue TopBid O.C.Mego

---

5 — 6-1

2:10⅘, G.M, '69 — Driver—ROBERT WILLIAMS. Trainer, Leonard Meehan — Purple-White

Bull Hill — B. g, 4, by Matador—Katherine H. — 1969 18 3 2 1 $2,071

Owner, Maurice T. Sullivan, Ludlow, Mass. — 1968 4 1 0 2 $583

Oct23-69 5Hol	1 :30⅘ 1:02⅗ 1:33⅗ 2:04⅗ ft	6½	6 7 8^{11} $5^{8\frac{1}{2}}$ 3^{6}	Wil'msR 6	Cd-1	2:05⅗	FrontierSue Blazit BullHill
Oct17-69 3Hol	1 :30 1:01⅗ 1:33⅗ 2:03⅗ ft	10	9 8 7^{7} 8^{9} $7^{7\frac{3}{4}}$	Wil'msR 9	Cd-1	2:05	T'x'sFr'ht R'y'lR'kHal R'sieF'v'l
Oct14-69 2Hol	1 :30⅗ 1:01⅕ 1:33⅘ 2:04⅘ ft	2¼ ▲	1 1 1^{1} 2½ 5^{6}	Wil'msR 4	Cd-1	2:06⅗	Y'keeM'd'm Tex'sFr't Fl'rDAm'r
Oct 7-69 4Hol	1 :30 1:01⅗ 1:33⅕ 2:04⅗ ft	3½	10^{0} 10 9^{15} $7^{9\frac{1}{2}}$ $5^{4\frac{3}{4}}$	Wil'msR 9	Cd-1	2:05⅗	IrishJ.W. Pet'rGoose Fl'rDAm'r
Oct 1-69 5Hol	1 :30⅘ 1:01⅗ 1:34 2:05 ft	43	2 3 3^{2} 2^{2} 2no	Wil'msR 2	Cd-1	2:05	BlazingRed BullHill RoyalBell
Sep24-69 2Hol	1 :30⅗ 1:03 1:34⅗ 2:03⅘ ft	60	4 5 6^{7} 7^{14} 6^{13}	G'shwaR 1	Cond	2:07	Marish Mr.Jazz PatchieGold

---

6 — 4-1

2:03⅘, Hol, '69 — Driver-Trainer—GLEN HOLT; Ass't, W. Rozier — Turquoise and White

Diamante Phil — Br. g, 3, by Junior Maplecroft—Shafter Queen. — 1969 5 2 0 1 $2,160

Owner, Glen Holt, Shafter, Calif. — 1968 0 0 0 0 ——

Oct20-69 4Hol	1 :31⅕ 1:03⅕ 1:34⅗ 2:04⅗ ft	9-5 ▲	8 5^{0} $4^{5\frac{1}{2}}$x7^{13} 7^{15}	HoltG 7	Cd-1	2:07⅗	F'k'nJew'l Bl'z'gRed Fl'shOnP'k
Oct16-69 2Hol	1 :30⅗ 1:02⅗ 1:33⅗ 2:03⅘ ft	8	7 5 4^{4} 2½ $1^{1\frac{1}{4}}$	HoltG 8	Cd-1	2:03⅘	Dia'tePhil ChillR'g'r AppleCus'r
Oct 8-69 3Hol	1 :31⅗ 1:03⅗ 1:36 2:06⅕ ft	4¾	x6 6 x7^{11} $6^{9\frac{1}{2}}$ $4^{3\frac{3}{4}}$	HoltG 2	Cd-1	2:06⅘	W'thyMedal ChillR'ng'r BigTime
Oct 1-69 2Hol	1 :31⅗ 1:04⅕ 1:34⅗ 2:05 ft	4-5 ▲	3 3 3^{5} 3^{4} 1¾	HoltG 2	Cd-1	2:05	DiamantePhil Status MisterRex
Sep26-69 1Hol	1 :30⅗ 1:02⅕ 1:34⅗ 2:05⅕ ft	3½	9 7 $7^{6\frac{1}{2}}$ $6^{8\frac{1}{2}}$ $3^{3\frac{1}{4}}$	HoltG 6	Cd-1	2:06	R'y'lBell G'ldWat'r Diam'ntePhil
Sep19-69 Hol	1 :32 1:05⅘ 1:37 2:08 ft		2 2 $2^{1\frac{1}{2}}$ 2^{1} 1^{1}	HoltG 1	Qua	2:08	D'm'tePhil P'c'ssEll'n R'cyC't'ss

---

7 — 10-1

No Record, '69 — Driver-Trainer—WAYNE SHORT — Purple and White

Heather Chance — B. g, 4, by Chance Play—Widow Ann. Owner, Alvin A. & Ernst Edward Berlin, Cudahy, Wisc. — 1969 14 0 2 0 $2,113 — 1968 13 3 1 3 $4,830

Oct22-69 3Hol	1 :30⅕ 1:01⅕ 1:32 2:02⅘ ft	19	2^{0} 1 $2^{3\frac{1}{2}}$ 2^{5} 5^{7}	ShortW 7	Cd-2	2:04⅗	WorthyByrd MaiTai DirectHome
Oct 8-69 Was	1 :30⅗ 1:01⅘ 1:33⅗ 2:04⅗ ft	4	3 5 8 $5^{5\frac{1}{2}}$ 4^{5}	ShortW 6	Cond	2:05⅗	PaintAway Mr.Vinc't Midn'tD'ny
Sep27-69 Was	1 :30⅕ 1:01⅗ 1:34 2:04⅗ ft	13	4 4 5 7^{6} $7^{3\frac{3}{4}}$	ShortW 2	Cond	2:05⅕	Ahgoo NobleDecis'n Mich'lJohn
Sep18-69 Was	1 :30 1:01⅕ 1:33 2:03⅗ ft	30	4 5 7 4^{2} $2^{2\frac{1}{4}}$	ShortW 4	Cond	2:03⅘	Tayl'sFarv'l H'th'rCh'ce St'gG'te
Sep 3-69 Was	1 :31⅕ 1:03⅕ 1:35⅗ 2:06 ft	13	1 2 8 $3^{1\frac{1}{2}}$ $5^{3\frac{1}{2}}$	ShortW 6	Cond	2:06⅘	Deac'nD'gt'n M'yWay Th'dM'ini
Aug26-69 Spk	1 :32⅘ 1:05⅘ 1:38⅗ 2:08⅗ ft	19	3 4 5 $4^{4\frac{1}{2}}$ $7^{4\frac{1}{4}}$	ShortW 2	7200	2:09⅗	Skinan ByeByeGen'l Even'gSky

---

8 — 3-1

2:04⅘, Hol, '69 — Driver—TOM WILBURN. Trainer, R. McGonagle — Gold and Green

Yankee Madam — B. m, 8, by Yankee Scott—Madam Dean. Owner, M. Heiden, M. Griess, R. McGonagle, San Gabriel, Calif. — 1969 26 1 3 4 $2,566 — 1968 38 7 9 2 $21,436

Oct27-69 6Hol	1 :31⅕ 1:02⅗ 1:33⅕ 2:04 ft	13	1 2 4^{4} 8^{11} 10^{11}	Wilb'nT 10	6000	2:06⅗	R'ym'dePris M'ksBoy B'b'rLaird
Oct20-69 7Hol	1 :30 1:01 1:33⅘ 2:04 ft	15	8 8 7^{7} $6^{5\frac{1}{2}}$ 3^{3}	Wilb'rnT 8	6000	2:04⅗	BoyTrust P'lyJinks Y'keeMadam
Oct14-69 2Hol	1 :30⅗ 1:01⅕ 1:33⅘ 2:04⅘ ft	3¾	6 6 4^{4} 4^{3} 1^{h}	O'Br'nJ 8	Cd-1	2:04⅘	Y'keeM'd'm Tex'sFr't Fl'rDAm'r
Oct 2-69 5Hol	1 :31⅗ 1:02⅘ 1:34⅗ 2:03⅘ ft	92	5^{0} 5 5^{6} $6^{8\frac{1}{2}}$ $7^{7\frac{1}{2}}$	McG'leR 8	6000	2:05⅕	TownMartial Galiss TopGunner
Sep26-69 5Hol	1 :30⅗ 1:01 1:33⅕ 2:03⅗ ft	21	8 8 5^{7} $5^{9\frac{1}{2}}$ 6^{12}	McG'leR 7	6000	2:06⅗	T'wnMart'l Sh'nHill Skip'rsSc't'r
Aug28-69 Spk	1 :31⅗ 1:06⅗ 1:37 2:07⅘ ft	5¾	1 1 4 $6^{4\frac{1}{2}}$ 7^{12}	LackeyJ 6	6000	2:10⅕	Fl'm'gP'ker M'lieByrd G'n'lJoy

---

9 — 20-1

2:07, F.P, '69 — Driver—JOE LIGHTHILL. Trainer, C. Marcotte — Green-White-Gold

Key Holder — Br. g, 5, by Keystoner—Iosola Scott. — 1969 28 2 3 4 $2,439

Owner, Clarence Marcotte, Chino, Calif. — 1968 31 3 4 4 $2,423

Oct23-69 5Hol	1 :30⅘ 1:02⅗ 1:33⅗ 2:04⅗ ft	19	4 6 $5^{6\frac{1}{2}}$ 7^{13} 7^{15}	L'hth'lJ 4	Cd-1	2:07⅗	FrontierSue Blazit BullHill
Oct17-69 3Hol	1 :30 1:01⅗ 1:33⅗ 2:03⅗ ft	49	8 9 $9^{9\frac{1}{2}}$ 9^{12} 8^{11}	L'hth'lJ 7	Cd-1	2:05⅘	T'x'sFr'ht R'y'lR'kHal R'sieF'v'l
Oct11-69 2Hol	1 :29⅗ 1:00⅕ 1:33 2:03⅗ ft	33	9 8 6^{9} 9^{14} 9^{14}	Light'llJ 6	5000	2:06⅗	TownMart'l Renard CarelessJoe
Oct 2-69 9Hol	1 :31⅗ 1:02⅕ 1:33⅕ 2:03⅕ ft	37	8 8 8^{7} 8^{11} 6^{11}	TisherK 6	Cd-1	2:05⅕	Hick'yD'l's FreeH'th'r B'nieL'k't
Sep25-69 2Pom	1 :34 1:06⅗ 1:39⅗ 2:11⅗ ft	5¼	2 1 2^{h} 2^{2} 5^{12}	M'c'teC 2	Cond	2:13⅘	Conniver SkyGold MissC.B.
Sep16-69 4Pom	1 :33⅗ 1:08⅘ 1:41⅘ 2:12⅗ ft	7½	4^{0} 4 5^{5} 4^{6} $4^{8\frac{1}{4}}$	M'c'teC 3	Cond	2:14	WeeCanD SeaTacChief NuJean

---

10 — 6-1

No Record, '69 — Driver—JACK WILLIAMS JR. Trainer, Joe O'Brien, Ass't, T. Caraway — Red-White

Teddy — Br. g, 3, by Royal Valley—Martys Miss. — 1969 16 0 2 3 $2,975

Owner, Nathan & Joanne I. Berlant, Narberth, Pa. — 1968 3 3 0 0 $800

Oct23-69 L.B	1 :31 1:02 1:32⅘ 2:05 ft	6½	4 5 4^{0} $6^{9\frac{1}{2}}$ 6^{9}	Gil'reW 1	Cond	2:06⅘	Overwhelm RichAx NobleRhyt'm
Oct 6-69 L.B	1 :30⅘ 1:02⅗ 1:33 2:05⅕ ft	2	6 6 6^{0} $4^{5\frac{1}{4}}$ 8^{24}	Gil'reW 5	Cond	2:10	JennieL.Frost Dudley DaveW's'n
Sep22-69 L.B	1 :30⅗ 1:02⅗ 1:33 2:03⅕ ft	4	4 4 4 $5^{4\frac{3}{4}}$ 5^{13}	Gil'reW 3	Cond	2:05⅘	Miracul'sStar Ballard M'nTarH'l
Sep 8-69 L.B	1 :30 1:01⅘ 1:32⅗ 2:03⅘ ft	6¼	5 3 2^{0} 2¼ 3¼	Gil'reW 2	Cond	2:03⅘	Wil'wBr'kSc't Roy'lDavid Teddy
Aug19-69 Brdwn	1 :31 1:03 1:34⅗ 2:05⅕ ft	3¼	8 6 5^{0} $3^{1\frac{1}{2}}$ $4^{3\frac{1}{2}}$	Gil'reW 6	Cond	2:05⅘	BlueHorseA. OurNibbler RichR'n

---

Declared—Irish J. W. ‡RACING WITHOUT HOPPLES.

HEAD NUMBER COLOR: BLACK—YELLOW NUMBER

ONE MILE TROT — 3rd RACE — PURSE $2,400

CONDITIONED. (Cd-1). FOUR-, FIVE- AND SIX-YEAR-OLDS THAT HAVE NEVER WON $3,500. ALSO ELIGIBLE: THREE-YEAR-OLDS THAT HAVE NEVER WON $5,000.

ASK FOR HORSE BY PROGRAM NUMBER

1 — Sirius (4-1)

2:07, Hol, '69 — Driver-Trainer—JAMES DENNIS — Green and White

B. c, 3, by Stars Pride—Ingrid Hanover. — 1969 5 2 1 0 $3,026
Owner, A La Carte Racing Stable, Inglewood, Calif. — 1968 0 0 0 0 ——

Oct28-69^{1}Hol	1	:30⅗ 1:02⅗ 1:35⅗ 2:07	ft	4-5 ▲	1^{0}	2	1^{1}	1½	1½	DennisJ^{6}	Cd-1	2:07	Sirius HastiAx TekeMon
Oct20-69^{3}Hol	1	:31⅕ 1:03 1:34⅘ 2:04⅗	ft	3¼	1	2	2^{2}	2^{2}	2^{3}	DennisJ^{6}	Cd-1	2:05⅕	OdetteAdios Sirius TrueChance
Oct13-69^{1}Hol	1	:30⅘ 1:02⅗ 1:34⅗ 2:05⅗	ft	4¼	4	6	$8^{7¼}$	6^{5}	$4^{2½}$	DennisJ^{4}	Cd-1	2:05⅘	StylishS's'n L'dysLady L'rP'c'ss
Oct 7-69^{1}Hol	1	:30⅗ 1:02 1:34⅘ 2:05⅘	ft	2¼ ▲	2^{0}	2	$2^{1½}$	$2^{1½}$x$9^{9¾}$		DennisJ^{2}	Cd-1	2:07⅗	L'b'rP'cess Zamb'nga L'dysLady
Oct 1-69^{3}Hol	1	:31⅗ 1:05⅗ 1:37⅗ 2:09	ft	1 ▲	2^{0}	1	1½	1^{2}	$1^{1¼}$	DennisJ^{6}	Cd-1	2:09	Sirius L'berPrinc'ss Wal'rAbbey
Sep25-69 Hol	1	:31⅘ 1:05⅗ 1:36⅘ 2:07⅗	ft		2	2	3^{3}	2^{2}	2½	DennisJ^{4}	Qua	2:07⅗	Q'n'sR'n'gade Sirius Seas'nsGift

2 — Odette Adios (2-1)

2:04⅗, Hol, '69 — Driver-Trainer—ROBERT FARRINGTON — Red and Grey

B. m, 5, by Greentree Adios—Odette Hanover. — 1969 2 1 0 0 $1,100
Owner, Farrington Stables, Inc., Richwood, Ohio. — 1968 RACED AS A PACER

Oct20-69^{3}Hol	1	:31⅕ 1:03 1:34⅘ 2:04⅗	ft	6-5 ▲	2^{0}	1	1^{2}	1^{2}	1^{3}	F'gtonR^{4}	Cd-1	2:04⅗	OdetteAdios Sirius TrueChance
Oct11-69^{1}Hol	1	:31⅗ 1:02⅕ 1:33 2:03	ft	3½	7	9	9^{11}	9^{13}	8^{13}	F'r't'nR^{3}	Cd-1	2:05⅗	B'tleLord A.C.'sHope L'b'rGal'n
Oct 6-69 Hol	1	:31 1:02⅕ 1:33⅗ 2:04⅗	ft		1	1	1^{3}	1^{3}	$1^{2½}$	Far'g'nR^{5}	Qua	2:04⅗	Od'teAd's K'yst'eSt'l't D'dyG'ne
Sep29-69 Hol	1	:32⅕ 1:04 1:35⅗ 2:06⅘	ft		1	1	1^{3}	1^{3}	1^{nk}	Far'g'nR^{3}	Qua	2:06⅘	OdetteAdios JohnColby SkyInky

3 — Stylish Season (3-1)

2:05⅖, Hol, '69 — Driver-Trainer—PHIL CORLEY — Red-White-Blue

Br. c, 3, by Seasons Catch—Fashion Deb. — 1969 3 2 0 0 $4,200
Owner, Peter J. Marengo III., Stockton, Calif. — 1968 0 0 0 0 ——

Oct24-69^{6}Hol	1	:29⅗ 1:00⅕ 1:32⅕ 2:02⅕	ft	16	1	3	3^{4}	2^{4}	$4^{7¼}$	CorleyP^{8}	Stk	2:03⅗	A'zinW'lie ArmbroJet Ar'eBl'ze
Oct13-69^{1}Hol	1	:30⅘ 1:02⅗ 1:34⅗ 2:05⅗	ft	6¾	7^{0}	4^{0}	3^{2}	2^{h}	1^{1}	CorleyP^{9}	Cd-1	2:05⅗	StylishS's'n L'dysLady L'rP'c'ss
Oct 1-69^{1}Hol	1	:31⅗ 1:03⅕ 1:35⅘ 2:06⅘	ft	8½	3^{0}	3^{0}	2½	$1^{1½}$	1^{1}	L'd'ciW^{4}	Cd-1	2:06⅘	StylishS's'n Bril'tSp'd Prev'ri'or
Sep25-69 Hol	1	:32⅕ 1:04⅕ 1:35⅕ 2:06	ft		1	1	1^{2}	1^{3}	1^{2}	CorleyP^{2}	Qua	2:06	Styl'hS'son B'k'rStr't L'dOffM'n
Sep19-69 Hol	1	:30⅘ 1:03⅗ 1:34 2:05⅘	ft		x 7	8	8^{16}	8^{15}	8^{14}	Land'ciT^{3}	Qua	2:08⅘	Arm'oInv'ta Z'mb'nga C'n'tC'tch

4 — Cant Catch (12-1)

2:16⅖, B.M, '69 — Driver-Trainer—CHARLES SHORT — White, Green and Gold

Br. m, 4, by Season's Catch—Nip and Tuck. — 1969 11 1 1 0 $1,213
Owner, Harold Rustigan, Los Angeles, Calif. — 1968 3 0 0 0 ——

Oct27-69^{5}Hol	1	:31 1:02⅗ 1:35 2:05⅘	ft	22	1	3	$2^{1½}$x9^{16}		9^{24}	ShortC^{4}	5800	2:10⅘	ShellCloud CleverOhio BillG.
Oct13-69^{1}Hol	1	:30⅘ 1:02⅗ 1:34⅗ 2:05⅗	ft	42	9	8	7^{7}	7^{7}	$7^{7¾}$	ShortC^{10}	Cd-1	2:07	StylishS's'n L'dysLady L'rP'c'ss
Oct 1-69^{1}Hol	1	:31⅗ 1:03⅕ 1:35⅘ 2:06⅘	ft	7½	4	4	5^{5}	7^{7}	$7^{7½}$	ShortC^{2}	Cd-1	2:08⅗	StylishS's'n Bril'tSp'd Prev'ri'or
Sep24-69^{1}Hol	1	:30⅘ 1:03⅗ 1:35⅗ 2:05	ft	27	7	4	2^{1}	2^{3}	2^{7}	ShortC^{5}	Cd-1	2:06⅗	BattleLord CantCatch Redeemer
Sep19-69 Hol	1	:30⅘ 1:03⅗ 1:34 2:05⅘	ft		5	6	$6^{7½}$	4^{7}	3^{4}	ShortC^{7}	Qua	2:06⅗	Arm'oInv'ta Z'mb'nga C'n'tC'tch
Aug18-69^{1}Stk	1	:34⅗ 1:11 1:46⅘ 2:22⅗	ft	3¾	6	6	$6^{3¼}$	$6^{5½}$	$5^{8½}$	ShortC^{3}	Cond	2:24⅗	D'm'nteTorre Quelette Mr.Vict'r

5 — Hasti Maid (8-1)

No Record, '69 — Driver-Trainer—LARRY GREGORY — Grey and Orange

B. f, 3, by Dial—Gayle Hall. — 1969 0 0 0 0 ——
Owner, Robert R. Buckley, Bakersfield, Calif. — 1968 0 0 0 0 ——

Oct16-69 Hol	1	:30⅕ 1:01⅗ 1:33⅗ 2:04⅗	ft		6^{0}	5	$5^{6½}$	$4^{7½}$	$4^{7½}$	Greg'ryL^{3}	Qua	2:06⅕	BakerStr't Royd'nJohn Quelette

6 — Hasti Ax (6-1)

No Record, '69 — Driver-Trainer—PHILIP CONROY — Blue and White

Br. g, 4, by Dial—Chara Hanover. — 1969 3 1 1 1 $990
Owner, Philip Conroy, lessee, San Mateo, Calif. — 1968 3 1 0 1 $124

Oct28-69^{1}Hol	1	:30⅗ 1:02⅗ 1:35⅗ 2:07	ft	9½	3^{0}	1	2^{1}	2½	2½	ConroyP^{8}	Cd-1	2:07⅕	Sirius HastiAx TekeMon
Oct23-69 Hol	1	:31 1:02⅗ 1:34⅘ 2:06⅗	ft		2	2	2^{h}	1^{2}	$1^{¾}$	ConroyP^{2}	Qua	2:06⅗	HastiAx LuringStar SharDee
Jly 15-69^{1}S.R	1	:34⅕ 1:09⅘ 1:44⅘ 2:17⅘	gd	7½	x7	2	$2^{1½}$	$4^{1¼}$	$3^{2¾}$	ConroyP^{4}	Cond	2:18⅗	Br'wnGoBoy Andy'sG'ge HastiAx
Jun25-69^{1}Sol	7 f	:34⅕ 1:08⅗ 1:44 2:03⅗	gd	18	1	1	1^{2}	1½	1no	ConroyP^{4}	Cond	2:03⅗	HastiAx TickTock Com'ncheP'tch
Feb13-69 B.M	1	:33 1:05⅕ 1:39⅘ 2:12⅗	ft		x6	5	5^{20}x5dis		5dis	ConroyP^{7}	Qua		Can'tC'tch C'm'cheP'tch M'sP'lly
Oct 4-68 Edm	1	:35 1:10 1:46⅘ 2:19⅘	m		6x	5	3	3^{4}	4^{11}	Gr'h'mRL^{4}	Qua	2:22	Nipp'rDir't Dir'tWay Princ'sB'g'n

7 — True Chance (8-1)

No Record, '69 — Driver-Trainer—EDWARD COBB — Blue and White

B. g, 4, by Amortizor—Fair Minnie. — 1969 6 0 0 1 $464
Owner, Robert J. McAllister (Lessee), Wantagh, N. Y. — 1968 RACED AS PACER

Oct28-69^{1}Hol	1	:30⅗ 1:02⅗ 1:35⅗ 2:07	ft	11	x10	10	10	10dis	10dis	CobbE^{9}	Cd-1		Sirius HastiAx TekeMon
Oct20-69^{3}Hol	1	:31⅕ 1:03 1:34⅘ 2:04⅗	ft	12	3	3	$3^{2½}$	3^{3}	3^{7}	CobbE^{1}	Cd-1	2:05⅘	OdetteAdios Sirius TrueChance
Oct13-69^{1}Hol	1	:30⅘ 1:02⅗ 1:34⅗ 2:05⅗	ft	9¾	8	7	$5^{4½}$x10^{16}		10dis	CobbE^{5}	Cd-1		StylishS's'n L'dysLady L'rP'c'ss
Oct 7-69^{1}Hol	1	:30⅗ 1:02 1:34⅘ 2:05⅘	ft	18	10	8	6^{5}	$9^{9½}$	5^{5}	CobbE^{8}	Cd-1	2:06⅘	L'b'rP'cess Zamb'nga L'dysLady
Sep29-69 Fhld	1	:31⅕ 1:03⅕ 1:35 2:07	ft	65	7	7	5x	6dis	6dis	McA'rR^{4}	Cond		PalmTr'dy AliceGr'y M'y'rMy'rs
Sep22-69 Fhld	1	:31 1:03⅘ 1:35⅕ 2:07⅘	ft	27	5	5	5	$5^{5¾}$	5^{12}	L'tm'nP^{6}	Cond	2:10⅕	PalmTr'dy M'y'rMy'rs AliceGr'y

8 — Prevaricator (20-1)

2:07⅕, Lex, '69 — Driver-Trainer—JOHN BENNETT — Red and White

Br. h, 6, by Galophone—Mary Main. — 1969 20 5 1 4 $2,398
Owner, Marian T. Brewer, Lexington, Ky. — 1968 RACED AS A PACER

Oct21-69^{1}Hol	1	:31⅗ 1:04⅘ 1:36⅗ 2:06⅘	ft	33	7	5^{0}	4^{3}	$5^{6½}$	$6^{6¾}$	WebbJH^{8}	Cd-1	2:08⅕	L'b'rGall'n CarolHoot L'dysLady
Oct11-69^{1}Hol	1	:31⅗ 1:02⅕ 1:33 2:03	ft	27	9	10	10^{12}	7^{10}	$7^{9¼}$	WebbJH^{4}	Cd-1	2:04⅘	B'tleLord A.C.'sHope L'b'rGal'n
Oct 1-69^{1}Hol	1	:31⅗ 1:03⅕ 1:35⅘ 2:06⅘	ft	21	8	8	8^{8}	$6^{5½}$	3^{3}	WebbJH^{5}	Cd-1	2:07⅕	StylishS's'n Bril'tSp'd Prev'ri'or
Sep29-69^{5}Hol	1	:30⅘ 1:01⅗ 1:33⅗ 2:03⅘	ft	44	7	7	8^{12}	8^{15}	$8^{8¾}$	WebbJH^{1}	7000	2:05⅗	JeanDaily CrownSong SmartSon
Sep24-69^{1}Hol	1	:30⅘ 1:03⅗ 1:35⅗ 2:05	ft	11	8	9	$9^{7½}$	$7^{9½}$	$4^{9¼}$	Benn'ttJ^{1}	Cd-1	2:06⅘	BattleLord CantCatch Redeemer
Sep 1-69 LouD	1	:31⅗ 1:04⅗ 1:37⅗ 2:10⅗	ft	2¼	5	4	5	$5^{1¾}$	1^{nk}	Benn'tJ^{1}	Cond	2:10⅗	Prevaric't'r D'styKing Ph't'mKid

9 — Ink (12-1)

2:10, B.M, '69 — Driver—CLYDE TISHER. Trainer, Kevin Tisher — All Blue

Ch. g, 5, by Hoot Mon—Chata. — 1969 9 1 1 1 $1,503
Owner, Clyde O. Tisher, Sherman Oaks, Calif. — 1968 5 1 0 1 $310

Oct20-69^{3}Hol	1	:31⅕ 1:03 1:34⅘ 2:04⅗	ft	14	4	4	$4^{5½}$	4^{7}	5^{14}	TisherC^{2}	Cd-1	2:07⅕	OdetteAdios Sirius TrueChance
Oct 1-69^{3}Hol	1	:31⅗ 1:05⅗ 1:37⅗ 2:09	ft	10	7^{0}	4	$7^{6½}$	6^{10}	$4^{4¼}$	TisherC^{8}	Cd-1	2:09⅘	Sirius L'berPrinc'ss Wal'rAbbey
Feb28-69^{3}B.M	1	:33⅕ 1:05⅘ 1:39⅘ 2:12⅕	sy	7¼	3	2x	6^{22}	6dis	6dis	TisherC^{4}	Cond		Sabetha VicArden PepperSteve
Feb11-69^{3}B.M	1	:33 1:06⅗ 1:39⅘ 2:12⅗	sy	5¾	3	1	$1^{1½}$	1^{2}	2¾	TisherC^{3}	Cond	2:13	SeasonsGift Ink Sabetha
Feb 6-69^{3}B.M	1	:32⅘ 1:04⅘ 1:38⅗ 2:11	sl	2¾	6	6	$6^{4¼}$	2^{5}	4^{7}x	TisherC^{4}	Cond	2:12⅗	CheerForMe SeasonsGift Sab'tha
Jan31-69^{3}B.M	1	:32⅗ 1:05 1:37⅕ 2:10	ft	5¼	2	2	$2^{1½}$	2^{h}	$1^{1½}$	TisherC^{1}	Cond	2:10	Ink Redeemer OurRoger

10 — Redeemer (15-1)

2:17⅘, B.M, '69 — Driver-Trainer—ANDY VAN ZANTEN — Pink and White

Br. m, 4, by Lumber Boy—Frosty Lady. — 1969 13 1 4 2 $2,355
Owner, Andy Van Zanten, Hanford, Calif. — 1968 2 0 0 1 $280

Oct28-69^{1}Hol	1	:30⅗ 1:02⅗ 1:35⅗ 2:07	ft	34	5	5	$7^{5½}$	$7^{7½}$	5^{2}	V'nZ'nA^{10}	Cd-1	2:07⅗	Sirius HastiAx TekeMon
Oct20-69^{3}Hol	1	:31⅕ 1:03 1:34⅘ 2:04⅗	ft	23	5	5	$5^{7½}$	$5^{7½}$	4^{11}	V'nZ'nA^{5}	Cd-1	2:06⅗	OdetteAdios Sirius TrueChance
Oct 7-69^{1}Hol	1	:30⅗ 1:02 1:34⅘ 2:05⅘	ft	5	9	9	7^{7}	10^{12}	6^{8}	O'Bri'nJ^{5}	Cd-1	2:07⅗	L'b'rP'cess Zamb'nga L'dysLady
Oct 1-69^{1}Hol	1	:31⅗ 1:03⅕ 1:35⅘ 2:06⅘	ft	12	6^{0}	5^{0}	4^{3}	$4^{4½}$	$8^{9¼}$	V'nZ'nA^{9}	Cd-1	2:08⅗	StylishS's'n Bril'tSp'd Prev'ri'or
Sep24-69^{1}Hol	1	:30⅘ 1:03⅗ 1:35⅗ 2:05	ft	12	4	7	$7^{4½}$	5^{7}	3^{8}	V'nZ'nA^{3}	Cd-1	2:06⅗	BattleLord CantCatch Redeemer

Declared—Ambassador and Dutch Special.

HEAD NUMBER COLOR: WHITE—BLACK NUMBER

ONE MILE PACE 4th RACE - - EXACTA PURSE $2,400

CLAIMING. ALL AGES. TOP CLAIMING PRICE, $6,000.

ASK FOR HORSE BY PROGRAM NUMBER

1 — 6-1
$4,000 2:06, H.P, '69 Driver—JAMES CURRAN. Trainer, John Curran Grey-Orange-Gold
Directnik B. g, 6, by Direct Spangler—Noodnik.
Owner, George N. Lewis, Detroit, Mich. 1969 31 7 7 1 $11,300 / 1968 34 3 2 6 $6,684
Oct29-69²Hol 1 1/16 :31 1:03⅗1:36⅖2:13⅗ft 3½ 9 7 33½ 55½ 65¼ Curr'nJa⁹ 4000 2:14⅘ RicksRoyal Jigsaw ToothPick
Oct20-69⁷Hol 1 :30 1:01 1:33⅖2:04 ft 6¼ 6 5⁰ 32½ 32½ 43 Curr'nJa² 5000 2:04⅗ BoyTrust P'lyJinks Y'keeMadam
Oct 1-69 H.P 1 :31⅗1:05⅗1:36 2:07 ft 8-5 ▲ 8 8 3⁰ 2½ 11¾ C'rr'nJa⁴ 4500 2:07 Directnik MikeAstra DaringDan
Sep25-69 H.P 1 :30⅗1:03⅗1:34⅖2:05⅗ft 2¼ ▲ 6 6 5⁰ 44½ 24 C'rr'nJa⁵ 4500 2:06⅗ M'nysFirst Directnik Roy'lRob't
Sep19-69 H.P 1 :31 1:04⅗1:35⅗2:06⅗ft 3-2 ▲ 5 5 4⁰ 2¹ 1¹ C'rr'nJa⁴ 4000 2:06⅗ Directnik KeyMaid DarkDemon
Sep11-69 H.P 1 :31 1:03 1:34⅗2:06 ft 6-5 ▲ 7 7 7 41¼ 12½ C'rr'nJa⁴ 3500 2:06 Directnik DarkDemon SunChief

2 — 15-1
$4,000 2:05⅘, Was, '69 Driver-Trainer—WAYNE SHORT Purple and White
X Pert Bert B. h, 7, by Walter McKlyo—Judy Jewell.
Owner, Graphique Stables, Chicago, Ill. 1969 28 5 1 3 $8.650 / 1968 4 0 0 0 $180
Oct28-69⁶Hol 1 :30⅗1:01⅗1:33 2:03⅗ft 16 6 8 8¹² 8¹⁶ 8dis ShortW⁵ 4000 A'roH'sky T'nM'rt'l Midn'tBr'ie
Oct 6-69 Was 1 :30⅗1:06⅗1:40⅗2:11⅓sy 5½ 6 5⁰ 4 52½ 56¾ ShortW⁴ 5000 2:12⅘ Invad'rWick Flam'gP'r P'ryWin
Sep27-69 Was 1 :31 1:03 1:36⅓2:05⅗ft 10 4 3 3 1² 1⁵ ShortW¹ 4000 2:05⅘ XPertBert BanjoMite S'rTraffic
Sep18-69 Was 1 :31⅓1:04⅗1:37 2:08 ft 9 6 8 9 75½ 6³ ShortW⁴ 4000 2:08⅗ HighReg'd Sil'rTraffic Shady'le
Aug 7-69 Spk 1 :30⅓1:02⅗1:33⅖2:04⅗ft 13 9 8 7 7¹⁸ 7¹⁵ ShortW⁹ 4000 2:07⅗ W'kC'nsel KarenG'y MaryTry'n
Jly 29-69 Spk 1 :31⅓1:05 1:35⅗2:07 ft 10 9x 9 9 9dis 9dis ShortW⁸ 4000 DukeGa'n HighReg'd MaryTry'n

3 — 9-2
$5,000 2:08⅕, Y.R, '69 Driver-Trainer—EDWARD COBB Blue and White
Logan Chance B. g, 4, by Adios Butler—Fai. Value.
Owner, Seal Stable, Garden City, N.Y. 1969 9 1 0 2 $2,712 / 1968 13 2 3 4 $5,070
Oct28-69⁶Hol 1 :30⅗1:01⅗1:33 2:03⅗ft 10 7 3 44½ 32½ 5³ CobbE⁷ 5000 2:04⅓ A'roH'sky T'nM'rt'l Midn'tBr'ie
Oct20-69 Hol 1 :30⅗1:02⅗1:35⅖2:06⅗ft 2 1 1½ 1¹ 2¹ CobbE⁵ Qua 2:06⅗ Pep'rAll Log'nChance SilverJac
Oct16-69 Hol 1 :30⅗1:01⅓1:33 2:04⅗ft 3 3 23½ 3⁴ 32½ CobbE³ Qua 2:05 NuJean M'd'wH'ther L'nChance
Mar22-69 R.R 1 :31 1:05 1:36⅗2:09 ft x7x 7x 6 6¹⁰ 67¾ CobbE³ Qua 2:10⅗ H'n'lsAbe Ad'r'sCl'p'r E'm'stQ'n
Mar11-69 R.R 1 :32⅗1:05⅗1:38⅖2:12⅗ft x7x 7x 7 43½ 4³ CobbE⁴ Qua 2:13⅓ S't'rFr'b'l M'st'rst'k M'tiniR'd'y
Mar 7-69 R.R 1 :30⅗1:04⅓1:34⅖2:06⅗ft 22 x7 5x 8 8¹² 87½ CobbE⁶ Cond 2:08⅗ Ch'mpR'b'w ColbyD'r's B'yl'rH'r

4 — 7-2
$4,800 2:03, Hol, '69 Driver-Trainer—JACK SHERREN Green, White and Black
Diamond Princess B. m, 7, by Lumber Boy—Shafter Queen.
Owner, Charles Fusco, Hawthorne, Calif. 1969 28 5 2 8 $5,914 / 1968 22 1 0 1 $1,578
Oct28-69⁶Hol 1 :30⅗1:01⅗1:33 2:03⅗ft 2½ 3 4 6⁷ 65½ 42½ Sherr'nJ² 4800 2:04⅓ A'roH'sky T'nM'rt'l Midn'tBr'ie
Oct17-69⁴Hol 1 :29⅗1:00⅗1:31⅖2:03 ft 5¼ 4 5 5⁵ 35½ 1¹ Sherr'nJ⁵ 4800 2:03 D'm'dPr'c's Mr.EdDir't G'meP'k
Oct 9-69⁵Hol 1 :30⅗1:01⅗1:33⅖2:04⅓ft 8½ 7 7 77½ 8⁸ 6³ Sherr'nJ³ 6000 2:04⅗ Dick'sDil'ma Fly'gD'ch'n Dante
Oct 3-69³Hol 1 :31⅗1:03 1:34 2:04 ft 8½ 3 6 4³ 4³ 11¼ Sherr'nJ³ 4800 2:04 D'm'dP'c's Dr'ndv'lle W'wK'thie
Sep26-69³Hol 1 :31 1:03⅓1:34⅖2:05⅗ft 3-2 ▲ 3 3 4⁴ ix65½ 33¾ Bail'yW⁴ c3600 2:06⅗ R'nieJ'yce Mr.Bissonay D'dP'c'ss
Sep23-69³Hol 1 :31 1:02⅓1:33⅖2:03⅗ft 16 3 2 1¹ 21½ 3⁴ BaileyW³ Cd-1 2:04⅗ S'tEst'heA. S'k'yBl'ze D'ndP'c's

5 — 3-1
$6,000 2:08⅕, Was, '69 Driver-Trainer—ORLANDO LARSON Gold-Green-Red
Jest Less Br. g, 3, by Don Adios—Maud Jester.
Owner, Eldon La Monte, Kirkland, Ill. 1969 45 7 7 9 $9,723 / 1968 27 5 9 3 $4,272
Oct28-69⁷Hol 1 :29⅗1:01⅗1:33⅖2:02⅗ft 13 2 3 4⁴ 54½ 74¾ Wilb'nT⁶ 11250 2:03⅗ Andy'sDon BoyTrust SatanTass
Oct23-69⁶Hol 1 :29⅗1:01⅗1:33 2:03⅗ft 9½ 3 4 2¹ 1² 52¼ Wilb'nT¹ 9000 2:04 Por'tiP'de RuthsS'p'r S'tEst'eA.
Oct17-69⁹Hol 1 :29⅗1:00⅗1:32⅖2:01⅗ft 18 1 2 2² 45½ 5⁸ Wilb'nT⁷ 7500 2:02⅘ B'kAmigo Car'l'sJoe D'k'sDil'ma
Oct10-69⁶Hol 1 :30⅗1:01 1:32⅖2:02⅓ft 60 10 10 88½10¹²10¹⁶ T'ppR¹⁰ 15000 2:05⅗ B'mb'rBay R'pertH. StarCarrier
Oct 3-69⁵Hol 1 1/16 :30⅗1:02⅗1:33 2:10⅗ft 38 6 7 76½ 7¹² 7¹⁴ TrippR⁶ Cd-2 2:14 W'yH'v'rN. P'p'rEd'e R'lByeBye
Sep27-69⁴Hol 1 :30⅗1:00⅗1:31⅓2:01⅓ft 58 6 6 6¹⁰ 65½ 4¹⁰ TrippR² Cd-3 2:03⅗ D'yH.F'bes Arl'eD'es M'rieSc't'n

6 — 20-1
$4,000 No Record. '69 Driver-Trainer—MARC GRENIER Red and White
Mount Eden B. g, 7, by Morris Eden—Queen Rani.
Owner, M. & A. Stable, Inc., Chicago, Ill. 1969 2 0 0 0 $160 / 1968 22 4 3 3 $6.896
Oct27-69²Hol 1 :30⅓1:03 1:34⅖2:05 ft 15 5 5 54½ 9¹² 47½ Gr'n'rM⁴ 3000 2:06⅗ Munchkin Abbeio RussetsBoy
Oct10-69²Hol 1 :31⅗1:02⅓1:33⅖2:04⅗ft 7¾ 1 2 21½ 8¹² 9²⁰ Greni'rJ¹ 3500 2:09⅗ H'r'uG'ne B'n'yB'k'ne R'm'deP's
Oct 2-69 Hol 1 :31⅗1:03⅗1:35⅓2:06⅗ft 3 1 1¹ 1½ 31½ GrenierJ⁷ Qua 2:07⅓ ArmbroJ'k Ir'hByeBye M'ntEd'n
Sep30-68⁹Hol 1 :30⅓1:03 1:34⅖2:04⅗ft 24 9 9 9¹² 9¹¹ 9⁹ GrenierJ⁶ 7000 2:06⅗ H'kTheD'ber St'myByrd F'stC'ig
Jly 6-68 Spk 1 :30 1:02 1:32⅗2:02⅗ft 38 6 6 6 88½ 8⁹ GrenierJ⁶ Cond 2:04⅗ Jereo CapeKennedy CarlessJoe
Jun28-68 Spk 1 :31⅗1:04⅗1:35⅖2:05⅗ft 15 9 7⁰ 7 6⁴ 5⁵ GrenierJ⁸ Cond 2:06⅗ B'ttleshipN. Q'n'sCadet JetC'sel

7 — 12-1
$4,000 2:09⅗, W.R, '69 Driver—ROBERT WILLIAMS. Trainer, M. Cunningham Purple and White
J. R. Mac B. g, 5, by Mac Wil—Ima Canuck.
Owner, Pearl Drake, Buckeye, Ariz. 1969 23 3 3 3 $3,678 / 1968 37 6 6 6 $5.565
Oct24-69¹Hol 1 :30 1:01⅓1:32⅖2:04 ft 10 2 4 33½ 3⁵ 55½ LaC'steL² 3500 2:05 F'r'gnP'rt R'kSp'gsBob BigD'vid
Oct16-69⁹Hol 1 :29 :59 1:30⅗2:01 ft 36 2 2 2³ 5⁷ 8¹⁰ LaC'teL¹ Cd-1 2:03⅓ BeagleBoy MiMargarita MaiTai
Oct10-69²Hol 1 :31⅗1:02⅓1:33⅖2:04⅗ft 27 9⁰ 9 78½ 9¹² 89¾ LaC'steL⁸ 3500 2:06⅗ H'r'uG'ne B'n'yB'k'ne R'm'deP's
Oct 3-69³Hol 1 :31⅗1:03 1:34 2:04 ft 22 9 8 89½ 89½ 77½ B'rkn'rG⁸ 4000 2:05⅗ D'm'dP'c's Dr'ndv'lle W'wK'thie
Sep27-69³Hol 1 :30⅗1:01⅗1:33⅖2:04⅗ft 18 4 6 5⁹ 53½ 3³ Berkn'rG² 3500 2:05⅗ RicksRoyal Shotgun J.R.Mac
Sep20-69¹Pom 1 :32 1:05 1:38⅗2:10⅗ft 21 1 2 2½ 2h 65½ B'rkn'rG⁵ Cond 2:11⅗ WeeJudyD. Sorrowful Gener'lJoy

8 — 6-1
$4,000 2:07, B.M, '69 Driver-Trainer—HAROLD WILSON Green and White
Hobbys Changer Br. g, 7, by Record Changer—Hobby Siskiyou.
Owner, H. J. & W. I. Wilson, Smith Center, Kansas. 1969 22 1 3 3 $3,579 / 1968 30 3 2 5 $5,316
Oct27-69⁶Hol 1 :31⅓1:02⅗1:33⅖2:04 ft 19 8 8 7⁸ 6⁸ 73¾ WilsonH⁷ 5000 2:04⅘ R'ym'dePris M'ksBoy B'b'rLaird
Oct16-69⁷Hol 1 :31 1:02 1:32⅗2:01⅗ft 52 6 6 88½ 7⁸ 89½ WilsonH⁵ 6000 2:03⅗ LandFr'ght B.D.Song Sorrowful
Oct 9-69⁷Hol 1 :31⅗1:02⅗1:32⅖2:02⅗ft 65 5 6 67½ 5⁷ 77¼ WilsonH⁵ 7500 2:04 EasterLind JoeParker RedEblis
Oct 1-69⁶Hol 1 :29⅗1:00⅓1:30⅖2:00⅗ft 73 7 7 8¹⁰ 9¹³ 9¹⁸ WilsonH² Cd-3 2:04⅗ Authentic ByeByeRoger LittleAl
Sep 2-69 ScD 1 :29⅗1:04⅗1:36⅖2:07⅗ft 3 5 6⁰ 5⁰ 63½ 2nk WilsonH² Cond 2:07⅗ BenChuck H'ysCh'g'r Tr'eD'ch's
Aug22-69 ScD 1 :31⅓1:03⅗1:35⅗2:05 ft 31 5 6 6⁰ 6⁵ 8⁷ WilsonH³ Cond 2:06⅗ F'sh'nGun Wing'tJill Tob'oR'der

9 — 8-1
$4,800 2:05⅕, Hol. '69 Driver-Trainer—JOE MARSH, JR. Grey, Red and Blue
Royal Bell B. m, 5, by Royal Blackstone—Genibel.
Owner, Louis Huegel & John S. Serra, Norwood Park, Ill. 1969 9 1 0 2 $1,727 / 1968 10 1 3 2 $1,337
Oct27-69⁴Hol 1 :29⅗1:02⅓1:34⅗2:03⅗ft 10 1 1 1² 2² 7¹³ M'shJJr⁵ Cd-1 2:06⅗ BigTime St'v'nAdios F'klinJ'w'll
Oct16-69²Hol 1 :30⅗1:02⅓1:33⅗2:03⅗ft 8¼ 1 1 11½ 1½ 59½ M'shJJr³ Cd-1 2:05⅗ Dia'tePhil ChillR'g'r AppleCus'r
Oct 1-69⁵Hol 1 :30⅗1:01⅗1:34 2:05 ft 4¾ 1 1 1½ 1² 32¼ M'shJJr¹ Cd-1 2:05⅗ BlazingRed BullHill RoyalBell
Sep26-69¹Hol 1 :30⅗1:02⅓1:34⅗2:05⅓ft 8 2 2 2h 13½ 1² M'shJJr⁷ Cd-1 2:05⅓ R'y'lBell G'ldWat'r Diam'ntePhil
Sep17-69 Was 1 :30 1:02⅓1:35 2:05⅗ft 18 1 1 1 2¹ 34¾ ShortW¹ Cond 2:06⅗ Pip'gTimes Gr'dEnt'g'ty R'y'lB'l
Sep 4-69 Was 1 :32 1:04 1:37⅓2:10⅗sy 25 x9 9 8 8²⁰x7dis C't'ldoH⁴ Cond McCl'nsM'sie DuMe'ns DinaH'v'r

10 — 9-2
$4,000 2:05, Was, '69 Driver-Trainer—MICHAEL JONES Red and White
Midnight Brownie Br. g, 7, by Huldah's Chief—Midnight Miss.
Owner, Clinton L. Jones, Oak View, Calif. 1969 31 1 3 6 $9,868 / 1968 36 4 6 6 $12,435
Oct28-69⁶Hol 1 :30⅗1:01⅗1:33 2:03⅗ft 4½ 4 6 56½ 5⁴ 31½ JonesM¹ 4000 2:04 A'roH'sky T'nM'rt'l Midn'tBr'ie
Oct17-69⁴Hol 1 :29⅗1:00⅗1:31⅖2:03 ft 10 9 9 9¹¹ 7¹² 42½ JonesM⁷ 4000 2:03⅗ D'm'dPr'c's Mr.EdDir't G'meP'k
Oct11-69²Hol 1 :29⅗1:00⅓1:33 2:03⅗ft 14 6 6 79½ 6⁸ 63¾ JonesM² 5000 2:04 TownMart'l Renard CarelessJoe
Oct 6-69⁹Hol 1 :30⅗1:01 1:32⅖2:03⅗ft 24 1 1 1¹ 1¹ 7⁶ JonesM⁵ 5000 2:04⅗ Lavina CarelessJoe TopGunner
Sep30-69⁹Hol 1 :31⅗1:04⅗1:36⅖2:05⅗ft 9½ 2 3 44½ 3⁵ 4⁵ JonesM¹ 5000 2:06⅗ Sorrowful HappyHal Lavina
Aug26-69⁶Spk 1 :32⅓1:05⅓1:38⅖2:08⅗ft 4¾ 6 6 6 5⁵ 42½ JonesM⁴ 6000 2:09⅓ Skinan ByeByeG'n'l EveningSky

Declared—Ricks Royal.

HEAD NUMBER COLOR: YELLOW—BLACK NUMBER

ONE MILE TROT **5th RACE** **PURSE $3,000**

CLAIMING. ALL AGES. NON-WINNERS OF FOUR RACES SINCE SEPTEMBER 22. TOP CLAIMING PRICE, $7,200.

ASK FOR HORSE BY PROGRAM NUMBER

1 — 10-1

$5,000 2:08, H.P, '69 Driver-Trainer—DONALD McILMURRAY Blue and Grey
Bill G. B. g, 10, by Florican—Bomb Star. 1969 24 3 7 8 $7,520
Owner, D. McIlmurray & J. C. Dillon, Detroit, Mich. 1968 9 0 1 1 $837
Oct27-695Hol 1 :31 1:02⅗1:35 2:05⅘ft 9½ 4 1 1½ 1²x 3²½ McIl'yD5 4000 2:06⅗ ShellCloud CleverOhio BillG.
Oct20-695Hol 1 :31⅗1:03⅗1:36 2:06⅘ft 15 3 30 2½ 2½ 6³ McIl'yD3 4000 2:07⅕ CleverOhio DevedasBoy AirShow
Oct13-697Hol 1 :30⅘1:01⅗1:32⅖2:04⅘ft 5½ 3 3 2²½ 2³ 6⁵¼ McIl'yD5 3500 2:05⅗ Tarp'tM't BillsSn'k'ms ShellCl'd
Oct 6-695Hol 1 :30⅗1:03⅕1:36⅖2:06⅘ft 9½ 1 1 1½ 1¹ 6⁵¼ McIl'yD7 6000 2:07⅘ Glid'nH'n'r His'yM'k'r T'rp'tM't
Sep30-695Hol 1 :31 1:03⅗1:36⅗2:06⅘ft 3½ 3 40 3¹½ 3²½ 2¹½ McIl'yD3 4000 2:07⅕ GliddenHan'er BillG. CleverOhio
Sep25-691Hol 1 :31⅗1:03⅗1:36½2:06⅘ft 4¾ 10 2 3¹ 2½ 3²¼ McIl'yD9 4000 2:07⅕ Glidd'nHan'r MySpecialty BillG.

2 — 6-1

$6,250 2:05⅘, Hol, '69 Driver-Trainer—DOUG ACKERMAN Blue and Grey
Shell Cloud Gr. g, 4, by Storm Cloud—Shelley Day. 1969 29 4 5 7 $7,427
Owner, Mrs. R. C. Ackerman, Galien, Mich. 1968 6 0 2 1 $735
Oct27-695Hol 1 :31 1:02⅗1:35 2:05⅘ft 6½ 2 2 3² 2² 1nk Ac'm'nD3 5000 2:05⅘ ShellCloud CleverOhio BillG.
Oct20-695Hol 1 :31⅗1:03⅗1:36 2:06⅘ft 5 5 1 1½ 1½ 4²¼ Ac'm'nD2 5000 2:07 CleverOhio DevedasBoy AirShow
Oct13-697Hol 1 :30⅘1:01⅗1:32⅖2:04⅘ft 16 9 9 9¹¹ 6⁹ 3²¼ Ac'm'nD9 5000 2:05⅕ Tarp'tM't BillsSn'k'ms ShellCl'd
Sep30-695Hol 1 :31 1:03⅗1:36⅗2:06⅘ft 28 7 7 8⁷½ 7⁸½ 6⁴¾ Ac'm'nD7 5625 2:07⅘ GliddenHan'er BillG. CleverOhio
Sep25-691Hol 1 :31⅗1:03⅗1:36½2:06⅘ft 32 7 6 4¹½ 5³½ 5³ Acker'nD8 5000 2:07⅕ Glidd'nHan'r MySpecialty BillG.
Jly 7-69 Nor 1 :32⅗1:05⅕1:37½2:09 ft 8½ 50 40 30 3¹½ 7⁷ HallD6 Hcp 2:10⅗ DutchDil'rd C'rlG'llon BaronCall

3 — 12-1

$5,000 2:06⅕, Y.R, '69 Driver-Trainer—GEORGE BERKNER Black and Red
Joe Brooke B. g, 7, by Way Yonder—Singing Brooke. 1969 16 2 1 1 $4,424
Owner, James K. Wetzel, Rancho Santa Fe, Calif. 1968 36 2 4 8 $7,840
Oct14-69 R.R 1 :31⅗1:04⅕1:37 2:08⅗ft 19 8 8 70 x7⁴¾ 7⁹½ S'M'aM7 Cond 2:10⅘ Atl'cFrost L'yCarlt'n Vic'rRod'y
Sep30-69 R.R 1 :31⅗1:04⅕1:36⅗2:08⅗ft 32 7 7 6 4⁵½ 4³ Mat'ciE8 Cond 2:09⅗ BiloxiH'v'r C'baLibre Vic'rRod'y
Sep23-69 R.R 1 :31⅗1:04⅗1:36⅗2:07⅗ft 8½ 7 7 7 6⁶½ 5⁶¾ Mat'ciE7 Cond 2:09⅕ Sm'keH'se CornMaid Vic'rRod'y
Aug27-69 R.R 1 :31⅗1:03⅗1:35⅗2:07⅗ft 4½ 5 4 40 6⁶ 8¹⁰ S'M'aM2 Cond 2:10 Corn'hM'n P'teSidn'y Nov'lBl'ze
Aug12-69 R.R 1 :32⅗1:05⅗1:36⅗2:07⅗ft 2½ ▲x7 7 6 6⁸¼ 6¹¹ S'M'aM1 Cond 2:10⅗ Mark'dP'k LittleSid Deb'teH'v'r
Jly 29-69 R.R 1 :32⅗1:04⅕1:35⅗2:08 gd 13 7 7 7 6⁴ 4²½ S'M'aM7 Cond 2:08⅗ Deb'teH'v'r LittleSid Ch'tteH'v'r

4 — 8-1

$5,000 2:04⅗, Hol, '69 Driver-Trainer—JACK SHERREN Green, White and Black
Tarport Mart Br. g, 9, by Thorpe Hanover—Meadow Lass. Owner, 1969 7 1 0 3 $2,306
Ann Sherren, Judy Carlsberg & Regina Marsh, Van Nuys, Calif. 1968 32 2 3 6 $7,030
Oct29-693Hol 1 :30⅕1:00⅗1:32⅖2:02⅕ft 33 20 20 2¹½ 9¹⁹ 9²⁴ Sher'nJ7 Cd-3 2:07⅕ T'nyVict'y T'rn'gPoint St'myLad
Oct21-691Hol 1 :31⅗1:04⅗1:36⅗2:06⅘ft 7½ 10 1 1h 1² 4²½ Sher'nJ6 Cd-1 2:07⅗ L'b'rGall'n CarolHoot L'dysLady
Oct13-697Hol 1 :30⅘1:01⅗1:32⅖2:04⅘ft 3¾ 1 1 1²½ 1³ 1nk Sherr'nJ8 4000 2:04⅘ Tarp'tM't BillsSn'k'ms ShellCl'd
Oct 6-695Hol 1 :30⅗1:03⅕1:36⅖2:06⅘ft 9½ 50 40 43 2¹ 3³¼ Sherr'nJ6 6000 2:07⅕ Glid'nH'n'r His'yM'k'r T'rp'tM't
Sep30-691Hol 1 :30⅕1:00⅗1:32 2:03⅕ft 41 1 1 1h 1½ 7¹¹ Sher'nJ8 Cd-1 2:05⅘ Fly'gTrip A.C.'sH'pe L'm'rGal'n
Sep26-692Pom 1 :32 1:04⅕1:37 2:09⅗ft 7-5 ▲ 2 4 4²½ 4⁵½ 3⁹ Sher'nJ1 Cond 2:11⅗ Br'veN'wp't VicArd'n T'rp'tM'rt

5 — 6-1

$5,000 2:11⅘, Pln, '69 Driver—ROBERT WILLIAMS. Trainer, T. Bartone Purple and White
Vic Arden Br. g, 7, by Jamie—Quick Victory. Owner, 1969 25 5 5 6 $6,899
Owner, Johnson-Martucci & T. Bartone, San Pedro, Calif. 1968 37 0 3 7 $6,901
Oct29-695Hol 1 :32⅗1:03⅕1:34½2:05⅕ft 46 x10 10 10¹⁹ 8¹⁶ 6⁶¾ B'rt'neT4 7000 2:06⅗ D'ttiesBoy Glid'nHan'r Cr'nSong
Oct20-695Hol 1 :31⅗1:03⅗1:36 2:06⅘ft 11 10 4 5⁵ 5⁴ 5²½ Wish'rdJ4 4000 2:07 CleverOhio DevedasBoy AirShow
Oct15-693Hol 1 :31 1:02⅗1:35⅗2:05⅗ft 5¾ 2 3 3²½ 3²¼ 4¾ O'Bri'nJ2 5000 2:05⅗ Glid'nH'n'r Kni'tValor Cl'v'rOhio
Oct 6-695Hol 1 :30⅗1:03⅕1:36⅖2:06⅘ft 8½ 30 20 2¹½ 5⁴½ 7⁶¼ Wish'dJ5 6000 2:08 Glid'nH'n'r His'yM'k'r T'rp'tM't
Sep29-695Hol 1 :30⅗1:01⅗1:33⅗2:03⅘ft 18 6 6 6⁹½ 7¹² 7⁶¾ Wish'rdJ4 8000 2:05 JeanDaily CrownSong SmartSon
Sep26-692Pom 1 :32 1:04⅕1:37 2:09⅗ft 4 3 3 3² 2⁴ 2⁹ Wish'dJ3 Cond 2:11⅗ Br'veN'wp't VicArd'n T'rp'tM'rt

6 — 4-1

$5,000 2:07, H.P, '69 Driver—JAMES CURRAN. Trainer, John Curran Grey-Orange-Gold
Devedas Boy B. g, 6, by Elby Hanover—Deveda. 1969 23 2 4 0 $6,438
Owner, John J. Curran, Jackson, Mich. 1968 27 3 1 3 $7,071
Oct20-695Hol 1 :31⅗1:03⅗1:36 2:06⅘ft 3½ 8 70 6⁵½ 6⁶ 2¹ Curr'nJa7 4000 2:06⅘ CleverOhio DevedasBoy AirShow
Sep30-69 H.P 1 :32⅗1:05⅗1:36⅗2:08 ft 2 ▲ 4 7 6 5³¾ 2nk C'rr'nJa7 4500 2:08 PicksC'l'te Dev'd'sB'y P'rlsChip
Sep22-69 H.P 1 :31⅕1:04⅗1:35⅗2:07⅘ft 6-5 ▲ 40 40 40 3³¾ 4¹½ C'rr'nJa7 4500 2:08 P'rlsChip P'ksC'l'te K'n'lw'dB'le
Sep15-69 H.P 1 :31⅗1:03⅗1:35 2:07 ft 4 6 6 40 2³ 1¹½ C'rr'nJa7 Cond 2:07 D'v'd'sB'y M'g'tAd's F'yL'tleS'g
Sep 5-69 H.P 1 :31⅗1:06 1:36⅗2:07⅗ft 4½ 3 4 40 4¹¾ 4⁴½ C'rr'nJa1 5000 2:08⅕ ChrisDares R'thmVolo L'ckyS'm
Aug19-69 H.P 1 :32 1:06 1:37⅗2:08⅗ft 3 x7x 5x 5 6⁵ 7⁸¼ C'rr'nJa4 Cond 2:10 Sp'c'lG. Eg'pt'nC's'd'r Arb'rW'y

7 — 9-2

$6,000 2:08⅗, B.M, '69 Driver-Trainer—LLOYD DAULTON Blue and Gold
Kelly's Mail Ch. g, 7, by Greentree Adios—Love Letters. 1969 15 3 4 2 $8,916
Owner, Kelly Katona, Milan, Mich. 1968 12 2 2 3 $3,343
Oct22-695Hol 1 :31⅗1:02⅕1:35 2:05⅘ft 16 8 7 8⁷½ 7⁶ 3h Da'ltonL2 7000 2:05⅘ Glid'nHan'r D'tiesBoy K'l'ysMail
Oct15-693Hol 1 :31 1:02⅗1:35⅗2:05⅗ft 8½ 60 6 5⁵ 6⁵½ 5²¾ Da'ltonL8 7000 2:06 Glid'nH'n'r Kni'tValor Cl'v'rOhio
Sep29-695Hol 1 :30⅗1:01⅗1:33⅗2:03⅘ft 22 5 1 1² 1² 6⁴¾ Da'ltonL3 8000 2:05 JeanDaily CrownSong SmartSon
Jun10-695Spk 1 :30⅕1:01⅗1:34 2:04⅘ft 11 4 4 4⁴ 3⁴½ 4⁴½ D'ltonL1 Cond 2:05⅘ R'thmD'ke Fort'neT'ler MarkRod
May27-696Spk 1 :30⅕1:01⅕1:32⅘2:03⅗ft 4¾ 40 30 2³ 2² 5⁷ D'ltonL7 Cond 2:05 G'lie'sR't'm W'taAm's'n F'llSp'd
May15-697Was 1 :31⅕1:02⅕1:34⅘2:05⅕ft 15 2 3 3¹ 1½ 3¹¾†D'ltonL6 Cond 2:05⅘†Pl]P'c'sR'ph M'tyP'r K'ly'sM'l

8 — 15-1

$7,200 2:08 LouD, '69 Driver-Trainer—JOHN BENNETT Red and White
Fair Vale Blk. m, 7, by Galophone—Mary Main. 1969 20 3 1 3 $2,676
Owner, Marian T. Brewer, Lexington, Ky. 1968 35 3 6 6 $6,109
Oct15-691Hol 1 :30⅗1:02 1:33⅗2:03⅘ft 24 5 6 7⁶½ 9¹⁰ 8⁷½ W'bbJH3 Cd-2 2:05 ArnieBlaze Partlow FamousTrip
Oct 4-691Hol 1 :31⅗1:03⅗1:35 2:05 ft 40 8 8 8⁹½ 9¹³ 8¹¹ WebbJH7 Cd-2 2:06⅗ ArnieBl'ze L'b'rGal'n M'wLest'r
Sep23-691Hol 1 :31⅕1:02⅗1:35⅖2:05⅘ft 25 9 8 7¹¹ 6⁷ 4³¾ Benn'tJ6 Cd-1 2:06⅕ JeanDaily CarolHoot FireBlaze
Sep 6-69 LouD 1 :30⅗1:02⅗1:34⅘2:06⅗ft 4 4 4 4 4³ ix4² Benn'tJ2 Cond 2:06⅗ D'tysFirst GanoVictor Ch't'rR'd'l
Sep 1-69 LouD 1 :31⅗1:04⅕1:35⅖2:07⅗ft 5 3 3 3 4²½ 3³½ Benn'tJ6 Cond 2:08 ToplandD. GanoVictor FairVale
Aug23-69 LouD 1 :31⅕1:02⅕1:34⅖2:06⅕ft 23 4 4 4 4¹½ 3¹¾ Benn'tJ3 Cond 2:06⅗ BonusBoy MelodySh't'n FairVale

9 — 7-2

$6,000 2:05⅗, H.P, '69 Driver—JOE LIGHTHILL. Trainer, F. Todd Sr. Green-White-Gold
Special Product Br. h, 5, by Something Special—Satin Hanover. 1969 24 3 3 4 $6,093
Owner, Hawley Todd, Miamiville, Ohio. 1968 26 3 4 2 $3,892
Oct22-695Hol 1 :31⅗1:02⅕1:35 2:05⅘ft 11 4 20 2² 3²½x9¹⁷ ToddF5 7000 2:09 Glid'nHan'r D'tiesBoy K'l'ysMail
Oct15-693Hol 1 :31 1:02⅗1:35⅗2:05⅗ft 3½ 40 20 2½ 2² 8⁹ ToddF7 7000 2:07⅕ Glid'nH'n'r Kni'tValor Cl'v'rOhio
Oct 7-697Hol 1 :31 1:02⅕1:32⅖2:03⅘ft 36 8 8 8⁹½ 8¹² 8⁹½ ToddF4 12000 2:05⅕ PrinceKam C'ftyLobell F'scoLad
Sep24-698Hol 1 :30⅗1:01⅗1:32⅖2:02⅘ft 37 9 9 9¹¹ 6⁷½ 6⁴¾†L'hthillJ8 Cd-4 2:03⅗†Pl5]Pop'rFr'ht P'ceKam Dor'lee
Sep11-69 H.P 1 :30⅗1:03⅕1:34⅗2:06 ft 7½ 30 1 1 1¹ 2½ T'ddJrF4 Cond 2:06 DevedaGirl Sp'cialProduct Affair
Sep 2-69 H.P 1 :30⅕1:02⅕1:34 2:05⅗ft 7-5 ▲ 40 4 30 2³ 1¹ Light'lJ4 Cond 2:05⅗ Sp'cialP'duct Sickle K'd'lw'dB'le

10 — 3-1

$6,000 2:04⅖, Spk, '69 Driver-Trainer—ROBERT FARRINGTON Red and Grey
Knight Valor B. g, 7, by Knight Dream—Vestas Worthy. 1969 8 2 1 0 $4,675
Owner, Farrington Stables, Inc., Richwood, Ohio. 1968 27 6 8 2 $36,145
Oct15-693Hol 1 :31 1:02⅗1:35⅗2:05⅗ft 2½ ▲ 8 8 7⁷½ 7⁷½ 2¾ Far'g'nR6 7000 2:05⅗ Glid'nH'n'r Kni'tValor Cl'v'rOhio
Oct 4-691Hol 1 :31⅗1:03⅗1:35 2:05 ft 8-5 ▲ 6 7 5⁵ 5⁶ 5³½ Far't'nR5 Cd-2 2:05⅗ ArnieBl'ze L'b'rGal'n M'wLest'r
Sep29-698Hol 1 :30⅗1:02⅕1:34 2:04⅕ft 13 8 7 6⁶½ 7⁸ 6⁴ F'gtonR6 Cd-3 2:05 Grig ArmbroInvicta Doralee
Aug13-694Spk 1 :30⅗1:02⅕1:33⅗2:04⅗ft 1 ▲ 40 30 2 2¹ 1nk F'ngt'nR9 8000 2:04⅗ KnightValor EyreYell AlfordKid
Aug 6-693Spk 1 :32⅕1:04⅕1:35⅗2:06 ft 2½ ▲ 8 40 1 1²½ 1²½ F'ngt'nR9 8000 2:06 KnightValor DukeLiner EyreYell
Jly 11-69 Spk 1 :30 1:01 1:32⅗2:03 ft 6¾ 8 8 8 9⁸ 8⁹½ F'gt'nR4 Cond 2:05 Ch'nceyGuy Colem'n M'th'sB'nda

HEAD NUMBER COLOR: GREEN—BLACK NUMBER

ONE MILE PACE — 6th RACE — PURSE $2,600

CONDITIONED. (Cd-2). THREE-YEAR-OLDS AND UPWARD, NON-WINNERS OF $5,000 IN 1969 THAT HAVE STARTED AND NOT WON $1,200 FIRST MONEY SINCE SEPTEMBER 22. ALSO ELIGIBLE: THREE-YEAR-OLDS AND UPWARD, NON-WINNERS OF $7.500 IN 1969 THAT ARE NON-WINNERS OF $1,000 FIRST MONEY IN LAST FOUR STARTS.

ASK FOR HORSE BY PROGRAM NUMBER

1 — Joe Blades — 6-1

2:02⅖, Spk, '69 — Driver-Trainer—MARC GRENIER — Red and White

B. g, 4, by Majestic Hanover—Nancy Blades.
Owner, A. B. Hanson, Santa Maria, Calif.

1969	21	3	3	2	$6,893
1968	31	2	6	8	$7,138

Oct27-69^{7}Hol	1	:30⅗1:01⅘1:32⅗2:02⅕ft	17	1	3	5^{6}	4^{4}	7^{7¾}	Gr'n'rM^{3}	Cd-3	2:03⅘	PressAg't L'aweeCreed TwoStep
Oct11-69^{4}Hol	1	:29⅕1:01⅕1:31⅗2:01⅗ft	15	5	9	8^{2}	6^{9½}	8^{7}	Gren'rM^{9}	Cd-3	2:03⅕	Shormar G'nysGene C'mp'sPoint
Oct 2-69^{6}Hol	1	:29⅘ :59⅘1:30⅗2:00⅗ft	3½	▲ 2	3	3^{1½}	4^{3½}	9^{12}	Gren'rM^{3}	Cd-3	2:02⅘	Lin'lnL'dB'k H'v'lyAir BriskRisk
Sep24-69^{7}Hol	1	:30⅕1:00⅗1:31⅗2:01⅘ft	8½	1	2	1^{2}	1^{2}	4^{4}	Gren'rM^{6}	Cd-3	2:02⅗	RedWave Pr'ssAg'nt Heav'nlyAir
Aug30-69^{6}Spk	1	:29⅗1:01⅗1:31⅘2:01⅗ft	3½	5°	4°	3	4^{3½}	8^{7}	Greni'rJ^{5}	Cond	2:02⅘	PressAgent Roswell ScotchDuke
Aug16-69^{4}Spk	1	:31 1:02 1:32⅗2:01⅘ft	2¼	3ix5	5		4^{5½}	4^{6}	†GrenierJ^{1}	Cond	2:03	†Pl3]Sp'd'rP'k Pr'sAg't S'leF'on

2 — John L. Purdue — 4-1

2:04⅘, Spk, '69 — Driver—NELSON WILLIS. Trainer, J. Cisna, Ass't, N. Willis — Maroon-Grey-White

Br. g, 4, by Purdue Hal—Sissy C.
Owner, Royal Wyn Stable, Springfield, Ill.

1969	21	2	3	0	$6,471
1968	30	6	2	4	$11,487

Oct27-69^{7}Hol	1	:30⅗1:01⅘1:32⅗2:02⅕ft	39	3	5	7^{9½}	7^{7}	5^{2½}	CisnaJ^{1}	Cd-3	2:02⅘	PressAg't L'aweeCreed TwoStep
Sep27-69 Was	1	:30⅗1:02⅘1:35⅕2:04⅗ft	6¾	4	5	8	5^{7}	4^{5¼}	WillisC^{2}	Cond	2:05⅗	HarryT.Hill BoBoR'r Pl'yY'rH'ch
Sep19-69 Was	1	:30⅗1:00⅗1:33⅗2:04⅗ft	6¼	6	6	8	5^{3}	2½	WillisN^{7}	Cond	2:04⅗	Mel'yWar'r J'hnL.P'due KipH'r
Sep 9-69 Was	1	:30⅗1:02⅕1:34⅗2:05 ft	13	1	2	2	3^{3}	6^{7¾}	CisnaJ^{6}	Cond	2:06⅗	PoplarC'kie M'rksBoy Keys'elris
Aug28-69 Spk	1	:31⅗1:04⅕1:35⅗2:06 ft	3¼	2°	1	1	1½	1no	WillisN^{8}	Cond	2:06	JohnL.Purdue Popl'rC'kie V'son
Aug20-69 Spk	1	:31⅕1:03⅗1:34⅗2:04⅘ft	8¾	6	5°	4	3^{1½}	2^{4}	WillisN^{8}	Cond	2:05⅗	Authentic JohnL.P'due P'tsm'th

3 — Scotch Duke — 5-2

2:01⅗, V.D, '69 — Driver-Trainer—EDWARD COBB — Blue and White

B. h, 8, by Duke of Lullwater—Grace Scott.
Owner, Ivanhoe Stables, Inc., Chicago, Ill.

1969	13	2	1	1	$4,378
1968	34	3	3	3	$14,240

Oct28-69^{9}Hol	1	:31 1:02 1:33⅘2:02⅗ft	2½	3	4	3^{2½}	3^{3½}	4^{6}	CobbE^{1}	Cd-3	2:03⅘	P'chieGold St'yBurkeN. Pan'che
Sep20-69 R.R	1	:29⅗1:01⅕1:34⅘2:06 ft	2¼	▲ 4°	4°	8	7^{6}	7^{5½}	CobbE^{3}	Cond	2:07⅕	Miz'leSm'k'y G'dShot SlyY'nkee
Sep12-69 V.D	1	:28⅘1:00⅗1:31⅗2:01⅗ft	3¼	1	1	1	1^{nk}	1^{nk}	CobbE^{8}	Pref	2:01⅗	ScotchDuke Shuffles GoldC'ntry
Sep 5-69 V.D	1	:30⅗1:03⅕1:32⅘2:02⅗ft	3	4	4	4	4^{1½}	2½	CobbE^{1}	Pref	2:02⅗	G'ldC'ntry Sc'tchDuke T.K.M'g'r
Aug30-69^{6}Spk	1	:29⅗1:01⅗1:31⅘2:01⅗ft	22	7	6°	6	5^{3½}	3^{4½}	CobbE^{8}	Cond	2:02⅘	PressAgent Roswell ScotchDuke
Aug23-69^{4}Spk	1	:29⅘1:01⅗1:32⅕2:03 ft	12	9	9	9	9^{9}	8^{5¼}	CobbE^{9}	Cond	2:04	W'tAFl'h Sm'k'yB'ze D'm'dJ'eN.

4 — Marish — 2-1

2:01⅕, Hol, '69 — Driver-Trainer—JOE MARSH, JR. — Grey, Red and Blue

Ch. g, 4, by Irish—Holly Wido.
Owner, Albert Mukdsi, Flint, Mich.

1969	13	3	1	0	$3,845
1968	6	2	0	1	$269

Oct21-69^{9}Hol	1	:29⅘1:00⅗1:31⅘2:01⅗ft	5¼	1	1	1^{2}	2½	x7^{13}	M'shJJr^{2}	Cd-2	2:04	RedWave Bew'ch'gAd's NipSp'r
Oct15-69^{7}Hol	1	:30⅗1:00⅘1:31 2:01⅕ft	1	▲ 2	1	1^{2}	1^{3}	1^{1}	M'shJJr^{2}	Cd-1	2:01⅕	Marish Mr.Jazz MissileTrip
Oct 9-69^{4}Hol	1	:30⅘1:02⅗1:33⅗2:02⅗ft	4	3	1	1^{2}	1^{2}	2½	M'shJJr^{2}	Cd-2	2:02⅗	P'chieGold Marish Imp's'veTime
Oct 3-69^{5}Hol	1 1/16	:30⅗1:02⅗1:33 2:10⅘ft	11	5	6	6^{4½}	6^{8}	6^{8}	M'shJJr^{4}	Cd-2	2:12⅗	W'yH'v'rN. P'p'rEd'e R'lByeBye
Sep24-69^{2}Hol	1	:30⅗1:03 1:34⅗2:03⅘ft	6-5	▲ 1	1	1^{2}	1^{2}	1^{4½}	M'shJJr^{7}	Cond	2:03⅘	Marish Mr.Jazz PatchieGold
Aug30-69^{2}Spk	1	:29⅘1:02 1:32⅗2:04⅗ft	2¼	7	7	2	6^{12}	ex6^{13}	M'shJJr^{5}	Cond	2:07⅕	ArmbroJeff Fairm'n Ruth'sCh'ce

5 — ‡Careless Joe — 10-1

2:06⅘, Spk, '69 — Driver-Trainer—ROBERT WILLIAMS — Purple and White

Ch. h, 6, by Irish—Nugget Wilson.
Owner, Gerald D. Lane, Chicago, Ill.

1969	13	1	3	2	$4,921
1968	15	3	1	4	$6.066

Oct29-69^{4}Hol	1	:30⅘1:02⅗1:34 2:02⅗ft	6¼	7	7	6^{7}	5^{7}	4^{9}	Wil'msR^{7}	Cd-2	2:04⅕	B'tleSt'rN. Pas'naN. ShadoT'vel
Oct22-69^{4}Hol	1	:31 1:03⅗1:35⅕2:04 ft	3½	3	4	4^{5}	4^{7}	3^{4¾}	Wil'msR^{1}	Cd-2	2:04⅘	S'k'yBlaze Dom'sStar C'lessJoe
Oct17-69^{9}Hol	1	:29⅗1:00⅗1:32⅗2:01⅗ft	12	8	8	6^{6½}	3^{5}	2^{1¼}	M'hJJr^{8}	c5000	2:01⅗	B'kAmigo Car'l'sJoe D'k'sDil'ma
Oct11-69^{2}Hol	1	:29⅗1:00⅕1:33 2:03⅗ft	2½	▲ 3	3	3^{4½}	2^{2½}	3^{1¼}	M'rshJJr^{1}	5000	2:03⅗	TownMart'l Renard CarelessJoe
Oct 6-69^{9}Hol	1	:30⅗1:01 1:32⅘2:03⅕ft	4½	3	3	3^{1½}	2^{1}	2½	M'shJJr^{1}	5000	2:03⅕	Lavina CarelessJoe TopGunner
Oct 2-69^{5}Hol	1	:31⅗1:02⅘1:34⅗2:03⅘ft	6½	8	8	6^{7}	5^{7½}	4^{3¾}	M'shJJr^{7}	5000	2:04⅗	TownMartial Galiss TopGunner

6 — Merrie Scotsman — 8-1

2:04, H.P, '69 — Driver-Trainer—TOM WILBURN — Gold and Green

B. h, 8, by Good Time—My Scotch Belle.
Owner, Paul F. Brune, St. Louis, Mo.

1969	31	5	5	2	$7,180
1968	22	0	1	3	$3,230

Oct27-69^{7}Hol	1	:30⅗1:01⅘1:32⅗2:02⅕ft	37	7	6	4^{4½}	5^{4½}	6^{4¼}	Wilb'nT^{6}	Cd-3	2:03	PressAg't L'aweeCreed TwoStep
Oct21-69^{7}Hol	1	:31⅗1:03⅕1:33⅗2:03⅕ft	28	8	4°	2½	4^{4½}	9^{4¾}	Wilb'nT^{6}	Cd-3	2:04⅕	LordB'tler P'rtiesF'ly D'teHan r
Oct16-69^{5}Hol	1	:30⅗1:02⅕1:33⅗2:02⅗ft	12	3	3	2^{1}	3^{1½}	7^{4½}	Wilb'nT^{3}	Cd-3	2:03⅗	SwingBye P'chieGold BradH'n'r
Oct11-69^{4}Hol	1	:29⅕1:01⅕1:31⅗2:01⅗ft	13	9	8	7^{7½}	8^{11}	7^{6½}	Wilb'nT^{7}	Cd-3	2:03	Shormar G'nysGene C'mp'sPoint
Oct 2-69^{6}Hol	1	:29⅘ :59⅘1:30⅗2:00⅗ft	12	7	7	7^{7½}	7^{6½}	7^{7}	Wilb'nT^{6}	Cd-3	2:01⅘	Lin'lnL'dB'k H'v'lyAir BriskRisk
Sep27-69^{4}Hol	1	:30⅕1:00⅕1:31⅕2:01⅕ft	10	3	3	3^{2}	4^{1½}	3^{6¼}	Wilb'nT^{3}	Cd-3	2:02⅗	D'yH.F'bes Ari'eD'es M'rieSc't'n

7 — Sandra Kay A. — 6-1

No Record, '69 — Driver-Trainer—GEORGE BERKNER — Black and Red

B. m, 7, by Scottish Note—Pirranuan.
Owner, Frank Douglas Hughes, San Diego, Calif.

1969	7	0	2	2	$2,282
1968	23	4	4	3	$2,642

Oct23-69 Y.R	1	:31⅘1:04⅗1:36⅕2:07⅗ft	6-5	▲ 1	1	2	2½	3¾	S'M'aM^{1}	Cond	2:07⅗	Fanfare Chukkah SandraKayA.
Oct14-69 R.R	1	:30⅗1:02⅕1:34⅕2:06⅗ft	2½	▲x8	8	6°	5^{4½}	2^{1½}	S'M'aM^{8}	Cond	2:07	T'tsieH'ver S'raKayA. H.T.Em'y
Sep30-69 R.R	1	:31⅕1:03 1:35⅕2:06⅗ft	2	▲ 6	6°	7°	7^{4¾}	3^{2}	Mat'ciE^{5}	Cond	2:07	W'thyPlay Chukkah S'draKayA.
Sep16-69 R.R	1	:30 1:04 1:34⅗2:06⅗ft	9-5	1	1	1	1^{1½}	2no	Mat'ciE^{5}	Cond	2:06⅗	B'aBrewst'r S'aKayA. W'hyPlay
Sep 5-69 R.R	1	:30⅗1:01⅘1:32⅗2:04 ft	50	8	8	8	8^{7¾}	6^{6¼}	S'M'aM^{8}	Cond	2:05⅘	ByeByeD'd RodAd's B'th'yH'ver
Aug30-69 R.R	1	:30⅘1:02⅗1:34⅗2:05⅕ft		2	2	4	4^{2}	4^{3}	S'M'aM^{1}	Cond	2:06	LowDia'd BlockT'lipN. JohnCr'g

EQUINE EMPORIUM

The Equine Emporium, a specialty shop dealing in gift and novelty items for the horse fans, is open every racing night and is located on the main floor of the grandstand.

EXACTA WAGERING

Western Harness will hold **Exacta** wagering on the fourth and ninth races each night. All **Exacta** tickets are for win and place combinations only. Each person purchasing an **Exacta** ticket shall designate the exact order in which the first two horses will finish in an **Exacta** race. For example, if number 3 is selected to finish first and number 6 is selected to finish second, they must finish number 3, first and number 6, second in order to win. Seller windows for $3.00 and $10.00 are available on the fourth race **Exacta** and windows for $5.00 and $10.00 are available on the ninth race **Exacta.** **Exacta** tickets will be sold nightly at all Nightly Double windows. Complete **Exacta** rules are posted throughout the plant.

‡RACING WITHOUT HOPPLES.

HEAD NUMBER COLOR: BLACK—WHITE NUMBER

ONE MILE PACE — 7th RACE — PURSE $3,000

CONDITIONED. (Cd-3). ALL AGES. NON-WINNERS OF $7,500 IN 1969 THAT ARE NON-WINNERS OF A RACE SINCE September 22. Also eligible: Non-winners of $12,500 in 1969 th^t are non-winners of $1,200 first money in last four starts.

ASK FOR HORSE BY PROGRAM NUMBER

1 ‡Lenawee Creed — 3-1

2:01⅗, Spk, '69 — Driver-Trainer—ROBERT WILLIAMS — Purple and White

B. g, 8, by Chief Lenawee—Easter Creed. — 1969 21 1 3 1 $7,716

Owner, Sol J. Lehtman, Highland Park, Ill. — 1968 33 7 4 8 $32,330

Oct27-697Hol	1 :30⅗1:01⅗1:32⅘2:02⅕ft	3½	6 7 67½ 65 2½	Wil'msR5	Cd-3	2:02⅗	PressAg't L'aweeCreed TwoStep
Oct21-697Hol	1 :31⅗1:03⅕1:33⅘2:03⅕ft	4¾	5 7 76½ 87½ 41¾	Wil'msR2	Cd-3	2:03⅗	LordB'tler P'rtiesF'ly D'teHan'r
Oct13-698Hol	1 :31⅕1:02⅗1:33⅕2:02⅗ft	11	9 7 57 56 76	Wi'msR9	15000	2:03⅗	SweepUp AmericoTass Instantly
Oct 7-698Hol	1 :30⅗1:02⅕1:34⅗2:03⅕ft	6¼	6 6 78½ 77½ 75	Wi'msR2	20000	2:04⅕	Vic'ysH'rn Del'xeH'n'r PressAg't
Sep30-698Hol	1 :30⅕1:00⅗1:31⅗2:00⅗ft	2 ▲	7 7 89½ 911 63¾	W'msR2	20000	2:01⅕	WayToGo Sc'tysColt Del'xeHan'r
Sep24-696Hol	1 :30⅗1:01⅕1:33⅕2:02⅕ft	16	8 8 77 65 2½	Wi'msR5	20000	2:02⅕	Del'xeH'v'r Len'weeCr'd Par'n'va

2 Toughie Direct — 6-1

2:00⅘, Spk, '69 — Driver-Trainer—WAYNE SHORT — Purple and White

B. g, 5, by Sampson Direct—Abbie Light. — 1969 23 3 4 0 $12,295

Owner, John W. Richards & James H. McMahon, Chicago, Ill. — 1968 7 2 1 0 $2,391

Oct29-697Hol	1 :30⅗1:00⅕1:32 2:01⅘ft	18	1 1 12½ 11½ 53¼	ShortW1	Cd-4	2:02⅗	P'ceButler RedWave Keyst'elris
Oct22-696Hol	1 :29⅗1:02 1:32⅘2:01⅗ft	20	3 5 97½ 1010 1010	ShortW8	Cd-4	2:03⅗	Tarp'tC'lter TheF'ler Arl'eD'res
Oct10-69 Was	1 :31⅕1:02⅗1:35⅕2:08 sy	7	2 2 2 42 53	Rap'neL2	Cond	2:08⅗	LaronMaid'n M'htyG.E. EdByrd
Sep26-69 Was	1 :29⅕ :59⅕1:30⅗1:59⅗ft	9¼	1 1 1 2¾ 65¾	Rap'neL4	Cond	2:00⅘	RightHonor EdByrd TomsChoice
Sep20-69 Was	1 :30 :58⅗1:29⅗1:59⅗ft	17	1 1 1 2½ 86¼	Rap'neL7	Cond	2:00⅘	ToodleyDu L'r'nMaid'n Sc'ysC'lt
Sep11-69 Was	1 :29 1:00 1:30⅘2:00⅗ft	3¾ ▲	1 1 1 11 44	Rap'neL4	Cond	2:01⅕	ChiefG.Dir't LadyAries M'tyG.E.

3 Dilly Davis — 4-1

2:07⅖, Brdwn, '69 — Driver—JOE LIGHTHILL. Trainer, E. Wheeler — Green-White-Gold

Br. h, 8, by Easy Adios—Fedors Jewel. — 1969 21 1 5 4 $9,547

Owner, Leo P. Van Rhoden, Mt. Vernon, Ohio. — 1968 33 4 2 7 $13,540

Oct24-699Hol	1 :30⅗1:01⅕1:30⅘2:00⅘ft	6	6 9 99 77 55	Wh'lerE3	Cd-3	2:01⅗	Q'ckProm St'lHome PatchieG'ld
Oct17-697Hol	1 :29⅗1:01⅕1:31⅗2:00⅕ft	2 ▲	4 4 56½ 56 34¼	Wh'lerE1	Cd-3	2:01	C'mp'ssPoint Q'kProm DillyD'vis
Oct14-697Hol	1 :29⅗ :59⅕1:29⅘2:00⅗ft	12	4 3 31½ 32 52	Wh'lerE1	Cd-3	2:01	T'myGene D'teH'n'r Keyst'eS's'n
Oct 7-696Hol	1 :29⅘1:00⅘1:33 2:02 ft	31	2 3 44 54½ 62	Ac'm'nD6	Cd-3	2:02⅗	AdiolaHanover I.V.P. LordButler
Sep30-697Hol	1 :31 1:02⅘1:34 2:02⅗ft	38	7 7 78½ 79 75¾	Ac'm'nD5	Cd-4	2:03⅗	Fash'nTip Pat'iaLouise RedW've
Sep24-697Hol	1 :30⅕1:00⅗1:31⅗2:01⅘ft	4¾	4 4 43½ 32½ 75¾	Wh'lerE2	Cd-3	2:03	RedWave Pr'ssAg'nt Heav'nlyAir

4 Freight Lawyer — 7-2

2:05⅕, Spk, '69 — Driver-Trainer—JAMES DENNIS — Green and White

B c, 3, by Torrid—Lusty Helen. — 1969 17 3 4 4 $8,103

Owner, ABC Stables, Inc., New York, N. Y. — 1968 5 0 1 0 $320

Oct29-696Hol	1 :30⅗1:01 1:32⅘2:00⅘ft	4½	3 3 34 32½ 22¼	DennisJ5	Cd-3	2:01⅕	B'ch'gAd's Fr'tLawy'r W'hyByrd
Oct22-699Hol	1 :30⅗1:01⅘1:34⅗2:04⅕ft	14	10 100 75½ 53 61½	D'nnisJ10	Cd-3	2:04⅗	Sc'tishD'sign ElMay'r'mo Tartar
Oct15-699Hol	1 :30 1:00⅕1:30⅗1:59⅘ft	5¼	8 8 813 713 57	DennisJ7	Cd-2	2:01⅕	AirBlazer Tartar Indication
Oct 9-699Hol	1 :30 1:01⅗1:33 2:02⅕ft	4½	3 3 44 45 31½	DennisJ2	Cd-2	2:02⅗	K'yst'nelris Ch'fRed Fr'htL'wy'r
Oct 2-696Hol	1 :29⅘ :59⅗1:30⅗2:00⅗ft	5	x9 8 99½ 99 64¾	DennisJ8	Cd-3	2:01⅗	Lin'lnL'dB'k H'v'lyAir BriskRisk
Sep26-692Hol	1 :30⅗1:01⅘1:33 2:02⅗ft	11	10 2 32½ 22½ 2no	DennisJ6	Cd-2	2:02⅘	Mr.MiteB. Fr'tL'wy'r B'tleSt'rN.

5 Two Step — 6-1

2:02⅘, Spk, '69 — Driver-Trainer—JOE MARSH, JR. — Grey, Red and Blue

B. m, 4, by Worthy Boy—Fascinator. — 1969 28 5 2 3 $12,134

Owner, Two Step Stable Inc., Chicago, Ill. — 1968 17 4 2 2 $643

Oct27-697Hol	1 :30⅗1:01⅘1:32⅗2:02⅕ft	7¼	20 2 21½ 32 31¼	M'shJJr8	Cd-3	2:02⅗	PressAg't L'aweeCreed TwoStep
Oct18-699Hol	1 :30 1:00⅗1:31 2:00 ft	20	9 9 89 912 913	M'shJJr9	Cd-4	2:02⅘	Wh'tAFl'sh Pat'iaLouise OsoSlo
Oct11-699Hol	1 :30 1:00⅘1:32⅗2:01⅘ft	8¾	6 6 67ix720 823	M'shJJr4	Cd-4	2:06⅗	AdiolaH'n'r Auth'ntic P'ceButl'r
Oct 4-697Hol	1 :30 1:01⅕1:33⅗2:02⅗ft	26	4 4 45 47 21	M'shJJr1	Cd-4	2:02⅘	PeppyTar TwoStep OsoSlo
Sep26-697Hol	1 :30⅕1:02 1:33⅘2:02⅘ft	24	1 1 1½ 1½ 87	M'shJJr2	Cd-5	2:04⅗	M'sL'styt'n Sh'r'nM'mie D'teK'g
Sep16-69 Was	1 :30⅗1:02 1:34⅘2:03⅗ft	34	8 7 8 810 87½	C't'ldoH6	Cond	2:05⅕	P'rm'ntW've N'nisH'v'r DeeBro'k

6 Poppa Rex — 8-1

2:07, B.M, '69 — Driver-Trainer—WILLIAM OLDS — Royal Blue and Chartreuse

B. g, 5, by Ashland—Meda Tass. — 1969 28 6 5 5 $11,817

Owner, W. Olds & G. B. Gason-Niebling II., Dresher, Pa. — 1968 29 6 4 3 $8,213

Oct29-698Hol	1 :29⅗1:01⅗1:32⅘2:01⅗ft	18	7 7 78 812 78¾	OldsW5	15000	2:03	SunSh'd'w S'raP'nter Tim'lyG'se
Oct22-698Hol	1 :29⅗1:00⅕1:30⅗2:00⅕ft	12	8 70 42 68 65¾	OldsW7	16000	2:01⅕	MayW't'n S'raP'nter SunSh'd'w
Oct15-698Hol	1 :31 1:02⅗1:32⅘2:01⅕ft	15	7 8 88 67 55¾	OldsW10	18000	2:02⅕	SunSh'dow MayW'st'n S'raP'ter
Oct 8-698Hol	1 :29⅗1:02⅗1:33⅕2:02⅕ft	17	5 5 77 76 2½	OldsW4	15000	2:02⅕	WeeHerb PoppaRex SaraPainter
Sep27-691Pom	1 :31⅕1:04⅕1:36⅗2:08⅗ft	1 ▲	20 2 11½ 12 14	OldsW2	Cond	2:08⅗	PoppaRex VernonAdios ArgoPat
Sep20-692Pom	1 :31 1:03⅗1:35⅗2:08⅗ft	4¾	3 3 33 22 32	OldsW5	Inv	2:08⅘	D'nteH'v'r D'styH.F'rbes P'paR'x

7 Stoney Burke N. — 10-1

2:06⅕, Spk, '69 — Driver—NELSON WILLIS. Trainer, J. Cisna, Ass't, N. Willis — Maroon-Grey-White

Br. g, 7, by Stormyway—Light Step. — 1969 26 2 6 1 $7,529

Owner, Royal Wyn Stable, Springfield, Ill. — 1968 18 1 0 2 $659

Oct28-699Hol	1 :31 1:02 1:33⅘2:02⅗ft	37	1 3 44½ 44½ 24½	CisnaJ6	Cd-3	2:03⅗	P'chieGold St'yBurkeN. Pan'che
Oct 3-69 Was	1 :31⅗1:02 1:33 2:02⅗ft	27	6 7 8 810 810	WillisN5	Cond	2:04⅗	HokeCr'd Emp'eLieut't Shormar
Sep23-69 Was	1 :30⅗1:01⅕1:33 2:03⅗ft	11	3 5 5 31½ 53¾	CisnaJ1	Cond	2:04⅕	M'sL'dyF'vel Ports'h Win'gCry'l
Sep15-69 Was	1 :30⅗1:01⅕1:32⅘2:01⅗ft	30	8 8 8 55½ 45¾	CisnaJ5	Cond	2:02⅘	Roswell MissPluto't M'sL'dyF'v'l
Sep 4-69 Was	1 :31⅗1:04 1:36⅘2:08⅕sy	25	x9 9 8 68½ 811	CisnaJ4	Cond	2:10⅗	Sp'derPick B'enoTi'po M'wRuby
Aug27-69 Spk	1 :31 1:05⅗1:35⅘2:06⅕ft	2½ ▲	6 6 4 32½ 1½	WillisN6	Cond	2:06⅕	St'yBurkeN. TopBid Maj'icLinn

8 Bye Bye Dannibyrd — 9-2

2:02⅗, Y.R, '69 — Driver-Trainer—ROBERT FARRINGTON — Red and Grey

Br. c, 3, by Bye Bye Byrd—Minniwashta. — 1969 18 4 4 4 $12,205

Owner, Dale D. & Floyd Miller, Archbold, Ohio. — 1968 0 0 0 0 ——

Oct27-697Hol	1 :30⅗1:01⅘1:32⅗2:02⅕ft	3¾	8 4 33 2½ 41¼	F'gtonR7	Cd-3	2:02⅗	PressAg't L'aweeCreed TwoStep
Oct22-696Hol	1 :29⅗1:02 1:32⅗2:01⅗ft	10	9 10 75 76½ 75½	F'gtonR9	Cd-4	2:02⅗	Tarp'tC'lter TheF'ler Arl'eD'res
Oct11-69 R.R	1 :30⅗1:02⅗1:32⅗2:03⅗ft	2½	7 50 40 41½x32¾	SholtyG4	Cond	2:04⅕	Dry'nSm'ke TheSc'f ByeB'eD'rd
Oct 6-69 R.R	1 :30⅕1:01⅗1:33⅕2:04⅘ft	2-5 ▲	4 4 40 42¼ 2nk	SholtyG3	Cond	2:04⅘	Kn'tRe'd ByeB'eD'rd AirN'wY'd
Sep26-69 R.R	1 :30⅗1:01⅗1:33⅗2:04⅕ft	5¼	8 80 70 52¼ 21¼	SholtyG8	Cond	2:04⅗	TheInlaw ByeB'eD'yrd N'sPride
Sep18-69 R.R	1 :30⅕1:01⅗1:32⅗2:04⅕ft	7-5 ▲	6 7 40 32 31½	InskoD4	Cond	2:04⅗	LawDr'nd High'dR'r ByeB'eD'rd

WHAT IS THE MORNING LINE?

The morning line is the opinion of an experienced handicapper and oddsmaker as to the possible estimated payoff on each entry, should it win. This is in the program, and is the first set of odds posted on the tote board before the race.

‡RACING WITHOUT HOPPLES.

HEAD NUMBER COLOR: BLACK—YELLOW NUMBER

ONE MILE PACE — **8th RACE** — PURSE $4,000

THE ENCINO

CLAIMING. ALL AGES. TOP CLAIMING PRICE, $15,000.

ASK FOR HORSE BY PROGRAM NUMBER

1 (8-1) — $12,500 — 2:03⅘, PcD, '69 — Driver-Trainer—JOE LIGHTHILL — Green, White and Gold

Dazzilum — B g, 4, by Widower Creed—Dazzlemade. Owner, Richard E. Mutz & George Schild, Monroeville, Ohio. 1968 29 4 7 3 $3,469; 1968 31 5 2 6 $3,419

Oct28-69 9Hol	1	:31 1:02 1:33⅘ 2:02⅗ ft	3¾	7 7 89½ 810 89½	L'hth'lJ5	Cd-3	2:04⅘	P'chieGold St'yBurkeN. Pan'che
Oct22-69 8Hol	1	:29⅗ 1:00⅕ 1:30⅗ 2:00⅕ ft	28	5 5 76½ 56 43	L'ht'llJ3	18750	2:00⅘	MayW't'n S'raP'nter SunSh'd'w
Oct13-69 6Hol	1	:29 :59 1:31⅗ 2:02⅕ ft	11	10 10 107½ 89 44½	L'ht'lJ10	11250	2:03	HappyHal TidalGale GypsyGoose
Oct 6-69 8Hol	1	:30⅕ 1:02⅗ 1:34⅕ 2:03⅕ ft	31	5 5 76½ 76½ 42	L'ht'llJ3	15000	2:03⅗	BillBlaine C.B.Sen'r LeS'gstr'ss
Sep29-69 7Hol	1 1/16	:30 1:00⅗ 1:31⅘ 2:09⅗ ft	5¼	30 1 22 46 711	L'hth'lJ9	12500	2:11⅗	BomberBay RainTime JustlySo
Sep25-69 9Hol	1	:30⅗ 1:03⅗ 1:33⅗ 2:02⅗ ft	27	3 3 64½ 65½ 43¾	L'thillJ2	15000	2:03	S'raP'nter M'sW'b'sh LeS'gstr'ss

2 (4-1) — $10,000 — 2:03⅘, Brdwn, '69 — Driver-Trainer—EDWARD COBB — Blue and White

Highland Raider — B. g, 9, by Morano—Tradition. Owner, Helm Wind Farm, Inc., Old Brookville, N. Y. 1969 38 5 7 4 $23,175; 1968 35 4 6 4 $15,685

Oct27-69 8Hol	1	:30 1:00 1:31⅘ 2:01⅘ ft	7½	6 6 78½ 67 64¾	CobbE2	12000	2:02⅗	Ar'brolnsko B'b'rBay D'k'sSister
Oct20-69 8Hol	1	:30⅕ 1:01 1:32⅗ 2:02⅕ ft	2½	▲ 20 1 13 11 55½	CobbE5	13000	2:03⅕	LeS'gstr's B'b'rBay M'ry'sDawn
Oct11-69 5Hol	1	:30⅗ 1:01 1:31⅘ 2:01⅗ ft	17	8 8 810 79½ 53½	CobbE8	Cd-5	2:02	Dick'sSister Cornell YellowBear
Oct 4-69 5Hol	1	:31 1:01⅗ 1:31⅘ 2:01⅗ ft	10	40 2 44 67½ 811	CobbE7	Cd-5	2:03⅗	Shia'seeSq'e H'l'nLee SunSh'ow
Sep18-69 R.R	1	:30⅕ 1:01⅗ 1:32⅗ 2:04⅕ ft	5½	7 6 20 21 2¾	CobbE5	Cond	2:04⅗	L'wD'm'd H'hl'dR'd'r B'eB'eD'd
Sep11-69 R.R	1	:30⅗ 1:02⅗ 1:33⅗ 2:04⅘ ft	5½	6 8 70 61¾ 2¾	CobbE3	Cond	2:05	A'ch'nc'g Highl'dR'd'r Bl'eAdios

3 (7-2) — $10,000 — 2:04⅕, Spk, '69 — Driver—JAMES CURRAN. Trainer, John Curran — Grey-Orange-Gold

The Voyager — B. g, 5, by Widower Paul—Bon Voyage. Owner, John Curran, David Garmel & George Lewis, Detroit, Mich. 1968 21 4 5 3 $8,853; 1968 21 4 5 3 $8,850

Oct24-69 9Hol	1	:30⅗ 1:01⅕ 1:30⅘ 2:00⅘ ft	33	7 10 1012 89 75¾	Cur'nJa5	Cd-3	2:01⅘	Q'ckProm St'lHome PatchieG'ld
Sep17-69 H.P	1	:31 1:02⅕ 1:33⅗ 2:03⅗ ft	2¼	8 8 8 824 823	C'r'nJo3	15000	2:08⅕	P'roWils'n L'tn'gL'd O.C.'sH't'e
Sep11-69 H.P	1	:31 1:06 1:37 2:07⅕ ft	2¼	x7 7 6 63 62¾	C'r'nJa5	15000	2:07⅘	P'roWils'n Tim'lyG'se M'yW'st'n
Sep 3-69 H.P	1	:30 1:03 1:34 2:04 ft	2	20 2 3 ix41¾ 512	C'r'nJa6	15000	2:06⅗	Midn'tJ'n'e M'yW't'n P'roWils'n
Aug30-69 H.P	1	:30⅗ 1:03 1:33⅗ 2:03⅗ ft	2¾	1 1 1 11 2h	C'r'nJo5	15000	2:03⅗	Tim'lyG'se TheV'y'g'r Q'nsC'd't
Aug22-69 H.P	1	:29⅘ 1:03⅗ 1:33⅗ 2:02⅕ ft	7	60 50 60 53½ 67¾	C'r'nJa7	17500	2:03⅘	P'chP'de Mid'tJ'nie H'meP'eL'y

4 (4-1) — $10,000 — 2:04⅗, L.B, '69 — Driver—ROBERT WILLIAMS. Trainer, Richard Rhoads — Purple and White

C. B. Senator — B. g, 7, by Adios Senator—Sister Mack. Owner, Richard H. Rhoads, West Lawn, Pa. 1969 19 3 4 2 $10,252; 1968 26 13 4 1 $34,150

Oct22-69 8Hol	1	:29⅗ 1:00⅕ 1:30⅗ 2:00⅕ ft	9½	6 6 87x 923 819	W'msR5	15000	2:04⅗	MayW't'n S'raP'nter SunSh'd'w
Oct18-69 9Hol	1	:30 1:00⅗ 1:31 2:00 ft	7¾	1 2 43½ 76½ 811	Wil'msR2	Cd-4	2:02	Wh'tAFl'sh Pat'iaLouise OsoSlo
Oct13-69 8Hol	1	:31⅕ 1:02⅗ 1:33⅕ 2:02⅗ ft	3¾	8 5 34 44½ 53¼	Rh'dsR7	15000	2:03	SweepUp AmericoTass Instantly
Oct 6-69 8Hol	1	:30⅕ 1:02⅗ 1:34⅕ 2:03⅕ ft	3	7 40 2½ 2½ 21¼	Rh'dsR7	15000	2:03⅗	BillBlaine C.B.Sen'r LeS'gstr'ss
Sep29-69 6Hol	1	:30⅕ 1:01 1:31⅗ 2:01⅕ ft	4½	8 8 64½ 66½ 31	Rh'dsR6	15000	2:01⅗	MissW'b'sh SunSh'd'w C.B.Sen'r
Sep25-69 4Hol	1	:31 1:03⅗ 1:34⅕ 2:03⅕ ft	5	1 1 11 12 2¾	RhoadsR3	Cd-4	2:03⅕	D'tyH.F'es C.B.S't'r H'byH'eL'pe

5 (5-2) — $15,000 — 2:04⅖, Was, '69 — Driver-Trainer—JAMES DOLBEE — Green and White

Bo Bo Ranger — B. g, 3, by Ranger Hanover—Baroness Byrd. Owner, Jimmy H. Dolbee & James L. McCann, Jackson, Mich. 1969 14 3 3 0 $7,535; 1968 11 2 1 5 $2,764

Oct29-69 6Hol	1	:30⅗ 1:01 1:32⅘ 2:00⅘ ft	5½	4 4 56½ 45 43¾	DolbeeJ7	Cd-3	2:01⅗	B'ch'gAd's Fr'tLawy'r W'hyByrd
Oct22-69 9Hol	1	:30⅗ 1:01⅗ 1:34⅗ 2:04⅕ ft	25	7 7 109 85 4½	DolbeeJ6	Cd-3	2:04⅗	Sc'tishD'sign ElMay'r'mo Tartar
Oct10-69 Was	1	:33⅗ 1:06 1:38⅗ 2:12 sy	2¾	▲x9 8 8 8dis 8dis	DolbeeJ5	Cond		Don'dByrd B'noT'mpo W'tCh'p'n
Oct 3-69 Was	1	:31⅘ 1:02 1:33 2:02⅗ ft	12	5 5 5 45 45	DolbeeJ4	Cond	2:03⅗	HokeCr'd Emp'eLieut't Sh'man
Sep27-69 Was	1	:30⅗ 1:02⅘ 1:35⅕ 2:04⅗ ft	2¾	▲ 2 2 2 2½ 22¼	DolbeeJ7	Cond	2:05	H'yT.Hill BoBoR'ger Pl'yY'rH'ch
Sep20-69 Was	1	:30⅘ 1:03⅕ 1:35⅗ 2:04⅗ ft	13	2 3 2 1h 11	DolbeeJ8	Cond	2:04⅗	BoBoR'ger Keys'elris Don'dByrd

6 (3-1) — $12,500 — 2:02, Hol, '69 — Driver-Trainer—KEVIN TISHER — All Blue

Hirams Bay — Ch. g, 4, by Hiram Hanover—Gracie Tass. Owner, J. Knight, D. Tullio & K. Tisher, Cardiff by the Sea, Calif. 1969 25 6 6 3 $11,456; 1968 6 2 0 0 $1,175

Oct24-69 5Hol	1	:30 1:01⅗ 1:33 2:02⅗ ft	2	▲ 2 2 22 32 2no	Tish'rK4	12500	2:02⅗	Wil'wPr'ce Hir'msBay MiteDr'm
Oct18-69 4Hol	1	:30⅕ 1:01⅗ 1:33 2:02⅗ ft	2½	▲ 4 4 76½ 78½ 51½	TisherK2	12500	2:02⅘	Tr'tw'dPaul StarC'ier E'st'rLind
Oct 8-69 9Hol	1	:30⅗ 1:01⅗ 1:32⅘ 2:02 ft	5½	3 3 44½ 32½ 1¾	TisherK8	11250	2:02	Hir'msBay JoJoLin'n Q'n'sCons't
Oct 1-69 7Hol	1 1/16	:31⅕ 1:03⅗ 1:34⅗ 2:11 ft	2¾	40 1 1h 12 24	TisherK7	12500	2:11⅗	D'k'sSis'r Hir'msBay Q'nsCons't
Sep25-69 5Hol	1	:30⅗ 1:01⅗ 1:32⅗ 2:02 ft	3¾	4 4 46 54½ 1¾	TisherK7	9375	2:02	HiramsBay DannyRip JoeParker
Sep13-69 Was	1	:30⅗ 1:01 1:31⅗ 2:02 ft	8¼	2 5 5 52¼ 54½	TisherK6	Cond	2:03	ArleneDares Assault Don'ldByrd

DRIVER STANDINGS THROUGH FRIDAY, OCTOBER 31, 1969

Driver	Starts	1st	2nd	3rd	Driver	Starts	1st	2nd	3rd
Robert Farrington	178	35	31	22	James Dennis	128	16	22	19
Robert Williams	131	26	22	13	Joe Marsh Jr.	124	16	17	16
Joe O'Brien	106	25	13	16	Joe Lighthill	116	15	15	9
Jack Williams Jr.	110	18	18	22	Edward Cobb	49	9	2	10
Tom Wilburn	134	17	20	11					

POST POSITION STATISTICS (Through Friday October 31, 1969)

Post	1	2	3	4	5	6	7	8	9	10
Starts	306	306	306	306	306	305	288	260	199	110
In the Money	132	124	126	99	100	112	78	79	49	23
Wins	43	37	43	37	32	46	24	25	13	4

Declared—Star Carrier.

HEAD NUMBER COLOR: WHITE—BLACK NUMBER

ONE MILE PACE — 9th RACE - - EXACTA — PURSE $2,400

CONDITIONED. (Cd-1). THREE-YEAR-OLDS AND UPWARD, horses that have started 10 or more times in 1969 and are non-winners of $3,650 in 1969. Also eligible: hnrses that hav started 20 or mnre times and are non-winners $5,000 in 1969.

ASK FOR HORSE BY PROGRAM NUMBER

1 Dominions Star — 10-1

2:04⅘, Nor, '69 — Driver—ROBERT STANSELL. Trainer, Doug Ackerman — Red and Blue
B. h, 5, by Dominion Boy—Lady Defense. — 1969 21 2 4 3 $4,873
Owner. Robert B. Stansell, Mason, Mich. — 1968 22 7 1 4 $3.490

Oct29-69^{4}Hol	1 :30⅗ 1:02⅗ 1:34 2:02⅗ ft	48	8	8	8^{8}	7^{9}	6^{11}	St'ns'IR^{8}	Cd-2	2:04⅗	B'tleSt'rN. Pas'naN. ShadoT'vel
Oct22-69^{4}Hol	1 :31 1:03⅗ 1:35⅕ 2:04 ft	39	1	2	2^{2}	$2^{1\frac{1}{2}}$	$2^{3\frac{1}{2}}$	St'ns'IR^{4}	Cd-2	2:04⅗	S'k'yBlaze Dom'sStar C'lessJoe
Oct16-69^{4}Hol	1 :30⅗ 1:01⅘ 1:33 2:02⅕ ft	20	7	4	$4^{2\frac{1}{2}}$	6^{11}	8^{12}	St'ns'IR^{7}	Cd-1	2:04⅗	Mr.MiteB. S'k'yBl'ze Sp'ishCh'f
Oct 9-69^{9}Hol	1 :30 1:01⅗ 1:33 2:02⅕ ft	56	9	9	9^{10}	8^{12}	$8^{8\frac{3}{4}}$	St'ns'IR^{8}	Cd-2	2:03⅘	K'yst'nelris Ch'fRed Fr'htL'wy'r
Oct 1-69^{6}Hol	1 :29⅗ 1:00⅕ 1:30⅘ 2:00⅗ ft	67	9	9	9^{12}	8^{9}	$6^{8\frac{1}{2}}$	St'ns'IR^{6}	Cd-3	2:02⅕	Authentic ByeByeRoger LittleAl
Sep24-69^{9}Hol	1 :30⅗ 1:02⅗ 1:33 2:02⅗ ft	50	9	9	$8^{9\frac{1}{2}}$	$8^{5\frac{1}{2}}$	5^{8}	St'ns'IIR^{8}	Cd-2	2:04	ChiefRed I.V.P. Ballock

2 ‡Dream Street — 12-1

2:03⅘, ScD, '69 — Driver-Trainer—JOE LIGHTHILL — Green, White and Gold
B. m, 5, by Good Time—Queens Dream. Owner, George H. North & Robert V. Rich, Cuyahoga Falls, Ohio.
1969 22 3 2 2 $3,337
1968 15 2 4 1 $2,589

Oct27-69^{9}Hol	1 1/16 :29⅗ 1:01 1:33 2:10⅘ ft	13	6	6	$5^{6\frac{1}{2}}$	$4^{5\frac{1}{2}}$	$5^{4\frac{1}{2}}$	L'hth'IJ^{6}	Cd-2	2:11⅗	Sp'nishCh'f Del'noKid H'pyOtto
Oct10-69^{4}Hol	1 :31⅗ 1:04⅗ 1:35⅗ 2:04⅘ ft	11	5	5	$5^{7\frac{1}{2}}$	4^{6}	$5^{5\frac{1}{4}}$	L'hth'IJ^{2}	Cd-1	2:05⅘	B'w'ch'gAd's WeeC'nD O.C.M'go
Oct 2-69^{4}Hol	1 :29⅘ 1:00⅗ 1:33⅗ 2:03⅕ ft	12	6	6x	8^{21}	8^{23}	7^{18}	L'hth'IJ^{8}	Cd-1	2:07⅕	SpanishChief DirectSue TopBid
Sep27-69^{9}Hol	1 :31⅕ 1:02⅗ 1:33 2:02⅗ ft	13	4	2	1^{2}	$2^{\frac{1}{2}}$	$7^{5\frac{1}{4}}$	L'hthillJ^{3}	Cd-1	2:03⅗	Popl'rEddie W'thyH'rN. MaiTai
Sep24-69^{5}Hol	1 :30 1:01⅗ 1:33⅗ 2:03 ft	5¾	8	8	6^{9}	$8^{9\frac{1}{2}}$	5^{6}	L'hth'IJ^{7}	Cd-1	2:04⅕	FrontierSue TopBid O.C.Mego
Sep19-69 H.P	1 :30⅗ 1:03⅗ 1:34⅗ 2:04⅘ ft	5	5^{0}	1	2	$3^{2\frac{3}{4}}$	$6^{3\frac{1}{4}}$	L'hth'IJ^{5}	Cond	2:05⅗	Spr'gFever BoyDiller SwiftKn'ht

3 Little Al — 3-1

2:05, F.P, '69 — Driver-Trainer—JOE VOLLARO — Green and Blue
Br. g, 7, by Waygale—Hoosier Maid. — 1969 26 1 1 6 $4,599
Owner, Joseph J. Vollaro, North Hollywood, Calif. — 1968 38 2 5 5 $16,032

Oct29-69^{9}Hol	1 :29⅘ 1:02⅗ 1:34 2:03⅗ ft	17	5	5	6^{8}	7^{7}	6^{2}	VollaroJ^{3}	3000	2:04	JoJoLin'n Q'n'sCons't Wil'wP'ce
Oct24-69^{5}Hol	1 :30 1:01⅗ 1:33 2:02⅗ ft	11	4	4	6^{7}	7^{6}	$8^{4\frac{1}{4}}$	Vol'roJ^{2}	10000	2:03	Wil'wPr'ce Hir'msBay MiteDr'm
Oct20-69^{9}Hol	1 1/16 :30 1:02⅕ 1:34⅗ 2:12⅕ ft	3½	9	9	10^{15}	6^{8}	$6^{4\frac{1}{2}}$	VollaroJ^{7}	Cd-2	2:13⅕	Indication ClinkerScott Kimpam
Oct13-69^{9}Hol	1 :31 1:01 1:31⅗ 2:01⅗ ft	6	6	1^{0}	1^{2}	$1^{\frac{1}{2}}$	$3^{5\frac{1}{4}}$	VollaroJ^{6}	Cd-3	2:02⅗	Ballock PacingBye LittleAl
Oct 6-69^{4}Hol	1 :30⅕ 1:00⅗ 1:31⅗ 2:01⅘ ft	6	3	4	6^{7}	$7^{6\frac{1}{2}}$	$3^{2\frac{1}{4}}$	VollaroJ^{2}	Cd-3	2:02⅕	Sc'tishD'sign TheG'mbl'r L'tleAl
Oct 1-69^{6}Hol	1 :29⅗ 1:00⅕ 1:30⅘ 2:00⅗ ft	16	1	1	$1^{\frac{1}{2}}$	$2^{1\frac{1}{2}}$	$3^{4\frac{3}{4}}$	VollaroJ^{9}	Cd-3	2:01⅗	Authentic ByeByeRoger LittleAl

4 Good Girl Wick — 10-1

2:09⅘, Spk, '69 — Driver—WILBUR LONG. Trainer, C. King; Ass't, W. Long — Blue-Silver
B. m, 4, by Gene Abbe—Good Girl. — 1969 20 1 2 4 $4,928
Owner, Bobby Ken Stable, Hamilton, Ohio. — 1968 26 3 9 6 $8,089

Oct28-69^{4}Hol	1 :31⅗ 1:03⅘ 1:35⅗ 2:05⅘ ft	37	9	9	9^{11}	9^{11}	8^{6}	LongW^{10}	Cd-2	2:07	Kimpam SisByrd LucineScott
Oct21-69^{9}Hol	1 :29⅗ 1:00⅗ 1:31⅘ 2:01⅗ ft	39	9	9	9^{19}	8^{15}	8^{15}	LongW^{9}	Cd-2	2:04⅗	RedWave Bew'ch'gAd's NipSp'r
Oct13-69^{4}Hol	1 :30⅘ 1:01⅗ 1:33⅗ 2:03⅗ ft	5¼	6^{0}	5^{0}	$5^{6\frac{1}{2}}$	7^{11}	9^{10}	LongW^{8}	Cd-2	2:05⅕	SisByrd SilverSing DirectSue
Oct 6-69^{6}Hol	1 :30⅕ 1:02⅗ 1:33 2:03 ft	8¼	2	2	$2^{1\frac{1}{2}}$	$2^{\frac{1}{2}}$	$2^{\frac{3}{4}}$	†LongW^{1}	Cd-3	2:03⅕†	DH P'n'che G'dG'lWick H'pyHal
Sep30-69^{6}Hol	1 :29⅗ 1:01⅗ 1:32⅗ 2:02 ft	54	4	4	7^{8}	8^{8}	$7^{3\frac{3}{4}}$	LongW^{3}	Cd-2	2:02⅘	I.V.P. Ballock KipHanover
Sep24-69^{4}Hol	1 :30⅗ 1:02⅗ 1:34 2:03 ft	10	3	3	3^{4}	$4^{5\frac{1}{2}}$	$7^{6\frac{1}{2}}$	LongW^{1}	Cd-2	2:04	BriskRisk ClinkerSc't MiMarg'ta

5 Saint Estephe A. — 12-1

2:03⅘, Hol, '69 — Driver—JOHN MEANS. Trainer, Irving De Witt — Brown and Tan
Ch. g, 7, by Fanfaron De Sequinel—Hermine VII. — 1969 29 3 5 4 $4,754
Owner, Irving De Witt, Reseda, Calif. — 1968 17 0 2 1 $1.617

Oct23-69^{6}Hol	1 :29⅗ 1:01⅗ 1:33 2:03⅗ ft	36	9	9	8^{9}	$8^{7\frac{1}{2}}$	$3^{1\frac{1}{2}}$	MeansJ^{8}	6000	2:04	Por'tiP'de RuthsS'p'r S'tEst'eA.
Oct16-69^{7}Hol	1 :31 1:02 1:32⅘ 2:01⅘ ft	12	2^{0}	1	2^{1}	4^{5}	6^{7}	Will'msR^{4}	6000	2:03	LandFr'ght B.D.Song Sorrowful
Oct11-69^{3}Hol	1 :30⅘ 1:02⅕ 1:33⅘ 2:03⅗ ft	12	6	6	5^{6}	6^{9}	$x4^{2\frac{1}{4}}$	Wil'msR^{3}	6000	2:03⅘	S'thPhillie B.D.Song Bl'kAmigo
Sep29-69^{9}Hol	1 :30⅕ 1:01 1:31⅕ 2:01⅗ ft	8¼	7	4^{0}	$4^{4\frac{1}{2}}$	8^{11}	$7^{8\frac{1}{4}}$	Wil'msR^{4}	6500	2:03	P'nc'rHan'r Sat'nT'ss F'styAbbe
Sep23-69^{3}Hol	1 :31 1:02⅕ 1:33⅕ 2:03⅘ ft	10	7	6	5^{3}	4^{5}	1^{1}	Wil'msR^{6}	Cd-1	2:03⅘	S'tEst'heA. S'k'yBl'ze D'ndP'c's
Sep 2-69^{2}Sac	1 :33⅗ 1:08 1:41⅗ 2:13⅕ ft	7	5	6	$3^{2\frac{1}{2}}$	$3^{3\frac{1}{2}}$	$2^{2\frac{1}{2}}$	DeWittI^{5}	Cond	2:13⅗	Fitm't S'tEst'pheA. SeaTacCh'f

6 Oakhampton — 8-1

No Record, '69 — Driver-Trainer—DENZIL BERRY — Red and Blue
B. g, 10, by Smokey Hanover—Characteristic. — 1969 10 0 0 1 $1,411
Owner, Roy A. McKenzie, Wellington, New Zealand. — 1968 10 1 1 0 $1,809

Oct29-69^{4}Hol	1 :30⅘ 1:02⅗ 1:34 2:02⅗ ft	15	4	4	$5^{5\frac{1}{2}}$	$4^{6\frac{1}{2}}$	5^{10}	BerryD^{3}	Cd-2	2:04⅗	B'tleSt'rN. Pas'naN. ShadoT'vel
Oct22-69^{4}Hol	1 :31 1:03⅗ 1:35⅕ 2:04 ft	6¼	2	3	3^{3}	$3^{5\frac{1}{2}}$	$4^{4\frac{3}{4}}$	BerryD^{3}	Cd-2	2:04⅗	S'k'yBlaze Dom'sStar C'lessJoe
Oct16-69^{9}Hol	1 :29 :59 1:30⅗ 2:01 ft	20	3	3	3^{5}	$2^{2\frac{1}{2}}$	$4^{2\frac{1}{4}}$	BerryD^{9}	Cd-1	2:01⅗	BeagleBoy MiMargarita MaiTai
Aug15-69^{4}Spk	1 :29⅗ 1:01⅗ 1:32⅕ 2:03⅕ ft	23	3^{0}	2^{0}	1^{h}	1^{nk}	3^{4}	BerryD5	Cond	2:04	TruH'n'v'r Hir'm'sBay O'kh'pton
Aug 8-69^{4}Spk	1 :30⅕ 1:02 1:32⅗ 2:03⅘ ft	32	9	9	$8^{4\frac{1}{2}}$	$8^{4\frac{1}{2}}$	$5^{4\frac{3}{4}}$	BerryD^{5}	Cond	2:04⅘	Sen't'rGlib East'rLind Ph't'mH'l
Jly 30-69^{7}Spk	1 :32⅗ 1:05⅕ 1:34⅗ 2:05⅗ ft	90	9	9	8^{7}	7^{7}	$7^{6\frac{1}{4}}$	BerryD^{8}	Cond	2:06⅗	R'sd'leCh'f R.B'tyLou Wh'tAFl'h

7 Texas Freight — 6-1

2:03⅗, Hol, '69 — Driver—TOM WILBURN. Trainer, A. Van Zanten — Gold and Green
B. g, 8, by Torpid—Trim Freight. — 1969 21 2 1 1 $3,356
Owner, Leonard C. VanBerg, Inglewood, Calif. — 1968 27 1 3 6 $4.148

Oct30-69^{7}Hol	1 :30⅘ 1:02⅕ 1:34 2:04 ft	5	4	4	4^{5}	$4^{3\frac{1}{2}}$	$4^{1\frac{3}{4}}$	Wilb'rnT^{2}	6000	2:04⅗	S'thPhillie P'c'rHan'r RolaC'st'r
Oct17-69^{3}Hol	1 :30 1:01⅗ 1:33⅗ 2:03⅗ ft	3½	6	6	$6^{6\frac{1}{2}}$	$5^{6\frac{1}{2}}$	1^{1}	Wilb'nT^{5}	Cd-1	2:03⅗	T'x'sFr'ht R'y'lR'kHal R'sieF'v'l
Oct14-69^{2}Hol	1 :30⅗ 1:01⅕ 1:33⅘ 2:04⅘ ft	7¼	8	7	7^{7}	$3^{2\frac{1}{2}}$	2^{h}	W'b'nT^{10}	Cd-1	2:04⅘	Y'keeM'd'm Tex'sFr't Fl'rDAm'r
Oct 7-69^{4}Hol	1 :30 1:01⅗ 1:33⅕ 2:04⅗ ft	3	1	2	$3^{5\frac{1}{2}}$	3^{5}	$4^{3\frac{1}{4}}$	Wilb'nT^{7}	Cd-1	2:05⅕	IrishJ.W. Pet'rGoose Fl'rD Am'r
Oct 2-69^{5}Hol	1 :31⅗ 1:02⅘ 1:34⅗ 2:03⅘ ft	45	9	9	9^{10}	7^{10}	$6^{6\frac{1}{4}}$	Wilb'nT^{9}	5000	2:05	TownMartial Galiss TopGunner
Sep25-69^{7}Hol	1 :31⅕ 1:03 1:34⅕ 2:03⅗ ft	70	3	3	3^{3}	3^{4}	$6^{7\frac{1}{4}}$	PettyA^{1}	6000	2:04⅗	RedEblis FrostyAbbe BoldWarr'r

8 Happy Otto — 12-1

2:08, Abion, '69 — Driver-Trainer—CHESTER MILLIGAN — All Blue
B. g, 3, by Otto—Miss Reynolds. — 1969 19 2 2 3 $3,036
Owner, KaCe Stock Farms, Tarzana, Calif. — 1968 16 2 1 2 $2,500

Oct27-69^{9}Hol	1 1/16 :29⅗ 1:01 1:33 2:10⅘ ft	56	7^{0}	7	$6^{8\frac{1}{2}}$	6^{8}	3^{3}	Mil'g'nC^{8}	Cd-2	2:11⅗	Sp'nishCh'f Del'noKid H'pyOtto
Oct16-69^{4}Hol	1 :30⅗ 1:01⅘ 1:33 2:02⅕ ft	36	x8	8	$8^{7\frac{1}{2}}$	8^{12}	7^{10}	Milli'nC^{2}	Cd-1	2:04⅕	Mr.MiteB. S'k'yBl'ze Sp'ishCh'f
Oct10-69^{9}Hol	1 :31 1:02 1:33⅗ 2:03 ft	26	2^{0}	3	3^{4}	3^{5}	$4^{7\frac{1}{4}}$	Milli'nC^{4}	Cd-1	2:04⅗	KipHanover MaiTai FreeHeather
Oct 2-69^{9}Hol	1 :31⅗ 1:02⅕ 1:33⅕ 2:03⅕ ft	7¾	1	3	$4^{2\frac{1}{2}}$	3^{6}	$4^{4\frac{3}{4}}$	Milli'nC^{8}	Cd-1	2:04	Hick'yD'l's FreeH'th'r B'nieL'k't
Sep24-69^{5}Hol	1 :30 1:01⅗ 1:33⅗ 2:03 ft	17	5	5	5^{8}	7^{9}	$6^{6\frac{1}{2}}$	Mil'g'nC^{3}	Cd-1	2:04⅗	FrontierSue TopBid O.C.Mego
Sep 8-69 Was	1 :30⅕ 1:03⅗ 1:34⅗ 2:04⅕ ft	13	4	5	6	6^{6}	6^{6}	Mil'g'nC^{2}	Cond	2:05⅗	Dir'ctSue H'yG'ne R'kSpringsH't

9 Nip Spencer — 4-1

2:10⅗, B.M, '69 — Driver-Trainer—WILLIAM LUTHER — All Green
B. h, 7, by Walter Spencer—Pussy Foot. — 1969 24 4 4 2 $4,787
Owner, Mr. & Mrs. L. J. Swanson, Tarzana, Calif. — 1968 36 7 2 3 $7,266

Oct27-69^{9}Hol	1 1/16 :29⅗ 1:01 1:33 2:10⅘ ft	7¼	8	8	7^{12}	7^{11}	4^{3}	L'th'rW^{9}	Cd-2	2:11⅗	Sp'nishCh'f Del'noKid H'pyOtto
Oct21-69^{9}Hol	1 :29⅗ 1:00⅗ 1:31⅘ 2:01⅗ ft	34	5	5	5^{10}	5^{8}	$3^{5\frac{3}{4}}$	L'th'rW^{3}	Cd-2	2:02⅗	RedWave Bew'ch'gAd's NipSp'r
Oct16-69^{4}Hol	1 :30⅗ 1:01⅘ 1:33 2:02⅕ ft	27	6	2	2^{h}	7^{11}	$6^{9\frac{1}{4}}$	Luth'rW^{3}	Cd-1	2:04	Mr.MiteB. S'k'yBl'ze Sp'ishCh'f
Oct10-69^{9}Hol	1 :31 1:02 1:33⅗ 2:03 ft	11	6^{0}	7	8^{9}	7^{13}	6^{11}	L'th'rW^{5}	Cd-1	2:05⅕	KipHanover MaiTai FreeHeather
Oct 3-69^{9}Hol	1 1/16 :30⅕ 1:03 1:34⅕ 2:11⅗ ft	16	5	5	6^{6}	$5^{6\frac{1}{2}}$	$4^{5\frac{1}{4}}$	L'th'rW^{1}	Cd-2	2:13⅗	Sh'll'sG'ld Fl'shOnP'k In'tPl's're
Sep26-69^{2}Hol	1 :30⅗ 1:01⅗ 1:33 2:02⅗ ft	31	5	6	$8^{9\frac{1}{2}}$	7^{8}	$6^{4\frac{1}{2}}$	LutherW^{1}	Cd-2	2:03⅗	Mr.MiteB. Fr'tL'wy'r B'tleSt'rN.

10 Delano Kid — 7-2

2:07⅘, B.M. '69 — Driver-Trainer—ROBERT WILLIAMS — Purple and White
B. g, 3, by Storm Cloud—Beauty Way. — 1969 21 4 4 1 $4,752
Owner, Frank A. Lucich, Delano, Calif. — 1968 4 1 1 1 $380

Oct27-69^{9}Hol	1 1/16 :29⅗ 1:01 1:33 2:10⅘ ft	7¼	2	2	2^{2}	$2^{\frac{1}{2}}$	$2^{2\frac{3}{4}}$	Wil'msR^{2}	Cd-2	2:11⅗	Sp'nishCh'f Del'noKid H'pyOtto
Oct20-69^{9}Hol	1 1/16 :30 1:02⅕ 1:34⅗ 2:12⅕ ft	7¾	7	7	6^{10}	7^{10}	8^{5}	Wil'msR^{3}	Cd-2	2:13⅕	Indication ClinkerScott Kimpam
Oct13-69^{4}Hol	1 :30⅘ 1:01⅗ 1:33⅗ 2:03⅗ ft	2½ ▲	8	7	7^{9}	8^{13}	7^{10}	Wi'msR^{6}	Cd-2	2:05⅕	SisByrd SilverSing DirectSue
Oct 7-69^{9}Hol	1 :30⅕ 1:01⅕ 1:32 2:03⅗ ft	7½	7	7	8^{12}	6^{8}	2^{h}	Wil'msR^{7}	Cd-2	2:03⅗	PollyJinks Del'noKid Bl'kAmigo
Sep29-69^{4}Hol	1 :30⅗ 1:01⅗ 1:32⅗ 2:02 ft	87	7	7	$8^{7\frac{1}{2}}$	7^{8}	5^{7}	Wil'msR^{7}	Cd-2	2:03⅗	ElM'yord'mo Sw'gBye M'dysBoy

Declared—Top Gene. ‡RACING WITHOUT HOPPLES.

HEAD NUMBER COLOR: YELLOW—BLACK NUMBER

18

Hollywood Park, NOVEMBER 3, 1969

THE ONE-MILE TRACK is dry and fast, the weather pleasantly cool. Drivers who have been winning 15 percent or more of their starts include Bob Farrington, Bob Williams, Joe O'Brien, Jack Williams and Eddie Cobb. During the 35 previous nights of the meeting, the outer post positions have been producing fewer winners than usual. As if Holly Park had become a half-miler, posts 7 through 10 have gone fallow. My guess is that this is nothing permanent. We should continue to take guidance from the long-range probabilities, as summarized on page 236.

The First Race

To help fans recognize boosts and drops in class, the program now grades conditioned races (see p. 45). This race is a Cd-1, the lowest grade.

I can find only one contender, Peter Goose. His October 27 effort was the not-bad-not-good kind that directs us to a horse's previous race. On October 20, this gelding went at least a quarter-mile on the outside, finishing second as favorite.

On To Fame, Copper Green Tree, Status, Princess Ellen, Frosty Woollen and Bewitching Goldie have shown little in the way of recent form. Pacing Bear's good qualifier of October 27 was not good enough to attract a bet. Sister Dares and Ruby Stormcloud are also returning to action from qualifiers.

RESULT: A tremendous favorite at 1 to 2, Peter Goose was far in the lead in the stretch but Pacing Bear wore it down and won by a half-length, paying $20.60.

The Second Race

Blazit's latest race might seem uninspired to persons accustomed to half-mile tracks. But the homestretch at Hollywood is 988 feet long. A horse must be fit and courageous to gain ground while racing close to the leader through that heart-burstingly long straightaway. Blazit is a contender.

So is Wee Johnny D., for roughing it. Sampson Frisco has broken stride in three of the four betting races on his list. Out he goes. So does Bull Hill, who raced a rapid final quarter on October 23, but finished too far behind the winner. His October 17 effort was altogether bad.

Diamante Phil, a three-year-old with gait problems, seems to produce a good race in every second attempt. Perhaps we had better excuse his galloping of October 20 (and his absence since), and see what kind of rating his October 16 victory yields us. Heather Chance raced well enough in his California debut against tougher company. His failure to win in 13 previous starts this year is a black mark, but note that he was competing in much better races than tonight's—a $7,200 claimer, for instance. We had better give him a rating, and see how he fits in here.

Yankee Madam and Key Holder have nothing, and the three-year-old Teddy probably needs a race before establishing local form.

Rating the contenders:

Blazit. Basic rating is 203. Might give an extra point for the stretch gain, making the final figure 204.

Wee Johnny D. Basic rating is 208. Add 5 for roughing it, 5 for the drop in class and 1 for the improved post. Total is 219.

Diamante Phil. Basic rating is 209, using the October 16 race. Add 2 for the stretch gain and 3 for the improved post. Total is 214.

Heather Chance. Basic rating is 212, plus 5 for roughing it and 5 for the drop in class. Total is 222.

Heather Chance has the highest rating and, in my opinion, is a worthwhile play at 10 to 1. Our standards of fitness make that last race a good one. Some of the Chicago races also were good, and were against much more formidable opposition.

RESULT: Teddy looked like a winner at 22 to 1, but broke into a gallop during the stretch drive. Heather Chance had been setting or pressing the pace all the way and now took over to win by four lengths. The payoff was $23.40 to win and $11.40 for place. Blazit (7 to 1) was third. Wee Johnny D. was 28 to 1 and finished next to last, ahead of the favored Diamante Phil (6 to 5), who had broken stride. The daily double paid $244.20.

The Third Race

None of the three-year-olds in this modest trotting race has the kind of class edge we seek in such youngsters. Sirius has not been moving up the ladder, having plenty of trouble in lowly conditioned races. Stylish Season won a couple of Cd-1 affairs at high odds (indicating that nobody saw too much in him, even after he had won). And then he was found wanting against better three-year-olds on October 24.

To me, the only choice here is Odette Adios, the former pacer whose October 20 race produced a higher rating than possibly could be computed for Sirius, Hasti Ax and Prevaricator, the other legitimate contenders.

RESULT: She led all the way and was extending her lead at the end. Paid $5.20. Sirius was second at almost 7 to 1, and Hasti Ax (10 to 1) was third. Prevaricator broke twice and finished last, justifying his 25 to 1 odds. Stylish Season, the 6 to 5 favorite, was fifth after breaking.

The Fourth Race

Unimpressive form eliminates everything but Diamond Princess and Midnight Brownie. The mare's last race was rather marginal, suggesting that we rate her performance of October 17:

Diamond Princess. Basic rating of 223, plus 7 for the big stretch gain. Total is 230.

Midnight Brownie. Basic rating of 213, plus 2 for the stretch gain, and 5 for beating Diamond Princess on October 28 (see p. 230), less 2 for the change in post position. Final rating is 218.

RESULT: Diamond Princess, the 5 to 2 favorite, beat everything but Mount Eden, which paid $50.20. Such things are expected. The trick is to become involved in as few as possible. Incidentally, the minimum bet on the exacta is $3. This one paid $711.

The Fifth Race

An interesting trot, with many possible contenders. We can eliminate the migrant, Joe Brooke, and the absentees, Fair Vale and Knight Valor.

The ratings:

Bill G. Not ordinarily a breaker, this one can be rated off its October race. The basic rating is 186. The rise in class cancels the credit for roughing. Final rating is 186.

Shell Cloud. Basic rating is 198. Deduct 5 for the rise in class, add 2 for the stretch gain and 10 for the topnotch driver, Doug Ackerman. Total is 205.

Tarport Mart. Basic rating is 202, plus 10 for racing on the outside. No credit for supposed drop in class. That race was no better than this one, and my file of result charts proves it. Final rating is 212.

Vic Arden. This gelding is not an habitual breaker and should be forgiven the October 29 gallop. Its October 20 performance yields a basic rating of 187, plus 5 for roughing it, 2 for the stretch gain and 10 for Bobby Williams, less 5 for the rise from a $4,000 claiming price to tonight's $5,000. Total is 199.

Kelly's Mail. Basic rating is 199. Add 5 for the drop in class and 6 for the stretch gain. Total is 210.

Special Product. Rate the October 15 performance, which earned a basic figure of 191. Add 5 for the drop in class and 10 for roughing it, but deduct 2 for the changed post position. Total is 204.

The selection is Tarport Mart.

RESULT: Bill G. won it, paying $29.20. Tarport Mart, a 9 to 1 shot, passed Special Product in the stretch to take second place by a neck. The place mutuel was a comfortable $12.00. Knight Valor, favored at 5 to 2, was never a factor and finished last. Vic Arden (7 to 1) was fourth.

The Sixth Race

No need to compute ratings for this race. Excusing Marish's break on October 28, his October 15 performance earns him far higher figures than could be generated for the only other possible contender, John L. Purdue. Besides which, Marish is driven by the eminent Joe Marsh.

RESULT: Bad. Joe Blades led from wire to wire, paying $19.40. John L. Purdue went off at better than 6 to 1 and finished second. Marish galloped again, and came in fifth. He was a 9 to 5 favorite.

The Seventh Race

An interesting situation which deserves a few minutes of study. We can eliminate Toughie Direct, whose record is that of a puller. If he had not been folding in the stretch in those Chicago races after cutting out rapid early fractions, his failure to hold his speed on October 29 could be excused on grounds of his 1:00:1 time to the half. But premature effort seems to be his style, so we write him off. Dilly Davis, Poppa Rex and Bye Bye Dannibyrd are dismissed for unimpressive form. The contenders:

Lenawee Creed. Basic rating of 219, plus 4 for the stretch gain, 1 for the better post and 10 for Bobby Williams. Final rating is 234.

Freight Lawyer. Basic rating of 229. Add 1 for the stretch gain, small though it was. Also add 10 for Jim Dennis. And deduct 5 for a rise in class. The boost is not evident in the record, which labels the October 29 race a Cd-3. However, the result chart of that race shows that it was for somewhat weaker stock with lower earnings than specified in the conditions of tonight's race. Final rating is 235.

Two Step. Basic rating of 219, plus 5 for roughing it, 1 for the stretch gain and 10 for Joe Marsh. Total is 235.

Stoney Burke N. This one's figures obviously will not compare with the others, so we need not do the arithmetic.

With two animals rated at 235 and another at 234, one needs to be an all-time-great hair-splitter to separate them. Lenawee Creed is favored at about 2 to 1, Freight Lawyer is 7 to 2 and Two Step is almost 9 to 1. What to do? I say that this is a race to sit out.

RESULT: Toughie Direct led from the first step to the last, paying $17.20. Pullers *do* win sometimes, you know. Lenawee Creed was second all the way. Two Step and Freight Lawyer were fourth and fifth behind Bye Bye Dannibyrd.

The Eighth Race

Don't let the claiming label fool you. These are pretty good pacers. And a $15,000 claiming price is nothing to be sneezed at.

Two possible contenders:

Bo Bo Ranger. In my opinion, the three-year-old is moving out of his class, regardless of the dramatic fact that he is being offered for claim after racing in conditioned events. That Cd-3 of October 29 was for cheaper stock than these, with a $2,700 purse. Most of the horses in tonight's field would have been ineligible for the race, having won too much purse money this year. However, let us proceed with the rating. The October 29 performance gets a basic figure of 227. Deduct 5 for the rise in class, add 1 for the stretch gain and subtract 1 for the changed post position. Total is 222.

Hirams Bay. This hard-knocking four-year-old looks like a shoo-in. His October 24 race produces a basic rating of 221. Add 2 for the stretch gain, 3 for the improved post and 5 for having been a beaten favorite. Final rating is 231.

RESULT: Hiram Bay paid $6.00. Bo Bo Ranger ended next to last.

The Ninth Race

The minimum bet on this exacta is $5. Eliminate Dominions Star (form), Dream Street (scratched), Little Al (poor winning percentage), Good Girl Wick (form), Oakhampton (form), Nip Spencer (no really good races) and Delano Kid (last race at a mile was dreadful). Now eliminate Happy Otto, whose last ratable performance at a mile (October 10) does not measure up in terms of class or speed. The survivors:

Saint Estephe A. Rate the latest performance. The footnote comment in the result chart of that race shows that the horse closed with a tremendous rush after being blocked earlier. *California Racegoers Should Collect Result Charts.* The basic rating is 213. Add 6 for the stretch gain and 5 for the drop in class from a claimer with a $3,000 purse and tougher livestock. Final rating is 224.

Texas Freight. The result-chart footnotes say that Tom Wilburn's gelding was a victim of traffic congestion on October 30. Perhaps we should use its previous performance. The basic rating is 214. Add 8 for the stretch gain, 1 for the better post position and 10 for the topnotcher, Wilburn. Final rating is 233.

Texas Freight is the choice. Readers may be wondering why we went to this horse's next-to-last race for a rating but used the latest race of Saint Estephe A. We did it because the result charts indicated that Texas Freight had not been able to get out of traffic soon enough to do his best on October 30, whereas the other horse had been able to perform representatively. Texas Freight would remain the choice even if Saint Estephe A.'s October 16 race were used for handicapping purposes. The switch from Bobby Williams to Means would undermine the higher speed rating.

RESULT: A lot of argument to no immediate avail. Good Girl Wick won it, Dominions Star was second and Texas Freight (4.40 to 1) was third, beating the 5 to 2 favorite, Little Al. Saint Estephe A. showed nothing, finishing sixth. The exacta paid $329.50.

We passed only one race, suggesting 11 plays, of which five were successful: Peter Goose (lost), Heather Chance ($23.40, $11.40), Odette Adios ($5.20), Diamond Princess (lost), Tarport Mart (lost, but paid $12.00 for place), Marish (lost), Hirams Bay ($6.00), Texas Freight (lost both win and place).

19

Rules and Regulations of the United States Trotting Association

RULE 1.
Mandate.

Section 1. The following Rules and Regulations, having been duly enacted, are hereby declared to be the Official Rules and Regulations of The United States Trotting Association which shall apply to and govern the Registration of Standard Bred Horses and the conduct of all racing by Members and upon Member Tracks.

All published conditions and programs of Member Tracks shall state that said races shall be conducted under and governed by the Rules and Regulations of The United States Trotting Association, with only such exceptions stated as are specifically authorized and permitted.

§ 2. In the event there is a conflict between the rules of The United States Trotting Association and the rules or conditions promulgated by any of its members, the rules of The United States Trotting Association shall govern.

§ 3. In the event USTA denies membership to any person for failure to meet the requirements of the By-Laws relative to membership, and in the event a State Racing Commission determines that such person fully meets its requirements and licenses such person to participate at meetings under the jurisdiction of such Commission, USTA will issue an eligibility certificate and/or a drivers license limited to such meetings and keep performance records on such person and his horses while racing at such meetings in the same manner and for the same fee as for members.

RULE 2.
Authorities and Terms.

Section 1. The term "President" or "Executive Vice-President" in these Rules refers to the President or Executive Vice-President of The United States Trotting Association. "Board of Review" refers to the Board comprised of the Directors from the Association District where the matter originated. The term "Association" when used in these rules refers to The United States Trotting Association.

RULE 3.
Violations.

Section 1. Any Member of this Association violating any of its Rules or

Regulations, shall be liable upon conviction, to a fine not exceeding One Thousand Dollars ($1,000.00) or suspension, or both, or expulsion from the Association, unless otherwise limited in the rules.

The conviction of any Corporate Member of this Association of a violation of any of its rules or regulations may also subject the Officers of the said corporation to a penalty not exceeding that which is hereinabove provided.

§ 2. Any attempt to violate any of the Rules and Regulations of this Association falling short of actual accomplishment, shall constitute an offense, and, upon conviction, shall be punishable as hereinabove provided.

RULE 4.
Definitions.

Section 1. *Added Money Early Closing Event.*—An event closing in the same year in which it is to be contested in which all entrance and declaration fees received are added to the purse.

§ 2. *Age, How Reckoned.*—The age of a horse shall be reckoned from the first day of January of the year of foaling.

§ 3. *Appeal.* — A request for the Board of Review to investigate, consider, and review any decision or rulings of Judges or officials of a meeting. The appeal may deal with placings, penalties, interpretations of the rules or other questions dealing with the conduct of races.

§ 4. *Claiming Race.*—One in which any horse starting therein may be claimed for a designated amount in conformance with the rules.

§ 5. *Classified Race.*—A race regardless of the eligibility of horses, entries being selected on the basis of ability or performance.

§ 6. *Conditioned Race.*—An overnight event to which eligibility is determined according to specified qualifications. Such qualifications may be based upon:

(a) Horses' money winnings in a specified number of previous races or during a specified previous time.

(b) A horses' finishing position in a specified number of previous races or during a specified period of time.

(c) Age.

(d) Sex.

(e) Number of starts during a specified period of time.

(f) Or any one or more combinations of the qualifications herein listed.

(g) Use of records or time bars as a condition is prohibited.

§ 7. *Dash.*—A race decided in a single trial. Dashes may be given in a series of two or three governed by one entry fee for the series, in which event a horse must start in all dashes. Positions may be drawn for each dash. The number of premiums awarded shall not exceed the number of starters in the dash.

§ 8. *Declarations.* — Declarations shall be taken not more than three days in advance for all races except those for which qualifying dashes are provided.

§ 9. *Disqualification.*—It shall be construed to mean that the person disqualified is debarred from acting as an official or from starting or driving a horse in a race, or in the case of a disqualified horse, it shall not be allowed to start.

§ 10. *Early Closing Race.*—A race for a definite amount to which entries close at least six weeks preceding the race. The entrance fee may be on the installment plan or otherwise, and all payments are forfeits.

No payments on 2-year-olds in early closing events are permissible prior to February 15th of the year in which the horse is a 2-year-old.

§ 11. *Elimination Heats.*—Heats of a race split according to Rule 13, Sections 2 and 3, to qualify the contestants for a final heat.

§ 12. *Entry.*—Two or more horses starting in a race when owned or trained by the same person, or trained in the same stable or by the same management.

§ 13. *Expulsion.* — Whenever the

penalty of expulsion is prescribed in these rules, it shall be construed to mean unconditional exclusion and disqualification from any participation, either directly or indirectly, in the privileges and uses of the course and grounds of a member.

§ 14. *Extended Pari-Mutuel Meetings.*—An extended pari-mutuel meeting is a meeting or meetings, at which no agricultural fair is in progress with an annual total of more than ten days duration with pari-mutuel wagering.

§ 15. *Futurity.*—A stake in which the dam of the competing animal is nominated either when in foal or during the year of foaling.

§ 16. *Green Horse.*—One that has never trotted or paced in a race or against time, either double or single.

§ 17. *Guaranteed Stake.*—Same as a stake, with a guarantee by the party opening it that the sum shall not be less than the amount named.

§ 18. *Handicap.*—A race in which performance, sex or distance allowance is made. Post positions for a handicap may be assigned by the Racing Secretary. Post positions in a handicap claiming race may be determined by claiming price.

§ 19. *Heat*—A single trial in a race two in three, or three heat plan.

§ 20. *In Harness.*—When a race is made to go "in harness" it shall be construed to mean that the performance shall be to a sulky.

§ 21. *Late Closing Race.*—A race for a fixed amount to which entries close less than six weeks and more than three days before the race is to be contested.

§ 22. *Length of Race and Number of Heats.*—Races or dashes shall be given at a stated distance in units not shorter than a sixteenth of a mile. The length of a race and the number of heats shall be stated in the conditions. If no distance or number of heats are specified all races shall be a single mile dash except at fairs and meetings of a duration of 10 days or less, where the race will be conducted in two dashes at one mile distance.

§ 23. *Maiden.*—A stallion, mare or gelding that has never won a heat or race at the gait at which it is entered to start and for which a purse is offered. Races or purse money awarded to a horse after the "official sign" has been posted shall not be considered winning performance or affect status as a maiden.

§ 24. *Match Race.*—A race which has been arranged and the conditions thereof agreed upon between the contestants.

§ 25. *Matinee Race.*—A race with no entrance fee and where the premiums, if any, are other than money.

§ 26. *Overnight Event.*—A race for which entries close not more than three days (omitting Sundays) or less before such race is to be contested. In the absence of conditions or notice to the contrary, all entries in overnight events must close not later than 12 noon the day preceding the race.

§ 27. *Protest.*—An objection, properly sworn to, charging that a horse is ineligible to a race, alleging improper entry or declaration, or citing any act of an owner, driver, or official prohibited by the rules, and which, if true, should exclude the horse or driver from the race.

§ 28. *Record.* — The fastest time made by a horse in a heat or dash which he won. A standard record is a record of 2:20 or faster for two-year-olds and 2:15 or faster for all other ages.

§ 29. *Stake.*—A race which will be contested in a year subsequent to its closing in which the money given by the track conducting the same is added to the money contributed by the nominators, all of which except deductions for the cost of promotion, breeders or nominators awards belongs to the winner or winners. In any event, all of the money contributed in nominating, sustaining, and starting payments must be paid to the winner or winners.

§ 30. *Two in Three.*—In a two in three race a horse must win two heats to be entitled to first money.

§ 31. *Two-Year-Olds.* — No two-year-old shall be permitted to start in a dash or heat exceeding one mile in distance. Except where elimination heats are required, two-year-olds may start only in races conditioned not to exceed two dashes or in a two in three race which shall terminate in three heats. Starting a two-year-old in violation of this rule shall subject the member track to a fine of not less than $25.00 and the winnings of such two-year-old shall be declared unlawful. In two year old races any colt may default the end of the second heat or dash and the remaining colt shall be declared the winner. Any colt withdrawing under this rule shall forfeit all right to the race winner's share of the purse or to the award of the trophy. Any arrangement between contestants for sharing purse money shall be a violation of Rule 5 Section 3 (Hippodroming). In the event all eligibles withdraw, the sponsor may retain the ten per cent and the trophy.

§ 32. *Walk Over.* — When only horses in the same interest start, it constitutes a walk over. In a "stake race" a "walk over" is entitled to all the stake money and forfeits unless otherwise provided in the published conditions. To claim the purse the entry must start and go once over the course.

§ 33. *Winner.*—The horse whose nose reaches the wire first. If there is a dead heat for first, both horses shall be considered winners. Where two horses are tied in the summary, the winner of the longer dash or heat shall be entitled to the trophy. Where the dashes or heats are of the same distance and the horses are tied in the summary, the winner of the faster dash or heat shall be entitled to the trophy. Where the dashes or heats are of the same distance and the horses are tied in the summary and the time, both horses shall be considered winners.

§ 34. *Wire.*—The wire is a real or imaginary line from the center of the judge's stand to a point immediately across, and at right angles to the track.

§ 35. *Contract Track.*—A pari-mutuel track, not a member of this Asso-

ciation, which receives data and services pursuant to Article VII, Section 7 (c) of the Association's By-Laws.

RULE 5.
Track Members.

Section 1.   Whenever races are conducted each member track shall display its certificate of membership in this Association for the current year and specified dates. Horses racing after January 1, 1940, upon due notice to members on tracks which are not in contract or which are not in membership with The United States Trotting Association or the Canadian Trotting Association, or racing on tracks in membership with the Association on dates that have not been sanctioned by the Association shall from the date of the first such race be ineligible to race in anything but a free-for-all, and he is barred from classified and claiming and conditioned races and no eligibility certificate will be issued on that horse in the future. In the event of a bona fide sale of the horse to an innocent party or upon satisfactory proof that the owner of such horse was deceived as to the absence of contract with such track, the non-membership of such track or failure to be sanctioned for such dates, the penalty hereinbefore provided may be limited in the discretion of the Board of Review. Such horse may be restored to eligibility and may be admitted to classified, claiming and conditioned races and may receive USTA eligibility certificate upon the payment of the sum of $10 per start with a maximum of $50 for any one meeting to cover the cost of establishing and verifying the racing performances of that horse on such non-member or non-contract track.

§ 2.   *Location of Judges' Stand.*— The Judges' stand shall be so located and constructed as to afford to the officials an unobstructed view of the entire track and no obstruction shall be permitted upon the track, or the center-field which shall obscure the officials' vision of any portion of the track during the race. Any violation of this section shall subject the member to a fine not exceeding $500 and immediate suspension from membership by the President or Executive Vice-President, subject to appeal.

§ 3. *Hippodroming Ban.* — All races conducted by Member tracks shall be bona fide contests with the winner receiving the largest share of the purse and the balance of the purse distribution made according to the order of finish. No hippodroming or other arrangement for equal distribution of the purse money among the contestants is permitted. Violation of this rule will subject the track member, officials in charge, and the owners and drivers to fine, suspension, or expulsion.

§ 4. *Default in Payment of Purses.* —Any member that defaults in the payment of a premium that has been raced for, shall stand suspended, together with its officers. No deduction, voluntary or involuntary, may be made from any purse or stake, or futurity other than for payments to be made to the owners, nominators, or breeders of money winning horses and clerical, printing, postage and surety bond expenses specifically related to such purse, stake or futurity.

§ 5. *Time to File Claims for Unpaid Purses.*—Unless claims for unpaid premiums shall be filed with this Association within sixty days after the date the race is contested the Association may release any performance bond that had been required.

§ 6. If at a meeting of a member a race is contested which has been promoted by another party or parties, and the promoters thereof default in the payment of the amount raced for, the same liability shall attach to the members as if the race had been offered by the member.

§ 7. *Dishonored Checks.* — Any member who shall pay any purse, or charges due The United States Trotting Association, or a refund of entrance fees by draft, check, order or other paper, which upon presentation is protested, payment refused, or otherwise dishonored, shall by order of the Executive Vice-President be subjected to a fine not exceeding the amount of said draft, check or order and shall be suspended from membership until the dishonored amount and fine are paid to the Executive Vice-President.

§ 8. *Minimum Advertised Purse or Schedule of Purses.*—When any member track advertises minimum purses or purses for a class and conducts any race for that class for less than said advertised minimum or class purse, such track member shall be fined by the Executive Vice-President the difference between the advertised minimum or advertised purse and the lesser purse for which such race was conducted unless there is a contract with a horsemen's association concerning purse distributions.

§ 9. *Removal of Horses From the Grounds.*—No horse shall be ordered off the grounds without at least 72 hours notice (excluding Sunday) to the person in charge of the horse.

§ 10. *Driver Awards.*—Except as herein stated, no member track in the United States shall advertise to pay or pay any awards other than to the Owners, Nominators, or Breeders of money winning horses. Awards may be made to drivers of horses breaking or equaling track or world records, or to leading drivers at meetings.

§ 11. *Paddock Rules.*—Every extended pari-mutuel track shall:

(1) Provide a paddock or receiving barn.

(2) The paddock or receiving barn must be completely enclosed with a man-tight fence and all openings through said fence shall be policed so as to exclude unauthorized personnel therefrom.

(3) Horses must be in the paddock at the time prescribed by the Presiding Judge, but in any event at least one hour prior to post time of the race in which the horse is to compete. Except for warm-up trips, no horse shall leave the paddock until called to the post.

(4) Persons entitled to admission to the paddock:

- (a) Owners of horses competing on the date of the race.
- (b) Trainers of horses competing on the date of the race.
- (c) Drivers of horses competing on the date of the race.
- (d) Grooms and caretakers of horses competing on the date of the race.
- (e) Officials whose duties require their presence in the paddock or receiving barn.

(5) No driver, trainer, groom, or caretaker, once admitted to the paddock or receiving barn, shall leave the same other than to warm up said horse until such race, or races, for which he was admitted is contested.

(6) No person except an owner, who has another horse racing in a later race, or an official, shall return to the paddock until all races of that program shall have been completed.

(7) No more than two members of a registered stable, other than the driver, shall be entitled to admission to the paddock on any one racing day.

(8) During racing hours each track shall provide the services of a blacksmith within the paddock.

(9) During racing hours each track shall provide suitable extra equipment as may be necessary for the conduct of racing without unnecessary delay.

(10) Each track shall see that the provisions of this rule are rigidly enforced and a fine not to exceed $500.00 for each violation of this rule may be imposed.

§ 12. *Photo Finish, Head Numbers — Starting Gate.* — At all member tracks where pari-mutuel wagering is allowed, a photo finish, head numbers, and starting gate must be used. Whenever the Judges use a photo to determine the order of finish, it shall be posted for public inspection. Photo finish equipment shall not be acceptable unless a spinner or target is used therewith.

§ 13. *Payment of Dues.* — If a member fails to pay the dues prescribed by the By-Laws of the Association within thirty (30) days of notice of the amount due, the member together with its officers and directors may be suspended from membership in the Association.

§ 14. *Driver Insurance.* — Each member conducting an extended pari-mutuel meeting shall prepare and prominently display, in the Race Secretary's office, a statement giving the name of the company with which they carry driver insurance.

§ 15. *Supervision of Meeting.*—Although members have the obligation of general supervision of their meeting, interference with the proper performance of duties of any official is hereby prohibited.

RULE 6.
Race Officials.

Section 1. *Officials Required.*—In every race over the track of a member, the Manager shall appoint or authorize the appointment of three men familiar with the rules to act as Judges, one of whom shall be designated as Presiding Judge, who shall be in charge of the stand. He shall also appoint a licensed Starter, three Timers, and a competent person to act as Clerk of the Course.

At all matinees there shall be at least one licensed official in the Judges' stand.

§ 2. No license shall be granted to any person not in membership with this Association.

§ 3. Any member track permitting an unlicensed person to officiate when a license is required shall be fined not exceeding $100 for each day such unlicensed person officiates. Any person officiating without being licensed as required by these rules or acting as an official at any meeting not in membership with this Association, or the Canadian Trotting Association, shall be fined not exceeding $100 for each day he acts as such an official; PROVIDED HOWEVER, that nothing herein contained shall prevent any person from officiating at a contract track.

§ 4. *Officials at Extended Meetings.* —No presiding Judge, Starter or Race Secretary shall be qualified to serve as such at an extended pari-mutuel harness race meeting or a grand circuit meeting without a license valid for pari-mutuel meetings or grand circuit meetings. An Associate Judge, Barrier Judge, Patrol Judge, Clerk of the Course, or Paddock Judge who serves at an extended pari-mutuel meeting or at pari-mutuel meetings totaling more than ten days during a race season must have a license valid for pari-mutuel meetings. Starters, Presiding Judges and Race Secretaries holding pari-mutuel licenses are authorized to officiate at all meetings, and Associate Judges holding pari-mutuel licenses are authorized to serve as Presiding Judges at pari-mutuel meetings of ten days or less and at non pari-mutuel meetings. No person shall serve as an Associate Judge at any pari-mutuel meeting in the United States unless he is a member of the USTA. The Executive Vice-President may permit an exchange of license in the various capacities above, upon proper application. The fee for each such license shall be $25.00 for all categories with the exception of the Patrol Judge and Clerk of the Course which shall be $15.00, which includes an active membership in this Association. The applicant for such license must satisfy the Executive Vice-President that he possesses the necessary qualifications, both mental and physical, to perform the duties required. Elements to be considered among others shall be character, reputation, temperament, experience, and knowledge of the rules and of the duties of a racing official. No official acting as Judge at a pari-mutuel meeting shall serve as a Race Secretary or Clerk of the Course at such meeting. No licensed official shall be qualified to act

as such at any pari-mutuel meeting where he is the owner or otherwise interested in the ownership of any horse participating at such meeting. Any refusal to grant this license to a person who had been so licensed in the past may be reviewed by the Board of Appeals as provided in Article IX of the By-Laws.

§ 5. *Disqualification to Act as Official.*—A person under suspension, expulsion, or other disqualification, or who has any interest in or any bet on a race or has an interest in any of the horses engaged therein, is disqualified from acting in any official capacity in that race. In the event of such disqualification the management shall be notified by the disqualified person and shall appoint a substitute. Any person who violates this restriction shall be fined, suspended or expelled.

§ 6. *Suspension or Revocation of Official's License.*—An official may be fined, suspended, or his license may be revoked or denied at any time by the President or Executive Vice-President for incompetence, failure to follow or enforce the rules, or any conduct detrimental to the sport including drinking within 4 hours prior to the time he starts work as an official. Such license may be reinstated by the President or Executive Vice-President in his discretion upon such terms as he may prescribe. Any revocation or suspension of license hereunder may be reviewed by the Board of Appeals as provided in Article IX of the By-Laws.

Breath Analyzer Test. — Any officials, when directed by a representative of this Association, shall submit to a breath analyzer test, and if the results thereof show a reading of more than .05 per cent of alcohol in the blood, a report shall be made to the respective State Racing Commissions and The United States Trotting Association for appropriate action.

§ 7. *Ban on Owning or Dealing in Horses.*—No employee of any pari-mutuel track whose duties include the classification of horses shall directly or indirectly be the owner of any horse racing at such meeting, nor shall he participate financially directly or indirectly in the purchase or sale of any horse racing at such meeting. Any person violating this rule shall be suspended by the Executive Vice-President.

§ 8. *Judges' Stand Occupants.* — None but the Judges, the Clerk of the Course, the Secretary, Starter and Timers, Official Announcer, and Officers, Officials, and Directors of this Association, and the State Racing Commission having jurisdiction shall be allowed in the Judges' stand during a race. Any association violating this rule shall be fined not to exceed $100.

§ 9. *Improper Acts by an Official.* —If any person acting as Judge or an official shall be guilty of using insulting language from the stand to an owner, driver, or other person, or be guilty of other improper conduct, he shall be fined not exceeding $500, or be expelled.

§ 10. *Presiding Judge.*—No person shall act as Presiding Judge where purses are raced for unless he is a member of and holds a license for the current year from this Association.

A Presiding Judge's license shall be issued by the Executive Vice-President upon payment of an annual fee of $25.00 which includes an active membership, when the applicant therefor has established that his character and reputation, knowledge of the rules, harness horse experience, temperament and qualifications to perform the duties required are satisfactory. Such application must be accompanied by the written approval of at least one Director of this Association from the district in which the applicant resides. However, a license limited to one public race meeting not exceeding five days in duration may be issued for $5.00 but no Judge shall receive more than one such limited license a year.

(a) The Presiding Judge shall have supervision over:

1) Associate Judges
2) Patrol Judges
3) Starters
4) Paddock Judge
5) Finish Wire Judge
6) Clerk of the Course
7) Timers

(b) Shall examine the official track license issued by the Association and if the license is not produced shall make public announcement that the meeting shall not proceed.

(c) Notify owners and drivers of penalties imposed.

(d) Report in writing to the Executive Vice-President violations of the rules by a member, its officers or race officials giving detailed information.

(e) Make such other reports as required by the Executive Vice President.

(f) Sign each sheet of the judges' book verifying the correctness of the information contained therein.

(g) Be responsible for the maintenance of the records of the meeting and the forwarding thereof to The United States Trotting Association except in cases of a contract track in which the contract provides otherwise.

Services of the Presiding Judge shall be paid for by the track employing him and he shall not act as a Starter, announcer or an officer at any meeting at which he officiates as Presiding Judge.

§ 11. The Judges shall have authority while presiding to:

(a) Inflict fines and penalties, as prescribed by these rules.

(b) Determine all questions of fact relating to the race.

(c) Decide any differences between parties to the race, or any contingent matter which shall arise, such as are not otherwise provided for in these rules.

(d) Declare pools and bets "off" in case of fraud, no appeal to be allowed from their decision in that respect. All pools and bets follow the decision of the Judges. Such a decision in respect to pools and bets shall be made at the conclusion of the race upon the observations of the judges and upon such facts as an immediate investigation shall develop. A reversal or change of decision after the official placing at the conclusion of the heat or dash shall not affect the distribution of betting pools made upon such official placing. When pools and bets are declared off for fraud, the guilty parties shall be fined, suspended or expelled.

(e) Control the horses, drivers, and assistants and punish by a fine not exceeding $100.00 or by suspension or expulsion, any such person who shall fail to obey their orders or the rules. In no case shall there be any compromise or change on the part of the Judges or members of punishment prescribed in the rules, but the same shall be strictly enforced. Members shall not remove or modify any fine imposed by the Judges of a race, review any order of suspension, expulsion, or interfere with the Judges performing their duties.

(f) Examine under oath all parties connected with a race as to any wrong or complaint. Any person required to appear before the Judges for a hearing or examination who shall fail to appear after due notice in writing shall be penalized as provided in (e) above.

(g) Consider complaints of foul from the patrols, owners, or drivers in the race and no others.

§ 12.   It shall be the duty of the Judges to:

(a) Exclude from the race any horse that in their opinion is improperly equipped, dangerous, or unfit to race, which shall include sick, weak, and extremely lame horses. No horse shall race with a tube in its throat.

(b) Investigate any apparent or possible interference, or other violation of Rule 18, Section 1, whether or not complaint has been made by the driver.

(c) Investigate any act of cruelty seen by them or reported to them, by any member towards a race horse during a meeting at which they officiate. If the Judges find that such an act has been committed, they shall suspend or fine the offending member not to exceed $500.00.

(d) Immediately thereafter or on the day of the race conduct an investigation of any accidents to determine the cause thereof, and the judges shall completely fill out an accident report and mail to the Association office.

(e) Observe closely performance of the drivers and the horses to ascertain if there are any violations of Rule 18; particularly, interference, helping, or inconsistent racing, and exhaust all means possible to safeguard the contestants and the public.

(f) Grant a hearing at a designated time before a penalty may be imposed upon any party. All three Judges should be present if possible, and at least the Presiding Judge and one Associate Judge must be present at all Judges' hearings. The Judges may inflict the penalties prescribed by these rules.

In the event the Judges believe that a person has committed a rule violation other than a racing violation and has left the grounds and they are unable to contact him, and hold a hearing thereon, they may make an investigation and send a detailed written report to the Executive Vice-President of this Association. The Executive Vice-President may impose a penalty not to exceed 10 days without a hearing based upon the report of the Judges. No penalty in excess of 10 days shall be imposed before a hearing is granted.

It shall be the duty of the Judges to submit in writing, a complete list of all witnesses questioned by them at any hearing, which list of witnesses, along with the testimony of such witnesses, shall be forwarded to the Executive Vice-President along with the reports required in Rule 6, Section 10.

The testimony of all witnesses questioned by the Judges shall be recorded by one of the following methods: written, signed statements, tape recorders or court reporter's transcript. At all extended pari-mutuel tracks Judges shall use tape recorders to record their hearings.

No decision shall be made by the Judges in such cases until all of the witnesses called by the Judges and the person so required to appear before the Judges have given their testimony. Any person charged with a rule violation shall be given at least until 12:00 noon of the following day to prepare his defense if he so requests.

All penalty notices will carry the exact reason why the penalty has been imposed together with the wording of the rule violated.

(g) It shall be the duty of the Judges to declare a dash or heat of a race no contest in the event the track is thrown into darkness during the progress of a race by failure of electricity.

§ 13. It shall be the procedure of the Judges to:

(a) Be in the stand fifteen minutes before the first race and remain in the stand for ten minutes after the last race, and at all times when the horses are upon the track.

(b) Observe the preliminary warming up of horses and scoring, noting behavior of horses, lameness, equipment, conduct of the drivers, changes in odds at pari-mutuel meetings, and any unusual incidents pertaining to horses or drivers participating in races.

(c) Have the bell rung or give other notice, at least ten minutes before the race or heat. Any driver failing to obey this summons may be punished by a fine not exceeding $100.00 and his horse may be ruled out by the Judges and considered drawn.

(d) Designate one of their members to lock the pari-mutuel machines immediately upon the horses reaching the official starting point. The Presiding Judge shall designate the post time for each race and the horses will be called at such time as to preclude excessive delay after the completion of two scores.

(e) Be in communication with the Patrol Judges, by use of patrol phones, from the time the Starter picks up the horses until the finish of the race. Any violation or near violation of the rules shall be reported by the Patrol Judge witnessing the incident and a written record made of same. At least one Judge shall observe the drivers throughout the stretch specifically noting changing course, interference, improper use of whips, breaks, and failure to contest the race to the finish.

(f) Post the objection sign, or inquiry sign, on the odds board in the case of a complaint or possible rule violation, and immediately notify the announcer of the objection and the horse or horses involved. As soon as the Judges have made a decision, the objection sign shall be removed, and the correct placing displayed, and the "Official" sign flashed. In all instances the Judges shall post the order of finish and the "Official" sign as soon as they have made their decision.

(g) Display the photo sign if the order of finish among the contending horses is less than half-length or a contending horse is on a break at the finish. After the photo has been examined and a decision made, a copy or copies shall be made, checked by the Presiding Judge, and posted for public inspection.

§ 14. *Patrol Judges.*—At the discretion of the Judges, patrol may be appointed by the member, but such patrols shall be approved by the Presiding Judge and work under his direction. At extended pari-mutuel meetings and at other meetings conducting one or more races with a purse value of $5,000 or over, at least two (2) Patrol Judges shall be employed. It shall be their duty to phone or repair to the Judge's stand and report all fouls and improper conduct. The result of a heat or dash shall not be announced until sufficient time has elapsed to receive the reports of the patrols. Where there is a Patrol car, only one Patrol Judge shall be required.

§ 15. *Emergency Appointment of Official.*—If any licensed official is absent or incapacitated, the member or director, or officer of the association, may appoint a substitute at such meeting, or until another licensed official can be procured. If such official acts for more than three days, he shall apply for a license in that capacity. Notice of any temporary appointment shall be wired immediately to the main office of this Association. This power may only be used in case of unavoidable emergencies. Any Director of this Association, in an emergency, may exercise any or all of the functions of any official or licensee.

§ 16.   *Starter.*—No person shall be permitted to start horses on a track in membership with this Association unles he holds a Starter's license for the current year. An application for such license must be accompanied by the written approval of at least one Director of this Association from the district in which the applicant resides. Upon sufficient information as to good character, knowledge of these rules and ability to do the work, a license to start horses may be issued by the Executive Vice-President upon payment of an annual fee of $25.00. However, a license limited to start horses in matinee races, or at one public race meeting not exceeding five days in duration may be issued to members upon payment of an annual fee of $5.00, but no starter shall receive more than one such license in any one year.

§ 17.   The Starter shall be in the stand or starting gate fifteen minutes before the first race. The Starter, prior to starting any race at a meeting, shall examine the official track license issued by this Association and in the event the same is not produced, shall make public announcement that the meeting shall not proceed. He shall have control over the horses and authority to assess fines and/or suspend drivers for any violation of the rules from the formation of the parade until the word "go" is given. He may assist in placing the horses when requested by the Judges to do so. He shall notify the Judges and the drivers of penalties imposed by him. He shall report violations of the rules by a member or its officers, giving detailed information. His services shall be paid for by the member employing him. An Assistant Starter may be employed when an association deems it necessary. At all meetings at which the premiums do not exceed three thousand dollars, the Starter may also act as an Associate Judge.

§ 18.   *Clerk of Course.*—The Clerk of the Course shall:

(a) At request of Judges assist in drawing positions.

(b) Keep the Judges' Book provided by the U.S.T.A. and record therein:

(1) All horses entered and their eligibility certificate numbers.

(2) Names of owners and drivers and drivers' license numbers.

(3) The charted lines at nonfair pari-mutuel meetings. At fairs, the position of the horses at the finish. At all race meetings, the money won by the horse at that track.

(4) Note drawn or ruled out horses.

(5) Record time in minutes, seconds and fifths of seconds.

(6) Check eligibility certificates before the race and after the race shall enter all information provided for thereon, including the horse's position in the race if it was charted.

(7) Verifying the correctness of the Judge's Book including race time, placing and money winnings, reasons for disqualifications, if any, and see that the book is properly signed.

(8) Forward the Judges' Book, charts and marked programs from all extended pari-mutuel meetings the day following each racing day and from fairs and other meetings not later than the last day of the meeting.

(9) Notify owners and drivers of penalties assessed by the officials.

(c) Upon request may assist Judges in placing horses.

(d) After the race, return the eligibility certificate to owner of the horse or his representative when requested.

Failure to comply with any part of this rule and make the above listed entries legible, clear and acurate, may subject either the Clerk or the Member, or both, to a fine of not to exceed $50.00 for each violation.

§ 19. *Timers.*—At each race there shall be three Timers in the Judges' or Timers' stand except when an electric timing device approved by the Executive Vice-President of the Association, is used, in which event there shall be one Timer. The chief timer shall sign the Judges' Book for each race verifying the correctness of the record. All times shall be announced and recorded in fifths of seconds. An approved electronic or electric timing device must be used where horses are started from a chute.

The Timers shall be in the stand fifteen minutes before the first heat or dash is to be contested. They shall start their watches when the first horse leaves the point from which the distance of the race is measured. The time of the leading horse at the quarter, half, three-quarters, and the finish shall be taken. If odd distances are raced, the fractions shall be noted accordingly.

§ 20. *Paddock Judge.*—Under the direction and supervision of the Presiding Judge, the Paddock Judge will have complete charge of all paddock activities as outlined in Rule 5 Section 10. The Paddock Judge is responsible for:

(a) Getting the fields on the track for post parades in accordance with the schedule given to him by the Presiding Judge.

(b) Inspection of horses for changes in equipment, broken or faulty equipment, head numbers or saddle pads.

(c) Supervision of paddock gate men.

(d) Proper check in and check out of horses and drivers.

Check the identification of all horses coming into the Paddock including the tattoo number if he does not personally recognize the horse.

(e) Direction of the activities of the paddock blacksmith.

(f) The Paddock Judge will immediately notify the Presiding Judge of anything that could in any way change, delay or otherwise affect the racing program.

The Paddock Judge will report any cruelty to any horse that he observes to the Presiding Judge.

(g) The Paddock Judge shall see that only properly authorized persons are permitted in the paddock and any violation of this rule may result in a fine, suspension or expulsion.

§ 21. *Program Director.*—Each extended pari-mutuel track shall designate a Program Director.

(a) It shall be the responsibility of the Program Director to furnish the public complete and accurate past performance information as required by Rule 7, Section 2.

(b) No person shall act as a Program Director at an extended pari-mutuel meeting unless he has secured a license from this Association. A license may be granted to any person who, by reason of his knowledge, experience and industry, is capable of furnishing accurate and complete past performance information to the general public.

(c) The annual fee for such license shall be $25.00 which includes an active membership.

§ 22. *Duties of Patrol Judges.*—The Patrol Judges shall observe all activity on the race track in their area at all times during the racing program. They shall immediately report to the Presiding Judge:

(a) Any action on the track which could improperly affect the result of a race.

(b) Every violation of the racing rules.

(c) Every violation of the rules of decorum.

(d) The lameness or unfitness of any horse.

(e) Any lack of proper racing equipment.

The Patrol Judges shall, furthermore:

(a) Be in constant communication with the Judges during the course of every race and shall immediately advise the Judges of every rule violation, improper act or unusual happening which occurs at their station.

(b) Submit individual daily reports of their observations of the racing to the Presiding Judge.

(c) When directed by the Presiding Judge shall attend hearings or inquiries on violations and testify thereat under oath.

§ 23. *Licensed Charter.* — The charting of races shall be done only by a licensed charter and he shall be responsible for providing a complete and accurate chart. A license may be granted only to a person who has the knowledge, training and industry to accomplish this. The annual fee for such a license shall be $15.00 which includes an active membership.

RULE 7.
Identification of Horses.

Section 1. *Bona Fide Owner or Lessee.*—Horses not under lease must race in the name of the bona fide owner. Horses under lease must race in the name of the lessee and a copy of the lease must be recorded with this Association. Persons violating this rule may be fined, suspended or expelled.

§ 2. *Program Information.* — A printed program shall be available to the public at all meetings where purses are raced for. All programs shall furnish:

(a) Horse's name and sex.

(b) Color and age.

(c) Sire and dam.

(d) Owner's name.

(e) Driver's name and colors.

At extended pari-mutuel meetings the following additional information shall be furnished:

(f) In claiming races the price for which the horse is entered to be claimed must be indicated.

(g) At least the last six (6) per-

formance and accurate chart lines. (See Rule 14, Section 2, Sub-Section (d). An accurate chart line shall include: Date of race, place, size of track if other than a half-mile track, symbol for free-legged pacers, track condition, type of race, distance, the fractional times of the leading horse including race time, post position, position at one quarter, one half, three quarters, stretch with lengths behind leader, finish with lengths behind leader, individual time of the horse, closing dollar odds, name of the driver, names of the horses placed first, second and third by the Judges. The standard symbols for breaks and park-outs shall be used, where applicable.

(h) Indicate drivers racing with a provisional license.

(i) Indicate pacers that are racing without hopples.

(j) Summary of starts in purse races, earnings, and best win time for current and preceding year. A horse's best win time may be earned in either a purse or non-purse race.

(k) The name of the trainer.

(l) The consolidated line shall carry date, place, time, driver, finish, track condition and distance, if race is not at one mile.

§ 3. *Failure to Furnish Reliable Program Information.*—May subject the track and/or Program Director to a fine not to exceed $500.00 and/or the track and/or the Program Director may be suspended until arrangements are made to provide reliable program information.

§ 4. *Inaccurate Information.* — Owners, drivers, or others found guilty of providing inaccurate information on a horse's performance, or of attempting to have misleading information given on a program may be fined, suspended, or expelled.

§ 5. *Check on Identity of Horse.*— Any track official, officer of this Association, owner or driver, or any member of this Association may call for information concerning the identity and eligibility of any horse on the grounds of a member, and may demand an opportunity to examine such horse or his eligibility certificate with a view to establish his identity or eligibility. If the owner or party controlling such horse shall refuse to afford such information, or to allow such examination, or fail to give satisfactory identification, the horse and the said owner or party may be barred by the member, and suspended or expelled by the President or Executive Vice-President.

§ 6. *False Chart Lines.*—Any official, clerk, or person who enters a chart line on an eligibility certificate when the race has not been charted by a licensed charter may be fined, suspended, or expelled.

§ 7. *Frivolous Demand for Identification.*—Any person demanding the identification of a horse without cause, or merely with the intent to embarrass a race, shall be punished by a fine not exceeding $100 or by suspension, or expulsion.

§ 8. *Tattoo Requirements.* — No horse will be permitted to start at an extended pari-mutuel meeting that has not been tattooed unless the permission of the Presiding Judge is obtained and arrangements are made to have the horse tattooed.

§ 9. *Withholding Eligibility Certificate.*—Any person withholding an eligibility certificate from the owner of a horse, after proper demand has been made for the return thereof, may be suspended until such time as the certificate is returned.

RULE 8.
Racing, Farm, or Stable Name.

Section 1. Racing, farm, corporate, or stable names may be used by owners or lessees if registered with this Association giving the names of all persons who are interested in the stable or will use the name. The fee for such registration is $100.00. All stockholders of a corporation formed after April 1, 1962 and racing a horse must be members of the Association. The Executive Vice-President shall be notified immediately if additional persons become

interested in a registered stable or if some person listed in a registration disassociates himself from the stable. Failure to do so will place the stable in violation of Rule 12, Section 2. Two stables cannot be registered under the same name and the Executive Vice-President may reject an application for a name that is confusing to the public, unbecoming to the sport, or exceeds 25 letters. All owners and persons listed in a registered stable, whether incorporated or not, shall be liable for entry fees and penalties against the registered stable. In the event one of the owners or persons listed in a registered stable is suspended, all the horses shall be included in accordance with Rule 22, Section 6. When a stable name is not in active use for a period of three consecutive years it will be placed on the inactive list.

§ 2. *Signature on Transfers and Other Documents Relating to Racing, Farm, Corporate and Stable Names.*— Only the signature of the corresponding officer of a racing, farm, corporate or stable name will be recognized on transfers and other documents pertaining to such organizations. Documents bearing the signature of the stable by the corresponding officer will be considered binding upon the members thereof.

Each member of a registered farm, corporate or stable should sign a document designating the name and address of the corresponding officer thereof—for future applications only.

RULE 9.
Eligibility and Classification.

Section 1. *Eligibility Certificate.*— There shall be an automatic fine of $10.00 on the owner if a horse is declared in without an eligibility certificate first being presented for the current year at the gait the horse is declared to race. The track member shall automatically be fined $5.00 for accepting a declaration without an eligibility certificate for the proper gait and a track member may refuse to accept any declaration without the eligibility certificate for the proper gait first being presented. Telegraphic or telephone declarations may be sent and accepted without penalty, provided the declarer furnishes adequate program information but the eligibility certificate must be presented when the horse arrives at the track and before he races, or the above fines will be imposed.

The Race Secretary or where the meeting is held at a contract track, the Association's authorized representative shall check each certificate and certify to the judges as to the eligibility of all the horses.

§ 2. *Fee for Eligibility Certificate and Replacement Certificate.*—The fee for an eligibility certificate shall be $5.00. In the event of the loss or destruction of an eligibility certificate, a replacement certificate may be issued to the same owner for $10.00 when the application therefor is accompanied by *a signed statement from the owner or trainer certifying that the certificate is lost or destroyed listing the starts together with all fair races,* qualifying races and matinee races made by the horse during the current year.

Applications for eligibility certificates must state the name and address of the owner, and the color, sex, age and breeding of the horse.

§ 3. *Issuance of Eligibility Certificate.*

(a) An eligibility certificate shall be issued only to an active member of this Association in good standing and shall not be issued to an owner or horse under penalty except as provided in Rule 1, Section 3.

(b) *Joint Ownership.* — When a horse is owned jointly by two or more parties, all owners must be members in good standing in this Association before an eligibility certificate will be issued.

(c) *Sale or Lease During Current Year.*—When a horse is sold or leased after an eligibility certificate is issued for the current year, the seller or his authorized agent duly authorized in writing shall endorse the eligibility certificate *and deliver it to the new owner or lessee immediately* who may use it providing he is a member for that year and providing he immediately sends the registration certificate in for a transfer or sends a copy of the lease, the eligibility certificate following the horse. If the new owner or lessee is not a member of this Association, he shall immediately apply for membership.

Failure to forward the registration certificate within 20 days after purchase of an animal which is racing, will subject the buyer to a fine not to exceed $100.00.

(d) *Leased Horses.*—Any horse on lease must race in the name of the lessee. No eligibility certificate will be issued to a horse under lease unless a copy of the lease is filed with the Association.

(e) *Procedure Where Eligibility Certificate Is Not Endorsed.*—If the eligibility certificate is not endorsed to him, the new owner or lessee must apply for an eligibility certificate, pay the regular fee, send satisfactory information on the starts made by the horse during the current year *which will include all fair races, qualifying races and matinee races.*

(f) *Information Required From Horses Racing at Canadian Tracks.*— Prior to declarations, owners of horses having Canadian eligibility certificates who are not in membership with the USTA shall furnish the Racing Secretary with a Canadian eligibility certificate completely filled out for the current year, which has a certificate of validation attached thereto. Residents of Canada under Canadian Trotting Association jurisdiction holding eligibility certificates who are members of this Association may obtain a validation certificate by filing an application with this Association. Residents of the United States and the Maritime Provinces holding Canadian eligibility certificates and who are members of this Association must have the horse registered in current ownership in The United States Trotting Association register before a validation certificate can be obtained by filing an application with this Association. The fee shall be the same as that for an eligibility certificate. This validation certificate may then be attached to the Canadian eligibility certificate and used at tracks in membership with this Association.

No validation certificate will be issued in the name of the lessee unless a copy of the lease is on file with either The United States Trotting Association or the Canadian Trotting Association.

(g) *Tampering With Eligibility Certificates.*—Persons tampering with eligibility certificates may be fined, suspended or expelled and winnings after such tampering may be ordered forfeited.

(h) *Corrections On Eligibility Certificates.* — Corrections on eligibility certificates may be made only by a representative of this Association or a licensed official who shall place on the certificate his initial and date.

(i) *Withholding Eligibility Certificates On Horses Not Tattooed.*—An eligibility certificate may be denied to any person refusing to permit his horses to be tattooed.

§ 4. *Information Required On Horses That Have Raced In A Country Other Than Canada.*—No eligibility certificate will be issued on a horse coming from a country other than Canada unless the following information, certified by the Trotting Association or governing body of that country from which the horse comes, is furnished:

(a) The number of starts during the preceding year, together wtih the number of firsts, seconds and thirds for each horse, and the total amount of money won during this period.

(b) The number of races in which the horse has started during the current year, together with the number of firsts, seconds and thirds for each horse and the money won during this period.

(c) A detailed list of the last six starts giving the date, place, track condition, post position or handicap, if it was a handicap race, distance of the race, his position at the finish, the time

of the race, the driver's name, and the first three horses in the race.

§ 5. (a) *Registration of Standard and Non-Standard Bred Horses.*—All foals of 1937 and thereafter shall be registered in current ownership either as Standard or Non-Standard. If registration is properly applied for and all fees paid, an eligibility certificate for one year may be issued and marked "registration applied for."

(b) *Horses 15 Years of Age or Older.*—No eligibility certificate shall be issued to any horse that is fifteen years of age or older to perform in any race except in a matinee.

(c) *Matinee Races Prior to April 1st.* — Permission may be given for horses and drivers to participate in matinees prior to April 1st in each year without having an eligibility certificate or drivers' licenses, respectively.

(d) *Use of Eligibility Certificates During the Month of January.*—Authorization may be granted to use eligibility certificates from the previous year during the month of January.

(e) *Bar On Racing of Yearlings.*— No eligibility certificate will be issued on any horse under two years of age.

§ 6. *Eligibility Certificates for Corporations.*—*Eligibility Certificates will be issued to a corporation only when the corporation is recorded with the Association to show the officers, directors and stockholders.*

No entity whether it be a partnership, a corporation or a registered stable, comprising more than ten (10) persons will be acceptable either to race or to lease horses for racing.

§ 7. *Eligibility.*—For purposes of eligibility, a racing season or racing year shall be the calendar year.

§ 8. *Time Bars Prohibited.* — No time records or bars shall be used as an element of eligibility.

§ 9. *Date When Eligibility Is Determined.* — Horses must be eligible when entries close but winnings on closing date of eligibility shall not be considered.

In mixed races, trotting and pacing, a horse must be eligible to the class at the gait at which it is stated in the entry the horse will perform.

§ 10. *Conflicting Conditions.* — In the event there are conflicting published conditions and neither is withdrawn by the member, the more favorable to the nominator shall govern.

§ 11. *Standards for Overnight Events.*—The Race Secretary should prescribe standards to determine whether a horse is qualified to race in overnight events at a meeting.

§ 12. *Posting of Overnight Conditions.*—Conditions for overnight events must be posted at least 18 hours before entries close at meetings other than extended pari-mutuel meetings.

At extended pari-mutuel meetings, condition books will be prepared and races may be divided or substituted races may be used only where regularly scheduled races fail to fill, except where they race less than 5 days a week. Such books containing at least three days racing program will be available to horsemen at least 24 hours prior to closing declarations on any race program contained therein.

§ 13. *Types of Races to be Offered.* —In presenting a program of racing, the racing secretary shall use exclusively the following types of races:

1. Stakes and Futurities.

2. Early Closing and Late Closing Events.

3. Conditioned Races.

4. Claiming Races.

5. Preferred races limited to the fastest horses at the meeting. These may be Free-For-All Races, JFA, or Invitationals. Horses to be used in such races shall be posted in the Race Secretary's office and listed with the Presiding Judge. Horses so listed shall not be eligible for conditioned overnight races unless the conditions specifically include horses on the preferred list. Twelve such races may be conducted during a 6-day period of racing at tracks distributing more than $100,000 in overnight purses during such period and not more than 10 such races shall be conducted at other tracks during a 6-day period of racing, provided that at least two of these races are for three year olds, four year olds, or combined three and four year olds. At tracks which race less than 5 days per week, not more than ten such races may be conducted during a 6-day period. Purses offered for such races shall be at least 15% higher than the highest purse offered for a conditioned race programmed the same racing week.

No two-year-old, three-year-old, or four-year-old, will be eligible to be placed on the preferred list to race against older horses until it has won five races at that member track during the year or has won a life-time total of $15,000 unless requested by the owner or authorized agent.

Where a meeting is in progress in December and continues in January of the subsequent year, races and earnings won at that meeting may be computed in determining whether a horse may be placed on the preferred list.

§ 14. *Limitations on Conditions.*— Conditions shall not be written in such a way that any horse is deprived of an opportunity to race in normal preference cycle. Where the word "preferred" is used in a condition it shall not supersede date preference. Not more than three also eligible conditions shall be used in writing the conditions for any overnight event.

§ 15. *Dashes and Heats.* — Any dash or any heat shall be considered as a separate race for the purposes of conditioned racing.

§ 16. *Named Races.*—Named races are not permitted except for preferred races for the fastest horses at a meeting as set forth in Section 13 (5) above, and invitational two, three or four-year-old races with a purse at least 15% higher than the highest purse offered for a conditioned race programmed the same racing week.

§ 17. *Selection or Drawing of Horses.* — For all overnight events, starters and also eligibles shall be drawn by lot from those properly declared in, except that a Race Secretary must establish a preference system for races as provided for in Rule 14 Section 5. However, where necessary to fill a card, not more than one *conditioned* race per day may be divided into not more than two divisions after preference has been applied and the divisions may be selected by the Racing Secretary. For all other overnight races that are divided the division must be by lot unless the conditions provide for a division based on performance, earnings or sex.

§ 18. *Posting Requirements.* — Names of all horses at the track ready to race shall be posted by gait in the declaration room, together with all the pertinent information concerning such horse which may be required to determine eligibility of such horse to condition races offered at the track. There shall be a separate posting of two, three and four-year-olds.

Supplemental purse payments made by a track after the termination of a meeting will be charged and credited to the winnings of any horse at the end of the racing year in which they are distributed, and will appear on the eligibility certificate issued for the subsequent year. Such distribution shall not affect the current eligibility until placed on the next eligibility certificate by this Association.

§ 19. *Rejection of Declaration.*—

(a) The Racing Secretary may reject the declaration on any horse whose eligibility certificate was not in his possession on the date the condition book is published.

(b) The Racing Secretary may reject the declaration on any horse whose past performance indicates that he would be below the competitive level of other horses declared, provided the rejection does not result in a race being cancelled.

§ 20. *Substitute and Divided Races.*—Substitute races may be provided for each day's program and shall be so designated. Entries in races not filling shall be posted. A substitute race or a race divided into two divisions shall be

used only if regularly scheduled races fail to fill.

If a regular race fills it shall be raced on the day it was offered.

Overnight events and substitutes shall not be carried to the next racing day.

§ 21. *Opportunities to Race.*—A fair and reasonable racing opportunity shall be afforded both trotters and pacers in reasonable proportion from those available and qualified to race. Claiming races may be carded to the proportion of each week's racing program as the number of claiming authorizations on file with the Racing Secretary bears to the total number of horses on the grounds which are qualified and available for racing.

§ 22. *Qualifying Races.*—A horse winning a qualifying race shall not be deprived by reason of such performance of his right to start in an event limited to maidens.

§ 23. *Definition of "Start".*—The definition of the word "start" in any type of condition unless specifically so stated will include only those performances in a purse race. Qualifying and matinee races are excluded.

§ 24. *Sandwiching Races.* — Not more than five races may be sandwiched.

RULE 10.
Claiming Races.

Section 1. *Who May Claim.*—An owner who has declared a horse programmed to start at that meeting. An authorized agent may claim for a qualified owner.

§ 2. *Prohibitions.*—

(a) No person shall claim his own horse nor a horse trained by him.

(b) No person shall claim more than one horse in a race.

(c) No qualified owner or his agent shall claim a horse for another person.

(d) No owner shall cause his horse to be claimed directly or indirectly for his own account.

(e) No person shall offer, or enter

into an agreement, to claim or not to claim, or attempt to prevent another person from claiming any horse in a claiming race.

(f) No person shall enter a horse against which there is a mortgage, bill of sale, or lien of any kind, unless the written consent of the holder thereof shall be filed with the Clerk of the Course of the Association conducting such claiming race.

(g) Any entry in a claiming race cannot declare for a subsequent race until after the claiming race has been contested.

§ 3.   Claiming Procedure.—

(a) *Owner's Credit.* — The owner must have to his credit with the track giving the race an amount equivalent to the specified claiming price.

(b) *Owner's Consent.*—No declaration may be accepted unless written permission of the owner is filed with the Race Secretary at the time of declaration.

(c) *Program.*—The claiming price shall be printed on the program and all claims shall be for the amount so designated and any horse entered in a claiming race may be claimed for the designated amount.

(d) *Claim Box.*—All claims shall be in writing, sealed and deposited at least 15 minutes before the race in a locked box provided for this purpose by the Clerk of the Course.

(e) *Opening of Claim Box.* — No official shall open said box or give any information on claims filed until after the race. Immediately after the race, the claim box shall be opened and the claim, if any, examined by the Judges.

(f) *Multiple Claims on Same Horses.*—Should more than one claim be filed for the same horse, the owner shall be determined by lot by the Judges.

(g) *Delivery of Claimed Horse.*—A horse claimed shall be delivered immediately by the original owner or his trainer to the successful claimant upon authorization of the Presiding Judge.

(h) *Refusal to Deliver Claimed Horse.*—Any person who refuses to deliver a horse legally claimed out of a claiming race shall be suspended together with the horse until delivery is made.

(i) *Vesting of Title to Claimed Horse.*—Every horse claimed shall race in all heats or dashes of the event in the interest and for the account of the owner who declared it in the event, but title to the claimed horse shall be vested in the successful claimant from the time the word "go" is given in the first heat or dash, and said successful claimant shall become the owner of the horse, whether it be alive or dead or sound or unsound, or injured during the race or after it.

(j) *Affidavit by Claimant.* — The judges may require any person making a claim for a horse to make affidavit that he is claiming said horse for his own account or as authorized agent and not for any other person. Any person making such affidavit willfully and falsely shall be subject to punishment as hereinafter provided.

(k) *Penalty for Thirty Days.*—If a horse is claimed it shall not start in another claiming race until thirty days have elapsed unless such horse is entered for a claiming price at least twenty per cent greater than the price at which it was claimed. The day following the date of claiming shall be the first day. If a horse is claimed no right, title or interest therein shall be sold or transferred except in a claiming race for a period of 30 days following the date of claiming.

(l) *Return of Claimed Horse to Owner or Stable.*—No horse claimed out of a claiming race shall be eligible to start in any race in the name or interest of the original owner for thirty days, nor shall such horse remain in the same stable or under the care or management of the first owner or trainer, or anyone connected therewith unless reclaimed out of another claiming race.

§ 4.   *Claiming Price.* — The track shall pay the claiming price to the owner at the time the registration certificate is delivered for presentation to the successful claimant.

§ 5. *Claiming Conditions.*—Whenever possible claiming races shall be written to separate horses five years old and up from young horses and to separate males from females. If sexes are mixed, mares shall be given a price allowance.

Optional claiming races shall not be used unless limited to horses six years old and up.

§ 6. *Minimum Price.*—No claiming race shall be offered permitting claims for less than the minimum purse offered at that time during the same racing week.

§ 7. Any person violating any of the provisions of this rule, shall be fined, suspended, or expelled.

RULE 11.
Stakes and Futurities.

Section 1. All stake and futurity sponsors or presentors, except contract tracks:

(a) Shall be members of this Association.

(b) Shall make an annual application for approval containing:

(1) Satisfactory evidence of financial responsibility.

(2) Proposed conditions.

(3) Sums to be deducted for organization or promotion.

(4) *Bond.*—An agreement to file with the Association a surety bond in the amount of the fund conditioned on faithful performance of the conditions, including a guarantee that said stake or futurity will be raced as advertised in said conditions unless unanimous consent is obtained from owners of eligibles to transfer or change the date thereof, or unless prevented by an act of God or conditions beyond the control of

the sponsor, segregation of funds and making all payments. Any association may deposit in escrow negotiable government securities in the amount of the fund and this may be accepted by The United States Trotting Association in lieu of a surety bond.

State Agency. — Where funds are held by a state or an authorized agency thereof, this provision will not apply.

Trust Funds.—Collections resulting from the forfeiting of any bond will be paid to the contestants according to the order of finish, or in the event the race is not contested, will be divided equally among owners of eligibles on the date the breach of conditions occurs.

(5) *Waiver of Bond.* — The requirement of a bond may be waived by the President of the Association upon written request of a sponsor who is a track member and whose financial statement shows a net worth of five times the amount of trust funds received from payments in stakes and futurities. Where this is permitted, the sponsor will furnish a certified copy of the bank deposit in lieu of the bond.

(c) *Rejection of Application.*—May appeal the rejection of an application to the Executive Committee within 20 days after the mailing of the notice of rejection by registered mail.

(d) *List of Nominations.* — Shall mail list of nominations within 30 days after the date of closing to this Association.

(e) *Financial Statement.* — Shall furnish this Association with an annual financial statement of each stake or futurity and, within 30 days following day of race, submit to this Association a final financial statement.

(f) *Failure to Fill.*—Shall notify all nominators and this Association within 20 days if the stake or futurity does not fill.

(g) *Lists of Eligibles.*—*Shall mail within 20 days a complete list of all horses remaining eligible, to this Association and shall mail within 20 days following the last payment before the starting fee, a complete list of all horses remaining eligible to the owners of all eligibles and to this Association together with a list of any nominations, transferred or substituted if such is permitted by the conditions.*

This list of eligibles shall also include a resume indicating the current financial status of the stake or futurity, or of each individual division thereof if there is more than one division, by listing the number of horses remaining eligible, the amount of money that has been paid in and the amount to be added. The purse shall constitute this amount plus starting fees, if any.

(h) *Nominating and Sustaining Payment Dates.*—Shall set the nominating date and the dates for all sustaining payments except the starting fee on the fifteenth day of the month, and there shall be no payments on yearlings except a nomination payment and such nomination payment shall be due not later than August 15th. Before taking any sustaining payments during the year the race is to be contested, the date and place of the race shall be stated. *No stake or futurity sustaining fee shall become due prior to February 15 of any year.* There shall be no conditions that call for payments in stakes or futurities to fall due after August 15th and before *February 15* of the following year.

No more than one sustaining payment on two-year-olds in stakes and futurities that do not have a two-year-old division will be permitted. No more than two sustaining payments on any horse of any age in any calendar year with the exception of the starting fee will be approved.

(i) *Notice of Place and Date of Race.*—Shall, if possible, advertise the week and place the stake or futurity will be raced before taking nominations. Otherwise announcement of the week and place shall be made as soon as the stake or futurity is sold or awarded.

(j) *Forms.* — All nominations and entry forms, lists of nominations and lists of eligibles shall be on standard 8½ x 11 paper. Such lists shall list the owners alphabetically.

(k) *Estimated Purse.* — No estimated purse shall be advertised or published in excess of the actual purse paid or distributed during the previous year, unless increased by guaranteed added money. No stake or futurity shall be raced for less than 75% of the average estimated purse.

§ 2. *Sponsor's Contribution.*—The sum contributed by a sponsor who is not a track member shall be considered forfeit and is to be included in the sum distributed in the event the stake or futurity is not raced.

Effective, with stakes and futurities opened in 1965 thereafter, no stake or futurity shall be approved for extended pari-mutuel meetings if the added money is not at least 20 percent of the purse and for all other meetings at least 10 percent of the purse shall be added.

In the event a stake or futurity is split into divisions, the added money for each division shall be at least 20% of all nomination, sustaining and starting fees paid into such stake or futurity.

§ 3. *Failure to Make Payment.*—Failure to make any payment required by the conditions constitutes an automatic withdrawal from the event.

§ 4. *Refund of Nomination Fee.*—In the event that a mare nominated to a futurity fails to have a live foal, the nominator shall receive a return on his payment upon notification by December 1st of the year of not foaling, or if the conditions so provide, he may substitute.

§ 5. *Registration of Names.* — *All names of stakes and futurities, includ-*

ing names of specific events which are raced as part of any stake or futurity, may be registered with this Association for a fee of $25. Such registered names shall not be used to identify any other stake, futurity, early closer, late closer or overnight event. Names of farms or active horses, including stallions and brood mares, may not be registered as names for stakes and futurities without written permission of the owner or owners. Names of living persons may not be used without written permission of the person involved. Names of inactive horses, farms or persons no longer living must be approved by this Association before being registered.

§ 6. If the sponsor has failed to comply with the provisions of the within rules, the Executive Vice-President shall be authorized to refuse renewals of such Stakes and Futurities.

RULE 12.
Entries.

Section 1.   All entries must:

(a) Be made in writing.

(b) Be signed by the owner or his authorized agent except as provided in Rule 14, Section 1.

(c) Give name and address of both the bona fide owner and agent or registered stable name or lessee.

(d) Give name, color, sex, sire and dam of horse.

(e) Name the event or events in which the horse is to be entered.

(f) Entries in overnight events must also comply with the provisions of Rule 14, Section 1.

§ 2. *Penalties.* — The penalty for noncompliance with any of the above requirements is a fine of not less than $5.00 nor more than $50.00 for each offense. If the facts are falsely stated for the purpose of deception, the guilty party shall be fined and/or suspended or expelled.

§ 3. *Sale of Horse With Entrance Due.*—If any person shall sell a horse to be free and clear and it appears thereafter that payments were due or to become due in races of any descrip-

tion and for which suspension has been or is subsequently ordered, such seller shall be held for the amount due with the penalty on the same and fined an amount equal to the amount of suspension. Unless the horse has been suspended prior to a sale, a subsequent suspension for unpaid entry fee will have no effect as against a bona fide purchaser for value without notice.

§ 4. *Receipt of Entries for Early Closing Events, Late Closing Events, Stakes and Futurities.*—All entries not actually received at the hour of closing shall be ineligible, except entries by letter bearing postmark not later than the following day (omitting Sunday) or entries notified by telegraph, the telegram to be actually received at the office of sending at or before the hour of closing, such telegram to state the color, sex, and name of the horse, the class to be entered; also to give the name and residence of the owner and the party making entry. Whenever an entry or payment in a stake, futurity, or early closing race becomes payable on a Sunday or a legal holiday that falls on Saturday, such payment is to be due on the following Monday and if made by mail the envelope must be postmarked on or before the following Tuesday. If a payment falls on a Monday that is a legal holiday, such payment is due on Tuesday, and if made by mail must be postmarked on or before the following Wednesday.

Postage Meter.—Where an entry is received by letter bearing the postage meter date without any postmark placed thereon by the Post Office Department, such postage meter date shall be considered to be a postmark for the purposes of this rule if the letter is actually received within seven days following the closing date of the event. Receipt subsequent to this time of an entry by letter bearing the metered postmark date shall not be a valid entry or payment to any event. The metered date, of course, must conform to the postmark date as set forth above in order to be valid.

§ 5. *Deviation from Published*

Conditions.—All entries and payments not governed by published conditions shall be void and any proposed deviation from such published conditions shall be punished by a fine not to exceed $50 for each offense, and any nominator who is allowed privileges not in accordance with the published conditions of the race, or which are in conflict with these rules, shall be debarred from winning any portion of the purse, and the said nominator and the Secretary or other persons who allowed such privileges shall be deemed to have been parties to a fraud.

§ 6.   *Where Ineligible Horse Races.* —A nominator is required to guarantee the identity and eligibility of his entries and declarations and if given incorrectly he may be fined, suspended, or expelled, and any winnings shall be forfeited and redistributed to eligible entries. A person obtaining a purse or money through fraud or error shall surrender or pay the same to this Association, if demanded by the Executive Vice-President, or he, together with the parties implicated in the wrong, and the, horse or horses shall be suspended until such demand is complied with and such purse or money shall be awarded to the party justly entitled to the same. However, where any horse is ineligible as a result of the negligence of the Race Secretary, the track shall reimburse the owner for the resultant loss of winnings.

§ 7.   *Transfer of Ineligible Horse.* —A horse entered in an event to which it is ineligible, may be transferred to any event to which he is eligible at the same gait.

§ 8.   *Withholding Purse on Ineligible Horse.* — Members shall be warranted in withholding the premium of any horse, without a formal protest, if they shall receive information in their judgment tending to establish that the entry or declaration was fraudulent or ineligible. Premiums withheld under this rule shall be forthwith sent to The United States Trotting Association to await the result of an investigation by the member or by the District Board

of Review, and if the eligibility of the horse is not established within thirty days he shall be barred from winning unless the case is appealed to the Board of Appeals.

§ 9.   *Effect of Death on Future Payments.*—All engagements shall be void upon the decease of either party or horse, prior to the starting of the race, so far as they shall affect the deceased party or horse, except when assumed by the estate or where the proprietorship is in more than one person, and any survive.

§10.   *Agreement to Race Under Rule.*—Every entry shall constitute an agreement that the person making it, the owner, lessee, manager, agent, nominator, driver, or other person having control of the horse, and the horse shall be subject to these Rules and Regulations, and will submit all disputes and questions arising out of such entry to the authority and the judgment of this Association, whose decision shall be final.

§ 11.   *Early Closing Events and Late Closing Races.*—

(a) *Date and Place.*—The sponsor shall state the place and day the event will be raced and no change in date, program, events, or conditions can be made after the nominations have been taken without the written consent of the owners or trainer of all horses eligible at the time the conditions are changed.

(b) *File Conditions.* — An entry blank shall be filed with the Executive Vice-President.

(c) *Payments on the Fifteenth of the Month.*—All nominations and payments other than starting fees in early closing events shall be advertised to fall on the fifteenth day of the month.

(d) *List of Nominations.*—A complete list of nominations to any late closing race or early closing event shall be published within twenty (20) days after the date of closing and mailed to each nominator and the Executive Vice-President.

(e) *Procedure If Event Does Not Fill.*—If the event does not fill, each nominator and the Executive Vice-President shall be notified within ten (10) days and refund of nomination fees shall accompany the notice.

(f) *Transfer Provisions—Change of Gait.*—Unless a track submits its early closing conditions to the USTA at least 30 days prior to the first publication and has such conditions approved the following provisions will govern transfers in the event of a change of gait. If conditions published for early closing events allow transfer for change of gait, such transfer shall be to the slowest class the horse is eligible to at the adopted gait, eligibility to be determined at time of closing of entries, the race to which transfer may be made must be the one nearest the date of the event originally entered.

Two-year-olds, three-year-olds, or four-year-olds, entered in classes for their age, may only transfer to classes for same age group at the adopted gait to the race nearest the date of the event originally entered, entry fees to be adjusted.

§ 12. *Subsequent Payments—Lists of Eligibles.*—If subsequent payments are required, a complete list of those withdrawn or declared out shall be made within fifteen (15) days after the payment was due and the list mailed to each nominator and the Executive Vice-President.

§ 13. *Trust Funds.*—All fees paid in early closing events shall be segregated and held as trust funds until the event is contested.

§ 14. *Early Closing Events by New Member.*—No early closing events may be advertised or nominations taken therefor for a pari-mutuel meeting that has not had its application approved by the President, unless the track has been licensed for the preceding year. Members accepting nominations to Early Closing Races, Late Closing Races, Stakes and Futurities will give stable space to any horse nominated and eligible to such event the day before, the day of, and the day after such race.

§ 15. *Limitation on Conditions.*—Conditions of Early Closing Events or Late Closing Races that will eliminate horses nominated to an event or add horses that have not been nominated to an event by reason of the performance of such horses at an earlier meeting held the same season, are invalid. Early Closing Events and Late Closing Events shall have not more than two also eligible conditions.

§ 16. *Penalties.* — Any official or member who fails to comply with any provisions of this rule shall be fined, suspended or expelled, unless otherwise provided.

§ 17. *Excess Entry Fees.* — When entry fees exceed 85% of the advertised purse value, such excess entry fees shall be added to the purse. Where the race is split into divisions, each division shall have a purse value of not less than 75% of the advertised purse. However, entry fees in excess of the amount prescribed above may be used toward the amount that must be added. In all cases the sponsor shall add at least fifteen per cent (15%) to the advertised purse.

RULE 13.
Entries and Starters Required Split Races.

Section 1. An association must specify how many entries are required for overnight events and after the condition is fulfilled, the event must be contested except when declared off as provided in Rule 15.

In early closing events, or late closing events, if five or more horses are declared in to start, the race must be contested, except when declared off as provided in Rule 15. (Pari-mutuel meetings may require five interests to start.) Stakes and Futurities must be raced if one or more horses are declared in to start except when declared off as provided in Rule 15.

In an early closing event, if less horses are declared in than are required to start, and all declarers are immediately so notified, the horse or horses declared in and ready to race shall be entitled to all the entrance money and any forfeits from each horse named.

§ 2. *Elimination Heats or Two Divisions.*—

(a) In any race where the number of horses declared in to start exceeds 12 on a half-mile track or 16 on a larger track, the race, at the option of the track member conducting same stated before positions are drawn, may be raced in elimination heats. No more than two tiers of horses, allowing eight feet per horse, will be allowed to start in any race.

(b) Where the race is divided, each division must race for at least 75% of the advertised purse.

In an added money early closing event the race may be divided and raced in divisions and each division raced for an equal share of the total purse if the advertised conditions so provide, provided, however, extended meetings shall add an additional amount so that each division will race for 75 percent of the advertised added money. These provisions shall apply to any stake with a value of $20,000 or less.

(c) In any stake race or futurity, where the conditions state that the event shall be raced one dash on a race track of less than a mile at an extended pari-mutuel meeting, and where the number of horses declared in to start exceed twelve, the race, at the option of the racing association conducting the same, stated before positions are drawn, may be divided by lot and raced in two elimination divisions with all money winners from both divisions competing in the final. Each division shall race one elimination heat for 20% of the total purse. The remainder of the purse shall be distributed to the money winners in the final.

§ 3. *Elimination Plans.*—(a) Whenever elimination heats are required, or specified in the published conditions such race shall be raced in the following manner unless conducted under another section of this rule. That is, the field shall be divided by lot and the first division shall race a qualifying dash for 30 per cent of the purse, the second division shall race a qualifying dash for 30 per cent of the purse and the horses so qualified shall race in the main event for 40 per cent of the purse. The winner of the main event shall be the race winner.

In the event there are more horses declared to start than can be accommodated by the two elimination dashes, then there will be added enough elimination dashes to take care of the excess. The per cent of the purse raced for each elimination dash will be determined by dividing the number of elimination dashes into 60. The main event will race for 40 per cent of the purse. In event there are three (3) or more qualifying dashes, not more than three (3) horses will qualify for the final from each qualifying dash.

Unless the conditions provide otherwise, if twelve horses declare to start, only the first four horses in each elimination dash qualify to continue. If thirteen horses declare to start the first four horses in the division with six horses and the first five horses in the division with seven horses qualify. If fourteen or more declare to start, only the first five horses in each elimination dash qualify to continue.

The Judges shall draw the positions in which the horses are to start in the main event, i.e., they shall draw positions to determine which of the two dash winners shall have the pole, and which the second position; which of the two horses that have been second shall start in third position; and which in fourth, etc. All elimination dashes and the concluding heat must be programmed to be raced upon the same day or night, unless special provisions for earlier elimination dashes are set forth in the conditions.

In the event there are three separate heat or dash winners and they alone come back in order to determine the race winner according to the conditions, they will take post positions according to the order of their finish in the previous heat or dash.

(b) In any race where the number of horses declared in to start exceeds 12 on a half-mile track or 16 on a mile track, unless other numbers are specified in the conditions, the race, at the option of the track members conducting the same, stated before positions are drawn, may be divided by lot and raced in two divisions with all heat winners from both divisions competing in a final heat to determine the race winner. Each division shall race two heats for 20% of the purse each heat. The remaining 20% of the purse shall go to the winner of the final heat.

(c) Whenever elimination heats are required, or specified in the published conditions of a stake or futurity, such race may be raced on the three heat plan, irrespective of any provisions in the conditions to the contrary, unless such published conditions provide otherwise. That is, the field shall be divided by lot and the first division shall race for thirty per cent of the purse, the second division shall race for thirty per cent, and the horses qualifying in the first and second divisions shall race the third heat for thirty per cent of the purse. If, after the third heat, no horse has won two heats, a fourth heat shall be raced by only the heat winners. The race winner shall receive the remaining ten per cent of the purse. The number of horses qualifying to return after each elimination heat will be the same as set out in Section 3 (a) of this rule.

§ 4. *Overnight Events.*—Not more than eight horses shall be allowed to start on a half-mile track in overnight events and not more than ten horses on larger tracks at extended pari-mutuel meetings.

Trailers are not permitted where the track has room to score all horses abreast.

§ 5. *Qualifying Race for Stake, Etc.*—Where qualifying races are provided in the conditions of an early closing event, stake or futurity, such qualifying race must be held not more than five days prior to contesting the main event (excluding Sunday) and omitting the day of the race.

RULE 14.
DECLARATION TO START AND DRAWING HORSES.

Section 1. *Declaration.*

(a) *Unless otherwise specified in the conditions, the declaration time shall be as follows:*

(1) *Extended pari-mutuel meetings, 9:00 a.m.*

(2) *All other meetings, 10:00 a.m.*

(b) *No horse shall be declared to start in more than one race on any one racing day.*

(c) *Time Used.*—In order to avoid confusion and misunderstanding, the time when declarations close will be considered to be standard time, except the time in use at an extended pari-mutuel meeting shall govern that meeting.

(d) *Declaration Box.* — The management shall provide a locked box with an aperture through which declarations shall be deposited.

(e) *Responsibility for Declaration Box.*—The declaration box shall be in charge of the Presiding Judge.

(f) *Search for Declarations by Presiding Judge Before Opening Box.*—Just prior to opening of the box at extended pari-mutuel meetings where futurities, stakes, early closing or late closing events are on the program, the Presiding Judge shall check with the Race Secretary to ascertain if any declarations by mail, telegraph, or otherwise, are in the office and not deposited in the entry box, and he shall see that they are declared and drawn in the proper event. At other meetings, the Presiding Judge shall ascertain if any such declarations have been received by the Superintendent of Speed or Secretary of the Fair, and he shall see that they are properly declared and drawn.

(g) *Opening of Declaration Box.*—At the time specified the Presiding Judge shall unlock the box, assort the declarations found therein and immediately draw the positions in the presence of such owners or their representatives, as may appear.

(h) *Entry Box and Drawing of*

Horses at Extended Pari-Mutuel Meetings.—The entry box shall be opened by the Presiding Judge at the advertised time and the Presiding Judge will be responsible to see that at least one horseman or an official representative of the horsemen is present. No owner or agent for a horse with a declaration in the entry box shall be denied the privilege of being present. Under the supervision of the Presiding Judge, all entries shall be listed, the eligibility verified, preference ascertained, starters selected and post positions drawn. If it is necessary to reopen any race, public announcement shall be made at least twice and the box reopened to a definite time.

(i) *Procedure in The Event of Absence or Incapacity of Presiding Judge.*—At non-extended meetings in the event of the absence or incapacity of the Presiding Judge, the functions enumerated above may be performed by a person designated by said Judge, for whose acts and conduct said Judge shall be wholly responsible. If a substitution is made as herein provided, the name and address of the person so substituting shall be entered in the Judges' Book.

(j) *Drawing of Post Positions for Second Heat in Races of More Than One Dash or Heat at Pari-Mutuel Meetings.*—In races of a duration of more than one dash or heat at pari-mutuel meetings, the judges may draw post positions from the stand for succeeding dashes or heats.

(k) *Declarations by Mail, Telegraph or Telephone.*—Declarations by mail, telegraph, or telephone actually received and evidence of which is deposited in the box before the time specified to declare in, shall be drawn in the same manner as the others. Such drawings shall be final.

(l) *Effect of Failure to Declare on Time.*—When a member requires a horse to be declared at a stated time, failure to declare as required shall be considered a withdrawal from the event.

(m) *Drawing of Horses After Declaration.*—After declaration to start has been made no horse shall be drawn except by permission of the Judges. A fine, not to exceed $500, or suspension may be imposed for drawing a horse without permission, the penalty to apply to both the horse and the party who violates the regulation.

(n) *Procedure on Unauthorized Withdrawal Where There Is No Opportunity for Hearing.*—Where the person making the declaration fails to honor it and there is no opportunity for a hearing by the Judges, this penalty may be imposed by the Executive Vice-President.

(o) *Horses Omitted Through Error.*—Such drawings shall be final unless there is conclusive evidence that a horse properly declared, other than by telephone, was omitted from the race through the error of a track or its agent or employee in which event the horse may be added to this race but given the outside post position. This shall not apply at pari-mutuel meetings unless the error is discovered prior to the publication of the official program.

§ 2. *Qualifying Races.*—At all extended pari-mutuel meetings declarations for overnight events shall be governed by the following:

(a) Within two weeks of being declared in, a horse that has not raced previously at the gait chosen must go a qualifying race under the supervision of a Judge holding a Presiding or Associate Judge's license for pari-mutuel meetings and acquire at least one charted line by a licensed charter. In order to provide complete and accurate chart information on time and beaten lengths, a standard photo-finish shall be in use.

(b) A horse that does not show a charted line for the previous season, or a charted line within its last six starts, must go a qualifying race as set forth in (a). Uncharted races contested in heats or more than one dash and consolidated according to (d) will be considered one start.

(c) A horse that has not started at a charted meeting by August 1st of a season must go a qualifying race as set forth above in (a).

(d) When a horse has raced at a charted meeting during the current season, then gone to meetings where the races are not charted, the information from the uncharted races may be summarized, including each start, and consolidated in favor of charted lines and the requirements of Section (b) would then not apply.

The consolidated line shall carry date, place, time, driver, finish, track condition and distance if race is not at one mile.

(e) The Judges may require any horse that has been on the Steward's List to go a qualifying race. If a horse has raced in individual time not meeting the qualifying standards for that class of horse, he may be required to go a qualifying race.

(f) The Judges may permit a fast horse to qualify by means of a timed workout consistent with the time of the races in which he will compete in the event adequate competition is not available for a qualifying race.

(g) To enable a horse to qualify, qualifying races should be held at least one full week prior to the opening of any meeting that opens before July 1st of a season and shall be scheduled at least twice a week. Qualifying races shall also be scheduled twice a week during the meeting.

(h) Where a race is conducted for the purpose of qualifying drivers and not horses, the race need not be charted, timed or recorded. This section is not applicable to races qualifying both drivers and horses.

§ 3. *Entries.—When the starters in a race include two or more horses owned or trained by the same person, or trained in the same stable or by the same management, they shall be coupled as an "entry" and a wager on one horse in the "entry" shall be a wager on all horses in the "entry." Provided, however, that when a trainer enters two or more horses in a stake, early closing, futurity, Free-For-All or other special event under bonafide separate ownerships, the said horses may, at the request of the association and with the approval of the Commission, be permitted to race as separate betting entries. The fact that such horses are trained by the same person shall be indicated prominently in the program. If the race is split in two or more divisions, horses in an "entry" shall be seeded insofar as possible, but the divisions in which they compete and their post positions shall be drawn by lot. The above provisions shall also apply to elimination heats.*

At non-betting meetings or at fairs where there is no wagering, the person making an entry of more than one horse in the same race shall be responsible to designate the word "entry" on the declaration blank, providing that the horses qualify as an entry.

§ 4. *Also Eligibles.* — Not more than two horses may be drawn as also eligibles for a race and their positions shall be drawn along with the starters in the race. Also eligibles shall be drawn from those horses having the least preference. In the event one or more horses are excused by the Judges, the also eligible horse or horses shall race and take the post position drawn by the horse that it replaces, except in handicap races. In handicap races the also eligible horse shall take the place of the horse that it replaces in the event that the handicap is the same. In the event the handicap is different, the also eligible horse shall take the position on the outside of horses with a similar handicap. No horse may be added to a race as an also eligible unless the horse was drawn as such at the time declarations closed. No horse may be barred from a race to which it is otherwise eligible by reason of its preference due to the fact that it has been drawn as an also eligible. A horse moved into the race from the also eligible list cannot be drawn except by permission of the Judges, but the owner or trainer of such a horse shall be notified that the horse is to race and it shall be posted at the Race Secretary's office. All horses on the also eligible list and not moved in to race by 9:00 A.M. on the day of the race shall be released.

§ 5. *Preference.*—Preference shall be given in all overnight events according to a horse's last previous purse race during the current year. The preference date on a horse that has drawn to race and been scratched is the date of the race from which he was scratched.

When a horse is racing for the first time in the current year, the date of the first declaration shall be considered its last race date, and preference applied accordingly.

This rule relating to preference is not applicable for any meeting at which an agricultural fair is in progress. All horses granted stalls and eligible must be given an opportunity to compete at these meetings.

§ 6. *Steward's List.*—(a) A horse that is unfit to race because he is dangerous, unmanageable, sick, lame, unable to show a performance to qualify for races at the meeting, or otherwise unfit to race at the meeting may be placed on a "Steward's list" by the Presiding Judge and declarations on said horse shall be refused, but the owner or trainer shall be notified in writing of such action and the reason as set forth above shall be clearly stated on the notice. When any horse is placed on the Steward's list, the Clerk of the Course shall make a note on the Eligibility Certificate of such horse, showing the date the horse was put on the Steward's list, the reason therefor and the date of removal if the horse has been removed.

(b) No Presiding Judge or other official at a nonextended meeting shall have the power to remove from the Steward's List and accept as an entry any horse which has been placed on a Steward's List and not subsequently removed therefrom for the reason that he is a dangerous or unmanageable horse. Such meetings may refuse declarations on any horse that has been placed on the Steward's List and has not been removed therefrom.

§ 7. *Driver.* — Declarations shall state who shall drive the horse and give the driver's colors. Drivers may be changed until 9:00 A.M. of the day preceding the race, after which no driver may be changed without permission of the judges and for good cause. When a nominator starts two or more horses, the Judges shall approve or disapprove the second and third drivers.

§ 8. It shall be the duty of the Presiding Judge to call a meeting of all horsemen on the grounds before the opening of an extended pari-mutuel meeting for the purpose of their electing a member and an alternate to represent them on matters relating to the withdrawal of horses due to bad track or weather conditions.

§ 9. In case of questionable track conditions due to weather, the Presiding Judge shall call a meeting consisting of an agent of the track member, the duly elected representative of the horsemen and himself.

§ 10. Upon unanimous decision by this committee of three, that track conditions are safe for racing, no unpermitted withdrawals may be made.

§ 11. (a) Any decision other than unanimous by this committee will allow any entrant to scratch his horse or horses after posting ten per cent of the purse to be raced for. In the event sufficient withdrawals are received to cause the field to be less than six, then the track member shall have the right to postponement of an early closing event or stake and cancellation of an overnight event.

(b) Said money posted shall be forwarded to The United States Trotting Association and shall be retained as a fine, or refunded to the individual upon the decision of the District Board hearing the case at its next meeting as to whether the withdrawal was for good cause.

THE ABOVE PROCEDURE APPLIES ONLY TO THE WITHDRAWAL OF HORSES THAT HAVE BEEN PROPERLY DECLARED IN AND DOES NOT RELATE TO POSTPONEMENT WHICH IS COVERED ELSEWHERE.

RULE 15.
POSTPONEMENT.

Section 1.   In case of unfavorable weather, or other unavoidable cause, members with the consent of the Judges shall postpone races in the following manner.

(a) Early Closing Races, Stakes, and Futurities. All shall be postponed to a definite hour the next fair day and good track.

(b) Any LATE CLOSING RACE, EARLY CLOSING RACE, and STAKE OR FUTURITY (except as provided in (d) and (e) below) that cannot be raced during the scheduled meeting shall be declared off and the entrance money and forfeits shall be divided equally among the nominators who have horses declared in and eligible to start.

(c) Any Late Closing Race or Early Closing Race that has been started and remains unfinished on the last day of the scheduled meeting shall be declared ended and the full purse divided according to the summary. Any such race that has been started but postponed by rain earlier in the meeting may be declared ended and the full purse divided according to the summary.

(d) Stakes and Futurities should be raced where advertised and the meeting may be extended to accomplish this. Any stake or futurity that has been started and remains unfinished on the last day of the scheduled meeting shall be declared ended and the full purse divided according to the summary except where the track elects to extend the meeting to complete the race.

(e) Unless otherwise provided in the conditions, in order to transfer stakes and futurities to another meeting unanimous consent must be obtained from the member and from all those having eligibles in the event.

(f) (1) At meetings of MORE THAN FIVE DAYS duration, overnight events may be postponed and carried over not to exceed two racing days.

(2) At meetings of a duration of FIVE DAYS OR LESS, overnight events and late closing races shall be cancelled and starting fees returned in the event of postponement, unless the track member is willing to add the postponed races to the advertised program for subsequent days of the meeting.

At the option of management any postponed races may be contested in single mile dashes. Where races are postponed under this rule, management shall have the privilege of selecting the order in which the events will be raced in any combined program.

RULE 16.
Starting.

Section 1.   With Starting Gate.—

(a) *Starter's Control.*—The starter shall have control of the horses from the formation of the parade until he gives the word "go".

(b) *Scoring.*—After one or two preliminary warming up scores, the Starter shall notify the drivers to come to the starting gate. During or before the parade the drivers must be informed as to the number of scores permitted.

(c) The horses shall be brought to the starting gate as near one-quarter of a mile before the start as the track will permit.

(d) *Speed of Gate.*—Allowing sufficient time so that the speed of the gate can be increased gradually, the following minimum speeds will be maintained:

(1) For the first ⅛ mile, not less than 11 miles per hour.

(2) For the next ¹⁄₁₆ of a mile not less than 18 miles per hour.

(3) From that point to the starting point, the speed will be gradually increased to maximum speed.

(e) On mile tracks horses will be brought to the starting gate at the head of the stretch and the relative speeds mentioned in sub-section (d) above will be maintained.

(f) *Starting Point.* — The starting point will be a point marked on the inside rail a distance of not less than 200 feet from the first turn. The Starter shall give the word "go" at the starting point.

(g) WHEN A SPEED HAS BEEN REACHED IN THE COURSE OF A START THERE SHALL BE NO DECREASE EXCEPT IN THE CASE OF A RECALL.

(h) *Recall Notice.*—In case of a recall, a light plainly visible to the driver shall be flashed and a recall sounded, but the starting gate shall proceed out of the path of the horses.

(i) There shall be no recall after the word "go" has been given and any horse, regardless of his position or an accident, shall be deemed a starter from the time he entered into the Starter's control unless dismissed by the Starter.

(j) *Breaking Horse.*—The Starter shall endeavor to get all horses away in position and on gait but no recall shall be had for a breaking horse except as provided in (k) (5).

(k) *Recall — Reasons For.* — The Starter may sound a recall only for the following reasons:

(1) A horse scores ahead of the gate.

(2) There is interference.

(3) A horse has broken equipment.

(4) A horse falls before the word "go" is given.

(5) Where a horse refuses to come to the gate before the gate reaches the pole ⅛ of a mile before the start, the field may be turned.

(l) *Penalties.*—A fine not to exceed $100, or suspension from driving not to exceed 15 days, or both, may be applied to any driver, by the Starter for:

(1) Delaying the start.

(2) Failure to obey the Starter's instructions.

(3) Rushing ahead of the inside or outside wing of the gate.

(4) Coming to the starting gate out of position.

(5) Crossing over before reaching the starting point.

(6) Interference with another driver during the start.

(7) Failure to come up into position.

A hearing must be granted before any penalty is imposed.

(m) *Riding in Gate.*—No persons shall be allowed to ride in the starting gate except the Starter and his driver or operator, and a Patrol Judge, unless permission has been granted by this Association.

(n) *Loudspeaker.* — Use of a mechanical loudspeaker for any purpose other than to give instructions to drivers is prohibited. The volume shall be no higher than necessary to carry the voice of the Starter to the drivers.

The penalty for violation of this section shall be a fine of not to exceed $500.00 or suspension not to exceed thirty days after a hearing by the President or Executive Vice-President.

§ 2. *Holding Horses Before Start.* —Horses may be held on the backstretch not to exceed two minutes awaiting post time, except when delayed by an emergency.

§ 3. *Two Tiers.*—In the event there are two tiers of horses, the withdrawing of a horse that has drawn or earned a position in the front tier shall not affect the position of the horses that have drawn or earned positions in the second tier.

Whenever a horse is drawn from any tier, horses on the outside move in to fill up the vacancy.

§ 4. *Starting Without Gate.*—When horses are started without a gate the Starter shall have control of the horses from the formation of the parade until he gives the word "go". He shall be located at the wire or other point of start of the race at which point as nearly as possible the word "go" shall be given. No driver shall cause unnecessary delay after the horses are called. After two preliminary warming up scores, the Starter shall notify the drivers to form in parade.

§ 5. The driver of any horse refusing or failing to follow the instructions of the Starter as to the parade or scoring ahead of the pole horse may be set down for the heat in which the offense occurs, or for such other period as the Starter shall determine, and may be fined from $10 to $100. Whenever a driver is taken down the substitute shall be permitted to score the horse once. A horse delaying the race may be started regardless of his position or gait and there shall not be a recall on account of a bad actor. If the word is not given, all the horses in the race shall immediately turn at the tap of the bell or other signal, and jog back to their parade positions for a fresh start. There shall be no recall after the starting word has been given.

§ 6. *Starters.*—The horses shall be deemed to have started when the word "go" is given by the Starter and all the horses must go the course except in case of an accident in which it is the opinion of the Judges that it is impossible to go the course.

§ 7. *Overhead Barrier.*—A member may use an overhead barrier or counting start in starting races and any driver who fails to obey the orders of the Starter or Assistant Starter operating same may be fined or ruled out of the race.

§ 8. *Unmanageable Horse.*—If in the opinion of the Judges or the Starter a horse is unmanageable or liable to cause accidents or injury to any other horse or to any driver it may be sent to the barn, but the entry and declaration fees on the horse shall then be refunded. When this action is taken the Starter will notify the Judges who will in turn notify the public.

§ 9. *Bad Acting Horse.*—At meetings where there is no wagering, the Starter may place a bad acting horse on the outside at his discretion. At pari-mutuel meetings such action may be taken only where there is time for the Starter to notify the Judges who will in turn notify the public prior to the sale of tickets on such race. If tickets have been sold, the bad acting horse must be scratched under the provision of Section 8 herein.

§ 10. *Snap Barrier.*—All handicaps shall be started with a snap barrier, unless a starting gate or walk-up start is used, and sprung simultaneously with the announcement of the word "go." Any driver allowing his horse to go into the barrier before the word "go" shall be fined $10 to $100.

§ 11. *Post Positions—Heat Racing.* —The horse winning a heat shall take the pole (or inside position) the succeeding heat, unless otherwise specified in the published conditions, and all others shall take their positions in the order they were placed the last heat. When two or more horses shall have made a dead heat, their positions shall be settled by lot.

§ 12. *Shield.* — The arms of all starting gates shall be provided with a screen or a shield in front of the position for each horse, and such arms shall be perpendicular to the rail.

RULE 17.
Drivers, Trainers and Agents.

Section 1. *Licensing of Drivers.*— No person shall drive a horse in any race on a track in membership with this Association without having first obtained from this Association an Active Membership including a driver's license. The proper license shall be presented to the Clerk of the Course before driving. Any person violating this rule shall be automatically fined $10.00 for each offense and no license shall be issued thereafter until such fines shall have been paid. In addition, thereto, the track member shall automatically be fined the sum of $5.00 for permitting a driver to start without a license. In the event of a driver's license being lost or destroyed, a replacement may be obtained upon payment of a fee in the sum of $1.00.

The Executive Vice-President shall require the applicant to:

(a) Submit evidence of good moral character.

(b) Submit evidence of his ability to drive in a race and, if he is a new applicant, this must include the equivalent of a year's training experience.

(c) Be at least 14 years of age for an (MA) or (M) license and 16 years of age for an (F) license.

(d) Be at least 18 years of age for a (P) license.

(e) Furnish completed application form.

(f) When requested submit evidence of physical and mental ability and/or to submit to a physical examination.

(g) Applicants, other than for an *M, MA or Fair license* shall submit to a written examination at a designated time and place to determine his qualification to drive or train and his knowledge of racing and the rules. In addition any driver who presently holds a license and wishes to obtain a license in a higher category who has not previously submitted to such written tests shall be required to take a written test before becoming eligible to obtain a license in a higher category.

A license will be issued in the following categories:

(A) A full license valid for all meetings.

No full license will be granted until the applicant has had, (1) at least one year's driving experience while holding a (P) Provisional license, and (2) 25 satisfactory starts at an extended pari-mutuel or Grand Circuit meeting.

(P) A Provisional license valid for fairs and for extended pari-mutuel meetings subject to satisfactory performance.

(Q) A license valid for fairs and a license for qualifying and non-wagering races at extended pari-mutuel meetings with the approval of the Presiding Judge. The Presiding Judge shall make a report to this Association relating to the performance of such a driver in a qualifying race. The Horsemen's Committee may appoint an Advisory Committee of three drivers at any meeting to observe the qualifications, demeanor and general conduct of all drivers and report in regard thereto to the Presiding Judge, copy of any such report to be in writing and forwarded to the Association.

(F) A license valid for fairs and all meetings with the exception of extended pari-mutuel meetings.

Drivers holding a license valid for fairs only who have driven at fairs must demonstrate an ability to drive satisfactorily before they will be granted a (Q) license valid for qualifying races.

(MA) A license valid for matinee meetings and amateur racing at other meetings providing he is an amateur at the time of the race.

(M) A license valid for matinee meetings only.

(V) A probationary license indicating that the driver has been guilty of rule violations and has been warned against repetition of such violations. When a driver with a probationary license commits more than one rule violation, or one major violation, proceedings may be started and he will be given a hearing either before the Executive Vice-President or the District Board of Review in the District where the last penalty was imposed, to determine if his license should be revoked.

(T) Trainer.

No Provisional license will be granted to women drivers for extended pari-mutuel meetings, and no full license will be granted to women drivers who have not previously held such a license for extended pari-mutuel driving.

Repeated rule violations shall be considered grounds for refusal to grant or grounds for revocation of any driver's license. A provisional, qualifying, or fair license may be revoked for one or more rule violations, or other indications of lack of qualifications, and the qualifications of drivers in these categories may be reviewed at any time, with written examinations if necessary, to determine if a driver is competent.

All penalties imposed on any driver will be recorded on the reverse side of his driver's license by the Presiding Judge.

§ 2. Any licensed driver who shall participate in a meeting or drive a horse at a meeting not in membership with this Association or the Canadian Trotting Association shall be fined not to exceed $100 for each such offense:

PROVIDED HOWEVER, that nothing herein contained shall prevent any person from driving at a contract track or from participating in a meeting conducted at such a track.

(a) No driver's license other than a matinee will be granted for the first time to any person 60 years of age, or over, until such application and the supporting papers have been submitted to the Driver's Committee of the Board of Directors and favorable recommendation made thereon.

(b) *Physical Examination.*—An applicant for a driver's license 65 years of age or over may be required to submit annually, with his application for a driver's license, a report of a physical examination on forms supplied by the Association. If the Association so desires, it may designate the physician to perform such examination. However, in such event, the cost thereof shall be paid by the Association.

(c) In the event any person is involved in an accident on the track, the Association may order such person to submit to a physical examination and such examination must be completed within 30 days from such request or the license may be suspended until compliance therewith.

§ 3.   The license of any driver or trainer may be revoked or suspended at any time after a hearing by the President or Executive Vice-President for violation of the rules, failure to obey the instructions of any official, or for any misconduct or act detrimental to the sport. The President or Executive Vice-President may designate a proper person as a hearing officer who will conduct a hearing and furnish a transcript to the President or Executive Vice-President. The license may be reinstated by the President or Executive Vice-President in his discretion upon application made to him and upon such terms as he may prescribe. Any suspension or revocation of license made hereunder may be reviewed by the Board of Appeals as provided in Article IX of the By-Laws.

§ 4.   The following shall constitute disorderly conduct and be reason for a fine, suspension, or revocation of a driver's or trainer's license:

(a) Failure to obey the Judges' orders that are expressly authorized by the rules of this Association.

(b) Failure to drive when programmed unless excused by the Judges.

(c) Drinking intoxicating beverages within four hours of the first post time of the program on which he is carded to drive.

(d) Appearing in the paddock in an unfit condition to drive.

(e) Fighting.

(f) Assaults.

(g) Offensive and profane language.

(h) Smoking on the track in silks during actual racing hours.

(i) Warming up a horse prior to racing without silks.

(j) Disturbing the peace.

(k) Refusal to take a breath analyzer test when directed by the Presiding Judge.

§ 5.   Drivers shall, when directed by the Presiding Judge, submit to a breath analyzer test and if the results thereof show a reading of more than .05 per cent of alcohol in the blood, such person shall not be permitted to drive, and an investigation will be started to determine if there has been a violation of Section 4 (c) of this rule.

§ 6.   Drivers must wear distinguishing colors, and shall not be allowed to start in a race or other public performance unless in the opinion of the Judges they are properly dressed.

No one shall drive during the time when colors are required on a race track unless he is wearing a type of protective helmet, constructed with a hard shell, and containing adequate padding and a chin strap in place.

§ 7.   Any driver wearing colors who shall appear at a betting window or at a bar or in a restaurant dispensing alcoholic beverages shall be fined not to exceed $100 for each such offense.

§ 8.   No driver can, without good

and sufficient reasons, decline to be substituted by Judges. Any driver who refuses to be so substituted may be fined or suspended, or both, by order of the Judges.

§ 9. An amateur driver is one who has never accepted any valuable consideration by way of or in lieu of compensation for his services as a trainer or driver during the past ten years.

§ 10. Drivers holding a full license, or registered stables participating at an extended pari-mutuel meeting, shall register their racing colors with this Association. Colors so registered shall not be taken by any other person. The fee for such registration is *$25.00* for lifetime registration. *The fee for a duplicate color registration card is $10.00 and the fee for changing a design once registered is $10.00.* All disputes on rights to particular colors shall be settled by this Association.

§ 11. Any person racing a horse at a meeting where registered colors are required by Section 10 hereof, using colors registered by any person or persons except himself or his employer, without special permission from the Presiding Judge, shall be fined $10.00.

§ 12. *Trainer.* An applicant for a license as trainer must satisfy the Executive Vice-President that he possesses the necessary qualifications, both mental and physical, to perform the duties required. Elements to be considered, among others, shall be character, reputation, temperament, experience, knowledge of the rules of racing, and duties of a trainer in the preparation, training, entering and managing horses for racing.

An applicant shall be required to:

(a) *Submit evidence of good moral character.*

(b) *Be at least 18 years of age.*

(c) *Furnish complete application form including photographs.*

(d) *Submit evidence of his ability to train and manage a racing stable which shall include at least three years experience working as a groom or second trainer, and satisfactory completion of a written examination.*

(e) *When requested, submit evidence of physical ability and/or to submit to a physical examination.*

(f) *Submit three copies of his fingerprints.*

RULE 18.
Racing and Track Rules.

Section 1. Although a leading horse is entitled to any part of the track except after selecting his position in the home stretch, neither the driver of the first horse or any other driver in the race shall do any of the following things, which shall be considered violation of driving rules:

(a) Change either to the right or left during any part of the race when another horse is so near him that in altering his position he compels the horse behind him to shorten his stride, or causes the driver of such other horse to pull him out of his stride.

b) Jostle, strike, hook wheels, or interfere with another horse or driver.

(c) Cross sharply in front of a horse or cross over in front of a field of horses in a reckless manner, endangering other drivers.

(d) Swerve in and out or pull up quickly.

(e) Crowd a horse or driver by "putting a wheel under him."

(f) "Carry a horse out" or "sit down in front of him," take up abruptly in front of other horses so as to cause confusion or interference among the trailing horses, or do any other act which constitutes what is popularly known as helping.

(g) Let a horse pass inside needlessly.

(h) Laying off a normal pace and leaving a hole when it is well within the horse's capacity to keep the hole closed.

(i) Commit any act which shall impede the progress of another horse or cause him to "break."

(j) Change course after selecting a position in the home stretch and swerve in or out, or bear in or out, in such manner as to interfere with another horse or cause him to change course or take back.

(k) To drive in a careless or reckless manner.

(l) *Whipping under the arch of the sulky, the penalty for which shall be no less than 10 days suspension.*

§ 2. All complaints by drivers of any foul driving or other misconduct during the heat must be made at the termination of the heat, unless the driver is prevented from doing so by an accident or injury. Any driver desiring to enter a claim of foul or other complaint of violation of the rules, must before dismounting indicate to the judges or Barrier Judge his desire to enter such claim or complaint and forthwith upon dismounting shall proceed to the telephone or Judges' stand where and when such claim, objection, or complaint shall be immediately entered. The Judges shall not cause the official sign to be displayed until such claim, objection, or complaint shall have been entered and considered.

§ 3. If any of the above violations is committed by a person driving a horse coupled as an entry in the betting, the Judges shall set both horses back, if, in their opinion, the violation may have affected the finish of the race. Otherwise, penalties may be applied individually to the drivers of any entry.

§ 4. In case of interference, collision, or violation of any of the above restrictions, the offending horse may be placed back one or more positions in that heat or dash, and in the event such collision or interference prevents any horse from finishing the heat or dash, the offending horse may be disqualified from receiving any winnings; and the driver may be fined not to exceed the amount of the purse or stake contended for, or may be suspended or expelled. In the event a horse is set back, under the provisions hereof, he must be placed behind the horse with whom he interfered.

§ 5. (a) Every heat in a race must be contested by every horse in the race and every horse must be driven to the finish. If the Judges believe that a horse is being driven, or has been driven, with design to prevent his winning a heat or dash which he was evidently able to win, or is being raced in an inconsistent manner, or to perpetrate or to aid a fraud, they shall consider it a violation and the driver, and anyone in concert with him, to so affect the outcome of the race or races, may be fined, suspended, or expelled. The Judges may substitute a competent and reliable driver at any time. The substituted driver shall be paid at the discretion of the Judges and the fee retained from the purse money due the horse, if any.

(b) In the event a drive is unsatisfactory due to lack of effort or carelessness, and the Judges believe that there is no fraud, gross carelessness, or a deliberate inconsistent drive they may impose a penalty under this sub-section not to exceed ten days suspension, or a $100.00 fine.

§ 6. If in the opinion of the Judges a driver is for any reason unfit or incompetent to drive or refuses to comply with the directions of the Judges, or is reckless in his conduct and endangers the safety of horses or other drivers in the race, he may be removed and another driver substituted at any time after the positions have been assigned in a race, and the offending driver shall be fined, suspended or expelled. The substitute driver shall be properly compensated.

§ 7. If for any cause other than being interfered with or broken equipment, a horse fails to finish after starting in a heat, that horse shall be ruled out.

§ 8. Loud shouting or other improper conduct is forbidden in a race.

Whipping a horse underneath the arch of the sulky shall be considered improper conduct and is forbidden.

After the word "go" is given, both feet must be kept in the stirrups until after the finish of the race.

§ 9. Drivers will be allowed whips not to exceed 4 feet, 8 inches, plus a snapper not longer than eight inches.

§ 10. The use of any goading device, chain, or mechanical devices or appliances, other than the ordinary whip or spur upon any horse in any race shall constitute a violation of this rule. In the discretion of the Judges, brutal use of the whip or spur or indiscriminate use of a whip or spur may be considered a violation punishable by a fine of not to exceed $100 or suspension.

§ 11.   No horse shall wear hopples in a race unless he starts in the same in the first heat, and having so started, he shall continue to wear them to the finish of the race, and any person found guilty of removing or altering a horse's hopples during a race, or between races, for the purpose of fraud, shall be suspended or expelled. Any horse habitually wearing hopples shall not be permitted to start in a race without them except by the permission of the Judges. Any horse habitually racing free legged shall not be permitted to wear hopples in a race except with the permission of the Judges. No horse shall be permitted to wear a head pole protruding more than 10 inches beyond its nose.

§ 12.   *Breaking.*

(a)   When any horse or horses break from their gait in trotting or pacing, their drivers shall at once, where clearance exists, take such horse to the outside and pull it to its gait.

(b)   The following shall be considered violations of Section 12 (a):

(1) Failure to properly attempt to pull the horse to its gait.

(2) Failure to take to the outside where clearance exists.

(3) Failure to lose ground by the break.

(c)   If there has been no failure on the part of the driver in complying with 12 (b), (1), (2), and (3), the horse shall not be set back unless a contending horse on his gait is lapped on the hind quarter of the breaking horse at the finish.

(d)   The Judges may set any horse back one or more places if in their judgment any of the above violations have been committed.

§ 13.   If in the opinion of the Judges,

a driver allows his horse to break for the purpose of fraudulently losing a heat, he shall be liable to the penalties elsewhere provided for fraud and fouls.

§ 14.   To assist in determining the matters contained in Sections 12 and 13, it shall be the duty of one of the Judges to call out every break made, and the clerk shall at once note the break and character of it in writing.

§ 15.   The time between heats for any distance up to and including a mile shall be not less than twenty-five minutes; for any distance between one and two miles, thirty minutes. No heat shall be called after sunset where the track is not lighted for night racing.

§ 16.   Horses called for a race shall have the exclusive right of the course, and all other horses shall vacate the track at once, unless permitted to remain by the Judges.

§ 17.   In the case of accidents, only so much time shall be allowed as the Judges may deem necessary and proper.

§ 18.   A driver must be mounted in his sulky at the finish of the race or the horse must be placed as not finishing.

§ 19.   Any violation of any sections of Rule 18 above, unless otherwise provided, may be punished by a fine or suspension, or both, or by expulsion.

RULE 19.
Placing and Money Distribution.

Section 1.   Unless otherwise provided in the conditions, all purses shall be distributed on the dash basis with the money awarded according to a horse's position in each separate dash or heat of the race.

Purse money distribution in overnight events shall be limited to five moneys.

§ 2.   *Dashes.* — Unless otherwise specified in the conditions, the money distribution in dashes shall be 45%, 25%, 15%, 10%, and 5%. In Early Closing Races, Late Closing Races or Added Money Events, if there are less than five (5) starters, the remaining premium shall go to the race winner unless the conditions call for a different distribution. In overnight events if there are less than five (5) starters the premium for the positions for which there are no starters may be retained by the track.

If there be any premium or premiums for which horses have started but were unable to finish, due to an accident, all unoffending horses who did not finish will share equally in such premium or premiums.

If there be any premium or premiums for which horses have started but were unable to finish and the situation is not covered by the preceding paragraph, such premium shall be paid to the winner.

§ 3. *Every Heat a Race.* — The purse shall be distributed as in dash races with nothing set aside for the race winner.

§ 4. *Placing System.*—If the placing system is specified in the conditions, the purse shall be distributed according to the standing of the horses in the summary. In order to share in the purse distribution, each horse must complete the race and compete in each heat to which he is eligible. A horse must win two heats to be declared the race winner and such horse shall stand first in the summary. In deciding the rank of the horses other than the race winner, a horse that has been placed first in one heat shall be ranked better than any other horse making a dead heat for first or any other horse that has been placed second any number of heats; a horse that has been placed second in one heat shall be ranked better than any other horse that has been placed third any number of heats, etc.; e.g., a horse finishing 3-6 would be ranked ahead of another horse finishing 4-4. A horse finishing in a dead heat would be ranked below another horse finishing in the same position and not in a dead heat. If there be any premium for which no horse has maintained a position, it shall go to the race winner, but the number of premiums awarded need not exceed the number of horses that started in the race. Un-

less otherwise specified in the conditions, the money shall be divided 50%, 25%, 15% and 10%.

§ 5. *Two In Three.*—In a two in three race, a horse must win two heats to win the race, and there shall be 10% set aside for the race winner. The purse shall be divided and awarded according to the finish in each of the first two or three heats, as the case may be. If the race is unfinished at the end of the third heat, all but the heat winners or horses making a dead heat for first shall be ruled out. The fourth heat, when required, shall be raced for the 10% set aside for the winner. If there be any third or fourth premiums, etc., for which no horse has maintained a specific place, the premium therefor shall go to the winner of that heat, but the number of premiums distributed need not exceed the number of horses starting in the race. In a two-year-old race, if there are two heat winners and they have made a dead heat in the third heat, the race shall be declared finished and the colt standing best in the summary shall be awarded the 10%; if the two heat winners make a dead heat and stand the same in the summary, the 10% shall be divided equally between them.

RULE 20.
Conduct of Racing.

Section 1. No owner, trainer, driver, attendant of a horse, or any other person shall use improper language to an official, officer of this Association, or an officer of an Association in membership, or be guilty of any improper conduct toward such officers or judges, or persons serving under their orders, such improper language or conduct having reference to the administration of the course, or of any race thereon.

§ 2. No owner, trainer, driver, or attendant of a horse, or any other person, at any time or place shall commit an assault, or an assault and battery, upon any driver who shall drive in a race, or shall threaten to do bodily injury to any such driver or shall address to such driver language outrageously insulting.

§ 3.   If any owner, trainer, or driver of a horse shall threaten or join with others in threatening not to race, or not to declare in, because of the entry of a certain horse or horses, or a particular stable, thereby compelling or trying to compel the Race Secretary or Superintendent of Speed to reject certain eligible entries it shall be immediately reported to the Executive Vice-President and the offending parties may be suspended pending a hearing before the District Board of Review.

§ 4.   No owner, agent or driver who has entered a horse shall thereafter demand of the member a bonus of money or other special award or consideration as a condition for starting the horse.

§ 5.   No owner, trainer, driver, agent, employee, or attendant shall bet or cause any other person to bet on his behalf on any other horse in any race in which a horse owned, trained, or driven or in which he in anywise represents or handles as a starter.

§ 6.   *Failure to report fraudulent proposal.*—If any person shall be approached with any offer or promise of a bribe, or a wager or with a request or suggestion for a bribe, or for any improper, corrupt or fraudulent act in relation to racing, or that any race shall be conducted otherwise than fairly and honestly, it shall be the duty of such person to report the details thereof immediately to the Presiding Judge.

§ 7.   Any misconduct on the part of a member of this Association fraudulent in its nature or injurious to the character of the turf, although not specified in these rules, is forbidden. Any person or persons who, individually or in concert with one another, shall fraudulently and corruptly, by any means, affect the outcome of any race or affect a false registration, or commit any other act injurious to the sport, shall be guilty of a violation.

§ 8.   If two or more persons shall combine and confederate together, in any manner, regardless of where the said persons may be located, for the purpose of violating any of the rules of this Association, and shall commit some act in furtherance of the said purpose and plan, it shall constitute a conspiracy and a violation.

§ 9.   In any case where an oath is administered by the Judges, Board of Review, or Officer of this Association under the rules, or a Notary Public, or any other person legally authorized to administer oaths, if the party knowingly swears falsely or withholds information pertinent to the investigation, he shall be fined, suspended, or both, or expelled.

§ 10.   *Financial Responsibility.* — Any participant who shall accumulate unpaid obligations, or default in obligations, or issue drafts or checks that are dishonored, or payment refused, or otherwise display financial irresponsibility reflecting on the sport, may be denied membership in this Association or may be suspended on order by the Executive Vice-President.

§ 11.   *Nerved Horses.—All horses that have been nerved shall be so designated on The United States Trotting Association registration certificate and be certified by a practicing veterinarian. It is the responsibility of the owner of the horse at the time the horse is nerved to see that this information is placed on the registration certificate. All horses that have been nerved prior to the adoption of this rule must also be certified and it will be the responsibility of the owner or the trainer of such horse to see that such information is carried on the registration certificate. No trainer or owner will be permitted to enter or start a horse that is high nerved. Low nerved horses may be permitted to start providing this information is published on the bulletin board in the Racing Secretary's Office.*

§ 12.   Any violation of any of the provisions of this rule shall be punishable by a fine, suspension, or both, or by expulsion.

RULE 21.
Stimulants, Drugs.

Section 1. At every meeting except as stated herein where pari-mutuel wagering is permitted, the winning horse in every heat and/or race shall be subjected to a saliva test for the purpose of determining thereby the presence of any drug, stimulant, sedative, depressant, or medicine. At any meeting where there is a pre-race blood test of all horses and where the Commission requires a post-race urine test of the winner, a saliva test will not be required. In addition, the Judges at any meeting may order any other horse in any heat or race to be subjected to the saliva test or any other test for the purpose of determining thereby the presence of any drug, stimulant, sedative, depressant, or medicine. Also, the Judges may order any horse in a race to be subjected to a urine test. At all extended pari-mutuel meetings and at Grand Circuit meetings at least 25% of the horses subjected to a saliva test shall be given a urine test. Such horses to be selected by the Presiding Judge by lot. Such tests shall be made only by qualified veterinarians and by laboratories approved by the Executive Vice-President. In addition to the above, the winning horse in every heat or dash of a race at any track with a total purse in excess of $5,000.00 shall be subjected to both a saliva and a urine test. However, such urine test shall be counted in determining the 25% required above.

§ 2. The Executive Vice-President may, in his discretion, or at the request of a member, authorize or direct a saliva, urine or other test of any horse racing at any meeting, whether or not tests are being conducted at such meeting, provided that adequate preliminary arrangements can be made to obtain proper equipment, and the services of a competent and qualified veterinarian and an approved laboratory.

During the taking of the saliva and/or urine sample by the veterinarian, the owner, trainer or authorized agent may be present at all times. Unless the rules of the State Racing Commission or other governmental agency provide otherwise, samples so taken shall be placed in two containers and shall immediately be sealed and the evidence of such sealing indicated thereon by the signature of the representative of the owner or trainer. One part of the sample is to be placed in a depository under the supervision of the Presiding Judge and/or any other agency the State Racing Commission may designate to be safeguarded until such time as the report on the chemical analysis of the other portion of the split sample is received.

Should a positive report be received, an owner or trainer shall have the right to have the other portion of the split sample inserted in with a subsequent group being sent for testing or may demand that it be sent to another chemist for analysis, the cost of which will be paid by the party requesting the test.

§ 3. Whenever there is a positive test finding the presence of any drug, stimulant, sedative or depressant present, in the post-race test, the laboratory shall immediately notify the Presiding Judge who shall immediately report such findings to the Executive Vice-President of this Association.

When such positive report is received from the State Chemist by the Presiding Judge, the persons held responsible shall be notified and a thorough investigation shall be conducted by or on behalf of the Judges. Then a time shall be set by the Judges for a hearing to dispose of the matter. The time set for the hearing shall not exceed four racing days after the responsible persons were notified. The hearing may be continued, if in the opinion of the Judges, circumstances justify such action. At County Fairs and non-parimutuel meetings, in the event the Judges are unable to perform this action, the Executive Vice-President shall forthwith set a date for a prompt hearing to be conducted by him or some person deputized by him for the purpose of determining all matters concerning the administration of such drug, stimulant, sedative or depressant and the care and the custody of the horse from which the positive sample was obtained.

The decision of the Executive Vice-President or the person deputized by him shall be reduced to writing and shall be final unless the person or persons aggrieved thereby shall within 30 days appeal in writing to the Board of Appeals as provided in Article IX of the By-Laws.

Should the chemical analysis of saliva, urine or other sample of the post-race test taken from a horse indicate the presence of a forbidden narcotic, stimulant, depressant, or local anesthetic, it shall be considered prima facie evidence that such has been administered to the horse. The trainer and any other person or persons who may have had the care of, or been in attendance of the horse, or are suspected of causing such condition, shall be immediately stopped from participating in racing by the Judge and shall remain inactive in racing pending the outcome of a hearing. The horse alleged to have been stimulated shall not run during the investigation and hearing, however, other horses registered under the care of the inactive trainer may, with the consent of the Judge of the meeting, be released to the care of another licensed trainer, and may race.

§ 4.   Any person or persons who shall administer or influence or conspire with any other person or persons to administer to any horse any drug, medicant, stimulant, depressant, narcotic or hypnotic to such horse within forty-eight hours of his race, shall be subject to penalties provided in Section 9 of this rule.

§ 5.   Whenever the post-race test or tests prescribed in Section 1 hereof disclose the presence in any horse of any drug, stimulant, depressant or sedative, in any amount whatsoever, it shall be presumed that the same was administered by the person or persons having the control and/or care and/or custody of such horse with the intent thereby to affect the speed or condition of such horse and the result of the race in which it participated.

§ 6.   A trainer shall be responsible at all times for the condition of all horses trained by him. No trainer shall start a horse or permit a horse in his custody to be started if he knows, or if by the exercise of reasonable care he might have known or have cause to believe, that the horse has received any drug, stimulant, sedative, depressant, medicine, or other substance that could result in a positive test. Every trainer must guard or cause to be guarded each horse trained by him in such manner and for such period of time prior to racing the horse so as to prevent any person not employed by or connected with the owner or trainer from administering any drug, stimulant, sedative, depressant, or other substance resulting in a post-race positive test.

§ 7.   Any owner, trainer, driver or agent of the owner, having the care, custody and/or control of any horse who shall refuse to submit such horse to a saliva test or other tests as herein provided or ordered by the Judges shall be guilty of the violation of this rule. Any horse that refuses to submit to a pre-race blood test shall be required to submit to a post-race saliva and urine test regardless of its finish.

§ 8.   All winnings of such horse in a race in which an offense was detected under any section of this rule shall be forfeited and paid over to this Association for redistribution among the remaining horses in the race entitled to same unless it is clearly shown that the horse was not stimulated. No such forfeiture and redistribution of winnings shall affect the distribution of the pari-mutuel pools at tracks where pari-mutuel wagering is conducted, when such distribution of pools is made upon the official placing at the conclusion of the heat or dash.

§ 9.   *Pre-Race Blood Test.*—Where there is a pre-race blood test which shows that there is an element present in the blood indicative of a stimulant, depressant or any unapproved medicant, the horse shall immediately be scratched from the race and an investigation conducted by the officials to determine if there was a violation of Section 4 of this rule.

§ 10. The penalty for violation of any sections of this rule, unless otherwise provided, shall be a fine of not to exceed $5,000, suspension for a fixed or indeterminate time, or both, or expulsion.

§ 11. All Veterinarians practicing on the grounds of an extended pari-mutuel meeting shall keep a log of their activities including:

(a) Name of horse.

(b) Nature of ailment.

(c) Type of treatment.

(d) Date and hour of treatment.

It shall be the responsibility of the Veterinarian to report to the Presiding Judge any internal medication given by him by injection or orally to any horse after he has been declared to start in any race.

§ 12. Any veterinarian practicing veterinary medicine on a race track where a race meeting is in progress or any other person using a needle or syringe shall use only one-time disposable type needles and a disposable needle shall not be re-used.

RULE 22.
Fines, Suspensions, and Expulsion.

Section 1. *Fines—Suspension Until Paid.*—All persons who shall have been fined under these rules shall be suspended until said fine shall have been paid in full.

Fines which have been unpaid for a period of five years may be dropped from the records of the Treasurer of the Association, however, such action will not affect the suspension.

§ 2. *Recording and Posting Penalties.*—Written or printed notice thereof shall be delivered to the person penalized, notice shall be posted immediately at the office of the member, and notice shall be forwarded immediately to the Executive Vice-President by the

Presiding Judge or Clerk of the Course. The Executive Vice-President shall transmit notice of suspension to the other members; and thereupon the offender thus punished shall suffer the same penalty and disqualification with each and every member.

§ 3. *Effect of Minor Penalty on Future Engagements.*—Where the penalty is for a driving violation and does not exceed in time a period of 5 days, the driver may complete the engagement of all horses declared in before the penalty becomes effective. Such driver may drive in Stake, Futurity, Early Closing and Feature races, during a suspension of 5 days or less but the suspension will be extended one day for each date he drives in such a race.

§ 4. *Disposition of Fines.* — All fines which are collected shall be reported and paid upon the day collected to the Executive Vice-President.

§ 5. *Effect of Suspension Penalty.* —Whenever the penalty of suspension is prescribed in these rules it shall be construed to mean an unconditional exclusion and disqualification from the time of receipt of written notice of suspension from the Member or the President, or Executive Vice-President, from any participation, either directly or indirectly, in the privileges and uses of the course and grounds of a member during the progress of a race meeting, unless otherwise specifically limited when such suspension is imposed, such as a suspension from driving. A suspension or expulsion or denial of membership of either a husband or wife may apply in each instance to both the husband and wife. The suspension becomes effective when notice is given unless otherwise specified.

§ 6. *Effect of Penalty on Horse.*— No horse shall have the right to compete while owned or controlled wholly or in part by a suspended, expelled, disqualified or excluded person. An entry made by or for a person or of a horse suspended, expelled or disqualified, shall be held liable for the entrance fee thus contracted without the right to compete unless the penalty is removed. A suspended, disqualified or excluded person who shall drive, or a suspended or disqualified horse which shall perform in a race shall be fined not less than $50, nor more than $100, for each offense.

§ 7. *Fraudulent Transfer.* — The fraudulent transfer of a horse by any person or persons under suspension in order to circumvent said suspension, shall constitute a violation.

§ 8. *Indefinite Suspension.*—If no limit is fixed in an order of suspension and none is defined in the rule applicable to the case, the penalty shall be considered as limited to the season in which the order was issued.

§ 9. *Suspended Person.* — Any member wilfully allowing a suspended, disqualified or excluded person to drive in a race, or a suspended or disqualified horse to start in a race after notice from the President or Executive Vice-President, shall be together with its officers, subject to a fine not exceeding $100 for each offense, or suspension or expulsion.

§ 10. *Expelled Person.* — Any member wilfully allowing the use of its track or grounds by an expelled or unconditionally suspended man or horse, after notice from the President or Executive Vice-President, shall be, together with its officers, subject to a fine not exceeding $500 for each offense, or suspension or expulsion.

§ 11. Whenever a person is excluded from a pari-mutuel track by the track member, this Association shall be notified.

§ 12. An expelled, suspended, disqualified or excluded person cannot act as an officer of a track member. A track member shall not, after receiving notice of such penalty, employ or retain in its employ an expelled, suspended, disqualified or excluded person at or on the track during the progress of a race meeting. Any member found violating this rule shall be fined not to exceed $500.

§ 13. *Dishonored Check, Etc.* — Any person being a member of this As-

sociation who pays an entry, a fine or other claim to this Association or an entry or fine to another member of this Association by a draft, check, order or other paper, which upon presentation is protested, payment refused or otherwise dishonored, shall be by order of the Executive Vice-President, subject to a fine not exceeding the amount of said draft, check or order, and the winnings of the horse or horses declared illegal and said persons and horses suspended until the dishonored amount and fine are paid and the illegal winnings returned.

§ 14. *Penalty of Racing Commissions.*—All penalties imposed by the Racing Commissions of the various states shall be recognized and enforced by this Association upon notice from the Commission to the Executive Vice-President, except as provided in Section 15 of this Rule 22.

§ 15. *Reciprocity of Penalties.* — All persons and horses under suspension or expulsion by any State Racing Commission or by a reputable Trotting Association of a foreign country shall upon notice from such commission or association to the Executive Vice-President, be suspended or expelled by this Association. Provided, however, that, for good cause shown, the Board of Appeals may, upon consideration of the record of the proceedings had before such State Commission or foreign Association modify or so mould the penalty imposed to define the applicability thereof beyond the jurisdiction of the State Commission or foreign Association. Provided further that, whether or not a penalty has been imposed by a State Racing Commission, the District Board may make original inquiry and take original jurisdiction in any case as provided in Sections 2 and 15 of Article IV of the By-Laws.

§ 16. *Modification of Penalty.* — Any suspension imposed by Judges can be removed or modified by the Executive Vice-President upon the recommendation of the Judges and Member on whose grounds the penalty was imposed.

§ 17. An application for removal of expulsion imposed for starting a horse out of its class or under change of name, or both, shall not be docketed for a hearing by the District Board until all the unlawful winnings are returned for redistribution and a fine of $250 is paid.

RULE 23.
Protests and Appeals.

Section 1. *Protests.*—Protests may be made only by an owner, manager, trainer or driver of one of the contending horses, at any time before the winnings are paid over, and shall be reduced to writing, and sworn to, and shall contain at least one specific charge, which, if true, would prevent the horse from winning or competing in the race.

§ 2. The Judges shall in every case of protest demand that the driver, and the owner or owners, if present, shall immediately testify under oath; and in case of their refusal to do so, the horse shall not be allowed to start or continue in the race, but shall be ruled out, with a forfeit of entrance money.

§ 3. Unless the Judges find satisfactory evidence to warrant excluding the horse, they shall allow him to start or continue in the race under protest, and the premium, if any is won by that horse, shall be forthwith transmitted to the Executive Vice-President to allow the parties interested an opportunity to sustain the allegations of the protest, or to furnish information which will warrant an investigation of the matter by the District Board of Review. Where no action is taken to sustain the protest within thirty days, payment may be made as if such protest had not been filed.

§ 4. Any person found guilty of protesting a horse falsely and without cause, or merely with intent to embarrass a race, shall be punished by a fine not to exceed $100 or by suspension or expulsion.

§ 5. When a protest has been duly made or any information lodged with the Judges alleging an improper entry or any act prohibited or punishable under these rules, the same shall not be withdrawn or surrendered before the expiration of thirty days, without the approbation of the Executive Vice-President. If any member shall permit such a withdrawal of protest or information with a corrupt motive to favor any party, the executive officers so permitting it may be expelled by the District Board of Review.

§ 6. *Appeals.* — All decisions and rulings of the Judges of any race, and of the officers of Member Tracks may be appealed to the District Board of Review within ten (10) days after the notice of such decision or ruling. The appeal may be taken upon any question in the conduct of a race, interpretation of the rules, decisions relative to the outcome of a race, application of penalties, or other action affecting owners, drivers, or horses, but it must be based on a specific charge which, if true, would warrant modification or reversal of the decision. In order to take an appeal under Rule 18, a driver must have first made a complaint, claim, or objection as required in Rule 18. The District Board of Review may vacate, modify, or increase any penalty imposed by the Judges and appealed to the Board. In the event an appellant fails to appear at the hearing of his appeal without good cause the District Board may impose a fine not to exceed $100.00 or a suspension not to exceed thirty days to be effective at the first meeting at which he has horses entered for racing.

§ 7. Nothing herein contained shall affect the distribution of the pari-mutuel pools at tracks where pari-mutuel wagering is conducted, when such distribution is made upon the official placing at the conclusion of the heat or dash.

§ 8. All appeals shall be in writing and sworn to before a Notary or one of the Judges of the Meeting. At the time the appeal is filed, a deposit of $100, or an agreement to forfeit the sum of $100 in the event the Board determines the appeal is not justified, must accompany the appeal. In the event the District Board of Review feels that the appeal was justified, it will refund the money to the appellant. This procedure does not apply to protests.

§ 9.   In case of appeal or protest to The United States Trotting Association, the purse money affected by the appeal or protest must be deposited with the Executive Vice-President pending the decision of the District Board of Review. Any purse or portion thereof withheld for any reason shall be forthwith sent to the Executive Vice-President together with a full statement showing the reason for such withholding.

§ 10.   Any track member that fails to send the Executive Vice-President, within one week of the date on which it was filed, any protest or appeal filed with the member or its Judges, may be fined or suspended.

§ 11.   The license of any Presiding Judge may be revoked for refusal to accept a protest or appeal, or for refusing to act as witness for a person seeking to swear to a protest or appeal.

RULE 24.
Time and Records.

Section 1.   *Timing   Races.* — In every race, the time of each heat shall be accurately taken by three Timers or an approved electric timing device, in which case there shall be one Timer, and placed in the record in minutes, seconds and fifths of seconds, and upon the decision of each heat, the time thereof shall be publicly announced or posted. No unofficial timing shall be announced or admitted to the record, and when the Timers fail to act no time shall be announced or recorded for that heat.

§ 2.   *Error in Reported Time.*—In any case of alleged error in the record, announcement or publication of the time made by a horse, the time so questioned shall not be changed to favor said horse or owner, except upon

the sworn statement of the Judges and Timers who officiated in the race, and then only by order of the District Board of Review, or the Executive Vice-President.

§ 3.   *Track   Measurement   Certificate.*—In order that the performances thereon may be recognized and/or published as official every track member not having done so heretofore and since January 1st, 1939, shall forthwith cause to be filed with the Executive Vice-President the certificate of a duly licensed civil engineer or land surveyor that he has subsequently to January 1st, 1939, measured the said track from wire to wire three feet out from the pole or inside hub rail thereof and certifying in linear feet the result of such measurement. Each track shall be measured and recertified in the event of any changes or relocation of the hub rail.

§ 4.   *Time for Lapped on Break.*— The leading horse shall be timed and his time only shall be announced. No horse shall obtain a win race record by reason of the disqualification of another horse unless a horse is declared a winner by reason of the disqualification of a breaking horse on which he was lapped.

§ 5.   *Time for Dead Heat.*—In case of a dead heat, the time shall constitute a record for the horses making the dead heat and both shall be considered winners.

§ 6.   *Timing Procedure.*—The time shall be taken from the first horse leaving the point from which the distance of the race is measured until the winner reaches the wire.

§ 7.   *Misrepresentation of Time— Penalty.*—(a) A fine not to exceed $500 shall be imposed upon any member of this Association on whose grounds there shall be allowed any misrepresentation of time, and time shall be deemed to have been misrepresented in any race, wherein a record of the same is not kept in writing. A fine imposed under this rule shall include the officers of the member.

(b) Any person who shall be guilty

of fraudulent misrepresentation of time or the alteration of the record thereof in any public race shall be fined, suspended or expelled, and the time declared not a record.

§ 8. *Time Performances.* — Time performances are permitted subject to the following:

(a) Urine and saliva tests are required for all horses starting for a time performance.

(b) An approved electric timer is required for all time performances. In the event of a failure of a timer during the progress of a time performance, no time trial performance record will be obtained.

(c) Time trial performances are permitted only during the course of a regular meeting with the regular officials in the Judges' stand.

(d) Time trial performances are limited for two-year-olds who go to equal or to beat 2:10, three-year-olds who go to equal or to beat 2:05 and aged horses that go to equal or to beat 2 minutes.

(e) In any race or performance against time excessive use of the whip shall be considered a violation.

(f) Any consignor, agent or sales organization or other person may be fined or suspended for selling or advertising a horse with a time trial record without designating it as a time trial or who sells or advertises a horse without showing the gait of its parents or grandparents.

(g) Time trial performance records shall not be included in a race program.

(h) Time trial performances shall be designated by preceding the time with two capital Ts.

RULE 25.
International Registration.

Section 1. The Executive Vice-President may appoint export agents at various ports of shipping who shall upon examination and identification of the horse to be exported, indorse the application for export certificate. Every application for an export certificate must be accompanied by a certificate of registration in the current ownership and a fee in the sum of $35.00. The export certificate shall be issued and signed by the Executive Vice-President *or Registrar* of the Association and the corporate seal affixed thereto. No such certificate will be issued for the export of any horse under expulsion nor for any horse currently under suspension by this Association. The fee for a duplicate certificate shall be $10.00.

§ 2. Any party or parties giving false information to procure an export certificate shall be deemed guilty of fraud and upon conviction thereof shall be fined or expelled and the horse in question may be expelled.

§ 3. If any horse registered with this Association is exported from the United States or Canada to any other country without making application for an export certificate, then the said horse will be stricken from the records of The United States Trotting Association.

§ 4. *Imported Horses.—Horses imported into the United States from countries other than Canada may be registered with this Association, Non-Standard, providing the following requirements are complied with by the person or persons seeking such registration.*

(a) *Horse must be registered in the country of birth and certificate of such registration must accompany application.*

(b) *Complete history of breeding including sire, and 1st, 2nd and 3rd dams and chain of ownership must accompany application if not fully set forth on registration of origin.*

(c) *Clearance or export certificate from country of origin including markings, positive identification of horse, and veterinarian certificate, must accompany application.*

(d) *If horse is leased, a valid executed lease signed by all parties must accompany application. If lease is signed by agents, written authorization from their principals must be submitted.*

(e) *Person or persons seeking such registration must be members of this Association and a fee of $25.00 in the case of horses which have not raced previously, and $50.00 in the case of horses which have previously raced, must accompany the application.*

RULE 26.
Registration of Horses.

Section 1. In order to register a horse the owner thereof must be a member of this Association.

§ 2. *Standard Bred.*—Horses may be registered as Standard bred with any of the following qualifications:

(a) The progeny of a registered Standard horse and a registered Standard mare.

(b) A stallion sired by a registered Standard horse, provided his dam and granddam were sired by registered Standard horses and he himself has a Standard record and is the sire of three performers with Standard records from different mares.

(c) A mare whose sire is a registered Standard horse, and whose dam and granddam were sired by a registered Standard horse, provided she herself has a Standard record.

(d) A mare sired by a registered Standard horse, provided she is the dam of two performers with Standard records.

(e) A mare or horse sired by a registered Standard horse, provided its first, second and third dams are each sired by a registered Standard horse.

(f) No horse over seven years of age is eligible for registration.

(g) The Standing Committee on Registration may register as Standard any horse which does not qualify under the above six rules, if in their opinion he or she should be registered Standard.

§ 3. *Non-Standard Bred.* — Any horse may be registered as Non-Standard upon filing application showing satisfactory identification of the horse for racing purposes. This identification may be accomplished by furnishing the name, age, sex, sire, dam, color and markings and history of the previous owners. A mating certificate must accompany this application, showing the sire to be some type of a registered horse.

§ 4. The breeder of a horse, for the purposes of registration, is the owner or lessee of the dam at the time of breeding, and when held under lease, bred on shares or in partnership, only such lease or partnership will be recognized for such purposes which is filed in the offices of The United States Trotting Association.

§ 5. *Mating Certificates.* — Mating certificates shall be signed by the owner or if the horse is under lease a letter must be filed with this Association signed by the owner of the horse stating to whom and for what period of time the horse is under lease. In addition to the letter signed by the owner a letter signed by the lessee stating that he will accept responsibility for the accuracy of the mating certificate during the period of time covered by the lease must be filed. In such event the lessee must sign the mating certificate. A mating certificate must be on file in the office of the Association before a certificate of registration will be issued.

§ *Artificial Insemination.* — A colt conceived by semen transported off the premises where it is produced is not eligible for registration.

§ 7. *Breeding Records.* — Stallion owners shall keep a stallion record showing the mare's name, sire and dam, color, markings, owner, breeding dates, and color, sex and foaling date of any foals born on the stallion owner's premises. The records shall be available for inspection by officers or authorized representatives of The United States Trotting Association, and shall be kept at least ten years or filed with The United States Trotting Association.

All persons standing a stallion at either public or private service shall file with this Association a list of all mares bred to each stallion, together with the dates of service. This list must be filed by *September 1st* of the year of breeding. In addition to the service report, a list of standardbred foals dropped on the farm with foaling dates and markings must be filed by August 1st. Failure to comply with this provision may subject the owner or lessee of the stallion to a fine of not less than $10.00 nor more than $50.00. Application for registration may be refused from any person not complying with this rule.

§ 8.   *Names.*—

(a) Names for proposed registration shall be limited to sixteen letters and three words.

(b) Horses may not be registered under a name of an animal previously registered and active.

(c) Names of outstanding horses may not be used again, nor may they be used as a prefix or suffix unless the name is a part of the name of the sire or dam. A prefix or a suffix such as Junior, etc., is not acceptable.

(d) Use of a farm name in registration of horses is reserved for the farm that has registered that name.

(e) Names of living persons will not be used unless the written permission to use their name is filed with the application for registration.

(f) No horse shall be registered under names if spelling or pronunciation is similar to names already in use.

(g) Names of famous or notorious persons, trade names, or names claimed for advertising purposes, except names, or parts of a name, of a registered breeding farm, will not be used.

(h) The United States Trotting Association reserves the right to refuse any name indicating a family or strain which may be misleading, or any name which may be misleading as to the origin or relationship of an animal, *or any name which might be considered offensive, vulgar or suggestive.*

(i) Horses may be named by January 1st, subsequent to their foaling, without penalty.

§ 9.   *Fees for Registration.*—Complete application submitted for foals prior to October 1st—$10.00. Com-

plete applications submitted subsequent to October 1st and prior to the date on which the foal becomes two years of age — $15.00. Complete applications submitted thereafter—$25.00. Horses registered with the Canadian Standard Bred Horse Society Records may be *registered or re-registered* with The United States Trotting Association upon presentation of the Canadian certificate in the applicant's name and a $5.00 fee.

§ 10.   *Fees for Transfer.*—For each change in ownership, if application is received within one month after date of sale $2.00; one to three months $5.00; three to six months $10.00; and (effective on sales after January 1, 1962) six months to one year $25.00; one to two years $50.00; over two years $100.00.

§ 11.   *Fee for Duplicate Registration Certificate.*—A duplicate registration certificate shall be issued for $5.00 upon receipt of a satisfactory written statement from the owner stating why duplicate papers are needed.

§ 12.   *Fees for Tattooing.*—The fee for tattooing horses foaled on or after January 1, 1960 will be $5.00.

§ 13.   *Fees for Re-registration to Change the Name.*—Fee for re-registration of a yearling prior to January 1st when it shall become two years old, which re-registration is solely for the purpose of a change of name, shall be $1.00. After a horse becomes a two-year-old the fee for change of name shall be $15.00. No change of name will be permitted once a horse has raced nor will any change of name be permitted for stallions or mares that have been retired for breeding purposes.

§ 14.   *Notice of Sale.*—Any party selling a registered horse shall immediately notify The United States Trotting Association, giving the full name and address of the new owner and the date of sale. No horse shall be transferred unless a registration certificate, together with a transfer signed by the registered owner, is filed with this Association.

§ 15. *Skipping Transfers.* — Any person who is a party, whether acting as agent or otherwise, to skipping or omitting transfers in the chain of ownership of any horse, may be subjected to the penalties and procedures set forth in Section 16 hereof.

§ 16. *Penalty for Executing False Application for Registration or Transfer.*—The President, Executive Vice-President, Registration Committee or District Board of Review may summon persons who have executed applications for registration or transfer that have become subject to question, as well as any other person who may have knowledge thereof. Failure to respond to such summons may be punished by a fine, suspension or expulsion. If the investigation reveals that an application for registration or transfer contains false or misleading information, the person or persons responsible may be fined, suspended or expelled, and in addition may be barred from further registration or transfer of horses in the Association and such animal may be barred from registration. The decision of the President, Executive Vice-President, Registration Committee or District Board of Review, as the case may be, shall be reduced to writing and shall be final unless the person or persons aggrieved thereby shall, within ten (10) days appeal in writing to the Board of Appeals as provided in Article IX of the By-Laws.

§ 17. *Fine for Careless Reporting of Markings.*—Any person filing an application for registration with incorrect information shall be fined $10.00 for each such incorrect application.

§ 18. *Cancellation of Incorrect Registration.* — If, upon any proceeding under the provisions of Section 16 of this Rule 26, it shall be determined that any outstanding registration is incorrect, the Executive Vice-President shall order immediate cancellation of such outstanding incorrect registration and shall forthwith forward notice of such cancellation to the owner of the horse which is incorrectly registered.

§ 19. Failure by a member to submit requested information relative to the breeding and/or transfer of a horse to this Association may subject the member to suspension by the Executive Vice-President.

§ 20. *The Board of Directors may designate a proper person as Registrar who may affix his signature on the Registration Certificates and documents relating to import and export of horses.*

INDEX TO RULES

Index